OUTBACK AUSTRALIA HANDBOOK

INCLUDING THE RED CENTRE, KAKADU NATIONAL PARK, AND THE KIMBERLEY

OUTBACK AUSTRALIA HANDBOOK

INCLUDING THE RED CENTRE, KAKADU NATIONAL PARK, AND THE KIMBERLEY

SECOND EDITION

MARAEL JOHNSON

MOON
PUBLICATIONS INC.

OUTBACK AUSTRALIA HANDBOOK
INCLUDING THE RED CENTRE, KAKADU NATIONAL PARK,
AND THE KIMBERLEY
SECOND EDITION

Published by
Moon Publications, Inc.
P.O. Box 3040
Chico, California 95927-3040, USA

Printed by
Colorcraft Ltd., Hong Kong

ISBN: 1-56691-047-1

ISSN: 1085-2670

Editor: Michael Ray Greer
Copy Editors: Deana Corbitt Shields, Gina Wilson Birtcil, Matt Orendorff
Production & Design: Carey Wilson
Cartographers: Bob Race, Brian Bardwell
Index: Deana Corbitt Shields

Front cover photo: Trephina Gorge National Park, Bill Bachman
All photos by Bill Bachman unless otherwise noted.

Distributed in the U.S.A. by Publishers Group West
Printed in Hong Kong

Please send all comments,
corrections, additions,
amendments, and critiques to:

OUTBACK AUSTALIA HANDBOOK
MOON PUBLICATIONS, INC.
P.O. BOX 3040
CHICO, CA 95927-3040, USA
e-mail: travel@moon.com

Printing History
1st edition — May 1992
2nd edition — June 1996

CONTENTS

MAPS

MAP SYMBOLS

WATER	STATE BORDER	**C.P.**	CONSERVATION PARK
DRY LAKE	BRIDGE	■	POINT OF INTEREST
NATIONAL HIGHWAY	FREEWAY	O	CITY
STATE HIGHWAY	MAIN HIGHWAY	o	TOWN
MOUNTAIN	OTHER ROAD		NOTE: CONDITION OF
ACCOMMODATION	UNPAVED ROAD		UNPAVED ROADS MAY VARY
	RAILROADS		

CHARTS AND SPECIAL TOPICS

ABBREVIATIONS

ACT—Australian Capital
    Territory
B&B—bed and breakfast
BHP—Broken Hill Proprietary
C—centigrade
CWA—Country Women's
    Association
4WD—four-wheel drive
NSW—New South Wales

NT—Northern Territory
P.O.—post office
RAA or **RAC**—Royal
    Automobile Association *or*
    Royal Automobile Club
QLD—Queensland
SA—South Australia
STA—State Transit Authority
    (South Australia) *or* Student
    Travel Association

tel.—telephone
WA—Western Australia
YHA—Youth Hostel Association
YMCA/YWCA—Young
    Men's/Women's Christian
    Association

ACKNOWLEDGMENTS

Thanks to everyone for helping me pull this masterpiece together: Cheryl Grant and Garuda Indonesia for generous help and support; my sister, Susan (a.k.a. The Good One), for her crackerjack contract negotiations; saving angels Andrew Hempstead and Nadina Purdon for unfaltering help above and beyond; Taran March, saintly editoress and all-around fall guy; guru Bill Dalton, for inspiring me to be a travel writer in the first place; Hamish Trumble and Macro The Wonder Dog for their contribution to this book's Introduction; Mike Greer, editor and Volvo mechanic; Bill Bachman, heaven-sent Outback photographer; Michael, for sorting countless illustrations of boomerangs, koalas, and big rocks; Moon computer whiz Asha Johnson, *artistes* Bob Race and Dave Hurst, all the other Moon Beams; and all my mates Down Under and my pals Up Top who put up with my bad moods and midnight appetites during this intense project, ESPECIALLY the Argyle Street gang (happy now?).

IS THIS BOOK OUT OF DATE?

Of course it is. What do you think—I wrote it last night, it was printed this morning, and you got the first copy hot off the press? Though we strive to be as accurate and current as possible, alas—things change.

If you discover an error, or something new and exciting (a walking trail, dinosaur footprint, cache of diamonds, a reflection of the man in the moon), please let me know. Other than routine updates, your contribution, if used, will be acknowledged. Also, send love letters and snapshots.

Outback Australia Handbook
c/o Moon Publications, Inc.
P.O. Box 3040
Chico, CA 95927 USA
e-mail: travel@moon.com

PREFACE

Almost every night, for ten years, I dreamed about the Outback. I was involved in every imaginable activity—walking about purposefully, running circles around myself, skipping down a long stretch of road. Time stopped still, eons flashed past—I was stuck in Dreamtime, not Aboriginal, but my own. When I finally *did* step onto Australian soil, I was not disappointed.

The Outback is an adventure through some of the oldest, most wondrous places on earth—Oz-spots where perhaps your only constraint will be your imagination. This is where reality is dream-like and Dreamtime is for real. You may have no idea of the mind-expanding and body-humbling experiences that await you in this land of unearthly enigmas and geological giants—but *I* do.

BOB RACE

INTRODUCTION

Australian history . . . does not read like history, but like the most beautiful lies. And all of a fresh sort, no mouldy old stale ones. It is full of surprises and adventures and incongruities, and contradictions and incredibilities; but they are all true, and they happened.

—MARK TWAIN

THE LAND

Australia is indeed made of contradictions and conundrums. Is it the smallest continent or the biggest island on earth? Is it the oldest place in the world? Indeed it is, and you can stroll over rocks that were formed four billion years ago. But geologists will remind you that Australia didn't separate from the Asian landmass to become its own continent until recent, almost modern times—a mere 50 million years ago.

Its isolation in the remote southern ocean meant that Australia, aside from Antarctica, was the last continent to succumb to human occupancy (Aborigines arrived about 40,000 years ago); but long before Europeans arrived, philosophers from Athens to Alexandria postulated the existence of the "antipodes" on the theory that

symmetry demanded a southern continent to balance the known world in the north.

Australia is a fragment of the ancient supercontinent Pangaea. Six hundred million years ago, South America, Africa, Antarctica, Australasia, and the Indian subcontinent were all hooked together. Over the millennia since, they have been drifting apart, as the massive tectonic plates float across the earth's mantle. Australia is riding in the middle of a plate whose leading edge in northern India is relentlessly smashing into central Asia, piling up the Himalayas. The eastern edge of the same plate runs alongside New Zealand, which experiences the volcanic consequences of two unimaginably vast slabs of rock grinding away at each other.

WELCOME TO THE OUTBACK BUFFET

Consider this your personal invite to the world's most enormous all-you-can-muster feast—the Australian Outback. Select anything—or everything—from the enclosed menu. Some travelers will swallow up the sweet and spicy cities, take a nibble at side trips; others will dig straight into the thick centre cut, chewing on every track and formation.

Pick and choose from unlimited condiments—refreshing dips, supernatural grounds, exotic relishes . . . I've even thrown in tantalizing islands and scrumptious beaches as starters, between-course palate pleasers, or for dessert.

Our banquet stretches from the affordable and do-able to the energetic and extravagant. Select prix fixe or a la carte, according to your budget, time frame, and desires (be they wild or simple)—you say "when."

Whether you go for meat and potatoes or truffles and caviar—savor every single bite. I expect to find you licking your fingers and coming back for more.

Being in the middle of this enormous plate has meant that the Australian continent has been comparatively free of volcanic and other cataclysmic upheavals. Consequently, Australia is the flattest of the continents; time and weather have eroded mountain ranges that once would have dwarfed Mt. Everest. Mount Kosciusko in New South Wales, Australia's highest mountain (2,228 meters above sea level), would barely pass muster as a respectable foothill elsewhere in the world. Australia has an average height of only 200 meters, and one of the most powerful impressions the traveler experiences in Australia is of awesome, mind-numbing flatness.

Another impression is dryness. Australia is the driest of the continents; some areas are subject to more evaporation than precipitation. While 40% of its landmass lies in the tropics, almost 70% is arid, with an annual rainfall below 25 centimeters. These parched conditions are accompanied by a *big* load of sand; some of the longest sand dunes in the world run parallel for up to 200 kilometers in the Simpson Desert. Where the sandy deserts give out, they are replaced by stony "gibber" deserts, relics of an ancient inland sea.

GEOGRAPHY OF THE OUTBACK

The Outback covers two of Australia's three main geographical zones. On the east side, Australia's Central Lowlands traverse the continent from north to south, and never rise more than a dizzying 350 meters. South Australia's northeastern corner is comprised in part of these lowlands. The rest of the Outback is Australia's Western Plateau, which covers almost three-quarters of the continent and is the quintessential flat, arid, harsh, empty, knock-your-socks-off, and alluringly beautiful Outback. The third zone, the Great Dividing Range, is in eastern Australia.

Notable geographical features include Uluru (or Ayers Rock), the largest monolith in the world. Like an iceberg, most of its bulk lies beneath the surface, and it rears so dramatically out of the landscape that it is little wonder that Aborigines regard it as a sacred site. Lake Eyre, usually Australia's largest salt pan, is also the country's largest lake when it fills a couple times per century. The Great Sandy, Gibson, and Great Victoria Deserts occupy much of the central Outback.

The Central Eastern Lowlands that bisect the continent along the 140th meridian contain the Great Artesian Basin, a vast underground water source tapped by some 9,000 bores, or wells. At the southern edge of this basin is the Murray-Darling river system that runs from New South Wales through northwest Victoria and into South Australia—really the only river system in the country. Many of Australia's rivers run only seasonally, and in times of drought dry up, leaving

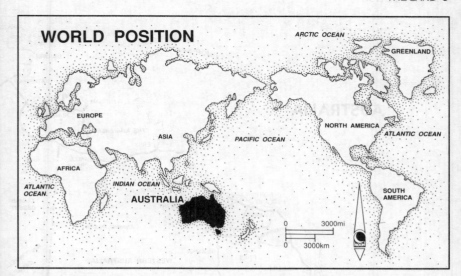

WORLD POSITION

ARCTIC OCEAN
GREENLAND
EUROPE
ASIA
NORTH AMERICA
ATLANTIC OCEAN
PACIFIC OCEAN
AFRICA
INDIAN OCEAN
ATLANTIC OCEAN
AUSTRALIA
SOUTH AMERICA

0   3000mi
0   3000km

stranded pools or lakes called "billabongs." Lake Eyre, in South Australia, is at the center of the largest internal drainage system on earth, more than twice as big as the Great Basin of Utah, Nevada, and California. When it fills, only a few times each century, it transforms the landscape with a spectacular explosion of birds and plantlife.

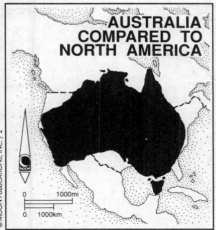

AUSTRALIA COMPARED TO NORTH AMERICA

0   1000mi
0   1000km

© MOON PUBLICATIONS, INC. / 2

The center of the continent is flat, sandy, and arid, except for the MacDonnell and Musgrave ranges. The sand and rock here are the color of terra-cotta, giving rise to the expression, the "Red Centre." More desolate yet is the Nullarbor Plain, which runs almost 1,500 km from east to west; it is famous for its utter flatness and for the limestone caves that lie hidden beneath its featureless face. The longest straight stretch of railway line in the world runs 468 km across the Nullarbor. The southern edge of the Nullarbor drops abruptly into the wild ocean from spectacular vertical cliffs that run along the Great Australian Bight. Drama and beauty aside, these cliffs proved a virtual hell for vessels with the bad fortune to be slammed against them, allowing little hope for survivors to climb to safety.

PROTECTING THE LAND

Land Protection Programs

The Register of the National Estate, compiled by the Australian Heritage Commission, provides annual grants for more than 200 projects within all states and territories. The 1990s have been dedicated the "Decade of Landcare" by the federal government, which has established environ-

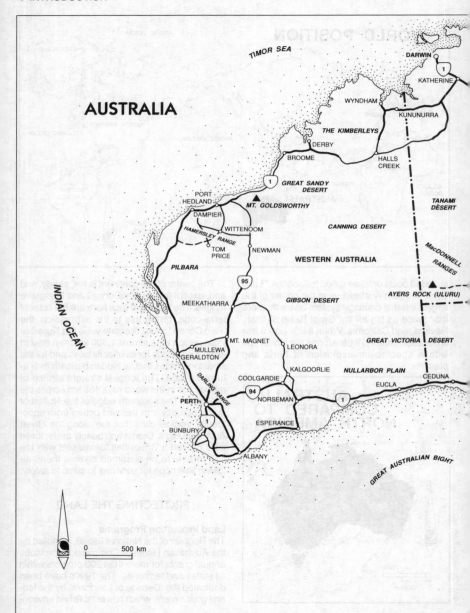

ARAFURA SEA

TORRES STRAIT

CORAL SEA

ARNHEM LAND

GULF OF CARPENTARIA

SOUTH PACIFIC OCEAN

LARRIMAH

DALY WATERS

CAPE YORK PENINSULA

ATHERTON TABLELAND

CAIRNS

GREAT BARRIER REEF

NORMANTON

BARKLY TABLELAND

87

TENNANT CREEK

66

TOWNSVILLE

CHARTERS TOWERS

78

PROSERPINE

MACKAY

MT. ISA

NORTHERN TERRITORY

WINTON

GREAT DIVIDING RANGE

LONGREACH

66

EMERALD

ALICE SPRINGS

QUEENSLAND

ROCKHAMPTON

71

GLADSTONE

SIMPSON DESERT

THE CHANNEL COUNTRY

CHARLEVILLE

MARYBOROUGH

54

17

MAROOCHYDORE

COOBER PEDY

LAKE EYRE

CUNNAMULLA

TOOWOOMBA

SUNSHINE COAST

BRISBANE

SOUTH AUSTRALIA

FLINDERS RANGES

LAKE TORRENS

87

BOURKE

NEW SOUTH WALES

71

DIVIDING RANGE

GOLD COAST

TAMWORTH

39

15

GRAFTON

PORT AUGUSTA

1

32

BROKEN HILL

DUBBO

PORT MACQUARIE

EYRE PENINSULA

MURRAY

MILDURA

39

32

NEWCASTLE

PORT LINCOLN

YORKE PENINSULA

20

RIVER

79

GREAT

SYDNEY

31

ADELAIDE

CANBERRA

VICTORIA

ALBURY

20

1

1

8

MELBOURNE

COOMA

MT. GAMBIER

31

TASMAN SEA

BASS STRAIT

BURNIE

DEVONPORT

LAUNCESTON

TASMANIA

HOBART

NATIONAL PARK CODE

The Australian Nature Conservation Agency (formerly the National Parks and Wildlife Service) asks you to follow a number of simple rules to protect both you and the parks.

- Guard against fire. Use fireplaces where provided. Native timber is the home of small animals, so please preserve it by using a portable stove. No fires, including gas barbecues and stoves, may be lit when a fire ban is in force.
- Do not disturb, collect, or damage animals, wildflowers, vegetation, or earth or rock formations.
- Do not disturb or collect artifacts from Aboriginal sites. Sites and items may have sacred, ceremonial, mythological, and historical significance to Aboriginal people, and have scientific value.
- Firearms are not permitted.
- Do not litter. Carry your rubbish out of the park when you leave, or use a litter bin.
- Leave your pets at home. Dogs and cats are not allowed in parks, as they disturb both native animals and park visitors.
- Drive carefully and observe all notices.
- Use of registered off-road vehicles is restricted to existing designated roads and tracks.
- Contact local rangers for camping permits and for information on local conditions for bushwalking.

mental and conservation protection programs throughout the country—with all levels of government participating. This is a feather in the Green caps of the estimated 800,000 members of Australia's conservation societies (numbering nearly 1,000—up from 50 in the '50s).

In 1974, Australia became one of the first signatories to the UNESCO World Heritage convention—signers and members are committed to identify, protect, and promote World Heritage properties. Australia's list consists of: the Great Barrier Reef, Kakadu National Park, the Willandra Lakes Region, the Tasmanian Wilderness, Lord Howe Island Group, the Australian East Coast Temperate and Sub-tropical Rainforest Parks, Uluru National Park, Wet Tropics of Queensland, Shark Bay in Western Australia, and Fraser Island in Queensland. State and territorial governments join with the federal entity to protect these ecologically diverse and magnificent regions.

Pollution-wise, the feds control dumping of waste in the sea, as well as imports and exports of hazardous waste, while state and territory governments hold main responsibility for pollution controls (though guidelines for permitted levels of pollution are a collaborative effort with the federal government). As for industrial pollution, the federal government offers "encouragement" for cleaner methods.

State and territory governments are accountable for native wildlife within their respective boundaries, with the federal government taking over for the critters inhabiting federal territories. The federal level also has the say-so regarding international import and export of wildlife, and holds the pen when it comes to international treaties and conventions dealing with nature conservation.

Conservation Organizations
Greenies and other concerned travelers have several ways to join or support Australia's environmental consciousness.

The **Australian Conservation Foundation** (ACF) is the country's largest private conservation organization. Often working in coalition with the Wilderness Society and other action groups, the ACF is concerned with ozone depletion and the greenhouse effect, rainforest preservation, logging, and land abuse. It even casts its (save-the) eagle eye on the fragile Antarctic region. Memberships, subscriptions, and individual donations constitute most of their funding (the government contributes only about 10%). For more information, contact ACF, 340 Gore St., Fitzroy (Melbourne), VIC 3065 (tel. 03-9416-1455).

The **Wilderness Society,** which began as the Tasmanian Wilderness Society in response to the forthcoming *damning* of the Franklin River, has expanded its causes to encompass the entire country. You can support their positions by purchasing goods such as T-shirts, posters, books, and postcards from shops in all states except the Northern Territory. For more information, contact the main office at 130 Davey St., Hobart, TAS 7000 (tel. 03-6234-9366).

National Parks

For information on Australia's more than 2,000 national parks, wildlife sanctuaries, and nature reserves, contact the following organizations.

Australian Capital Territory, Parks and Conservation Service, G.P.O. Box 1119, Tuggeranong, ACT 2901 (tel. 06-237-5222)

New South Wales, National Parks and Wildlife Service, 43 Bridge St., Hurstville, NSW 2220; G.P.O. Box 1967, Hurstville, NSW 2220 (tel. 02-9585-6444)

Queensland, Queensland Department of Environment and Heritage, 160 Ann St., Brisbane, QLD 4000; P.O. Box 155, North Quay, Brisbane, QLD 4002 (tel. 07-3227-7111)

South Australia, Department of Environment and Natural Resources, 77 Grenfell St., Adelaide, SA 5001; G.P.O. Box 667, Adelaide, SA 5001 (tel. 08-8204-1910)

Victoria, Department of Conservation and Natural Resources (DC&NR), 240 Victoria Parade, East Melbourne, VIC 3002; P.O. Box 41, East Melbourne, VIC 3002 (tel. 03-9412-4011)

Northern Territory, Conservation Commission of the Northern Territory, P.O. Box 496, Palmerston, Darwin, NT 0831 (tel. 08-8999-5511)

Northern Territory, Australian Nature Conservation Agency, Smith St., Darwin, NT 0800; G.P.O. Box 1260, Darwin, NT 0801 (tel. 08-8981-5299)

Western Australia, Department of Conservation and Land Management, 50 Hayman Rd., Como, WA 6152 (tel. 09-334-0333)

Tasmania, Department of Environment and Land Management, 134 Macquarie St., Hobart, TAS 7000; P.O. Box 44a, Hobart, TAS 7001 (tel. 03-6230-8011)

For countrywide information, contact the **Australian Nature Conservation Agency** (formerly National Parks and Wildlife Service), G.P.O. Box 636, Canberra, ACT 2601 (tel. 06-250-0200).

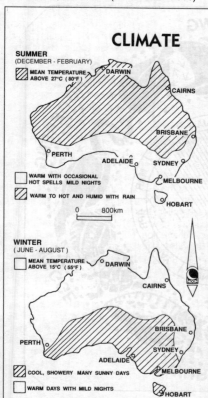

CLIMATE

SUMMER
(DECEMBER - FEBRUARY)

MEAN TEMPERATURE ABOVE 27°C (80°F)

DARWIN

CAIRNS

BRISBANE

PERTH

ADELAIDE

SYDNEY

MELBOURNE

HOBART

WARM WITH OCCASIONAL HOT SPELLS MILD NIGHTS

WARM TO HOT AND HUMID WITH RAIN

0   800km

WINTER
(JUNE - AUGUST)

MEAN TEMPERATURE ABOVE 15°C (55°F)

DARWIN

CAIRNS

BRISBANE

PERTH

ADELAIDE

SYDNEY

MELBOURNE

HOBART

COOL, SHOWERY MANY SUNNY DAYS

WARM DAYS WITH MILD NIGHTS

CLIMATE

The Seasons

Visitors from the Northern Hemisphere will immediately be struck by Australia's topsy-turvy seasons: summer officially begins on 1 December and winter on 1 June. This means that the academic and calendar years coincide, and both end with the summer holidays, in December. It also means you may experience the novelty of sitting down to a piping-hot Christmas dinner, perhaps of roast turkey or baked ham with all the trimmings, in the sweltering heat of high summer. And don't forget—here the sun rides across the northern sky and new rules apply. If you get lost and look for the mossy side of trees, just remember you're pointed south instead of north.

SEASONS

Seasons in the Southern Hemisphere are the reverse of those in the Northern Hemisphere.

Spring: September-November
Summer: December-February
Fall: March-May
Winter: June-August

Australia straddles the Tropic of Capricorn, and climatic conditions range from temperate in the south to tropical in the north. Adelaide enjoys a mild, almost Mediterranean climate, with moderate winters and dry summers. Perth's weather is some of the best: sunny, mild, and not too humid (conditions are mild by run-for-the-thermal-undies standards). South Australia's northern half and Queensland's and New South Wales' inner reaches share the same hot, semi-arid Outback conditions that characterize the Northern Territory's southern reaches. Top End weather, which occurs in the northern part of Western Australia and the Northern Territory, favors distinct wet (Oct.-March) and dry (May-Sept.) seasons.

Winters are extremely comfortable, particularly near the coast, with dazzling days and dreamy nights. However, summer brings tropical rains and cyclones, some of which have been devilishly savage. In 1974, Cyclone Tracy—like a

The Aborigines who live around Kakadu National Park recognize six annual seasons rather than the usual four.

lover on a rampage—destroyed Darwin overnight, and most other coastal cities have suffered extensive damage from cyclones in the past. While traveling in these regions during the summer cyclone season, keep your ears open for radio weather reports, which give frequent updates on the movements of cyclones as they develop.

The Aboriginal Seasons

The Aborigines who live around Kakadu National Park recognize six annual seasons rather than the "usual" four. The terms come from the Gundjeidmi (Maiili) language. *Gunumeleng,* the early storm season, is marked by hot, increasingly humid weather, along with building thunderstorms and scattered showers; *gudjewg,* the early monsoon season (known as the Wet), is usually a time of thunder and lightning, heat and humidity, and blossoming plant and animal life; *bangereng* is late monsoon season (also referred to as "knock 'em down" season) with violent storms, intense humidity, and a riot of flora and fauna; *yegge,* late storm season, brings early morning mists and water lilies, as well as strong winds and the first fires; *wurrgeng,* the cool, dry season, sees continuing burning, drying billabongs, dewy nights, and the relatively low humidity and temperatures that bring prolific bird- and wildlife as well as flocks of tourists; *gurrung,* the hot dry season, is *very* hot with some wind, rapidly traveling fires, and building thunderheads, which signal the return of *gunumeleng.*

Droughts, Fires, and Floods

The vast interior is arid; this makes for clear skies, warm to hot days, and chilly (and amazingly starry) nights. Rain rarely falls in the Outback, but when it does the landscape responds spectacularly as dormant vegetation bursts into life. Australia's aridity is such that many areas are subject to drought, and it is common for some regions to struggle for as much as seven years without a drop of rain. Even the wetter coastal areas are not immune to occasional droughts, and water restrictions are something that most Australians are familiar with. In 1994, the weather reversed its geographical pattern, bringing bizarre summer rains to the Red Centre and South Australia and devasting drought (the worst in Australian history) to the east coast. The farming community was hard hit as cattle, crops, and wildlife bit the dust and farmers were forced both to slaughter livestock early and refrain from planting summer crops. The drought was so serious, in fact, that the Sydney Water utility launched an official campaign to encourage water-rationing: "Save Water, Shower with a Friend."

In the normally dry summer months in the south, bushfires are an annual danger, and the consequences of uncontrollable outbreaks have been devastating for some time. In 1982, incalculable damage was caused by the terrible fires that broke out, ironically enough, on Ash Wednesday of that year, in Victoria and South Australia. And, certainly, few Australians will forget 1994's out-of-control wildfires (the worst since European colonization 200 years ago), which snuffed out more than a half-million hectares of bush and grasslands, destroyed 100-or-so homes, and roared within several miles of central Sydney. Ash and haze left the city's famous opera house a shade of dismal orange rather than its customary blinding white— but at least it was left.

The opposite side of the drought-and-fire coin is flood. Many agonizingly long droughts have been broken by catastrophic floods that can isolate outlying communities for weeks.

The Outback is a land of periodic extremes. The highest recorded temperature was a brain-frying 53.1° C (127° F) in Cloncurry, Queensland, in 1889, while Marble Bar, in Western Australia, had 160 sweltering days over 37° C (98° F) in 1923-24, still a world record. The highest rainfall in a 24-hour period was 108 cm in 1979 at Bellenden, Queensland, which also holds the Australian record for the highest annual rainfall—over 10 meters.

The best time to visit the tropical north is in the winter, when rainfall and humidity are at a minimum and temperatures are comfy for most travelers.

The temperate south is enjoyable year-round although spring in South Australia's wine country is hard to beat and fall also has its advocates, particularly those interested in bushwalking or cycling tours. Spring is also the season of choice for Western Australia, when the 8,000 or so species of wildflowers, for which the state is famous, are in bloom. For more detailed information on local weather, see "Climate" in the Introduction to each state.

Sunshine and Ozone

Australia is exposed to more hours of sunshine than most countries. This has two important consequences. First, the anxiously observed hole in the protective ozone layer over the South Pole has extended at times to expose southern parts of the continent, and it is expected that the hole will only enlarge further. Scientific opinion about the negative effects of this startling development is divided. There is no doubt, however, about the consequences of exposure to high levels of sunshine on humans. Even before the rent in the ozone layer became a concern, Australia's rate of skincancer cases was abnormally high. The combination of a fashion for bronze suntans, an addiction to sunbathing, a beach culture, and a love of outdoor activities has led to a national health problem of major proportions. It is worth remembering the simple creed propounded in a recent public health campaign: Slip, Slop, Slap (slip on a shirt, slop on some sunscreen, and slap on a hat).

Harsh climatic conditions have helped to shape the national character, and, far from resenting the forces of nature that so often blight the lives of Australians, especially in the bush, many people have a strangely sentimental attachment to this rigorous and inhospitable land. The words of Dorothy Mackellar in this poem, which most Australians learn at school, sum up their ambivalent affection:

> *I love a sunburnt country,*
> *A land of sweeping plains,*
> *Of rugged mountain ranges,*
> *Of droughts, and flooding rains.*
> *I love her far horizons.*
> *I love her jewelled sea.*
> *Her beauty and her terror;*
> *A wide brown land for me.*

FLORA AND FAUNA

In wilderness is the preservation of the world. We need the tonic of wilderness, to wade sometimes in the marshes . . . we can never have enough of nature.

—HENRY THOREAU

Australia's 50 million years of geographic isolation has led to the evolution of a bewildering array of indigenous plant and animal life that has little in common with life-forms in relatively nearby parts of the world. It is one of the fascinations of travel in the Outback to be continually confronted with animals and plants that might easily spring from the fevered brains of science fiction writers.

FLORA

"The great quantity of plants Mr. Banks and Dr. Solander found in this place occasioned my giving it the name of Botany Bay." This brief entry in Captain Cook's 1770 journal does little justice to the excitement the two botanical gentlemen in his company must have experienced. The flora they collected was certainly novel and was the subject of lively academic interest in Europe. The following overview highlights some of the botanic marvels that Banks and Solander probably observed, species also prevalent on the other side of the continent.

The Bush

The term "bush," which Australians bandy about so loosely, covers a variety of terrains and broad vegetation types, including rainforests, both temperate and tropical, mangrove swamps, savannahs, rolling scrub-covered hills, forests of eucalypt or conifer, grasslands,

and deserts. Australian plants and trees are generally nondeciduous, and many species bear fragrant blossoms. After a desert rainstorm, the air is cloyingly sweet, and sailors say they can smell the sharp medicinal scent of gums (eucalypts) far out to sea.

Myrtles and Gums

The largest and most famous of Australian plant groups is the myrtle family. It contains over 1,000 native species, from the ground-hugging heathlike kunzeas to the 500-odd species of

OFFICIAL FLORA AND FAUNA EMBLEMS

FLORA

The golden wattle *(Acacia pycnantha)* is Australia's national floral emblem. Individual state emblems are:

New South Wales; waratah *(Telopea speciosissima)*
Northern Territory; Sturt's desert rose *(Gossypium sturtianum)*
Queensland; Cooktown orchid *(Dendrobium bigibbum)*
South Australia; Sturt's desert pea *(Clianthus formosus)*
Tasmania; Tasmanian blue gum *(Eucalyptus globulus)*
Victoria; common heath *(Epacris impressa)*
Western Australia; kangaroo paw *(Anigozanthos manglesii)*

FAUNA

New South Wales; platypus *(Ornithorhynchus anatinus);* laughing kookaburra *(Dacelo novaeguineae)*
Northern Territory; red kangaroo *(Macropus rufus);* wedge-tailed eagle *(Aquila audax)*
Queensland; koala *(Phascolarctos cinereus)*
South Australia; hairy-nosed wombat *(Lasiorhinus latifrons)*
Tasmania; none (not even the Tasmanian tiger or devil)
Victoria; helmeted honeyeater *(Meliphaga cassidix)*
Western Australia; numbat *(Myrmecobius fasciatus);* black swan *(Cygnus atratus)*

eucalypt. It includes the tea-tree (so named by Captain Cook's crew, who made a tea-colored drink from its leaves) the picturesque paper-bark with its white papery trunk, and the brilliantly colored bottlebrush. The hundreds of species of eucalypt, or gum tree, many with colorful scarlet, coral, and white blossoms, are now the most transplanted trees in the world. More than 100 years ago these fast growers, well-suited to arid climates, were planted in California and Arizona as windbreaks, and you can find Australian eucalypts in well over 70 countries, a tribute to their hardy adaptability.

Fewer than 100 species of eucalypt are found in the country's arid climes, many of them shorter and squatter than their relatives living in the bush, highlands, or coastal regions. These varieties have developed an ability to resist heat and preserve moisture. Many gum trees have leaves that turn their edges to the sun's rays to reduce evaporation, which, incidentally, makes them poor shade trees on scorching afternoons. Gum leaves are generally thick-skinned and equipped with oil glands to provide an oily film to resist the heat.

Commonly sighted Outback eucalypts include: the ghost gum with sheeny, bleached-out bark and vibrant green leaves, a haunting vision around central Australia and the tropical north; the river (or "red") gum, a large-limbed giant of a tree with slick bark tattooed in tans and greys, found rooted in the region's waterways; coolabahs, another water- and swamp-dweller, recognizable by its gnarly shape, lackluster leaves, and tough bark; mallee, scrubby tangled little growths common throughout the southeastern Outback; and the Darwin woollybutt, a tall lumbering tree with a two-toned, dual-textured trunk and seasonal orange blossoms, scattered coast-to-coast across the Top End.

Other Plants and Shrubs

The wattle, Australia's floral emblem, belongs to the acacia family, which is represented by some 600 species across Australia with about one-fifth of those growing in the Outback. Mulgas, the most common arid-zone wattle, can grow in sparse clumps or thick groupings and look somewhat like scrawny eucalypts. In early days, colonists made wattle-and-daub huts, an ancient building technique involving interwoven saplings covered with mud, and the name "wattle" was attached to this profusely blooming species with its either spikey or rounded yellow flowers. Like a good Aussie football player, the wattle is extremely hardy and fast growing, and can thrive in the arid, bare interior where even eucalypts cannot compete, but its career is not long-lived. Some species have adapted to sand dunes drenched with salt spray, some to soggy ill-drained swamps, and others to stony exposed ridges. And like many Australian plants, they have adapted to fire.

The bushfire did not come to Australia with the Europeans. Since ancient times, lightning has started many a blazing inferno, and Aborigines used fire to flush animals out of dense foliage. Many species of Australian plants have developed a remarkable resistance to fire. Eucalypts have dormant buds beneath their bark that open immediately after a bushfire to restore foliage to a burnt tree. The seeds of other plant species do not readily germinate until the first rains after a fire, when great quantities of acacia seedlings spring up from the charred earth. The woody fruits of hakeas and banksias actually require the heat of fire before they will burst open and release the seeds.

The ubiquitous banksia trees and shrubs are named after Sir Joseph Banks, and they have a special place in the nightmares of Australian children after the artist May Gibbs created the wicked Banksia men for her popular bush fairy tales. Banksias belong to the Protaceae family, which has developed most abundantly in Australia. It is named after Proteus, the shape-changing Old Man of the Sea in Greek mythology, and it points to the enormous diversity of the family. Some banksias, for instance, grow half submerged in the sand, while others grow into trees

KAREN McKINLEY

15 meters tall. Leaves and flowers of this family vary tremendously from the so-called spider flowers of the *Grevillea* genus to the dense heads of the waratahs. The most commercially valuable members of the family are the macadamia, which are grown in Queensland for their rich, yummy nut, and the silky oak, which produces a fine cabinet wood.

And yet there are still *more* wildly beautiful, utterly strange trees and shrubs to stumble across: spinifex, a hardy, prickly, spiky plant—and favorite reptilian hiding place—that blankets much of central Australia; some 30 varieties of saltbush, a staple in the diets of Outback livestock, that has a special fondness for the Birdsville and Oodnadatta tracks; the boab tree, a squatty, gnarly-branched oddity with a bloated, water-retaining trunk, and a relative of the African baobab, expat-ing it in the northeastern Northern Territory and the southwestern Kimberley; the desert oak, a tall, shady drama queen of a breed prevalent around arid spots like Ayers Rock and King Canyon; and a species of red cabbage palms, known as *Livistona mariae,* which has not been identified any place else on the planet! Groves of the palms as well as cycads—all left over from prehistoric times—are alive and well in the Northern Territory.

KAREN McKINLEY

Late and Early Bloomers

The Outback's native plants include profuse bloomers. Sturt's desert pea stretches like a red carpet across vast tracts of inland desert. More than 600 varieties of orchids, including the only two underground species in the world, lend their sensuous beauty to the steamy rainforests of the north, while water lilies float gently and dreamily atop Top End lagoons.

Western Australia alone grows more than 6,000 species of wildflowers and flowering shrubs and trees. For many eons, the southwest corner of Australia was virtually a floral island, isolated from the world by the Indian Ocean and the deserts to its north and east. Among the most colorful of Western Australia's flowers are the kangaroo paw, the Geraldton wax flower, the scarlet coccinea, the exquisitely scented boronias, and the pine grevillea with its enormous deep orange spikes that grow to six meters. Australia's Christmas tree is not a conifer, but a relative of the mistletoe, a parasite that blooms at Christmas in masses of orange balloon-like blossoms.

One reason for the very different configurations of Australian flowers, in which petals are often tiny or nonexistent while stamens and pistils are prominent, is that many have evolved in isolation where they are pollinated by birds, not bees, and have had to adapt to the demands of a host of honey-eaters' beaks.

The sight of Western Australian wildflowers, covering the earth as far as the eye can see, like the prolific blue leschenaultia (which Aborigines called "the floor of the sky"), is worth the cost of a dozen trips there. But there are fantastic botanical eye-poppers to be found elsewhere: the stately kauri and jarrah forests; the majestic mountain ash and beech myrtle of the temperate rainforests; ghost gums silhouetted against the setting sun; grass trees spiked with flowers; primitive tree ferns slowly inching their way up from the mossy, mist-shrouded forest floor; the sparse but fascinating vegetation of the Nullarbor Plain—so inhospitable but so alive; and for the ghoulish, two carnivorous species, the pitcher plant and the rainbow plant. The isolation and stress of a harsh climate have created plant life in Australia that is unique, extraordinary, and well worth investigating.

FAUNA

The Extinct

Carnivorous lizards standing nine meters tall, eight-meter ichthyosaurs (or fish lizards), and three-meter labyrinthodonts (or frog lizards) in-

FOSSILS, FOOTPRINTS, AND OLD BONES

The land of Oz was home to some of the earth's earliest life-forms, many of them uncovered in the Outback (and probably more waiting to be discovered). These are some discoveries and their finding spots.

TYPE OF FIND IN: NEW SOUTH WALES	WHERE FOUND
Cretaceous-period carnivorous theropod	Lightning Ridge
a monotreme—the country's oldest fossil of a mammal	Lightning Ridge

NORTHERN TERRITORY	
Ordovician-period vertebrate fish	Amadeus Basin
Miocene-period fossils including enormous flightless birds, meat-eating thylacinids, a huge diprotodontid, and a marsupial lion	Alcoota Station, near Alice Springs
extinct marsupials	Bullock Creek

QUEENSLAND	
Permian-period fish	Blackwater
Australia's first therapsid	Carnarvon Gorge
the sauropod, Australia's first Jurassic-period discovery	near Roma
Jurassic-period pliosaurs	Mount Morgan area
plesiosaurs	north of Wandoan
"Mutta," an Ornithopoda-period dinosaur— unalive and well in Queensland Museum	Thomson River near Muttaburra
possibly the largest known marine reptile, from the Cretaceous period	near Hughenden
Cretaceous-period ichthyosaurs	Richmond
many dinosaur footprints	Lark Quarry, south of Winton
pterosaurs	near Boulia and Richmond
extinct marsupials, kangaroos and other mammals	Riversleigh

habited prehistoric Australia. These creatures died out in the cataclysmic worldwide extinction of the dinosaurs, long before humans arrived. Their most dangerous descendants are the saltwater crocodile, the great white shark, and a gallery of the world's deadliest snakes. A class of creature known as megafauna, however, still roamed the land when the first Aborigines came ashore. The bones of gigantic wombats bigger than buffalos, huge saber-toothed marsupial lions, and outsized kangaroos that would dwarf their puny descendants have been found, and some of these creatures

may well have entered the racial memory of the Aborigines, in the form of Dreamtime myths.

The Extraordinary

Some of Australia's native fauna are candidates for *Ripley's Believe It Or Not*. The silver barramundi, found in the Northern Territory's Kakadu National Park, spends the first six years of its life as a male and the rest as a female. Australia has the world's largest and most ferociously destructive termites, some of which build nests as high as six meters. The grand champion of termite mounds is near Hayes Creek in the

TYPE OF FIND IN: SOUTH AUSTRALIA	WHERE FOUND
"Eric," a Cretaceous-period opalized pliosaur— usually on tour	Coober Pedy
carnivorous theropod of the Cretaceous period	Andamooka
Miocene-period river dolphins	Lake Frome region
extinct marsupials	Lake Eyre basin
Pleistocene-period wombats	Cooper Creek, Lake Eyre, and Lake Callabonna

WESTERN AUSTRALIA	
Archaean-era stromatolites, the planet's oldest life form	Shark Bay
Devonian-period fish	The Kimberley
Devonian-period placoderms	Gogo Station, near Fitzroy Crossing
Triassic-period fish predators	Erskine Range, between Derby and Fitzroy Crossing
dinosaur footprints	Gantheaume Point, near Broome

Northern Territory, and others are scattered about the central deserts. The world's most venomous snake is the taipan, and its kissing cousin, which inhabits northeastern South Australia and southwestern Queensland, carries enough venom to kill more than 200,000 mice.

The rather unsavory platypus frog deserves a mention; the female carries her young in her stomach and gives birth by regurgitating them. Personally, this seems like a much more humane method than the labor-and-delivery hell that most women go through! Hmpf, Mother Nature must never have been pregnant.

Marsupials

The most famous of Australian animals are the marsupials—mammals that lack a placenta, give birth to offspring still in the gestative stage, and carry them in a pouch. Almost all the 150-odd marsupial species—most notably kangaroos, wallabies, possums, koalas, and wombats—are found in Australia.

Kangaroos, or "'roos," are the country's national symbol, and the largest of the marsupials. They are also the most widespread; since the arrival of Europeans, their numbers have increased as pastoralists cleared land and drilled water bores for sheep and cattle. Australians

now resort to "culling," a euphemism for massacring large numbers of native animals that interfere with graziers' interests and thereby earn the title of pest.

Despite the increasing numbers of some kangaroo species, it is a misconception that kangaroos can be seen loping down the main street of any town in Australia. In fact, they are timid creatures—usually hiding about in open plains and forest—often most active at night, and they are seen about as often as a deer is in North America.

Kangaroos are hunted for their skins and meat by Aborigines, for whom they form an important food source. It used to be that most culled kangaroos would end up as dog food, but recent initiatives have allowed kangaroo steaks and burgers onto the menus of sophisticated (and some not-so-sophisticated) city restaurants. Reputedly, kangaroo meat is highly nutritious, containing no cholesterol and very little fat. So, dear travelers, you and your canine mates can now feast on the same chow.

The largest recorded kangaroo was 3.2 meters tall and weighed nearly 100 kilograms. Far from being the harmless, inoffensive creature gazing doe-eyed from a glossy tourist brochure, kangaroos are ready and able to defend themselves. When attacked, by dingoes or a rival kangaroo, they use their forepaws to immobilize their opponent and, rearing up on their powerful tail, they attempt to rip open their adversary's belly with knifelike hind claws.

The kangaroo has evolved a remarkably efficient means of locomotion: jumping. It cannot walk or run, though it can swim surprisingly well, but it can achieve speeds of up to 50 km per hour by just hopping along. The sight of a group of kangaroos loping across an open field in full flight is exquisite.

Kangaroos' powerful hind legs are cunningly structured with a system of counterweighted tendons and muscles that conserve the energy expended in motion, thus enabling the animal to travel at high speeds for prolonged periods. Some rural racetracks have stories to tell about kangaroos bounding onto the track and beating a field of thoroughbred race horses.

The female kangaroo, like some other marsupials, is able to control her reproductive cycle depending on the availability of food and water. A female can carry a "joey," or immature kangaroo, in her pouch and one in her uterus. Should conditions become unfavorable, she will terminate her unborn joey in utero. The joey at birth is about one inch long and must drag itself from the birth canal to the mammary gland in the pouch, a perilous journey during which the mother offers no assistance. Hairs on the mother's belly grow in a pattern that gives the joey directional aid, but should the joey fall off the

mother, she will abandon it. Once the joey puts its mouth to the mammary gland, the nipple swells up and effectively locks the joey onto the teat until it has grown sufficiently to suck for itself. The joey will stay in the pouch for six to eight months until it is weaned, but it will continue to use its mother's pouch for safety and transportation until it is almost ridiculously big— a big, old pouch potato.

Kangaroo species range in size from the five-centimeter dusky hopping mouse to the giant two-meter red kangaroo. "Wallaby" usually denotes smaller kangaroos, while "wallaroo" usually denotes kangaroos that prefer a rocky or densely wooded habitat.

The sleepy, cuddlesome **koala,** beloved star of so many Australian tourist promotions, is not a bear but another marsupial. Despite its endearing good looks, koalas prefer not to be handled by kootchy-kooing humans, and they frequently outrage distinguished visitors, who pose for photo opportunities, by piddling on them. They are also equipped with formidable claws and are really much better left dozing in the trees where they belong, well-hidden atop a gum tree.

Koalas rarely drink water; they obtain their moisture from the 37 species of eucalypt leaves that form their sole diet. Their sleepy attitude is due in part to the sedative and hypnotic effect of a naturally occurring barbiturate in the eucalypt leaves. Koala numbers have rapidly declined since European settlement, and now they are a protected species. No longer hunted for their

nobody's teddy bear

pelts, they are still under threat from loss of habitat and a venereal disease similar to chlamydia. Needless to say, that stuffed bear you take home will—hopefully—be a fake.

Wombats are stocky, thickset marsupials slightly bigger than the koala. They make their home in burrows on the forest floor. They are nocturnal animals, and consequently the headlights of cars upset their night vision.

Other marsupials include the tree kangaroo, the monkeylike cuscus, batlike flying foxes, a host of tree-dwelling possums (which are really the only marsupial to have adapted to city life), marsupial rats and mice.

One disturbing sight for drivers on Outback roads is passing countless carcasses of wombats and other native animals. Road signs warn motorists of frequent crossing points, and not just for the animals' protection. Many drivers have cracked a radiator—or worse—in a collision with a kangaroo.

Monotremes

Monotremes are egg-laying mammals. There are only two in the world and they are both in Australia: the platypus and the echidna. The **duck-billed platypus** is perhaps the most intriguing of all Australia's odd creatures. The first specimens sent to the British Museum were dismissed as a hoax. Scientists thought that the web-footed, duck-billed creature with fur and claws had been intricately stitched together from the various parts of several animals, like so-called mermaids made of monkey heads attached to fish bodies that travelers brought back from time to time from the East. However, the platypus is genuinely odd. It represents a possible link in the evolutionary chain between reptiles and mammals, since it both lays eggs and suckles its young. Its choice of home is also peculiar. The platypus, living within the confines of eastern Australia and Tasmania, seems equally happy whether basking in a tropical river or freezing its bill off in a nippy mountain stream.

The platypus is extremely shy and sensitive to pollution or any disturbance to its habitat. Naturally, since European settlement, its numbers are well down; so, now it is a protected species. It lives in burrows in the banks of streams and feeds off the streambed. The platypus must close its eyes and ears under water and uses a

mysterious electric sense to locate food. For protection against natural predators, the adult male has venomous spurs on its hind legs. It's not too likely that you'll see a platypus in the wild, but if you do, remember that these creatures are enormously sensitive and their existence is utterly dependent on being left alone.

The other monotreme, the **echidna,** or spiny anteater, is much more accessible and a reasonably common sight in the bush, deserts, and mountains. It is named after Echidna, a monster of Greek mythology—part beautiful woman, part voracious serpent—whose offspring were even more monstrous than her own sweet self. The echidna resembles a North American porcupine, with a spine-covered body, a protruding snout, and a distinctive waddling gait, as it rolls along on its knuckles. It also has sharp claws, but its usual response to disturbance is to roll into a ball with its quills flexed.

Dingoes, Bats, and Bandicoots

Australia's native dog is the dingo, which was actually introduced from Southeast Asia about 6,000 years ago, well after the Aborigines arrived. Traditionally, Aborigines used dingoes for several activities, including sleeping beside them for warmth on cold nights—hence the expression "a three-dog night" for a particularly cold night. Nowadays the dingo roams the Outback in packs, and it is a difficult, though not impossible, animal to domesticate. The dingo earned worldwide notoriety through the Azaria Chamberlain case (wherein a dingo allegedly snatched—and, later, gnawed to death—baby Azaria from her family's Ayers Rock campsite), which only reinforced the need to take precautions when traveling in the more remote regions of the Outback. (Those dark-of-night dingo howls hardly inspire dreamy-bye lullabies.) Actually, sheep have more to worry about than newborn babes. Dingoes are known to wreak havoc (i.e. feast upon) whole flocks of sheep, inspiring a "shoot-to-kill" stance among many graziers. The famous Dingo Fence—the world's longest fence—stretches from the bottom of South Australia up to northwest Queensland. Inspectors regularly patrol about one-half of the fenceline, mending holes and setting traps, keeping the dingoes to the north and west of the barrier and out of southeastern Australia.

Australia is home to about 50 species of bats, including the colossal fruit bat. These large bats congregate in huge colonies, often in the tops of trees, and feed at night. Watching a colony wake up at sunset is a spectacle not to be missed: there is an all-pervading batty smell, and the sound of their bat cries as they fly in bat formation 'round the treetops is quite eerie. Gradually they disperse in search of fruit. Many species can be found grouped inside caves, and the rare golden horseshoe bat can be viewed at the Cutta Cutta Caves south of Katherine in the Northern Territory.

Both feral and domestic cats, unfortunately, have taken a vampire-ish liking to the rare—and getting rarer—rat-ish, little bandicoot. The mostly nocturnal bandicoots, however, prefer a diet of insects with perhaps a bit of plant fiber to aid digestion. The short-nosed bandicoot, found around both eastern and western Australia, is the most common breed, while the rabbit-eared (bilby) is a scarce sight in the Northern Territory.

Introduced Species

These are "the animals that ate Australia." Feral dogs, cats, pigs, goats, rabbits, and a host of other nonnative species, introduced by a series of intentional and accidental blunders, have brought with them economic and environmental devastation and a wave of extinctions unparalleled in the 50 million years since Australian life was cut off from outside influence by plate tectonics. Scores of native animals have been driven to near or complete extinction by competition with or attack from introduced species. Unique and irreplaceable creatures like the eastern hare-wallaby, the golden bandicoot, and the short-tailed hopping mouse have disappeared forever.

Australia's 200-300 million rabbits were introduced by English colonists soon after settlement for the purpose of sport. The spry hippity-hops adapted marvelously to the semiarid areas that were cleared for pasture, and they soon out-ate the resident animals. Now, rabbit infestations regularly break out, producing tens of millions of rabbits at a time. Huge amounts of money and effort have been poured into the control and eradication of the rabbit, most notably for the construction of the "rabbit-proof fence," which extended for thousands of miles across the continent, and for the hideous virus myxomatosis, which wiped out millions of rabbits in the 1930s. These days rabbits are largely immune to myxomatosis and vast research programs seek new and more virulent solutions to the rabbit problem.

An estimated 10 million feral pigs cause in excess of $100 million worth of damage annually and pose a nightmarish threat to Australia's lucrative livestock industry should they contract and spread diseases like foot-and-mouth disease or rinderpest.

Feral cats and dogs create havoc in national parks. In the trees, gorgeously colored native parrots, parakeets, and lorikeets are fighting a losing battle against introduced sparrows and starlings (the sparrows and starlings, however, have not yet made it into Western Australia, thanks to the sharp-shooters on watch at the state's borders). Wild horses and feral goats roam at will, ravaging remote areas of wilderness. More than 70,000 feral donkeys are shot each year. Foxes—also introduced deliberately for sport—are a pest for farmers, but they are steadily wiping out native species as well.

In the arid zones, wild camels—one-hump dromedaries, descendants of animals brought here for cartage purposes—are actually captured for export to the Middle East; Australia now has the dubious distinction of being home to the last wild camels (approximately 100,000 of them) on earth.

Until the arrival of Europeans, Australia had never known a cloven-hoofed beast; the hard impact of hoofs breaks up the dry crusted earth in the arid regions so that annually millions of tons of topsoil simply blow away. In the Northern Territory, herds of wild buffalo and semiwild cattle roam across a fragile landscape that struggles to recover from the devastation.

Where feral animals encroach on the interests of agriculture, enormous efforts are made to control the situation. But where human population is thin, and livestock (and, consequently, livelihoods) are not affected, feral animal populations are quite literally out of control. Paradoxically, in areas that are declared national parks—and there are more than 500 of them—feral animals often thrive because they are no longer subject to the control mechanisms of agriculture, and park authorities rarely have sufficient resources to take over.

Birds

Australia's birds are a wonderful and unexpected surprise for many visitors—about 700 species, of which approximately 500 are endemic and 200 migrate to all parts of the world. Watchers in the Outback will spot a large and exotic assortment of multicolored parrots (including the raucous cockatoo), budgerigars, and galahs. If you're hanging around the termite mounds you might glimpse the rare hooded parrot. Of the kingfishers, the largest is the kookaburra, found near permanent water sources. Its infectious laughing cry has earned it the nickname "the laughing jackass."

On the open plains, often inside the Dingo Fence, the flightless emu roams, its natural curiosity often piqued by the passing traveler. It's slightly smaller than the ostrich. The male emu has sole responsibility for child-rearing from the time the eggs are laid. Most recently, the emu—part of the country's coat-of-arms, along with the kangaroo—is becoming trendy in the skin/feather/nouvelle cuisine arena.

Most of Australia's 18 types of finch inhabit the tropic regions, but two renegades, the painted fireball and the zebra finch, have managed to adapt in the arid zone, usually close to permanent water sources. (Hint to Outback travelers: zebra finches = nearby water.) The exquisitely colorful Gouldian finch, once a common sight across the Top End, is now almost extinct.

When rain falls in the interior and long-dry watercourses and lakes fill for a few months, millions of birds appear, from black swans, ducks, and geese to pelicans and cormorants. They feed on the long-dormant creatures that lie for years under the scorched clay.

Curvy-billed honeyeaters—67 species that range from small and colorful to big and drab—not only frequent the watercourses but are regulars around Outback scrub, plains, and woodlands.

Around the coast, seabirds congregate in large numbers. Gulls and terns, the fairy penguins of Adelaide and Kangaroo Island, the mutton bird—even the lonely albatross—may be seen in the southern oceans.

The bowerbird constructs an elaborate "bower" or display for mating purposes. It collects all manner of shiny and colorful objects for inclusion in its display, from flowers and berries to jewelry stolen from campsites. Some bowerbirds mix various substances into a form of paint to enhance their overall concept of interior decorating. The females select their mates from the most resourceful and tasteful males.

The lyrebird, so named after the fabulous lyre-shaped display feathers of the male, is a great mimic and will deliver prolonged concerts imitating the sounds of the forest, other birdcalls, and even a tractor or a chainsaw. A single concert may contain up to 40 different calls.

The stately brolga (a large crane) is famous for its courtship dance, a spectacle of immense beauty.

Of the birds of prey, the keen-sighted, wedge-tailed eagle is the largest, and hawks and kites are a common sight, hovering motionlessly above their intended victims or wheeling in pairs high over their territory. White-bellied sea eagles and ospreys do their preying along the remote coasts.

A fashion for native gardens that swept Australia in the '60s has meant that many species of native birds have returned to the suburbs of Outback gateway cities to feed on the flowering shrubs that replaced the hedges and annuals imported from Europe. Many previously unsighted species of native birds are now common in suburbs that once knew only sparrows and pigeons.

Unfortunately, many of Australia's exotic birds are highly prized by collectors overseas and, since the birds are protected, a cruel and illicit smuggling industry has developed. Snaring threatens to wipe out some species, especially of parrots, and the smuggling process itself kills more of these sensitive creatures than can satisfy this objectionable market.

Reptiles and Amphibians

Love lizards and snakes? Then you've come to the right place. Select from about 230 species of lizard, from the extraordinary frill-necked lizard to the lethargic two-meter-long goanna, plus 140 species of snake and two species of crocodile. Relatively few people are killed annually by snake bites, and occasionally an incautious swimmer is taken by a crocodile—sometimes beside a sign warning against swimming (or, worse, beside a sign that *used* to be there but was pinched by a thoughtless tourist!).

Fewer than 20 species of Australian (and Outback) **snakes** have the potential to kill humans. The taipan is the deadliest, although its bite is not necessarily fatal if an antivenin is administered soon enough. Other snakes to be wary of include the tiger snake, the copperhead, the death adder, the common brown, and the common red-bellied black snakes. Additionally, more than 30 species of poisonous sea snakes frequent coastal waters, though they are rarely encountered by humans. Remember that snakes are no more delighted to meet you than you are to meet them. Most snake bites are the result of humans trying to kill the snake, or stumbling across one suddenly and startling it into attack. When hiking in the bush or Outback it's sensible to wear boots, thick socks, and long pants. Never stick your fingers into holes and be especially careful when poking around wood or rocks (did I really have to tell you that?). Tromp and stomp and any nearby snakes should sense your approach well in advance; most will simply move away—hopefully in the opposite direction.

The two types of **crocodiles** found in Australia, freshwater and saltwater (or "salties"), are now protected since hunting severely depleted their numbers. The salties, inhabitants of tidal estuaries along Australia's northern coastline, occasionally creep into freshwater territory and are *extremely dangerous.* Big and bulky, and growing up to seven meters long, salties viciously attack and kill humans. And make no mistake—they move *fast!* More finely built, shorter in length (three to four meters), and with smaller teeth, the freshwater croc usually sticks to a diet of fish and frogs. It has, however, been known to attack humans, especially to defend its nests.

Good advice: No matter how inviting the river or pool, and no matter how tantalizing the prospect of diving into its limpid depths, if there are crocodile warning signs, *always* resist the temptation to swim there. Most victims of crocodile attacks have ignored the warnings. It is worth going out of your way to see these magnificent creatures, but always treat them with the greatest respect and give them a wide berth!

Outback **lizards** are harmless to humans, but you might not believe that when you look at them. The very size of the giant perentie goanna, almost 2.5 meters long, is enough to

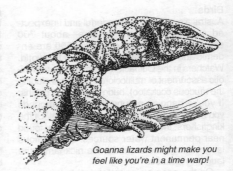

Goanna lizards might make you feel like you're in a time warp!

BOB RACE

keep most of its foes at bay. The goanna inhabiting central Australia is a sleek-appearing critter with distinctive yellow spots on its back; its large grey cousin hangs out around northern riverbanks.

Lazing about the western arid zone, the fierce-looking thorny, or mountain, devil dragon can change color to a limited extent and is covered with spines so sharp that no predator would contemplate eating it. *It,* on the other hand, has a fetish for eating nothing except heaps of black ants. The Top End's frill-necked lizard is another whose hiss is worse than its bite; when threatened, it unfurls a vividly colored ruff of membrane, which makes it appear much larger, and sways menacingly from side to side, spitting and hissing with gusto. The bearded dragon has the ability to flatten its body while sunbathing in its favorite arid-zone turf.

Giant leatherback turtles (one of Australia's dozen or so species of freshwater tortoise and five types of marine turtle) breed on some northern beaches, but they are under threat from driftnet fishing and suffocation from floating plastic bags that impersonate their favorite kind of jellyfish.

You can pick out 130 species of **frogs.** In the arid claypans where rains come only once every few years, some croakers survive by filling their bladders with water and burrowing into the mud just before it dries. There they coat their bodies with a mucilaginous secretion that seals in their juices for the next few years until rain falls again. In this way they might live for 40 years—unless they are dug up by Aborigines who use them as a source of fresh water.

Insects and Arachnids

Just as there are numerous bird species across Australia, there are some 50,000 insect species for them to feed on. These include 350 species of butterflies, 7,600 varieties of moths, and 18,000 types of beetles. New insect species are discovered with almost monotonous regularity.

Australia's 9,000 kinds of ants make it the mecca for ant scientists around the world. In some arid areas of Western Australia, there are more ant species in half a hectare than there are in the rest of the world.

Termites, also called "white ants" though they are not ants at all, are hard to miss; their humongous mounds, some in the shapes of pillars or tombstones, actually the topsides of nests, are eye-popping sights in the tropical north.

The various types of flies will soon become all too familiar to visitors with no interest in natural history, as will the staggering array of mosquitoes, midges, and other biting mites. Native bees and wasps are present as are the generally larger and more vicious European varieties. And, if the human race were to die out, cockroaches are already established in Australia, poised to take our place.

Mosquitoes cause the usual grief and are most bothersome in tropical areas. Ward them off with your choice of poisons, keep skin well covered, and sleep beneath netting; mosquito coils may or may not work. The rare but potentially fatal Ross River fever is a mosquito-induced malady with mononucleosis-like symptoms.

Thousands of spider species reside here, many of them large and hairy enough to feature in the most horrific Hollywood fantasy, but the only two which pose a threat to life and limb are the infamous red-back (kin to the black widow) and funnel-web spiders. Popular mythology places the red-back squarely under the seats of outdoor lavatories so that uneasy thoughts of tiny red spiders haunt many Australians' more intimate moments. Scientists tell us that only the female red-back is venomous, but it is hard to tell the difference in a creature so small. The funnel-web spider is the most toxic in the world and is confined to Sydney and its environs. Still, very few people in Australia have died from spider bites in the last two decades. Other Outback species to watch out for are the three varieties of scorpion, which like to hide inside shoes and clothing (clean or not), and the trap-door spider, which lives in underground holes.

The most ubiquitous, infuriating, and unsavory creature in the Australian biosphere is without a doubt the fly. In hotter months or after rains, Outback bushflies descend like a nightmarish scene out of a Hitchcock film. They are relentless: they want your sweat, they want your tears, they want your moistest orifice and live for the moment you drop your drawers. They will irritate you into resorting to the most ridiculous contrivance of a hat fitted with dangling corks, or covering your head with a fly net, drawstring tied snugly around your neck (it's amazing how the sadistic creatures know exactly when you're going to sneak a bite of food or sip a drink!). Repellents, such as Aerogard, are moderately effective. Blessedly, the little devils dissipate at nightfall. Tip: Both fly nets and repellents sell out fast in the Outback; try to stock up in one of the gateway cities. Or simply resort instead to waving your hand constantly in front of your face, like everybody else. This is known as the Great Australian Salute.

Marinelife

Australia's seas are filled with such diversity and abundance that this topic deserves its own book. The first sea creature that most Aussies would think of is the **shark.** Australians love the beach and the danger of shark attack is instilled into all swimmers from a tender age. Consequently, the shark has been hunted mercilessly and undeservedly, without regard to the vital part it plays in the overall marine ecology. As a result, the existence of some shark species is threatened. The largest sharks inhabit southern waters, the home of the white pointer which starred in *Jaws.* The best place to ogle these monsters is Dangerous Reef (hence the name) on South Australia's Eyre Peninsula. By the way, smaller sharks are the staple fish in fish 'n' chips shops, where they are called "flake."

Swimmers should also beware of the deadly **box jellyfish** (a.k.a. sea wasp or stinger), prevalent along tropical coastal waters and estuaries between late October and May. Unfortunately these are the exact spots and months when the beach looks oh-so-inviting. Steer clear! The translucent box jellyfish is very difficult to see and its potentially fatal bite elicits horrific pain, red welts, possible collapse, and the need for emergency medical help. Why do you think the locals stay away?

Fishing addicts, don't worry that Australia's aridity will prevent you from finding a catch of the day (or year). Whether your taste runs to game fishing a la Hemingway or dropping a line off the end of a pier, a fish waits for you! Surfing beaches usually provide space enough for surf fishing, and the reefs, bays, estuaries, and Outback rivers and pools are full of fish. Among the most sought-after Outback catches is the barramundi in northern Australia; abalone, crayfish, oysters, and prawns are also delicious and lucrative resources. Arid-zone fish are plentiful, though generally on the small side. The yellowbelly, or golden perch, found in Cooper Creek and the Diamantina River, defies the norm by growing as large as 20 kilograms. The spangled perch, a common catch throughout most of the country's coastal waters and inland streams as well as central Australia's Finke River, is one of the largest of its kind, growing up to one-half kilogram. Three other species of perch are found at Dalhousie Springs, near the Simpson Desert.

Most coastal areas of Australia are visited by **dolphins,** and surfers often tell of schools of dolphins frolicking with them while they surf. An isolated beach in Western Australia called Monkey Mia has become quite famous for the intimacy of its regularly visiting dolphins. Humans flock to this remote spot in such droves that there is a danger of the dolphins being frightened away or getting sick from too much human contact.

From June through October **southern right whales** can be seen during their annual breeding migration along the coastline between Yalata and the border. (See "Crossing the Nullarbor" in the South Australia chapter.)

southern right whale

BOB RACE

HISTORY

FIRST SETTLERS

Contrary to the assertion of most Australian school textbooks published before 1980, Australia was not discovered by Europeans, and certainly not by the intrepid Captain Cook. Australia's first settlers were the Aborigines, who arrived from Asia at least 40,000 years ago, and possibly as early as 100,000 years ago.

At that time the sea levels were very much lower than they are today, and the Australian landmass was connected to Papua New Guinea in the north and Tasmania in the south. Nevertheless, the water distance separating what was then Asia from this extended Australian continent was 100 km at its very shortest. The sea journey necessary to reach and colonize Australia was a remarkable achievement, especially when you consider that early Europeans had not yet reached some Mediterranean islands where the distances involved were a lot shorter. Aborigines had arrived and populated the entire continent millennia before the great expansionary movements of either the Europeans or the Polynesians.

At least 1,800 generations of Aborigines have lived in Australia with a simple but appropriate technology—a stark contrast to the eight or nine generations of Europeans with their highly inappropriate mechanical and agricultural technologies.

Early Aboriginal Society

Much of the archaeological evidence revealing Aboriginal history comes from places like Lake Mungo, an ongoing living excavation in southwest New South Wales. Sites like this are natural treasures because their remoteness and aridity has left the fossil record undisturbed. Lake Mungo used to lie on the edge of a vast inland sea, even at the time of the earliest Aboriginal relics, and huge piles of discarded bones and seashells (known as "middens") found there provide a fairly detailed peek into the daily life of the Aborigines.

Aborigines dwelt in hunter-gatherer societies, following the kangaroos, wallabies, goannas, and fish and collecting "bush food" like witchetty grubs, roots, seeds, honey, nuts, and berries. Conditions in Australia seem to have been so favorable and the bounties of nature so prolific that Aborigines never developed permanent agricultural settlements as their cousins in Papua New Guinea did. Their main tools were spears, three types of boomerang, sharpened stones for digging and shaping wood, and a spear-thrower called a woomera. They fished with nets, traps, and hooks. Controlled fires were started to flush game and, it has been suggested, as a land-management practice, since some forests have adapted to periodic bushfires. The remnants of elaborate stone weirs designed to trap fish can be seen in parts of Victoria and New South Wales. In northern Australia's wetlands bamboo-and-cord nets trapped end-of-wet-season fish, while woven nets were employed to snag wallabies and 'roos galavanting the Queensland tablelands.

Aborigines were split up into clans—a practice that still occurs today. Clan members were considered to be descendants of a common ancestor, bound by ritual, tradition, law, and—most importantly—to designated spiritual sites. Their religious belief decrees that, after death, clan members' spirits will return to these sites. Consequently, clan rituals to honor their Dreamtime creators and ancestral spirits are supremely important events, as are their spiritual links to the land. Designated members of the clan are responsible for keeping the ancestral spirits happy by protecting the sacred sites (hardly an easy task with white settlers and, later, tourists trampling upon them) or else risk traditional punishments and/or the wrath of the ancestral ones—disasters, sicknesses, and droughts are often signs that the spirits are mighty annoyed.

Parts of the Outback contain the harshest and most inhospitable environments on the planet, yet the Aborigines developed an affinity with the land that is a testament to their knowledge and skill. As recently as the mid-1980s, an Aboriginal family arrived at a remote Outback station, never before having had contact with whites. Their only possessions were two stone

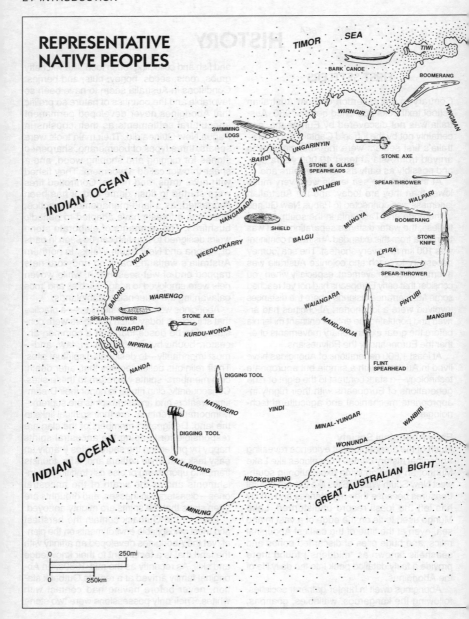

REPRESENTATIVE NATIVE PEOPLES

TIMOR SEA

TIWI

BARK CANOE

BOOMERANG

WIRNGIR

YUNGMAN

SWIMMING LOGS

UNGARINYIN

STONE AXE

BARDI

STONE & GLASS SPEARHEADS

WOLMERI

SPEAR-THROWER

NANGAMADA

WALPARI

MUNGYA

BOOMERANG

INDIAN OCEAN

SHIELD

BALGU

STONE KNIFE

WEEDOOKARRY

ILPIRA

SPEAR-THROWER

NOALA

WAIANGARA

PINTUBI

WARIENGO

MANDJINDJA

MANGIRI

BAIONG

SPEAR-THROWER

STONE AXE

INGARDA

KURDU-WONGA

INPIRRA

FLINT SPEARHEAD

NANDA

DIGGING TOOL

YINDI

NATINGERO

MINAL-YUNGAR

WANBIRI

DIGGING TOOL

WONUNDA

INDIAN OCEAN

BALLARDONG

NGOKGURRING

GREAT AUSTRALIAN BIGHT

MINUNG

0   250mi

0   250km

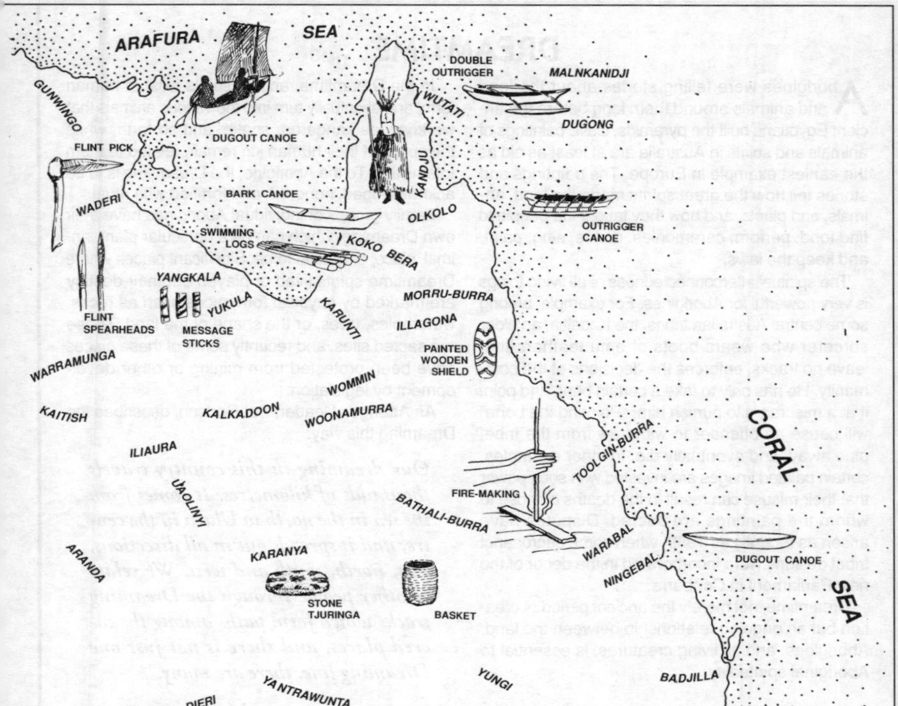
ARAFURA
SEA
DOUBLE OUTRIGGER
MALNKANIDJI
GUNWINGO
WUTATI
DUGONG
DUGOUT CANOE
FLINT PICK
KANDJU
WADERI
BARK CANOE
OLKOLO
OUTRIGGER CANOE
SWIMMING LOGS
KOKO BERA
YANGKALA
YUKULA
MORRU-BURRA
KARUNTI
FLINT SPEARHEADS
MESSAGE STICKS
ILLAGONA
PAINTED WOODEN SHIELD
WARRAMUNGA
WOMMIN
KAITISH
KALKADOON
WOONAMURRA
CORAL
ILIAURA
TOOLGIN-BURRA
UAOLINYI
FIRE-MAKING
BATHALI-BURRA
ARANDA
WARABAL
KARANYA
DUGOUT CANOE
NINGEBAL
SEA
STONE TJURINGA
BASKET
YUNGI
BADJILLA
YANTRAWUNTA
DIERI
GEEBRA
BARUNGA
SHIELD
KOMBAINGA
CARVED TREES
KAMILAROI
WIRANGO
WONGAJDYA
BAKANDI
INITIATION GROUND (BORA)
SPEAR-THROWER
MELJURNA
RED GUM CANOE
SPEAR-THROWER
KURIAL
HUMAN SKULL WATER VESSEL
WAWURUNG
WATER VESSEL FROM TREE KNOT
BARK CANOE
TANGANALUN
HAND USED FOR OMENS
BIDUELLI
TASMAN SEA
MOON

DREAMTIME

Aborigines were telling stories about the land and animals around them long before the ancient Egyptians built the pyramids. Cave paintings of animals and spirits in Australia are at least as old as the earliest example in Europe. The paintings and stories tell how the great spirits made the land, animals, and plants, and how they taught the people to find food, perform ceremonies, dance, sing, paint, and keep the laws.

The spiritual interconnectedness of all living things is very powerful for Aborigines. For example, among some central Australian tribes, the Kadaitja, an elder sorcerer who wears boots of emu feathers that leave no tracks, enforces the decisions of the community. He has only to take a certain bone and point it at a miscreant to punish him. "Pointing the bone" will cause an offender to withdraw from the tribe, pine away, and eventually die. In other examples, certain painted images are invested with such power that their misuse can result in the deaths of those to whom the paintings are sacred. Disputes have arisen as recently as 1989, when some sacrosanct tribal designs were incorporated in the decor of the new Parliament in Canberra.

Dreamtime, not merely the ancient period of creation but an ongoing relationship between the land, Aborigines, and all living creatures, is essential to Aboriginal spirituality.

In the Dreamtime, animal spirits exist in human form, and eventually turn into the various animals that we know as kangaroo, snake, and so forth, while the spirits of their human kin remain related to them totemically. To the Aborigine, the Dreamtime is to be acknowledged, honored, and fortified with ritual.

Family groups or individual Aborigines have their own Dreaming, which can be a particular plant, animal, place, or natural force. Significant places where Dreamtime spirits lived or played out their destiny are marked by physical formations such as rocks, waterholes, trees, or the shape of the land. These are sacred sites, and recently some of these places have been protected from mining or other development by legislation.

An Aboriginal leader, Pat Dodson, describes the Dreaming this way:

Our dreaming in this country travels thousands of kilometres. It comes from the sea in the north to Uluru in the centre, and it spreads out in all directions, east, north, south and west. We relate to other people through the Dreaming tracks which form paths among the sacred places, and there is not just one Dreaming line, there are many.

knives, two rubbing sticks to make fire, a container of dried worms, a boomerang, a spear, a woomera, and a dingo. In contrast, automobile clubs today advise travelers in the same terrain to carry the following equipment in their 4WD vehicles: long-range fuel tanks, water tanks, food for twice the expected stay, two spare wheels and tires, spare battery, tools, medicine, cooking gear, mosquito nets, blankets, maps, compass, and a radio!

Long before Captain Cook sailed into Botany Bay and formally "took possession" of their land on behalf of the British Crown, there were 700 Aboriginal tribal groups using some 300 different languages. Their population then is estimated at anywhere up to a million people, distributed in subgroups of up to 40. By that time theirs was an ancient, complex culture, rich and finely tuned to the environment. Like their American Indian counterparts, the Aborigines lived in a spiritual communion with the land. Concepts of land ownership (like that icon of European social order—the fence) implicit in Captain Cook's first act of possession, are alien to Aborigines: "We don't own the land," says Aboriginal poet Oodgeroo. "The land owns us."

European Contact

Like white Americans, European Australians have historically accorded the native culture and heritage little or no value. This attitude was encapsulated in the earliest recorded commentary on the Aborigines by a European, the gentleman pirate William Dampier, when he wrote in 1688: "The Inhabitants of this country are the Miserablest People in the World . . . they are long visaged and of very unpleasing Aspect, having no one graceful Feature in their Faces."

The complexity of the Dreamtime for most non-Aborigines is not simply that it is obscure. Many aspects of the culture are accessible only by initiation, and taboos forbid some ceremonial and spiritual practices to be even discussed. Men and women often have separate and exclusive ceremonies. Non-Aborigines often can only guess at the real significance and experience that underlies the Dreamtime stories. Here is a world where giant marsupials carve out the hills, the hills themselves are age-old marsupials frozen in moments of significance, the rivers are the tracks of the rainbow serpent, and the Milky Way is the river of the sky where, after the rainbow serpent has swallowed the sun, people fish for stingrays and turtles, and the stars are their campfires.

The Southern Cross is an especially significant constellation for all Australians. One Dreamtime myth gives this account of its creation: A father had four daughters. When he was old, he told his daughters that they had no one else to protect them and that when he died they might have to marry men they did not like. They agreed to meet him in the sky after he was dead. With the aid of a sorcerer, he spun a silver rope from the strands of his hair, and when he died, his four daughters climbed the rope to take up their positions as the four bright points of the Southern Cross. Their father is the brightest of the nearby pointers, Alpha Centauri, still watching over them.

The balance and harmony that Aborigines had developed and refined in their world was doomed to destruction with the first contact with land-owning Europeans who quickly "pioneered" beyond their first few coastal settlements. They brought in sheep and cattle, subsequently annihilating the waterholes that for millennia had supported many plants and animals—staples of the Aboriginal diet. Those sheep and cattle started looking mighty tempting to Aborigines, empty bellies growling with hunger. Thus the spears went a-flying, the cow pies hit the fan, and savage retaliation by the settlers left many Aborigines dead. The dispossession of the Aborigines came with brutal suddenness and more from epidemics of introduced diseases to which they had no immunity than from gunfire and violence. Aborigines died by the thousands from smallpox, sexually transmitted diseases, tuberculosis, measles, and influenza, all of which spread rapidly through the nonresistant native community. In addition there was a policy of "dispersal," in which Aborigines were cynically cleared like any other pest from areas valuable to the pastoralists—a sickening practice tantamount to massacre. Aborigines were even hunted "for sport"—an unofficial sport, of course—as recently as the 1950s in isolated parts of Australia.

The Tasmanian example illustrates the deliberate policy of genocide instigated by the invading Europeans. Aborigines were either killed or simply rounded up and shipped to small island colonies "for their protection," where they died of disease, malnutrition, and mistreatment. Tasmania's Aboriginal population declined from an estimated 4,000 to fewer than 500 between 1800 and 1830. By 1847 only 40 remained.

Truganini, the last Tasmanian, died in 1876. Her body was preserved and displayed in a museum. Hers was not the only body to receive such ignominious treatment. Scientists in the learned universities of Europe were excited by the search for a "missing link" to demonstrate Darwin's novel theories of evolution, and thought that the Tasmanian Aborigines might prove to be that link. Bodies were purloined from burial sites to enhance the anthropological collections of faculties from Dublin to Leipzig. In 1803, the governor of New South Wales presented the preserved head of the Aboriginal warrior Pemulwoy to botanist Sir Joseph Banks, who wrote that the head "caused some comical consequences when opened at the Customs House but when brought home was very acceptable to our anthropological collections." Today, the remains of some 3,000 Aborigines, together with objects of immense cultural value, lie moldering in British museums; Aboriginal groups have been negotiating for some time, with little success, to retrieve the bodies for proper burial.

Not everybody contributed to this genocide. There were well-meaning, sometimes enlightened, but usually ineffectual efforts to help. Reservations were created, rations issued, and religious missions established, many of which are still the focus of Aboriginal settlements today. However, by the beginning of the 20th century, most Aborigines were beggars in their own country, dependent on handouts of food and clothing (without the latter they were not allowed in the white man's towns), or they worked for white bosses without pay. (Not too long ago, I saw a newspaper photo of several Aboriginal entertainers on tour in America. Posing in costume, i.e., nearly naked, they were being presented with brand new suitcases.)

White society, if it thought at all about Aborigines, took a paternalistic approach, which resulted in legislation aimed at the "benevolent" protection of an inferior race for its own good. Aborigines were under the control of official guardians in the bureaucracy until very recent times. Children were sometimes taken from their families to be raised within the "civilizing" influence of urban, Christian folk. A form of segregation, with limits to movement, property restrictions, separate employment conditions, and regulated marriage, has existed in different forms from state to state until the last few decades. In fact, the infamous South African apartheid laws grew in part from the observations of a delegation, early this century, to Queensland, where the treatment of Aborigines was at its worst.

Up until 1939, official policy was still predicated upon the inhuman thesis that the Aborigines were a self-solving problem, meaning they would eventually die out. It was not until 1967 that Aborigines were granted the vote and the Department of Aboriginal Affairs was created by the government to legislate their needs. Australians are traditionally suspicious of attempts to alter the Constitution by referendum, and most referenda fail. So it is to Australia's credit that one of the very few to succeed was this landmark 1967 vote to grant Aborigines the same status as the rest of the community. Too bad it had to take so long. The full horror of the dispossession of the Aborigines is difficult for many Australians to grasp, and there is still an enormous gulf that separates the lives of white Australians from the ugly realities that Aborigines are laboring under even today.

ABORIGINES TODAY

Why change our sacred myths for your sacred myths?

—OODGEROO

Of the 18 million people who live in Australia today, fewer than two percent are Aborigines. The largest population of Aborigines (about 40,000) is in the Northern Territory where the first land-rights legislation returned some lands to their original owners. Altogether there are some 300 Aboriginal reserves totaling about 286,000 square kilometers.

Most Australians seldom ever see an Aborigine, but political pressure from Aboriginal groups means that they are no longer psychologically invisible. Issues like land rights, unlawful discrimination, and Aboriginal deaths in custody are much more likely to gain media attention today than just 10 years ago. Hand in hand with increased political struggle is a renaissance of Aboriginal identity through art, dance, and music. The 1988 Bicentennial celebrations, which marked two hundred years since the establishment of the first penal colony, saw protests and demonstrations from highly visible and vocal Aboriginal groups who tried to point out that the country was a bit older than that. Still, there's a long struggle ahead.

In most states Aborigines make up 25-40% of prison populations; infant mortality among Aborigines is twice the national average; Aboriginal children are affected by serious diseases like trachoma and hepatitis B at rates well above the national average; Aborigines are still more vulnerable to sexually transmitted disease; Aborigines have a life expectancy 20 years below the national average; unemployment among Aborigines is four times the national average; access to education and health services in remote areas, where most Aborigines live, is minimal; racial discrimination, while outlawed theoretically, is a constant reality for many Aborigines. Under these demoralizing conditions many (especially young and middle-aged men) are vulnerable to alcohol abuse, or worse, petrol-sniffing. Not surprisingly, domestic violence follows in the heavy footsteps of substance abuse.

But thanks largely to Aboriginal women who have been victimized, many communities now ban booze, and rehab programs have been implemented. Inroads have also been made by the Royal Commission into Aboriginal Deaths in Custody which, in its report to the federal Parliament, acknowledged the need for big changes in police practice and the justice system as they pertain to Aborigines. The Aboriginal and Torres Strait Islanders Commission (ATSIC), created in 1990, authorizes elected Aboriginal representatives to give input and exercise some control over a number of federally funded employment and social-works programs.

Land Rights

Advances on the land-rights issue are slow but have gained momentum since the '60s when the Yolngu people of Yirrkala in northeastern Arnhem Land had the audacity to present a petition (on a sheet of bark, no less) to the federal government, demanding recognition of their original ownership. As you might imagine, that action was dismissed quickly. But the Yolngu people—a tough-nut bunch—fought the matter all the way to court where (surprise) it was quashed in the Yirrkala Land Case of 1971, wherein the courts upheld the Australian government's credo of *terra nullius,* i.e., no one had lived in the island-continent before 1788. This outrageously racist stance eventually pressured the government into passing the Northern Territory Aboriginal Land Rights Act of 1976.

Three Aboriginal Land Councils were established to reclaim Aboriginal lands; however, the act applied only to the dregs of the Territory, deserts or semideserts, nothing within town boundaries or owned or leased by anyone else, i.e. *anyone* else. Even Kakadu and Uluru-Kata Tjuta (Ayers Rock and the Olgas) were declared exceptions, albeit *big* exceptions, because the land fell within boundaries already designated as conservation reserves. Thus the

ABORIGINAL ARCHAEOLOGICAL SITES

Lake Mungo, a World Heritage site in the Willandra Lakes region of southwestern New South Wales, is the undisputed badass of Aboriginal archaeological discoveries. Though the lake has been dried up for about 20,000 years, the site itself is an active excavation. Muddy, sandy embankments have eroded with time and weather, unearthing a treasure trove of human and animal remains that date back about 38,000 years. Other relics, such as fireplaces, tools, and leftover food (!) provide a good glimpse into the Aborigines' daily life. One extraordinary find was the 25,000-year-old cremated remains of a young woman—the world's first recorded cremation.

Northern Victoria's Kow Swamp has yielded a bounty of 10,000-12,000-year-old remains, while Keilor (near Melbourne and the international airport) has uncovered evidence of human occupation 40,000 years back. A relative baby (maybe 7,000 years old) was dredged up around Lake Nitchie in western New South Wales.

Tools and other artifacts, 20,000-40,000 years old, have been plucked from rock shelters at Miriwun on the Kimberley's Ord River, Mt. Newman in the Pilbara, and Malangangerr in Arnhem Land. Significant sites in southwestern Australia are the Swan Valley, where the oldest implements have been found, and Devil's Lair, near Cape Leeuwin in the very southwesternmost corner (near good surfing and vineyards).

Some of the oldest petroglyphs (Ice Age rock engravings) are located on the Nullarbor in South Australia's Koonside Cave. Other petroglyph-viewing spots include the Lightning Brothers locale (Delamere, Northern Territory), Early Man shelter (Laura, Queensland), Mootwingee National Park (far western New South Wales), and Burrup Peninsula (Damper, Western Australia).

Do I hear *terra nullius,* anyone?

lands were handed over with the provision that they were to be leased back to the Australian Nature Conservation Agency. The Aborigines do, however, constitute a majority of the management board and hold 99-year leases that are renegotiated in five-year increments. The co-managers, intrinsically knowledgeable about the delicate ecology and precious conservation of their formerly sacred sites, are snappy in their ranger uniforms as they give directions to ogling tourists.

The complex rules and regulations of the claiming process have meant years of haggles and hassles butting against the Territorial government, mining companies, and the federal conservation agency. Still, about one-half of the Northern Territory has or is being "processed." Some enterprising Aborigines have started small businesses and, as for those mining rights, the Aboriginal owners have accepted the majority of the mining companies' proposals. This is progress, no?

In South Australia, the semi-obscure Aboriginal Land Trust Act of 1966 established small reserves with but few rights. More far-reaching was the Pitjantjatjara Land Rights Act of 1981, which bestowed the Anangu Pitjantjatjara and Yankunytjatjara people with title to the Anangu Pitjantjatjara Lands in the far north, about 10% of the state's area. This was followed by the Maralinga Tjarutja Land Rights Act of 1984, which returned another eight percent of the state known as the Maralinga Lands to the Anangu people. This parcel, though conveniently located just south of the designated Anangu Pitjantjatjara Lands, is hardly choice property; it was widely contaminated in the 1950s and '60s by British nuclear testing. The Anangu retain the right to regulate liquor availability as well as access to their land. Mining is another story: an arbitrator makes the ultimate decision in any dispute between the Anangu people and the mining companies.

Land rights in the rest of Australia are still very limited. In Western Australia, where Aboriginal land constitutes about 13% of the state, the Aboriginal Affairs Planning Authority exercises dominion over only two-thirds of the Aboriginal reserves; they are granted 99-year leases for the remainder. Queensland allots less than two percent of that state to Aborigines, many of whom, because of the Queensland Aboriginal Land Act of 1991, are unable to claim their land. The Queensland Nature Conservation Act of 1992 commands that, should a claim to one of that state's parks prove successful, the Aboriginal owners must immediately lease it right back to the government—no future lease negotiations, no majority representation on the park management team, pretty much no nothing. New South Wales is not much better. That state's Aboriginal Land Rights Act of 1983 merely turned over the titles to already established Aboriginal reserves, with the possibility to claim a few other clumps of land as well as receiving some piddling privileges to the national parks. Provisions for land rights in Tasmania and Victoria are minuscule. (There are no Aborigines in Tasmania, you say? Guess what? They're back—well at least about 6,000 descendants are—and they're pushing to reclaim their land and heritage.)

On the national level, however, recent measures have been taken, if not to actually bond the Aborigines and the white folk, to at least reconcile them to one another's presence on the same land. A legal battle initiated in 1982 by Eddie Mabo and four other Torres Islanders over Queensland's Murray Islands culminated 10 years later with the ground-breaking Mabo Decision in which the High Court of Australia actually rejected terra nullius. This effectively acknowledged that Aborigines were the original owners of the land—yes, before the British! Nothing of the kind was ever done in the past. Despite adverse hoopla from pastoralists, mining, and other "special interest" groups, the Native Title Act was passed by federal Parliament in 1993 and implemented in 1994, paving the way for Aborigines to claim their rightful title. Sounds good, doesn't it? Don't kid yourself. There are so many limitations and complexities surrounding this law that claims will no doubt be tangled up in legal mumbo jumbo far into the future. And somehow those mining companies (and "significant others") don't seem to be whining as much; maybe because the small print reads that existing leases and ownership supersede Aboriginal land claims.

If the Aborigines believe the Australian government will truly return their land—well, they'd better keep on dreaming.

EUROPEAN SETTLEMENT

The ancient Greeks, who were quite comfortable with the notion that the earth was round, proposed without any concrete evidence that a large southern continent was necessary to preserve the earth's equilibrium. In the 2nd century A.D., the mathematician Ptolemy, conjecturing, mapped the "Terra Incognita," the Unknown Land. It was not until the great age of European exploration, more than a thousand years later, that these intuitions were confirmed. Following the sea routes opened up by Magellan, who entered the Pacific while exploring South America, Portuguese navigator Cristoval de Mendonca made an unauthorized trip to map much of the north and east coasts of Australia. This expedition violated the treaty between Spain and Portugal, which gave Spain all the lands west of Brazil, and so the discovery was kept hush-hush. As a result no European saw the east coast of Australia until Cook's expedition 240 years later.

As early as 1606, the Spanish navigator Torres, approaching from the west around southern Africa, sailed through the straits that separate Australia from Papua New Guinea and now bear his name. Willem Janzoon followed in the same year and entered the Gulf of Carpentaria. Seventeen years later, Jan Carstensz followed Janzoon's route and mapped the western coast of Cape York. In 1642, the Dutch almost completed the coastal surveillance of Australia when Abel Tasman circumnavigated Tasmania calling it "Van Diemen's Land," but he could see little potential for the mercantile interests that he largely represented.

By the end of the 17th century, the Dutch had poked about every part of Australia but the east coast. This was partly because they caught the prevailing westerlies as they rounded Cape Horn in Africa, sweeping them on to the lucrative markets of the East Indies. Interesting enough, many of the Europeans who found their way to Australia had simply overshot their mark on the way to the Spice Islands to the north.

The first Englishman to visit Australia, William Dampier, landed near King Sound on the northwest coast in 1688 with a rather disreputable company that had lost its way and needed to stop for repairs. He was so unimpressed with the desolate country that he could see no reason to return or to encourage his countrymen to do so.

It was not until 82 years later that the celebrated navigator Captain James Cook visited Australia and dragged it into the modern world. Cook had been sent to the South Pacific primarily to make astronomical observations of Venus and, while he was about it, to explore a region that was receiving more and more attention from the great powers of the day. After accomplishing his scientific mission, he returned, circumnavigating New Zealand. On 20 April 1770, he sighted the southeast coast of Australia. He turned north and charted the length of the east coast. His first landfall was "a fine bay," which Cook later called "Botany Bay" because of the numerous botanical specimens they were able to collect there.

Cook continued north for 3,000 kilometers until his ship *Endeavor* ran aground on a coral reef near what is now Cooktown in north Queensland. It took his crew two months to repair the damage before they sailed north through Torres Strait. On an island three kilometers off Cape York, which he named Possession Island, Cook raised the Union Jack and formally took possession of the eastern part of the continent. British law enabled him to do this as long as the land was regarded as *terra nullius* or unoccupied. This legalistic form of finders-keepers could only be sustained subsequently if the Aborigines were ignored or, worse, considered as less than human. And so it was all the way up to 1992, when the High Court of Australia finally rejected *terra nullius,* and acknowledged that the Aborigines were the original title-holders. (See "Land Rights," above.)

Colonization

Cook's discovery of Australia was timely for British interests in more than one way. Cook was excited by the tall straight trunks of the Norfolk pine that grew in this new land, thinking they would make excellent masts for the expanding British navy. As it turned out they were not suitable, but Britain had recently lost its colonies in the American War of Independence, and so with them went a cheap and easy way of disposing of the convicts that were clogging

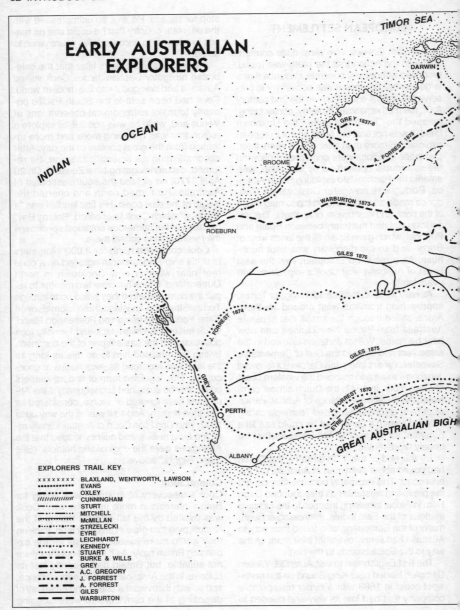

EARLY AUSTRALIAN EXPLORERS

TIMOR SEA

DARWIN

INDIAN OCEAN

GREY 1837-8

A. FORREST 1879

BROOME

WARBURTON 1873-4

ROEBURN

GILES 1876

J. FORREST 1874

GILES 1875

GREY 1839

J. FORREST 1870

PERTH

J. FORREST 1870

EYRE 1840

GREAT AUSTRALIAN BIGH

ALBANY

EXPLORERS TRAIL KEY

xxxxxxxx	BLAXLAND, WENTWORTH, LAWSON
••••••••••	EVANS
• •• •• ••	OXLEY
///////////	CUNNINGHAM
— •• — ••	STURT
— • — •	MITCHELL
⌐⌐⌐⌐⌐⌐	McMILLAN
— •••• —	STRZELECKI
▪▪▪▪▪▪▪	EYRE
••••••••	LEICHHARDT
•• •• ••	KENNEDY
••••••••••	STUART
— • — •	BURKE & WILLS
— •• — ••	GREY
— ••• —	A.C. GREGORY
▪ ▪ ▪ ▪	J. FORREST
••••••••	A. FORREST
•••••••••	GILES
— — — —	WARBURTON

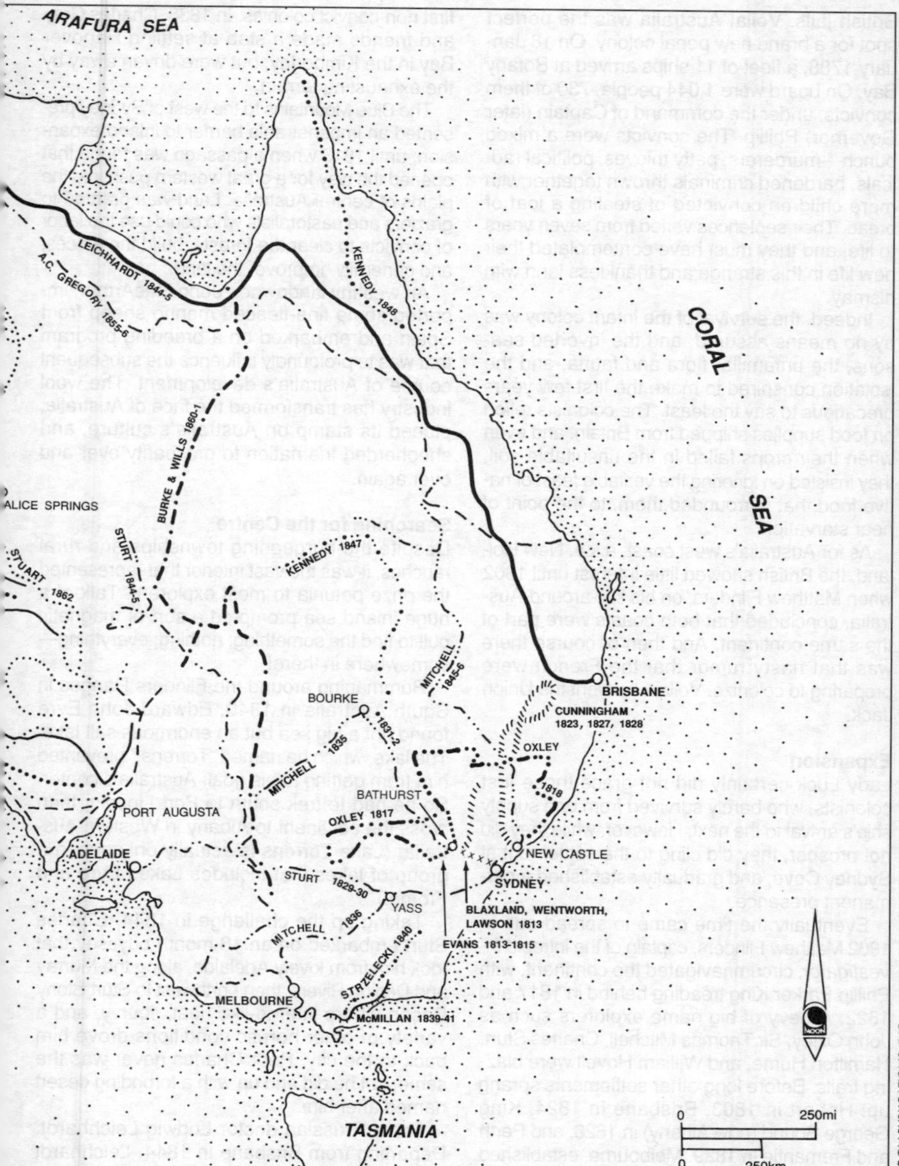

ARAFURA SEA

CORAL SEA

LEICHHARDT 1844-5

A.C. GREGORY 1855-6

KENNEDY 1848

ALICE SPRINGS

STUART 1862

STUART 1844-5

BURKE & WILLS 1860-1

KENNEDY 1847

BOURKE

MITCHELL 1831-2

MITCHELL 1845-6

BRISBANE

CUNNINGHAM 1823, 1827, 1828

OXLEY 1818

MITCHELL 1835

BATHURST

OXLEY 1817

NEW CASTLE

PORT AUGUSTA

STURT 1829-30

SYDNEY

ADELAIDE

BLAXLAND, WENTWORTH, LAWSON 1813

MITCHELL 1836

YASS

EVANS 1813-1815

STRZELECKI 1840

MELBOURNE

McMILLAN 1839-41

TASMANIA

250mi

250km

0

British jails. Voila! Australia was the perfect spot for a brand new penal colony. On 18 January 1788, a fleet of 11 ships arrived at Botany Bay. On board were 1,044 people, 730 of them convicts, under the command of Captain (later Governor) Phillip. The convicts were a mixed bunch—murderers, petty thieves, political radicals, hardened criminals thrown together with mere children convicted of stealing a loaf of bread. Their sentences varied from seven years to life, and they must have contemplated their new life in this strange and thankless land with dismay.

Indeed, the survival of the infant colony was by no means assured, and the inverted seasons, the unfamiliar flora and fauna, and the isolation conspired to make the first few years precarious to say the least. The colonists relied on food supplies shipped from Britain, and even when their crops failed in the unsuitable soil, they insisted on ignoring the veritable feast of native food that surrounded them, to the point of near starvation.

As for Australia's west coast, a.k.a. New Holland, the British showed little interest until 1802 when Matthew Flinders, on his sail-around-Australia, concluded that both coasts were part of the same continent. And then of course there was that nasty rumor that the French were preparing to colonize. Voila—up went the Union Jack.

Expansion

Lady Luck certainly did not grace those first colonists, who barely survived from one supply ship's arrival to the next. However, while they did not prosper, they did cling to the settlement at Sydney Cove, and gradually established a permanent presence.

Eventually the time came to spread out. In 1802 Matthew Flinders, captain of the intrepid *Investigator,* circumnavigated the continent, with Phillip Parker King treading behind in 1817 and 1822. A bevy of big name explorers such as John Oxley, Sir Thomas Mitchell, Charles Sturt, Hamilton Hume, and William Hovell were blazing trails. Before long other settlements sprang up: Hobart in 1803, Brisbane in 1824, King George Sound (now Albany) in 1826, and Perth and Fremantle in 1829. Melbourne, established in 1835, and Adelaide, in 1836, were Australia's first non-convict colonies. In 1838, Charles Grey and friends made a stab at settling Hanover Bay in the Kimberley, but were driven away by the exhausting terrain.

The Blue Mountains to the west of Sydney presented an impenetrable barrier to inland expansion, until 1813 when a passage was found that opened the way for a great western push into the plains of central Australia. Land was granted to graziers and pastoralists who could use the labor of convicts to clear the forests, build the fences, and generally "improve" the land.

An wealthy landowner, John MacArthur, imported some fine-fleeced merino sheep from Spain and embarked on a breeding program that was to profoundly influence the subsequent course of Australia's development. The wool industry has transformed the face of Australia, placed its stamp on Australia's culture, and shepherded the nation to prosperity over and over again.

Searching for the Centre

Despite the burgeoning townships and rural ranches, it was the vast interior that represented the prize petunia to most explorers. Talk of a huge inland sea prompted a sort of magnetic pull to find the something; nothing; everything—somewhere in there!

Rummaging around the Flinders Ranges in South Australia in 1840, Edward John Eyre found not a big sea but an enormous salt lake. The lake, which he named "Torrens," prevented him from getting to his goal: Australia's center. So he had to trek south to Port Lincoln, then cross the continent to Albany in Western Australia. (Lake Torrens is actually only one in a group of lakes that includes Lakes Eyre and Frome.)

Taking up the challenge in 1844, Charles Sturt embarked on an 18-month odyssey that took him from lovely Adelaide, along the Murray and Darling Rivers, then northwest to Sturt Stony Desert where inferno-like heat, scurvy, and a variety of other horrific conditions drove him back to the city. Poor Charles never was the same, but he did end up with a forboding desert named after him.

Enter Prussian doctor Ludwig Leichhardt. Departing from Brisbane in 1844, Leichhardt and his men made an historic 14-month crossing between Darling Downs and Port Essington, near Darwin, and were credited with finding potential farmlands for pastoral expansion. Unfortunately, the heroic Leichhardt vanished two years later while attempting another crossing. In the same year that Leichhardt went poof, the Edmund Kennedy expedition also met a dismal demise. Trekking from Rockingham Bay, south of Cairns, to Cape York in northern Queensland, a combination of bad strategy, illness, and Aboriginal attack wiped out Kennedy and most of his men.

In 1860 the Burke and Wills expedition was running neck-in-neck with that of John Mac-Douall Stuart, as they raced to conquer Australia's mysterious center and to forge the best route for the overland telegraph line soon to begin in Darwin.

Explorers Robert O'Hara Burke and William John Wills had money, men, and equipment aplenty, but still they did not fare very well. Departing Melbourne, Burke and Wills left most of their men at Menindee, southeast of Broken Hill. After establishing a depot at Coopers Creek, only four members of the expedition headed any farther: Burke, Wills, John King, and Charles Grey.

Summer. Ah, a marvelous time for a 1,100 kilometer stroll through central Australia up to the Gulf of Carpentaria. They eventually achieved their goal—it was the return journey that was the killer. Grey bit the dust first, followed by Burke and Wills, who actually made it back to the Coopers Creek depot only to find their loyal mates had split back to Menindee that same morning. You can still visit the Dig Tree with its carved message on the Cooper Creek banks. John King, however, survived, thanks to nursing by local Aborigines.

Meanwhile, John MacDouall Stuart turned out (in some ways) the big winner. A much better planner, Stuart had traveled roundtrip from Adelaide to Chambers Bay on the north coast, east of Darwin—a route eventually mimicked by the original road, railway, and overland telegraph lines. He went down in history as the first explorer to reach Australia's geographical center, but then he just went down, period, losing his vision, memory, and his life soon after his journey.

As for that big inland sea, it turned out to be the vast, dry Outback interior. No oasis, just a *big* mirage.

Western Exploration

Except for settlements at Perth and Fremantle, the western half of Australia remained virtually undiscovered by The White Man until the latter part of the nineteenth century when a handful of intrepid explorers ventured into the region: William Gosse, aiming west from the Alice Springs telegraph station, stumbled upon Uluru (Ayers Rock); Ernest Giles bumped into Kata Tjuta (the Olgas) on his crossing attempt, then made a later expedition from between the Gascoyne River to Kata Tjuta and the telegraph line; Major John Warburton, also trying to locate a westward route from Alice Springs, eventually forged his way to the Oakover River; from the west coast, John Forrest made expeditions from Geraldton to the Overland Telegraph Line, and from Perth to Fowlers Bay in South Australia.

The 1890s brought a series of scientific expeditions into the region to check out flora and fauna, rocks and minerals, and lifestyles of the local Aborigines. Explorations were conducted northeast of Coolgardie by David Lindsay (in charge of the Elder Scientific Exploring Expedition), while the territory west and south of Alice Springs was covered by the Horn Expedition. Prospector David Carnegie staked a route from Coolgardie to Halls Creek while, around the same time, the Calvert Expedition did not survive its foray around Western Australia's Great Sandy Desert.

It was Alfred Canning, in 1906, who mapped out his famous Canning Stock Route southwest from Halls Creek to Wiluna in Western Australia—a barren, treacherous track through the Great Sandy and Gibson deserts and a thumbs-up favorite with diehard four-wheel-drivers.

Gold and the Australian Psyche

The discovery of gold in the 1850s sparked a gold rush that brought huge numbers of hopeful prospectors from around the world.

Edward Hargraves began the fury in 1851. The news of even his relatively small find at Ophir, near Bathurst in New South Wales, was all it took to start the fever. Diggers came flocking, first to Ophir, and then to Turon. The Victorian government, none to happy with the migration to its neighboring state, offered a reward for gold discovery closer to, say, their own

Melbourne. Within a month gold was discovered at Clunes, followed by the extraordinary finds at Ballarat, Castlemaine, and Bendigo, thereby establishing Victoria as a center of wealth and influence.

Spawned by an 1887 find in Southern Cross, Western Australia, the rush rushed westward. Five years later, Arthur Bayley staked an astoundingly huge claim near Coolgardie, then came an even larger find by three Irish prospectors at neighboring Kalgoorlie. This so-called "Golden Mile" is supposedly the world's richest area of gold-bearing earth. Once the country's poorest and most undeveloped state, Western Australia's population soared; the place was on the map—even European opera stars traveled to the wild mining settlements to have gold nuggets thrown at their feet. Even today, Western Australia is the country's richest state.

The opulence and grandeur of Melbourne and the cities that grew up around the gold mines were the exuberant expressions of an unprecedented boom. Vast fortunes were made and Australian society was transformed almost overnight. Gold fever brought Prussians, Americans, Italians, Chinese, and—of course—more English, Irish, Scottish, and Welsh. Today, Darwin's mix of over 50 ethnic groups reflects the demographic wealth brought about by the gold rush. A tiny provincial society was inundated with intellectuals, merchants, entrepreneurs, professionals, artists, and adventurers ready to take advantage of new opportunities that seemed to be opening up everywhere.

Economic and social consequences aside, the gold rush gave birth to a peculiarly Australian ethos, that of "mateship." In many other parts of the English-speaking world, "mate" means a marriage partner; in Australia it also means a friend, and as a form of address, it carries an unspoken appeal to deep levels of devotion, loyalty, and affection that come from a tradition of interdependence that was born in the crucible of the goldfields. This fraternal tradition remains deeply entrenched in the Australian psyche.

It was on the goldfields near Ballarat that the Eureka Stockade incident took place. With easily extractable ore already mined, the "diggers" were forced to sink deeper and more elaborate shafts, causing mining costs to increase. As a result the gold miners' license fee became the subject of outraged protest. The dispute between the miners and the government agents became so heated that a group of diggers who refused to pay the fee built a stockade at a place called Eureka, and fought government troops on 3 December 1854. Thirty diggers died and the incipient rebellion was quashed, but the event remains significant as an expression of what author Thomas Keneally calls "that most Australian of birthrights, the Fair Go." This is a central concept for Australians, involving a sense of natural justice based on common sense, equality, and a healthy disregard for authority and ideology.

The Bushrangers

A passion for the "fair go" flows on as a sympathy for the underdog, the "battler." This accounts for the affection—almost reverence—rogues and outlaws command in the popular imagination, particularly the 19th-century bushrangers. The most famous of them was Ned Kelly, whose distinctive homemade helmet and suit of armor have become icons of Australian culture. Kelly came from an Irish family of small selectors (cockatoo farmers, or "cockies") whose frequent conflict with wealthy pastoralists, or "squatters," and the authorities led them into a miniature revolt. After seeing their mother imprisoned and serving time themselves for uncommitted crimes, the Kelly brothers took to the bush and began a brief but spectacular career as bank robbers. Ned Kelly often brazenly and single-handedly captured entire townships for days at a time. His reputation grew until he was captured after a siege at Glenrowan in which he received 28 gunshot wounds. He was taken to Beechworth where a sensational trial took place, then transported to Melbourne to be hanged. "Tell them I died game," he said, awaiting execution. On the gallows his last words summed up the battler's philosophy: "Such is life."

There were many other bushrangers—Bold Ben Hall, Mad Dog Morgan, Frank Gardiner, Martin Cash (who was one of only a few to escape the infamous Port Arthur penal colony in Tasmania), Bogong Jack, Midnight—and it is interesting to note that much of the mythology about them centers around the unfair and treacherous circumstances of their capture and death. Traditionally, Australians have tolerated almost every kind of social aberration, but they draw the line at the arbitrary exercise of power and privilege by the strong over the weak.

Social Reform

By the end of the 19th century the scene was set for further social upheaval. Labor was organizing itself and leading the world in a militant struggle for workers' rights. The Australian Labor Party was founded over 100 years ago in 1891, and that same year a wave of strikes for better wages and conditions culminated in the famous Shearers' Strike, which was ruthlessly put down by the wealthy landowners who employed scabs, or "blacklegs," to bring in the all-important wool clip (crop). Labor leaders were imprisoned, which led to the cry: "If they jail a man for striking, it's a rich man's country yet." If the cardinal virtue in Australia is mateship, the two deadly sins are scabbing and dobbing—informing against one's mates.

On 1 January 1901, after a decade of debate and negotiation, the six Australian colonies were joined in a federation of states with the passage of the Constitution by the British Parliament. The new federal government met in Melbourne until moving to the new capital, Canberra (designed by the fashionable architect Walter Burley Griffin), in 1927. Australia continued to pioneer policies of social reform that did not go unnoticed elsewhere in the world. For example, Australia was the first country to elect Labor representatives and the first country to elect a Labor government. It was one of the first countries to grant women the vote.

These notable developments came to the attention of Lenin, who wrote a tract on the Australian Labor Party. He concluded that it was a tool of the bourgeoisie. Nevertheless, a number of progressive developments were enshrined in Australian legislation long before they were achieved elsewhere. The old-age pension, the eight-hour workday, the right to strike—all these became realities in Australia when other nations would not even tolerate their advocacy.

While Australia achieved its independence from Britain without bloodshed, it still remained emotionally and psychically bound to the mother country. Britain remained Australia's chief trading partner and military ally through two world wars. The decline of the British Empire

and the emergence of the United States as a world power meant merely that dependence was transferred from one to the other. More recently, however, talk of breaking with the monarchy and creating a brand new Republic of Australia is rife in the air from Outback pubs to city clubs. Many Australians would like to see this change instigated by the year 2000—possibly as an Olympic event?

World Wars

The first world war terribly scarred the generation that took part in it. Australia's first action was at Gallipoli in the Dardanelles, where, hopelessly outnumbered and outpositioned by a firmly entrenched Turkish army, thousands of young Australians were slaughtered. The incident was so profoundly shocking to a young nation that the sacrifice and suffering of those Anzacs (Australia and New Zealand Army Corps) has never been forgotten.

Perhaps the most moving story of that conflict concerns a young soldier, Simpson, who with his donkey rescued the injured and dying without regard for his own safety. Eventually he fell to a sniper's bullet, but Simpson and his donkey have an honored place in the national consciousness.

Australians went on to fight on the battlefields of Europe and, if nothing else, their experiences helped to open the eyes of an insular and isolated community to the wider world. This process was terribly gradual and, despite its proximity to Asia, Australia for years regarded itself as an outpost of the British Empire.

The 1920s brought increased prosperity, largely through the export of primary produce. Refrigeration had made possible the shipment of frozen meat over the enormous distances necessary to reach markets in Europe; Australia was said to ride once again on the sheep's back. Unable to avoid the worldwide depression of the 1930s, Australians suffered all the hardships that were familiar to people in America and Europe, and—with the outbreak of WW II— once again took up arms for king and country. This time, however, there was a direct threat from Japan and, while Australians fought in Europe and Africa, they also had to defend their own land. An air raid on Darwin by Japanese bombers created an unprecedented response and helped cement a military alliance with the United States that continues today. General Douglas MacArthur's proud boast that he would return to the Philippines was made possible in part by retreating and regrouping on the Australian mainland.

Changing Times

After the war, social change picked up tempo. A positive immigration drive replaced the infamous White Australia Policy, which had restricted entry to Australia largely to white Anglo-Saxons. Displaced refugees from Europe were recruited to come for a new start in the land of opportunity. For many, the realities did not measure up to the promise, but, nevertheless, ever-increasing numbers of Italians, Greeks, Hungarians, Yugoslavs, and peoples from a host of other countries began to make their presence felt.

It is often hard now for Australians to appreciate just how staid, unimaginative, and limited their society was only a few decades ago. The isolated Outback, as might be expected, has almost always possessed a typically anarchic "we make our own rules" nature, while the Western Australians are plain and simply "laid back," like their Southern California geographic counterparts. Other parts of the country, particularly the east coast, were slightly on the uptight side. In Melbourne, for example, no alcohol could be sold after six o'clock, which led to the degrading "six o'clock swill," as patrons rushed into hotels after work and downed as many beers as quickly as they could. "Wowserism," or puritanism, ensured that virtually no activity of any kind, except church-going, could take place on Sunday. A combination of the influx of more sophisticated migrants and the liberating influence of the youth culture of the '60s has irreversibly transformed the face of Australian society over the past two or three decades.

During the same period, Australia's traditional allegiance to Britain became more and more irrelevant. Meanwhile, Britain has gradually divested itself of its colonial heritage and turned more and more toward a future in Europe. With Britain's entry into the Common Market, Australia lost automatic access to its traditional markets and was forced to face the reality of its location on the edge of Asia. The increasing numbers of European and, later, Asian migrants felt

no sentimental attachment to the British institutions that had figured so largely in the minds of Anglo-Saxon Australians.

Finally, Australia's strategic position in the South Pacific brought it into the sphere of American influence. Since the 1950s, Australian troops have answered the call from Washington, not London, first in the Korean War and more disastrously in the Vietnam War. Australia's longest-serving prime minister, Sir Robert Menzies, once said of Queen Elizabeth, "I did but see her passing by, and yet I love her till I die," much to the dismay of independence-minded Australians. Nothing could better illustrate the dramatic shift in cultural focus that has taken place in Australia than the words of his successor, Harold Holt, at the height of the Vietnam War: "All the way with L.B.J."

AUSTRALIA TODAY

Australia describes itself as a multicultural society, and it is perhaps the most cosmopolitan society in the world, with almost one quarter of its present population having been born elsewhere. The benefits of such a wide mix of ethnic, cultural, and religious backgrounds are immense and, although the potential for social discord undoubtedly exists, somehow the friction that characterizes similarly heterogeneous communities has rarely occurred in Australia. Whether this is due to a tradition of easygoing tolerance, or to an ambience of apathy which infects all new arrivals, Australia's numerous ethnic communities have achieved a harmony that would be unthinkable in many parts of the world.

That is not to say that discrimination and prejudice do not exist, but most Australians have grown to appreciate the differences that succeeding waves of migrants bring to their society—from the novelty of new foods (Australia boasts some fabulous—and tony—ethnic restaurants) to the challenge of learning new languages, customs, and ways of thinking.

It would be wrong to suggest that Australians are a race of Paul Hogans laconically tossing prawns onto barbies, or Greg Normans playing endless rounds of golf (though it would be terrific if *Strictly Ballroom* hearthrob Paul Mercurio, in his skimpy ad-campaign briefs, represented all the men). Beneath the gloss of tourist promotions is a dark side—Australians consume more alcohol and pain killers per capita than any other English-speaking country. Like other developed countries, Australia is plagued by recession, unemployment, a blowout of foreign debt, natural disasters, and pressing environmental degradation. Having a small population, and a tax base that is minuscule compared to that of larger industrialized countries, Australia is helpless in the face of international economic developments. For decades, the country has relied on the export of primary produce and now finds that its markets are increasingly unreliable, while prices are out of control. A new drive to turn the "Lucky Country" into the "Clever Country" has been launched to stop the flight of its scientists and technicians to the universities and research companies of America and Europe, and at the same time develop the "sunrise" industries necessary for a high-technology future. New high-technology cities, or the "Multi-function Polis," are planned in partnership with the Japanese, the first having already been approved at a site near Adelaide.

Aborigines have made strides because of the Native Titles Act, and through international recognition of their art, music, and culture. The harsh Outback has become romanticized through films and books—and the more far-fetched the better.

Australians have developed a unique laissez-faire attitude, embodied in the expressions "no worries" and "she'll be right," and it seems difficult to rouse them to action. The advantage of this approach is that life in Australia is remarkably relaxed and stress-free, even in the cities. Violence and the social blight of drug abuse have not quite reached the heights that most Americans would consider normal. Access to a comfortable standard of living is easier in Australia than almost anywhere else on earth. The price for such a self-satisfied lifestyle is indolence, apathy, and procrastination, and Australians are only just beginning to realize how precarious their delightful existence is.

Australia is changing, and never more so than now. The past has forced Australians to be innovative and adaptable because of their extreme isolation. Air travel, which so many Australians helped to pioneer, and the information superhighway have meant that Australia no longer must labor under the "tyranny of distance."

Despite its very real problems, Australia still has a refreshing, overriding sense of optimism—hey, South Australia still has its festivals; Northern Territory and Outback, their mystique; Queensland, the reef; New South Wales, its harbor; Victoria, her restaurants; Tasmania, its wild beauty; and Western Australia, the surfers and prospects of gold. So, what's the problem, mate?

GOVERNMENT

For a country of only 18 million people, Australia has an awful lot of government. It is a measure of Australians' political apathy that they have allowed themselves to become, according to some commentators, one of the most over-governed peoples in the free world. Australians labor under three tiers of government—federal, state, and shire or municipal. There are six state governments, two assemblies for the territories, and 900 local government bodies. All are accompanied by the appropriate bureaucracies, red tape, and seals of approval (or disapproval).

STRUCTURE

Australia follows the American example in the separation of powers, whereby the executive, legislative, and judiciary are independent. The federal government is an odd mix of the British Westminster system and the American congressional system. Australia's Constitution is an Act of the British Parliament, passed in 1901, which provides for a House of Representatives, whose 147 members (divided on the basis of population) are elected every four years, and an upper house, the Senate, whose function is to act as a house of review and provide equal representation for each state, thereby preserving state rights. The political party with most members in the House of Representatives becomes the governing party and the prime minister is elected from within that majority. Regional breakdowns for house members are: New South Wales, 50; Victoria, 38; Queensland, 25; Western Australia, 14; South Australia, 12; Tasmania, 5; Australian Capital Territory, 2; and Northern Territory, 1.

Canberra (Australian Capital Territory, or ACT) is home to the federal Parliament and other government agencies, as well as foreign embassies. Surrounded on all sides by New South Wales and on its own piece of land, Canberra resembles Washington D.C., but it's not nearly as exciting.

The formal head of state is still the Queen of England, although her powers are vested in the governor-general, who is nominated by the Australian government of the day. (With all the current buzz about ditching the monarchy, however, the title Governor-General may soon transmute into President of the Republic of Australia.) Under the Australian Constitution, the governor-general, being the chief executive, has the power to dissolve Parliament, ratify legislation, appoint ministers of the government, command the armed forces, and appoint judges to the high court. Under an unwritten convention, the governor-general acts, in a mainly titular capacity, under the instructions and advice of the prime minister, as does the queen.

Many Australians remember with outrage the events of 11 November 1975, when Governor-General Sir John Kerr dismissed the Labor government of Prime Minister Gough Whitlam, thus bucking the customary hierarchy. Right before a general election Whitlam couldn't pass supply bills through the hostile Senate, agitated by the governor-general. The intricacies and implications of that decision still reverberate in the corridors of Parliament House and the case is still a hotly debated point for many Australians.

The Senate is made up of 12 senators from each state and two from each territory. State senators are elected for six years, but only half the Senate faces the electorate every three years. Territory senators serve a maximum of three years, their terms coinciding with those of House members. Because the popular mandate only affects those senators who stand for reelection, this has often led to the situation in which the House of Representatives faces a hostile Senate. The Senate, while theoretically a house of review, is able to block legislation—as it did in the crisis of 1975.

State governments are microcosms of the federal structure and are bicameral, with the exception of Queensland, which disbanded its upper house as soon as it could. Numerous attempts in other states to follow that example have all been met with the in-built suspicion with which Australians treat politicians who start tinkering around with the system: it is axiomatic that politicians are not to be trusted, so if they want to do something it is much safer not to let them do it. Consequently, most states are lumbered with unwieldy edifices of government. With the exception of the Northern Territory, which is governed by a chief minister, the states are run by individual premiers. Aside from renegade Queensland and the Northern Territory, upper houses in the states are known as the Legislative Council; lower houses in New South Wales, Victoria, and Western Australia are the Legislative Assembly; lower houses in South Australia and Tasmania are the House of Assembly. The state governments are based in each capital city.

The struggle between the state and federal governments is ongoing. The Constitution gave the states considerable powers, many of which have been whittled away by the federal government over the years. States have responsibilities for health, housing, education, justice, and transport, but they have lost much of their power to raise revenue and must receive grants from Canberra, which controls the power of taxation. The control of natural resources is under the jurisdiction of the states, but the federal government has used its powers to make foreign policy (particularly by entering the World Heritage Treaty) to block development in environmentally sensitive areas of Tasmania and Queensland. Other federal controls consist of the usual matters concerning defense, foreign policy, immigration, the economy, and the postal service.

Australia has a plethora of local governments, responsible for collecting rubbish, mending holes in the road, giving out parking tickets, and holding up homeowners' plans to renovate their kitchens. Councilors are mostly unpaid, except for the widely publicized case of the mayor of Brisbane who, it turned out, was earning more than the prime minister.

POLITICS

Parties

Historically, Australian politics has been effectively dominated by a two-party system. The Australian Labor Party (ALP) has traditionally drawn its support from the union movement but in recent times has extended its base to white-collar workers and liberals. The Liberal Party (LP), drawing its support from private enterprise, small business, and the professions, is the principal partner in a conservative coalition with the rural-based National Party. Recently, the Australian Democrats (AD), a centrist party with a strong environmental platform, and various Green Independent parties have made inroads into the two-party system. (But in 1984, some Greens supported Midnight Oil rock singer Peter Garrett as he tried for a Senate seat under the Nuclear Disarmament Party banner; after he lost, the party pretty much disbanded.) In 1996 the Australian Labor Party and the Liberal Party were running neck-in-neck in Senate representation, while in the House of Representatives the ALP had stretched way ahead. The Australian Democrats currently hold seven Senate seats.

The drive to make the final break with Britain and declare Australia a republic has recently intensified. Former Prime Minister Paul Keating pushed hard for it, and the Queen didn't object! (Is this good or bad?) A government-established Republic Advisory Committee is advising details on the changes involved, including the flag (currently with the Union Jack in the upper left corner) and the national anthem. The turnover, which will require a referendum, is poised to become reality by the year 2000, when the Olympic athletes flame their way into Sydney.

Voting

Because of the huge variations in population density across Australia, it has never been possible to achieve "one vote, one value." Rural electorates can be quite enormous in area but still have fewer electors than inner-city seats, so there is an inevitable gerrymander that favors rural communities, traditionally the most conservative voting block.

Voting is mandatory for all citizens over 18; electors who fail to vote are liable for a fine. Voluntary voting was tried in the '20s, but the turnout was so abysmally low that it was abandoned. Voting is preferential and candidates on the ballot must be numbered in order of the elector's preference. This has made it necessary for political parties to produce "how to vote" cards and hand them out at polling booths, to instruct their supporters in the best manner of distributing their preferences. Some Senate ballot papers have had over 60 candidates, and voters have had to number each one for their vote to be valid. This system has given rise to the "donkey vote" in which a lazy, bored, or hurried voter will simply number the candidates in order down the page. So widespread did this practice become that it has decided the outcomes of several close ballots, and candidates with names at the beginning of the alphabet enjoyed such an advantage that they have been known to change their names to secure the donkey vote. To counter this practice, candidates' positions on the ballot are now determined by random selection.

International Relations

The Australian government is signatory to a number of international treaties including ANZUS, a joint-defense pact between Australia, New Zealand, and the United States. Recently, New Zealand was suspended from this arrangement because of its refusal to allow nuclear-armed ships into their ports; still the Aussies haven't abandoned the Kiwis—they have other agreements. Strategic commitments are also active in Papua New Guinea and nearby southwest Pacific islands.

The United States maintains three top-secret military bases in Australia—at Pine Gap, the North West Cape, and Narungar. No rental is charged for these facilities (unlike U.S. bases in the Philippines); while they are described as joint facilities, access for Australians is limited. Many Australians believe these bases are first-strike targets and have lobbied for their removal.

The North West Cape facility has currently been turned over to the Australians.

Australia is one of the senior members of the Commonwealth of Nations and has a long history of concerned involvement in international affairs through the United Nations and, more recently, the South Pacific Forum. The country lays claim to the largest area of the Antarctic and has been instrumental in ensuring that Antarctic Treaty nations agree to prevent mining and damaging development of the continent. Australia has also campaigned vigorously against French nuclear testing in the Pacific.

Acknowledging its identity as Asia-Pacific (and not part of the United States or Europe), Australia is taking steps to build relations with its northern neighbors. One example is dispassionate work for a solution to the terrible problems that beset Cambodia; e.g., the Khmer Rouge. Australia's "good guy" reputation for being the first country to recognize the early 1970s Beijing government has been used to persuade the Chinese government to improve civil rights for its people. Similarly, relations with close neighbor Indonesia have been helped through two 1992 events: the creation of the Australia-Indonesia Ministerial Forum and the signing of the Timor Gap Treaty, which recognizes Timor's sovereignty and legitimacy as an Indonesian country. The government is also increasing dialogue regarding security and defense with important nations such as Malaysia, Singapore, and Indonesia, and continues to pursue mutual arrangements and agreements with Japan, China, the Republic of Korea, and Vietnam.

Relations with independent African nations are relatively friendly, as they are in parts of Latin America and the Carribean, and of course Europe. Australia is a supporter both of peace negotiations in the Middle East and the Israeli-Palestine Liberation Organization peace accord.

But don't think for a minute that Australia has softened its allegiance with the United States, despite occasional tensions over wheat subsidies and airline routes. Australia sent a battalion to join the U.S.-guided task force in Somalia and was also the first country to back the Gulf War. In fact, at this very moment I am staring at a photo of Bill Clinton and Paul Keating practically holding hands, side-by-side, on a boat during a break at a 1993 economic conference in Seattle. Mr. Keating's hair is tousled, President Clinton's is picture-perfect. It is a windy day and the Stars and Stripes billow colorfully behind a smiling Mr. Keating. Ah, one picture's worth . . .

ECONOMY

Official embassy statistics peg Australia twelfth from the top of the world's economies, with a GDP (Gross Domestic Product) around 70% that of the United States. Agriculture and mining still account for much of Australia's wealth, but, increasingly, other sectors such as tourism, manufacturing, and service industries have shown big promise as "econo-boosters."

Life wasn't looking so rosy during the world recession of the early 1990s, which dragged Australia down with it. The usual greed, corruption, and rah-rah investments of the booming 1980s—most of them instigated by a few megarich Western Australian tycoons—lost big bucks for many—trusting senior citizens and hyped-up spendthrift yuppies alike. Few went unscathed. The result of those high-profile entrepreneurs shuffling worthless pieces of paper back and forth was the same: huge stockmarket losses, wiped-out savings accounts, building societies and banking institutions gone belly-up.

Times were tough on the farm those days—not just because of the recession but because of an international trade war with potentially disastrous consequences for the land of Oz. Even the Outback, while it might seem removed from the rest of the planet's concerns, gets heavily spun up in the buy-and-sell trade-war web. Cattle, wool, and mining (and now tourism) are major Outback commodities, and the Outback comprises a big chunk of Australia, which relies heavily on global trade.

Australia has been working diligently to establish an internationally competitive economy, enabling it to compete with the United States and Europe, but most particularly with the rapidly exploding Asia-Pacific markets (Japan, which purchases more than one-fourth of the country's merchandise exports, remains the largest single export market). To enable primary export commodities to compete, Australia has greatly reduced tariffs on once heavily protected industries.

Overall, the increased-trade plan seems to be working and, happily, the country is pitting its growth against that of the top industrialized nations. (In 1995 the economy grew by four percent and, at this writing, is expected to jump another one-half percent.) The knocking-down of the high tariff walls means that Australian manufacturers, production having increased about 25%, now compete with traditional commodities to bring export revenue into the country. Latest statistics show that manufacturing and services exports have increased threefold, while overall exports have doubled.

An annual average inflation rate that hovered at about eight percent in the 1980s has slid to about two percent, equal to or below that of most of the country's largest trading partners. Interest rates have dropped to their lowest level in two decades. Official short-term rates plunged from about 18% in 1989 to below five percent in late 1993; long-term rates of around seven percent are at their lowest since the early 1970s. This is certainly good news in a country that boasts one of the highest levels of home ownership in the world.

Unemployment, however, has not fared too well in the numbers game. And, while a substantial number of jobs were created in the manufacturing and services sectors (1.4 million 1983-1990), the traditional arena saw massive layoffs and cutbacks. Optimists point to signs of a strengthening job market in these mid-1990s, but the reality is that unemployment, which ranked a whopping 11% in late 1992, still drifts within the double-digit range. As of late 1993, just under six million people worked full-time, with women making up 41% of the labor force. Most employment fell within manufacturing, construction, community services, and wholesale and retail trade.

The pressure of international competition has inevitably eroded the hard-won conditions that a century of union activity had established. At one time more than 50% of the labor force belonged to one of 227 unions, affiliates under the umbrella of the national Australian Council of Trade Unions (ACTU). And even though membership has dropped some 10%, industrial relations—and the ubiquitous strikes—continue to be a thorny issue in Australian politics.

Employment discrimination because of race, color, sex, marital status, pregnancy, descent, or national or ethnic origin is illegal throughout Australia, and age discrimination is now squeaking its way onto the list as well. The average work week is 38 hours and almost every employee is entitled to four weeks per year of paid holiday time. But, how about wage discrimination? Women's average weekly earnings equal a whopping two-thirds of men's earnings. As for the Aborigines—do you even have to ask?

In the Outback, as well as throughout much of Australia, volatile prices have alternately wreaked havoc and created glory with the economy. The massive mining and agricultural enterprises usually get by nicely while the "independent" gold- and opal-miners, small-scale ranchers ("cockies"), and bourgeoning Aboriginal-owned businesses struggle for survival.

Bear in mind that the picture presented by government stats on laser-printed spread sheets may appear much brighter than the black-and-white images of battlers barely scraping by and the all-too-invisible Aborigines focused in the corners of a harsh, shadowy landscape.

Major Trade Agreements

GATT (General Agreement on Tariffs and Trade): Australia has been a GATT member since the organization's inception in 1948 as a vehicle for strengthening international trade and resolving related disputes. When the Uruguay Round met in 1991, Australia lobbied heavily for the removal of all agricultural trade barriers. It is allied in this endeavor with the Cairns Group—named for its initial 1986 meeting in North Queensland. The Cairns Group, chaired by Australia, includes Argentina, Brazil, Canada, Chile, Colombia, Fiji, Hungary, Indonesia, Malaysia, New Zealand, the Philippines, Thailand, and Uruguay, and altogether these nations provide about 20% of the world's agricultural exports. The group aims to reduce protection and subsidy practices by the big industrial-

ized nations, including those granted under the U.S. Export Enhancement Program (i.e., recall the sale of subsidized wheat by the United States to China and Yemen).

APEC (Asia Pacific Economic Cooperation): Initiated by Australia to facilitate economic cooperation within the region, a group of 12 ministers representing Australia, New Zealand, the United States, the Philippines, Singapore, Thailand, Indonesia, Japan, Canada, Brunei, and the Republic of Korea met in Canberra in 1989; two years later China, Hong Kong, and Taipei joined the group. In 1992 APEC positioned a secretariat in Singapore and has become a high-level forum for dialogue and consultation on regional economies and trade policies.

ASEAN (Association of South East Asian Nations): Though most economic matters with the member nations are conducted through APEC, Australia still keeps its foot in the door of this group. Mutual trade issues negotiated at the Uruguay Round, particularly those regarding agriculture, have established a strong link (let's not forget that Indonesia, Malaysia, the Philippines, and Thailand are part of the Cairns Group). At the regularly held ASEAN-Australia Forum, senior officials put their heads together on matters of education, trade, science, technology, and telecommunications.

ANZCERTA or CER (Australia New Zealand Closer Economic Relations Trade Agreement): This 1983 pact between neighbors opened the way for important trade and investment expansion when all restrictions were abolished, enabling each country to open up service operations and manufacturing concerns on each other's turf.

Papua New Guinea: Papua New Guinea, recipient of an estimated 2,500 Australian products, relies heavily on Australian trade, services, and foreign investment funds. The Joint Declaration of Principles of 1987 is the umbrella under which a number of bilateral agreements fall, including those ensuring duty free and unrestricted access for most PNG exports, investment protection, and development cooperation.

Japan: As the country's strongest single export market, Japan is accorded most-favored-nation status. Formal arrangements between the two countries date back to the Agreement on Commerce signed in 1957 and renegotiated in 1963.

Double taxation agreements hold as do those with shipping, air services, and investment.

Indochina: The dramatic rise in petroleum imports from Vietnam was the major factor behind Australia's almost $400 million worth of trade with Indochina during 1994-95; other large imports from the area are coffee and seafood. Australia provides crude petroleum, ore processing machinery, zinc, wheat, and telecommunications equipment to Indochina. Power generating machinery is targeted for Cambodia and nonmonetary silver and gold head to Laos.

South Pacific: SPARTECA (South Pacific Regional Trade and Economic Cooperation Agreement) comprises individual trade agreements between Australia and the South Pacific Forum countries of New Zealand, Fiji, Federated States of Micronesia, Cook Islands, Solomon Islands, Papua New Guinea, Republic of the Marshall Islands, Kiribati, Nauru, Niue, Tuvalu, Tonga, Vanuatu, and Western Samoa.

Women: Finally, women are trading instead of *being* traded! In 1994 a delegation of almost 100 Australian female executives journeyed to Singapore to join 130 other women from 14 Asian countries in the Australia/ASEAN Women Leaders conference. Supported by the Australian government's Office of the Status of Women and the Department of Foreign Affairs and Trade, the groundbreaking mission finally allowed businesswomen entree into the male-dominated South East Asia trade arena. For three days the Australian women liaised and networked—the outcome being an invitation to establish a branch of the Women for Women support group, the creation of a women's investment fund for small-business start-up costs, and the decision to build a joint venture cosmetics factory in Vietnam. (I said *entree,* not *equality.*)

AGRICULTURE

Agricultural products account for nearly one-fourth of Australia's export revenue. Not too bad, considering that only about two-thirds of the country is suitable for any kind of agricultural or ranching enterprise, and half of *that* area can only handle pastoral activities. Nevertheless, advanced know-how in crop yields, pastoral output, and soil fertility, along with the related equipment and machinery, have inaugurated and/or boosted cultivation at many desert and semidesert stations (rural ranches). And, of course, Australia's so-called "cattle kings" of the late 1800s were instrumental to the inland's pastoral development; Sir Sidney Kidman, Nat Buchanan, the Durack family—all of them were successful cattle-station pioneers.

Stations are enormous. Numbering about 125,000, they encompass 60% of the country's total land area and are the breeding grounds for most of the cattle and sheep. South Australia's Anna Creek Station, for example, totals 31,000 square kilometers and is the size of some European countries. Typically each station has a homestead, or headquarters, where the owners, managers, and other staff tend to, eat, and knit their livestock. (Overnight station-stays have also become de rigueur on some tourist circuits.)

Australia is the world leader in wool production and, with the majority of its sheep being that fine merino breed, most of that wool eventually threads its way into (warm) apparel, while skins off the sheeps' rears often end up cozying those of humans riding in cars or sprawled in front of a fireplace. Australia's major wool markets are Germany, Italy, France, Japan, and China.

In case any of you thought we were entering some sort of "cut your cholesterol, curtail your meat intake" era—forget it. As of the 1990s, Australia knocked out the entire European Community as the largest international exporter of veal and beef, with mutton and lamb following behind. And although exports are sent to more than 100 countries, guess who's stuffing down the most? Yes, the new "fat-free" United States. Skinny Japan, however, is the biggest spender. (Some consolation: Japan and the United States are also the main export markets for fish and seafood.) The Aussies, coming in third as the world's biggest meateaters, support their own country by consuming approximately 100 kilograms per person annually of beef, veal, chicken, lamb, mutton, and pork.

Dairy concerns, situated mainly around the high-rainfall southwestern and southeastern mainland coasts and northern Tasmania, pump out billions of liters of whole milk; two-thirds are made into cheese, butter, milk powders, and other related products.

Australia's massive wheatbelt, stretching across all five mainland states, produces more than 15 million tons of the grain, with nearly two-thirds exported to big buyers like India, Egypt, Japan, Korea, and China. Wheat production accounts for almost half of farmers' total income from field crops, but also important are rice, cotton, barley, sugarcane, oats, oilseeds, and field peas.

Fruit and vegetables are practically devotional commodities in Australia, and the country enshrines approximately 125,000 hectares of vegetables and 25 million fruit trees. Vineyards, planted on 65,000 hectares, produce millions of liters of wine annually and are receiving recognition— and occasional raves—from rapidly growing export markets in the United States, United Kingdom, New Zealand, Canada, Japan, and Sweden. Major wine-growing regions are in South Australia and New South Wales, but Victoria and Western Australia each have noteworthy cellars. Australian beer has also been hopping.

Forestry, as in many other parts of the world, is a touchy subject. Three-quarters of Australia's native forests (mainly eucalypt forests, but significant areas of rainforest as well) have disappeared since the arrival of Europeans. Some have been destroyed by fire, but the majority have—as elsewhere—simply been logged. Parts of Tasmania look positively ravaged. Plantation forests are usually pine, which offer no food or habitat to native bird and animal life. Logging in native forests and reserves, the "national estate," has been increasingly opposed by environmental groups on the grounds that such activities are unsustainable, and bitter disputes rage between the Greens and proponents of the timber industry, who see their jobs and livelihoods threatened.

The government has ostensibly recognized the environmental concerns and designated the 1990s the "Decade of Landcare." National programs include rainforest and soil conservation, biodiversity, and the reversal of tree decline by planting an estimated one *billion* trees.

MINING

You name it, Australia probably mines it—the country has been mined for well over a century.

Once the only mineral of any interest to the prospector was gold, gold, and more gold; this is still one of the principal targets of the mining industry (after all, Australia is still the world's third-largest producer), and gold miners have tax-exempt status. There's still gold lurking (and luring) in the hills; every now and again some lucky fossicker trips over a nugget and sells it to a Las Vegas casino for a million dollars.

Now miners have turned their attention to the host of other valuable minerals still underground. Prices fluctuate and mining has its slumps and booms, but the only check on mining activities for the past decade has been the combination of environmental and Aboriginal land rights issues.

Australia is the world's largest producer of bauxite, which is mined mostly in Queensland's Cape York, the mainland's northernmost point. The principal source of aluminum, bauxite is also a major player in the iron ore business, of which Australia, along with Brazil, is the world's largest exporter. Much of Australia's bauxite is mined from the remote Pilbara region of Western Australia and is a big reason for the state's wealth. Iron ore launched BHP (Broken Hill Proprietary) on the path that has made it Australia's largest company and a multinational corporation.

Australia has some of the world's largest reserves of black coal, most of it mined in Queensland and New South Wales where it was discovered in 1791. It's an energy source that becomes more significant as global supplies of oil are depleted. Like so many of Australia's raw materials, minerals are generally shipped offshore to the industrial powerhouses of Europe, Japan, and other Asian countries to be turned into consumer products like cars, television sets, and computers, and sold back to Australia, aggravating the problems of foreign debt and balance of trade. (The government's "Buy Australian" admonishment is taken quite seriously by citizens.)

Australia is a major producer of copper, which is mined in all states except Victoria. The largest deposits are at Queensland's Mount Isa and South Australia's Olympic Dam, with refineries in South Australia, Queensland, and New South Wales.

Nickel, another huge output, is mined largely in Western Australia, followed by Queensland. Groote Eylandt, in the Northern Territory, is home to one of the world's largest manganese mines, while Kunwarara in Queensland is a major cryptocrystalline magnesite reserve.

More mega-producers are the wealth of mineral sands that contain titanium minerals and byproducts such as zircon and monazite, minerals important in the development of new technology ceramics. These sands have traditionally been found and mined on the nation's beaches, and pristine areas of environmental importance have been ravaged in the past. Public pressure has resulted in the preservation of Fraser Island, Moreton Island, and other sensitive areas, while places like the Shelbourne Bay wilderness in Cape York, where mineral sands have been identified, are the subject of ongoing disputes.

Australia contains an estimated one-third of the world's known uranium ore, with the major deposits situated in South Australia, Western Australia, and the Northern Territory. The government allows the mining and export of uranium from Northern Territory's Ranger mine and South Australia's Olympic Dam—export conditions being that the raw "yellowcake" is to be used for peaceful purposes only. This is a dubious restriction when one buyer is the French government, which until recently persisted in a program of nuclear testing at Moruroa Atoll in the Pacific, at Australia's back door. Further exploration for uranium threatens parts of Kakadu National Park in the Northern Territory, where environmentalists and Aboriginal activists have joined to oppose development.

Other mining activities bring much happier thoughts of future use: Australia is the world's leading producer of diamonds, sapphires, and opals. Sparkly, happy things!

ENERGY

Australia is ideally situated to take advantage of the development of solar energy, although progress in this field is slow; fewer than 10% of Australian homes are equipped with solar hot-water units, but the figure is growing. In the Northern Territory and Western Australia, where cloudless days are as numerous as anywhere on earth, the figure is much higher. Locally developed silicon solar cells power remote railway crossings. Telecom, the national telephone authority, has installed solar-powered telephones in isolated communities in the Outback. Interest in solar power is getting stronger in Australia, which is running low on traditional energy sources. In 1993, Perth (Western Australia) was designated the first United Nations Centre for Applications of Solar Energy, giving it a leading edge in international research.

Wind provides another environment-friendly energy option, particularly in the high-wind coastal areas of South Australia, Western Australia, Tasmania, and the Bass Strait. Its main uses are to power windmills and small turbine generators and is now the preferred choice over diesel at Outback homesteads.

Most of Australia's energy requirements are still supplied by coal, which is also exported in the millions of tons along with large quantities of liquefied natural gas and light crude oil. Australia is roughly two-thirds self-sufficient in oil and produces plenty of natural gas. Most petroleum comes from the Bass Strait and Timor Sea regions, while Western Australia's North West Shelf—Australia's largest development project—is pumping out millions of tons of liquefied natural gas (LNG). (More areas, showing potential for large gas and oil discoveries, have yet to be fully explored.) Light crude oil as well as LNG represent in-

An old mine attests to early settlers' interest in precious metals.

BOB RACE

creasingly significant exports, most of it slicking toward the South Pacific and Japan. Heavy crude, however, is still on the import list, supplied by the Middle East but refined domestically.

Huge, easy-access coal reserves give Australia the benefit of substantial, low-cost electricity, most of it produced by coal-fired power plants bolstered by hydroelectric systems and natural gas-fired units. State public utilities have been the suppliers for most of the country's electricity; however, the federal government is geared up for a soon-to-come national electricity grid to provide a competitive market for business consumers.

Gas is becoming increasingly more important as a power source in Australia. The federal government's National Gas Strategy is encouraging free and fair trade between states, the dismissal of a lot of red-tape approvals, and a "casual" approach to pipeline regulations. Natural gas is supplied to all mainland capital cities via pipelines from producing fields.

Environmental Concerns

The looming greenhouse effect from carbon gas emission is becoming more critical, even to the normally apathetic Australian public. Several neighboring nations in the South Pacific face the prospect of literally sinking beneath the waves should global warming cause sea levels to rise even a meter or two.

Substantial hydroelectric systems operate in Tasmania and the Snowy Mountains between New South Wales and Victoria, but it is unlikely that further development of this energy source will be acceptable to a public that, thankfully, is growing more environmentally aware. It was the planned flooding of the Gordon River for hydroelectricity that placed environmental issues firmly on the agenda of every political party in Australia early in the 1980s.

And, remember that little problem with the ozone layer . . .

The good news is the politicians have been listening and maybe even *care* (at least about reelection). Concerned Greenies, innocent islanders, gasping asthmatics—help may be on the way!

In 1994 the Commonwealth Environment Protection Agency in Australia signed an agreement with the United States Environmental Protection Agency to help each other with mutual environmental concerns. This global stance will encourage joint research-and-development projects and an information-and-personnel network that will benefit both countries and thereby extend to the rest of the world, hopefully. Both countries are part of the Montreal Protocol on Substances that Deplete the Ozone Layer, which regulates trade in, and production of, ozone-depleting substances. Also, Australia is a signatory to the Climate Change Convention. Too, the federal government has developed a National Greenhouse Response Strategy and is preparing a National Strategy for the Conservation of Biological Diversity (for preservation of ecosystems, plants, and animals).

Ocean Rescue 2000, a 10-year program (due to end . . . guess when?) promotes conservation and sustainable use of Australia's marine environment; the Antarctica Treaty protects that region's fragile environment; and—hang on you sinking South Pacific islands—Australia is a spirited member of the South Pacific Regional Environment Program, which hopes to promote conservation, protection, and sustainable development in the South Pacific countries.

TOURISM

Beloved travelers, *you* are the brightest stars in Australia's economic Southern Cross. Over the past decade, tourism has boomed, driven by the success of Big Croc Dundee and an aggressive marketing campaign in which juicy shrimp were tossed on the barbies of Europe, Japan, and the United States. Also helpful were the 1987 America's Cup Challenge at Fremantle (near Perth) and Expo 88 in Brisbane, both of which brought large numbers of tourists—and their large wallets—streaming into the country. And, though Paul Hogan's overused shrimp has been replaced by *Strictly Ballroom* star Paul Mercurio's attention-grabbing buns, tourist-wise, Australia is still cookin'.

Tourism has consistently been the highest growth sector of the economy, and tourist dollars promise to be the country's largest source of foreign income. (The setbacks of a crippling pilots' strike, which adversely affected many resorts in the late 1980s and nearly devastated Tasmania tourism, thankfully are over.)

The Australian Tourist Commission (ATC), tourism-marketing arm of the government, has offices throughout the world from which it promotes Australia's glories as a tourist destination. Marketing endeavors have been particularly successful in Asia and Europe, with North Asia accounting for nearly one-third of short-term visitors. And Sydney's successful bid for the summer Olympics in 2000 is certain to bring a soar of inbound tourists.

The ATC hardly has a tough job—the land of Oz is an easy sell. It's safe, healthy, friendly, and full of spectacular scenery, fabulous beaches, and natural wonders. The Outback, especially, has become a choice destination in recent years. The Outback represents a myriad of take-me-there qualities: the mysterious and mesmerizing Aboriginal culture, a rough-and-tumble pioneering lifestyle, night skies to die for (or under), and flora, fauna, and geological forms to boggle the mind. And it has become a mecca for followers of New Age bestsellers with their phantasmagorical walkabouts and spirit channeling. Most importantly, in these Type-A personality days, the Outback represents the ultimate get-me-as-far-away-from-pressure destination—unless, of course, you happen to be a guidebook writer working on deadline.

The federal government, in fact, is aiming to promote the country's unique natural sites, and yet wants to ensure manageable eco-tourism. Substantial funds have already been committed to spur regional tourism and expand opportunities for the rural and backpacker markets, prompting the Bureau of Tourism Research to project accommodation shortages by the late 1990s in the outback areas of the Northern Territory, Perth, Brisbane, Far North Queensland, and the Gold Coast.

Australians are an amiable people and easygoing, but they've had to learn the rudiments of a service industry like tourism from the ground up—trying to master the "art" of commercial hospitality in a culture that does not readily distinguish between service and servility. So don't always expect them to do a kangaroo hop whenever a demanding tourist snaps his fingers (note to reader: If *you're* a finger-snapper, please don't carry my book around). For the most part, tourists are treated with great openness and friendliness, and the delight that visitors generally take in Australia has stimulated the Aussies to take new interest in the natural wonders of

their own country—wonders that had previously been taken for granted in a country that's a mix of Stone Age, New Age, and the year 2000.

MANUFACTURING

Australia's manufacturing industry has boomed during the past decade, since trade barriers and economic regulations have been dropped to make the country a more productive and competitive exporter. Manufacturing, which has seen a rapid rise of about 16% per year, now comprises about 15% of the country's GDP (Gross Domestic Product), with about one-fifth of the goods being exported, mainly to Asian countries.

The broad range of manufactured items includes: iron and steel products (BHP, the predominant producer, is Australia's largest company), engineering equipment and tools, telecommunications and electronic equipment, small- to medium-sized ships and vessels, chemicals and plastics, aerospace equipment, information technology, motor vehicles, processed foods, paper and woodchips, and aluminum.

Australia would like you to know that it is behind the scenes where least expected. The Swiss Stock Exchange and Frankfurt-based Lufthansa's ticketing system use Australian software; Aussie software also manages Heathrow, Schipol, and Manchester airports. Many BMW gearboxes are Australian-made, as are most of Europe's high-speed ferries and *all* of the public transport "smart cards" in Scandinavia and the United Kingdom.

Smaller entrepeneurs are cashing in also. One fast-growing company ships large cryogenic gas storage tanks to Thailand and other Asian markets, another supplies "Ronald on a Park Bench" figures to McDonald's outlets around the globe, and one outfit sends off hundreds of thousands of individually wrapped cheesecake slices to Japan every year.

Increasing numbers of international companies already active in, or about to pounce upon, the booming Asian markets have already set up regional headquarters in Australia. Two such companies are Mars and Kellogg Australia. (Lifesaving Tip: Down Under, your Mars and Snickers bars remain the same, but your Rice Krispies and Raisin Bran masquerade as Rice Bubbles and Sultana Bran.)

THE PEOPLE

Just under 18% of Australia's approximate 18 million people live in Outback regions, and that includes the cities of Darwin, Adelaide, Perth, and Alice Springs. Australia's population is about the same as Texas, and would fit between Los Angeles and San Diego, except it is spread over a continent roughly the size of the United States. Mostly the people are concentrated along the two widely separated coastal regions: the eastern coastal area between Cairns and Adelaide and Western Australia's "high-density" corner from Perth down to the southwest coast.

Almost the entire population lives in six or seven cities, most of them congested enough so that you'd scarcely sense that vast emptiness outside the urban limits. The current population breakdown is as follows: 6,008,000 in New South Wales; 4,465,000 in Victoria; 3,116,000 in Queensland; 1,677,000 in South Australia; 1,676,000 in Western Australia; 471,000 in Tasmania; 299,000 in Australian Capital Territory; and 169,000 in the Northern Territory. Aborigines and Torres Strait Islanders make up about 1.6% of the total population, with the majority of them residing in the Northern Territory.

Before World War II, the majority of Australians were of British and Irish origin. That mix, however, has changed drastically. After the war,

migrants came in droves and the island continent soon included significant numbers of Italians, Greeks, Yugoslavs, Dutch, Germans, Lebanese, Turks, and Maltese. Melbourne is said to be the second-largest Greek city in the world, after Athens, and has the largest population of Italians outside Italy, with Sydney having the second-largest; Germans made stakes in the Barossa Valley; Chinese pearled around Broome; and Darwin is just one big cosmopolitan city, with people from just about everywhere.

Waves of migration occurred in the 1850s, 1880s, early 1900s, and 1920s. The Great Depression and World War II restricted immigration, and a low birth rate made necessary a renewed migration drive in the 1950s. This campaign brought three million people to Australia (mostly to the major cities) between 1947 and 1974.

The scrapping of the White Australia Policy along with Australia's humanitarian refugee program after the Vietnam War has brought a steady increase in Asian immigration, particularly Vietnamese refugees. Also, Hong Kong's reversion to China in 1997 is looming and many Hong Kong nationals are looking to Australia for possible emigration.

Presently, as home to almost five million migrants from approximately 160 countries, Australia is rich in cultural and ethnic diversity. Nearly 13% of Australians have parents who were both born in another country; four out of ten Australians are first-generation children of migrants—or migrants themselves—and many come from non-English speaking households. Southeast and Northeast Asia contributed 41% of new immigrant arrivals in the early 1990s and thousands more resettlement places have been allotted to refugees and displaced persons throughout the decade.

BIG STUFF

Size *does* make a difference—well, they must think so in big ol' Oz. Travelers will find a kitschy array of humongous "Big Things" popping up in various towns and cities throughout the country. Most are mega-life-sized replicas of fruits or creatures that house, or sit in front of, souvenir shops or tourist offices. Some notable examples are the Big Lobster, Big Orange, Big Pineapple, Big Banana, Big Penguin, Big Cow, Big Gold Panner, and Big Apple (move over, New York City). Whatever your proclivity, you'll undoubtedly find yourself trampling over others to snap some photo of a regular-sized human snuggling up to a big hunk of fiberglass.

THE OUTBACK DWELLERS

Outback residents *are* rugged individualists taming a savage wilderness, *and* they are a unique breed. Hey, life in the middle of nowhere isn't especially easy—most residents live 500 kilometers or more from the nearest corner store, and even farther from a school or physician.

The Royal Flying Doctor Service high-frequency radio network (see "Outback Health and Education," below) handles more than just rural medical calls: it also provides an important social forum. Regular open broadcasts, called "galah sessions," allow far-apart residents to gab and gossip, share information, keep up on events, and send or receive telegrams.

In general, Outback men are very brusque and very strong, with too many tattoos and too few teeth. They sweat, drink, sweat again, and drink some more. They work in the mines, operate big rigs and heavy equipment, tend to heated beasts (who sweat and drink), and they party hard—usually in the remote pubs where they spin dubious tales until they pass out. The Outback women are saints.

ABORIGINES AND TORRES STRAIT ISLANDERS

Though white Australians often refer to themselves as the "world's newest people," the Aborigines who began living there at least 50,000-60,000 years ago (and maybe as far back as 100,000 years ago) are surely the world's oldest people. The most current census shows that Aborigines and Torres Strait Islanders number 265,459, or about 1.6% of Australia's total population. The majority are concentrated in the remote Outback, many still living (or trying to live) according to their traditional ways; even Aborigines living in or near towns hang out primarily with their own people.

There is dispute among anthropologists over the exact number of Aboriginal cultural groups: it could have been 11, it could have been twice that. Basically, groups were linked by common language, tools, art forms, social structure, and their environment—most of them lived in the desert or its fringes, along the coast or down in Tasmania. Political activism over the last two decades has inspired a cultural revival among surviving groups with a renewed commitment to those traditional common links. Consequently, these days many Aborigines prefer to be called by their self-designated names: Kooris (Victoria and New South Wales); Murris (Queensland);

Anangu (western desert); Yappa (Warlpiris); Nunga (coastal South Australia); Nyoongah (southwest Australia); and Yolngu (northeast Arnhem Land). If you have any doubts about correct affiliation, it's probably best to simply refer to the traditional people as "Aborigines"—and that goes for those of mixed descent, as well. The terms "abo" and "coon" are hideously derogatory and unacceptable.

Though often lumped together with the Aboriginal people, the estimated 10,000 Torres Strait Islanders are mainly Melanesian and represent a separate cultural group with two distinct languages. Residing on the islands separating New Guinea and Cape York, the eastern islanders work the rich soil while the western islanders remain semi-nomadic. Thursday Island, a regularly scheduled ferry ride from Queensland's Cape York, is administrative center of Torres Strait. The gone but never-to-be-forgotten Eddie Mabo neoned the speck-size islands on the map when he had the gumption to suggest the Australian government acknowledge the Merriam people as rightful, traditional owners of Murray Island, sparking the landmark Mabo Decision and Native Title Act.

The Aboriginal and Torres Strait Islander Commission (ATSIC), established in 1990, is the major policy-making agency that allows indigenous people to make decisions about important matters such as education, housing, and employment; the ATSIC is also responsible for administering federal government programs. (See "Aborigines Today" in the "History" section, above.)

OUTBACK HEALTH AND EDUCATION

Medical care is provided by the Royal Flying Doctor Service (RFDS), which, since the 1920s, has been coming to the rescue of the Outback's sick and injured in an area equal to about two-thirds of the United States. Established in 1912, the service is now a sophisticated network of 15 bases with twin-engine aircraft and a large staff of doctors, nurses, radio operators, pilots, aircraft engineers, and other personnel, with the capacity to arrive on the scene within a few hours. Funded by donations and government subsidies, the RFDS does not charge patients

ROYAL FLYING DOCTOR SERVICE

CORAL SEA

DARWIN

WYNDHAM

DERBY

CAIRNS

PORT HEDLAND

MOUNT ISA
CLONCURRY

GIBSON

ALICE SPRINGS

DESERT

CHARLEVILLE

CARNARVON

MEEKATHARRA

MAREE

BRISBANE

GERALDTON

KALGOORLIE

BELTANA

BROKEN HILL

PERTH

PORT AUGUSTA

GREAT AUSTRALIAN BIGHT

SYDNEY

ADELAIDE

CANBERRA

INDIAN OCEAN

MELBOURNE

0   500 km

HOBART

© MOON PUBLICATIONS, INC.

unless they have workers' compensation or accident insurance coverage. About 40% of RFDS patients are Aborigines.

High-frequency radio networks enable Outback residents to be in contact with doctors around the clock. Besides fly-in-and-out emergency evacuations to base hospitals, the RFDS also supervises small nurse-run hospitals and community clinics and provides remote clinics, reserves, and homesteads with comprehensive first-aid and medicine chests. (Ah, how comforting to know a friend or relative could perform emergency surgery while getting radio instructions!)

Since 1951, when the first facility opened in Alice Springs, School of the Air has been edu-

cating school-age children living on Outback stations or in other remote parts of Australia. Lessons are a combination of high-frequency radio transmissions, correspondence courses (including audio and video materials), once-a-week "private" radio sessions, and at least one annual personal visit—when teachers swoop in via light planes or heavy vehicles.

RELIGION

The First Fleet brought to Australia the alien concept of the separation of church and state in the form of an Anglican minister to service the religious needs of the convicts and their keepers. It was well over a week after their arrival before the immigrants got around to performing their first religious ceremony, however, and religion seems to have been consigned to the backseat of Australian life ever since. In this regard, Australia offers a curious contrast to America's pilgrim fathers, who knelt in prayer as soon as they stepped ashore.

This is not to say that religion doesn't play any part at all in Australian life—it's just not a starring role. Adherents of every major world religion practice their faith in an environment of freedom and tolerance. Not surprisingly, Christianity in all its variants and deviants is the principal religion. The largest group belongs to the Roman Catholic Church, followed by the Anglican. Anglicans have declined in number, possibly because the days when the establishment and Anglican Church went hand-in-hand are over. The Uniting Church now encompasses most of the Protestant sects. Roman Catholic numbers have been boosted since the war, with the arrival of Catholic migrants from Europe. However, the overall membership of any formal religious group is in decline in Australia, due in

part to a secular, almost hedonistic, culture. Nevertheless, visitors who want to practice their religion and contact the Big Boss up top from the land Down Under will find plenty of opportunity.

Australia's major non-Christian faiths are Judaism, Buddhism, and Islam, but there are growing leagues of just about every California-meets-The East, New Age religion—replete with channelers, UFO-watchers, and surfing nudists.

Aboriginal Religion

To cast off the Aborigines' religion in a paragraph or two (or a century or two) is a real sacrilege. The early Christian missionaries couldn't fathom their beliefs at all; they simply assumed the Aborigines, without any seeming belief in a white God and his crucified son, were Judgment Day goners.

Australia's first inhabitants, in isolation, had a spirituality that was inseparable from their way of life. In a sense their religion was and is an all-encompassing experience in which their life, their tribe, the land, the plants and animals around them, the past, and the great Dreamtime legends are inextricably interwoven. (See the special topic "Dreamtime.")

BOB RACE

LANGUAGE

English, with its distinct Australian accent and vocabulary, is the predominant language spoken throughout Australia. Of course, that's aside from hundreds of Aboriginal languages and dozens of other languages—Italian, Greek, Vietnamese, Turkish, you name it!—spoken within various immigrant communities.

One advantage to visitors is that regional variants are very subtle, so if you can understand someone in Perth, you can understand someone in Cairns or Melbourne. Class-linked distinctions are more noticeable than regional ones; the upper middle classes affect a plummier accent closer to their English cousins, while the working classes are prone to exaggerate the idiosyncratic earthy tones that distinguish the Australian accent. But even these distinctions are much less dramatic than those that Americans are used to amongst themselves.

However, be warned. The Australian accent can be tricky for American or British visitors, at least at first. Australians love to tell stories about their compatriots traveling overseas and failing to make themselves understood; tales of Australians trying to explain to bewildered American barkeepers that all they want is a beer, or British hotel receptionists calling for the house translator to cope with Australian tourists.

One common misconception is that all Australians use a profusion of colorful idiomatic words and phrases, such as those that are regularly listed in travel books. Such words are well known to all Australians, but have a currency that may exist solely in the minds of the compilers of Australian slang dictionaries. Some Australians will live their whole lives without ever saying "fair dinkum" or "chunder," even though they know perfectly well what these terms mean. Treat such words with caution! People using them may be doing so facetiously or ironically. "Bastard," for example, can mean several different things, depending on context: a bad bastard is someone who's bigger than you; good bastard, someone who's lent you money; lucky bastard, someone who has a better job than you; greedy bastard, someone with a better

house; and a lucky, of course, is someone who has the weekend off. "Mate" may be the cheery greeting of long-lost chums *or* the signal for a barroom brawl. With the proviso that the words are often the fossilized relics of an Australia that may never have existed, and that they can sound quite peculiar in an American accent, refer to this book's glossary (but don't write me if you're laughed at).

You *won't* go wrong, however, if you shorten just about any word to one- or two-syllables and then add a "y," "ie," or "o" to the end. Examples: "television" becomes "telly"; "journalist," "journo"; and "surfers," "surfies."

Transatlantic variations that exist between English and American usage often occur in Australia, where generally the English version is preferred. However, from being regularly bombarded by American film, music, and television, Australians are familiar with all things American, and most people will understand that when you say "cookie" you really mean biscuit, and so on.

In some parts of Australia a variant of the Cockney rhyming slang is used and this can lead to profound confusion for the visitor. Often the rhyming part of the expression is left out altogether, which confounds the uninitiated even more. Examples are far too numerous to give more than a few of the most common and relevant instances:

Arra—Aristotle, bottle (of beer)
Captain Cook—a look
china—china plate, mate
rubbity—rubbity dub, pub
septic tank—Yank

If it seems from these examples that Australians use only the most insulting and derogatory terms for almost everything except alcohol and for everyone except themselves, be assured that for most Australians the use of many of these expressions would be unthinkable. The visitor to Australia will find a language with its own unique flavor that is riddled with delightful idioms while remaining basically English.

Aboriginal Languages

If you thought the shortening and rhyming and unique idioms discussed above were confusing, just wait! Aboriginal languages number at least 100 and have many dialects. This isn't quite so overwhelming when you realize that before the Europeans barged in the number was in the ballpark of 250 languages and 700 dialects—all thought to stem from just one language that changed and expanded as the traditional people broke off into groups and spread around the continent. Most languages were exclusively oral, not written, and subsequently died out along with their speakers. Others, such as Pitjantjatjara—the most common dialect of the western desert language group—were painstakingly transcribed. Pitjantjatjara (also known as Pitjantjara) is spoken in Uluru National Park (where visitors find it written phonetically on park signs), in Aboriginal communities from the Northern Territory/Western Australia border to the Simpson Desert's eastern border, and within the Anangu Pitjantjatjara traditional lands in South Australia. Pitjantjatjara contains three vowels (each having an additional long form) and 17 consonants, some of which require some tricky curling-tongue action.

Most Aboriginal languages contain about 10,000 words and some of these have also merged with Australian English: dingo, boomerang, kangaroo, kookaburra, barramundi, galah, mulga, mallee, and wallaby should be recognizable to most readers. Conversely, some English has found its way into Aboriginal speech, particularly in the relatively new Aboriginal Kriol, the "adopted" language of a growing contingency of younger people.

Many Outback Aborigines speak little or no English—they don't learn it in their communities, nor do they need to. Even on shopping trips to town, the Aborigines seem to get by, communicating adequately via fistfuls of money. Nonetheless, when speaking to Aborigines, use your normal English words and voice tones. The Aborigines will probably do the same for you—in their own language. Hopefully, *someone* will understand.

By the way, most Aboriginal languages do not contain words that mean "hello," "please," or "thank you," but if you need any kind of plant or animal, are looking for water, or want to say "sorry," you're in business.

CONDUCT AND CUSTOMS

Rule number one: bring alcohol or flowers if you're invited to a dinner or party. Other than that, say "please" and "thanks," and you're in business—at least in the cities. In country and Outback areas, well, it's a different story. They take care of things *themselves,* if you catch my drift.

The concept of "fairness" is always a prime consideration. "Whatever's fair," "fair enough" and, yes, "fair dinkum." The only problem is, "fair dinkum" for the cocky, allegedly innocent, or downright guilty foreigner can quickly become "fair dinkum stinkum." Play it by ear and don't get in over your head. It's fine standing up for principles and such, but the reality is—when you're in the middle of nowhere with no one to jump to your aid—who cares? Tell them you'll sue and they'll laugh (tell them you'll call the cops and they *won't*). Think about survival first and foremost. This goes ditto for feminists; though it's tempting to barge into a redneck pub and demand equal rights from macho men with too many tattoos and too few teeth, use common

sense and a bit of restraint. (For those of you who've seen *Thelma and Louise,* I know you're going to ignore me anyway.)

My Aussie friends will hate me for saying this, but all that hype you've heard about Australia being 15 or so years behind the U.S. is, in many ways, true. Not everyone is fast, fast, fast, nor is everything mega-modern or high-high-tech. But that's good? It also means that people still count; that in a country so far from other urban centers and with such a comparatively small population human life is not so expendable.

Outback dwellers are hardworking, down-to-earth, and take well-earned pride in being self-sufficient and in control of their lives. They have to be, in such vast, far-from-anywhere spaces. The mail arrives via plane or truck every week or two, and shopping is usually a day-or-so's drive away. No 7-Eleven's, no McDonald's. The compensation is an envious sense of independence as well as freedom from city blights like traffic and smog (and 7-Elevens and McDonald's).

Entertainment usually takes the form of special events and community social gatherings.

OUTBACK LAND ETIQUETTE

It cannot be stressed enough that just because the Outback *looks* deserted much of the land is actually station property, or Aboriginal-owned (see "Aborigines Today" under "History," above). If you decide to detour off the main road to camp or cavort on private property, then do the right thing: contact the station owner or manager for permission. Most have phones and faxes. Never stop at a station expecting handouts; bring your own food, booze, sunscreen, and styling gel (you'll make points if you bring some practical items for the station owner).

Basic rules apply to visitors on pastoral lands. Please heed them so you don't wreck things for future travelers.

Always leave gates exactly as you find them—no matter how you think they should be, and no matter how difficult they are to maneuver. Open gates often mean that livestock are passing in and out for water.

Do not pollute water supplies by washing yourself, your clothes, or dishes in them; use some alternative container.

Don't camp near watering areas. Stock need to have primary access to the watering hole and usually won't come around if people are nearby.

Take rubbish with you when you break camp. Wrap it in heavy plastic bags until you can dump it in an appropriate place. Wildlife will usually dig up buried food scraps.

Prevent bushfires. Build small campfires and douse them with dirt, making sure all embers have died before you leave the scene.

Stay off flooded roads. If you're caught in heavy rain, either stay on high ground or get out quickly to avoid gashing 4WD prints in the roads. If you *must* bring Fido along, keep him leashed when near livestock areas.

ABORIGINAL LAND ETIQUETTE

You need to obtain an advance permit from the traditonal owners before entering Aboriginal land, and you should be prepared for rejection! Normally, permits are not granted to travelers,

but if you are part of an organized tour or have a relative working on the land, authorization will probably be approved. Tours are easy—the tour company ordinarily handles the tedious red tape (don't assume this though, check first). Otherwise, if you're doing it yourself, allow plenty of time for the application process. Make sure to apply for all states and territories in which you will be traveling, including dates of journey, expected route, purpose of the visit, and names of all fellow travelers.

Permits are not required for travel on public roads that cross Aboriginal land, but if you have to stop for fuel along the way, you'll still need a transit permit. Entering Aboriginal land without a permit can result in a fine of up to $1000. (See the special topic "Permits for Outback Travel" in the On the Road chapter.)

Appropriate conduct for travelers on Aboriginal lands should be stringently followed. When you come across larger communities, you'll probably find a store—staffed by English-speakers—where you can buy fuel, provisions, souvenirs, and locally produced artwork (*no bargaining, please*—you are not in Mexico or India where such behavior is part of the art; here it's offensive). If you arrive at an isolated or smaller community, park your vehicle well away from any shelter or gathering and wait for someone to approach you; otherwise call out. If you're ignored, take it as a hint to go away. *Do not intrude* in a gathering or business meeting. Also, upon encountering any Aborigine, do not come on like you've just come from a "networking" seminar. Eyes lowered slightly and a soft hand-clasp will work far more wonders than the aggressive direct-stare and firm-shake method.

Sacred sites are places or objects that hold special meaning for the Aboriginal people and, as such, are protected by law. Show respect for their significance and do not enter, damage, or deface these areas. You'll need advance permission for any commercial photography on traditional lands, but not for personal snapshots. However, *do not* snap away at individual Aborigines without asking first (and don't expect a jovial response, either).

Liquor is restricted in many Aboriginal communities; check with the permit-issuing land council for particulars. Also, please heed signs posted at some Outback pubs and shops asking that travelers not buy or pass alcohol on to Aborigines.

BOB RACE

ON THE ROAD

SPORTS AND RECREATION

Australians love sport. They love it so much that it's tempting to include this section under the "Religion" heading. They have a tradition of competitive sport that goes back to the earliest days of colonization, and they'll travel anywhere on earth if there's someone willing to play against them. Australia is one of the few countries to have been represented at every modern Olympiad. The Olympic Games were held in Melbourne in 1956, where Australians won the third-most medals, an extraordinary feat for a nation with such a tiny population. Yet that is a measure of how seriously Australians treat athletic achievement. Australian champions regularly crop up in sports as diverse as golf, tennis, weightlifting, squash, yachting, cycling, and swimming.

A significant number of champion athletes enter public office after their sporting career is over, and political leaders of all persuasions find it necessary to publicize their allegiance to particular sporting clubs. Personal appearances at matches are a prerequisite to a successful career in politics. The Grand Final of the Australian Football League in Melbourne drives all other news from the headlines for weeks beforehand. The Melbourne Cup is an occasion for a public holiday. Australians can name past or present world champions in almost every sport, a phenomenon that causes their chests to swell with pride, even though sporting involvement for many Australians is confined to watching their idols on the telly.

Water Sports

Swimming is particularly important in a land where so much social activity takes place on the beach, and most Australian children are taught to swim very early. Let's face it—the country is filled with spectacular beaches. And, while the beaches are deserted and beautiful, the water may be dangerous. In surf areas, strong "rips" can sweep an unwary swimmer out to sea. Most popular beaches are patrolled by Surf Life

Saving Clubs, which post flags to indicate safe swimming areas. (Swim between the flags.) For specific recommendations for the Outback's virtually limitless swimming options, both coastal and freshwater, check the "Recreation" and "Sights" sections in the travel chapters.

Once the Hawaiians introduced the surfboard to Australia, it was hang-ten fever, and surfies soon made their own innovations to the clumsy Malibu, creating a generation of smaller, more maneuverable short boards. Superb surfing beaches surround the country, fronting the Pacific, Great Southern, and Indian Oceans. And, like surfers almost everywhere, the Aussie variety has developed its own subculture, complete with fashion statements, lingo, mores, and surf-turf.

Australians are equally at home in boats, and the America's Cup created national heroes out of the team that wrested it briefly from the grip of the New York Yacht Club. Most water-lovers have their sights set a bit lower than 12-meter racing, however, and are content to go fishing, skin diving, and waterskiing on the country's bountiful oceans, rivers, lakes, and streams.

Barramundi Fishing

Fishing for the highly prized barramundi (or "barra") seems to reel in all types—from local pros and holiday-making Aussies to big-shot Hollywood celebrities and international politicians; catching it is a challenge and eating it is a treat. The barra teases fishers in coastal and river waters of the Top End, Kimberley region (Northern Territory), Cape York, and Gulf Country (Queensland). Enthusiasts seem to have very individual ideas regarding method, timing, and season—which is just as well or they'd be trampling over each other. Both novices and pros will find a myriad of organized fishing trips (see "Tours" later in this chapter). For information regarding bag and size limits, permits, seasonal and other restrictions, contact: Amateur Fishermen's Association of the Northern Territory, P.O. Box 41512, Casuarina, NT 0810 (tel. 08-8999-5096); Fisheries Service of the Queensland Department of Primary Industry, Cairns, QLD (tel. 070-35-1580); Northern Territory Game Fishing Association, G.P.O. Box 128, Darwin, NT 0801 (tel. 08-8999-5605); or Western Australia Department of Fisheries, 108 Adelaide Terrace, East Perth, WA (tel. 09-220-5333).

Spectator Sports

Australians love and excel at many competitive sports and flock in droves to watch their favorites. So important is sport in Australia that federal and state governments appoint quite senior ministers to Departments of Sport. The federal government sponsors a kind of athletic university in Canberra, called the Institute of Sport, where promising atheletes are coached. Tennis, golf, basketball, and soccer are all played and followed with keen interest, and the feats of champions are heralded on the television and analyzed in the press.

The most important game, especially in Victoria (some say exclusively)—and one which visitors must not miss—is Australian Rules football. Australian Rules (or footy) is the passion of all Australians except a few deadbeats who have lost their love for life. Developed on the goldfields of central Victoria well over a century ago, it is Australia's gift to the world.

Footy is an anarchic game, played with an oval ball on an oval field, with no offside rule—where eternal Truth, Courage, Imagination, Honor, and Justice are acted out in front of an audience whose good taste and discernment are proverbial. Strongest in Melbourne, the

---

SYDNEY 2000

Word came in September 1993 that Sydney had been chosen to host the Summer Olympic Games in the year 2000, and Sydneysiders have been celebrating—and preparing—ever since. (Talk about optimism—some 65% of competition sites had already been constructed, or were underway, when the announcement was made!)

With the exception of four of the 25 Olympic sports, all games (with about 85% of athletes participating) will take place in two areas, just 14 km apart.

Athletes Village, within 30 minutes' travel of all game venues, will actually become a new Sydney "suburb." The estimated 15,000 athletes will be housed in one village—a "first" in modern Olympic Games history.

The games will take place from 16 September until 1 October. Mark your calendars. The year is 2000.

game is currently in the throes of a titanic struggle to create a national league. Visitors can look forward to witnessing the game being played at the very highest levels in all the major capitals around Australia. The rival rugby league and rugby union (principally concentrated in New South Wales and Queensland), while perhaps being more accessible to Americans used to gridiron football, cannot claim the hearts of Australians in quite the same way as footy. Remember, footy is more than a game, it is a barometer of the culture of a particular society. Footy is life.

Unfortunately, footy is only played in the winter months, and Australians turn their attention in summer to their other great passion—cricket. Cricket is a relic of a colonial past and, although many Americans might be surprised to learn that the U.S. even has a national team, it is strongest in those Commonwealth countries like India, the West Indies, New Zealand, Sri Lanka, and Pakistan, as well as Australia, which left the British Empire only this century.

Cricket is a leisurely, cerebral sport, which ideally suits it to the thoughtful and aesthetic Australian public. Important games last five days, and to the novice whole days may pass with very little actually happening. This provides the spectator with ample time to chat (and drink) with a neighbor and discuss the Byzantine intricacies of past controversies. A livelier version of the game takes place in one day and is guaranteed to end in a result; this provides a more suitable introduction to the game.

Other Sports

The natural beauties of the Australian bush make bushwalking (or hiking) a popular activity for anyone who wants to see the wildlife up close. City, country, and Outback cycling is another favorite pursuit, and Australia has a history of producing champions in world competitions (see "Cycling" under "Getting Around" later in this chapter). Golf, tennis, horseback riding, camel trekking, hot-air ballooning, hang gliding, even baseball—all have their adherents and various Outback venues. Fossicking (searching for gold and gemstones) is a unique Outback activity and, for some, the main reason to travel to this destination.

OUTBACK ENTERTAINMENT AND EVENTS

Like other Western industrialized nations, Australia is replete with the wonders of modern technology: television, films, popular music, and so on. Americans will find that much of their culture has preceded them and taken root to the point that Australia is beginning to export its own version of America's late-20th-century global techno-culture back to the United States—with the exception of film.

Filmmakers Peter Weir, Gillian Armstrong, Paul Cox, Jocelyn Moorehouse, Bruce Beresford, Baz Luhrmann, and P.J. Hogan, along with film stars Mel Gibson, Paul Mercurio, Judy Davis, Bryan Brown, and Toni Collette lead a coterie of Australian artists who have dazzled starbright Hollywood. They learned their craft in the domestic Australian industry, offering entertainment with not merely an Australian accent but with some fabulously quirky characters and fresh, innovative themes. Thankfully, in this respect, Australia does not lean heavily on the traditional box-office, crass-market models (*Crocodile Dundee* excepted) normally provided by the U.S. film industry. Some of the many well-known films with Outback locations include not only *Crocodile Dundee*, but *Mad Max II, My Brilliant Career, Evil Angels, Breaker Morant, Walkabout, Chant of Jimmie Blacksmith,* and the delightfully fashionable *Priscilla, Queen of the Desert*.

Australia also has a vital and dynamic music industry, very much in evidence in the major cities and towns in the Outback. Hundreds of hopeful young musicians play nightly in every style you can name—and some you can't. Not long ago it was possible to see bands like Midnight Oil, AC/DC, Men at Work, and INXS playing in small suburban pubs, and you can bet the bands that play there now have big ambitions. Australian contemporary music embraces a dynamic diversity from jazz to hip-hop, rock to heavy metal. Other international headliners include Sexing the Cherry, Single Gun Theory, My Friend the Chocolate Cake, Trout Fishing

DO-IT-YOURSELF MINING

Fossicking is a favorite Outback adventure. Seek your pot of gold or cache of gems in river deposits, rock bars, along the bases of rock outcrops, or around old mine dumps. Stay out of old or abandoned mines!

Basic tools will suffice: pick and shovel, prospecting dish, small crowbar, sledgehammer, a gravel-washing container, and varied aluminum sieves.

All fossickers must have a fossicking permit or miner's right from either the state or territorial government, or, on private land, permission must be obtained from the landowner or leaseholder.

The following agencies will provide you with specific info on mining laws and can point you to fossicking guides and geological maps:

New South Wales, Dept. of Mineral Resources, P.O. Box 536, St. Leonards, NSW 2065 (tel. 02-9901-8888)

Northern Territory, Dept. of Mines and Energy, P.O. Box 2901, Darwin, NT 0800 (tel. 08-8999-5511)

Queensland, Dept. of Minerals and Energy, 61 Mary St., Brisbane, QLD 4000 (tel. 07-3237-1435)

South Australia, Dept. of Mines and Energy, P.O. Box 151, Eastwood, SA 5063 (tel. 08-8274-7500

Western Australia, Dept. of Minerals and Energy, 100 Plain St., East Perth, WA 6004 (tel. 09-222-3333)

Victoria, Dept. of Energy and Minerals, P.O. Box 98, East Melbourne, VIC 3002 (tel. 03-9651-7799)

in Quebec, silverchair, and Vince Jones. Adelaide and Perth both have major international arts festivals (see "Holidays and Festivals," below).

Outback music tends toward a strange concoction of country and bush ballad, with some Irish jig tossed in for good measure. Aboriginal music—an inspiring mix of political and racial statements, contemporary electronics, and traditional didgeridoo (a large wooden trumpet)—has been garnering international acclaim in recent years. Two of the best-known Aboriginal entertainment troupes are Tjapukai Aboriginal Dance Theatre and the rock band Yothu Yindi (lead singer Mandawuy Yunupingu was named 1993 Australian of the Year). Both groups were part of 1994's Festival Australia, a 12-day per-

formance and cultural extravaganza held at The Kennedy Center in Washington D.C.

Aboriginal dance is another resurgent art form, and new performances of established companies are eagerly awaited—particularly those of the Tjapukai company. Corroborees are ceremonial dances accompanied by the unearthly music of the didgeridoo. Non-Aborigines are rarely invited to authentic corroborees, but you can catch tourist versions at Darwin and a few other spots.

Finally, Australia offers one superb entertainment that you won't see in the Northern Hemisphere—the brilliant glow of a million stars lighting up the unfamiliar constellations of a strange southern sky, an impossibly classy act to follow.

Gambling

Australians love to gamble—you can bet on it. Each of the three major cities in the Outback has its glitter-and-flash gambling mecca: the Adelaide Casino, Perth's Burswood Island Resort, and the Diamond Beach Hotel and Casino in Darwin; other states sport gambling venues as well. A huge industry has also grown up around horse racing, harness racing (pacing or trotting), and greyhound racing. Billions of dollars are invested annually either with trackside bookmakers or off-course government-run totalizators. Champion thoroughbred horses occupy as exalted a position in the galaxy of Australian sporting heroes as champion human athletes, and a racing subculture has long been established in which the uninitiated quickly find themselves lost in a strange land. The passion for horses culminates in the fabulous Melbourne Spring Carnival; the prized petunia of that meet is the Melbourne Cup, a race that few Australians fail to bet on—and a declared local holiday.

HOLIDAYS AND FESTIVALS

Australia is partyland, folks, and *any* excuse for a long weekend or a raucous rage is welcomed. Most public holidays fall on Monday, allowing for what is called a "long weekend." You can pretty much count on everything being closed for all three (or, in some instances, four) days.

Major National Holidays

New Year's Day: 1 January

Australia Day: 26 January

Good Friday, Easter Saturday, Easter Sunday, and Easter Monday: varies

Anzac Day: 25 April

Queen's Birthday: second Monday in June (Western Australia celebrates in late September/early October)

Melbourne Cup Day: first Tuesday in November (the whole country stops in its hooves for this all-important race—Melbourne stops for the entire day!)

Christmas Day: 25 December

Boxing Day: 26 December

Regional Holidays

Labour Day: first or second Monday in March (Victoria)

Labour Day: first Monday in March (Western Australia)

Labour Day: first Monday in May (Queensland)

May Day: 1 May (Northern Territory)

Adelaide Cup Day: third Monday in May (South Australia)

Foundation Day: first Monday in June (Western Australia)

Show Days: four days throughout July (Northern Territory)

Bank Holiday: first Monday in August (New South Wales)

Picnic Day: first Monday in August (Northern Territory)

Labour Day: first Monday in October (South Australia, New South Wales, and Australia Capital Territory)

School Holidays

These are scheduled four times a year and fall on different dates throughout all the states and territories. Basically they run mid-December to early February, mid-April to mid-May, late June to late July, and mid-September to mid-October. It is especially important to book transport and accommodations ahead during school holiday periods, as that's when most Aussies hit the road or take to the skies.

Festivals and Seasonal Events

January: The **Schützenfest** goes full guns in Hahndorf, South Australia's German community. At Lake Jabiru, in the Northern Territory, the **Jabiru Regatta** features offbeat games and races.

February: The two-day **Kangaroo Island Racing Carnival** comes to Kangaroo Island's Kingscote (South Australia). In the Northern Territory, **race meetings and rodeos** take place at Alice Springs, Tennant Creek, and Darwin.

March: The **Australian Formula One Grand Prix** burns rubber through Melbourne streets for four days (the race is on the last day). South Australia's famed **Adelaide Arts Festival** (even-numbered years) offers three weeks of premier theater, music, dance, arts exhibitions, and fringe events. The **Festival of Perth** is a similar cultural extravaganza in Western Australia, beginning the end of February and lasting a month. Also in Western Australia, at Bindoon, is the **Bindoon Rock Festival,** a Woodstock-wannabe music fest.

April: In odd-numbered years, South Australia's **Barossa Valley Vintage Festival** is a major weeklong taste-till-you-waste celebration in honor of the local grapes and vintners. Also in April Coober Pedy hosts its **Opal and Outback Festival.**

May: In the Northern Territory, Alice Springs' **Bangtail Muster** features a float parade and other events. Other Alice Springs festivals include the **Alice Springs Cup** annual horse race and the **Lions Camel Cup** with races, fireworks, and—of course—camel races. **May Day** in Darwin signals the end of those treacherous box jellyfish and the beginning of beach parties.

June: Darwin's **Bougainvillea Festival** offers two weeks of flowery events. The **Katherine**

Gorge Canoe Marathon (Northern Territory), is a 100-km race along the Katherine River, organized by the Red Cross. Grab the opportunity to celebrate (non-alcoholically) with the traditional people at Barunga Festival, at the Northern Territory's Beswick Aboriginal Land.

July: Darwin is at the forefront again with its Beer Can Regatta, comprised of sailing "craft" constructed entirely from empty beer cans. Almond-lovers will want to attend the Almond Blossom Festival, in Willunga, South Australia, with assorted nutty activities.

August: Shinju Matsuri ("Festival of the Pearl") is a weeklong Asian-theme event held in Broome, Western Australia's old pearling port. The Darwin Rodeo is a well-attended international competition. And Darwin's Mud Crab Tying Competiton is another must on the cultural calendar.

September: The tiny Outback community at Birdsville, Queensland, hosts the hot-to-trot Birdsville Races. The AFL Grand Final, Australian football's final game, is in Melbourne but religiously followed by almost everyone in the country. Watch it on the telly from your favorite pub. Also, Perth blossoms over its Western Australia Wildflower Festival.

October: The Henley-on-Todd Regatta in Alice Springs (late August or early September) features bizarre and creative mock-ups of boats propelled by the racers' feet as they run along the dry Todd River bed. South Australia's

McLaren Vale Bushing Festival commemorates the release of a new vintage with a variety of events including the crowning of a Bushing King and Queen. The Kalgoorlie Cup horse race is held in Western Australia's eponymous mining town.

December: And all's right with the world.

Bush Bashes

Rodeos are favorite Outback entertainments. You'll see stockmen who are dead ringers for cowboys, Americano-style—10-gallon hats, chaps, spurs, struts, the whole shebang. Flies, dust, lots of beer, and monstrous steak sandwiches lend that unique Aussie flavor. The range of events includes calf roping, steer wrestling, bull riding, and saddle- and bareback broncing.

The other live-to-die-for event is the B&S Ball. The B&S have nothing to do with what's left after the rodeo—it actually stands for "bachelor and spinster," though the event is no longer confined to just single folk. The balls are grand social occasions where rural dwellers can socialize, renew old aquaintances, and kick up their dusty heels. In true Aussie style, the balls are one big, long party, with lots of drinking, eating, and carousing. Despite the fact they're held in big barns or open fields, ball-goers dress to the hilt. Balls can be located via fax info sheets. For more info, fax (005) 52-5281 or (005) 56-5902).

ARTS AND CRAFTS

Australians have long been noted for a "cultural cringe," meaning they look to London and New York in matters of taste and style, slavishly following their lead. Although this attitude dies hard, Australians are making real advances in the creation of a national culture. Bolstered by the success of expatriates in all artistic endeavors (Dame Joan Sutherland, Nobel Laureate Patrick White, artist Sir Sydney Nolan—not to mention the Bee Gees and INXS), artsy Aussies are growing more confident and ready to take their work to the outside world.

Each state capital has its own symphony orchestra, opera company, ballet company, theater, and art gallery, which are recipients of generous arts funding. Lovers of traditional Western art forms will be happily surprised at the high standards and support from a quite sophisticated public at the end of the earth.

Australia also is home to a lively "fringe" arts scene, mainly centered in the bohemian suburbs of Sydney, Melbourne, and Adelaide. Adelaide's Fringe Festival, which runs concurrently with the city's renowned and highbrow Festival of the Arts, honors the more avant-garde contributions to theater, music, art, and literature. And while it isn't Times Square or Haight-Ashbury, the low-key local color can be a lot of fun. The cultural melting pot of Australia's cities has meant that artists no longer need to travel to Europe or America to eke out a penurious living in a squalid garret; they can do it here!

The "Heidelberg School" of young artists who resided near Melbourne in the 1930s, along with a group of artists living up around Sydney Harbour, established the first uniquely Australian painting style. Working in oils and watercolors, using natural light to its full advantage, the painters captured the magic, starkness, and intensity of Australian life and landscape. Notable artists of that period were Julian Ashton, Louis Abrahams, Charles Conder, Frederick McCubbin, Tom Roberts, and Arthur Streeton. A later revolution in the 1940s brought fame and acclaim to Sir Sidney Nolan and Arthur Boyd—probably Australia's most well-known painters—and a bevy of other talents, including Pro Hart, who still strokes Outback images from his Broken Hill studio.

VISUAL ARTS

SCULPTURE

LIVING TOGETHER
AUSTRALIA 75c

Aboriginal Art

Aboriginal art has its own aesthetics, which reflect the profound experience of life in Australia. Recently "discovered" by the West, Aboriginal paintings can command substantial prices on the world market.

Most Aboriginal art forms are spiritually based and concerned with the myths and totemic beliefs of the Dreamtime. Painting on bark and, more recently, canvas, Aboriginal artists employ a decorative dot technique that to Western eyes appears quite abstract, and representational images of animals and spirits are painted in the style of an X-ray, revealing internal organs. These techniques are incredibly ancient. Extremely old examples are found on the walls of caves in Arnhem Land. Often the actual rendering of these works is accompanied by songs that instruct the artist in the progress of the work and invest him with spiritual power. The full significance of such works is sacred and available only to the initiated. Aborigines also craft exquisite implements, from the aerodynamically perfect boomerang to ceremonial belts and headdresses.

Australia's most famous Aboriginal artist, Albert Namatjira (1902-59), hailed from Hermannsburg Lutheran Mission, west of Alice Springs. Learning European-style watercolor techniques from a non-Aboriginal painter, Namatjira became comparatively successful for what were considered to be European-style, Central Australian landscapes; eventually he became the first Aborigine to "achieve" Australian citizenship. This achievement, however, did not accord him blanket privileges. Just one year later, in 1958, Namatjira was arrested for buying alcohol for other Aborigines; one year after that, he died. Still, he inspired other would-be artists with his technique, use of color, imagery—and his image.

The 1970s weren't exclusively prime time for American and European artists—the creative renaissance of that period also surfaced at Papunya, a tiny impoverished Aboriginal community northwest of Alice Springs. There, the painting of a mural—a children's school project—turned into a cross-generational creation when elders (with mixed feelings about their traditional symbols being splattered across a public wall) joined in and helped complete the piece. The result, Honey Ant Dreaming, became the first art piece in which traditional images were displayed on something other than a rock or human body. Pretty soon the community was passionately painting away and, though more murals were produced, acrylic paints on canvas eventually became the preferred medium. Central Australian painting has since evolved as an important source of religious and traditional instruction for Aboriginal children.

Other distinctive contemporary Aboriginal arts and crafts include: batiks, pottery, wooden sculptures and carvings in Central Australia; bark paintings, painted log coffins, fiber art, Ngukurr acrylics on canvas in Arnhem Land; paintings and engraved pearl-shell pendants in the Kimberley; spears, bark baskets, carved and painted burial poles, sculptures, and bark paintings on the Tiwi Islands.

As some of us might expect, the works of city-dwelling Aboriginal artists tend to reflect either European influences or deep, raging, racially themed anger. In fact, the beginnings of Aboriginal urban art can be traced to the land-rights issues of the 1970s.

If you'd rather view Aboriginal art from earlier times, drawn or engraved on rocks rather than hanging on gallery walls, significant sites open to visitors are: Chambers Gorge and Cooper Creek (South Australia); Ewaninga (Northern Territory); and Mootwingee (New South Wales). The South Australian Museum, in Adelaide, also houses one of the country's most outstanding collections of Aboriginal artifacts.

SHOPPING

It is possible to buy Aboriginal art from cooperatives run by local communities; these are often the best sources. Much of what is passed off as Aboriginal art in the cities is worthless imitation and souvenir schlock. Some excellent Aboriginal-owned or -managed shops and galleries are the Papunya Tula Gallery in Alice Springs, Maruku Arts and Crafts Centre in Uluru National Park, and Mt. Ebenezer Roadhouse on the Lasseter Highway, en route to Uluru. Most buyers will be able to take home a print, small carving, or T-shirt, but be prepared to pay dearly for gallery originals.

Aside from Aboriginal arts and crafts, Australia is not shop-till-you-drop territory. I'm afraid it's basic and boring—malls, Kmarts, and a few chic international- and local-designer boutiques plunked about the major city centers. In all the cities and most smaller towns, you will find everything you need, from flyscreens to condoms. The Outback, however, is another story. Stock up on provisions before you start out. You'll find necessary and desired gear and clothing in most cities around Australia. Prices for most items are just a bit higher than in the U.S., but books and records are much more expensive. Either bring books with you or buy them secondhand.

Distinctly Australian items include Blundstone boots (elastic sides; Aussie Doc Marten's), Akubra hats, and Driza-bone overcoats. You will just have to purchase at least one sheepskin item, a bottle of Australian wine, and an opal (or 10).

Be cautious when buying opals; try to get recommendations from tourist bureaus, and definitely comparison-shop. The three types of solid opal are: black opal, the most valuable, found at Lightning Ridge, New South Wales, and Mintabie, South Australia; white opal, also called "light" or "fire" opal, found at Coober Pedy and Andamooka, South Australia; and boulder opal, found in southwestern Queensland. A "triplet" is a thin slice of opal layered between a clear dome capping of dark opal potch and crystal quartz.

A not-to-be-missed shopping experience is at the mostly outdoor, sometimes indoor markets held almost everywhere in the country. In Adelaide, the Central Market near Victoria Square is a prime example, as is Darwin's Big Flea Market, the city's oldest. These usually take place on weekends, though some city markets are open during the week. Depending on where you are and the type of market it is, you'll be able to pick up bargains on fruits and veggies, furniture, secondhand clothing, used tools, camping gear, and various bric-a-brac, like the ubiquitous plastic fish and fake handcuffs from Asia.

Normal shopping hours are Mon.-Fri. 9 a.m.-5 p.m., Saturday 9 a.m.-noon. One night a week—usually Thursday or Friday—is often a designated "late shopping night" with doors staying open until 9 p.m. Darwin and Perth offer late-night shopping on Thursday; Adelaide's is Saturday. In the Outback and in rural towns, shops basically open and close whenever.

ACCOMMODATIONS

Australian lodging is well represented by the cliche, "myriad of possibilities." Choices range from backpackers' dorms to penthouse suites in luxury hotels—with motels, pubs, guesthouses, bed and breakfasts, holiday flats, caravan parks, and Outback stations tossed in between. You can get accommodation guides with up-to-date prices at branches of the automobile clubs or, often, at state tourist bureaus. It is advisable to book ahead during public and school holidays. (See "Tourist Information" under "Maps and Tourist Information," later in this chapter.)

Hotels

These come in a few varieties—the big Hyatt-type places, older-style pubs, and private hotels. Worldwide, national, and regional hotel chains and resorts are of international standard and feature all the requisite luxuries and amenities—pools, saunas, spas, room service, complimentary toiletries, phones next to the toilet. Pubs are called "hotels" because originally they were required to provide lodging for travelers. Thus they are usually rather old (and, in some cases, magnificent), with simple rooms and "facilities" down the hall. The private hotel (versus the licensed hotel) does not serve alcohol and is more like a guesthouse.

Motels

As in the U.S., motels are prevalent throughout Australia, owned either by independent operators or chain establishments (Flag, Budget, Country Comfort, and Golden Chain are the biggies). Rooms—usually doubles—are serviced daily and have private bathrooms, radios, televisions, refrigerators, and the ubiquitous electric jug accompanied by packets of instant coffee and tea bags. Motels often have a swimming pool and attached restaurant, and some have family suites with cooking facilities.

Serviced Apartments and Holiday Flats

Serviced apartments are usually found in the cities, while holiday flats (or units) are in resort or vacation areas. They range from basic motel-style rooms with kitchenettes to full-on posh apartments with several rooms. Cutlery, dishes, and cooking utensils are provided but, unless you're staying in one of the upmarket pads with daily or weekly maid service, plan on doing the cleaning yourself. Rented by the week or month, they cater mainly to those who plan an extended stay in one place, and can be an exceptionally good value for a group traveling together.

Guesthouses

Guesthouses, bed and breakfasts, and private hotels are all basically the same—small establishments with shared facilities and "brekkie" thrown into the deal. Other meals can often be arranged. Again, these can be anything from simple residences to elegant mansions. This style isn't for everyone—for instance, if you're secretive or reclusive. Be prepared to hear the other guests' life stories or have your own dragged out of you over the morning's bacon and eggs.

ACCOMMODATION TYPES AND PRICES

Here's the breakdown of accommodations costs listed in this handbook, give or take a few Aussie dollars either way:

> **Inexpensive**—under $35
> **Moderate**—$35-70
> **Expensive**—$70 and way up

Hotels: Chain and independent establishments with all the creature comforts range from $70 up to $350, and higher, for international resorts.

Motels: Chain or locally owned, and ubiquitous throughout Australia; can be had for $35-55, single or double.

Serviced Apartments: Good options for families, groups, and long-termers. Fully equipped at a variety of prices, but usually located in cities or resort areas.

Pub "Hotels": Older rooms with simple furnishings and shared baths, often in renovated or once-glorious buildings—in cities or country towns. Priced around $25-45.

Guesthouses and Bed and Breakfasts (B&Bs): Intimate sharing experiences (sometimes *too* intimate). Can be cheap ($25) or way up there ($100).

Home and Farm Stays: Again, a wide variety, from basic down-home to yuppy-ish pseudo-farms—$50-150ish per day.

Camping and Caravanning: Figure campsites at around $8-15 per day, on-site caravans or cabins at $16-$65 (prices are for two).

Youth and Backpacker Hostels: Average $10-18 per night.

Youth Hostels and Ys

If you're over the age of 12, don't let the word "youth" scare you off. Instead, think of it as meaning "young at heart." Youth hostels are the ultimate for budget travelers (about $10-18 per night), to say nothing of a superb clearing-house for local information, job possibilities, ride-sharing, juicy gossip, et cetera. (You'll hear them referred to as "backpacker lodges," but not all backpacker lodges are youth hostels, and may not operate with the same standards.) Accommodations are in dormitories or bunk-rooms (though sometimes double rooms are available to couples), and usually offer communal cooking and laundry facilities. "Extras" might include bicycle, surfboard, and equipment rentals, as well as organized excursions and tour bookings.

Youth Hostel Association

(YHA) hostels are internationally known, well organized, and efficiently run. They operate from an incredible variety of locations, including tiny shelters, railway cars, suburban mansions, and country churches. Unlike some countries which impose lockouts and curfews, all Australian YHA hostels provide 24-hour access. One across-the-globe requirement, however, is the regulation sheet sack (a couple of sheets sewn together), which is used as a light sleeping sack or sleeping bag liner. Sometimes you can rent these for a few bucks at individual hostels; otherwise purchase them from YHA offices or larger hostels.

You must be a YHA member ($24 per year, plus $16 to join), but you can sign up at any state office and at many individual hostels. The joining fee is not charged if you're not an Australian resident. Also, if you're a YHA member in your home country, it will entitle you to reciprocal rights in Australia. Pick up the handy booklet, *YHA Accommodation Guide,* at any YHA office in Australia. YHA hostels are affiliated with Hostelling International.

For more information, contact: YHA, 38 Sturt St., Adelaide, SA 5000 (tel. 08-8231-5583); YHA, Darwin Hostel Complex, 69A Mitchell St., Darwin, NT 0821 (tel. 08-8981-3995); YHA, 65 Francis St., Northbridge, WA 6003 (tel. 09-227-5122); 422 Kent St., Sydney, NSW 2000 (tel. 02-9261-1111); 154 Roma St., Brisbane, QLD 4000 (tel. 07-3236-1680); 205 King St., Melbourne, VIC 3000 (tel. 03-9670-9611); or 28 Criterion St., Hobart, TAS 7000 (tel. 002-34-9617). In Australia, the **head office** is in Sydney, at 10 Mallett St., Camperdown, NSW 2050 (tel. 02-9565-1699).

In the United States, contact **American Youth Hostels** (AYH), P.O. Box 37613, Washington,

D.C. 20013-7613 (tel. 202-783-6161). In Canada, contact Canadian Hostelling Association, 1600 James Naismith Dr., Suite 608, Cloucester, ON K1B 5N4 (tel. 613-748-5638). In the U.K., contact **Youth Hostel Association,** Trevelyan House, St. Stephen's Hill, St. Albans, Herts. AL1 2DY (tel. 0171-836-1036). In New Zealand, contact **Youth Hostels Association of New Zealand,** P.O. Box 436, Christchurch 1, New Zealand (tel. 03-79-9970).

Non-YHA **backpacker hostels** vary in standards, and usually cost about the same as YHA hostels. They have no membership requirements and offer round-the-clock access, but they might also be a bit scruffy. The smaller, owner-managed establishments are the better bets. Check out the other occupants before you bed down.

Backpackers Resorts of Australia (BRA), a group of about 120 independently owned hostels offer accommodations in historic properties, terrace houses, and the like, offering such divine amenities as pools, spas, tennis, bars, and bistros. To receive a guide to member properties, send $5 to Backpackers Resorts of Australia, P.O. Box 1000, Byron Bay, New South Wales 2481 (tel. 018-66-6888).

The **YMCA** and **YWCA** offer good-value city residences with plain rooms and shared bathrooms. Some Ys have dorm rooms for travelers; others are occupied mainly by permanent residents. You don't need to be a member to stay. The **CWA** (Country Women's Association), somewhat akin to the Y, has both city and country locations, and sometimes allows men and couples.

Camping and Caravanning
Australia has plentiful caravan (trailer) parks which offer powered and unpowered campsites, on-site vans

---

HOME AND FARM STAYS

It's easy—you stay with Aussies in their homes or on their farms. In homes, you're treated like one of the family. You'll have a private bedroom, though you'll probably share bathroom facilities with your Aussie parents and siblings. Breakfast is almost always included, and other meals can often be arranged.

Farm stays (usually on very large sheep or cattle stations) can mean anything and—if you're fussy—should be checked out thoroughly in advance. You might be lodged in the bunkhouse or shearers' quarters and expected to work alongside the jack-and-jilleroos. Particularly on Outback stations, life is simple and often tough. Then again, you might arrange a motel-style farm stay, where you sit back on the veranda with a cold beer (probably *many* cold beers) and breathe in the scent of fresh cow and sheep dung. Ah, nature!

Book home and farm stays through state tourist centers or the following North American representatives: B**ed and Breakfast Australia** (Adventure Center, tel. 800-227-8747, U.S.); **Farmstays** (Sprint Australia, tel. 800-423-2880 U.S.); **Inta-Aussie Accommodation Service** (Inta-Aussie Tours, tel. 800-531-9222 U.S.); **Austravel** (tel. 800-633-3404 U.S.); **Goway Travel** (tel. 800-387-8850, Canada); and **SoPac** (tel. 800-551-2012 or 213-871-0747, U.S. and Canada).

(a caravan that stays on its site), and cabins. Parks are located along highways, near beaches and rivers, in country towns, and on the city fringes. Basic facilities include showers, toilets, hot and cold water; fancier sites might have swimming pools, playgrounds, and recreation rooms. Caravanning is a very popular travel mode for Aussies, so book ahead during peak periods.

Other Accommodations
During academic holidays (usually November through February, plus May and August), you might try scoring a room at one of the universities or colleges. It isn't that easy—you must book in advance and most of the places are inconveniently located. Students are given first preference and cheaper rates (about $20 for B&B, double for nonstudents).

For longer stays, check bulletin boards at hostels, bookshops, and cafes, as well as the local newspaper's classified ads.

FOOD AND DRINK

TUCKER

With the exception of major cities, tucker (food) in the Outback is basic meat and potatoes fare. Just keep in mind that the "meat" may be crocodile, kangaroo, camel, or buffalo! Seafood, especially the prized barramundi, John Dory, yabbies (freshwater crayfish), and Moreton Bay bugs (a local crustacean), is popular around the coastal areas. Though most supermarkets are well stocked, don't expect to find very fresh fruits and veggies in Australia's Red Centre.

Breakfast is an all-important meal Down Under, and Vegemite, a dark yeast mixture, is the national spread. Whatever you do, don't malign Vegemite in Australia—it's worse than desecrating the flag.

Although some progress has been made in recent years, this is *not* an easy country for cholesterol watchers—many foods are fried, breaded, cheesed, and buttered. Food labeling is not very detailed. For example, a label may proclaim "100% vegetable oil" but does not elaborate on what kind of vegetable.

The bigger cities have supermarkets that rival even those in the United States, and even smaller communities have a passable assortment of shops. It's a very good idea to stock up before you go bush or Outback; otherwise you'll be at the mercy of roadhouses—far apart and high-priced. Don't forget that quarantine regulations prohibit fruits, veggies, plants, and some other agricultural products from crossing state lines— eat them, plant them, or prepare to relinquish them at each border.

Favorite takeaway items include roast chicken, fish and chips, chips and chips, pies, pasties, sausage rolls, and hamburgers with "the lot" (meaning with egg, cheese, lettuce, and a slice of red beet). And, thanks to the ethnic population, you'll find a large number of luscious Italian, Greek, Lebanese, Turkish, and Asian establishments for sit-down meals or takeaways.

Takeaways are cheap, pub meals are cheap to moderate ($4-9), and restaurant meals run the price gamut ($10 and *way* up).

FOOD AND DRINK GLOSSARY

You say toe-mate-oh and I say toe-motto! Here are some common Aussie words, translated for your dining pleasure:

barbie—barbecue
billy tea—bush tea boiled in a tin container
biscuit—cookie
brekkie—breakfast
BYO—Bring Your Own (booze)
chips—French fries
chook—chicken
cuppa—tea or coffee
damper—bush bread
Darwin stubby—Darwin's two-liter beer bottle (mainly a tourist item)
flagon—two-liter wine bottle
flake—shark meat (usually the fish that goes with your chips)
floater—meat pie floating in pea soup

lollies—candy
middy—medium-size beer glass
milk bar—local convenience shop
pavlova—traditional cream-and-meringue dessert
piss—booze
pissed—drunk
plonk—wine, especially rotgut
pot—large mug of beer
schooner—large beer glass
serviette—napkin
slab—four six-packs of tinnies/stubbies
snag—sausage
takeaway—takeout
tea—evening meal
tinny—can of beer
tomato sauce—ketchup
tucker—food

THE EDIBLE DESERT

These notes (provided by the Northern Territory Conservation Commission) are a brief introduction to the traditional lifestyle and bush foods of central Australian Aborigines.

You should not eat any bush foods unless they have been positively identified as being edible. The desert areas contain many poisonous plants, some of which look just like their edible relatives.

Aboriginal Lifestyle

Aborigines have survived the harsh conditions of semiarid and desert lands for thousands of years. The secret to their survival lies in their detailed knowledge of the plants, animals, and water sources available in the country.

The women and children gathered fruits, roots, witchetty grubs, and small animals, while the men hunted larger game such as kangaroos and emus. Many of the traditional foods are still collected and eaten today.

BOB RACE/2

cyclorana

Water

Knowledge of all available water sources is passed down from old to young. Water is not only found in local water holes and under the dry surface of creekbeds, but also in a variety of plants and certain animals. The succulent leaves of the parakeelya plant can be eaten in time of emergency. The graceful desert oak tree holds a secret store of water in its roots and in hidden hollows amongst its upper branches.

The water-holding frog, **cyclorana,** burrows beneath the ground with an abdomen full of water and waits for the next heavy rains to fall. With their detailed knowledge of the land, the Aborigines can dig these frogs from their burrows and squeeze them for a thirst-quenching drink.

witchetty grub

Protein

Witchetty grubs live in the roots of certain acacia bushes. These grubs, the juvenile stage of a large moth, contain large amounts of protein and fat, and can be eaten either raw or cooked. When roasted, the grub has a pleasant nutty flavor.

Both the **perentie** and its eggs are valuable sources of protein. The perentie is roasted whole in

(continues on next page)

Restaurants

One of the best things about Australian dining is this: when you book a table in a restaurant, it's yours for the whole night. No one hovers vulture-like, intimidating you to gulp your meal so the table can be turned over to other diners. That's where the no-tipping stance really shines—no tips involved, no need to hurry the patrons. Consequently, dining out is popular entertainment for most Aussies.

Other things to know: A licensed restaurant serves alcohol (though sometimes only beer

and wine), while a BYO restaurant, though unlicensed, allows you to bring your own bottle; dinner is often called "tea"; entree means appetizer, and main course means entree; pub counter meals (commonly veal, chicken, steak, or sausages, with salad and chips) are normally available noon-2 p.m. and 6-8 p.m., and can be eaten either at the counter or at a table in the adjoining lounge (if there is one); many pubs now have attached "bistros"—but be aware that the word "bistro" will probably add an extra digit to the tab!

THE EDIBLE DESERT
(continued)

hot coals with the eggs, which are pierced to remove the whites before cooking.

Flour

The seeds of the **woollybutt** grass and **hakea** tree are just two of the many seeds that can be mixed with water to make damper or seed cake. The seeds are dehusked, ground, mixed with water, and then baked on hot coals. The result is a highly nutritious seed cake.

Fruits and Vegetables

The arid lands of central Australia provide an abundant supply of native fruits. The **ruby saltbush** bears a small red berry that can be eaten. The yellow **bush tomato** is very high in vitamin C and can be dried and stored for long periods. **Bush onions** can be peeled and roasted on hot coals before being

hakea

eaten, perhaps with seed cake or witchetty grubs.

Honey

There are many sources of honey in the bush. The tiny lac scale insects that live on the branches of the **mulga tree** appear as red bumps that exude sweet sticky honeydew. The dew is usually sucked directly from the mulga branch.

The flowers of the **honey grevillea** produce quantities of sweet nectar, which can be sucked straight from the flower or mixed with water in a *mimpu* (wooden bowl) to make a sweet drink.

A different source of honey comes from **honey ants.** These ants live in nests several meters underground and have honey-filled abdomens the size of small grapes. The honey can be eaten by biting off the honey pot or by mixing the whole ant with flour to make a sweet damper.

BOB RACE

DRINK

Australians love to drink. Walk into someone's house and the kettle is instantly put on the stove; make a deal and you'll invariably seal it at the local pub. Favorite nonalcoholic drinks include mineral waters, Coca-Cola, fresh juices, flavored milk, tea, and *lots* of coffee. "White" tea or coffee has milk in it; "flat white" or "flat black" coffee has milk in it, but no froth, as opposed to a cappuccino. Despite the ubiquitousness of the almighty espresso machine, Outback tea- and coffee-drinkers may have to resort to the trusty teabag and instant coffee powder.

Australian Beer

Ice cold and plenty of it! Aussies love their beer, and each state and territory has its favorite brand, though Foster's is the best known worldwide. In addition, boutique breweries have popped up in the major cities, but you'll only be able to taste their efforts at the hotel where they're made. Beer comes in a dizzying variety of containers—tin-

nies, twisties, stubbies, middies, pots, schooners, ponies, goblets, and plain old glasses. The containers and glasses vary by location, so it's best to ask advice from the publican or a friendly local.

Each state or territory has its own special brew, though most are available Australia-wide: **Swan** and **Emu** (Western Australia), **Coopers** (South Australia), **XXXX** (pronounced "FOUR-ex") and **Powers** (Queensland), **Tooheys** (New South Wales), **Victoria Bitter** (Victoria), and **Brogues** (Tasmania). Some of the best boutique varieties are: **Redback** and **Matilda Bay** (Western Australia), **Eumundi** and **Cairn's Draught** (Queensland), and **Cascade** (Tasmania). Try 'em all.

Locals prefer draught (draft) beer straight from the tap. Keep in mind that Australian beer is higher in alcohol content than American varieties (even the Foster's you buy in the U.S. has been watered down), so gauge your consumption accordingly. "Drink-driving" laws are tough in Australia; on-the-spot sobriety checks and booze buses (Breathalyzer vans) are common in urban areas. (See "Laws and Licenses" under "Getting Around," below.)

Australian Wine

South Australia's McLaren Vale, Barossa and Clare Valleys, and Western Australia's Swan and Margaret River Valleys produce excellent domestic wines, as do the Hunter Valley, on the east coast of New South Wales, and a smaller vineyard in Queensland and Victoria. Barossa has some divine reds, and Western Australia excels with its dry riesling. Some common varietals are shiraz, hermitage, and cabernet (reds); riesling, semillon, chardonnay (whites). Australian champagne (oops—I mean *methode champenois*) is widely imbibed and a good value. Tour the vineyards for free tastings, then buy a bottle or two of your favorite wine or bubbly. Less expensive wines can be purchased in two- or four-liter casks.

Spirits

If you're on a budget, you'd best stick to beer and wine—spirits down here are expensive, at least compared to prices

in the Unites States. If money is no object, you'll find most of your favorite brands readily available at bottle shops and bars. Australia also produces port, brandy, and sherry, as well as two types of Queensland rum (but beware of the alcohol content, which could be considerably more than the normal 33%).

Drinking Laws

You must be 18 or older to buy alcohol or consume it. Liquor licenses vary from state to state (and territory). Pubs normally stay open for 12 hours (10 a.m.-10 p.m., or variations thereof) seven days a week. Other bars, clubs, and restaurants can offer alcohol until 2 or 3 a.m. Many establishments can serve you only if you're eating food, or else they are designated BYO (Bring Your Own). Beer, wine, and spirits can be purchased at bottle shops (often attached to a pub) or liquor stores. It is illegal to bring alcohol into an Aboriginal community or reserve.

GETTING THERE

Fly. It's the only way to get Down Under, unless you opt for an expensive cruise with a couple of one- or two-day port stops. Most international airlines operate wide-body aircraft to Australia. Gateway cities are Adelaide, Brisbane, Cairns, Darwin (from Asia), Hobart (from New Zealand), Melbourne, Perth (from Europe, Asia, and Africa), Port Hedland (from Bali), Sydney, and Townsville. Sydney and Melbourne are the two busiest international airports, and customs and immigration formalities can seem endless, particularly when many flights arrive around the same time. If you can avoid flying in over Christmas, Easter, or the middle of Australia's summer or school holiday periods, do so. Otherwise book well ahead as these are Australia's heaviest travel periods. Flights to Sydney from Singapore or Hong Kong are especially popular and often overbooked. Also, try to avoid weekend arrivals.

Travel Agents

If you're looking for the most economical fare, make sure you have a travel agent who doesn't

COUNCIL TRAVEL OFFICES

IN THE UNITED STATES

Austin, 2000 Guadalupe St., Austin, TX 78705 (tel. 512-472-4931)

Berkeley, 2486 Channing Way, Berkeley, CA 94704 (tel. 510-848-8604)

Boston, 729 Boylston St., Suite 201, Boston, MA 02116 (tel. 617-266-1926)

Chicago, 1153 N. Dearborn St., 2nd Fl., Chicago, IL 60610 (tel. 312-951-0585)

Los Angeles, 10904 Lindbrook Dr., Los Angeles, CA 90024 (tel. 310-208-3551)

New Orleans, Joseph A. Danna Center, Loyola University, 6363 St. Charles Ave., New Orleans, LA 70118 (tel. 504-866-1767)

New York, 205 E. 42nd St., New York, NY 10017 (tel. 212-661-1450); New York Student Center, 895 Amsterdam Ave., New York, NY 10025 (tel. 212-666-4177); 148 West 4th St., New York, NY 10012 (tel. 212-254-2525)

Portland, 7155 W. Morrison, Suite 600, Portland, OR 97205 (tel. 503-228-1900)

San Diego, 953 Garnet Ave., San Diego, CA 92109 (tel. 619-270-6401); UCSD Price Center, 9500 Gilman Dr., La Jolla, CA 92093 (tel. 619-452-0630)

San Francisco, 530 Bush St., San Francisco, CA 94108 (tel. 415-421-3473); Suite 102, 919 Irving St., San Francisco, CA 94122 (tel. 415-566-6222)

Seattle, 1314 N.E. 43rd St., Suite 210, Seattle, WA 98105 (tel. 206-632-2448); 219 Broadway Ave. East, the Alley Building, Suite 17, Seattle, WA 98102 (tel. 206-329-4567)

Washington, D.C., 3300 M St. NW, 2nd Fl., Washington, D.C. 20007 (tel. 202-337-6464)

For other U.S. cities, phone (800) 226-8624.

ELSEWHERE

France, 22, rue des Pyramides, 75001 Paris (tel. 1-44-55-55-65); 16, rue de Vaugirard, 75006 Paris (tel. 1-46-34-02-90)

Germany, Düsseldorf (tel. 211-36-30-30); Munich (tel. 089-39-50-22)

Japan, Tokyo (tel. 3-3581-5517)

Singapore (tel. 65-738-7066)

Thailand, Bangkok (tel. 66-2-282-7705)

U.K., 28A Poland St., London W1V (tel. 0171-437-7767)

STUDENT TRAVEL ASSOCIATION OFFICES

IN THE UNITED STATES

Berkeley, 2nd Floor, ASUC Building, UC Berkeley, Telegraph at Bancroft Way, Berkeley, CA 94720 (tel. 510-642-3000

Boston, 297 Newbury St., Boston, MA 02115 (tel. 617-266-6014)

Cambridge, 65 Mt. Auburn St., Cambridge, MA 02138 (tel. 617-576-4623)

Chicago, 429 S. Dearborn St., Chicago, IL 60605 (tel. 312-786-9050)

Los Angeles, 7202 Melrose Ave., Los Angeles, CA 90046 (tel. 213-934-8722); 920 Westwood Blvd., Los Angeles, CA 90024 (tel. 310-824-1574); 120 Broadway #108, Santa Monica, CA 90401 (tel. 310-394-5126)

New York, 10 Downing St., New York, NY 10014 (tel. 212-627-3111); 103 Ferris Booth Hall, Columbia University, New York, NY 10027 (tel. 212-854-2224)

Philadelphia, 3730 Walnut St., Philadelphia, PA 19104 (tel. 215-382-2928)

San Francisco, 51 Grant Ave., San Francisco, CA 94108 (tel. 415-391-8407)

Seattle, 4341 University Way NE, Seattle, WA 98105 (tel. 206-633-5000)

Washington, D.C., 2401 Pennsylvania Ave., Suite G, Washington, D.C. 20037 (tel. 202-887-0912)

IN AUSTRALIA

Adelaide, 235 Rundle St., Adelaide, SA 5000 (tel. 08-8233-2426)

Brisbane, Shop 25, Brisbane Arcade, 111-117 Adelaide St., Brisbane, QLD 4000 (tel. 07-3221-9388)

Cairns, Shop 2, Central Court, 43 Lake St., Cairns, QLD 4870 (tel. 070-31-4199)

Canberra, Ground Floor, 13-15 Garema Pl., Canberra, ACT 2601 (tel. 06-247-8633)

Darwin, Darwin Transit Centre, 69 Mitchell St., Darwin, N.T. 0800 (tel. 08-8941-2955)

Melbourne, 222 Faraday St., Carlton, VIC 3053 (tel. 03-9349-2411)

Sydney, First Floor, 732 Harris St., Ultimo, Sydney, NSW 2007 (tel. 02-281-2604)

Perth, 100 James St., Northbridge, Perth, WA 6003 (tel. 09-227-7569)

ELSEWHERE

Germany, Leipzigerstrasse 17a, 60487 Frankfurt/Main (tel. 069-979-0760)

Japan, 7th Floor, 1-16-20 Minami-Ikebukuro, Toshima-Ku, Tokyo 171 (tel. 03-5391-2889)

Netherlands, Schipholweg 101, 2316 XC Leiden (tel. 071-68-8888)

New Zealand, 10 High St., Auckland (tel. 09-309-9723)

Singapore, 02-17 Orchard Parade Hotel, 1 Tanglin Rd., Singapore 1024 (tel. 734-5681)

Thailand, 14th Floor, room 1406, 33 Surawong Rd., Bangrak, Bangkok 10500 (tel. 02-233-2582)

U.K., 6 Wrights Lane, London W8 6TA (tel. 071-938-4711)

mind doing a little work on your behalf. **Council Travel** and **STA** (Student Travel Association)—both student-oriented agencies, often with university locations—usually offer the cheapest deals with the fewest restrictions, and student status is not a prerequisite for many of their fares. In London, bucket shops (advertised in *Time Out, City Limits* and *TNT*) offer discounted fares; reliable agencies include: **Campus Travel,** 52 Grosvenor Gardens, London SW1 (tel. 071-730-8111); **Quest Worldwide,** 29 Castle St., Kingston, Surrey KT1 (tel. 081-547-3322) and **Trailfinders,** 42-50 Earls Court Rd., London W8 (tel. 071-938-3366). Me—I rarely use a travel agent. Instead, I call individual airlines myself and do the comparison-shop routine; consequently, for about half a day's telephone inquiries, I have saved a *lot* of money by doing my own research. Important questions to ask include applicable standby fares, special promotions, allowed stopovers, and restrictions and penalties.

If you're not fussy about travel dates, say so. You can save plenty of bucks by traveling in the low or shoulder season instead of sky-high peak time. **Fare seasons** from the Northern Hemisphere are: 1 May-31 August, low; 1 December-28 February, high; everything else, shoulder. Some airlines vary these periods by a few weeks.

FARES

Scads of fares are available—from rock-bottom, off-season economy to super-luxe, super-bucks first class. Business class, an upgraded economy and downgraded first class, is available on most airlines. Advance-purchase excursion (APEX) fares are usually the best value, though some (and, occasionally, many) restrictions apply. These might include minimum and maximum stays, and nonchangeable itineraries (or hefty penalties for changes); tickets may also be nonrefundable, once purchased—and most airlines are not buying the "medical excuse" bit anymore.

Other travel options to consider are Round-the-World or Circle-Pacific fares. **Round-the-World tickets**—usually combining two airlines—allow travel in the same direction (with no backtracking) around the world anywhere on their combined route systems. Tickets ordinarily require that the first sector be booked in advance and that travel be completed within one year. The number of stops permitted may vary, and cancellation penalties may apply. **Circle-Pacific** tickets work pretty much the same as round-the-worlders except that they circle only the Pacific rather than the whole world. A sample itinerary might encompass San Francisco, Honolulu, Auckland, Sydney, Singapore, Bangkok, Hong Kong, Tokyo, then back to San Francisco. Contact travel agents for participating airlines and current fares; both types of tickets can be an exceptionally good value.

At the time of this writing, the average low-season, roundtrip APEX fare from either Los Angeles or San Francisco—with one stopover allowed—is $1150 to Sydney and $1700 to Perth; high season is $1450 to Sydney, and $2000 to Perth.

AIRLINES

Garuda Indonesia

An easy and exotic way to enter the Outback (or Australia, for that matter) is to hop over to Darwin from Bali.

From North America, Garuda flies out of Los Angeles, via Honolulu, to Bali and Jakarta. From Europe, Garuda takes off from London, Amsterdam, and a host of other major capitals; just a few of the many Asian options are Tokyo, Beijing, Seoul, Hong Kong, Bangkok, Singapore, Kuala Lumpur, and Manila (for **Circle-Pacific** ticket holders, Garuda's partners are Delta and Cathay Pacific). The airline serves more than 40 international destinations; Meripati, Indonesia's domestic carrier, provides connections within the archipelago. (Naturally, you will want to explore the country with Moon's *Indonesia Handbook*—Bill Dalton's bible to the country—or with *Bali Handbook,* Dalton's smaller epistle.) At the time of this writing, the average low-season, roundtrip APEX fare from Los Angeles to Darwin is $1770, and that will allow you a six-month stay in both Bali and Darwin; high season (June-August and December) will cost $100 more. Besides to Darwin, Garuda also flies from Bali or Jakarta into Adelaide, Brisbane, Cairns, Melbourne, Perth, Sydney, and Townsville. For reservations in the United States, phone (800) 342-7832; in Canada, phone (800) 663-2254; and, in London, phone (071) 486-2644 or 486-3011.

International Carriers from North America

Air New Zealand, Canadian International, United Airlines, and Qantas Airways will all get you from the west coast of North America to the eastern shores of Australia, via a variety of routes. However, **be forewarned:** Fares, airlines, and routes are continually changing. Call your travel agent or the individual airlines for up-to-date info and fares.

Many nonstop flights now operate between Los Angeles or San Francisco and Sydney (flying time about 15 hours). Other flights offer some attractive stopover possibilities: Honolulu/Western Samoa/Tahiti/Fiji Islands/Cook Islands/Tonga/Auckland with Air New Zealand; Honolulu/Tahiti/Fiji Islands/Auckland with Qan-

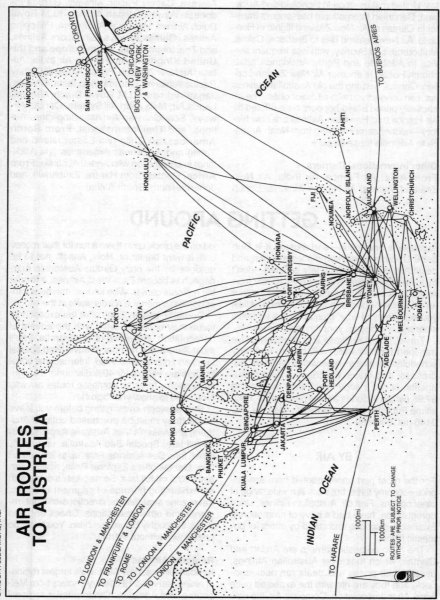

AIR ROUTES
TO AUSTRALIA

© MOON PUBLICATIONS, INC.

ROUTES ARE SUBJECT TO CHANGE
WITHOUT PRIOR NOTICE

1000mi
1000km

TO LONDON & MANCHESTER
TO FRANKFURT & LONDON
TO ROME
TO LONDON & MANCHESTER
TO LONDON & MANCHESTER

TO HARARE

TO BUENOS AIRES

INDIAN
OCEAN

PACIFIC

OCEAN

TO TORONTO

LOS ANGELES
SAN FRANCISCO
VANCOUVER

TO CHICAGO, NEW YORK,
BOSTON, NEW YORK,
& WASHINGTON

HONOLULU

TAHITI

FIJI
NOUMEA
NORFOLK ISLAND
AUCKLAND
WELLINGTON
CHRISTCHURCH

HONIARA
PORT MORESBY
CAIRNS
BRISBANE
SYDNEY
MELBOURNE
HOBART
ADELAIDE
DARWIN
PORT HEDLAND
DENPASAR
PERTH

TOKYO
NAGOYA
FUKUOKA

MANILA

HONG KONG

BANGKOK
PHUKET

KUALA LUMPUR
SINGAPORE
JAKARTA

tas; United makes stops in Honolulu and Auckland; Canadian International passengers transfer to Qantas or Air New Zealand flights in Honolulu. Air New Zealand flies to Brisbane, Cairns, Melbourne, and Sydney, with less frequent service to Adelaide and Perth; Auckland/Christchurch/Hobart is another Air New Zealand option. Qantas, wearing the old Australian Airlines hat, can connect you with all major cities. The attractively priced island-hoppers once offered by Air France and Hawaiian Airlines are now history—neither carrier is flying from North America to Australia these days.

Other International Carriers

From Asia: Air France, Air India, Air New Zealand, Alitalia, All Nippon Airways, British Airways, Cathay Pacific Airways, Garuda Indonesia Airways, Japan Airlines, KLM Royal Dutch Airlines, Malaysian Air System, Philippine Airlines, Qantas Airways, Singapore Airlines, and Thai International. **From Europe and the United Kingdom:** Air France, Air India, Alitalia, Air New Zealand, British Airways, Cathay Pacific Airways, Garuda Indonesia Airways, Japan Airlines, KLM Royal Dutch Airlines, Lauda Air, Malaysian Air System, Qantas Airways, Scandinavian Airlines, Singapore Airlines, and Thai International. **From South America:** Lan Chile (via Easter Island and Tahiti) and Aerolineas Argentinas (via Auckland) in conjunction with Ansett Australia. **From Africa:** Qantas (from Harare, Zimbabwe, and Johannesburg, South Africa).

GETTING AROUND

Australia is enormous—and most of it is Outback. Distances between places are vast and destinations often completely isolated—don't try to see the whole continent on a 10-day tour. Australia is also not a dollar-a-day country, nor an especially good one for hitchhiking. Allow yourself plenty of time, plan at least a tentative itinerary, and budget your funds accordingly.

Travel Times Australia is a comprehensive transport timetable with rail, coach, and ferry schedules, as well as reservation numbers, addresses, and maps. Purchase it from newsagents, or get a copy in advance by sending $7.95 (which includes airmail postage) to Traveltime Publishing, 3 Goodwin St., Glen Iris, VIC 3146 (tel. 03-9889-3344).

BY AIR

For the most part prices quoted here are full-price economy fares, but there is a wide range of other options. First off, Australian airlines, since deregulation, have had a bevy of promotional, excursion, discount, and stand-by offers for domestic flights.

The main domestic carriers are Ansett and Qantas, which took over Australian Airlines; usually their prices and deals run neck-and-neck, and they are rife with the expected price wars. After deregulation, Compass Air, the new kid on the block, gave them a run for their money until it went bankrupt. Now, Ansett, not to be outdone by the cozy Qantas/Australian marriage, has bought East-West Airlines, a former big regional carrier. Who knows, maybe another domestic ménage à trois waits in the wings.

Domestic passes don't offer the exceptional value they once did, what with the advent of deregulation. Once you're in Australia, you'll most likely see a number of advertised special fares and promotions. Also, international ticket holders are eligible for 40% discounts off regular economy fares on domestic routes anyway (you have to show your ticket).

Passes worth investigating before you leave home (they must be purchased outside Australia) are Ansett's Visit Australia Airpass, 55% off full fare, Special See Australia, up to 40% off full fare, See Australia Fare, up to 25% off full fare; Qantas offers Explorer Pass, which averages 50% off full fare. Some passes come with an exhausting barrage of segment coupons, travel zone separations, directions-of-flight, regional and other restrictions. Check dos and don'ts thoroughly before purchase. You might do just as well without them.

Regional Airlines

Kendell Airlines, now Australia's largest regional airline, services 19 country centers from Melbourne and Adelaide. Other smaller regional

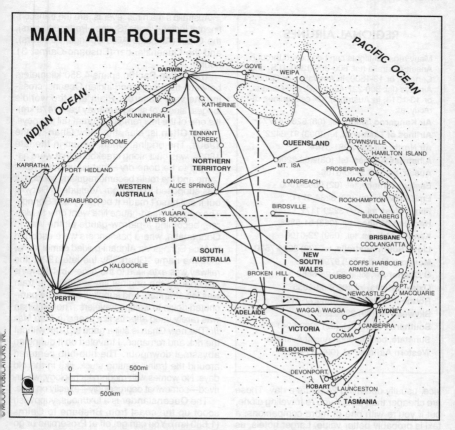

MAIN AIR ROUTES

INDIAN OCEAN

PACIFIC OCEAN

DARWIN
GOVE
WEIPA
KUNUNURRA
KATHERINE
CAIRNS
BROOME
TENNANT CREEK
QUEENSLAND
TOWNSVILLE
HAMILTON ISLAND
KARRATHA
PORT HEDLAND
NORTHERN TERRITORY
MT. ISA
PROSERPINE
MACKAY
PARABURDOO
WESTERN AUSTRALIA
ALICE SPRINGS
LONGREACH
ROCKHAMPTON
YULARA (AYERS ROCK)
BIRDSVILLE
BUNDABERG
BRISBANE
COOLANGATTA
KALGOORLIE
SOUTH AUSTRALIA
NEW SOUTH WALES
COFFS HARBOUR
ARMIDALE
BROKEN HILL
DUBBO
PT. MACQUARIE
NEWCASTLE
PERTH
ADELAIDE
WAGGA WAGGA
SYDNEY
CANBERRA
VICTORIA
COOMA
MELBOURNE
DEVONPORT
HOBART
LAUNCESTON
TASMANIA

0   500mi
0   500km

carriers provide scheduled service between cities, provincial towns, and Outback areas—some only travel within individual states or territories, others cross borders. Most can be booked from North America through Qantas or Ansett. Within Australia, contact individual airlines at their local numbers (see chart).

Regional carriers, with their booking contacts, are: In **New South Wales,** Aeropelican (Ansett), Australian Airlink (Qantas), Eastern Airlines (Qantas), Hazelton Airlines (Ansett), and Impulse Airlines (Ansett); in **Northern Territory,** Air North (Ansett); in **Queensland,** Flight West (Ansett), Sabair (Ansett), and Sunstate (Qantas); in **South Australia,** Southern Australia Airlines (Qantas);

in **Tasmania,** Airlines of Tasmania (Ansett); in **Victoria,** Kendell Airlines (Ansett); and in **Western Australia,** Skywest (Ansett).

North American contacts are: **Ansett Australia** (tel. 800-366-1300 in the U.S. and Canada, 13-1300 in Australia); and **Qantas Airways** (tel. 800-227-4500 in the U.S. and Canada, 13-1313 in Australia). Both Australian numbers are toll-free, countrywide (no area code is necessary).

From the Airport
Major cities offer inexpensive public bus service to, from, and between international and domestic airports. A variety of shuttle companies operate convenient door-to-door minivan ser-

REGIONAL AIRLINES

Many regional flights can be booked through Ansett Australia (tel. 800-366-1300, U.S. and Canada, or 13-1300, in Australia), or Qantas Airways (tel. 800-227-4500 U.S. and Canada, or 13-1313, in Australia). Or call airlines directly, at:

Air Kangaroo Island, tel. (08) 8234-4177
Airlines of Tasmania, tel. (003) 91-8422
Air North, tel. (08) 8981-5144
Albatross Airlines, tel. (08) 482-2296
Ausair, tel. (03) 9580-6166
Eastern Airlines, tel. (02) 9693-1000
Emu Airways, tel. (08) 8234-3711
Flight West, tel. (07) 3229-1177
Hazelton Airlines, tel. (063) 61-5888
Kendell Airlines, tel. (069) 22-0100
Lloyd South Australia, tel. (08) 8224-7500
Monarch Air, tel. (02) 9790-0899
O'Connor Air, tel. (087) 25-6666
Oxley Airlines, tel. (065) 83-1955
Rottnest Airlines, tel. (09) 277-4198
Skywest, tel. (09) 334-2288
Southern Pacific, tel. (07) 3229-5041
Sunstate, book through Ansett Australia
Western Airlines, tel. (09) 277-4022

vice, usually operating 24 hours a day. These are cheaper than taxis if you're traveling alone, but if you're with one or more companions, a taxi is probably better value. Larger hotels, as well as many motels, provide free pick-up service for their guests. In smaller towns, you'll have to rely on whatever you can—a taxi, passing local, or your good looks.

BY TRAIN

Frequent commuter and suburban trains link most capital cities with inner-city, outlying, and country areas. Some of the few Outback areas accessible by rail are Alice Springs, Broken Hill, Charleville, Longreach, Mount Isa, the vast Nullarbor Plain with stops at Port Augusta and Kalgoorlie, as well as Adelaide and Perth.

Australia's main rail "events" are the transcontinental Indian-Pacific (Sydney-Perth, 64 hours), the Ghan (Adelaide-Alice Springs, 20 hours), and the Queenslander (Brisbane-Cairns, 31 hours).

The **Indian-Pacific** spans 4,350 kilometers between the Pacific and Indian Oceans, crossing the vast Nullarbor Plain and the world's longest length of straight railway track (478 km). It's one of the few remaining great rail journeys.

The **Ghan** is, alas, the "new Ghan" of the 1980s. The original Ghan, begun in the late 1800s, was built along creekbeds that were assumed to be bone-dry—that is, until the rains came and the route became regularly flooded. It was supposed to run from Adelaide to Darwin, but it still hasn't made it beyond Alice Springs. The original broad-gauge line went only to Marree, becoming a narrow-gauge all the way to Oodnadatta, where passengers were escorted to Alice Springs via Afghani-guided camel trains, thus the name "Ghan." By the late 1920s the railway was extended to the Alice—but the rains still flooded the original lines. Often the train was left stranded, and supplies had to be parachuted down to waiting travelers. The old Ghan was rarely used after its film scene in *Mad Max III.* The new Ghan is still a good trip, but without the risk and romance. I traveled on it during an abyssmal downpour. The hub-bub centered around the train's getting stuck, like in the old days. No worries with modern technology; we arrived—somewhat depressingly—exactly on time.

The **Queenslander** is a luxurious, yuppy-ish scoot up the coast from Brisbane to Cairns (1,680 km). You can get off at Proserpine or go to the end of the line. You'll be pampered with great views, gourmet cuisine, and sophisticated entertainment.

Other rail services include the **Sunlander** (Brisbane-Cairns, 31 hours), the **Spirit of the Tropics** (Brisbane-Cairns, 31 hours), the **Spirit of the Outback** (Brisbane-Longreach, 24 hours), the **Westlander** (Brisbane-Cunnamulla-Quilpie, 22 hours), the **Inlander** (Townsville-Mount Isa, 19 hours), the **XPT** (Sydney-Brisbane, 14 and one-half hours), the **Overland** (Adelaide-Melbourne, 12 hours), the **XPT** (Sydney-Melbourne, 10 and one-half hours), the **XPLORER** (Sydney-Canberra, four and one-half hours), the **Prospector** (Perth-Kalgoorlie, eight hours), and the **Silver**

City Link (Melbourne-Mildura, Broken Hill, 13 hours). The **Daylink** and **Speedlink** provide train-coach combination travel from Melbourne and Sydney (respectively) to Adelaide.

First- and economy-class seats and berths are available on all long-distance services and must be booked in advance. First-class twinette cabins have seats that turn into two sleeping berths; most have en suite shower, toilet, wash basin with hot and cold water, and electric shaver outlet. First-class single cabins only have toilets and basins—showers are down the hall. Economy-class sleepers in Queensland accommodate three people, with toilets and showers available in each car. Available on the Ghan

and Indian-Pacific only, "holiday class" offers two-berth cabins with economy sleepers. Coach-class cars feature reclining seats and, on many hauls, also provide showers. Meals are included with first-class accommodation fares. All long-distance trains have dining cars, bars, buffet cars, and lounges with a variety of entertainment. The Spirit of the Tropics (Brisbane-Townsville-Cairns) is famed for Club Loco, its high-tech "Rock 'n' Rail" disco on wheels. Meals are included with first-class accommodations.

In Australia, trains can be booked through **Rail Australia** (tel. 13-2232, toll-free). State railways can also book long distance, interstate, or intrastate trains, and many offer a variety of in-

RAIL AUSTRALIA ~ MAJOR SERVICES

teresting one-day or longer trips. For more information contact: Australian National, Keswick Rail Terminal, Adelaide (tel. 08-8231-7699); Countrylink, Central Station, Eddy Ave., Sydney (tel. 02-9217-8812); Queensland Rail, Roma Street Station, Brisbane (tel. 07-3235-1122); V/Line, Spencer Street Station, Melbourne (tel. 03-9619-5000); or Westrail, East Perth Terminal, West Parade, East Perth (tel. 09-326-2813 or 13-2232 toll-free).

Rail Passes

Austrailpasses allow unlimited rail travel, including metropolitan trains, and are good deals if you plan to do a lot of rail travel. They, too, must be purchased outside Australia. Costs in Australian dollars are: 14 days, $725 first class, $435 economy; 21 days, $895/$565; 30 days, $1100/$685; 60 days, $1535/$980; 90 days, $1765/$1125.

The **Austrail Flexi-Pass** allows limited travel within a six-month period. Costs are: eight days, $560 first class, $340 economy; 15 days, $790/$500; 22 days, $1100/$700; 29 days, $1400/$900. The eight-day pass does not allow travel on the Ghan or Indian-Pacific from Adelaide to Perth. Passes do not cover charges for sleeping berths or meals. For more information or reservations, phone **Rail Australia** (tel. 800-423-2880 U.S., or 800-387-8850 Canada).

If you want to catch a train but don't have a railpass, inquire about **Caper Fares.** If booked seven days ahead, they can save you some 30% off regular rail fares.

BY COACH

Modern air-conditioned coaches (buses) are an easy and comfortable way to see the country. Most of them have bathroom facilities, overhead video monitors, piped-in music, on-board hostesses, and drivers who double as tour guides. Buses are usually the cheapest way to travel *and* they go to a far wider range of places than trains and planes—to all capital cities, country towns, provincial centers, and most Outback regions. If there's a place they don't travel, they can usually hook up with a local bus system (which might be a mail truck) that will get you where you're going.

The big coach lines, Greyhound, Pioneer, and Bus Australia, have merged as Greyhound Pioneer Australia (don't be confused by the old logos still painted on the buses). Other large companies are McCafferty's (tel. 07-3236-3033), based in Brisbane, traveling the east coast, Townsville, Darwin, Alice Springs, and Adelaide; Premier Roadlines/Stateliner (tel. 08-8415-5544), offering Adelaide regional service, including the Flinders Ranges; Westrail (tel. 09-326-2813 or 13-2232 toll-free), operating within the Western Australia region; and Tasmanian Redline Coaches (tel. 03-6334-4442), which traverse most of that state. A plethora of small local companies venture just about everywhere else.

Coach travel is a good way to kick back and relax, see the countryside, and meet other Aussie and international travelers. On the downside, you might find yourself locked up with some madding crowd.

Daily express routes include: Sydney-Adelaide (24 hours, $95); Sydney-Canberra (four and one-half hours, $30); Sydney-Melbourne (14 and one-half hours, $61); Canberra-Melbourne (nine and one-half hours, $55); Melbourne-Adelaide (nine and one-half hours, $55); Adelaide-Alice Springs (20 hours, $142), Adealide-Perth (35 hours, $189); Adelaide-Brisbane (33 and one-half hours, $155); Darwin-Alice Springs (19 hours, $142); Darwin-Kakadu (three and one-half hours, $155); Alice Springs-Ayers Rock (six hours, $77); Cairns-Brisbane (25 hours, $137); Cairns-Darwin (42 hours, $261); Brisbane-Sydney (17 hours, $73); Brisbane-Melbourne (25 hours, $129); Perth-Darwin (33.5 hours, $347).

Contact Greyhound Pioneer Australia at 13-2030 (toll-free, in Australia); consult the telephone books or *Travel Times Australia* for other phone numbers.

Bus Passes

Again, you have an almost infinite assortment of bus passes—local, regional, national, and bus and train combination passes—explorer passes, backpacker discounts, bargain fares, etc. Some you have to buy outside Australia; others you can only buy once you're there.

Aussie Passes offer unlimited travel on the Greyhound Pioneer Australia national network, using the "flexi-pass system." Travel days consist of 24-hour periods. Costs are: seven days in one month, $380; 10 days in one month, $540; 15 days in one month, $635; 21 days in two months, $890; 30 days in two months, $1080; 60 days in three months, $1610; 90 days in six months, $2225.

For more information for both Greyhound Pioneer Australia and McCafferty's, phone (800) 531-9222, U.S. and Canada.

Alternative Buses

A new breed of "adventure" buses has spawned within Australia. They head off the beaten path, carry small groups, and ease—rather than rush—you along. For more information, contact: **Oz Experience,** Sydney-Cairns adventure travel (tel. 02-9977-2688); **Straycat,** Melbourne-Sydney high country adventure (tel. 1800-800-840); or **Wayward Bus,** with a range of city, Centre, and transcontinental journeys (tel. 1800-882-823).

BY BOAT

Spirit of Tasmania ferries cruise three times each week between Port Melbourne, Victoria, to Devonport, Tasmania. The 14-hour overnight trip offers everything from sleeper seats to private cabins, but even the basic seats sometimes cost more than an airline flight. The ferries do take vehicles, but, unless you own one, this isn't very practical either as most rental agencies prohibit sea transport of their fleet. Also, be forewarned, the Bass Strait can be a very rough ride!

The **Kangaroo Island Sealink** operates two roll-on roll-off ferries daily between Cape Jervis, South Australia, to Kangaroo Island.

Western Australia's Rottnest Island is serviced daily by **Boat Torque.**

PUBLIC TRANSPORTATION

Simply put, there is no public transportation in the Outback. In the big cities, however, you'll have a choice of sleepy trams, frequent buses, efficient ferries, commuter trains, or light rail service. See the "Transport" sections in the destination chapters.

Many companies offer money-saving daily, weekly, or monthly commuter passes—if you're

a student or senior, this is the time to pull out your i.d. and grab the concession fares.

BY CAR OR CARAVAN

Outside the major cities, cars are about the only practical way to go. Rentals are not cheap, but if you're with a group the cost can work out more favorably. Avis, Budget, Hertz, and Thrifty are well represented and can be booked ahead from North America, but you'll often get a better deal from smaller, independent concerns after you've arrived. One advantage of the big conglomerates is that you can pick up and return your car at the airport and, in many cases, drop your car off at a destination other than your pick-up place (one-way rentals are not usually available in Western Australia, the Northern Territory, or other remote locations).

Before renting a car, find out if it includes unlimited kilometers. Daily rates range from about $75 for a small car (Toyota Corolla, Ford Laser), $90 for a medium size (Toyota Camry, Holden Camira), and $105-plus for a larger vehicle like the Holden Commodore. These rates include insurance, but if you're paying by credit card, check with your company to see if you qualify for CDW (Collision Damage Waiver), which can save you considerable money. For U.S. residents, your regular auto insurance policy also might cover this charge. For more information, contact: Avis (tel. 800-831-2847, U.S.); Budget (tel. 800-283-4382, U.S.); or Hertz (tel. 800-654-3001, U.S.). Territory Rent-A-Car, with six Northern Territory branches, can now be booked from the U.S. (tel. 800-423-2880). Also see the "Transport" sections in each travel chapter.

If you take a car into Outback regions you will be charged a hefty premium. Four-wheel-drive vehicles are available for more adventurous travel, but they are costlier than conventional cars ($100-150 daily, many with limited kilometers). Also, insurance can add considerably to the cost. When tallying up the cost and equipment of a 4WD journey, travelers may find that organized tours are more economical and less stressful. Reputable rental agencies include: Brits: Australia (tel. 800-641-8772, U.S.); Oz Rentals (tel. 03-9877-2986, Victoria); and

ROAD WARNING SIGNS

CROSSING HERE
NEXT 15 km
SPEED LIMIT ENDS

WARNING SIGNS

South Perth 4WD Rentals (tel. 09-362-5444, Western Australia).

Campervans (two to three berths) and **caravans** (four to six berths) range in price from $900 to $1400 per week, with unlimited mileage. Most come equipped with refrigerator, sink, gas stove, and water tank, and some have showers and toilets. Caravans are not recommended for Outback travel—they fall apart, get stuck, are difficult to control. Also, they're not even allowed into some of the national parks. Camper and motorhome rental agencies include: Apollo Motorhome Holidays (tel. 800-286-2147, U.S.); Inta-Aussie Tours (tel. 800-531-9222 U.S.); and Koala Camper Rentals (tel. 800-423-2880 U.S.).

Whatever type of vehicle you rent, make sure you take out adequate insurance.

Purchasing a Car

Buying a car, especially for the short-term visitor, can be a pain—an *expensive* pain. New ones, whether locally manufactured or imported, are not cheap; used ones can turn out to be unreliable lemons. This is not like going to Sweden or Germany to pick up a shiny new Saab or Porsche and drive off into the sunset. Buying a car, particularly a used one, can be the same kind of arduous, time-consuming hell in Sydney or Perth as it is in Los Angeles or Detroit. And, as you ride off into that central Australian sunset, and the car blows its head gasket or cracks the block, your salty tears will do nothing more than blur your written guarantee.

The **buy-back** plan is another option: you buy a car (or motorcycle) at a fixed rate, put down a deposit equal to the vehicle's value, return it after a specified period, and get your money back, less the agreed-upon fee. Most prices include a set number of kilometers, limit-ed warranties, and short-term insurance. One company that specializes in both car and motorcycle buy-backs is **Car Connection Australia,** RSD Lot 8, Vaughan Springs Rd., Glenluce, VIC 3451 (tel. 054-73-4469, fax 73-4520).

Highways and Byways

City expressways and thoroughfares are just about as hectic and expletive-inspiring as those in any other first world metropolis and come complete with rush-hour (peak) traffic, which, increasingly, seems to last early morning until late at night. The major highways are sealed (called "bitumen") with asphalt or tar and well-maintained—though they are often only two-lane affairs (in the Outback, bitumen roads can barely accommodate even one vehicle). Only since the 1980s have Highway 1 (the 'round-Australia road) and the Stuart Highway (up the center) been completely surfaced.

Filling stations are plentiful in cities, suburbs, and townships, but can be few and far between in the Outback. Petrol, sold by the liter, comes in leaded and unleaded grades and works out to $3-3.50 per gallon, though in desolate areas prices can go much higher (what are you going to do, shop around?). Diesel and leaded premium are usually available, but remote service stations may not have unleaded in stock—and, occasionally, they have *no* stock. Distances between petrol pumps can be considerable; check with each roadhouse and service station before assuming a fill-up will be available at your next stop.

For Outback travel you must follow special driving laws (a brochure detailing them can be obtained from any branch of the Royal Automobile Association) and have an appropriate vehicle with spare parts and other supplies in tow. Outback "roads" are like no others (off-roading in Baja on a summer weekend does not compare—or prepare you) and a rented 4WD does not come equipped with inherent immortality. You must learn about such matters as low and high ratios, free-wheeling hubs, speed and flotation, key- or stall-starting, and how to use them properly on steep hills, corrugated roads, water crossing, sand dunes, and deep mud. Drivers inexperienced with Australia's harsh driving conditions should not attempt any

EQUIPMENT

The Royal Automobile Club suggests you take the following equipment on your Outback tour:

Vehicle Equipment
good condition spare wheel
spare tire
jack, jack base
tow rope
fan belt
radiator hose
extra ignition key
fuses, spark plugs
spare bulbs for headlights and tail lights
petrol in jerry cans
engine oil (sufficient for complete change)
container of brake fluid
lubricating spray
insulating tape
epoxy resin putty
tube of silicone rubber gasket
bottle of Bars-Leak
tube of Bostik
two meters of bailing wire
welding wire or copper wire
set of disc brake pads (if fitted)
brass brake-lining rivets
spare air-cleaner element

spare engine oil/fuel filter cartridge
sufficient automatic transmission fluid for a
    complete change

Minimum Tool Kit
hacksaw
hammer
set of box- and open-ended spanners and socket
    spanner set to suit your vehicle
cold chisel
set of screwdrivers
pliers
file
tire pump
wheel chocks
vulcanizing clamp and patches
tire levers
valve key
pressure gauge
jumper cables
two meters of 6.35-mm-inside-diameter
    reinforced fuel-resistant plastic hose
two meters of four-mm low-tension wire

---

expeditions without a tour operator or experienced companion.

A good option is to join a "tag-along" tour in which you join other 4WD travelers in a caravan, tagging along behind an experienced lead vehicle. Some tours carry passengers and provide food; all have radio equipment, emergency provisions, secret camping places, and required permits. Call a tourist office or a Youth Hostel Association travel office to find out more about tag-along tours.

Laws and Licenses

First rule to remember: Drive on the left side of the road! (And for you four-on-the-floorers, this means you shift with your *left* hand.) Second rule: The vehicle on your right has right-of-way, though there are some variations to this rule that seem to confuse locals and tourists alike. Play it safe and watch carefully.

The maximum **speed limit** in cities and towns is 50-80 km/h, increasing to 100-110 km/h on

country roads and highways, unless signs say otherwise. **Seat belts** are mandatory and must be worn by the driver and all passengers; small children must be harnessed into a safety seat. **Motorcyclists** need a special license, as well as a helmet (check with state automobile clubs). **"Drink-driving" laws** are strict and spot checks, including Breathalyzer tests, are commonplace. Drivers having blood-alcohol levels 0.05 percent or higher (0.08 percent in the Northern Territory) will incur large fines, a court appearance, and loss of driving privileges.

Tourists can get away with using their valid overseas driver's license (along with a passport) if driving the same class of vehicle. International Driver's Licenses are only recognized if used in conjunction with a valid driver's permit (so, why bother?)

If you're a member of the American Automobile Club, bring your membership card to receive reciprocal rights from Australian automobile clubs.

CYCLING

Both long-distance and round-the-city cycling are popular in Australia. Most cities have designated bike routes, and flat country roads can be sheer heaven. Remote areas and Outback tracks require careful planning, extra equipment, and excellent health—always check with locals and notify police or park rangers before venturing into desolate regions. Make certain to drink heaps of water, wear plenty of sunscreen, and use a bicycle helmet (mandatory). You can bring your own bike from overseas (check with your airline regarding packing and costs) or buy a touring or mountain bike once you get to Australia.

For route maps, trail suggestions, and information on bicycle touring, contact **Bicycle Institute of New South Wales,** 82 Campbell St., Surry Hills, NSW 2010 (tel. 02-9212-5628); **Pedal Power ACT,** P.O. Box 581, Canberra, ACT 2601 (tel. 06-248-7995); **Bicycle Institute of South Australia,** 11 Church Rd., Mitcham, SA 5062 (tel. 08-8271-5824); **Bicycle Victoria,** 29 Somerset Pl., Melbourne, VIC 3000 (tel. 03-9328-3000); **Cycle Touring Association,** P.O. Box 174, Wembley, WA 6014 (tel. 09-349-2310); **Bicycle Institute of Queensland,** The Web, 142 Agnew St., Norman Park, QLD 4101 (tel. 07-3899-2988); or **Pedal Power Tasmania,** c/o Environment Centre, 102 Bathurst St., Hobart, TAS 7000 (tel. 002-34-5566).

OTHER OPTIONS

Motorcycles

Read the info above regarding car purchases; the same applies to motorcycles. You can ship your own over (special permit necessary, and expensive) or buy one out of the classifieds—April or May, the beginning of the Australian winter, is a good time to shop. Rentals are usually available only in the cities, but the same buy-back scheme for cars (see above) can be had for motorcycles. A favorite is the Yamaha Ténéré, a long-distance cruiser and off-road beauty.

It is *not* recommended that bikers solo into the Outback. Tag-along tours, similar to those for 4WD vehicles (see "By Car and Caravan" above) are also available for motorcylists. Rates for motorcycles range $60-95 per day and $300-500 per week, depending on engine size; a refundable deposit—around $500—is required.

Hitchhiking

The official word is: "Hitchhiking is illegal in most states and strongly discouraged throughout Australia. It is definitely not recommended."

Since I feel confident that lawbreakers and renegades make up at least a small percentage of my readers, I am including some do-it-at-your-own-risk tips.

Use common sense. Outback areas are isolated and not well-traveled. Be prepared for very long waits. Best hitching combo is a man and a woman. Women should not hitch alone. If you're traveling solo, check hostel and backpacker lodging bulletin boards for partners and/or rides. In any case, make sure before you get in the car or truck that you are not going to be dumped at the end of some lonely track.

Hitching a truck ride only works if the driver can stop and start quickly, so pick your spot accordingly (probably the top of some hill). Try to stay awake in the truck and be a congenial companion; if the driver doesn't like you or you bore him (or her), you might get booted in a very inopportune spot!

NATIONAL HIGHWAY   NATIONAL ROUTE   STATE ROUTE   TOURIST DRIVE

Write your destination on a sign, aim for a clean but unmonied look and—most importantly—leave word with a trusted friend or a hostel or hotel manager as to your intended destination so someone can check on you (especially important for women).

Mail Trucks and Mail Planes

Outback mail runs, whether by truck or plane, are one of Australia's most enduring traditions. For Outback dwellers, the weekly runs—covering hundreds or thousands of kilometers—often provide the only outside human contact. Besides being a reliable source for important information and juicy gossip—and, of course, the mail—the service also delivers everything from Vegemite to spark plugs.

Travelers can ride the mail truck every Monday and Thursday for its 600-kilometer route around Coober Pedy, Oodnadatta, and William Creek. Fare is $50-60. For information, call (1800) 802-074 (toll-free), or contact Underground Books, 1 Post Office Hill Rd., Coober Pedy (tel. 086-72-5558). Mail planes are costlier ($150-300). For information, contact Augusta Airways, Port Augusta, SA (tel. 086-42-3100); Air Mount Isa, QLD (tel. 077-43-2844); or Cape York Air Services, QLD (tel. 070-35-9399).

TOURS

The range of tours available in Australia is as vast as the country, as wild as your imagination, as extravagant or economical as you wish, and as environmentally conscious or politically correct as you choose. The place to begin is at each state or territory's government tourist office (see "Maps and Tourist Information" later in this chapter). These offices are glorious resources for all kinds of information, and will not only recommend and seek out a suitable tour for you, but will book it as well. Major cities offer the usual tourist-friendly range of commercial "city sights," "by day," and "by night" tours, either in a big bus, minivan, or hop-on-and-off shuttle.

Recommended tour operators in North America are: **Inta-Aussie Tours,** an Australian-owned concern with a vast range of Outback, value, wilderness, and coach expeditions, as well as city, coastal, reef, and island adventures (tel. 800-531-9222, U.S. and Canada) and **Globus,** dating from 1928, specializing in escorted and independent first-class tours to Australia (tel. 800-221-0090 U.S., or 800-268-1639 Canada). Or try **Adventure Express** (tel. 800-443-0799 U.S.) and **American Wilderness Experience** (tel. 800-444-0099 U.S.) for adventure holidays. Other tour operators specializing in a broad spectrum of Australian tours include: **ATS Tours** (tel. 800-423-2880 U.S.), **SoPac** (tel. 800-551-2012 U.S. and Canada), and **Swain Australia** (tel. 800-227-9246 U.S. and Canada). **Rascals in Paradise** (tel. 800-872-7225 U.S.) organizes Australian adventures geared to the whole family. Youth Hostel Association travel offices are also excellent sources for inbound tours, including 4WD and motorcycle Outback tag-alongs.

Aerial Tours

From the comfort of a six- or 10-seater Piper, fly high above the Outback, peering down at the ant-appearing climbers at Uluru or the Bungle Bungles. Tours from a few days to a few weeks can be arranged through the state tourist offices, **Air Adventure Australia** (tel. 1800-033-160), **Aircruising Australia** (tel. 02-9693-2233), **Aviatour** (tel. 03-9589-4097), or **Outback NT Air Safaris** (tel. 08-8979-2411). Also see "Mail Trucks and Planes" under "Getting Around" earlier in this chapter.

Riverboats, Camel Treks, And Greased Lightning

Captain Cook Cruises (tel. 02-9206-1144) and **Proud Australia Holidays** (tel. 08-8231-9472) will cruise you along the Murray River. **Frontier Camel Tours** (tel. 08-8953-0444) will take you for a day's outing near Alice Springs, or a longer trek; **Frontier Outback** (tel. 800-227-8947 U.S.) also offers extended safaris. Explore the Alice Springs area with **Harley Davidson Scenic Tours** (tel. 08-8953-4755).

Fishing Tours

Catch the big one with **Angling Adventures Australia** (tel. 800-356-6982 U.S.), **Fishing International** (tel. 800-950-4242 U.S.), or, in Australia, phone **Arafura Safaris** (tel. 08-8927-2372, Northern Territory) and **Big Barra Fishing Tours** (tel. 08-8932-1473, Northern Territory). The latter is permitted to fish in Arnhem Land. Also call **Budget Barra Tours** (tel. 08-8927-2572, Northern Territory), **Croc-Spot Fishing Tours** (tel. 08-8975-8722, Northern Territory), and **Kimberley Sport Fishing** (tel. 091-68-2752 WA).

ABORIGINAL TOURS

Certainly one of the most rewarding opportunities of Outback travel is to visit one or more of the Aboriginal lands. As in all of Australia, tourism plays an important economical role for the Aborigines. The tour companies listed below are owned, managed, and/or led by the traditional people. Focus might be on religion, the rudiments of "Dreaming," art and culture, the use of plants and animals, or bush tucker. Be prepared to abide by special customs and rules of behavior (e.g., do not spit out the food—unless you're *supposed* to).

NORTHERN TERRITORY

Ipolera Community (tel. 08-8956-2299): short culture-oriented walks and talks

Kurkara Tours (tel. 08-8956-7442): tours of Watarrka (Kings Canyon) National Park

Ntaria Aboriginal Community (tel. 08-8956-7402): self-guided tours of historical Hermannsburg

Oak Valley Day Tours (tel. 08-8956-0959): day tours to areas south of Alice Springs

Walala Bush Tucker Tour (tel. 08-8962-3388 or 62-1353): Aboriginal women led, March-November, in Tennant Creek

Wallace Rockhole Aboriginal Community (tel. 08-8956-7415): short walks and talks about culture and rock art

NORTHERN TERRITORY—TOP END

Aussie Safaris (tel. 08-8981-1633): day tours of Peppimenarti Aboriginal Community

Manyallaluk and Travel North (tel. 08-8972-1044): tours and meetings with Jawoyn traditional owners, leaving from Katherine

Tiwi Tours (tel. 08-8981-5144): trips to Vathurst and Melville Islands, off of Darwin

Umorrduk Aboriginal Safaris (tel. 08-8948-1306): flying and driving art-and-culture tours of northwest Arnhem Land and Kakadu National Park

Wilderness Experience (tel. 08-8941-2899): Aboriginal guided tours, leaving from Katherine

QUEENSLAND

AngGnarra Aboriginal Corporation (tel. 070-60-3214): guided tours of Split Rock Gallery and other rock sites, departing from Laura

Munbah Aboriginal Culture tour (tel. 070-60-9173): north of Cooktown, Hopevale Aboriginal community will give you a tour and let you bed down in a traditional hut

SOUTH AUSTRALIA

Desert Tracks (tel. 08-8956-2144): excellent—but costly—cultural tours of Anangu-Pitjantjatjara Lands, departing from Uluru (Ayers Rock) Resort

WESTERN AUSTRALIA

Derby Tourist Bureau (tel. 091-91-1426): arrangements can be made to cruise Geikie Gorge with Bunuba traditional people

Karijini Walkabouts (tel. 09-309-1395): backpacking trips in the Pilbara's Karijini National Park.

Flack Track Tours (tel. 091-92-1487): Aboriginal community visits departing from Broome

Point Inbound Tours (tel. 09-388-2210): Aboriginal artist, Shane Pickett, will accompany you to the Kimberley or Pilbara

Volunteer and "Green" Tours
WWOOF (Willing Workers On Organic Farms), will trade you bed and board in exchange for several hours' daily work. The farms, numbering more than 300, are not always organic, nor are they always farms; an occasional pottery or other enterprise might sneak in there. Some farms are in Outback areas, though most are in more built-up regions. Membership ($25 outside Australia, $20 within the country) is required. Send the fee and you'll receive a membership number and WWOOF directory in return. For more information, contact WWOOF, Mt. Murrindal Co-op, Buchan, VIC 3885 (tel. 051-55-0218).

Volunteer conservation projects are available through **ATCV** (Australian Trust for Conservation Volunteers). This is a wonderful opportunity for travelers to do something constructive with the environment, meet other like-minded souls, and visit some roads less traveled. Projects are often situated in the Outback and can include track construction, tree planting, and cataloging natural habitation. Volunteers make a contribution to help cover costs and, in return, are supplied with transportation, accommodations, and food. You can join for a week, weekend, or several weeks. For more information, contact ATCV, P.O. Box 423, Ballarat, VIC 3350 (tel. 053-33-1483).

Volunteers can also help out the **ANZSES** (Australian and New Zealand Scientific Exploration Society). One hundred or so assistants are sent annually with an experienced guide into remote parts of the country, usually to collect flora and fauna specimens. For more information, contact ANZSES, P.O. Box 174, Albert Park, VIC 3206 (tel. 03-9690-5455).

Operators specializing in organized ecotours include **Ecotour Travel Agency** (tel. 02-9223-2811) and **Eco-Adventures Australia** (tel. 800-724-4880 U.S.). **Tailored Tours** (tel. 08-8363-0068) and **Wait-A-While Rainforest Wildlife Tours** (tel. 070-33-1153) take small groups on wildlife safaris.

VISAS AND OFFICALDOM

Keep up to date on current red tape by contacting the nearest embassy or consulate, as well as your country's customs service. See "Australian Embassies and Consulates" below for addresses.

PASSPORTS AND VISAS

Every visitor must have a valid passport for entry into Australia. In addition, visas are required for everyone except holders of Australian and New Zealand passports.

Tourist visas are issued free of charge, for stays of three months or less, at Australian consulates and embassies and, for U.S. and Canadian citizens, are generally valid for one year. For a US$24 fee, you can request an additional three months or multiple-entries for a period of four years (or the life of your passport, if it is less than four years)—if you're planning more than one trip to Australia, this can cut down considerably on bureaucracy and keep your passport updated for spontaneous travel.

If applying in person, a visa will probably be issued on the spot; if applying by mail, be sure to enclose the completed application, any necessary fees, and a stamped, self-addressed envelope large enough to accommodate your passport. Also, allow at least 21 days for processing. If you want special services, such as your documents returned via first-class, certified, registered, or express mail, enclose the appropriate forms and postage. Mail that is marked "insufficient postage" will be returned, unprocessed.

Whether applying in person or by mail, you must present your passport and a signed application form (they don't seem to want your photograph anymore).

Within Australia, visas can be extended (often on the whim of the official you approach) at Department of Immigration and Ethnic Affairs offices in major cities. Do this well ahead of your visa expiration date, as the process can be lengthy. The application fee for the further extension of either a three-month (short-stay) or six-month (long-stay) visa is $135. These fees are *not* returned should your extension be denied. You may be required to have a personal interview and produce bank statements and other proof of financial solvency, including medical insurance and an onward ticket. The maximum stay, including extensions, is one year.

The tourist visa, no matter how long it's good for, does not allow you to be employed or take formal study in Australia. If you want to reapply as a resident, you'll probably have to go home and do it—the old pay-someone-to-marry-you-and-stay-forever technique is pretty much a thing of the past.

Visitors from Britain, Ireland, Canada, Japan, or the Netherlands, aged 18 to 26 (sometimes a bit older), may be eligible for a **Working Holiday visa.** This visa, which should be applied for in the applicant's home country, allows casual employment for a period of three months, though the visa is good for up to 12 months. **Student visas** entitle the holders to study full-time and work part-time, up to 20 hours per week. Application must be made in person—and in advance—at an Australian consulate or overseas Australian Education Centre. Individ-uals who have approved sponsorship from an employer or organization in Australia can apply for a **temporary working visa** at their nearest Australian consulate—be forewarned, the requirements are stringent.

WORK

Regular tourist visas clearly state that *no* employment of *any* kind is allowed during your stay. A lot of travelers used to think, "sure, sure—I'll just work 'under the table.'" Unfortunately, with Australia's unemployment rate in the double digits, this is no longer a reliable option—there are too many "legit" citizens looking for jobs. Also, it is now required that workers have a "Tax File Number" (i.e., a Social Security card) in order to receive earnings; forms are available at the Taxation Department office or post office (be prepared to show your passport and visa).

PERMITS FOR OUTBACK TRAVEL

I know it looks big and empty—still, you may need special permits to enter, pass through, or camp.

Aboriginal Lands
The laws vary—on some lands you can pass through on "main roads" or stop in a community for fuel, on others you need a permit just to put your little toe on the land. If you're on an organized tour, the operator or guide will probably have taken care of all the red tape, otherwise apply well in advance (allow a couple of months) to the following land councils (you must apply to each state or territory that you wish to visit): Permits Officer, Aboriginal Affairs Planning Authority, P.O. Box 628, West Perth, WA 60005 (tel. 09-483-1222, fax 321-0990); Administration Officer, Maralinga-Tjarutja Inc., P.O. Box 435, Ceduna, SA 5435 (tel. 086-25-2946); Permits Officer, Central Land Council, P.O. Box 3321, Alice Springs, NT 0871 (tel. 089-51-6320, fax 53-4345), for central and southern areas; Permits Officer, Northern Land Council, P.O. Box 42921, Casuarina, NT 0811 (tel. 089-20-5172, fax 45-2633), for northern areas and Arnhem Land; Aboriginal Coordinating Council, P.O. Box 6512, Cairns Mall Centre, QLD 4870 (tel. 070-31-2623); Permits Officer, Tiwi Land Council, Ngulu, Bathurst Island via Darwin, NT 0822 (tel. 089-78-3966), for Melville and Bathurst Islands.

National Parks and Desert Parks
Obtain camping and visitor permits in advance (see destination chapters for more info). If you're planning a visit to Simpson Desert Conservation Park, Simpson Desert Regional Reserve, Lake Eyre National Park, Innamincka Regional Reserve, and/or Witjira National Park in South Australia, you'll require a Desert Parks Pass. The pass, which costs around $50 per vehicle, includes camping and visiting permits, essential maps, and mini-travel guides. Purchase one at various shops in the northern part of the state, or through Flinders Ranges-based South Australian National Parks and Wildlife Service, Far Northern Region (tel. 086-48-4244).

Holders of "Working Holiday" visas are officially allowed to work for three out of 12 months, and can take advantage of the CES (Commonwealth Employment Service), the government employment agency that has branches or representatives in virtually every city and town. Casual labor is what you'll probably be offered—Outback possibilities are the usual domestic chores at roadhouses or stations, bar and restaurant work, as well as some skilled positions for carpenters, electricians, plumbers, mechanics, and such. Check bulletin boards at hostels and cafes, and also ask around.

Harvesting is another possibility. Best opportunities are: South Australia—Barossa Valley grapes (Feb.-April), Riverlands citrus and soft fruits (all year); Western Australia—west coast seafoods (March-Nov.), Kununurra-area fruit and vegetables (May-Oct.), southwest-region grapes (Oct.-June); Queensland—central coast fruit and vegetables (May-Dec.), New South Wales border area grapes and orchard fruits (Dec.-March), Bundaberg-area fruits and vegetables (all year), northern coast bananas, tobacco, and sugarcane; New South Wales—northern coast bananas (all year), central eastern-area asparagus, cottons, onions, orchard and other fruits (Nov.-April); Victoria—Shepparton-area orchard and soft fruits, grapes, tobacco, and tomatoes (Nov.-April); Tasmania—grapes, hops, orchard and soft fruits (Dec.-March).

AUSTRALIAN CONSULATES AND EMBASSIES

United States
You'll find Australian consulates in the following cities:

Atlanta, Suite 2920, 303 Peachtree St. NE, Atlanta, GA 30308 (tel. 404-880-1700)

Honolulu, 1000 Bishop St., Penthouse, Honolulu, HI 96813 (tel. 808-524-5050)

Houston, Suite 800, 1990 Post Oak Blvd., Houston, TX 77056 (tel. 713-629-9131)

Los Angeles, Century Plaza Towers, 2049 Century Park East, 19th floor, Los Angeles, CA 90067 (tel. 310-229-4800)

New York, Suite 420, 630 Fifth Ave., New York, NY 10111 (tel. 212-408-8400)

San Francisco, 7th floor, 1 Bush St., San Francisco, CA 94108 (tel. 415-362-6160)

The **Australian Embassy** is at 1601 Massachusetts Ave. NW, Washington, D.C. 20036 (tel. 202-797-3000)

Canada
Ottawa, Suite 710, 50 O'Connor St., Ottawa, Ontario K1P 6L2 (tel. 613-236-0841)

Toronto, Suite 314, 175 Bloor St. East, Toronto, Ontario M4W 3R8 (tel. 416-323-1155)

Vancouver, Suite 602, 999 Canada Place, Vancouver, British Columbia V6C 3E1 (tel. 604-684-1177)

New Zealand
Auckland, 32-38 Quay St., Auckland 1 (tel. 09-303-2429)

Wellington, 72-78 Hobson St., Thorndon, Wellington (tel. 04-473-6411)

Asia
China, 21 Dongzhimenwai Dajie, San Li Tun, Beijing (tel. 10-532-2331)

Indonesia, Bali, Jl. Prof. Moh Yamin 51, Renon (tel. 0361-235-092); Jakarta, Kav. c 15-16; Jl H.R. Rasuna Said, Jakarta Selatan (tel. 021-522-7111)

Hong Kong, 25 Harbour Rd., Wanchai (tel. 2827-8881)

India, No. 1/50-G Shantipath, Chanakyapuri, New Delhi 110021 (tel. 011-688-8223)

Japan, Osaka, 2-1-61 Shiromi, Chuo-ku 540 (tel. 06-941-9271); Tokyo 2-1-14 Mita, Minato-ku (tel. 03-5232-4111)

Malaysia, 6 Jalan Yap, Kwan Seng, Kuala Lumpur 50450 (tel. 03-242-3122)

Papua New Guinea, Independence Dr., Waigani, Port Moresby (tel. 675-325-9333)

Philippines, 104 Paseo de Roxas, Makati, Metro Manila (tel. 02-817-7911)

Singapore, 25 Napier Rd., Singapore 1025 (tel. 737-9311)

Thailand, 37 S. Sathorn Rd., Bangkok 10120 (tel. 02-287-2680)

Europe
Denmark, Kristianagade 21, 2100 Copenhagen (tel. 035-26-2244)

France, 4 rue Jean Rey, Paris 15 (tel. 01-40-59-33-00)

Germany, Godesberger Allee 107, 5300 Bonn 1 (tel. 0228-81-030)

Greece, 37 Dimitriou Soutsou St., Ambelokipi, Athens 11521 (tel. 01-644-7303)

Ireland, Fitzwilton House, Wilton Tce., Dublin 2 (tel. 01-676-1517)

Italy, Via Alessandria 215, Rome 00198 (tel. 06-85-2721)

Netherlands, Carnegielaan 14, 2517 KH The Hague (tel. 070-310-8200)

Sweden, Sergels Torg 12, Stockholm (tel. 08-613-2900)

Switzerland, 29 Alpenstrasse, Berne (tel. 031-351-0143)

United Kingdom

Edinburgh, 25 Bernard St., Leith EH6 6SH (tel. 0131-555-4500)

London, Australia House, The Strand, London WC2B 4LA (tel. 171-379-4334)

Manchester, Chatsworth House, Lever St., Manchester M1 2DL (tel. 161-228-1344)

South Africa

Pretoria, 292 Orient St., Arcadia, Pretoria 0083 (tel. 012-342-3740)

FOREIGN CONSULATES AND EMBASSIES

Canberra (Australian Capital Territory), Australia's equivalent to Washington D.C., is where you'll find the foreign embassies. Wieldy connections such as New Zealand, the United Kingdom, the United States, and significant others, maintain consulates in other capital cities such as Sydney and Melbourne; an Indonesian consulate resides in Darwin. Canberra offices include:

Austria, 12 Talbot St., Forrest (tel. 06-295-1533)

Canada, Commonwealth Ave., Canberra (tel. 06-273-3844)

Germany, 119 Empire Circuit, Yarralumla (tel. 06-270-1951)

Indonesia, 8 Darwin Ave., Yarralumla (tel. 06-250-8600)

Ireland, 20 Arkana St., Yarralumla (tel. 06-273-3022)

India, 3 Moonah Pl., Yarralumla (tel. 06-273-3999)

Japan, 112 Empire Circuit, Yarralumla (tel. 06-273-3244)

Malaysia, 7 Perth Ave., Yarralumla (tel. 06-273-1543)

Netherlands, 120 Empire Circuit, Yarralumla (tel. 06-273-3111)

New Zealand, Commonwealth Ave., Yarralumla (tel. 06-270-4211)

Norway, 17 Hunter St., Yarralumla (tel. 06-273-3444)

Papua New Guinea, Forster Crescent, Yarralumla (tel. 06-273-3322)

Singapore, 17 Forster Crescent, Yarralumla (tel. 06-273-3944)

South Africa, State Circle, Yarralumla (tel. 06-273-2424)

Sweden, 5 Turrana St., Yarralumla (tel. 06-273-3033)

Switzerland, 7 Melbourne Ave., Forrest (tel. 06-273-3977)

Thailand, 111 Empire Circuit, Yarralumla (tel. 06-273-1149)

United Kingdom, Commonwealth Ave., Yarralumla (tel. 06-270-6666)

CUSTOMS

Australian Customs

Visitors may bring personal clothing and effects into Australia duty-free. If you're over 18 years old, you're also allowed 250 cigarettes or 250 grams of cigars or tobacco, in addition to one liter of wine, beer, or spirits (you must carry these items on you to qualify). Other taxable goods (up to $400 worth per adult and $200 per child under 18 years old) may be admitted duty-free if included inside personal baggage.

Drugs, weapons, and firearms are prohibited or restricted in Australia. Eager (and possibly kinky) German shepherds will be sniffing you as you wait to clear immigration. Drug laws are strictly enforced. Also, certain quarantined items such as meats, vegetables, fruit, and flowers will be confiscated. Forget about bringing in items made from endangered species (an ivory mojo man in a polar bear fur pouch, for example), live animals (endangered or not), and certain types of nonapproved telecommunication devices. If you're not sure of something, *don't* try to smuggle it in—ask a customs agent. And if that doesn't suit you, drop the questionable article in the amnesty box.

Since you will probably not want to drop cash into the amnesty box, you should also know that persons carrying or sending cash and coins valuing A\$5000 or more (in *any* country's currency) into or out of Australia must declare the money and fill out a report with the Australian Customs Service at the airport. Traveler's checks in any amount of Australian or foreign currency are exempt from this rule.

Aside from international customs, quarantines on fresh fruit, vegetables, and plants are in effect between states and territories. Eat everything up before you reach the state line.

International Customs
Each family member is allowed to bring back up to US\$400 in duty-free goods; that is, if you're out of the U.S. for a minimum of 48 hours and haven't taken any other international journey in 30 days. Family members may combine their exemptions. Goods between \$400 and \$1400 are assessed at a flat 10% rate. If you're at least 21 years old, your allowance may include 100 cigars (no Cuban brands), 200 cigarettes, and one liter of wine, beer, or spirits. You may mail

gifts, valued under \$50, duty-free to friends or relatives—but don't send more than one package per day to any one person.

Canadians who have been abroad for less than eight days may bring back up to C\$100 of goods duty-free. Those who have been away for eight days or more are allowed up to C\$300 in merchandise. The duty-free allowance for Canadians includes up to 1.1 liter of spirits, one carton of cigarettes, and fifty cigars. Tax rates vary by item.

Travelers from the United Kingdom may bring home up to £32 of goods duty-free. In addition, goods such as wine, tobacco, and perfume are duty-free, and so is anything you've owned for longer than six months. The same regulations apply to items that are mailed home. The standard value-added tax rate for the U.K. is 17.5%.

Departure Tax
Unless you're a transit passenger who's been in the country less than 24 hours (in which case you probably wouldn't be reading this book), every person 12 years and older must pay a \$27 departure tax when leaving Australia. To offset the cost of insulating houses under a new flight path, all passengers departing from Sydney must also pay an airport Noise Levy of \$3.40. In most cases, departure tax for all countries you visit is added to (or hidden in) the cost of your ticket.

DISTINCT INTERESTS

WOMEN

What can I tell you? Most Aussie men come off as being pretty brusque and gruff—though they're not always that way deep under Down Under. In the Outback—too few teeth, too many tattoos, remember?—they are macho and oftentimes big, mean, and hard-drinking. City men are easier to deal with but, in the end, women still must endure the usual cat-call and sexually explicit verbal assault. And worse— *much worse.*

Aussie men still consider their mates, cars, and sports atop the pecking order, with the women coming in last. The men are usually anything but gallant, but the Aussie women seem to take this in stride.

Always exercise common sense: Don't walk alone late at night in the city (also city trains at night are not particularly safe); try to avoid bars and pubs—particularly Outback pubs; don't hitchhike alone.

Conditions for women are slowly improving: less sexism in the media, more career opportunities, et al. There are women's resource centers, health clinics, and hotlines in every major city for help and assistance.

GAY AND LESBIAN

Well, *Priscilla, Queen of the Desert*, managed quite well, thank you, in her Outback travels. But, will *you* if you're gay or Lesbian?

Oddly enough, despite all of Australia's

machismo, the country enjoys a lively, large, friendly, and active gay and (lipstick) Lesbian scene. Sydney is the major mecca, with Melbourne a close runner-up. Other cities and many country areas have gay-and-Lesbian havens. Parades, gatherings, networks, and club-life are all part of the open lifestyle.

The Outback, however, is not quite so accepting—those miners, ranchers, and truckers have been known to be a wee bit intolerant. Consequently, it might be best to keep your sexual preference under wraps in those circumstances.

Monthly gay and Lesbian mags such as *Outrage* and *Campaign* provide current information as well as lists of services and resources. The Australian Gay and Lesbian Tourism Association (P.O. Box 429, North Sydney, NSW 2060, tel. 02-9957-3811) publishes a homosexual-friendly accommodation guide.

TRAVELERS WITH DISABILITIES

Many of Australia's accommodations, restaurants, cinemas, and tourist attractions provide facilities and access for travelers with disabilities. Most newer buildings are equipped with wheelchair access. Guides and booklets for travelers with disabilities, which include state and local organizations and travel specialists, can be obtained from *National Information Communication Awareness Network* (NICAN), P.O. Box 407, Curtin, ACT 2605 (tel. 06-285-3713, fax 285-3717).

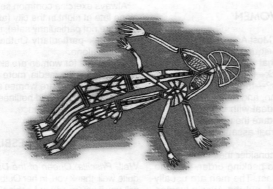

HEALTH AND SAFETY

Yes, you can drink the water and eat your fruit unpeeled—Australian hygiene standards are high. Most city hospitals are well equipped, though you might run into problems in country towns, particularly on weekends, when some hospital laboratories are closed.

If you're in the middle of the Outback, you can have the well-trained Royal Flying Doctor Service soar to your aid (see "Outback Health and Education" under "The People" in the Introduction chapter).

Pharmacies (chemists) are readily available and stock most drugs, though often by their generic name. If you're taking medication, bring a supply and duplicate prescriptions with generic equivalents with you—and that goes for eyeglasses, too.

Take it easy until you get acclimated, especially if the weather is hot or humid, if you're traveling into the Outback, or if you're planning any strenuous physical activities. Go slow, and work up to a pace you're comfortable with. Always carry a good first-aid kit and handbook for Outback expeditions (auto clubs and St. John ambulance service sell a selection of kits; and consider taking Moon Publications' *Staying Healthy in Asia, Africa, and Latin America,* an informative, practical first-aid handbook).

The **International Association for Medical Assistance to Travellers** (IAMAT) provides a list of doctors worldwide with U.S. standards of medical training. For more information, contact IAMAT, 417 Center St., Lewiston, NY 14092 (tel. 716-754-4883). If you find yourself in a real medical nightmare, contact your country's consulate or embassy for emergency help.

Vaccinations

Vaccinations are not necessary if you're traveling from the United States, Canada, or the United Kingdom. If you've visited a yellow fever-infected country within six days of your arrival in Australia, you'll need appropriate inoculations.

Health Hazards

This is a country with one of the highest rates of skin cancer in the world. The sun is intense and the hole in the ozone layer is *wide*—wear sunblock and a hat whenever you're outdoors. Also, drink plenty of fluids to ward off possible dehydration. When traveling in Outback areas, check in first with the automobile club, local police, or park rangers.

Other potential dangers include Australia's infamous poisonous snakes, those faster-than-you'd-care-to-imagine saltwater crocs, a few poisonous spiders, and the box jellyfish (see "Flora and Fauna" in the Introduction chapter). Obey all warning signs and, when in doubt, ask the locals.

Animals on the road, particularly at night, can also be deadly. When walking on coral reef, protect your feet with sturdy shoes. Seek prompt medical treatment for any coral cuts.

Health Insurance

Though a visit to the doctor's office might only cost $25 or so, other medical expenses can be quite hefty (for example, if you need an ambulance or search-and-rescue team). Make sure you have health insurance to adequately cover possible accidents and illness before you leave home; if you plan to take part in any dangerous sport or activity, make sure the policy covers it. Both Council Travel Services and STA offices, as well as most travel agents, can recommend reliable insurance companies. Coverage can also be obtained for emergency transportation, lost luggage, and trip cancellation. Holders of International Student Identity Cards receive automatic coverage up to certain limits. In any case, be sure to read all fine print.

Travel insurers include: **Travel Assistance International,** Suite 400, 1133 15th St. NW, Washington, D.C. 20005 (tel. 202-347-2025 or 800-821-2828); and **TravelGuard International,** 1145 Clark St., Stevens Point, WI 54481 (tel. 715-345-0505 or 800-782-5151).

FIRST AID

For expert first-aid information, see Moon Publications' *Staying Healthy in Asia, Africa, and Latin America,* by Dirk G. Schroeder, ScD, MPH.

Prevention

Be sensible! The ultraviolet rays are intense, the ozone hole wide, and the skin cancer rate very high. Even cloudy skies can cause a bad burn and—as for the super-bright Outback—wow! Wear a hat and sunblock, drink plenty of water to avoid dehydration, go easy on booze and cigarettes, and you should be right, mates.

Exhaustion and Heat Exposure

It's *hot* in the Outback. Keep a slow pace until you get acclimated. Get lots of rest, fill up on water, make sure you have enough salt in your diet, and avoid overexposure to the harsh sun. Wear loose, cotton clothing and your hat, of course. Beware of heatstroke. Symptoms include increased body temperature, a reduction in sweat, and occasional vomiting or nausea. Heatstroke is an emergency situation: the victim should be taken to a cool place, then doused, fanned, and sponged with cold water until body temperature drops to at least 39° C (102° F).

Traveler's Diarrhea

It doesn't matter how clean the place is, unfamiliar foods, overeating, too much drinking, and a variety of other factors can cause the runs. Again, be sensible until you get used to your new environment. If you do come down with Bali Belly or Montezuma's Revenge, ward off dehydration by drinking lots of fluids such as clear broth or soup, weak tea, or juice (*no* alcohol or coffee). Gradually add bland and boiled grub to your diet—rice, biscuits, bread, bananas.

Stings and Bites, Snakes and Beasties

Oz is renowned for its numerous evil snakes. Most won't attack unless provoked, but exceptions are the "fierce" tiger and taipan snakes (the most dangerous). For bites, apply a pressure bandage and splint, keep the victim calm and immobilized, and get medical help fast. Don't move the victim if at all possible; make sure someone stays behind in case artificial respiration is required.

Spiders to watch out for are the red-back (usually found in dunnies and toilets), the trap-doors (usually lurking in holes, with or without trap-door lids), and the funnel-web (only in Sydney!). Place ice on the affected area and seek prompt medical attention.

Know your nasty sea critters before you wiggle your toes in the water. The box jellyfish can inflict a fatal sting. Douse the area with vinegar, pull out tentacles, and procure immediate medical attention. Some other poisonous marine dwellers are the sea snake, the blue-ringed octopus, the scorpion fish, and the stonefish (which masquerades as a harmless piece of rock). Treat stings as for snake bites.

Finally, if you're attacked by a saltwater croc, well . . . *adios.*

Sexually Transmitted Diseases

There is AIDS in Oz, and this includes the Outback. Use condoms. Period.

Help!

To summon emergency help, dial 000 (a free call) from any telephone. The Royal Flying Doctors can be contacted any time, any day, via HF (high-frequency) radios. These units can and should be rented by anyone venturing into very remote areas.

MONEY

Note: All prices quoted in this guide are in Australian dollars (A$) unless otherwise noted.

Currency
Australian currency is based on the dollars-and-cents decimal system (100 cents equal one dollar). Notes, of different colors, come in denominations of $5, $10, $20, $50, and $100. Unfortunately the majority of $5, $10, and $50 notes are new and improved, i.e., plasticky and indestructible; the paper notes are rapidly disappearing. Coins are in denominations of 5 cents, 10 cents, 20 cents, 50 cents, $1, and $2.

You may bring in or take out any amount of personal funds; however, if you're carrying or sending $5000 or more in Australian or foreign currency, you must file a form with the Australian Customs Service. You may also be required to furnish a report with customs agents in other countries.

Changing Money
Currency exchange facilities are available at all international airports, though many open only for incoming and outgoing flights. Larger hotels and most banks will also exchange foreign cash and traveler's checks (traveler's checks fetch a slightly higher exchange rate). Traveler's checks are

---

CURRENCY EXCHANGE

As of May 1996, the Aussie dollar was trading at about US80 cents to A$1 (exchanging at about A$1.25 per US$1). Travelers with currency other than the almighty greenback should be able to exchange funds at most banks and airport money-changing facilities without problem. Current exchange rates (per A$) for other major currencies are:

C$1 = 91 cents
DM1 = 82 cents
HK$10 = $1.61
NZ$1 = 86 cents
UK£ = $1.90
¥100 = $1.19

---

easily cashed in the city (have identification with you) but can be a pain in rural communities.

Outback areas and smaller towns may only deal in hard cash; have a good stash of it before you head Outback.

Banking hours are generally Mon.-Thurs. 9:30 a.m.-4 p.m., Friday 9 a.m.-5 p.m. A few of the larger city banks are open on Saturday morning—but don't count on it.

Credit Cards
The most commonly accepted credit cards are American Express, Bankcard, MasterCard, and Visa, and it shouldn't be a problem using them anywhere in Australia, including the Outback. Also, many rental agencies will only rent vehicles to customers with recognized credit cards.

Another advantage to the credit card is the ability to pull cash advances from ATMs (Automatic Teller Machines), which are prevalent throughout Australian cities and towns.

Bank and Passbook Accounts
Another way to handle your funds (and to ensure easy access) is to open a local bank account, especially if you'll be in the country for several months. Commonwealth, National, ANZ, and Westpac are located nationwide. If you're a foreigner, you can open an account within six weeks of arrival in Australia, using just your passport for identification. After that the ante is upped—you'll need your passport, birth certificate, driver's license, credit cards, etc. Make sure to apply for an ATM (or cash) card. It takes about a week (you'll need an Australian address for delivery). Many of the banks accept each other's cards, so you'll have access to plenty of ATM machines across the country. Also, as in the U.S., many establishments such as petrol stations and supermarkets accept cash cards for payment.

Your home ATM card should work in Australia if it is designated for one of the following systems: Star, Cirrus, or Plus. Check with your issuing bank regarding use and service charges.

You can also open a passbook account at the Commonwealth Bank. They'll give you a funky little booklet that you can use at all Australian post offices or post office agencies (as well as the Commonwealth Bank). A passbook with a blacklight signature is important, as some offices may require it. Also, the account normally has to be closed at the same branch where it was opened (if you're not planning to return to Australia for a long time, just use up the money in the account).

Costs

You've probably guessed, transport is the most expensive. The country is huge and transportation costs are comparatively high. Buying a rail, air, or coach pass, or going in on a car with others can be a real money saver. Fuel is more expensive than in the U.S. and Canada, but cheaper than in Europe; however, you'll probably use large quantities of it. Clothing is also fairly expensive. On the other hand, food and accommodations are both relatively cheap.

Outback prices are higher for almost everything due to increased freight costs. Taking advantage of discount passes and sharing with other travelers should compensate, at least partially.

Tipping and Bargaining

Tipping is not mandatory in Australia. Your waitperson will not follow you into the street, meat cleaver in hand, for the extra 15-20%. Normally, tipping is done only in an expensive restaurant, or when service has been extra good—and then 10% will suffice. Leave taxi drivers the extra change to make the tab an even amount and they'll be happy.

Bargaining is confined to flea markets and some of the larger secondhand shops. It is extremely uncool to bargain in the Outback, and downright offensive to do so with Aborigines for their arts and crafts.

Student and Senior Discounts

Students and seniors, with proper photo identification (such as an International Student Identity Card) are eligible for "Concession" rates on many transportation services and at attractions, cinemas, and entertainment venues.

Check with the ticket office before you purchase your ticket.

COMMUNICATIONS AND MEDIA

COMMUNICATIONS

Postal Services

The mail averages a whopping seven to 10 days or longer between Australia and North America or Europe—going either direction. Domestic service, however, is relatively efficient (barring postal strikes).

General post offices and branches will hang onto your mail, free of charge, for up to a month. Alternatively, American Express cardholders can have mail sent to city American Express offices, to be held for later pick-up.

Post office hours are Mon.-Fri. 9 a.m.-5 p.m. There is no Saturday mail delivery. Stamps can also be purchased at some hotels, motels, and from newsagents. A domestic stamp costs 45 cents; to the U.S. and Canada, stamps are 95 cents for postcards and $1.05 for letters.

Main post offices have philatelic desks, which sell sets of souvenir stamps ranging from poignant and historical to political and colorful.

Outback mail runs operate weekly via truck or plane (see "Getting Around" earlier).

Telephone

Australian Telecom has followed the deregulation path of AT&T. A second company, Optus, now offers alternative service—on long-distance and international calls—in the big-user cities. The result is the same kind of confusion, special access codes, varying rates, and endless advertising perks and bribes that occurred after U.S. telephone deregulation.

Basically, if you're not a player in the Telecom/Optus game, the telephone system is easy to master and efficiently operated. Most of the Outback is still part of Telecom.

Local calls from pay phones (i.e., coin boxes) cost 40 cents. Telecom phone cards can also be purchased in $2, $5, and $10 amounts from chemists (pharmacies), newsagents, and other shops. Some phones accept only credit or bank cash cards and, though convenient, are more expensive.

Almost all public phones are equipped for STD (subscriber trunk dialing) and ISD (international subscriber dialing). Just keep feeding coins into the slots (you can use one-dollar pieces, if you like). There is no three-minute

TELEPHONE ALERT

As of this writing, AUSTEL (Australian Telecommunications Au thority) is in the process of changing the country's tele- phone-number system. The restructuring process, begun in 1994 and due for completion by 1999, will shrink Australia's previous 54 area codes down to a paltry four: New South Wales and Australian Capital Territory, 02; Victoria and Tasmania, 03; Queensland, 07; South Australia, Western Australia, and the Northern Territory, 08. Ultimately all telephone numbers will consist of eight digits. In larg- er cities, where numbers are currently seven digits, an additional digit will be attached to the front. In country and rural regions, existing six- digit numbers will receive two extra digits (probably the last two digits of what was the previous area code). The point of this is to make more telephone numbers available. (For what, the exploding population???) Anyway, for six months callers will be able to reach both old and new numbers; for another few months, a recorded message will inform callers to "let their fingers do the walking."

Toll free numbers have the prefix 1800; companies such as airlines and other transport services often have six-digit numbers beginning with 13, meaning it is charged as a local call even if it's cross-country; the prefix 018 is an example designation for mobile phones; and nine-digit numbers, begin- ning with 0055, are usually psy- chic, sex, lonely-hearts, or do-it- yourself lines.

In this land of few and far be- tween, **fax** machines are used everywhere, including the Out- back. Almost every post office provides a fax calling and re- ceiving service.

In remote Outback locations, both CB and HF (high-frequen- cy) radios play an important part in communi- cations. CBs are used mainly for vehicles to keep in contact with each other, while HF ra- dios are used to summon medical help, provide education, spread community information—and gossip. Licenses are necessary for both types of radio. Telstra (OTC), with government-controlled frequencies, will most likely take over future com- munications for the Royal Flying Doctor Service.

In **emergencies,** dial 000 to summon help.

minimum and unused change will be returned when you hang up. Don't forget to dial the "zero" before the city code when making STD calls, then dial the number you want.

When placing international calls, dial 0011 (the international access code), the country code, the city code, and then the desired phone number (from private phones it's about $1.50 per minute to the U.S. or U.K.; on pay phones it's much more). Use the appropriate area code for long-distance calls between states in Australia.

Operator-assisted calls can be placed from any phone, though fees for reverse-charge (col- lect) and person-to-person calls run $6-8. Cred- it card phones are now installed in many air- ports, hotels, and post offices. Refer to the front pages of the local telephone book for dialing in- formation and charges. Try not to make any long-distance calls from big hotels—the sur- charges are usually astronomical and can dou- ble or triple the actual cost of the call.

Country Direct allows travelers to access operators in their home countries (more than 40 countries are hooked up to the service) for easier, and maybe cheaper, credit card, calling card, or collect calls. To the U.S. operator, call (1800) 881-011 (AT&T), (1800) 881-877 (Sprint), or (1800) 881-100 (MCI). To Canada, call (1800) 881-150. For other countries, refer to the local telephone book or call the international operator.

MEDIA

Newspapers and Magazines

The most respected daily newspapers are *Syd- ney Morning Herald* and Melbourne's *Age.* Or- dinarily available in the major cities and many small towns (even if a day or so old), they might not hit the Outback stands at all. Other city news- papers are Adelaide's *Advertiser,* Darwin's *Northern Territory News,* and Perth's *West Aus- tralian.* The monthly *Adelaide Review* lists the- ater, gallery, and restaurant reviews while *Rip it Up* and *dB* are free music and street-happening mags available at bars, clubs, and record shops. For entertainment news in Perth, pick up a free copy of *X-Press,* Australia's biggest weekly music magazine, also available at record shops as well as many other locations. Australia has two national dailies: *The Australian* and *The Australian Financial Review.*

Australian editions of *Time, Vogue, Cosmopolitan,* and other international magazines, plus worldwide newspapers (like *USA Today*) and foreign-language press are sold at many news agencies. Most newsagents, in fact, stock an astonishing array of specialty magazines. Two "women's mags," *New Idea* and *Woman's Weekly,* will assure that you never are out-of-touch with the U.K.'s latest royal scandals.

Radio and Television

The independent, government-funded ABC (Australian Broadcasting Corporation) is the national television and radio network. Often its programs are all you will hear or see in rural areas, though the major cities and towns will feature two or three regionally based commercial stations. Stations frequently televise nearly-first-run movies, as well as some excellent foreign films. The gov-

ernment-sponsored SBS beams excellent multicultural news and entertainment, along with uncensored films, to all state capitals.

American look-alike programming includes the *Today Show, 60 Minutes,* and several genre dating game, newlywed, quiz, and love connection shows—plus MTV. You can also catch the U.S. *Today Show, Oprah, Entertainment Tonight,* and *Late Show with David Letterman* in many locales, and—never fear—*Roseanne* is part of the regular programming (although it's about a year or so behind).

Alice Springs-based Imparja is an Aboriginal-run station that broadcasts many types of programs, including some produced by and for Aborigines, over about one-third of Australia.

The ABC, which operates radio stations in many of the cities, can be picked up in all parts of Australia. Other listening options (AM and FM) include everything from rock and Muzak to talk shows and community services.

MAPS AND TOURIST INFORMATION

MAPS

Tourist offices and automobile clubs are gold mines for free and cheap maps. Other excellent suppliers include: Rand McNally, 595 Market St., San Francisco, CA 94105 (tel. 415-777-3131); 150 E. 52nd St., New York City, NY 10022 (tel. 212-758-7488); 444 N. Michigan Ave., Chicago, IL 60611 (tel. 312-321-1751); and Eliot Bay Book Company, 101 S. Main St., Seattle, WA 98104 (tel. 206-624-6600). Other good sources are Magellan Travel Books (tel. 800-303-0011 U.S.) and South Pacific Travelers Booksource (tel. 800-234-4552 U.S.)

For Outback travel, you might want to obtain topographic sheets from AUSLIG (Australian Surveying & Land Information Group), the country's mapping agency. For information or a catalog, contact AUSLIG, Department of Administrative Services, P.O. Box 2, Belconnen, ACT 2616 (tel. 06-201-4300).

TOURIST INFORMATION

Tourist Offices

There's no lack of tourist information centers in Australia. All of the states and territories have branch offices in major city centers—veritable treasure troves of details on tours, attractions, sports, accommodations, package deals, car and campervan rentals, and local and interstate transportation. Most of these centers will make bookings for you, and all will load you with brochures. Additionally, almost every country town has an information center—albeit an office, petrol station, or museum—marked by the international "I" sign. Hours are usually Mon.-Fri. 9 a.m.-5 p.m., Saturday 9 a.m.-1 p.m. Centers in heavily touristed areas are often open on Sunday as well.

Main **state tourist offices** are:

Canberra Tourist Bureau, Jolimont Centre, Northbourne Ave., Canberra, ACT 2601 (tel. 1800-026-166, toll-free)

New South Wales Government Travel Centre, 19 Castlereagh St., Sydney, NSW 2000 (tel. 02-9231-4444)

Darwin Regional Tourism Association Information Centre, 33 Smith St., Darwin, NT 0800 (tel. 08-8981-4300)

Central Australian Tourism Industry Association, Ford Plaza Building, Todd Mall, Alice Springs, NT 0871 (tel. 08-8952-5199)

Queensland Travel Centre, 196 Adelaide St., Brisbane, QLD 4000 (tel. 07-3221-6111)

Far North Queensland Promotion Bureau, 36-38 Alpin St., Cairns, QLD 4870 (tel. 070-51-3588)

South Australian Tourism Commission Travel Centre, 1 King William St., Adelaide, SA 5000 (tel. 08-8212-1505)

Tasmanian Travel Centre, 80 Elizabeth St., Hobart, TAS 7000 (tel. 002-30-0250)

RACV Victorian Tourism Centre, 230 Collins St., Melbourne, VIC 3000 (tel. 03-9650-1522)

Western Australia Tourist Centre, corner Forrest Place and Wellington St., Perth, WA 6000 (tel. 09-483-1111)

Overseas Tourist Offices

For information on travel to Australia *before* your trip, contact the nearest office of the **Australian Tourist Commission.**

United States, Suite 1200, 2121 Avenue of the Stars, Los Angeles, CA 90067 (tel. 310-552-1988); 31st floor, 489 Fifth Ave., New York, NY 10017 (tel. 212-687-6300). Also, you may contact the South Australian Tourism Commission at 1600 Dove St., Suite 215, Newport Beach, CA 92660 (tel. 714-852-2270, toll-free 800-546-2155, fax 714-852-2277)

United Kingdom, Gemini House, 10-18 Putney Hill, London, England SW15 6AA (tel. 081-780-2227)

Germany, Neue Mainzerstrasse 22, D60311 Frankfurt am Main (tel. 069-274-0060)

New Zealand, Level 13, 44-48 Emily Place, Auckland 1, New Zealand (tel. 09-379-9594)

Hong Kong, Suite 1006, Central Plaza, 18 Harbour Rd., Wanchai, Hong Kong (tel. 802-7700)

Singapore, Suite 1703, 17th floor, United Square, 101 Thomson Rd., Singapore 1130 (tel. 255-4555)

Osaka, 4th floor, Yuki Building, 3-3-9 Hiranomachi, Chuo-ku, Osaka 541, Japan (tel. 06-229-3601)

Tokyo, 8th floor, Sankaido Building, 1-9-13 Akasaka, Minato-ku, Tokyo, 107 Japan (tel. 03-3582-2191)

For the **head office** of the Australian Tourist Commission, contact: Level 3, 80 William St., Woolloomooloo (Sydney), NSW 2011 (tel. 02-9360-1111).

The tourist commission also produces *Destination Australia,* a free, magazine-format guide with tempting photos, sample itineraries, and listings of transport companies and tour operators. To order, phone (800) 333-0262 (U.S.).

Aussie Helplines
Aussie Helplines work in conjunction with the Australian Tourist Commission to answer questions, offer travel tips, assist with itinerary planning, and mail out brochures. Free travel information sheets are available on many aspects of Australia, including sports, beaches, diving, Aboriginal Australia, nightlife, backpacking, surfing, etc. For more information in the U.S. and Canada, phone (708) 296-4900, Mon.-Fri. 8 a.m.-7 p.m. central standard time.

Other Helpful Information
Hostels, airports, and coach depots carry quite a few free publications and brochures for travelers—everything from fruit-picking information to accommodation options. Especially useful are *For Backpacker By Backpackers, Aussie Backpacker, Backpacker's Guide,* and *Go Oz-YHA Magazine.*

Available for purchase at newsagents is *Travel Times,* an inexpensive timetable of all coach, train, and ferry schedules throughout Australia.

Automobile Associations
Australian automobile clubs offer reciprocal rights to members of the American Automobile Club and the United Kingdom's RAC and AA (bring your membership card with you). The **Australian Automobile Association's** services include free roadside emergency breakdown service (within certain city limits), route maps, touring information, discounted travel guides, and accommodations and camping directories. Many offices will make tour and accommodations reservations for you.

The **main state offices** are: **Australian Automobile Association** (AAA Head Office), G.P.O. Box 1555, Canberra, ACT 2601 (tel. 06-247-7311); **Royal Automobile Association of South Australia** (RAA), 41 Hindmarsh Square, Adelaide, SA 5000 (tel. 08-8223-4500); **Royal Automobile Club of Queensland** (RACQ), 300 St. Pauls Terrace, Fortitude Valley, QLD 4006 (tel. 07-3361-2444); **Royal Automobile Club of Victoria** (RACV), 550 Princes Hwy., Noble Park, VIC 3174 (tel. 03-9790-2627); **Automobile Association of the Northern Territory** (AANT), 79-81 Smith St., Darwin, NT 0800 (tel. 08-8981-3837); **Royal Automobile Club of Tasmania** (RACT), corner Patrick and Murray Streets, Hobart, TAS 7001 (tel. 002-38-2200); **National Roads and Motorists Association** (NRMA), 92 Northbourne Ave., Canberra, ACT 2601 (tel. 06-243-8826); **Royal Automobile Club of Western Australia** (RACWA), 228 Adelaide Terrace, Perth, WA 6000 (tel. 09-421-4444); **National Roads and Motorists Association** (NRMA), 151 Clarence St. Sydney, NSW 2000 (tel. 02-9260-9222).

WHAT TO TAKE

Clothing
Australians are casual dressers—except in the major cities (especially Melbourne and Sydney), where you might wish to keep up with the trendy set in your very best '60s-70s garb, *or* if you're headed to one of the Outback's formal-attire B&S balls.

Follow the old, basic rule: Dress for comfort and climate. If you're going to the tropical north, take lightweight cottons, which are suitable year-round. (Shorts are okay most places.) The southern temperate regions also call for cottons and other natural fibers during summer months; winters can be very cold there, so pack a heavy sweater and jacket. The Outback will be searing during the summer, giving way to chilly nights in winter. And rain can drop any time, unexpectedly, and in great torrents; you might want to include a light raincoat and an umbrella in your suitcase. It's always well advised to dress in layers, particularly due to rapidly changing weather conditions in many regions.

Outback Clothing
For the authentic Outback Aussie look in warmer months, outfit yourself in a singlet (sleeveless T-shirt), a pair of shorts (Stubbies are the Oz favorite), heavy socks, and Blundstone boots (they have elastic sides, last forever, but are somewhat costly) or a good pair of sturdy (well broken-in!) hiking boots. You'll definitely need a hat, so, if you still have some clothing budget left, pick up an Akubra (the Aussie working-bloke's Stetson).

Et Cetera
Other articles to bring along are a sunhat, sunglasses, sunscreen, sturdy walking shoes (again, broken-in *before* arrival), and waterproof sneakers for coral reef-walking. You might also want to pack a voltage converter, adapter plugs, insect repellent, prescription medications, and an extra pair of eyeglasses or contact lenses. Most brands of cosmetics, toiletries, and over-the-counter medications are readily available at chemist shops (pharmacies).

Et Cetera Et Cetera
Pack light. Leave room in your backpack or luggage for necessities (and souvenirs) that you'll collect along the way. Bring a sheet sack if you'll be doing the hostel routine, as well as your usual camping gear. Don't forget any required permits (which you should have obtained beforehand), maps, and a good, ahem, *guidebook.* Special equipment, swags or other camp bedding, cooking equipment, first-aid kits and such, can all be purchased in Australia—and may be better suited to the unique environment than the closer-to-civilization gear you may be used to. Often you can pick up good deals on used equipment from departing travelers at hostels. If you sign up for an organized tour, many operators provide many needed items. You can pick up the fly net to wear over your face after you arrive in Australia.

FILM AND PHOTOGRAPHY

Film and Processing
Film, processing labs, and photo equipment are easy finds in Australian cities. Bring your own 35mm camera and lenses. Unless you're coming in via Singapore or Hong Kong, it's unnecessary to stock up on film beforehand; Australian film costs about the same as in North America or Europe. You'll also find many "one-hour" photo shops with speedy processing for those on the move.

Photo Tips
Special conditions to be aware of are: intensity of light, particularly in the Outback; temperature extremes (try to keep film cool and dry); Outback dust; and, in the country's far north, tropical humidity.

Best times for taking photos in the Outback are early morning and late afternoon. A polarizing filter will help minimize washout.

As for those airport X-ray machines—if you're worried about your film (especially any over 400 ASA), carry it in a lead-lined bag and/or request hand inspection.

Photo Etiquette
Do not photograph Aboriginals without their permission—which you probably won't get. They do not like having their photos taken—and that includes crowd and distance shots.

WEIGHTS AND MEASURES

Measurements
Australia uses the metric system, like almost every other country in the world. Temperatures are in Celsius (C). (See the conversion tables at the back of this book.)

Electrical Voltage
Australia's electrical current is 240/250 volts, 50Hz AC. You'll need a **three-pin adapter plug** (different from the British three-pronger) for any 110-volt appliances you intend to bring, as well as the appropriate **voltage converter.** It's best to purchase adapter plugs and converters before arrival, though both are available in the larger cities. If you're bringing a computer or other specialized equipment, be sure to check with the manufacturer for exact requirements.

Time Zones
Australia has three time zones. New South Wales, Australian Capital Territory, Victoria, Tasmania, and Queensland operate on **eastern standard time** (EST); South Australia and the Northern Territory use **central standard time** (CST); and Western Australia has its very own **western standard time** (WST).

Here is the confusing part: central standard time is half an hour behind eastern standard

time, while western standard time is two hours behind eastern standard time. And all of the states except Western Australia, Queensland, and the Northern Territory go on **summer time** (daylight saving time) from October to March, when clocks are set ahead one hour. And Tasmania keeps to daylight saving time one month longer than the others. It's no wonder the Aborigines keep to Dreamtime!

© MOON PUBLICATIONS, INC.

BOOMERANG LOVE

*If you won't
let me go,
then I'll never
come back.*

—EXCERPT FROM *LULU, QUEEN OF
EVERYTHING,* BY MARAEL JOHNSON
(MANILA: CACHO PUBLISHING
HOUSE, 1994)

BOB RACE

SOUTH AUSTRALIA
INTRODUCTION

License plates proclaim it "The Festival State." Border-crossing signs herald it "The Grand Prix State" and, underneath, warn that speeding laws are strictly enforced (those signs, however, don't announce the Grand Prix's moving to Melbourne in 1996). Fact decrees it the driest state in Australia. And the Tourism Commission banners it—most accurately—"The State of Surprise." The surprises are many, for, dry as most of its 984,200 square kilometers may be, South Australia is definitely not dull.

Flanked by Victoria and New South Wales on the east, by Western Australia on the west, and neatly tucked beneath the Northern Territory, this land has almost as many ripe attractions to pick from as it does grapes growing on its famous vines. Most people have heard about the Barossa and Clare Valleys, famous for fine wines and the warm feelings that go with them; and about Adelaide, the "pretty" capital city, where nearly two-thirds of the state's 1.4 mil-

lion inhabitants live from one festival to the next—and, without a doubt, the mere mention of the huge Outback part of the state sends shivers down the spines of those who dream of scorching in their boots. Coober Pedy, the opal-mining town so hot that homes and shops are built underground, has also received its share of publicity (though it's often depicted as the end of the earth).

Not so popularized by films, jewels, or wine labels are South Australia's lesser-known gems: Hahndorf, a German settlement where you can pick up streusel on the corner instead of meat pie; Burra, an exquisitely preserved copper center with miners' dugouts, Cornish cottages, and the "monster mine"; Kangaroo Island, abundant in 'roos and other wild-and-woollies, with picnic areas that keep the humans fenced in so the animals can watch *them* eat and perform; the Flinders Ranges, spectacular multicolored rock formations, about 1.6 billion years old, with

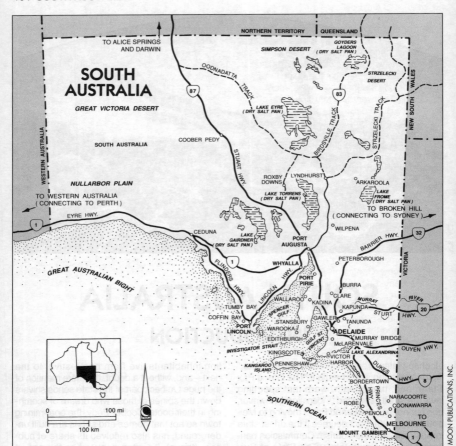

deep gorges and endlessly changing vistas; the Blue Lake, which is actually gray but turns bright blue at the exact same time each year; Lake Eyre, a (usually) dry salt pan that is Australia's largest lake; and the mighty Murray, the country's most important river, which stretches more than 2,000 kilometers from the Snowy Mountains to Lake Alexandrina.

These, of course, are just a few tidbits to whet your appetite. You will also discover heritage towns with exquisitely crafted sandstone buildings, little sleepy fishing villages, bustling beach resorts, reputed UFO landing sights, and Outback tracks to test the heartiest, nerviest, and possibly craziest souls. Naturally, there are some dry spots, but think of them merely as crackers to clear your palate between sips (or gulps) of the sweetest wine.

Most places are easily accessible by a variety of transport. Hop a vintage tram to the beach or catch the Ghan and train it up to the Red Centre. To get around cities, between towns, or across the Nullarbor Plain, hire an air-conditioned luxury car, a 4WD jeep, or use your thumb and feet.

Float along the Murray in your own houseboat, or sign up for a paddle steamer cruise. (Incidentally, some of the gurgly ferries-'cross-the-Murray will pang the nostalgic hearts of early '70s travelers who once clutched tattered copies of *Siddhartha* against their searching breasts.)

There is one forthcoming development, however, which may very well turn The State of Surprise into a State of Shock—the Multi-functional Polis, proposed for Adelaide's northwestern suburbs.

The MFP, as it is called, is billed a "city of the future." The 3,500-hectare site will accommodate some very high-tech industries, housing for a hundred thousand people, as well as health, education, and recreation facilities, and it will be financed by Japanese yen. The controversies are many and politicos, environmentalists, and average citizens continue to form committees. Some of the pros: The MFP will give Australia prestigious international standing while providing a much-needed boost to the ailing economy. Opponents insist that the project will be an environmental nightmare, citing possible seepage of toxic chemicals, higher risk of earthquakes, and death of the all-important mangroves as just a few ramifications of filling in the land. *And* there is fear and consternation that the Japanese may well be using their yen only to satisfy their own cravings.

The project, originally slated for Queensland's Gold Coast area but nixed by that state due to problems with private land acquisitions, was shunted down to Adelaide, the alternate choice (don't ever say second choice—they're touchy about it!).

Amid all the hoopla comes this unique view expressed by South Australia's UFO expert, Colin Norris: "We must stop knocking the Multi-functional Polis because visitors from other galaxies are waiting for it. This is the sort of place that will attract other beings. It's the sort of place they've been waiting for to come to."

So, on that enticing note—welcome, aliens, to South Australia!

CLIMATE

There is good reason why more than 99% of the state's population lives south of the 32nd parallel—it is the only part that isn't hot, harsh, and desolate.

Adelaide is frequently described as having a "Mediterranean-like" climate. The short, mild winters (June-Aug.) average 17° C (62° F). Even with occasional downpours and some very chilly nights, most days are bathed in plenty of sunshine. Summers (Dec.-Feb.) are very dry and range from a warm 29° C (84° F) to a downright hot 38° C (100° F). Autumn (March-May) and especially the spring months (Sept.-Nov.) are delightful times to visit the wine country or plan a bushwalk.

Adelaide's surrounding hills and vineyards are fertile and well irrigated. The southeast corner of the state and Kangaroo Island are cooler and greener yet. And, though snow is a rarity in South Australia, an occasional spatter of white has been sighted atop the Mt. Lofty Ranges.

The Outback, which makes up most of the state's northern region, blisters in summer. Searing temperatures of 51° C (124° F) have been recorded in the Oodnadatta area—and that was in the *shade.* The yearly rainfall is less than 25 cm, but an occasional fierce storm can prompt sudden, violent downpours.

In 1989, the Nullarbor Plain actually flooded, even halting the fabled Indian Pacific train in its tracks! I made the crossing several months after the rains and saw so many pools of water and bits of scrub popping up out of the normally cracked, parched, and stark earth that I feared I was hallucinating multiple oases. Lake Eyre, normally a huge salt pan, has also been getting its fill. For world weather-watchers, these unusual occurrences probably seem all too usual.

HISTORY

There was life before Light—Colonel William Light, that is, the British surveyor general who laid out the site for the capital city.

Thousands of years prior to Britain's colonization of South Australia, small tribes of Aboriginal hunters and gatherers lived a nomadic lifestyle in the environs of what is now Adelaide. Part of the coastline was charted as early as 1627 by Dutch explorer Peter Nuyts, but it was British navigator Matthew Flinders who in 1802 actually became the first white man to fully explore the coast. (Amazingly, American sealers, who established a base on nearby Kangaroo Island only one year later, stayed right where they were and minded their own business.)

Meanwhile, Charles Sturt, a hotshot who'd been exploring the country's interior, began making his way south along the Murray River, being spit out of its mouth at Lake Alexandrina in 1830. The London tabloids reported the exciting news of his discovery—a rich, fertile riverland. This inspired a fellow named Edward Gibbon Wakefield to come up with a great idea for reducing Britain's unemployment crisis: colonize this bountiful new land and raise much-needed money by selling off parcels. In other words—move in, run out the natives, and start subdividing. Sound familiar? Best yet, they would not need any of those nasty convicts because the settlers, having the "pride of ownership" carrot dangling over their noses, would be motivated to do their own hard labor. To this day, South Australians are pretty haughty about the fact that theirs is the only state in the country that was not begun as a convict colony.

In 1836 the British established their settlement, naming Captain John Hindmarsh as its first governor. Colonel William Light, responsible for laying out the capital city, called it Adelaide, in honor of King William IV's wife.

The new settlers were supposed to be religious, morally upright, and hardworking. However, as soon as they arrived in "their" new land, the Aboriginal population quickly dwindled. Many were killed by the white men, others died from the diseases the settlers brought, and the remainder were forced out to the hostile territory up north. There were the inevitable squabbles, bickering, red tape, and claims of incompetent government. There was a shortage of labor; bankruptcy loomed. Then in 1842 rich copper deposits were discovered, and South Australia quickly bounced back. Besides the mining boom, crops flourished. Soon Adelaide became an agricultural mecca for wheat, fruits, and wool. Shortly after, European refugees settled in the Barossa Valley, bringing with them their considerable talent for winemaking. Though the state's economy is still based mainly on its agricultural products—wine, citrus fruit, merino wool, wheat, barley, and fishing—other important industries include shipbuilding and automobile manufacturing.

A Crown colony in 1842, with its own legislative assembly elected by ballot in 1856, South Australia was made a state of the Commonwealth of Australia in 1901.

The state's staid image has greatly diminished since the advent of the Adelaide Festival of the Arts in 1960, not to mention some rather liberal legislation in the areas of homosexuality, marijuana usage, and Aboriginal land rights.

KAREN McKINLEY

ADELAIDE

Approaching Adelaide from Melbourne, we left the train and were driven in an open carriage over the hills and along their slopes to the city. It was an excursion of an hour or two and the charm of it could not be overstated.

The road wound through gaps and gorges and offered all variety of scenery and prospect—color, color everywhere and the air fine and fresh, the skies blue and not a shred of cloud to mar the downpour of the brilliant sunshine.

And finally the mountain gateway opened, and the immense plain spread out below, stretching away into the dim distance on every hand, soft and delicate and dainty and beautiful.

On its near edge reposed the city; with wide streets compactly built; with fine houses everywhere, embowered in foliage and flowers and with imposing masses of public buildings nobly grouped and architecturally beautiful.

—MARK TWAIN

Colonel William Light has practically been beatified for his foresight in planning South Australia's capital city (pop. 1.1 million). The man loved straight lines and broad boulevards. He wanted Adelaide to reflect both simplicity and elegance and he had a magnificent site on which to realize his vision: a flat plain, centrally located on the southern coastline, with the glorious backdrop of rolling hills and dales and the Mt. Lofty Ranges.

Light designed a one-square-mile central business district composed of grid-patterned streets bisecting at right angles and five perfect city squares interspersed at regular intervals. One of these, Victoria Square, is the designated heart of the city (you'll find the general post office across the street and the central bus station about a block away). Gouger Street, on one perimeter, has not only the bounty-filled Central Market but a bevy of international cuisines and a mini-Chinatown.

Running north and south, skirting around Victoria Square, is King William Street, the center for business and commerce and supposedly the widest city street in any Australian capital. (Light named the main thoroughfare after his king, but it was his Queen Adelaide who took the whole city and, eventually, a wine label as well.)

Heading north up King William Street, you'll come to the intersection of Hindley Street on the west and Rundle Mall on the east—same street, but it changes names. Hindley Street is lined with restaurants, discos, and nightclubs, a couple of strip joints, and an adult book shop or two. This is Adelaide's "racy" quarter, if the occasional street brawl, broken beer bottle, or risqué book jacket justify the term.

Rundle Mall is the no-cars-allowed main shopping promenade that sports arcades with specialty shops, art galleries, department stores, outdoor cafes, occasional street vendors and buskers, and the much-debated stainless-steel sculpture of an enormous pair of balls. One block farther up King William St., on your right, is the **South Australian Tourism Commission Travel Centre.**

Rundle Street East, an "add-on" of Rundle Mall, is the student sector, replete with grunge and retro shops, alternative everything, the fabulous new East End Market, and an energetic street scene with many outdoor cafes at which to hide behind a tattered copy of Kerouac or Proust.

The city center is bounded in a neat little parcel by broad tree-lined terraces, aptly named North, South, East, and West Terrace. North Terrace, just another block up from the Travel Centre, is where you'll find most of the city's architectural and cultural attractions—Parliament House, the museums, Festival Arts Centre, University of Adelaide, and such. The terraces, in turn, are bordered by expansive parklands with

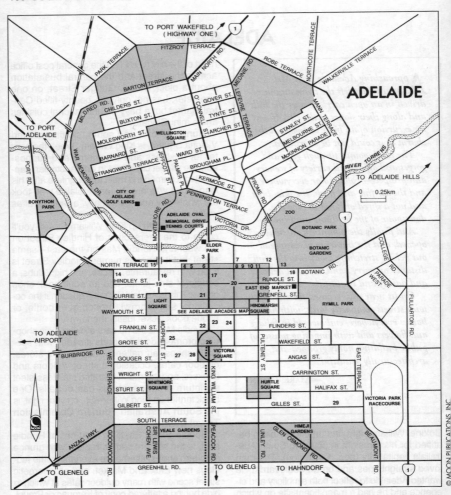

ADELAIDE

lovely greenbelts, towering eucalyptus trees, picnic areas, and recreation facilities.

The River Torrens, navigated by rowboats, motor launches, and a variety of other putt-putts, separates the business district from North Adelaide, one of the oldest sections of the city. North Adelaide is yet another of Colonel Light's babies—the Chosen Suburb, an exclusive residential grid built around a perfectly regular town square, surrounded by lots of greenery. Melbourne Street, part of the plot, is famed for its too-chic-to-be-believed boutiques and eateries.

Now, don't start thinking that all these well-organized grids and squares mean this is a metropolis full of unimaginative boxes. The architecture is *brilliant*—at least most of it—luscious stone churches, ornate and filigreed mansions, superb colonial buildings. As in most big cities,

1. St. Peter's Cathedral
2. Light's Vision
3. Adelaide Festival Centre
4. Convention Centre
5. Adelaide Casino (and Railway Station)
6. Parliament House
7. Migration and Settlement Museum
8. State Library
9. Mortlock Library
10. South Australian Museum
11. Art Gallery of
    South Australia
12. University of Adelaide
13. Royal Adelaide Hospital
14. Newmarket Hotel
15. Lion Arts Centre
16. Qantas Airways
17. South Australian Tourism Commission
    Travel Centre
18. Ayers House
19. Hindley St. Restaurant and Entertainment
    Area
20. Rundle Mall Shopping Area
21. Edmund Wright House
22. general post office
23. Adelaide Town Hall
24. YMCA
25. central bus station
26. Glenelg Tram Terminal
27. Central Market
28. Hilton International Hotel
29. Adelaide Youth Hostel

however, the old and beautiful structures do sometimes sit beside new and tasteless office blocks. But in Adelaide a movement is well underway to preserve as much of the original architecture as possible, or at least to keep the original facades.

Because of its compactness and methodical layout, Adelaide is easy to explore on foot. And, though it lacks the street action of many major cities, the small-town atmosphere and almost pastoral spaciousness make this state capital unique.

You're likely to hear a string of adjectives rattled off whenever Adelaide is mentioned—"calm," "stately," and, occasionally, "staid." The slightly more than one million residents like to think of themselves as sophisticated and infinitely more cultured than those beer-guzzling, telly-watching,

footy-fiend louts who inhabit the rest of the country. In Adelaide they drink fine wines, follow the cricket matches, attend the theater, and put on a world-class Festival of the Arts.

Calm, stately, staid? In 1988, Mick Jagger opened his solo world concert tour in Adelaide. Let someone try to grid and square *that* one.

ON THE TERRACE

North Terrace, wedged between the city hustle-bustle and the gentle River Torrens, is Adelaide's historic and cultural heart. This easy walk begins at the corner of West Terrace and North Terrace and ends at the corner of East Terrace. Conveniently, you start off at the **Newmarket Hotel** and finish up at the **Botanic Hotel,** two of Adelaide's most sumptuous pubs, which date back to the late 19th century.

Lion Arts Centre

Many of the Adelaide Arts Festival fringe events are held in this old Lions Club building at the corner of Morphett Street. Performance stages, galleries, arts and crafts workshops, and casual eating areas are the core of this vibrantly renovated factory. It is usually open during the daytime for a wander or coffee and a sandwich, otherwise hours depend on scheduled events. For more information, phone (08) 8231-7760.

Holy Trinity Church

The foundation stone for the state's oldest Anglican church, beside the Morphett St. bridge, was laid by Governor Hindmarsh himself in 1838. The present building is actually about 50 years newer, but the original clock still remains.

Adelaide Casino

You can bet that more people cross the threshold of the swanky casino than of the church across the street! Built atop the classic sandstone railway station with its majestic colonnades and balconies (still used by commuters), the casino offers two floors of gaming tables—roulette, craps, blackjack, baccarat—plus Keno, a Money Wheel, and Two-Up, an Aussie invention that has something to do with tossing coins in a ring. For those of you who prefer one-armed bandits, you're already out of luck: you'll find no poker or slot machines here. High rollers, however, can try to get a pass into the exclusive International Room. Even if you don't gamble, this is a good spot to people-watch. Also, there are five bars and two restaurants, the **Pullman** and the less formal **Carvery.**

Security is tight—photography is not allowed. In addition, a dress code is enforced: dressy or "smart casual." Guards will scrutinize you from head to toe as you cross the marble hall to the entrance, although I'm not at all sure they know what they're looking for—I sashayed in wearing a man's faded tee, a denim mini, and moth-eaten fishnets.

The casino is part of Adelaide Plaza, which also houses the Adelaide Convention Centre and Festival Centre, as well as the Hyatt Regency Hotel. It is open Mon.-Fri. 10 a.m.-4 a.m., Sat.-Sun. 24 hours, closed Christmas Day and Good Friday (when you can probably lay odds that more people are over at the church). Automatic-teller machines are on the premises, and visitors under 18 are *not.* For more information, phone (08) 8212-2811.

State History Centre
Sandwiched between the casino and the new Parliament House, South Australia's original Parliament house is one of the state's oldest and most historic buildings. In 1855 it was home to the first Legislative Council. Painstaking renovations were completed in 1980 and it is now the **Constitutional Museum,** which presents audiovisual displays and exhibits depicting the state's history, from Dreamtime to the present. The museum's **House of Assembly** is reputedly the world's oldest surviving chamber of democracy. A bookshop specializes in South Australian history, and there's a relaxing restaurant in the garden courtyard.

New Parliament House, next door, was a 56-year-long construction project, begun in 1883 and completed in 1939. Built out of grey Kapunda marble with high Corinthian columns in neoclassical style, it is a sharp contrast to its simpler predecessor. The public is invited to watch proceedings when Parliament is sitting and tours are available at various times. For more information, phone (08) 8237-9100.

The State History Centre is open Mon.-Fri. and public holidays 10 a.m.-5 p.m., Sat.-Sun.

noon-5 p.m., closed Christmas Day and Good Friday. Admission is $4. For more information, phone (08) 8207-1077.

The Adelaide Festival Centre
On King William Street, just behind the houses of Parliament and banking the River Torrens, the Adelaide Festival Centre, built in 1972, is home to the three-week Adelaide Festival of Arts, held in March of even-numbered years. Ranked as one of the world's top international multi-arts festivals, it draws diverse and big-name talents like Eartha Kitt, Yehudi Menuhin, the Royal Shakespeare Company, Japan's Kabuki Theatre, Twyla Tharp, and Mick Jagger. In addition, the Fringe Festival, which takes place simultaneously, presents innovative theatrical productions, performance events, poetry readings, art exhibitions, and a writers' week. Fringe events are held at the Lion Arts Centre and a host of other venues around town. The local newspapers' daily listings will keep you informed of when and where.

The Adelaide Festival Centre comprises a 2,000-seat multipurpose theater and concert hall, a drama theater (home to the State Theatre Company), an additional flexible performance space, an open-air amphitheater, a piano bar, and two restaurants. A variety of entertainment is presented year-round, including professional productions of successful musicals like *Cats* and *Evita,* chamber orchestra symphonies, and an informal late-night cabaret.

You can tour the Festival Centre Mon.-Fri. 10 a.m.-5 p.m., Saturday 1-5 p.m. Tours depart hourly and the cost is $3, payable at the enquiry counter in the foyer. For more information, phone (08) 8216-8729.

Government House
Back on North Terrace and east across King William Street is the Regency-style official residence of South Australia's governor. The first governor, John Hindmarsh, lived on the same site in 1836, but not in the same house. Governor Hindmarsh lived in a mud hut. It was George Gawler, the second governor (1838-41), who decided it was time to build a more suitable residence and, in 1839, began construction of the east wing. The midsection was added in 1855 and by 1878 the house as you see it was completed.

On either side of Government House are two **war memorials:** to the west is a bronze infantryman, commemorating South Australians who died in the Boer War; to the east is the National War Memorial, honoring those who died in WW I; plaques along the wall of Government House pay tribute to the dead of WW II.

Royal South Australian Society of Art
Across Kintore St., the Society, founded in 1856, exhibits at least six major members' works per year, its own permanent collection, and works of various individual artists. The archives and reference library are available for research. Hours are Mon.-Fri. 11 a.m.-5 p.m., Sat.-Sun. 2-5 p.m., closed Christmas, New Year's Day, and Easter weekend. Admission is free. For information, phone (08) 8223-4704.

State Library
This place is just a bit confusing: the State Library, which was originally in the old wing, is now in the Angaston white marble building next door; the **Mortlock Library,** restored to Victorian grandeur, is actually the original state library. To put it another way: the State Library carries all the regular books and overseas newspapers; the Mortlock has all the special collections—memorabilia relating to South Australia, a Historic Treasures Room with Colonel Light's surveying equipment on display, a family history research library, and a cricketing memorabilia collection. Both libraries are open Mon.-Fri. 9:30 a.m.-6 p.m., Wednesday and Friday until 8 p.m., Sat.-Sun. noon-5 p.m., closed public holidays. For information, phone (08) 8207-7200.

Migration and Settlement Museum
Next to the State Library, on Kintore Ave., is Australia's first multicultural museum. The building itself is Adelaide's restored Destitute Asylum. Exhibits and an audiovisual program give a realistic picture of what life was like for the early settlers. You can even visit the dark cells built back in the 1870s after a riot. The bookshop specializes in South Australian history. **Mrs. Gifford's** is a cafe in the courtyard. The museum is open Mon.-Fri. 10 a.m.-5 p.m., Sat.-Sun. and public holidays 1-5 p.m. Closed Good Friday and Christmas Day. Except for special traveling exhibits, admission is free. Guided

tours are available. For information, phone (08) 8207-7570.

Police Barracks and Armory
Tucked in a courtyard, near the Migration and Settlement Museum, the small **South Australian Police Museum** displays 1860s law enforcement memorabilia. Open Sat.-Sun. and public holidays 1-5 p.m., closed Christmas Day and Good Friday. Donations are requested. For information, phone (08) 8218-1228.

South Australian Museum
A distinctive North Terrace landmark, with whale skeletons in the front window, this museum is especially noteworthy for its extensive collections of Aboriginal, New Guinean, and Melanesian native artifacts. The museum shop stocks natural history and anthropology books, as well as related gift items. The museum is open daily 10 a.m.-5 p.m., closed Good Friday and Christmas Day. Except for special exhibitions, admission is free. For information, phone (08) 8207-7500.

Art Gallery of South Australia
Next door to the museum, a comprehensive collection of Australian, European, and Asian art is housed in two wings of the gallery. Highlights include examples of Australian impressionists, colonial works (including furniture, silver, and other decorative arts), 20th-century works by important painters like Arthur Boyd, Sir Sidney Nolan, and Russell Drysdale, recent Aboriginal landscapes, and an interesting collection of Southeast Asian ceramics. Changing exhibitions of contemporary art and Australian and international touring shows are also on display. The bookshop has a good collection of art books, periodicals, cards, some jewelry, and other related items. A pleasant coffee shop in the rear sells small cakes and sandwiches. The gallery is open daily 10 a.m.-5 p.m., closed Good Friday and Christmas Day. Admission is free, but there is often a charge for special exhibitions. Tours leave from the front entrance Mon.-Fri. 11 a.m. and 1 p.m., Sat.-Sun. 11 a.m. and 3 p.m. For information, phone (08) 8207-7000.

Museum of Classical Archaeology
The Mitchell Building, a striking Gothic edifice on the **University of Adelaide** campus, is a fitting

site for this collection of Greek, Egyptian, and Etruscan relics—some more than 5,000 years old. The museum, on the first floor, is open Mon.-Fri. noon-3 p.m., closed for two weeks at Christmas. Admission is free. For information, phone 303-5226. (There are many fine examples of 19th-century architecture on this 10-hectare campus. Of particular interest is castle-like Bonython Hall.)

Ayers House

Across Frome Rd. and opposite the Royal Adelaide Hospital, this former residence of Sir Henry Ayers, former premier of South Australia, is now headquarters of the **National Trust.** Construction on the elegant bluestone manor was begun in 1846 and took 30 years to complete. Carefully preserved and refurnished, Ayers House is a lovely specimen of gracious Victorian living, with special displays of fine silver, crystal, nursery toys, and an early kitchen. You can inspect the house Tues.-Fri. 10 a.m.-4 p.m., Sat.-Sun. and holidays 2-4 p.m., closed Good Friday and Christmas Day. Admission is $4. For information, phone (08) 8223-1655.

OTHER CITY SIGHTS

King William Street

You'll find several more noteworthy attractions as you stroll along King William Street, between North Terrace and Victoria Square.

Edmund Wright House, 59 King William St., was built in 1876 for the bishop of South Australia. These days the ornate Renaissance-style residence is used for government offices and offical functions. Take a peek inside during normal business hours. Free lunchtime music performances are held here every Wednesday during autumn and spring.

The **Telecommunications Museum,** in Electra House at 131 King William St., features working displays and original equipment that trace South Australia's technology from past to present. Open Sun.-Fri. 10:30 a.m.-3:30 p.m., closed Saturday. Admission is free. For information, phone (08) 8225-6601.

Approaching Victoria Square, on the opposite side of the street is **Adelaide Town Hall.** Built in 1863, the freestone facade is carved

with the faces of Queen Victoria and Prince Albert. You can take a free one-hour guided tour on Tuesday and Wednesday 2:30 p.m., Thursday at 10:30 a.m. and 2:30 p.m.. A two-week advance booking is requested. For information, phone (08) 8203-7777.

The post office, across the street, is another fine example of stately colonial architecture. For postal history buffs, the **Postal Museum** next door (on the Franklin St. side) has a reconstructed turn-of-the-century post office, as well as archival philatelic displays. Open Mon.-Fri. 11 a.m.-2 p.m. Admission is free. For information, phone (08) 8216-2225.

More Museums and Manors

You can view historic transport vehicles as well as ride on restored trams at the **Australian Electrical Transport Museum** in St. Kilda (about 30 km northwest of the city center). Open Sunday and Wednesday during school holidays, closed Good Friday and Christmas Day. Admission is $4. For information, phone (08) 8261-9110.

Carrick Hill, 46 Carrick Hill Dr., Springfield (a 10-minute drive from the city), was built in 1939 in the fashion of a late Elizabethan-era English manor house. Set on nearly 39 hectares of English gardens and surrounded by native Australian bush, the estate features a superb collection of Australian, English, and French paintings, as well as silver, pewter, and English oak furniture. The grounds also include a sculpture park and picnic area. Devonshire tea is served in the tearooms. The home and grounds are open Wed.-Sun. and public holidays 10 a.m.-5 p.m., closed the month of July. Admission is $6. For information, phone (08) 8379-3886.

Botanic Gardens

The Botanic Gardens sit on 16 hectares near the junction of North and East terraces. Besides the usual and unusual Australian and exotic species, the Adelaide gardens house Australia's only **Museum of Economic Botany** and the **Tropical Conservatory,** the largest conservatory in the Southern Hemisphere. The museum, housed inside a Grecian-style heritage building, exhibits an array of plants used for commercial, medicinal, and artistic purposes. The conservatory, built with the help of NASA tech-

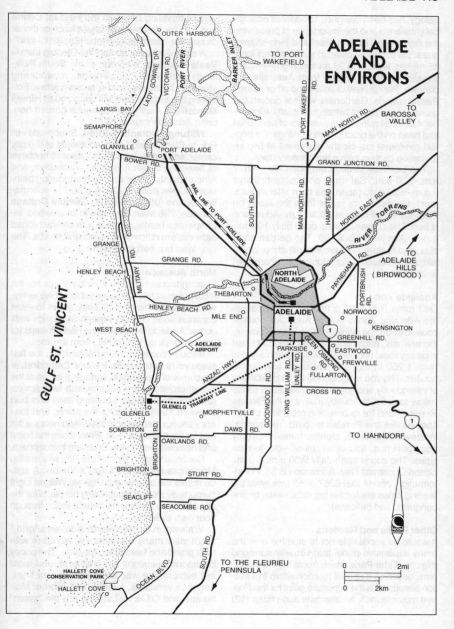

ADELAIDE AND ENVIRONS

TO PORT WAKEFIELD

TO BAROSSA VALLEY

TO ADELAIDE HILLS (BIRDWOOD)

TO HAHNDORF

TO THE FLEURIEU PENINSULA

OUTER HARBOR

BARKER INLET

PORT RIVER

LADY GOWRIE DR.

VICTORIA RD.

LARGS BAY

SEMAPHORE

GLANVILLE

PORT ADELAIDE

BOWER RD.

RAIL LINE TO PORT ADELAIDE

GRANGE

GRANGE RD.

HENLEY BEACH

MILITARY RD.

HENLEY BEACH RD.

THEBARTON

MILE END

NORTH ADELAIDE

ADELAIDE

PORT WAKEFIELD RD.

MAIN NORTH RD.

GRAND JUNCTION RD.

MAIN NORTH RD.

HAMPSTEAD RD.

NORTH EAST RD.

SOUTH RD.

RIVER TORRENS

PAYNEHAM RD.

PORTRUSH RD.

NORWOOD

KENSINGTON

GREENHILL RD.

EASTWOOD

FREWVILLE

FULLARTON

CROSS RD.

GULF ST. VINCENT

WEST BEACH

ADELAIDE AIRPORT

ANZAC HWY.

PARKSIDE

GLEN OSMOND RD.

UNLEY RD.

KING WILLIAM RD.

GOODWOOD RD.

GLENELG TRAMWAY LINE

GLENELG

MORPHETTVILLE

SOMERTON

BRIGHTON RD.

OAKLANDS RD.

DAWS RD.

BRIGHTON

STURT RD.

SEACLIFF

SEACOMBE RD.

SOUTH RD.

OCEAN BLVD.

HALLETT COVE CONSERVATION PARK

HALLETT COVE

0   2mi

0   2km

MOON

nology, has been designed to address ecological imbalance and the importance of preserving the rainforests. Built of steel and lens-shaped glass, the building—measuring 100 meters long, 45 meters wide, and 27 meters high—encompasses rainforest plants from Australia, Indonesia, Papua New Guinea, and other nearby Pacific islands. Gardeners will not disturb the growth of any plants (which eventually will number 4,000), allowing leaves and bits of bark to fall and heap on the ground. The workings of a tropical rainforest are clearly explained at two information centers within the conservatory.

The Botanic Gardens are open Mon.-Fri. 7 a.m.-5:30 p.m., Sat.-Sun. and public holidays 9 a.m.-5:30 p.m. (open one hour later in summer). Guided tours leave from the kiosk on Tuesday and Friday at 10:30 a.m. Admission is free. The conservatory is open daily 10 a.m.-4 p.m. Admission is $2.50. The garden complex also features a book and gift shop, and a lakeside restaurant. For information, phone (08) 8228-2311.

Adelaide Zoo

On Frome Rd., next to the Botanic Gardens, the Adelaide Zoo is one of Australia's oldest zoos. Set on the banks of the River Torrens, the animals, birds, and reptiles are contained in grassy moat enclosures, walk-through aviaries (with 1,200 birds), and nocturnal and reptile houses. The zoo is acclaimed for its exhibitions of infrequently seen native animals, such as the yellow-footed rock wallaby (native of the Flinders Ranges), and for its breeding programs of rare species like the Persian leopard, red panda, Prezewalski's horse, ctontop tamarin, pygmy hippopotamus, and other roll-off-your-tongue types. The zoo is open daily 9:30 a.m.-5 p.m., closed Christmas Day. Admission is $8. For information, phone (08) 8267-3255 (ask what the feeding times are for the big cats, seals, bears, penguins, and pelicans).

Other Parks and Gardens

It would be impossible not to stumble onto the many expansive parks that virtually surround this city. **Elder Park,** which fronts the River Torrens, deserves a special mention within this section because it is the departure point for the *Popeye* motor launch, an alternate and cheap ($2)

way of traveling between the Festival Centre and the zoo. You can also take a lunch or dinner cruise. For information, phone (08) 8295-4747.

A short ride away aboard the Glenelg tram is **Veale Gardens,** a portion of the South Parklands with lovely flowerbeds, meandering streams, fountains, and a conservatory. Following the terrace east will bring you to **Himeji Gardens,** a traditional Japanese garden honoring Adelaide's sister city.

Wittunga Botanic Garden, Shepherds Hill Rd., in Blackwood, 14 km southeast of the city center, and dating from 1901, offers 15 hectares of flowering South Australian, Australian, and African plants, accessed via meandering pathways. Open daily 9 a.m.-5 p.m. For information, phone (08) 8228-2311. **Gamble Cottage Garden,** 296 Main Rd., also in Blackwood, intersperses heritage roses with old-fashioned perennials and flowering plants and shrubs. The rear lawn is a delightful picnic area.

North Adelaide

Outstanding architecture and ritzy shops are the focal points of this exclusive suburb. Like everywhere else in the city, it's easy to get to—just continue north up King William St., a nice walk across Adelaide Bridge and the River Torrens (or you can walk up Frome Rd., from the zoo).

If you're coming up King William St., the first place you'll notice is **St. Peter's Cathedral,** at the corner of Pennington Terrace. It is one of the few churches in the country with twin spires, and though the church building itself was built between 1868 and 1876, the spires and towers were not erected until 1902. And here's a fun fact for your almanac—St. Peter's has the finest and heaviest bells in the Southern Hemisphere.

Continue west to Montefiore Rd., where atop Montefiore Hill stands **Light's Vision.** A statue marks the spot where Colonel William Light purportedly started blueprinting his plans for the city. Here you can see his beatific vision through your own eyes.

Walking about the North Adelaide "grid," you'll view many architectural wonders with their grand and fascinating touches. The pricey bluestone mansions are well kept, and most are quite ornate with eye-catching roof lines, iron lace verandas, towers, and filigree. Melbourne and O'Connell streets are the "smart"

(top) Aboriginal Tiwi culture is particularly rich and relatively unscathed by colonial encroachment.
(bottom) a wallaroo, Queensland

(top) coastal heath near Cape Leeuwin, Western Australia
(bottom) fig roots and sandstone, Edith Creek, Katherine Gorge National Park, Northern Territory

shopping districts, with equally pricey boutiques, restaurants, and hairdressing salons, along with some interesting little pubs peppered in between. Many of the commercial buildings are renovated Victorian workers' cottages.

Port Adelaide

Port Adelaide, about 25 minutes from the city center (buses leave from North Terrace), is South Australia's first heritage area. The 19th-century wharf district, an important hub for coastal steamers until World War II, has been preserved as the **Maritime Museum,** spread over seven historic sites. Main display galleries are inside the **Bond** (1854) and **Free** (1857) stores; **Weman's Building** (1864) is the old sailmaker's shop; the **Lighthouse** (1869), first erected at the entrance to the Port River, was shifted over to South Neptune Island in 1901, then, in 1986, re-sited to its present location. The **Customs House, police station,** and **courthouse** complete the museum buildings. You'll soak up lots of atmosphere just wandering the streets. Many of the facades, ranging from modest houses to ornate banks (particularly those along Lipson St.), have been restored to old port-days splendor. At **No. 1 Wharf** you can hop aboard the *Nelcebee* (1883), an old coastal ketch, or the *Yelta* (1949), the last tug to steam in the port. The museum buildings are open Tues.-Sun. and daily during school holidays 10 a.m.-5 p.m. Admission is $8. For information, phone (08) 8240-0200.

Port Dock Station Railway Museum, also on Lipson St., has one of the country's largest collections of locomotives and carriages, as well as lots of memorabilia, an audiovisual theaterette, and model railways. Go on the weekend when you can take a ride on one of two different steam trains. A railway cafeteria car houses tearooms. Open Sun.-Fri. and public holidays 10 a.m.-5 p.m., Saturday noon-5 p.m. Admission is $6. For information, phone (08) 8341-1690.

Rather trains than planes? The **Historical Aviation Museum,** 11 Mundy St., exhibits various aircraft as well as engines and aero-memorabilia. Open Sat.-Sun. and public holidays 10 a.m.-5 p.m. Admission is $3. For information, phone (08) 8264-2199.

If you visit on Sunday, be sure to visit **Port Adelaide Market** in a huge warehouse on

Queens Wharf. Junk, junque, and Asian food-stalls are among the offerings. Open 8 a.m.-5 p.m.

Got your sea legs and find the salt air flaring your nostrils? Check at the dock for available cruises.

Glenelg

This is the most popular of Adelaide's suburban beaches. Though not equal to the famed beauties on the east and west coasts, there's water (sometimes blue), sand (at low tide), shark netting (to keep out South Australia's deadly white pointer), a water slide, amusement park, pie carts, and wienie wagons. What more do you want? History? Then you've come to the right place—Glenelg is where South Australia began, the landing place of Governor Hindmarsh and the first settlers back in 1836. Over at the **Patawalonga Boat Haven,** you can climb aboard a replica of the HMS *Buffalo,* from which Captain Hindmarsh stepped ashore and proclaimed South Australia a colony. (Unlike the original, however, this buffalo is fitted with a restaurant, bar, and small museum.) Open daily 10 a.m.-5 p.m. Admission is $2.50. For information, phone (08) 8294-7000.

The **Old Gum Tree,** on MacFarlane St., marks the exact spot where the Union Jack was raised. You can witness a reenactment each year on Proclamation Day, 28 December.

A large shell display, including circa-1930s shell art and crafts, is on exhibit at **Shell Land,** 17 Mary Street. Open Tues.-Sun. 10:30 a.m.-noon and 1-4:30 p.m. For information, phone (08) 8294-5837.

The **tourist information center,** on the foreshore (tel. 08-8294-5833), provides walking and cycling maps. Open daily, weather permitting, 9 a.m.-5 p.m.

Adelaide's only tram makes a sentimental journey from Victoria Square directly to Jetty Rd., Glenelg's main street, taking approximately 30 minutes. Cost is $2.20 one-way.

Other Options

Favorite local beaches north of Glenelg are West Beach, Henley Beach, Grange, West Lakes, Glanville, Semaphore, and Largs Bay; south of Glenelg (where the surf is decent) are Somerton, Brighton, and Seacliff. Nude bathing is allowed at

Maslin Beach, about 40 km south of the city. Between Seacliff and Maslin is **Hallett Cove Conservation Reserve,** where the landscape has been fabulously molded and colored by a glacial movement some 270 million years ago.

At Grange, you can visit **Sturt's Cottage,** where the famous explorer, Captain Charles Sturt, lived between 1840 and 1853 (when he was home, that is). The house contains his family memorabilia and is furnished in that period's style. Sturt's Murray River campsite has been re-created on the grounds—in case you need some pointers. The home is open Wed.-Sun. and public holidays 1-5 p.m. Admission is $2.50. For information, phone (08) 8356-8185.

Fort Glanville, in Semaphore, was built in 1878 and restored in the 1980s. You can blast your ears out on the third Sunday of each month, 1-5 p.m., when reenactments of rifle drills and cannon firings (two 64-pounders!) are staged. Admission is $3. For information, phone (08) 8242-1978.

For a gentler pursuit, visit **Bower Cottages,** 200 Bower Rd., where you can watch local craftspeople and their works-in-progress. The cottages were built in 1897 to commemorate Queen Victoria's Diamond Jubilee. Open Wed.-Fri. noon-4 p.m., and tours are available. For information, phone (08) 8449-2959.

ACCOMMODATIONS

As in most large cities, accommodations in Adelaide run the spectrum from cheap and basic to ritzy and plush—except here, quite often, the two ends sit side by side and back to back. It's usually easy to find a room unless you arrive at festival time. Keep in mind that the Adelaide Festival of the Arts (first three weeks of March, in even-numbered years) and the spillover from the Barossa Valley Vintage Festival (Easter week, in odd-numbered years) are peak periods. If you plan to attend any of these events, or to be in the Adelaide area at those times, you'd be well advised to book a room *way* in advance.

City Accommodations

Words of caution: If you or your traveling companions are unaccustomed to city noises, you may not want to bed down on occasionally

Adelaide's only tram chugs from Victoria Square to seaside Glenelg, where South Australia began.

MIKE WELLINS

rowdy Hindley Street. Prices in Adelaide, as might be expected, run somewhat higher than in rural areas.

Inexpensive (under $35): Centrally located **West's Private Hotel,** 110B Hindley St. (tel. 08-8231-7575), is cheap ($20 per room), and more of a guesthouse than a hotel. Linen is included, but not much else. Backpackers are welcome, but women alone should pass on this one. The **Metropolitan Hotel,** 46 Grote St. (tel. 08-8231-5471), near Victoria Square, has basic accommodations with shared facilities. Over at the **Plaza Private Hotel,** 85 Hindley St. (tel. 08-8231-6371), rooms come with washbasins. The Plaza is an old-timer, once nicely kept but now down the tubes. Some of the costlier rooms ($50) have private facilities. The **Austral Hotel,** 205 Rundle St. (tel. 08-8223-4660), has clean and simple pub accommodations with shared facilities. **The Clarice,** 220 Hutt St. (tel. 08-8223-3560), is both a hotel and motel, near the East Terrace side of town. Rooms with shared facilities start low. It'll cost you $10-20 more to stay in the newer motel wing, with your own shower and toilet.

Moderate ($35-70): Accommodations at **City Central Motel,** 23 Hindley St. (tel. 08-8231-4049), have private facilities and include continental breakfast. At the corner of Gawler Place and Flinders St., the **Earl of Zetland Hotel** (tel. 08-8223-5500) offers good value in pub accommodations. Rooms are air-conditioned and have private showers and toilets. The pub downstairs puts out a decent buffet spread at lunch (about $6). **Directors Studio Suites,** 259 Gouger St. (tel. 08-8231-3572), offers roomy apartment-style digs close to the Central Market. Near the Festival Centre and casino, try the **Festival Lodge Motel,** 140 North Terrace (tel. 08-8212-7877), **The Strathmore,** 129 North Terrace (tel. 08-8212-6911), or the **Grosvenor Hotel,** 125 North Terrace (tel. 08-8231-2961). This trio is well located and has all the modern amenities. Deluxe rooms at the Grosvenor (the city's former grand dame hotel) can climb as high as $120.

Expensive ($70 and way up): The Mansions, 21 Pulteney St. (tel. 08-8232-0033), is a really good deal especially if you're sharing. Spacious studios or one-bedroom apartments in this circa-1910 building feature cooking facilities as well as a rooftop spa and sauna. If you're a big spender (or you've just hit it big at the casino), Adelaide's two luxury high-rise hotels are the **Hilton International,** 233 Victoria Square (tel. 08-8217-0711), peacefully situated over the center city square, and the super-glitzy **Hyatt Regency** (tel. 08-8231-1234) on North Terrace, smack dab in the middle of the fun side. Basic doubles at either hotel are around $200, and go way up.

On the Outskirts

If you've got your heart set on staying in lovely North Adelaide, the moderately priced **Princes Lodge Motel,** 73 Lefevre Terrace (tel. 08-8267-5566), on the outer edge of the suburban grid, is your best bet ($35 including continental breakfast). If you like to spread out, **Greenways Apartments,** 45 King William Rd. (tel. 08-8267-5903), offers one-, two-, and three-bedroom flats with cooking facilities and parking. The more deluxe **Adelaide Meridien,** 21 Melbourne St. (tel. 08-8267-3033), sits on North Adelaide's prestigious shopping street. **Adelaide Heritage Apartments** (tel. 08-8272-1355) can book you in a lovely heritage apartment or cottage—all fully equipped, many with fireplaces or spas. Rates are expensive if you're alone, a great deal if you're with one or more companions.

If you're coming in from the southeast, Glen Osmond Rd., which heads straight into the city,

is Adelaide's motel row. Some good choices include **Princes Highway Motel,** 199 Glen Osmond Rd., Frewville (tel. 08-8379-9253); **Fullarton Motor Lodge,** 284 Glen Osmond Rd., Fullarton (tel. 08-8379-9797); **Sands Motel,** 198 Glen Osmond Rd., Fullarton (tel. 08-8379-0079); and **Powell's Court,** 2 Glen Osmond Rd., Parkside (tel. 08-8271-7033). (Don't be confused—the suburbs change names frequently along this thoroughfare.) All of these motels are in the moderate range. Powell's Court has cooking facilities. Just two km from the city, **Parkway Motor Inn,** 204 Greenhill Rd., Eastwood (tel. 08-8271-0451), is well-located, has a pool and restaurant, and costs slightly more than the others. **Adelaide Heritage Apartments** (tel. 08-8272-1355) has two cottages in Eastwood, cheaper than the North Adelaide properties.

Glenelg and the Beaches

Glenelg has oodles of places to stay, most at reasonable prices—particularly during off-seasons, when many of the holiday flats offer attractive weekly rates. The tourist office on the foreshore can provide a list of available flats.

St. Vincent Hotel, 28 Jetty Rd. (tel. 08-8294-4377), a cozy, locally popular establishment has rates of $30-40 per room and that includes continental breakfast. **Colley Motel Apartments,** 22 Colley Terrace (tel. 08-8295-7535), and the **South Pacific,** 16 Colley Terrace (tel. 08-8194-1352), both opposite Colley Reserve, are good midrange choices for holiday flats. Priced slightly higher, but still excellent value for two or more traveling together, are the holiday flats at **Coral Seaside Units,** 2 South Esplanade (tel. 08-8295-1592), and **La Mancha,** 8 Esplanade (tel. 08-8295-2345). The big ticket in town is the beachfront **Ramada Grand,** Moseley Square (tel. 08-8376-1222), a high-priced high-rise with highfalutin frills.

In Glenelg South, the **Bay Hotel Motel,** 58 Broadway (tel. 08-8294-4244), not far from the beach, has rooms with color television and private facilities, as does the **Norfolk Motor Inn,** 71 Broadway (tel. 08-8295-6354). Prices at both are moderate.

West Beach and Henley Beach are also packed with holiday flats. In West Beach, try **Cootura Holiday Flats,** 8 West Beach Rd. (tel.

08-8353-3210), **Marineland Village Holiday Villas,** Military Rd. (tel. 08-8353-2655), or **Tuileries Holiday Apartments,** 13 Military Rd. (tel. 08-8353-3874). A best bet in Henley Beach is **Meleden Villa,** 268 Seaview Rd. (tel. 08-8235-0577), an atmospheric, seafront bed and breakfast. Down the way, **Allenby Court,** 405 Seaview Rd. (tel. 08-8235-0445), offers fully equipped, two-bedroom holiday flats. Keep in mind that holiday flats are moderately priced but often require minimum stays of two or more nights. Farther north in Semaphore, the **Semaphore Hotel,** 17 Semaphore Rd. (tel. 08-8449-4662), is your *very* basic pub with shared facilities. A better choice is a few doors away at the moderately priced **Federal Hotel,** 25 Semaphore Rd. (tel. 08-8449-6866).

Hostels

Adelaide's hostels, like everything else in the city, are centrally located and easy to find. Three of the hostels are in the South Terrace district and can be reached by foot or by bus from Pulteney Street). The 50-bed **Adelaide YHA Hostel,** 290 Gilles St. (tel. 08-8223-6007), has a friendly atmosphere and helpful staff. The office is closed Mon.-Sat. 10 a.m.-1 p.m., Sunday 10 a.m.-5:30 p.m., but hostel guests have 24-hour access. The 40-bed **Backpackers Hostel Adelaide** is nearby at 263 Gilles St. (tel. 08-8223-5680) and has two sections: one closes 11 a.m.-3 p.m.; the other section stays open all day but costs a buck more. Office hours are 8-11 a.m. and 3-10 p.m. Both of these hostels have kitchen facilities and lounges where you can meet up with other travelers.

Another hostel, closer to the center of town, is **Backpackers Inn,** 112 Carrington St. (tel. 08-8223-6635). This former pub is run by the same folks at Backpackers Hostel Adelaide and offers both dorm beds and double rooms ($20). **Adelaide City Backpackers,** nearby at 118 Carrington St. (tel. 08-8232-4774), is shabby and best avoided.

Backpack Australia Hostel, 128 Grote St. (tel. 08-8231-0639), makes up for the small dorms with friendly atmosphere, a bar, and inexpensive meals. **East Park Lodge,** 341 Angas St. (tel. 08-8223-1228), is a private family-run hostel, also near the city center. Dorm beds, double rooms, and some meals are available.

Both men and women are welcome at the **YMCA,** 76 Flinders St. (tel. 08-8223-1611), conveniently near Victoria Square and the central bus station. Dorm beds run $11, singles are $18, doubles are priced at $28. Office hours are Mon.-Fri. 9 a.m.-9 p.m., Sat.-Sun. 9 a.m.-noon and 4-8 p.m.

In Glenelg, **Backpackers Beach Headquarters,** 7 Moseley St. (tel. 08-8376-0007), offers home-style accommodations in a heritage building with kitchen, laundry, and even car rental facilities. Dorm beds and some single and double rooms are available.

Homestays

The **South Australian Tourism Commission Travel Centre,** 1 King William St., Adelaide 5000 (tel. 08-8212-1505), will provide you with a list of homestay properties, which include city homes, historic cottages, health resorts, villas, and farms. Prices range from budget to luxury.

Camping

South Australia has a large number of camping facilities, though some accept only caravans, not tents. Most provide a number of powered and unpowered sites, as well as on-site cabins and vans. The state's caravan parks are generally of a very high standard—clean and comfortable. Many have swimming pools, game rooms, and tennis courts. The South Australian Tourism Commission Travel Centre can provide maps and brochures and assist with bookings. The following is a sampling of some of the more convenient and interesting locales.

Adelaide Caravan Park, Bruton St., Hackney (tel. 08-8363-1566), is the nearest park to city attractions. **Brownhill Creek Caravan Park,** Brownhill Creek Rd., Mitcham (tel. 08-8271-4824), set in 120 acres of bushland, is only seven km from Adelaide. **Belair Caravan Park,** Belair National Park (tel. 08-8278-3540), is just 11 km from the city center.

West Beach Caravan Park, Military Rd., West Beach (tel. 08-8356-7654), sits on a good swimming beach and is surrounded by playing fields and golf courses. And, for those of you who want to be near Fort Glanville's big cannons, there's **Adelaide Beachfront Van and Tourist Park,** 349 Military Rd., Semaphore Park (tel. 08-8449-7726), also on the beach.

FOOD

Adelaide does not have the "foody" scene so prevalent in its sister capital cities, Melbourne and Sydney. Though there are some "nouvelle" gourmet establishments sprinkled about, the emphasis here is on casual, outdoor dining—a terrace restaurant along the river, a picnic in the park, takeaways to eat in one of the city squares. Many of the restaurants are licensed, no doubt to keep those famous South Australian wines flowing. Adventurous eaters will often find dishes made from kangaroo meat on the menu—so if you want to try it in some form other than an old Jumbo Jack, keep your eyes peeled. In fact, this is the only state where it's a common meal selection. If you prefer to pass on the braised 'roo, you'll find plenty of fresh fish and seafood. Especially commendable are King George whiting and the local crayfish (sometimes called lobster).

Moored at Glenelg, this replica of the HMS Buffalo features a restaurant and museum.

Most of the ethnic restaurants are on Gouger Street, also home to the Central Market and Chinatown. Noisier dining can be had on Hindley Street, lodged above, between, or beneath the strip joints and sex shops and their accompanying sounds. Rundle Street East is where the fashionable avant garde dine indoors or out in chichi, trendy, and tony establishments; the fashionable old guard usually hang out on North Adelaide's Melbourne Street. Outdoor cafes on Rundle Mall can fix you up with a caffeine buzz so you don't drop before you shop. Many Adelaide restaurants are closed on Sunday, so plan accordingly.

Inexpensive

The **Adelaide University** campus has two informal eating places that are popular with students, faculty, and travel types. Both are in the Union Building. The cafeteria, on the ground floor, serves all the typical "uni" fare—sandwiches, apples, weak coffee, a few miscellaneous hot meals. The **Bistro** offers better quality at higher prices, about $5-9 for main dishes. The cafeteria has the customary casual class-in class-out hours; the Bistro is open Mon.-Fri. noon-2:30 p.m. for lunch, 5:30-8:30 p.m. for dinner.

Students and grungers tend to adore **Exeter Hotel**, 246 Rundle St., for both its good-value prices and wine list. Another hot spot for cheap eats is **Bijou**, 208 Hindley Street. Down the street, at 273 Hindley St., **Marcellina Pizza Bar** serves delicious pizzas all night, every night except Sunday. **Al Frescoes**, 260 Rundle St., is a superb late-night cafe, usually packed with Italians eating the Italian food—always a good sign. **Minim's Café**, 199 Hutt St., near the hostels, is popular both for breakfast and burgers. Fifties-style **Ruby's Café**, 255B Rundle St., with changing art exhibitions and a cocktail bar, is famed for its all-day Sunday breakfasts.

Vegetarian travelers will be happy at **Clearlight Café**, 203 Rundle St., with its clean environment and excellent food. The health food store, adjacent, offers a good selection and has a notice board with useful info. Nearby, **Vego and Lovin' It**, 240 Rundle St., is a super-cheap vegan cafe. **Carrots**, 62 Pulteney St., at Hindmarsh Square, is open weekdays for cheap vegetarian fare.

You can get a plain, simple **counter meal** at pubs throughout the city. Usually there's a blackboard outside the door that states meal times (around noon-2 p.m.) and prices (as low as $3). Menus are often bland and occasionally heavy on the grease. Typical choices are fish and chips, chicken schnitzel, and gravy-covered beef and lamb. Some Adelaide pubs now offer more "nouvelle" and international cuisine (which also boosts the prices). Some best bets include: **Old Queen's Arms,** 88 Wright St.; **Hotel Franklin,** 92 Franklin St.; **Austral Hotel,** 205 Rundle St.; and the **Park Tavern,** corner of Hindmarsh Square, at Grenfell Street.

Pick and choose from some of the city's international food centers, where different eateries are positioned around one central dining area. You can mix and match Indian, Thai, Chinese, Australian, and other cuisines for about $5 (more if you get carried away). Centrally positioned food centers are: **Hawker's Corner,** corner of Wright St. and West Terrace; **City Cross Arcade,** off Grenfell St.; **Gallerie of International Cuisine,** Renaissance Tower Center, Rundle Mall; **The Food Affair,** basement level, Gallerie Shopping Centre (between North Terrace and Gawler Place); and the **International Food Plaza,** on Moonta St. next to the Central Market. Most of the foodstalls stay open during shopping hours.

The **Central Market,** between Grote and Gouger streets (near Victoria Square), is a great spot to put together a meal or a picnic. The many colorful stalls in this historic old building feature fresh fruit and vegetables, meat, bread, cheese, and a variety of other foods. Or you can get a ready-made cheap (under $6) meal at **Malacca Corner,** a restaurant housed inside the market. Market hours are Tuesday 7 a.m.-5:30 p.m., Thursday 11 a.m.-5:30 p.m., Friday 7 a.m.-9 p.m., and Saturday 7 a.m.-1 p.m.

East End Market, on Rundle Street, redeveloped at the site of the original old market, features a huge central food court with stalls selling a delectable array of Asian and continental cuisine, and seating for 200. Fruit, vegetables, meats, cakes, nuts, breads, and other tasty treats are also on sale.

Don't forget about the cafes at the historic sites on **North Terrace.** You can get snacks and simple meals at the Botanic Gardens, Art Gallery, State History Centre, and the Lion Arts Centre.

Moderate
The **Red Ochre Grill,** 129 Gouger St. (tel. 08-8212-7266), is the buzz of the town with its unlikely, but nonetheless successful, marriage of typical Outback bush tucker with anything-but-typical gourmet flair. Diners can eat in the swank restaurant, cafe, or outdoors under the vines.

Main courses run $13-18. Open Mon.-Fri. lunch, Mon.-Sat. dinner; the cafe is open daily.

Jasmin Indian Restaurant, 31 Hindmarsh Square (tel. 08-8223-7837), has terrific North Indian dishes for about $14. Specialties include tandoori oven dishes and biryani rice plates. Open Tues.-Fri. lunch, Tues.-Sat. dinner.

North Adelaide's **Oxford,** 101 O'Connell St., has been running strong since the 1980s and, in 1995, was South Australia's most awarded restaurant. The fetching cuisine is created from the best and freshest ingredients. The service is dependable and the wine list is outstanding. Open Tues.-Sat. lunch and dinner.

The popular and casual **Boltz Café,** 286 Rundle St. (tel. 08-8232-5234), offers everything the youngish trend-setters could ask for: pseudo-industrial styling, a menu to please most appetites (pizzas, focaccias, curries, salads—in the $10-12 range), live music, and late hours. Open Mon.-Sat. lunch and dinner.

One of my special finds (which I hesitatingly share) is the **Grecian Taverna,** 89 O'Connell St., North Adelaide (tel. 08-8267-1446). This intimate restaurant provides beautifully presented, delectable Greek specialties in enormous portions, *plus* it's open for lunch and dinner every day of the week (yes, including Sunday). Average cost for main courses is $10.

Expensive
Splurgers should head directly for **Chloe's,** 36 College Rd., Kent Town (tel. 08-8363-1001), comprised of several grandly furnished dining rooms within a stunning restored villa. Classic French food and a superb wine list (choose from a 20,000-bottle cellar!) are standout features here. Without wine, you can expect to pay about $50 per person. Book ahead for Mon.-Fri. lunch, Mon.-Sat. dinner.

Peasant-Mediterranean-turned-flamboyant-South-Oz is an apt description for **Mezes,** 247 Rundle St. (tel. 08-8223-7384). The menu is limited but only in selections—not in imagination. The surroundings are simple, which only makes it more of a knockout once you taste the food. Plan on spending about $40 per person. Open Friday lunch, Tues.-Sun. dinner.

Nediz Tu, 170 Hutt St. (tel. 08-8223-2618), creates exotic and sublime Vietnamese delicacies, in a purifying white room filled with glorious floral arrangments—a sacred environment for the almost prayer-inducing cuisine. Dinner is approximately $40 per person. Open Tues.-Sat. dinner.

Jarmers, 297 Kensington Rd., Kensington Park (tel. 08-8332-2080), just east of the city, is another $50-per-header (again, without wine). Jarmers presents creative Australian cuisine (watch for that kangaroo!) in an elegant atmosphere for Mon.-Sat. dinner.

For fabulous—and fabulously expensive—hotel restaurants, try **The Grange Restaurant and Brasserie,** at the Hilton International (tel. 08-8217-0711), or **Blake's,** at the Hyatt Regency (tel. 08-8231-1234).

Late-Night Eats

It's slim pickings for late-night refrigerator raiders. If you're desperate you might try the **pie carts,** which set up outside the post office on Franklin Street and at The Parade, Norwood, every night from 6 p.m. until the wee hours. They sell that infamous Adelaide gastronomic *specialité,* the "floater"—an Australian meat pie floating (sort of like a rock) inside a bowl of thick green pea soup, topped with tomato sauce (catsup).

Maybe you'd prefer some harmless pancakes. The **Pancake Kitchen,** 13 Gilbert Place (tel. 08-8211-7912), on the South Terrace side of the city grid, is open every day, 24 hours. Also, don't forget **Marcellina Pizza Bar** on Hindley Street (see "Inexpensive" above). And, if you're dressed "correctly," there's always the casino.

For late-night food you're probably best off tucking some tucker in your backpack, satchel, or motel fridge to tide you over until morning.

ENTERTAINMENT AND EVENTS

Adelaide has all the usual amusements of a city its size—cinemas, art galleries, discos, pubs and clubs with live music, theater and concert performances, plus a couple of extras—the hustle-bustle casino and a really special festival of the arts. Newspapers, particularly Thursday's *Advertiser,* provide up-to-date information. Another good source is the monthly *Adelaide Review,* with lots of reviews and announcements of literary, arts, and theatrical happenings. *Rip It Up* and *dB,* free local music and street mags, can be

picked up at pubs, clubs, and record stores. Radio SA-FM operates a **club and concert line** (08-8272-1990) or, for jazz venues, try the **Jazz Line** (08-8303-3755). You can also call in at the South Australian Tourism Commission Travel Centre, on King William St. (08-8212-1505), for current entertainment listings and booking assistance. And don't forget about Adelaide University where, during school sessions, there's always something on.

Cinemas

If you're looking for commercial cinema (with releases that are ordinarily three to six months behind the U.S.), the four-, six- and eight-plexes are scattered around Hindmarsh Square, Hindley St., and Rundle Mall, and on Jetty Rd. in Glenelg. For artier films, try the **Capri,** 141 Goodwood Rd., Goodwood (tel. 08-8272-1177), the **Chelsea,** 275 Kensington Rd., Kensington (tel. 08-8431-5080), **Mercury Cinema,** 13 Morphett St. (tel. 08-8410-1934), **New Trak Cinema,** 375 Greenhill Rd., Toorak Gardens (tel. 08-8332-8020), or Adelaide University.

The annual **Adelaide Film Event,** held at the Chelsea from mid-July to mid-Sept., presents a good series of international films (past programs have included the reconstructed version of *Lawrence of Arabia,* along with *Do The Right Thing, Jesus of Montreal,* and *Roger and Me,* and a Glasnost Film Festival). You can either subscribe in advance for a series of tickets, or purchase a single admission ($12) on the night of performance, if seats are still available.

Or curl up in front of the telly and watch some really terrific classic, contemporary, and cutting-edge films on SBS. Check the newspaper for times.

Pubs and Clubs

You can do an easy—albeit tacky—pub crawl along **Hindley Street,** between King William Street and West Terrace. You'll find mega-discos at **Jules,** 94 Hindley St., a "real Aussie Pub" (and a real Aussie meat market), and across the street at **Rio's,** 111 Hindley St., which also has a bistro and piano bar and is open 24 hours.

City pubs that regularly feature music are: **Austral Hotel,** 205 Rundle St.; **Earl of Aberdeen,** Hindmarsh Square; **Seven Stars Hotel,** 187 Angas St., and, promising "no renovations, no bullshit," the **Exeter Hotel,** 246 Rundle Street. Both the Austral and Exeter hotels are popular with students and the artsy crowd.

A few of Adelaide's trendiest upmarket musical pubs (where you may well run into renovations and bullshit) are **Bull and Bear Ale House,** 91 King William St.; **Office Bar and Bistro,** 110 Pirie St.; **The Oxford,** 101 O'Connell St., North Adelaide; and, on Melbourne St., also in North Adelaide, the **Old Lion Hotel.** Still trendier are the bars and discos housed inside the **Hilton International** and **Hyatt Regency** hotels.

You'll pay a cover charge of $4-8 to hear music in the city pubs; about $12-16 at the big hotels.

Too-hip-to-be-believed (mainly) dance clubs are: **Cargo Club,** 213 Hindley St.; **Heaven,** 7 West Terrace, in New Market Hotel; and **Synagogue,** Synagogue Place, off Rundle Street.

Le Rox, 9 Light Square, is a large (two-room), late-night, groovy, mixed gay club. Also popular is the perenniel **Mars Bar,** 120 Gouger St., with weekend drag shows.

Serious **winetasters** should not miss the stylish **Universal Wine Bar,** 285 Rundle St., which offers not only an extensive wine list (including many wines-by-the-glass), but winetastings and workshops. **Mecca,** 290 Rundle St., also draws tasters to its bar and bistro.

Beer lovers can sample house-made brews at **Earl of Aberdeen,** Hindmarsh Square; **Old Lion Hotel,** North Adelaide; and **Port Dock Brewery Hotel,** Port Adelaide.

Theater and Concerts

The **Adelaide Festival Centre** is the city's major venue for theater, stage musicals, opera, concerts, and most other performing arts. For information, phone the box office at (08) 8216-8729, Mon.-Sat. 9:30 a.m.-8:30 p.m.; for credit card bookings, phone BASS at 13-1246 in South Australia, or 1800-88-8327 toll-free Australia-wide. The celebrated **Late Show,** in the Centre's Fezbah every Friday night from 11 p.m. until late, features cabaret acts. Free and casual jazz as well as classical and chamber music performances are often held on Sunday afternoon in the Festival Theatre Foyer.

The **Adelaide Symphony Orchestra** and **Australian Chamber Orchestra** perform at the old Adelaide Town Hall on King William Street.

For information, phone BASS at the numbers above. BASS also handles bookings for many other events, including Baroque and Renaissance music concerts at St. Peter's Cathedral.

Adelaide has a very active performance and contemporary theater scene. If you don't find what you're looking for at the Festival Centre, check with the Lion Arts Centre (tel. 08-8231-7760). Other good tries are **La Mama,** 4 Crawford Lane, Hindmarsh (tel. 08-8346-4212), a small venue showcasing experimental works, and **Little Theatre,** University of Adelaide (tel. 08-8228-1664), for student productions.

Events

The **Adelaide Festival of the Arts,** the oldest in Australia and one of the best in the world, attracts top international talent. During the first three weeks of March, in even-numbered years, the festival brews such mixes as Shakespearean tragedies with avant-garde performances, Beethoven symphonies with fusion jazz, Yehudi Menuhin with Mick Jagger.

The Fringe Festival, which is often even more exciting, coincides with the main event. During festival time, the city is agog over theater, dance, music, and art. Writers' Week attracts a wide array of poets, novelists, playwrights, and journalists to swig and tipple as they excerpt and expound. Make bookings for the festival well in advance by writing Adelaide Festival, G.P.O. Box 1269, Adelaide, SA 5001 (tel. 08-8216-8600).

For information on the **Barossa Valley Vintage Festival,** contact Barossa Wine and Tourism Association (tel. 085-62-1866). For information on the **McLaren Vale Bushing Festival,** phone (08) 8323-8999.

SPORTS AND RECREATION

Locals take advantage of the mild weather, gorgeous parklands, and nearby beaches, and spend a lot of time outdoors—if not participating in something themselves, then watching others who are. The parklands, particularly, are full of recreational areas. Meander too long in one grassy spot and you'll probably be commandeered into a game of soccer or cricket. Walkers and joggers will take happily to the many park pathways with their peaceful vistas and gentle climbs. Those of you who are more interested in a hike or bushwalk, stay tuned for "Hills and Vales," below. For useful info on almost every activity, contact the **Department of Sport and Recreation,** 11 Hindmarsh Square (tel. 08-8226-7301). **The Hire Life,** 139 Brebner Dr., Westlakes (tel. 08-8356-1911), rents out just about every type of sports equipment, including cycles, canoes, windsurfers, and rollerblades.

Cycling

Cycling about this nitty-gritty city, and the nine tracks that surround the parklands, is smooth and trouble-free. Rent bikes from **Super Elliott,** 200 Rundle St. (tel. 08-8223-3946); **Action Moped Hire,** 400 King William St. (tel. 08-8211-7060); or **Pulteney Street Cycles,** 307 Pulteney St. (tel. 08-8223-6678). All are open Mon.-Saturday. In Glenelg, contact **Bike and Beach Hire,** next to the tourist information office.

Scuba Diving

Diving is best off Kangaroo Island and the Yorke Peninsula, but boat diving isn't bad at Port Noarlunga Reef Marine Reserve, 18 km south of Adelaide, or Aldinga, 43 km south. You'll need proof of diving experience before you can rent equipment. For information, contact the **Scuba Divers Federation of South Australia,** 1 Sturt St. (toll-free tel. 13-0666).

Swimming

Swim along the beaches of Gulf St. Vincent, or dip into the **Adelaide Aquatic Centre,** Jeffcott Rd., North Adelaide (tel. 08-8344-4411), in the north parklands. The pool's open daily 9 a.m.-5 p.m. A gym, sauna, and spa are also available.

Tennis

Both grass and hard courts, as well as tennis rackets, are available for rent at **Memorial Drive Tennis Club,** War Memorial Dr. (tel. 08-8231-4371), and **Roseland's Tennis World,** 323 Sturt Rd., Bedford Park (tel. 08-8231-3033). **Adelaide City Courts** are in the parklands.

Golf

Guests are welcome to tee off at **City of Adelaide Golf Links,** Memorial Dr., North Adelaide (tel. 08-8231-2359). Equipment is available for hire.

Sailing

Adelaide's shoreline is fine for sailing. All the city beaches have yacht clubs, and most welcome casual visitors.

Skating and Skiing

You can ice skate 'round the rink, on either a beginner- or Olympic-size arena, or ski down the 12-meter-high indoor slope (covered in Permasnow, a real snowlike Australian product), at **Thebarton Ice Arena,** 23 East Terrace, Thebarton (tel. 08-8352-7977). Cost is $8, including skate hire, and both ski and skating instruction is available. Hours are Mon.-Fri. 9:30 a.m.-4:30 p.m., Wednesday and Friday 7-11 p.m., Sat.-Sun. 12:30-4 p.m. and 7:30-11 p.m.

Spectator Sports

Adelaide Oval, north of the city on King William St., is the main location for **cricket** matches, the country's favorite summer sport. International and interstate test matches are played Oct.-March.

The big winter sport, **Australian rules football,** is played—usually on Saturday—at both Adelaide Oval and Football Park, West Lakes. Soccer, rugby, and rugby union are also played during the April-Sept. season.

You can play the ponies or the pups year-round. The **South Australian Jockey Club** conducts meetings at Victoria Park, Morphettville, and Cheltenham; **Adelaide Greyhound Racing Club** is the venue for those flying dogs. Check local newspapers for meeting times.

SHOPPING

It's doubtful you'll ever "shop 'til you drop" in this city, but you will find the basics, maybe a few bargains, and possibly some baubles. **Warning:** Be especially careful when purchasing opals—take your time and shop around for reputable dealers. City shopping hours are generally Mon.-Fri. 8:30 a.m.-5:30 p.m., Saturday 8:30 a.m.-noon, late-night trading Friday until 9 p.m. (late-night trading is held on Thursday in the suburbs).

Rundle Mall, with its branches of arcades, offers standard mall-isms—John Martin's and Myer department stores, specialty shops that are really nothing special, a handful of com-

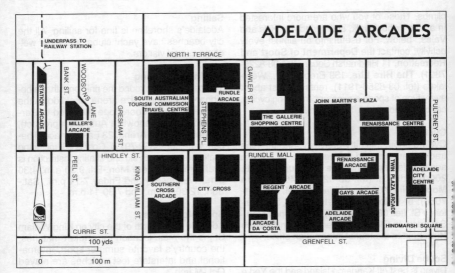

ADELAIDE ARCADES

mercial art galleries, a cinema complex, photo developers, jewelry stores, sandwich shops, a few buskers, and flower carts. **Rundle Street East** is far more exciting, with retro shops, alternative clothing and jewelry, New Age trinkets and nose rings, and black, black, and more black. For bookstores, see "Information," below.

For more chic and boutiques, North Adelaide's exclusive **Melbourne Street** will fill your Louis Vuitton luggage until you make it back to Rodeo Drive.

Markets
For far less sterile shopping, **Central Market** (see "Food" above) has colorful stalls stocked with food, produce, flowers, and bazaar items. The **East End Market** (also see "Food" above) has the same plus bizarre items. **Orange Lane Market,** off The Parade in nearby Norwood, is open Sat.-Mon. for seekers of imported fabrics, retro clothing, antiques, and full-body massages.

The **Brickworks Market,** 36 South Rd., Thebarton, is about three km from the city center. Hundreds of stalls sell everything from food and clothing to arts and crafts to junk and junque. Take the bus from Grenfell and Currie Streets in the city. The market is open Fri.-Sun. 9 a.m.-5 p.m.

Arts and Crafts
Local craftspeople create and sell jewelry, fabric, leather, glass, wood, ceramics, and other handmade wares at the **Jam Factory Craft and Design Centre,** 1 Morphett Street (tel. 08-8410-0727). The gallery features monthly changing exhibitions. Open Mon.-Fri. 9 a.m.-5 p.m., Sat.-Sun. and public holidays 10 a.m.-5 p.m.

Contemporary and traditional Aboriginal arts and crafts are sold and displayed at **Tandanya Aboriginal Cultural Institute,** 253 Grenfell St. (tel. 08-8223-2467). The institute, representing 50 traditional Aboriginal groups of South Australia, also sponsors performing and visual arts and houses a museum. Items for sale include Aboriginal artifacts, T-shirts, backpacks, and books. Open Mon.-Fri. 10:30 a.m.-5 p.m., Sat.-Sun. and public holidays noon-5 p.m. Admission is $4. **Otherway Aboriginal Arts and Crafts,** 185 Pirie St. (tel. 08-8232-1001), operated by Aborigines, also features a good range of arts and crafts, and all profits are channeled back into the community. Open Mon.-Fri. 10 a.m.-5 p.m.

See a broad spectrum of postmodern exhibitions by local and interstate artists, changing every few weeks, at **Union Gallery,** Level 6, Union Building, Adelaide University (tel. 08-8228-5013). Open Mon.-Fri. 10 a.m.-5 p.m.

Chic rustic kitchen accessories made from recycled wood and environmentally friendly Kangaroo Island swamp gums can be purchased at **D.Lux Homewares,** 238A Rundle St., while **Bimbo,** a few doors away at 279 Rundle St., offers pickings for metal- and wire-lovers.

SERVICES

King William Street is lined with **banks** and other financial institutions. Business hours are Mon.-Thurs. 9:30 a.m.-4 p.m., Friday 9:30 a.m.-5 p.m. When changing traveler's checks, be sure to carry your passport or driver's license for identification. Many city and suburban banking facilities have automatic teller machines that accept international credit cards.

Change money at Thomas Cook, 45 Grenfell St. (tel. 08-8212-3354), or American Express, 13 Grenfell St. (tel. 08-8212-7099).

The **general post office,** 141 King William St., provides the full range of postal services, including a philatelic bureau. Another convenient branch of Australia Post is in Rundle Mall. Hours of operation are Mon.-Fri. 8 a.m.-6 p.m., Saturday 8:30 a.m.-noon.

Just about every hotel, motel, and hostel provides **laundry facilities** for guests. Launderettes are dispersed around the city and suburbs. **Adelaide Launderette,** 152 Sturt St., is open daily 7 a.m.-8 p.m., and provides wash and iron service Mon.-Sat. 8 a.m.-5 p.m.

Stow your bags at any of the hostels, the YMCA residence hotel, the railway station, or central bus station—but not at the airport. The small fee will vary according to how many bags you stash and how long they're left.

Fruit pickers should have luck finding **casual labor** (during harvest time). Check at wineries in the Barossa and Clare valleys, as well as the Southern Vales, Riverland, and Coonawarra. The Murray River fruit-bearing districts of Berri, Renmark, and Loxton may also yield seasonal work.

INFORMATION

Bring an extra suitcase for all the literature you're sure to accumulate. Your first stop should be at the **South Australian Tourism Commission Travel Centre,** 1 King William St. (tel. 08-8212-1505), where you'll be handed an assortment of brochures, planners, maps, booklets, pamphlets, leaflets, and the like. The center is open Mon.-Fri. 9 a.m.-5 p.m., Sat.-Sun. 9 a.m.-2 p.m. **The Royal Automobile Association,** 41 Hindmarsh Square (tel. 08-8223-4500), is an invaluable source for detailed maps (particularly of Outback areas). They also have accommodations guides and a selection of books available for purchase. If you're a member of the American Automobile Association or the U.K.'s RAC and AA, you have full reciprocal privileges, but you must show your membership card as proof (that's what they say, but I've never been asked).

For literature, maps, and camping and hiking information on specific parks, contact the **Department of Environment and Natural Resources,** 77 Grenfell St., Adelaide, SA 5001 (tel. 08-8207-2000).

The **Disability Information Centre,** 195 Gilles St. (tel. 08-8223-7522), is open Mon-Fri. 9 a.m.-5 p.m.

Adelaide's **YHA** office is at 38 Sturt St. (tel. 08-8231-5583). Hours are Mon.-Fri. 9:30 a.m.-5:30 p.m.

Emergencies

To contact the **police, fire brigade,** or **ambulance,** phone 000. **Royal Adelaide Hospital,** corner of North Terrace and Frome Rd. (tel. 08-8223-0230), is a full-service facility with 24-hour emergency services. Also on Frome Rd. is **Adelaide Dental Hospital** (tel. 08-8223-9211). **Burden Chemist,** 41 King William St. (tel. 08-8231-4701), is open daily 8 a.m.-midnight for your pharmaceutical needs.

Bookstores, Newspapers, And Other Information

Read all about it on North Terrace. The Mortlock Library and bookshops in the museums, historic sights, and Adelaide University can provide inquiring minds with all they want to know about South Australian history, anthropology, archaeology, art, botany, and politics, both past and present.

Two levels of the **Third World Bookshop,** 103 Hindley St., are "literally" crammed with all subjects of secondhand books, radical literature, records, and alternative periodicals. The shop is open daily 9 a.m.-1 a.m.-ish. Another good secondhand bookshop is **O'Connell's,** 23 Gilbert Pl. (tel. 08-8231-5188).

Murphy Sisters Bookshop, 240 The Parade, Norwood (08-8332-7508), specializes in books by, for, and about women, as well as nonsexist and nonracist children's books. This shop is an excellent resource and meeting place for women. Hours are Mon.-Sat. 9 a.m.-5 p.m. (Thursday until 8 p.m.), Sunday 1-4 p.m.

Adelaide University Bookshop, on the campus, sells textbooks, plus general fiction, nonfiction, and children's books. The shop is open to the public. For information and hours, phone (08) 8223-4366.

The large mainstream bookshop is **Angus and Robertson,** 112 Rundle Mall, where you'll find an enormous range of titles, including many on Australian and regional topics. **The Mind Field Bookshop,** over on happening Rundle Street (no. 238), features a large selection of Australian fiction and is open late every night.

Psychic sciences, astrology, women's spirituality, health, and healing are some of the selections at **Quantum, The Metaphysical Bookshop,** 113 Melbourne St., North Adelaide. You can also pick up quartz crystals and relaxation music. Hours are Mon.-Fri. 9 a.m.-6 p.m. (Thursday until 9 p.m.), Saturday 9:30 a.m.-5 p.m., Sunday 1-5 p.m.

The coffee-and-newspaper crowd can choose from the morning *Advertiser* and the *Sunday Mail.*

The Wilderness Society is an Australian conservation group dedicated to addressing important and timely issues, such as preservation of rainforests, harmful effects of logging, and other environmental concerns. They also operate wilderness shops in each state, which sell books, T-shirts, badges, and other "collectibles." In Adelaide, you'll find them at 66 Grote St. (tel. 08-8231-6586). The **Conservation Council of South Australia,** 120 Wakefield St., is another clearinghouse for eco-info and has a bookshop, notice board, and library.

For **women,** the Murphy Sisters Bookshop (see above) is an excellent contact spot. Other resources include: the **Women's Information Switchboard** (tel. 08-8223-1244); the **Wom-**

en's **Studies Resource Centre,** 64 Pennington Terrace, North Adelaide (tel. 08-8267-3633); and **Adelaide Women's Community Health Centre,** also at 64 Pennington Terrace (tel. 08-8267-5366).

South Australia, being the first state to legalize homosexuality, offers a range of hassle-free services. Pick up a copy of the *Adelaide Gay Times* for news on current events, resources, and the club scene. **Lesbian Line** (tel. 08-8223-1982) and **Gay and Lesbian Counseling Service** (tel. 08-8362-3223) can also provide help and information.

TRANSPORT

Getting There by Air

Qantas, 144 North Terrace (tel. 08-8208-8877, or 13-1313 toll-free), is the only international airline that flies into Adelaide from North America (and that's with a change of aircraft in Sydney); both Qantas and **Singapore Airlines** have nonstop service from Singapore; **Garuda Indonesia** flies nonstop from Bali. **British Airways** operates two-stoppers from the United Kingdom.

The two major domestic airlines, **Ansett,** 205 Greenhill Rd., Eastwood (08-8208-4101 or 13-1300 toll-free), and **Qantas,** 144 North Terrace (tel. 08-8208-8877 or 13-1313 toll-free), provide daily direct and connecting service from all major Australian cities. Sample fares to or from Adelaide are: Melbourne, $175; Sydney, $260; Brisbane, $320; Perth, $380; Alice Springs, $285; Darwin, $365. These prices reflect the 40% discount accorded international ticket holders, but you can get about the same fare by going standby. There are other passes and discounts available depending upon your route and length of time traveling. **STA Travel,** 235 Rundle St. (tel. 08-8233-2426), is your best source for info and bargains.

Getting There by Train

Keswick Railway Terminal, on Railway Terrace, near the city center, is the arrival and departure point for interstate trains. The **Indian Pacific,** between Sydney and Perth, passes through both Adelaide and Broken Hill on its twice-weekly run. From Sydney to Adelaide, the 25-hour journey costs $110 economy, $199

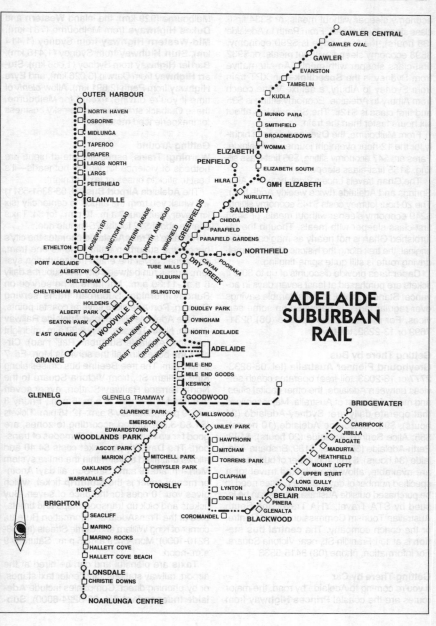

ADELAIDE SUBURBAN RAIL

GAWLER CENTRAL
GAWLER OVAL
GAWLER
EVANSTON
TAMBELIN
KUDLA
MUNNO PARA
SMITHFIELD
BROADMEADOWS
WOMMA
ELIZABETH
ELIZABETH SOUTH
GMH ELIZABETH
NURLUTTA
SALISBURY
CHIDDA
PARAFIELD
PARAFIELD GARDENS
NORTHFIELD
POORAKA
CAVAN
DRY CREEK
KILBURN
ISLINGTON
DUDLEY PARK
OVINGHAM
NORTH ADELAIDE

PENFIELD
HILRA
GREENFIELDS
WINGFIELD

OUTER HARBOUR
NORTH HAVEN
OSBORNE
MIDLUNGA
TAPEROO
DRAPER
LARGS NORTH
LARGS
PETERHEAD
GLANVILLE
ROSEWATER
JUNCTION ROAD
EASTERN PARADE
NORTH ARM ROAD
ETHELTON
PORT ADELAIDE
ALBERTON
CHELTENHAM
CHELTENHAM RACECOURSE
HOLDENS
ALBERT PARK
SEATON PARK
E AST GRANGE
GRANGE
WOODVILLE
WOODVILLE PARK
KILKENNY
WEST CROYDON
CROYDON
BOWDEN

TUBE MILLS

ADELAIDE
MILE END
MILE END GOODS
KESWICK
GOODWOOD

GLENELG
GLENELG TRAMWAY

CLARENCE PARK
EMERSON
EDWARDSTOWN
WOODLANDS PARK
ASCOT PARK
MARION
OAKLANDS
WARRADALE
HOVE
BRIGHTON
SEACLIFF
MARINO
MARINO ROCKS
HALLETT COVE
HALLETT COVE BEACH
LONSDALE
CHRISTIE DOWNS
NOARLUNGA CENTRE

MILLSWOOD
UNLEY PARK
HAWTHORN
MITCHAM
TORRENS PARK
CLAPHAM
LYNTON
EDEN HILLS
COROMANDEL

MITCHELL PARK
CHRYSLER PARK
TONSLEY

BRIDGEWATER
CARRIPOOK
JIBILLA
ALDGATE
MADURTA
HEATHFIELD
MOUNT LOFTY
UPPER STURT
LONG GULLY
NATIONAL PARK
BELAIR
PINERA
GLENALTA
BLACKWOOD

economy sleeper without meals, or $334 first-class sleeper with meals. From Perth to Adelaide (38 hours), the fare range is $290 economy, $598 economy sleeper without meals, or $932 first-class sleeper with meals. An alternative from Sydney is the **Speedlink**—an XPT train from Sydney to Albury, a deluxe V-line coach from Albury to Adelaide. Economy sitting is $95 and first class is $125. The Speedlink is about six hours faster than the train.

From Melbourne, the **Overland** departs nightly for the 12-hour overnight journey to Adelaide. Fares are $47 economy sitting, $95 first-class sitting, $155 first-class sleeper.

The **Ghan** travels once a week between Alice Springs and Adelaide (twice weekly April-Jan.). The 20-hour journey costs $145 economy sitting, $249 economy sleeper without meals, or $456 first-class sleeper with meals. Though the refurbished Ghan is not nearly as magical as the original, the trek along the historic Afghan camel-driving route is still quite spine-tingling.

Caper fares provide discounts of up to 30% if tickets are purchased at least seven days in advance. Standby travel, at considerable savings over regular fares, is permitted on some services. For rail information, phone (08) 8231-7699 or 13-2232, toll-free.

Getting There by Bus

Greyhound Pioneer Australia (tel. 08-8233-2777 or 13-2033, toll-free) operates coach services between Adelaide, the other capital cities, and most of the rest of Australia. Major services that operate daily are: Sydney-Adelaide (24 hours), $95; Melbourne-Adelaide (10 hours), $55; Alice Springs-Adelaide (20 hours), $142; Perth-Adelaide (35 hours), $189; Brisbane-Adelaide (34 hours), $155. A number of bus passes are available, allowing unlimited travel for a specified number of days. Some passes need to be purchased outside Australia; others can be issued by STA Travel, YHA Travel, the South Australian Tourism Commission Travel Centre, or the coach company. The **central bus station** is at 111 Franklin St., near Victoria Square. For information, phone (08) 8415-5533.

Getting There by Car

If you're coming to Adelaide by road, the major routes are the coastal **Princes Highway** from Melbourne (929 km), the inland **Western** and **Dukes Highways** from Melbourne (731 km), **Mid-Western Highway** from Sydney (1,414 km), **Sturt Highway** from Sydney (1,418 km), **Barrier Highway** from Sydney (1,666 km), **Stuart Highway** from Darwin (3,026 km), and **Eyre Highway** from Perth (2,691 km). Allow *plenty* of time if you're driving; except for Melbourne, these Outback stretches can be risky business for inexperienced motorists.

Getting Around

Warning: Trains, especially late at night, are hotbeds of violence for violent hotheads—it's best to stick to buses or taxis at night.

The **Adelaide Airport Bus** (tel. 08-8381-5311) will whisk you from the airport to center city (six km) every half-hour 7 a.m.-10 p.m., for $4. Taxis charge about $12 for the 25-minute ride.

Adelaide's **TransAdelaide** operates the city's buses, the suburban trains, and its one tram, and prices cover the entire transportation system. Buses run between city and suburbs daily 6 a.m.-11:30 p.m., but there is no service on Sunday morning. Suburban trains serving Glenelg, Port Adelaide, several coastal points, and the Adelaide Hills depart Adelaide Railway Station, North Terrace, daily 5:30 a.m.-midnight (see the "Adelaide Suburban Rail" map). **Circle Line** buses link all the services Mon.-Fri. 7 a.m.-6 p.m. The free **Beeline** bus cruises along King William St., from Victoria Square to the North Terrace Railway Station, every seven minutes Mon.-Thurs. 8 a.m.-6 p.m., Friday 8 a.m.-9 p.m., Saturday 8 a.m.-12:15 p.m. Tickets ($1.80-3.50), priced according to zones, are good for up to two hours on all modes of transport. The **Day Tripper** ticket costs $4.40 and allows unlimited travel within the entire system Mon.-Fri. after 9 a.m., Sat.-Sun. all day. Another money-saver is the **Multitrip** ticket, which gives you 10 rides for the price of seven. Buy tickets and pick up transport maps and timetables at the TransAdelaide Information Bureau, corner of King William and Currie Streets (tel. 08-8210-1000), Mon.-Fri. 9 a.m.-5 p.m., Saturday 9 a.m.-noon.

Taxis are plentiful and can be hired at the airport, railway stations, city center taxi stands, or by phoning direct. Companies include **Adelaide Independent** (tel. 08-8224-6000), **Sub-**

urban (tel. 08-8211-8888), and **United Yellow** (tel. 08-8223-3111).

All the big-name car-rental firms are represented in Adelaide, with offices at the airport, the major hotels, and along North Terrace. Several lesser-known and cheaper firms are **Moke Rent-a-Cars** (tel. 08-8352-7044), **Action Rent-a-Car** (tel. 08-8352-7044), **Rent-a-Bug** (tel. 08-8234-0911), and **Hire-a-Hack** (tel. 08-8271-7820). For moped and bicycle rentals, see "Cycling" under "Sports and Recreation" above. Mopeds will run about $28 per day, $8 per hour (be prepared to pay a $50 deposit). Mountain bikes average $20 per day, while 10-speeds are in the $12-14 bracket.

The **Adelaide Explorer Bus** (tel. 08-8212-1505) departs from 18 King William St. daily 9:10 a.m., 10:25 a.m., 12:20 p.m., 1:35 p.m., 2:55 p.m., and 4:10 p.m. (except Christmas Day and Good Friday), for sightseeing trips to eight popular city spots, including Glenelg. One $19 ticket permits you to get on and off at will, so if one place strikes your fancy, you can spend as much time there as you like, reboarding the bus next time around. Many tour operators offer City Sights, Adelaide Hills, Mt. Lofty Ranges, and Adelaide by Night junkets. Check with the tourist office for the current list of contenders.

Getting Away

Intrastate air carriers include **Kendell Airlines, August Airlines, Air Kangaroo Island, Whyalia Airlines, Eyre Commuter, Albatross Airlines, Emu Airways, O'Connor Airlines, Lincoln Airlines,** and **Southern Australia Airlines.** The smaller carriers will take you to communities such as Ceduna, Mount Gambier, Port Lincoln, Whyalla, Coober Pedy, Broken Hill, Olympic Dam, Woomera, American River, Kingscote, Parndana, Wudinna, Cummins, Tumby Bay, Port Lincoln, Renmark, and Mildura. Make bookings through Ansett or Qantas, or contact the South Australian Tourism Commission Travel Centre. (see "Getting Around" in the On the Road chapter)

The **MV *Philanderer III*** and **MV *Island Navigator*** (toll-free tel. 13-1301) passenger ferries operate service from Cape Jervis to Penneshaw, Kangaroo Island. Fares are $32 one-way for the one-hour journey. The **K.I. Connection** (tel. 08-8384-6860) is a coach service connecting Adelaide with the Cape Jervis departure point.

Country trains depart Keswick Railway Terminal for Peterborough, Port Pirie, and Mt. Gambier. For information, phone (08) 8217-4455.

Aside from the Greyhound Pioneer Australia conglomerate mentioned above under "Getting There by Bus," several smaller bus companies service the state's country towns, coastal villages, and remote stations. The **Country Passenger Depot,** 101 Franklin St., is next door to the central bus station. For information, phone (08) 8231-4144.

If you're hitching to Melbourne, the bus from Pulteney St. will take you to Old Toll Gate on Mt. Barker Rd., a good thumb-and-sign post. If you're headed far away to Perth, across the very barren Nullarbor Plain, it's easiest to begin in Port Augusta, at the petrol station nearest to town. Catch the bus from King William St. to Port Wakefield Rd., Gepps Cross, where you can walk to Carvans Petrol Station—your hitching point. Once you get to Port Augusta, be prepared to wait—sometimes days. Try to hit it on Friday night or Saturday morning when the truckies are coming through. **Warning:** Women should *not* hitch alone! **Bigger warning:** Hitching in Australia is illegal, remember?

HILLS AND VALES

Less than half an hour's drive from grid-and-square Adelaide are rambling hills and rolling vales, secluded hollows and hideaway valleys, nook-and-cranny villages and lush green terrain smothered in wildflowers, delicate orchids, and bold yellow wattle, and bathed in the fragrance of almond, apple, pear, and cherry orchards, and strawberry patches. Euphoric names such as Happy Valley, Tea Tree Gully, Basket Range, Mount Pleasant, and Chain of Ponds will ring in your ears with the distant echo of a near-forgotten, favorite fairy tale.

Adelaide is the perfect base for short excursions into the hills; or do the reverse—nestle into some cozy dell and day-trip down to the city.

ADELAIDE HILLS

The hills, part of the Mt. Lofty Ranges, can be explored by a number of meandering scenic routes. There's something for everyone—endless vistas for tourists in buses, scads of secluded picnic spots for lovers and loners, 1,000 kilometers of walking tracks for hikers. One exceptionally pretty itinerary that leads you around and through conservation parks and lookout spots with a bird's-eye view of the city begins at **Windy Point** on Belair Rd. (reached from the city via Fullarton Rd.). Skirt around Upper Sturt Rd. to **Belair National Park,** one of the world's oldest national parks (established 1891). Facilities include tennis courts, football ovals, cricket pitches, a popular golf course, bushwalking tracks, and camping sites. Admission is $3 per vehicle. For information, phone (08) 8278-5477.

Continue along Upper Sturt Rd., cross the South Eastern Freeway, and you'll be on Summit Road. Take the turnoff to **Mt. Lofty,** the ranges' highest point (771 meters). At road's end, a monument pays tribute to Colonel Matthew Flinders, and a large lookout area affords a panoramic view of Adelaide and the surrounding hills and plains. Near the summit, **Mt. Lofty Botanic Gardens** covers more than 42 hectares with exotic cool and subalpine plants.

The gardens are closed in winter and are most colorful in autumn. For information, phone (08) 8228-2311.

Cleland Conservation Park, on the slopes of Mt. Lofty, features koalas (cuddling daily 2-4 p.m.), emus, kangaroos, native birds, and other wildlife, as well as many enticing walking tracks along its 972 hectares of bushland. For information, phone (08) 8339-2444.

Back on Summit Rd., you'll pass pear and apple orchards until you reach **Norton Summit,** where there's a restaurant and yet another view.

Turning toward the city will bring you into **Morialta Conservation Park,** noted for its waterfalls, deep gorge, and excellent bushwalking. Trails lead to the gorge and several waterfalls (and some pretty spectacular views), as well as points like Pretty Corner, Kookaburra Rock, and the Giant's Cave. For information, phone (08) 8281-4022.

Magill Rd. runs into Payneham Rd., which leads back to Adelaide. An alternate route is Marble Hill Rd. (turn off before Norton Summit) to Montacute, toward the city through Morialta and the **Black Hill** Conservation Parks, then to Payneham Road.

Para Wirra Recreational Park, 40 km northeast of Adelaide, is a wooded plateau with steep gullies, kangaroos, birds, spring wildflowers, and more good walking trails and picnic areas. Admission is $3 per vehicle. For information, phone (08) 8280-7048.

Accommodations and Food
See the Adelaide **YHA** for information on its five limited-access hostels in the Mt. Lofty Ranges. Advance bookings are required.

Belair National Park (tel. 08-8278-3540) rents campsites, on-site vans, and inexpensive cabins with cooking facilities. Guestrooms at **Drysdale Cottage,** Debneys Rd., Norton Summit (tel. 08-8390-1652), are moderate to expensive and include breakfast. **Happy's Nest,** Summit Rd., Mt. Lofty, opposite the entrance to Cleland Conservation Park, is a moderately priced bed and breakfast.

Really big spenders and splurgers should consider a stay at **Mt. Lofty House,** 74 Summit Rd., Crafers (tel. 08-8339-6777). The exquisitely furnished house, built between 1852 and 1858, has sumptuous bedrooms, sitting rooms, and two luscious restaurants. Prices are hefty—$215-430 per double—and the breakfast is light.

You'll find tearooms and pubs tucked cozily away in the hills and valleys. At Norton Summit, the **Scenic Hotel,** hanging onto the hill, is a thrill for meals and drinks.

BIRDWOOD

Once upon a time Birdwood, less than 50 km northeast from Adelaide, was a gold-mining center. Today its claim to fame is the **National Motor Museum,** which displays more than 300 vintage, veteran, and classic motor cars and bikes. Housed inside an 1852 flour mill, the museum is open daily 9 a.m.-5 p.m., closed Christmas Day. Admission is $7. For information, phone (085) 68-5006.

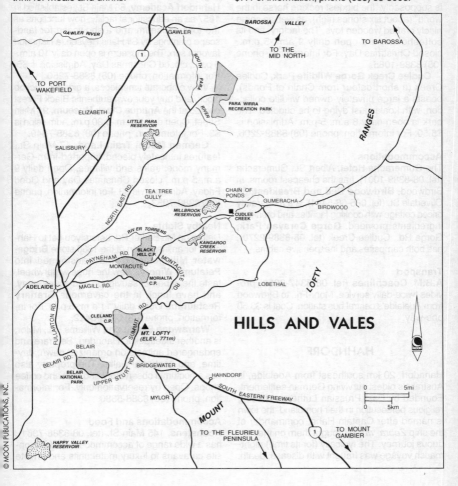

HILLS AND VALES

Cromer Conservation Park, Cromer Rd., has more than 70 species of birds flying around its 50 hectares.

Reached via Lobethal (and the River Torrens Gorge), or through Chain of Ponds and Gumeracha, Birdwood is both a convenient day-trip from Adelaide or a stop on the way to the Barossa Valley.

Nearby Sights

The **Toy Factory** of Gumeracha features what is supposedly "the biggest rocking horse in the world" (about six stories high), as well as some nicely crafted wooden toys. The factory, and its coffeehouse, are open daily 9 a.m.-5 p.m., closed Christmas Day. For information, phone (08) 8389-1085.

Cudlee Creek Gorge Wildlife Park, Cudlee Creek (a short detour from Chain of Ponds), boasts a large privately owned wildlife collection, with koalas just dying to be cuddled. The park is open daily 8 a.m.-5 p.m. Admission is $5.50. For information, phone (08) 8389-2206.

Accommodations

The **Gumeracha Hotel,** Albert St., Gumeracha (tel. 08-8389-1001), has the cheapest rooms. In Birdwood, **Birdwood Bed and Breakfast,** 38 Olivedale St. (tel. 085-68-5444), is a moderately priced cottage with cooking facilities and breakfast ingredients provided. **Gorge Caravan Park,** Gorge Rd., Cudlee Creek (tel. 08-8389-2270), has both campsites and inexpensive cabins.

Transport

A.B.M. Coachlines (tel. 08-8347-3358) provides twice-daily service, Mon.-Fri., to Birdwood from Adelaide's central bus station. Cost is $3.50 one-way.

HAHNDORF

Hahndorf, 20 km southeast from Adelaide, is Australia's oldest surviving German settlement. Founded by East Prussian Lutherans fleeing religious persecution in their homeland, the town is named after Captain Hahn, commander of the ship *Zebra,* which brought them on their arduous journey. The typically (for its time) nightmarish voyage was fraught with disease, death,

ripped sails, and killer heat; nonetheless the *Zebra* arrived safely at Port Adelaide in 1839. Today Hahndorf (pop. 1,300) is a popular daytrip from the city, drawing tourists to its historic buildings and well-preserved town to buy slices of streusel and *typisch* folk crafts, to partake of some oldy-worldy charm (albeit on the cutesy side). Stop by for a cuppa *kaffee* and you're apt to be greeted with a *"Guten Tag,* mate."

Sights

Hahndorf Academy, 68 Main St., established in 1857 as an educational facility, now functions as the town museum and a showcase for landscape paintings by Sir Hans Heysen, a Hahndorf favorite son. The museum is open daily 10 a.m.-5 p.m., closed Christmas Day. Admission is $5. For information, phone (08) 8388-7250.

View elaborate timepieces, a gigantic cuckoo clock, and buy your own authentic Black Forest cuckoo at the **Antique Clock Museum,** 91 Main Street. Open daily 9 a.m.-5:30 p.m. Admission is $3. For information, phone (08) 8388-7349.

German Model Train Land, 47 Main St., features intricately pieced, imported-from-Germany model trains and villages. Open daily 9 a.m.-5 p.m., closed Christmas Day and Good Friday. Admission is $3. For information, phone (08) 8388-7953.

Nearby Sights

Detour on Mt. Barker Rd. before you get to Hahndorf for an inspection of the 1860 stone **Bridgewater Mill,** restored and transformed into **Petaluma Winery.** View the huge waterwheel, taste the cabernet sauvignon and chardonnay, and have lunch in the cavernous **Granary Restaurant.** Open daily 11 a.m.-5 p.m. For information, phone (08) 8339-3422.

Warrawong Sanctuary, Williams Rd., Mylor, is another sidetrack to Hahndorf. See rare and endangered animals on organized dawn, daytime, and nocturnal walks. The property also has a nocturnal observatory and craft and coffee shops. Open by reservation only. For information, phone (08) 8388-5380.

Accommodations and Food

Hochstens, 145 Main St. (tel. 08-8388-7361), has a wide range of accommodations, from onsite caravans to luxury motel units and private chalets. Prices also vary from budget to expensive. **Hahndorf Old Mill Motel and Restaurant,** 98 Main St. (tel. 08-8388-7888), has moderate to expensive rooms with all the creature comforts. **Elderberry,** Old Mt. Barker Rd. (tel. 08-8388-7997), is a one-bedroom cottage with cooking facilities, fireplace, and high-moderate prices.

You can get stick-to-your-bones German food all over town. The **German Arms Hotel,** 50 Main St., dating from 1834, serves pub meals in historic surroundings. Along Main St., **Otto's Bakery, Karl's German Coffee House, Gretchen's Coffee Shop,** and **The German Cake Shop** will keep you going with good coffees and fresh cakes.

Do-it-yourselfers will want to pack the homemade wurst at **Hahndorf Gourmet Foods** and

pick the homegrown berries at either the **Berry Farm** on Tischer Rd. (tel. 08-8388-7071) or **Beerenberg Strawberry Farm,** Mt. Barker Rd. (tel. 08-8388-7272).

Events
Hahndorf's big event is the annual mid-January **Schützenfest,** a traditional shooting festival with German folk dancing, entertainment, cuisine, and beer—*lots* of beer.

Transport
To get to Hahndorf, catch the twice-daily bus from the Franklin Street depot in Adelaide. The ride takes 40 minutes, and the fare is $4. For information and schedules, phone Mount Barker Passenger Service (08-8391-2977).

This 1860 Bridgewater mill is the home of Petaluma Winery.

KAREN MCKINLEY

THE BAROSSA VALLEY

South Australia's most famous wine district lies in a shallow valley just 29 kilometers long and eight kilometers wide, amid gently rounded hills, icy-cold brooks, neat-as-a-pin grape-staked fields, pseudo chateaus and castles, and authentic Lutheran churches.

Less than an hour's drive north of Adelaide, most of the 50 or so wineries are situated in the 20-kilometer span from Lyndoch to Nuriootpa, with the town of Tanunda in between. Serious connoisseurs or occasional tipplers can follow their noses or their whims to both commercial mega-complexes and family-run boutique wineries for a gargle or a swallow of full-bodied reds, crisp whites, sherries, ports, and sparkling wines.

Two routes will get you to the Barossa—a rather boring, but quicker and more direct road through Gawler, or the longer, winding, picture-postcard way via Birdwood and Torrens Gorge. Assuming that you'll start off on the scenic route and by day's end will be wishing for the straight highway with the dividing lines, the following towns have been geographically arranged to reflect that. Also, not all of the wineries have been listed below, only some of the most historical and interesting. Well-placed signposts will lead you to others off the beaten path—it's fun to make a wrong turn here or there, up or down, to make your own vintage discoveries. You can do the Barossa in a day-trip from Adelaide, but if your feet get a little wobbly—or you haven't had your fill—consider bedding down for the night at a hostel, guesthouse, or motel along the way.

History

The Barossa was settled in 1842 by the same persecuted East Prussian Lutherans who arrived on the good ship *Zebra* with Captain Hahn. Their expedition had been funded by Englishman George Fife Angas, one of the original colonizers, in the hopes he was snagging good, hardworking folk whose skills would benefit South Australia. The new arrivals who didn't go to Hahndorf followed their pastor, August Kavel, to the Barossa Valley and put down roots in Lyn-

doch, Tanunda, Angaston, and Bethany. A few years earlier, the same region had been explored by Silesian mineralogist Johannes Menge, who passed the word that the area, similar to parts of Poland, was a grape-grower's heaven. By the late 1840s the new settlers had planted their vines and were soon turning out vintages ambrosial enough to knock their lederhosen off. At the same time they constructed beautiful stone churches, cottages, and town buildings, which you'll see on your tour of the valley.

The actual name "Barossa" came from our man Colonel Light, back in 1837. Twenty-five years earlier he had squared off in a battle in Barrosa, Spain, under the command of Lord Lynedoch. Feeling nostalgic because of the similar-looking terrain, Light named the Barossa "Barrosa" and the town of Lyndoch, "Lynedoch."

Springton

You've heard of the old woman who lived in a shoe? Well, pioneer settlers Caroline and Friedrich Herbig lived inside a gigantic hollow gum tree 1855-60. Caroline even bore two of their children there. The **Herbig Gum Tree** is just before Hamiltons Road.

Springton Gallery, Miller St. (tel. 085-68-2001), has a selection of Australian and international crafts. The gallery, formerly the old settlers' store and post office, is open daily except Tuesday 11 a.m.-5 p.m.

For winetastings, check out: **Craneford Wines,** Main St. (tel. 085-68-2220); **Karl Seppelts Grand Cru Estate,** Ross Dewells Rd. (tel. 085-68-2378); and **Robert Hamilton Winery,** Hamiltons Rd. (tel. 085-68-2264). All are open daily.

Keyneton

This tiny village was once called "North Rhine" because of its resemblance to the settlers' homeland. **Henschke Wines** (tel. 085-64-8223), established 1868, is a small fifth-generation family-run winery with some of the oldest shiraz vines in the region. Specialties are premium red and white table wines. Hours are Mon.-Fri. 9 a.m.-4:30 p.m., Saturday 9 a.m.-noon.

BOB RACE

Angaston

Named for George Fife Angas, landholder and financial backer for the *Zebra* voyage, who settled near the town (pop. 1,950) in 1851. Fife's son built **Collingrove Homestead** (tel. 085-64-2061), where family members lived until turning it over to the National Trust in 1976. It now serves as a museum for Angas memorabilia, a restaurant, and elegant country accommodation. Open daily 10 a.m.-5 p.m., closed Christmas Day and Boxing Day.

Angaston Galleria, 18 Murray St. (tel. 085-64-2648), features local and imported arts and crafts inside a 125-year-old former church building. Open Tues.-Sun. and public holidays 10 a.m.-5 p.m.

See how fruits are dried and then buy them on-site at **Angas Park Dried Fruit Centre,** 3 Murray St. (tel. 085-64-2052). Open Mon.-Sat. 9 a.m.-5 p.m., Sunday and public holidays 11 a.m.-5 p.m., closed Christmas Day and Good Friday.

Yalumba Winery, Eden Valley Rd. (tel. 085-61-3200), established 1849, is built of Angaston marble and topped with a clock tower. Specialties are premium red and white table wines and champagnes. Open Mon.-Fri. 8:30 a.m.-5 p.m.,

Saturday and holidays 10 a.m.-5 p.m., Sunday noon-5 p.m.

Saltram Winery, Nuriootpa-Angaston Rd. (tel. 085-63-8290), founded in 1859, is another old-timer in the Barossa, featuring red and white table wines and ports. Hours are Mon.-Fri. 9 a.m.-5 p.m., Sat.-Sun. noon-5 p.m., holidays 10 a.m.-5 p.m.

Nuriootpa

Once upon a time this town was an important Aboriginal bartering center (Nuriootpa translates to "A Meeting Place"). After William Coulthard, a pioneer settler, laid out his acre in 1854, the town grew around his red-gum-slab hotel. Today, Nuriootpa (pop. 3,200), at the northern end of the Barossa Valley, is the district's commercial heart, with a wide range of facilities, services, and government agencies. Coulthard's hotel is gone, but his home has been preserved and serves as the main information center for the Barossa Valley. Aside from the many clusters of wineries, Nuriootpa has some lovely parks and picnic grounds banking the North Para River which meanders through town.

Buildings to take note of along Light Pass Rd., are **Immanuel Lutheran Church** (1886), **Luhr's Pioneer German Cottage** (1841), and **Strait Gate Lutheran Church** (1861).

Penfolds Winery, Tanunda Rd. (tel. 085-62-0389), established in 1812, is a huge commercial complex (particularly after merging with Kaiser Stuhl) specializing in a full range of red and white table wines and fortified wines. This property can store more than 22 million liters of wine! Hours are Mon.-Fri. 9 a.m.-5 p.m., Saturday and holidays 10 a.m.-5 p.m., Sunday 1-5 p.m. Admission is $4.

Elderton Wines, 3 Tanunda Rd. (tel. 085-62-1058), established 1906, has red and white table wines, sparkling wines, *and* bicycles and mokes for hire. Hours are Mon.-Fri. 8:30 a.m.-5 p.m., Sat.-Sun. 11 a.m.-4:30 p.m.

Wolf Blass Wines (tel. 085-62-1955), along the Sturt Highway, was only established in 1973, yet practically started out winning Australia's most coveted red-wine prize three years in a row. Specialties are premium red and white table wines and champagne. Hours are Mon.-Fri. 9:15 a.m.-4:30 p.m., Sat.-Sun. and holidays 10 a.m.-4:30 p.m.

BAROSSA VALLEY

KEYNETON RD

TO RENMARK

KEYNETON

SPRINGTON

EDEN VALLEY

TO MURRAY BRIDGE

HAMILTONS RD

HERBIG GUM TREE

KAISERSTUHL CONSERVATION PARK

PENRICE RD

PENRICE

ANGASTON

ANGASTON RD

COLLINGROVE HOMESTEAD

LIGHT PASS RD

VINE VALE RD

MENGLER HILL

SCENIC RD

WIRRA WIRRA RD

BUNKHAUS BAROSSA

SIEGERSDORF RD

KEV ROHRLACH COLLECTION

BETHANY

TOURIST INFORMATION CENTRE

NURIOOTPA

MARANANGA

SEPPELTSFIELD

SEPPELTSFIELD RD

GREENOCK

BAROSSA VALLEY WAY

TANUNDA

ROWLAND FLAT

LYNDOCH

SANDY CREEK CONSERVATION PARK

SANDY CREEK

COCKATOO VALLEY

ROSEDALE

NORTH PARA RIVER

RAILWAY LINE

STUART HWY

MAIN NORTH RD

GAWLER

BAROSSA VALLEY HWY

TO ADELAIDE

ELIZABETH

TO THE MID NORTH

4mi

4km

= WINERY

© MOON PUBLICATIONS, INC.

1. Barossa Settlers
2. Basedow Wines
3. Bernkastel Wines
4. Bethany Wines
5. Burge Family Winemakers
6. Charles Cimicky Wines
7. Charles Melton Wines
8. Chateau Dorrien Wines
9. Chateau Yaldara Estate
10. Elderton Wines
11. Gnadenfrei Estate
12. Grant Burge Wines
13. Hardy's Siegersdorf
14. Henschke Wines
15. Heritage Wines
16. High Wycombe Wines
17. Kellermeister Wines
18. Kies Estate Cellars
19. Krondorf Wines
20. Leo Buring Wines
21. Lindner McLean Vineyards
    (St. Hallett Wines)
22. Orlando Winery
23. Penfolds Winery
24. Peter Lehmann Wines
25. Rockford Wines
26. Rovalley Estate
27. Saltram Winery
28. Seppeltsfield Winery
29. Tarac Distillers
30. Tarchalice Wine Co.
31. Tolley Pedare Winery
32. Veritas Winery
33. Wards Gateway Cellar
34. Willows Vineyard
35. Wolf Blass Wines
36. Yalumba Winery

Bored with wine? Check out **Tarac Distillers,** Tanunda Rd. (tel. 085-62-1522), for brandy, rum, gin, bourbon, vodka, whiskey, and tequila. Hours are Mon.-Fri. 8:30 a.m.-4:30 p.m.

Marananga

Gnadenfrei ("Freed by the grace of God") was the original name given to this little town by its settlers in the 1840s. In 1918, when Germanic names were being changed, it was christened Marananga, Aboriginal for "My Hands."

It's worth making the turn off the main road to see the old schoolhouse, cottages, and splendid

Gnadenfrei Church, begun in 1857, with additions in 1873 and 1913.

Heritage Wines (tel. 085-62-2880) is small and new-ish (established 1984), with interesting dry red and white table wines. Hours are daily 11 a.m.-5 p.m.

Seppeltsfield

Take the out-of-place-looking, date-palm-fringed road from Marananga to Seppeltsfield, founded by Silesian migrant Joseph Seppelt in 1851. Seppelt, who started off as a tobacco farmer, discovered that his crop was too rank for sale. He experimented with winemaking and the rest, as they say, is history. And history, as reported in the 1892 *London Gazette,* called Seppelt's cellars and stores "the most modern in the world." Those "modern" buildings have been carefully preserved and make for an interesting tour between sips of red and white table wines, fortified wines, and champagnes. Hours are Mon.-Fri. 9 a.m.-5 p.m., Saturday 10:30 a.m.-4:30 p.m., Sunday 11 a.m.-4 p.m. For information, phone (085) 62-8028.

Barossa Valley Way

It only takes about five minutes to get from Nuriootpa to Tanunda along this stretch of road, but you'll probably get hung up for hours if you stop at the **Kev Rohrlach Collection** (tel. 085-63-3407), a private museum of science, transport, and technology. More than 3,000 mechanical exhibits collected by Mr. Rohrlach (a builder) from all over South Australia will amaze, amuse, confound, and confuse you. The transport collection alone includes a maharaja's barouche and the 1955 Australian Grand Prix-winning car. Don't miss it! Hours are daily 10 a.m.-5 p.m. Admission charge is $5.

Tanunda

Established in 1843, Tanunda (pop. 2,860) was the second German settlement in the valley. Many of the traditional early stone buildings line the main avenue, as well as **Langmeil Road,** one of the back streets. **Goat Square,** sight of the first town market, is bordered by original cottages, preserved and classified by the National Trust.

Tanunda is home to four of the valley's most exquisite Lutheran churches: **Langmeil Church,** on the main drag, has Pastor Kavel's remains buried in the adjacent cemetery; **St. John's,** Jane St., is home to life-size wooden statues of Jesus, Moses, and selected apostles; **Tabor Lutheran Church,** north end of Murray St., is notable for its orb-topped spire; **St. Paul's,** corner Murray St. and Basedow Rd., features fine stained glass.

Brauer Biotherapies, 1 Para Rd. (tel. 085-63-2932), welcomes visitors to its laboratories where homeopathic medicines are concocted. Hours are Mon.-Fri. 8:30 a.m.-4 p.m., with guided tours at 2 p.m.

Rather watch performing dogs? You can applaud (or cry over) 25 trained canines at **Norm's Coolie Sheep Dog Performance,** Gomersal Rd. (tel. 085-63-2198). Show times are Monday, Wednesday, and Saturday 2 p.m. Admission is $6.

The numerous wineries in this area should obliterate both homeopathic remedies and bad dog memories.

Bethany

Bethany was the first German settlement in the Barossa, founded in 1842 by a group of Silesian families. This peaceful, pretty village is still home to old stone houses, cottage gardens, and farmlets, as well as Australia's smallest hotel. The old village common has been transformed into **Bethany Reserve,** a haven for picnickers along bubbling Bethany Creek. The church bells still ring at dusk on Saturday to signal the end of the work week in case anyone forgets. The **Landhaus,** on Bethany Rd. near the railway tracks, claims to be Australia's smallest licensed motel.

Opposite Bethany Reserve, **Bethany Art & Craft Gallery** (tel. 085-63-2614) is an outlet for handmade textiles, pottery, glass, and wooden wares. The gallery is open daily 10 a.m.-5 p.m.

Rowland Flat

Commercial winemaking began at Jacobs Creek in 1847 when Johann Gramp planted his first vines. Nowadays the **Orlando Winery,** which dominates the town, pays its tribute by carrying an excellent claret with the Jacobs Creek label. The complex is enormous and pretty sterile, but it does offer a very good, educational $1 winery tour. If you visit February through April you'll get to view the grape-crushing process. Red and white table wines and champagnes are the spe-

cialties. Hours are Mon.-Fri. 9:30 a.m.-5 p.m., Sat.-Sun. and holidays 10 a.m.-4 p.m. For information, phone (085) 21-3140.

Rockford Wines (tel. 085-63-2720) is on Krondorf Rd., about three km from Rowland Flat. If you've just been to Orlando, this tiny establishment, with its tasting room inside a former stable, may underwhelm you—but the spectacular vintages won't. Specialties are traditional full-bodied Australian wine styles (premium regional wines). Hours are daily 11 a.m.-5 p.m.

Lyndoch

Lyndoch (pop. 705), at the southern edge of the valley, was originally settled in 1839 as a farming community; the first winery was installed in 1896 in a converted flour mill. All of the 10 or so wineries in this district are family-owned. The largest is **Chateau Yaldara,** Gomersal Rd. (tel. 085-24-4200), established in 1947 on the remains of that same converted flour mill. Besides red and white table wines, sparkling wines, and port, the "chateau" displays a collection of porcelain and antiques. Hours are daily 9 a.m.-5 p.m.

Along the Barossa Highway, the **South Australian Museum of Mechanical Music** (tel. 085-24-4014) features antique music boxes, automatic accordions, barrel pianos, player organs, an 1840s musical church, and singing birds. The museum is open daily 9 a.m.-5 p.m., closed Christmas Day. Admission is $5.

Cockatoo Valley

Detouring off the Barossa Highway, you'll pass through this small village with a general store (for petrol and provisions), remnants of goldfields, and an 1870s miner's cottage (converted to accommodations). The big attraction, down the road, is Barossa Reservoir (built in 1898) and its famed **Whispering Wall,** a retaining wall with peculiar acoustics that enable you to stand on one side and hear whispers all the way from the opposite side of the dam.

Gawler

Gawler (pop. 15,000), founded in 1839, was South Australia's second country town after Port Adelaide. Superb bluestone architecture, dating from the late 19th and early 20th centuries, is reflected in the town hall, post office, and various churches. Other fine buildings are the **Old**

Telegraph Station (home of the National Trust), constructed of One Tree Hill sandstone, and homes and fences crafted from local limestone.

PRACTICALITIES

Accommodations

Angaston: Barossa Brauhaus Hotel, 41 Murray St. (tel. 085-64-2014), has both a cozy dining room and a saloon bar. Rates are $20 per person including continental breakfast. Historic Angaston Hotel, 59 Murray St. (tel. 085-64-2428), is known for the Bacchus mural in its lounge. Both hotels are inexpensive. Collingrove Homestead, Eden Valley Rd. (tel. 085-64-2061), is the Angas family ancestral home where guests can spend the night in converted servants' quarters. Prices are moderate and include continental breakfast.

Nuriootpa: Barossa Gateway Motel, Kalimna Rd. (tel. 085-62-1033), has plain, inexpensive rooms, and a bed in the hostel section only costs $10. Karawatha Guest House, Greenock Rd. (tel. 085-62-1746), is a much homier environment. Moderately priced rooms include breakfast. The modern Vine Inn Hotel/Motel, 14 Murray St. (tel. 085-62-2133), is in the center of town. Rooms run moderate to high and include continental breakfast.

Marananga: The Hermitage of Marananga, corner Seppeltsfield and Stonewell Roads (tel. 085-62-2722), features spacious suites overlooking the property's vineyards. Expensive rates include breakfast in the popular country restaurant.

Seppeltsfield: You have your choice between the comfy, modern, and moderately priced Holiday Cabins, Seppeltsfield Rd. (tel.

085-62-8240), for $41-50 double, or the sumptuous Lodge, Main Rd. (tel. 085-62-8277), where for about $210 you can live in the old Seppelt family digs. (A room with all meals will set you back $360!)

Barossa Way: Barossa Bunkhaus Travellers Cottage, Barossa Hwy. (tel. 085-62-2260), is a friendly backpackers' hostel with kitchen facilities, TV room, swimming pool, and bicycle rental. Dorm beds cost $11 per night, and a cottage with cooking facilities and fireplace is $30 for two. Barossa Junction Resort, Barossa Hwy. (tel. 085-63-3400), offers motel-style accommodations inside converted railway cars, including lounge and dining carriages. Rates, with continental breakfast, are inexpensive to moderate. Light Pass Farm House, four km east of the post office (tel. 085-62-1641), offers expensive cottage accommodations.

Tanunda: Tanunda Hotel, 51 Murray St. (tel. 085-63-2030), with shared facilities, is inexpensive and has a restaurant and swimming pool. Weintal Hotel/Motel, Murray St. (tel. 085-63-2303), with bars, a bistro, restaurant, underground cellar, tennis courts, swimming pool, and sauna, is moderately priced. In the expensive range is rural Lawley Farm, Krondorf Rd. (tel. 085-63-2141), where the farm cottage and barn have been converted into lovely country rooms. Rates include breakfast.

Bethany: The Landhaus, Bethany Rd. (tel. 085-63-2191), may be Australia's smallest licensed motel, but the price is a big $100, including breakfast.

Lyndoch: About 20 km south of Lyndoch, Kersbrook YHA Hostel, Roachdale Farm (tel. 08-8389-3185), rents bunks for $7, but there is no public transport to the facility. If you're sharing, Barossa Country Cottages, 55 Gilbert St.

Collingrove Homestead, an elegant country manor

(tel. 085-24-4426), is in the moderate range for fully equipped cottage accommodations that include continental breakfast and a community spa. **Chateau Yaldara Estate,** Barossa Valley Hwy. (tel. 085-24-4268), has a restaurant, swimming pool, and expensive rates.

Cockatoo Valley: The old 1870 **Miner's Cottage,** Goldfields Rd. (tel. 085-24-6213), has private accommodations comprised of living room with open fireplace, bedroom, and bathroom. Rates are expensive and include continental breakfast.

Gawler: Prasad's Gawler Motel, 1 Main North Rd. (tel. 085-22-5900), features good rooms, a swimming pool, spa, and sauna. Rates are moderate but double during festival season. **Gawler Arms Hotel,** 102 Murray St. (tel. 085-22-1856), doesn't have all the fancy amenities, but the moderate prices are steady.

Camping

Barossa Valley Tourist Park, Penrice Rd., Nuriootpa (tel. 085-62-1404), is a very large park with swimming pool, barbecue, playground, tennis courts, a recreation lake, and reserve. **Tanunda Caravan Park,** Barossa Valley Way, Tanunda (tel. 085-63-2784), features full-service grass sites in a sheltered setting. **Barossa Caravan Park,** Barossa Valley Hwy., Lyndoch (tel. 085-24-4262), is fairly plain, but near the Whispering Wall and other hot spots. **Hillier Park,** Hillier Rd., Gawler (tel. 085-22-2511), has a quiet rural setting, with swimming pool, playground, sheltered picnic and barbecue areas.

Most of the caravan parks offer campsites, onsite vans, and cabins.

Food

You mean you want something besides bread and cheese? You'll easily find tearooms, coffee shops, pub meals, bakeries, and takeaways, as well as some gourmet restaurants with food to match the local wines.

Angaston: Angas Park Dried Fruit Centre, 3 Murray St. (tel. 085-64-2052), has a wide selection of dried fruit and nuts for your picnic basket. The **Angaston Hotel,** 59 Murray St. (tel. 085-64-2428), is a favorite for counter meals as well as more expensive a la carte dining. **Barossa Bistro,** 37 Murray St. (tel. 085-64-2361), is a best bet for upmarket bush tucker.

The Vintners Restaurant, corner Nuriootpa and Stockwell roads (tel. 085-64-2488), is another expensive choice, popular with winemakers so you can be sure of a good menu and exceptional wine list.

Nuriootpa: Family-owned **Linke's Bakery,** 40 Murray St. (tel. 085-62-1129), has been turning out cakes and breads for more than 50 years. The tearooms serve sandwiches and other lunch items. The dining room at the **Vine Inn Hotel/Motel,** 14 Murray St. (tel. 085-62-2133), serves standard bistro fare as well as cheap counter meals. Big splurgers hunting interesting game dishes should look at **The Pheasant Farm,** Samuel Rd., off Seppeltsfield Rd. (tel. 085-62-1286), where menu choices include glazed kangaroo, rabbit-stuffed sausage, and, naturally, pheasant. The restaurant is closed during February.

Marananga: Marananga Restaurant, Seppeltsfield Rd. (tel. 085-62-2888), serves large portions of simple food inside a one-room rustic stone cottage with open beams and a fireplace. Prices are middle-of-the-road.

Tanunda: Stock up on delicious bakery items any day but Sunday at **Apex Bakery,** Elizabeth St. (tel. 085-63-2483). **Zinfandel Tearooms,** 58 Murray St. (tel. 085-63-2822), features inexpensive light lunches and cakes. Moderately priced German cuisine is the specialty at **Die Gallerie,** 66 Murray St. (tel. 085-63-2788), where you eat in the courtyard when it's warm, or next to the open fire when it's cold. **Tanunda Hotel,** 51 Murray St. (tel. 085-63-2030), serves hearty counter meals at reasonable prices. The stylish **1918 Bistro and Grill,** 94 Murray St. (tel. 085-63-0405), housed in a villa, is known for its regional cuisine and superb wines.

Lyndoch: Get your counter meals at **Lyndoch Hotel,** Gilbert St. (tel. 085-24-4211). **Lyndoch Bakery,** on Barossa Valley Hwy., offers terrific baked goodies, plus good, moderately priced meals in the adjoining restaurant.

Events

With all that wine around, you can well imagine that denizens of the Barossa Valley are ready to party at the drop of a grape. The big event, of course, is the **Barossa Valley Vintage Festival,** held over Easter week in odd-numbered years. Activities and amusements that fill the valley include grape-picking and -crushing contests, brass bands, maypole dancing, tug-o'-wars, gourmet dinners, arts and crafts exhibitions, and winetastings up the shiraz. For information, phone (085) 62-1866.

Some other prominent annual events include January's **Oom Pah Festival** in Tanunda (tel. 085-65-2674), the March **Essenfest** in Tanunda (tel. 085-63-2211), **Seppeltsfield Balloon Regatta** in May (tel. 08-8389-3195), and **Barossa Classic Gourmet Weekend** also in May (tel. 085-62-1866). Needless to say all of these events feature *a lot* of food and grog!

Information
Barossa Wine and Tourism Association, 66 Murray St. (inside Coulthard House), Nuriootpa (tel. 085-62-1866), is the regional information hub for the entire Barossa Valley. You can pick up maps to the vineyards, inquire about guided tours, etc., Mon.-Fri. 8:30 a.m.-5 p.m., Sat.-Sun. and holidays 9:30 a.m.- 1:30 p.m. The **Gawler Tourist Association,** Murray St. (tel. 085-22-6814), is open daily 10 a.m.-4 p.m. (Heritage bus tours of Gawler leave from the tourist office at 10 a.m. every Tuesday.)

For police, medical, and fire **emergencies,** dial 000. **Hospitals** are located at Angaston (tel.

64-2065), Tanunda (tel. 085-63-2398), and Gawler (tel. 085-22-1677). **Police stations** are at 61 Murray St., Nuriootpa (tel. 085-62-1111), and 23 Cowan St., Gawler (tel. 085-22-1088).

Transport
If you're driving, the scenic route can be reached via Chain of Ponds, through Birdwood, to Springton. The direct route is straight up Main North Rd. from Adelaide, through Elizabeth, to Gawler.

Barossa Adelaide Passenger Service (tel. 085-64-3022) leaves Adelaide's central bus station for Lyndoch, Tanunda, Nuriootpa, and Angaston. Service runs four times Mon.-Fri., one time only on Saturday. The fare is about $6 one-way.

Rent bicycles by the day or the hour from the **Bunkhaus,** corner Barossa Valley Hwy. and Nuraip Rd., Nuriootpa (tel. 085-62-2260), **Elderton Winery,** Nuriootpa (tel. 085-62-1058), or **Keil's Gift Centre,** 63 Murray St., Tanunda (tel. 085-63-2177).

Cars can be rented from **BP Service Station,** 8 Murray St., Nuriootpa (tel. 085-62-3022) or Elderton Winery. Rent mopeds at **Caltex Service Station,** Murray St., Tanunda (tel. 085-63-2677). Elderton Winery also rents mini-mokes.

FLEURIEU PENINSULA

The Fleurieu bills itself "South Australia's Holiday Playground." Like the Adelaide Hills and the Barossa Valley, the Fleurieu is easy day-tripping distance south of the city center. Aside from rolling hills, clustered vineyards, and pastoral farmlands, there are beaches—lots of beaches—from the Gulf St. Vincent, around Cape Jervis, along the pounding Southern Ocean, to Encounter Bay and the mouth of the Murray River—beaches to surf at, fish from, swim off, jog along, glide above, sail aside, and sun worship on.

Bushwalkers and nature lovers can explore more than 20 coastal, wetland, and woodland parks inhabited by native birds and animals. Hiking trails are plentiful, particularly within Deep Creek Conservation Park between Cape Jervis and Victor Harbor, where you super-adventurous hikers can hit the Heysen Trail and follow it all the way to the Flinders Ranges. Cape Jervis is also the jumping-off spot for Kangaroo Island, or you can island-hop to Granite Island off Victor Harbor for a glimpse of the fairy penguins, or to Hindmarsh Island, off Goolwa, to boat, fish, or waterski.

Less sporty travelers will enjoy tasting and tippling at the Wine Coast vineyards (especially noteworthy for reds), admiring early buildings, browsing the many antique shops and crafts cottages, holing up in a secluded cove, or maybe taking the plunge at clothing-optional Maslin Beach.

History

All the big-name explorers—Sturt, Light, Barker—traversed the Fleurieu, but it was French explorer Nicholas Baudin who, in 1802, named the area for Napoleon's Minister of the Navy, Charles Pierre Claret Comte de Fleurieu. In the same year, Baudin "encountered" rival Matthew Flinders at a site that was appropriately named Encounter Bay—the Encounter Coast becoming a natural legend thereof. Interestingly, neither Baudin nor Flinders spotted the sand-covered mouth of the Murray, Australia's largest river, a stone's throw away.

It was at Encounter Bay, in 1837, that South Australia's first whaling station (and first successful industry) was created.

THE WINE COAST

About 20 km south of Adelaide, the Wine Coast stretches from old Reynella, home of Cellar Number One, to Old Willunga, with its own share of historic buildings.

Most of the Fleurieu wineries sprouted in the 1850s when individual farmers harvested small vineyards for their personal use. It was Thomas Hardy who, in 1876, put the area on the map with his purchase of Tintara Vineyards (which subsequently evolved into a dynasty) in McLaren Vale. In the early 1900s, after the all-important London market accepted the Australian wines into their cellars and down their gullets, the local vintners began growing vines with a more serious bent. In 1973, the first annual bushing festival, celebrating the release of the year's vintage, furthered the Wine Coast's popularity. Today the district is comprised of more than 40 (mostly family-owned) wineries.

Reynella

Old Reynella, at the turnoff from Main South Rd., marks the start of the Wine Drive.

This is the town where John Reynell, South Australia's first commercial winegrower, planted his vines in 1839 and created Cellar Number One (also known as the Old Cave Cellar). See Reynell's original cellar and his home, Chateau Reynell, on the grounds of **Hardy's Reynella Winery**, Reynell Rd. (tel. 08-8381-2266). The winery, established in 1853, is open daily 10 a.m.-4:30 p.m., except Christmas Day and Good Friday.

Reynella's first school, erected in 1858 and since renovated, is on Peach Street.

Morphett Vale

South Australia's first Roman Catholic church, St. Mary's, was built here in 1846. To view other historic buildings, turn off of Main South Rd., at the Noarlunga turnoff, for **Pioneer Village** at Hackham, where they've built a rather hokey re-creation of other old structures, furnished in period style. Hours are Wed.-Sun.

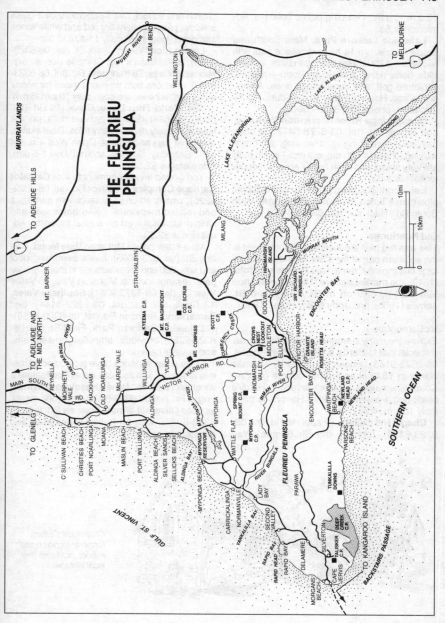

10 a.m.-5 p.m., including public holidays. Admission is $3.

Lakeside Leisure Park, Main South and Brodie Roads, is a 14-hectare hillside park with two lakes, a 700-meter tobaggan track, a water slide, horse riding, and—in mini form—railways, miniature golf, and dune buggy rides. Admission is free. Hours are daily 10 a.m.-dusk. For information, phone (08) 8326-0200.

Onkaparinga River Recreation Park, Piggott Range Rd. (tel. 08-8278-5477), is open daily for birdwatching, gum-viewing, and bushwalking (check in with rangers first—some trails are very steep, and flash floods are another potential hazard).

Eat a pork pie, plum pudding, or traditional plowman's lunch at **James Craig Inn,** Main South Rd., Hackham (tel. 08-8384-6944).

Old Noarlunga

This was the oldest concentrated settlement in the southern part of the state. Some of the heritage buildings that remain are **Horseshoe Hotel** (1840), the **market square** (1841), **Horseshoe Mill** (1844), **Church of St. Philip and St. James** (1850), and **Jolly Miller Hotel** (1850).

McLaren Vale

Explore the many surrounding wineries, but pay a special visit to **Hardy's Wines,** Main Rd. (tel. 08-8323-9185), whose purchase by Thomas Hardy in 1876 changed the course of Wine Coast winemaking. (Author's favorite is Hardy's black-bottle-pot-still brandy.) Hardy's is open daily 10 a.m.-4:30 p.m.

Chapel Hill Cellars, Chapel Hill Rd. (tel. 08-8323-8429), formerly the Sir Samuel Way church and school, has a superb stained-glass window, plus excellent dry red and white wines and ports. Hours are daily 11 a.m.-5 p.m.

Luong Rice Winery, Park St. (tel. 08-8323-8156), is Australia's first Chinese rice-winery. **Maxwell Wines,** 26 Kangarilla Rd. (tel. 08-8323-8200), produces both wine and mead (or honey wine). Both wineries are open daily 10 a.m.-5 p.m.

The **World Thru Dolls,** Chalk Hill Rd. (tel. 08-8323-8624), displays antique dolls, portrait figures, nursery rhymes, fairy tales, Bible stories, and other toys and dollies. Open Wed.-Fri. 1-4 p.m., Saturday, Sunday, and holidays 1-5 p.m. Admission is $2.50.

You'll need an appointment to visit **Camelot Carriage Complex,** 8 Pethick Rd. (tel. 08-8323-8225), where 40-or-so horsedrawn carriages and related memorabilia (like harnesses and whips) are displayed on a rural property. Admission is $2.50.

Moderately priced **McLaren Vale Motel,** Caffrey St. (tel. 323-8365), has a swimming pool and spa. Bed and breakfasts in the moderate-expensive range include: **McLaren Vale,** 56 Valley View Dr. (tel. 08-8323-9351); **Southern Vales,** 13 Chalk Hill Rd. (tel. 08-8323-8144); and **Samarkand,** Branson Rd. (tel. 08-8323-8756).

Lakeside Caravan Park, Field St. (tel. 08-8323-9255), provides campsites, on-site vans, and several cabins.

Quite a few wineries have picnic and barbecue areas, as well as restaurants that feature a winetaster's lunch. **James Haselgrove Wines,** Foggo Rd. (tel. 08-8323-8706), has good meals, as does **Oliverhill Wines,** Seaview Rd. (tel. 08-8323-8922), with an Italian winemaker and homemade pasta.

Chapel Hill Cellars, formerly a church and school, produces fine local vintages.

BOB RACE

McLaren Vale Bushing Festival (tel. 08-8323-8999), celebrating the release of a new vintage, occurs over several days in October. Activities include tastings, tours, a ball, fairs, toasting and crowning of the Bushing King and Queen, and an Elizabethan feast.

For help, call 000, or **McLaren Vale Hospital** (tel. 08-8323-8606), **police** (tel. 08-8323-8330), or **fire brigade** (tel. 08-8323-8393).

Willunga

Willunga, derived from Willa-unga, Aboriginal for "Place of the Green Trees," was first laid out in 1839. These days the town is one of Australia's most important almond-growing regions, with 4,500 acres planted. Several old bluestone buildings preserved by the National Trust include the courthouse and police station, dating from 1855. Many of the roof slates have been quarried locally.

View approximately 1,000 different rose varieties (when in season), all clearly labeled, at the **Rose Display Garden,** St. Andrews Terrace (tel. 085-56-2555). Hours are daily during daylight, and tours can be arranged.

If you'd rather smell the horses than the roses, make an appointment to see Arab, Pinto, and Clydesdales at **Rondoro Clydesdale Stud,** Yundi Rd., Yundi (tel. 085-56-0234).

Vanessa's Restaurant Motel, 27 High St. (tel. 085-56-2379), has moderately priced rooms with continental breakfast included. The restaurant is on the expensive side. **Willunga House,** 1 St. Peters Terrace (tel. 085-56-2467), offers B&B accommodations (some with fireplaces) in the upper-moderate category.

Rosella Café, Upper High St. (tel. 085-56-2258), serves light lunches and homemade European cakes. The **Salopain Inn,** on Old Willunga Rd. before town (tel. 08-8323-8769), features daily lunch in a restored 1861 hotel.

In late July, Willunga celebrates the start of spring with an **Almond Blossom Festival.**

Conservation Parks

South of Willunga, take the Hope Forest turnoff to **Kyeema Conservation Park,** which has an active bird population and walking trails, including a special trail that explores park animals' homes.

Also southeast of Willunga, the Yundi turnoff will lead you to **Mt. Magnificent Conservation Park,** where a portion of the Heysen Trail makes a steep ascent to the top of the mount.

GULF ST. VINCENT BEACHES

Heading south of Adelaide, past Hallet Cove, the first beach you come to is **O'Sullivan's,** with its breakwater-protected swimming and boating facilities. Next is **Christies Beach,** a popular family resort with safe swimming, sailing, and reef fishing. **Port Noarlunga,** circled by steep cliffs and sandhills, features a lovely reef (at low tide), fishing jetty, and the **Onkaparinga River Recreation Park,** a natural aquatic reserve with many types of water birds.

A favorite with surfers is **Moana,** where you can drive (cautiously!) onto the beach. **Moana Beach Tourist Park,** on the Esplanade (tel. 08-8327-0677), has on-site vans and campsites. The park has a boat ramp, tennis courts, gymnasium, sauna, and spa.

Maslin Beach, South Australia's first legal nude beach, is exceptionally popular for its, er, scenery and bodysurfing. Be aware that only the 1.5-km southern strip of the beach is clothing-optional (*trust* me). **Maslin Beach Caravan and Camping Ground,** 2 Tuit Rd. (tel. 085-56-6113), rents campsites and on-site vans. Features include swimming pool, tennis court, coin-operated barbecue, and laundry facilities.

Port Willunga is a historic spot with offshore reefs, occasional good surf, scuba diving to the shipwrecked *Star of Greece,* swimming, and sandy beaches.

Aldinga Beach also has good scuba diving, swimming, and sometimes surfing. Remnant plains scrub, wildflowers, and birdlife are features of **Aldinga Scrub Conservation Park,** off Cox Road. Walk through the scrub to the beach at **Aldinga Holiday Park,** Cox Rd. (tel. 085-56-3444). On-site vans and campsites are available, and there are also five yurtlike cottages and a swimming pool.

There's good fishing from offshore boats at **Silver Sands,** swimming at **Sellicks Beach,** and decent surf at sheltered **Myponga Beach.** Three conservation parks near the town of Myponga are **Myponga,** nine km southwest, **Spring Mount,** 13 km southeast, and **Nixon-Skinner,** behind Myponga Reservoir.

Be careful of the rips at **Carrickalinga.** A better choice is **Normanville,** where there's excellent swimming, both jetty and boat fishing, snorkeling on the offshore reef, and paraflying during the summer. A river runs through the **Normanville Beach Caravan Park,** Jetty Rd. (tel. 085-58-2038). Rent an on-site van or campsite there, or at **Beachside Caravan Park,** Willis Dr. (tel. 085-58-2458).

High Country Trails, Willis Dr., Normanville (tel. 085-58-2507), organizes horseback rides, from an hour's trot along the beach to three-day pack trips, for learners or experienced riders.

The beaches get pretty rocky from here on out. Try **Lady Bay** for snorkeling, **Second Valley** for boat and jetty fishing, and **Rapid Bay** for excellent scuba diving. (Colonel Light first landed in Rapid Bay.) In Second Valley, **Leonard's Mill** (tel. 085-98-4184), a restored 1849 stone mill, is open daily for a la carte meals, light snacks, and drinks at indoor or outdoor courtyard bars.

The tiny town of **Delamere,** inland along Main South Rd., has a number of historical buildings including the Uniting Church (1858), rural school (1861), St. James Church (1871), and council offices (1878).

CAPE JERVIS TO VICTOR HARBOR

Rounding the cape, the coast becomes more rugged as the waves of the Southern Ocean pound the shores and branch roads lead through weathered terrain to isolated and occasionally ferocious beaches below.

At the tip of the peninsula, **Cape Jervis** is both the jumping-off point to Kangaroo Island, 13 km across the Backstairs Passage, and the Heysen Trail, which passes through many different conservation parks on its faraway way to the Flinders Ranges. The coastal waters are noted for jetty and deep-sea fishing as well as scuba diving, and the tall cliffs and powerful breezes make it an ideal base for hang gliding. The **Cape Jervis Lighthouse** was in operation from 1871 to 1972. **Old Cape Jervis Station Homestead,** Main Rd. 9 (tel. 085-98-0233), offers inexpensive B&B accommodations, cheap bunkhouse beds, and a tennis court. **Cape Jervis Tavern Motel,** Main Rd. (tel. 085-98-0276), has moderate rates that include continental breakfast.

Back on Range Rd., turn into **Talisker Conservation Park,** where you can fossick about the 1862 silver and lead mine. You'll pass through the old mining town of **Silverton** on your way to the park. **Warning:** Watch out for those mine shafts!

Deep Creek Conservation Park is nothing short of spectacular—rugged cliffs form sheer drops downward to the raging sea, profusions of delicate orchids and luxuriant ferns tangle along cool running streams, native birds and wildlife sweep from steep terrain to secluded coves. Accessed from Range Rd., Deep Creek offers a number of exciting trails for hikers—everything from casual strolls to challenging bushwalks. It is essential that you check in at Park Headquarters before embarking on any of the walks, particularly the strenuous, long-distance Heysen Trail, which is closed outside the conservation parks in summer. You can also pick up trail maps, camping permits, and other detailed information from the park headquarters, or phone (085) 52-3677.

Due to powerful rips and changing currents, only very experienced surfers and strong swimmers should tempt their fate at isolated **Parsons** and **Waitpinga** Beaches, both part of **Newland Head Conservation Park,** reached from Range Road. The park also has walking trails and camping facilities. **Rosetta Harbor,** on the northern side of the Bluff in Encounter Bay, has good snorkeling and scuba diving.

VICTOR HARBOR

Situated on the shores of Encounter Bay, Victor Harbor (pop. 5,300) is the largest town on the Fleurieu Peninsula. Being a close 83 km from Adelaide makes it exceptionally popular with city folk who invade the town during summer and school holidays. Two unique natural formations are the Bluff, a 100-meter-high headland, and—protecting the bay from the Southern Ocean's wild surf—Granite Island, connected by causeway to the shore.

History
Victor Harbor's whaling stations bustled with activity from 1837 (when the first station was established) until 1869, attracting both small

(top) Step into the picture at this ruined hut in the Aroona Valley, Flinders Ranges National Park.
(bottom) Quelltaler Winery, near Watervale, South Australia
(following page) Tanami Desert termite mounds on Spinifex Plain, near Fiddlers Lake, Northern Territory

and large vessels to its port, making it one of the state's most important export terminals. Assuming that Victor Harbor would not only become *the* river port, but possibly the state capital, a railway was built in 1864, linking the town to Goolwa, at the mouth of the Murray River. Unfortunately, big ship owners, scared off by the Southern Ocean's erratic and stormy seas, searched for safer spots to drop anchor and the port soon became obsolete.

Sights
The **Museum of Historical Art,** Yankalilla Rd., three km from Victor Harbor (tel. 085-52-1546), has a large private collection of shells, rocks, coins, medals, firearms, and miniature cars. Open Sundays and school holidays 1-5 p.m. Admission is $2.

Historic buildings include the **Railway Station, Telegraph Station** (1867), **Newland Memorial Congregational Church** on Victoria St. (1869), and **St. Augustine's Church of England** on Burke St. (1869). The **Victor Harbor Tourist Information Centre,** located in the original primary school on Torrens St., will provide maps and direct you.

If you climb to the top of the rather steep **Bluff,** you'll get a stupendous view of the bay where Baudin and Flinders had their famous meeting in 1802, and below to Rosetta Bay and Whale Haven, where the whaling stations operated.

Ride to **Granite Island** on Australia's only horse-drawn tram. Gentle giant Clydesdales commute from Victor Harbor to the island daily 10 a.m.-4 p.m. Fare is $2 one-way. Buy tickets at the causeway on the Victor Harbor foreshore. During South Australian school holidays and good-weather weekends, chairlifts operate to the top of the peak for expansive views of the town and bay. Summertime visitors to the island might spy fairy penguins as they waddle toward their rocky homes each night after dusk.

Urimbirra Wildlife Park, Adelaide Rd., five km from Victor Harbor (tel. 085-54-6554), is a 16-hectare open-range park with dingoes, crocs (there's one named Aunty Jack), koalas, kangaroos, bats, wombats, bettongs, bandicoots, snakes, eels, and a nocturnal house. Hours are daily 10 a.m.-5 p.m. Admission is $6.

Opposite Urimbirra, the one-hectare **Nagawooka Flora Reserve** is planted with almost 1,000 named trees, shrubs, and groundcovers from all over Australia. The park is open daily during daylight hours.

Safe swimming beaches are on either side of the Causeway to Granite Island, good snorkeling at **Oliver's Reef,** and bodysurfing at **Chiton Rocks,** between Victor Harbor and Port Elliot.

Accommodations
You have a choice of simple guesthouses, motel rooms, or fully equipped holiday flats. Check with the tourist office for long-term selections. If you're visiting during peak periods, book far in advance, and expect rates to increase (and often double).

Anchorage Guest House, 21 Flinders Parade (tel. 085-52-5970), is a nearly-century-old traditional establishment, set right on the sea with terrific views. Inexpensive rates include breakfast. Both the **Grosvenor Hotel,** Ocean St. (tel. 085-52-1011), and **The Clifton,** 39 Torrens St. (tel. 085-52-1062), have inexpensive to low-moderate rooms. **Villa Victor,** 59 Victoria St. (tel. 085-52-4258), charges $45 single, including full breakfast. More luxurious (and expensive) is centrally located **Apollon Motor Inn,** 15 Torrens St. (tel. 085-52-2777). **Kerjancia Motor Lodge,** 141 Hindmarsh Rd. (tel. 085-52-2900), also expensive, offers self-contained apartments with a solar pool and spa.

Victor Harbor Holiday Centre, Bay Rd. (tel. 085-52-1949), has on-site vans, cabins, and campsites, as well as moderately priced motel units with cooking facilities.

Food
You'll find the usual resort town takeaways. **Fine Foods International,** Coral St. (tel. 085-52-3732), has yummy imported picnic goodies, nuts, dried fruits, and chocolates. **Higgy's Victor Harbor Bakery,** Albert Pl. (tel. 085-52-3515), bakes fresh pies and pasties and concocts custom-made sandwiches. The **Sub Station,** Ocean St., is another good sandwich-maker, and **South Coast Fish Café,** also on Ocean St., is a good spot for fresh catches. **Anchorage Guest House** serves moderately priced home-style meals in historic surroundings. The **Hotel Crown,** Ocean St., is the cheap pub-meal stop. For finer and costlier meals, try the restaurants

at **Apollon Motor Inn, Bayview Motel, Ocean Crest Motel,** or **Whalers Inn.**

Information

Dial 000 for emergencies. **Victor Harbor Hospital** (tel. 085-52-1066) and **police** (tel. 085-52-2088) serve the immediate area. For maps and other road information, contact the **Royal Automobile Association** (tel. 085-52-1033).

PORT ELLIOT

Farther along the Encounter Coast, on Horseshoe Bay, the historic township of Port Elliot (pop. 1,050) attracts body and board surfers to its fabled beaches and tourists to its picturesque shores with views of the Murray mouth and Coorong National Park.

History

Proclaimed a town in 1854—with the opening of South Australia's first iron railway on its inaugural Port Elliot-to-Goolwa link—Port Elliot was named by Governor Young after his buddy, Sir Charles Elliot. Like neighboring Victor Harbor, Port Elliot did not fare very well as a port. Though the first ship anchored in 1851, and traffic grew to a busy 85 arrivals in 1855, by 1864 seven ships had been sunk and strewn about the bay. So much for Port Elliot—in that same year, another railway link was built to Victor Harbor, and for a short time traffic was redirected.

Sights

Historic structures lining **The Strand** include the **police station** (1853), **courthouse** (1866), **council chamber** (1879), and nearby **St. Jude's Church** (1854). The National Trust has set up a historical display in the **Port Elliot Railway Station,** built in 1911.

For excellent **coastal views,** take the scenic walk from just above Horseshoe Bay and follow the cliffs to Knight's Beach, or look out from **Freeman Knob,** along The Strand at the main Victor Harbor-Goolwa Rd. junction.

West of town, **Boomer Beach** is where experienced bodysurfers come for large, dumping waves. Small, sheltered **Green Bay,** on Freeman Knob, is good for sunbathing, but

swimming is dangerous in the rocky bay with its strong riptides. Swimmers will find very good facilities at **Horseshoe Bay,** with small surf at the Commodore Point end. **Middleton Beach,** on the way to Goolwa, is one of the best surfing beaches on the Encounter Coast. **Big Surf Australia,** Main Rd., Middleton (tel. 085-54-2399), sells bodyboards, swimwear, and accessories, rents quality gear, and is open daily. Flagstaff Hill Rd. leads from central Middleton to another inspiration point, a winery, and a mushroom farm.

Accommodations

Royal Family Hotel, 32 North Terrace (tel. 085-54-2219), has simple, inexpensive rooms with shared facilities. Also inexpensive, **Hotel Elliot,** on The Strand by the railway station (tel. 085-54-2218), has more of a family-type atmosphere. Moderately priced **Cavalier Inn Motel,** The Strand (tel. 085-54-2067), has good views and a swimming pool. **Thomas Henry's House,** 8 Charteris St. (tel. 085-54-2003), offers 1930s-style B&B accommodation at high-moderate rates. If you're staying put, the following spots can set you up in a holiday unit at inexpensive weekly rates: **South Seas Townhouses,** 18 Merrilli Pl. (tel. 085-54-2029); **Lifeplan,** 4 The Strand (tel. 08-8212-3636); and **Dolphins Court,** Strangways Terrace, Horseshoe Bay (tel. 085-54-2029).

Port Elliot Caravan Park, Horseshoe Bay (tel. 085-54-2134), has on-site vans, campsites, and moderately priced cottages. **Middleton Caravan Park,** Middleton (tel. 085-54-2383), rents on-site vans and campsites.

Food

Royal Family Hotel and **Hotel Elliot** both serve inexpensive counter meals. **Sitar Indian Restaurant,** The Strand (tel. 085-54-2144), has moderately priced dinners and takeaways. **Arnella Restaurant,** North Terrace, on the main Victor Harbor-Goolwa Rd., has country-style dinners (lunch, in season, and on Sunday) in the higher price bracket. And higher yet is the continental cuisine at **Thomas Hardy's Restaurant.**

The **Middleton Fish Shop** (tel. 085-54-2688) and **Middleton General Store and Post Office** (tel. 085-54-2064) are both open daily for takeaway food and snacks.

GOOLWA

Situated where the Murray River meets the great Southern Ocean, Goolwa (pop. 2,360) draws railway buffs and river rats who come to ride Australia's first iron public railway, to cruise up and down the Murray or around Lake Alexandrina, or to laze away the days by the historic old wharf. Hindmarsh Island, a ferry ride away, sits between the mighty mouth and the entrance to Lake Alexandrina.

History

Prosperous paddle steamer trade along the Murray River made Goolwa an important port from the mid- to late 1800s. The opening of the railway line to Port Elliot gave the town true, though shortlived, notoriety. Alas, a new line extending all the way to Adelaide and built in the 1880s caused Goolwa's final fizzle as port extraordinaire.

Over on Hindmarsh Island, an obelisk marks the place where Charles Sturt, in 1830, squinted past the sand hills and into the Murray mouth, as did Captain Collett Barker, another explorer, who must have opened *his* eyes a little too wide before he got speared to death by the natives.

Sights

The **Goolwa Hotel** (1853), Cadell St.; **post office** (1857), Cadell St.; **Corio Hotel** (1857), Railway Terrace; and **police station** (1859), Goolwa Terrace, are some of the old buildings still in use today. (The Goolwa Hotel has a figurehead from the wrecked ship *Mozambique* on its parapet.)

Other historic sights are the **Railway Superintendent's House** (1852), **Railway Horse Stables** (1853), the **Saddlery** (1867), **Town Mechanics Institute** (1868), and **Church of England** (1867), all on Cadell Street.

The **Goolwa National Trust Museum** (1870), Porter St., is housed inside a former blacksmith shop. The museum has many exhibits focusing on Goolwa's early beginnings, including a "Port of Goolwa" room. Hours are Tues.-Thurs., Sat.-Sun., school and public holidays 2-5 p.m. Admission is $1.

Signal Point, The Wharf (tel. 085-55-3488), opened in 1988 by the illustrious Prince of Wales, is the River Murray Interpretive Center. High-

tech computerized displays show what the river was like before the Europeans came as well as the impact of modern industry and development on the important waterway. Climb aboard *Oscar W,* a restored paddle wheeler built in 1908, which sits alongside the wharf. Hours are daily 10 a.m.-5 p.m., except Christmas Day.

The only way to get to **Hindmarsh Island** is by the free 24-hour ferry near the wharf. Walking trails and lookouts enable you to see the Murray mouth on one side and Lake Alexandrina on the other. The Sturt Memorial granite obelisk is about three km from the ferry landing, on the right side of the main road. Boat ramps on the island will launch you into salt or fresh water.

Built between 1935 and 1940, **Goolwa Barrage,** an enormous concrete structure atop a multitude of wooden piles pounded into the riverbed, crosses the lower Murray—from Hindmarsh Island to Sir Richard Peninsula—and separates the salty sea from the fresh river water. A bird blind, off Barrage Rd., lets watchers view the area birdlife.

Currency Creek, an eight-km drive up Cadell St., has an Aboriginal canoe tree alongside the road, picnic areas, and a walking trail that will take you to a waterfall, old copper mine, and short detour to the cemetery.

Goolwa Beach often has big surf, crosscurrents, and some rips—recommended for experienced swimmers only.

Accommodations

Two of the town's oldest buildings, **Goolwa Hotel,** Cadell St. (tel. 085-55-2012), and **Corio Hotel,** Railway Terrace (tel. 085-55-2011), have inexpensive rooms with shared facilities. For cheap home-style accommodations, try **Graham's Castle,** corner Castle Ave. and Bradford Rd. (tel. 085-55-2182).

South Lakes Motel, Barrage Rd. (tel. 085-55-2194), features moderately priced rooms with kitchenettes, swimming area, and adjacent golf course. Other choices include **Kenmaur House,** Saratoga Dr. (tel. 085-55-3494), and **Goolwa Cottage,** 3 Hays St. (tel. 085-55-1021), with slightly higher rates in the heart of the wharf area, which is a "smoke-free zone." For motel-style accommodations, try **Goolwa Central,** 30 Cadell St. (tel. 085-55-1155), where rates include continental breakfast, a pool, spa, and rec room.

Narnu Pioneer Holiday Farm, Monument Rd., Hindmarsh Island (tel. 085-55-2002), features self-contained cottages in a rural setting for $50-60 per double, with horse riding and aquatic equipment available.

On-site vans and campsites are available at **Goolwa Camping and Tourist Park,** Kessell Rd. (tel. 085-55-2144), and campsites only at **Hindmarsh Island Caravan Park,** Madsen St., Hindmarsh Island (tel. 085-55-2234).

Food
Counter meals and a la carte fare are served daily at both the **Goolwa** and **Corio** hotels. A coffee shop at **Signal Point** serves light lunches, snacks, and cakes. **South Lakes Motel** has a comparatively pricey restaurant at the water's edge. Otherwise, it's the usual takeaways, chicken joints, and a Chinese restaurant.

Information
The **Goolwa Tourist and Information Centre,** Cadell St. (tel. 085-55-1144), provides information on all area facilities, as well as maps for historic walking tours. Hours are daily 10 a.m.-4 p.m., closed Christmas Day and Good Friday.

Reach out and touch the **police** (tel. 085-55-2018), **ambulance** (tel. 085-52-2111), or **fire brigade** (tel. 085-55-2000). The **Royal Automobile Association** (tel. 085-55-2009) will assist with maps and driving-related questions.

STRATHALBYN

Approximately 30 km north of Goolwa, beautiful Strathalbyn (pop. 1,925), a designated heritage township, was settled by Scottish immigrants in 1839. Examples of architecture which reflect Scottish influence are the **Angus Flour Mill** (1852), **20 High Street Crafts** (1854), **London House** (1867), and **Argus House** (1868). **Saint Andrew's Church** (1848), overlooking the river, is one of Australia's most fabled country churches.

The River Angus, which flows through town, is bordered by **Soldiers Memorial Gardens,** a peaceful setting for picnicking, duck-feeding, swan-songing, and gentle strolls. Several Aboriginal canoe trees line the water's edge and gum trees hover above lush lawns and rambling bridges.

Many arts and crafts, antique, and secondhand shops are scattered about the town. A walking-tour book ($1) to Strathalbyn's two shopping areas is available at many locations. You can also pick up tourist literature at 20 High Street Crafts.

Milang, 20 km southeast of Strathalbyn, is another former river port, now used as a launching point for boating, windsurfing, and waterskiing on Lake Alexandrina. **Langhorne Creek,** 60 km northeast from Milang, is a grape- and almond-growing district on the way to **Wellington,** farther east yet, on the banks of the Murray River. Don't miss a ride on the 24-hour free ferry, operating since 1839 (when it was the only access across the river between South Australia and the eastern states).

Accommodations
Two fine old pubs are **Robin Hood Hotel,** 18 High St. (tel. 085-36-2608), and the **Terminus Hotel,** 17 Rankine St. (tel. 085-36-2026). Both offer inexpensive rooms with shared facilities.

Strathalbyn Caravan Park, Coronation Rd. (tel. 085-36-3681), has on-site vans and campsites.

Food
Both the Robin Hood and Terminus hotels have reasonably priced counter meals. **Strath Eats,** 10 Dawson St. (tel. 085-36-3582), dishes up pizza, pasta, chicken, and chips. **Bonnie MacGregor's,** Dawson St. (tel. 085-36-3535), features gourmet foods and light meals at moderate prices.

Events
The **Penny Farthing Challenge Cup,** held annually in March, is an international event in which more than 30 riders race through the township on pennyfarthings and other vintage bicycles. Accompanying hooplah consists of parades, band performances, barbecues, a pancake brekky, arts and crafts displays, and Scottish street entertainment. For more information, phone (085) 36-3212.

Information
For **emergencies,** dial 000. For other assistance, phone the **police** (tel. 085-36-2044), **ambulance** (tel. 085-36-2333), **fire brigade** (tel. 085-36-2000), or local **Royal Automobile Association** (tel. 085-36-2066).

TRANSPORT

All buses to the Fleurieu Peninsula depart from Adelaide's Country Passenger Depot, 101 Franklin Street. **Premier Roadlines** (tel. 08-8415-5544) travels the Adelaide-Willunga-Victor Harbor route three times daily Mon.-Fri., twice daily Saturday and public holidays, once on Sunday. Fare to Victor Harbor is about $12 one-way. **Kangaroo Island Connection** (tel. 08-8231-5959) departs twice daily for Cape Jervis via Aldinga and Normanville. Fare to Cape Jervis is $12 one-way. **Johnson's Motor Service** (tel. 08-8231-5959) provides transportation to Goolwa, twice daily, Mon.-Friday. Fare is $10 one-way. **Mt. Barker Passenger Service** (tel. 08-8391-2977) leaves for Strathalbyn three times daily, Mon.-Friday. Fare is $11 one-way. **TransAdelaide** (tel. 08-8210-1000) serves outer suburbs within the Fleurieu area.

Railway buffs should board the steam-powered **Cockle Train,** which follows the historic Victor Harbor-Goolwa route at least three times daily on school holidays, long weekends, and Sundays. The one-hour-and-45-minute roundtrip costs about $12. For information, phone (08) 8231-1707.

The **MV _Philanderer III_** (tel. 13-1301, toll-free from S.A.) provides ferry service from Cape Jervis to Kangaroo Island up to five times daily for $30 one-way.

Huck Finn-ers and river queens can choose from a variety of Murray River cruises departing from Goolwa. **PS _Mundoo_** makes two-and-a-half-hour paddle steamer cruises to North Goolwa, Hindmarsh Island, and Currency Creek every Thursday and Saturday at 11:30 a.m. Fare, including bus transfer, is $35. **MV _Aroona_** has a luncheon cruise downstream to the Murray mouth, Tuesday and Saturday, for the same rates. For information, phone Goolwa Cruises (tel. 085-55-2203).

KANGAROO ISLAND

After Tasmania and Melville (off Darwin's coast), Kangaroo Island (pop. 4,000), approximately 145 km by 60 km, is Australia's third largest island. Though the climate is temperate, with only rare frosts and highs not usually exceeding 38° C, the island is at its best (and most crowded) during the summer months.

Dramatic cliffs, sheltered beaches, untamed coastline, untouched scenery, and flourishing wildlife lure tourists to this popular holiday resort, a relatively close 113 km southwest of Adelaide and just a short hop off the Fleurieu Peninsula. Families enjoy swimming and sunning, camping and hiking in their choice of 16 conservation parks. Divers have a grand time exploring the 40-plus ships reported wrecked around the coastal waters, beginning with the _William,_ in 1847. Anglers drop their lines from jetties, rocks, and boats, into surf, rivers, and the deep blue sea. Naturalists are enthralled by the plentiful wildlife—kangaroos, natch, plus koalas, seals, fairy penguins, emus, sea lions, echidnas, possums, and an occasional platypus—unscathed by such predators as foxes or dingoes, which are nonexistent on the island. On the western side, you can still see the kin of wild pigs, reputedly set ashore by French explorer Nicholas Baudin as feed for shipwrecked sailors. Besides all the critters, you can tiptoe through more than 700 native wildflower species, and about 150 others brought in from elsewhere in the world. _And,_ if you're into the birds and the bees, keep your eyes and ears perked for crimson rosellas, purple-gaped honeyeaters, ospreys, sea eagles, the rare glossy black cockatoo, and the unique Ligurian honeybee.

Kingscote, on Nepean Bay, is the island's commercial center and the city nearest the airport. Other communities with holiday facilities are American River, Penneshaw, and Parndana. The north coast flaunts calmer waters, with stretches of beach for swimming, sunning, and lazy-day fishing. Dudley Peninsula, along the Backstairs Passage, boasts fairy penguins, pelicans, stunning views, and the Cornwall-style village of Penneshaw. The south coast is the wild side, with sand dunes, crashing waves, and three conservation parks. And Flinders Chase National Park, on the south and west coasts, is Kangaroo Island's spectacular wildlife sanctuary.

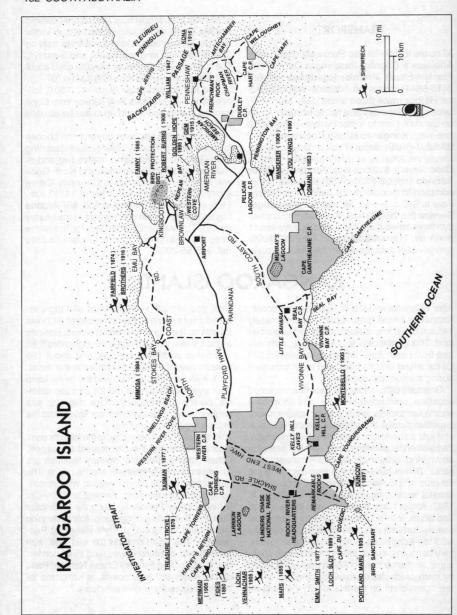

KANGAROO ISLAND

FLEURIEU PENINSULA

CAPE JERVIS

BACKSTAIRS PASSAGE

WILLIAM (1847)

KOMA (1916)

ANTECHAMBER BAY

CAPE WILLOUGHBY

CAPE HART

PENNESHAW

FRENCHMAN'S ROCK

CHAPMAN RIVER

CAPE HART C.P.

DUDLEY

PENNINGTON BAY

FANNY (1885)

BIRD PROTECTION DIST.

ROBERT BURNS (1908)

GOLDEN HOPE

GEM (1915)

BEACH

AMERICAN RIVER

WANDERER (1906)

YOU YANGS (1890)

OSMANLI (1853)

FAIRFIELD (1874)

BROTHERS (1916)

EMU BAY

KINGSCOTE

NEPEAN BAY

WESTERN COVE

BROWNLAW

AIRPORT

PELICAN LAGOON C.P.

CAPE GANTHEAUME C.P.

CAPE GANTHEAUME

MURRAY'S LAGOON

MIMOSA (1884)

STOKES BAY

EMU RD

PARNDANA

SOUTH COAST RD

COAST

NORTH

COAST

SOUTH

RD

PLAYFORD HWY

LITTLE SAHARA

SEAL BAY

SEAL BAY C.P.

VIVONNE BAY C.P.

VIVONNE BAY

MONTEBELLO (1905)

SOUTHERN OCEAN

TASMAN (1877)

WESTERN RIVER COVE

SNELLINGS BEACH

WESTERN RIVER C.P.

KELLY HILL C.P.

KELLY HILL CAVES

CAPE YOUNGHUSBAND

CAPE TORRENS

CAPE TORRENS C.P.

SHACKLE RD

WEST END HWY

FLINDERS CHASE NATIONAL PARK

ROCKY RIVER HEADQUARTERS

LARRIKIN LAGOON

REMARKABLE ROCKS

DUNCON (1897)

HARVEY'S RETURN

TREASURE (TROVE) (1878)

CAPE BORDA

MERMAID (1905)

FIDES (1860)

LOCH VENNACHAR (1905)

MARS (1855)

EMILY SMITH (1877)

LOCH SLOY (1899)

CAPE DU COUEDIC

PORTLAND MARU (1935)

BIRD SANCTUARY

INVESTIGATOR STRAIT

10 mi

10 km

= SHIPWRECK

History

Not much is known about the Aboriginals who originally inhabited the island; stone tools thought to be more than 10,000 years old are about the only sign of their presence. Anyway, they were long gone by 1802 when Matthew Flinders, voyaging on the *Investigator,* "discovered" Kangaroo Island for himself (and his king). But French explorer Nicholas Baudin was also nosing about, doing some circumnavigating of his own. By the time the two sailors faced off shortly afterward in Encounter Bay, Flinders had named the island—this time in tribute to the many kangaroos he'd seen, instead of for a compatriot—while Baudin had christened the places *he'd* charted *en français.* Consequently, you'll find French names attached to many island sights, reflecting the French vs. English "tug-of-words."

The island has an American influence also. In 1803, one year after Matthew Flinders had taken the island, a group of American sealers arrived at a site eventually named "American River." Using native pine, they built the *Independence,* South Australia's first boat.

It wasn't until 1836 that the first 400 settlers, sponsored by the South Australian Company, arrived from England aboard the *Duke of York* to formally establish a township at Reeves Point, north of Kingscote. The lack of fresh water kept this from being a viable colonial settlement and, by 1840, except for a few lingering souls, most of the population had shifted over to the mainland. The fact is, though, that Reeves Point was South Australia's first official European settlement, and the present inhabitants are tremendously proud of that bit of history.

Early industries on the island were yacca gum production, salt mining, and eucalyptus oil distilling (eucalyptus oil was Australia's first export product). Agriculture, however, was in a slump until the 1930s when cobalt and copper were added to the soil. After that, crops flourished and, before long, one-half the island had become productive farmland. Today Kangaroo Island's most vital industries are agriculture, fishing, and tourism.

KINGSCOTE

On the shores of Nepean Bay, Kingscote (pop. 1,450) blends its historical significance with modern-day necessities. Sheer cliffs to the north afford terrific views of the harbor and Western Cove, while cliffs to the south provide a languid drop to the Cygnet River swamp and bird lands. Kingscote is the island's major shipping port and trade center.

Sights

Reeves Point Historic Site is where the *Duke of York* anchored in 1836 and South Australia officially began. You'll find remnants of the first post office, the state's oldest cemetery and, farther north, the state's oldest introduced tree—a mulberry, planted around 1836, that still bears edible fruit! (You can buy jam made from the berries.)

Hope Cottage, the National Trust Museum, on Centenary Ave., is housed in an 1850s building built by two pioneering brothers. Displays include working exhibits, maritime history, family histories, photographs, and early newspapers. Open daily 2-4 p.m., closed mid-July through August. Admission is $2. For information, phone (0848) 22-151.

St. Alban's Church, built in 1884, is Kingscote's oldest public building. Stained-glass windows, memorials to pioneer families, and graffiti from when the church was used as a schoolroom are worth seeing.

Memorial Park, on the seafront close to the town center, has memorials to Flinders and the war dead, as well as barbecue and picnic areas for when your nostalgia gives way to hunger pangs.

Fairy penguins parade to their homes at dusk on most nights. Best viewing places are between the swimming pool and jetty, or among rocks near the jetty. At **Bay of Shoals,** see pelicans and other birds fed daily at 4 p.m.

Heritage Walking Trails explore Kingscote's natural history and heritage sights. Pick up maps at the tourist information center on Dauncey Street. For information, phone (0848) 22-381.

Family **beaches** with shallow swimming and wading facilities can be found in front of the Ozone Hotel and at Little Brownlow Beach, in front of the Yacht Club. Another spot for safe swimming is the rockbound **seawater pool.**

Accommodations

Be sure to book ahead, especially during school holiday periods. **Kangaroo Island Youth Hos-**

tel (also known as Hillfarm Hostel), Brownlow Beach (tel. 0848-22-778), has dorm beds for $12 per night, plus bicycle rentals, transportation from Kingscote, and meal service.

Kangaroo Island Holiday Village, 9 Dauncey St. (tel. 0848-22-225), has self-contained family units with kitchens at moderate prices. **Parade Units,** adjacent to Brownlow Beach (tel. 0848-22-565), is another decent choice. For a cottage-y experience, try **Nepean Heights Cottage,** 38 Franklin St. (tel. 0848-22-061).

Slightly higher-priced are the **Island Resort,** Telegraph Rd. (tel. 0848-22-100), with an indoor heated pool, sauna, and spa, and **Ellison's Seaview Motel,** Chapman Terrace (tel. 0848-22-030), featuring seafront motel units and guesthouse rooms. **Ozone Seafront Hotel,** the foreshore (tel. 0848-22-011), at the high end of the moderate range, has great views.

Both **Nepean Bay Caravan Park,** the foreshore, Brownlow Beach (tel. 0848-22-394), and **Kangaroo Island Caravan Park,** on the Esplanade (tel. 0848-22-325), rent campsites, onsite vans, and cabins.

Food
Good takeaways are **Pelican Pete's Takeaway Eats,** Main St. (tel. 0848-22-138), and **Nev's Tucker Box,** 3 Kingscote Terrace (tel. 0848-22-585). **Port of Call Restaurant,** the foreshore (tel. 0848-22-834), serves seafood, steak, and pasta in an intimate setting overlooking Nepean Bay. The **Ozone Seafront Hotel** features an a la carte dining room, bistro, and informal coffee shop with meals at all prices.

THE DUDLEY PENINSULA

Kangaroo Island's eastern tip, the Dudley Peninsula, starts as a narrow neck at Pelican Lagoon Conservation Park and white-sand beaches then rounds northeast to Cornish-influenced Penneshaw, over to rugged Cape Willoughby, south to Cape Hart, and then west to Dudley Conservation Park.

American River
This tiny village, midway between Kingscote and Penneshaw, is named for the American sealers who lived here for four months in 1803.

It's a favorite spot for fishermen who come not only for a fresh catch-of-the-day, but for the scenic beauty of gum and she-oak forested hills as they dip to meet the calm waters of Eastern Cove. Try to arrive at the end of August, when the freesias cover every knoll, dell, and pathway with brilliant blossoms.

The nearby aquatic reserve, Pelican Lagoon Conservation Park, is abundant with pelicans, swans, and Cape Barren geese.

Linnetts Island Club Resort (tel. 0848-33-053) has a choice of rooms, suites, villas, or holiday flats, ranging in price from inexpensive to expensive. **American River Motel,** Wattle Ave. (tel. 0848-33-052), overlooks the American River and has a pool, spa, and sauna. Prices are moderate to expensive and include continental breakfast. Rates are expensive at **Wanderers Rest,** corner Government and Bayview roads (tel. 0848-33-140), a guesthouse on a hillside with sweeping views of American River. All of these accommodations have restaurants or dining rooms.

Pennington Bay
Just one kilometer off the Kingscote-to-Penneshaw road, very near American River, Pennington Bay is a popular swimming and surfing beach—but only for the experienced. Otherwise, you can take a hike (more of a climb, actually) to the top of Mt. Thisby for views of both Pelican and Pennington Bays.

Dudley Conservation Park, near Pennington Bay, is one of the island's many wildlife havens where you may see the dama wallaby, Kangaroo Island kangaroo, purple-gaped honeyeater, echidna, and the fairy wren.

Penneshaw
Passing along the sandy-white Island and American Beaches, you'll come to Penneshaw, a Cornish-like hamlet, only 16 km across the Backstairs Passage from mainland South Australia. Tourists are drawn here for the safe bathing beach, excellent fishing off Hog Bay Jetty, and the parade of fairy penguins nesting (returning home each evening) in the cliffs and sand hills near town.

Captain Flinders landed near **Christmas Cove** in 1802. Also known as "The Basin." The granite boulders there had a slightly earlier arrival than the good captain—they were deposited by a glacier more than 200 million years ago.

Frenchman's Rock, at Hog Bay, marks the spot where, in 1803, Captain Baudin, who'd just "encountered" Captain Flinders, came ashore to fill his empty water casks. The two seamen, unaware that their respective countries were waging war, unwittingly became water brothers.

Penneshaw Museum, housed inside the 1922 school, features maritime and other historic and folk exhibits. Hours are Monday, Wednesday, and Saturday 3-5 p.m., daily in January and during Easter. Admission is $1.50. For information, phone (0848) 31-108.

Hog Bag Jetty, built 1902-09, is not only a famous fishing locale, but home port for the MV *Philanderer III.*

Bookings are essential at **Penneshaw Youth Hostel,** 43 North Terrace (tel. 0848-31-284, or 1800-01-8258 toll-free), where dorm beds cost $12 per night. Facilities include scooter, bicycle, and boat rentals, kitchen facilities, launderette, swimming beach, nature walks, slide and video presentations, and a range of organized tours of the island.

Tandarra Holiday Lodge, 33 Middle Terrace (tel. 0848-31-018), offers moderately priced holiday flats and a bunkhouse with $12 beds. **Sorrento Resort** (tel. 0848-31-028) features modern motel suites, cottages with kitchenettes, and alpine chalets with kitchenettes, ranging from moderate to expensive. The resort, set on two acres of seafront gardens, has a safe swimming beach, swimming pool, poolside bar, half-court tennis facilities, spa, and sauna, and offers a variety of island tours.

Penneshaw Caravan Park, Talinga Terrace (tel. 0848-31-075), with campsites and on-site vans, is opposite a safe beach and close to town.

Condon's Takeaway Foods, 43 North Terrace (tel. 0848-31-173), serves breakfast, chicken, chips, and rooburgers. You can also buy souvenirs, gas, ice, bait, and tackle, and get your laundry done here. The **Old Post Office Restaurant** (tel. 0848-31-063), in one of Penneshaw's oldest commercial buildings, on the first corner away from the ferry, gives you a choice of a la carte dining or more relaxed (and inexpensive) bistro meals in the enclosed courtyard. It's open every night except Monday.

Antechamber Bay

This long, sweeping stretch of beach meets the ocean, backdropped by the mainland and bisected by Chapman River as it runs into Lashmar Lagoon. Though this area is famous for canoeing and bream fishing, you'll also find hiking tracks leading to bushland, sandhills, and lagoons.

Antechamber Bay Farmhouse (tel. 0848-33-020) provides inexpensive guest accommodations.

Cape Willoughby

The first flicker of light was emitted from Cape Willoughby Lighthouse (South Australia's first) in 1852. Built of local limestone, the tower measures 27 meters high and sits 73 meters above sea level. Just below the lighthouse the rocky, wild, crashing coastline is aptly named Devil's Kitchen. The lighthouse is open to visitors daily 10 a.m.-4 p.m. For information, phone (0848) 22-381.

Cape Hart Conservation Park, four km southwest of Cape Willoughby, sports massive granite boulders and sandstone cliffs with drops to the Southern Ocean.

THE SOUTH COAST ROAD

From Kingscote to Flinders Chase National Park, ride the wild side in search of shells, shipwrecks, seals, and scenery, scenery, scenery.

Murray's Lagoon

Kangaroo Island's largest freshwater lagoon is encompassed within **Cape Gantheaume Conservation Park,** a favorite spot for birders. At D'Estrees Bay, on the east side of the park, you can catch fish or collect shells—both line the shores.

Seal Bay

Take the turnoff from South Coast Rd. to **Seal Bay Conservation Park,** a famous breeding colony of rare sea lions whose ancestors escaped the early sealers. Guided tours, led by the National Parks and Wildlife Service, will take you within a few meters of sunbathing sea lions. Tours run regularly year-round, and times are posted just off the road.

Little Sahara
Back on South Coast Rd., the first road on the left (immediately before the bridge) will take you down to Little Sahara desert, where ridge upon ridge of bleached white dunes blend into the surrounding bushland.

Vivonne Bay
The only safe harbor on this side of the coast, Vivonne Bay has a long, curvy beach with dazzling scenery and a variety of activities—beach, boat, and jetty fishing, beachcombing, swimming, picnicking. Students of all ages can take part in the **Outdoor Education Living Classroom,** a series of guided tours to enhance knowledge of the island and its history.

Make inquiries before you take a dip. Normally, safe swimming areas are near the jetty, boat ramp, and Harriet River—other parts of the bay have an undertow.

Correa Cottage (tel. 0848-31-233) and **Honeymyrtle Cottage** (tel. 0848-94-279) are available at moderate-expensive rates.

Kelly Hill Conservation Park
The Kelly Hill Conservation Park has an extensive network of limestone ridges, dense mallee, and a coastal trail that winds its way seaward. Kelly Hill shelters sinkholes, caverns, and caves molded from ornately shaped calcite that casts eerie shadows in the tricky light. The largest cave is open to visitors.

At the park's western boundary and sheltered at each side by ocean reefs and rocky headlands, **Hanson Bay** is another top spot for swimming and fishing.

Continuing along South Coast Rd. you'll soon approach Rocky River Headquarters in Flinders Chase National Park.

FLINDERS CHASE NATIONAL PARK

South Australia's largest national park consists of 73,662 hectares of protected sanctuary for Kangaroo Island's rare and opulent wildlife. Taking up the entire western end of the island, Flinders Chase is a mecca of unspoiled wilderness for friendly kangaroos (the distinctive Kangaroo Island kangaroo has dark, sooty brown fur), emus, Cape Barren geese, koalas, glossy black cockatoos, and possums riding piggy on their mother's back. The natives are so plentiful and friendly that at Rocky River humans picnic in enclosed areas while the animals scratch their chins and ogle at *them.*

South of Rocky River Headquarters you can reach the huge, oddly sculpted **Remarkable Rocks,** not to mention **Admiral's Arch,** another intriguing formation, and **Cape du Couëdic Lighthouse,** an "automatic" opened in 1906. (The island's largest shipwreck, that of the *Portland Maru,* occurred near the cape in 1935.)

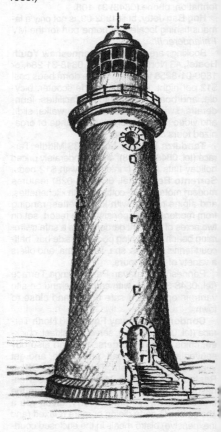

the "automatic" Cape du Couëdic Lighthouse

On the north side of the park, **Cape Borda Lighthouse,** opened in 1858, stands 155 meters above the sea. Before radio communication, the nearby cannon was used to signal ships of impending dangers. These days the meteorological station, nearby, is a quieter guide—and, no doubt, preferred by the wildlife inhabitants.

The **Rocky River Headquarters** (tel. 0848-37-235) will provide you with maps, necessary permits, and all the information you require for your park visit. Be sure to check in with the rangers before embarking on any lengthy hikes along isolated trails. Camping in the park is permitted and, if you like, you can spend a night or two at the Cape du Couëdic and Cape Borda Lighthouses (for a moderate fee). Admission to the park is $6.50 per vehicle.

THE NORTH COAST ROAD

The West End Highway, which borders the eastern edge of Flinders Chase National Park, will take you to the Playford Highway, a smooth run through grazing country back to Kingscote. The North Coast Rd. leaps and jogs off the beaten path to smooth beaches, rocky points, snug coves, and more stunning scenery.

Harvey's Return

This rugged, rocky cove, east of Cape Borda, was once a camp for American sealers. Later, after the lighthouse was built, it was used as a drop-off point for supplies. You can visit the graves of shipwrecked sailors and lighthouse-keepers at the nearby cemetery.

Cape Torrens Conservation Park

Towering cliffs hanging more than 200 meters above the sea make this a dazzling spot for bushwalkers who like trails with drop-dead views, or for birders in search of the rare glossy black cockatoo. Be sure to check in with the rangers at Rocky River Headquarters before setting out.

Western River Cove

This popular swimming and fishing beach, at the mouth of the Western River, is a steep descent from **Western River Conservation Park.** If you don't feel like hitting the beach, the park is full of stringy bark forests, wildlife, and excellent gorge, water, and valley views from its many high cliffs.

Snellings Beach

Swim, surf, dive, or fish at this peaceful protected bay, situated at the mouth of the Middle River (but be careful of the river's hidden snags and weeds). **Constitution Hill,** above the beach, affords great views of the area.

Accommodations at **Middle River Homestead** (tel. 0848-22-357) range from moderate to expensive (cheap if you're with several other travelers).

Stokes Bay

Farther east along the coast road, this white sandy beach draws families to its secluded shores, reached by walking through a tunnel within enormous limestone boulders. Though Stokes Bay is an excellent surf spot and fishing hole, its special feature is the large rock-enclosed pool, which provides a safe swimming area.

Paul's Place, between Stokes Bay and Amen Corner, has horse riding, a large aviary (on the off-chance you haven't seen enough birds in the wild), and a glass-fronted beehive where you can get a close-up look at the island's special Ligurian honeybee.

Remarkable Rocks, near Flinders Chase National Park

Stokes Bay Holiday House (tel. 0848-96-977) provides moderately priced accommodations.

Parndana

You have to head inland, back to the Playford Highway, if you want to visit this little farming community.

Though an experimental farm had been set up in 1938, development was hindered when the area became a soldiers' settlement during World War II. Eventually, 174 soldier-settlement farms were established and, in 1950, a government research center was set up on the experimental property. Today, the area is used mainly for sheep and cattle grazing.

For moderately priced holiday house accommodations try **Kelly's Pioneer Bend Homestead,** Pioneer Bend Rd. (tel. 0848-36-256), or **Coora Cottage,** Wetheralls Rd. (tel. 0848-96-027). **Gum Valley Resort** (tel. 0848-93-207) is a B&B in the expensive category.

Emu Bay

In the early 1900s (and up until the 1970s) the town was named Maxwell. Once it was discovered that the bay was both too shallow and too exposed, the port was moved over to Kingscote. Emu Bay is now a top-notch spot for safe swimming and boat or jetty fishing.

INFORMATION

Kangaroo Island Tourist Information Centre, 37 Dauncey St., Kingscote (tel. 0848-22-381), can help with tours, trails, and treks, and direct you to dive shops and bait stores. Be sure to pick up maps that detail the roads branching off main highways. The center is open Mon.-Fri. 9 a.m.-5 p.m., closed public holidays. (The public library and council office are in the same building.)

The information center can also provide brochures, issue permits, and arrange guided tours of the island's many conservation parks. Or, contact the **Department of Environment and Natural Resources** at Murray's Lagoon Headquarters (tel. 0848-28-233), Seal Bay Conservation Park (tel. 0848-28-233), Rocky River Headquarters (tel. 0848-37-235), Kelly Hill Con-

servation Park (tel. 37-231), or Cape Borda (tel. 0848-93-257). Be sure to pick up a copy of the national park code, and follow all rules to protect the island's sacred wildlife.

Do not fish without first finding out regulations and acquiring the necessary licenses. The tourist information center can help with these, as well as recommend and organize fishing expeditions. For more information, phone the **Fisheries Officers** at tel. 0848-22-130. At no time is fishing, or *any* disturbance of the seabed, permitted at the Pelican Lagoon and Seal Bay aquatic reserves.

Most of the island's emergency facilities are based in Kingscote, though park rangers provide assistance within their jurisdiction. In the case of an emergency, call the local ranger station, dial 000, or, in Kingscote, call the **ambulance** (tel. 0848-22-028), **police** (tel. 0848-22-018), and/or **fire brigade** (tel. 0848-22-200).

Island Stationery, 9 Osmond St., Kingscote (tel. 0848-22-625), stocks a selection of books about the island.

TRANSPORT

For information on getting to Kangaroo Island by plane or ferry, see "Getting Away" in the "Adelaide" section.

Getting Around

Airport Coach Service (tel. 0848-22-678) operates a bus from the Kingscote airport into town for $4, and also provides taxi and tour services. **Kangaroo Island Sealink** (toll-free tel. 13-1301) runs buses between Penneshaw, American River, and Kingscote, to connect with ferry departures. The Penneshaw and Kangaroo Island youth hostels also provide airport pick-up and some coach services for guests.

If you don't bring a car over with you on the ferry, you can rent one once you arrive. The Kangaroo Island Tourist Information Centre in Kingscote or your accommodation hosts can help you; otherwise, try **Kangaroo Island Car Hire,** corner Telegraph and Franklin Streets (tel. 0848-22-390), or **Budget,** 76 Dauncey St., Kingscote (tel. 0848-23-133). Expect to pay $75 and up per day (weekly deals are cheaper). Again, advance bookings are strongly recommended.

Rent bicycles at **Condon's Takeaway** (home of the rooburger), Penneshaw (tel. 0848-33-173), **Penneshaw Youth Hostel** (tel. 0848-31-284), or **Wisteria Lodge Motel,** Kingscote (tel. 0848-22-707); rent scooters at both Condon's and the Penneshaw Youth Hostel.

With nearly 1,600 kilometers of roads on the island, only the major highways are sealed. The extensive maze of off-the-beaten-paths range from bush tracks to gravel roads. The combination of dust and gravel makes driving at high speeds very hazardous. Even the most experienced cyclists can find road conditions exhausting. Allow plenty of time to cover the distance you expect to travel. Except during peak holiday

periods, the roads have very little traffic, making it unwise to depend on catching a lift. If you're driving, keep your petrol tank full (fill it at Kingscote, American River, Penneshaw, Parndana, and Vivonne Bay, year-round). Bushwalkers must inform rangers before embarking on remote or dangerous trails. And whether driving, hiking, or cycling, carry plenty of water with you.

For those who'd rather sit back and relax, sign up for an organized coach tour. Both youth hostels offer an interesting selection of one- and two-day jaunts. **Penguin Tours** (tel. 0848-22-844) depart nightly from Penneshaw and Kingscote for ranger-led observations of penguin lifestyles. Cost is $3.50.

THE SOUTHEAST

On the map, South Australia's southeast region doesn't appear to be more than a couple of major highways along the Adelaide-Melbourne route. Those "in the know" read between the thick black lines and head straight for the juicy parts—swamplands and wetlands, bird sanctuaries and wildlife preserves, sandy dunes and beaches, yawn-away fishing ports (including one marked by a giant walk-in lobster, named Larry), thick-as-thieves pine forests, pastoral farmland, weathered limestone caves, volcanic lakes and craters, a right-regular share of "ye old" buildings, and some downright extraordinary red wines.

Aside from bountiful fishing (especially Oct.-April, when it's lobster season) and delectable wines produced from rich *terra rossa* soil, this area also sustains timber and farming industries. Good annual rainfalls yield lush landscapes and, combined with neighboring western Victoria, this district is known as the Green Triangle.

TAILEM BEND

Both the Dukes and Princes Highways, principal routes between Adelaide and Melbourne, converge at Tailem Bend, along with the less-traveled Ouyen Highway. The inland Dukes Highway (which becomes Western Highway at Victoria's border) passes through a lot of flat farmland and is often referred to as the "boring road." The Princes Highway, running along the coast, is the preferred passage, as coastal roads usually are. If you're not in a rush to get to Melbourne, or if you're not going there at all, you can make a complete tour of the southeast by taking Princes Highway from Tailem Bend to Mt. Gambier; then, detouring north through wine and cave country, join up with the Dukes Highway at Keith and loop back to Tailem Bend.

Sights

Tailem Bend's most noteworthy attraction is **Old Tailem Town**, another one of those authentic turn-of-the-century villages. The township, five km north of Tailem Bend, features the usual pio-

neering cottages, butcher, barber, and bootmaker shops, emporium, church, one-room schoolhouse, and "real" general store. Old Tailem Town is open daily 10 a.m.-5 p.m. Admission is $7. For information, phone (085) 72-3838.

Accommodations

If you need more time to decide which road to take, inexpensive **River Bend Motel,** 110 Princes Hwy. (tel. 085-72-3633), will put you up for the night. **Westbrook Park River Resort,** Princes Hwy. (tel. 085-72-3794), on the banks of the Murray, has campsites, cabins, and on-site

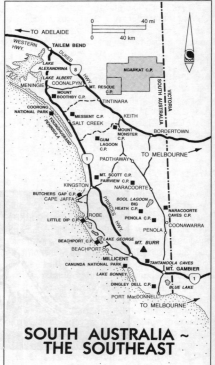

SOUTH AUSTRALIA ~ THE SOUTHEAST

vans. **Tailem Bend Rivers Edge Caravan and Tourist Park,** Princes Hwy. (tel. 085-72-3307), also on the Murray, features a boat ramp and canoes for hire.

MENINGIE

At the northern edge of the Coorong National Park, and the southern side of Lake Albert, Meningie (pop. 900) offers water sports, bird-watching, and easy access to the Coorong. The town is nothing special, but it is a decent place to overnight and stock up on provisions for your Coorong exploration. From Trigg Hill you can look out on Lakes Albert and Alexandrina, which comprise 746 square km of fresh water. **Melaleuca Centre,** 76 Princes Hwy., displays a variety of arts and crafts and also serves as the tourist information center. Hours are Mon.-Fri. 9 a.m.-5 p.m., Saturday 9 a.m.-12:30 p.m., Sunday and public holidays 11 a.m.-3 p.m. For information, phone (085) 75-1259.

Accommodations
The motels along Princes Highway are all in the inexpensive to low-moderate range. **Lake Albert Caravan Park,** Narrung Rd. (tel. 085-75-1411), offers bike, canoe, and sailboard hire, and a nice lakeside location.

THE COORONG

If you've seen the film *Storm Boy,* the poignant tale of a boy and his pelican, then you should have no trouble visualizing the Coorong, for it was filmed here. If you missed the flick, well, imagine a long, narrow, and shallow saltwater lagoon stretching 132 km from the Murray mouth to that big lobster Larry's mouth, just north of Kingston. Separated from the Southern Ocean by the shimmering sand dunes on Younghusband Peninsula (an average of two km wide), the Coorong is a haven for approximately 400 species of birds, including cormorants, terns, shags, ducks, swans, and pelicans. You can get from the Coorong across to the peninsula at Salt Creek during summer months; otherwise there's a year-round road about 75 km south, toward Kingston.

Pelicans and hundreds of other bird species find sanctuary in the Coorong.

A large Aboriginal tribe lived on the Coorong for thousands of years (the name is derived from "Kurangh," Aboriginal for "Long Neck of Water"), subsisting on fish, seafood, reptiles, birds, kangaroos, and wombats. You'll also come across wells built in the 1800s by Chinese immigrants who landed in Robe and, instead of joining their compatriots who headed for Victoria's goldfields, strayed northward to Adelaide. Australia's first oil well was drilled near Salt Creek in the 1890s, after Coorongite (a derivative of surface algae) was discovered.

In 1966, the Coorong was designated a national park and since then the National Parks and Wildlife Service has been responsible for its 43,500 hectares, as well as for **Messent Conservation Park,** six km northeast of Salt Creek.

The Coorong is an ideal location for fishing, boating, and hiking. Walking trails are marked throughout the park (try the three-km Lakes Nature Trail at Salt Creek) and, during Easter, Christmas, and New Year's holidays, rangers lead informative walks. Camping is permitted in the park, but you must obtain a permit first. The **De-**

partment of Environment and Natural Resources has offices at Salt Creek (tel. 085-75-7014) and Noonameena (tel. 085-75-1200).

KINGSTON

When you come upon a 17-meter-tall, four-ton, pre-fab lobster named Larry, you've arrived in Kingston (pop. 1,370), "gateway to the southern ports." Larry, presumably "the world's biggest (fake) lobster," stands watch over the entrance to this popular fishing port and beach resort. The town was established in 1856 by the Cooke brothers, who had procured government land grants near Maria Creek (so named for the vessel *Maria,* which wrecked near the Cape Jaffa Lighthouse in 1840; the crew and the passengers survived the shipwreck, only to be massacred by Aboriginals after they went ashore). The original jetty was too short and too shallow to make it useful for loading goods and, in 1876, was replaced by another—much longer, sitting in much deeper water—but even that one ceased being practical with the advent of modern roads and railways.

Sights
The **National Trust Museum,** 15 Cooke St., originally a timber mill built in 1872, presents items of local interest, including nautical memorabilia. Hours are daily 3-4 p.m. during school and public holidays. Admission is $2. For information, phone (087) 67-2114.

Cape Jaffa Lighthouse, moved from its 100-year-old post on Margarent Brock Reef, has been re-erected nearby on Marine Parade and is open to visitors. Other historic buildings are the post office, courthouse, and police station (now an antique shop). Hours are daily 2-5 p.m. during school and public holidays. Admission is $3. For information, phone (087) 67-2114.

Aside from the Coorong to the north, Kingston is near three other national parks: **Butchers Gap Conservation Park,** six km southwest, off Wyomi Rd., is another natural bird sanctuary where coastal vegetation thrives in the wetlands; part of a former coastal dune, **Mt. Scott Conservation Park,** 20 km east of Kingston, on Keith Rd., has good bushwalks through stringy bark forest inhabited by mallee fowl, sugar gliders, and wombats; and **Jip Jip Conservation Park,** 50 km

northeast of Kingston, features a variety of wildlife amid big exotically shaped granite boulders. You can also see unusual rock formations much closer to town at the **Granites,** off the highway north of Kingston, along the beach.

The fish are jumping in Kingston; anglers can cast lines from beach, boat, or jetty, either at Kingston or Cape Jaffa, a wee fishing village to the south. The foreshore and Wyomi and Pinks Beaches provide safe swimming, while Lacepede Bay is popular for sailing.

Accommodations
Crown Inn Hotel, Agnes St. (tel. 087-67-2005), has simple, inexpensive, pub-style rooms. Moderately priced **Bayview Motor Inn,** Marine Parade (tel. 087-67-2444), is near the jetty on the foreshore. **Kingston Caravan Park,** Marine Parade (tel. 087-67-2050), is situated on a sand beach. The usual range of campsites, on-site vans, and cabins are offered.

Events
If you're visiting the area in January, you can catch the annual **Yachting Carnival** and Cape Jaffa-to-Kingston race.

Information
Larry, the Big Lobster (tel. 087-67-2555), is not just another pretty face, but a tourist complex with a bistro, cafeteria, takeaways, souvenir and bottle shops, *and* tourist information. You can also pick up tourist info at **Wood Hut Craft Shop,** Kingston District Hall, Agnes St. (tel. 087-67-2151). Both places are open daily.

ROBE

In 1802, French explorer Nicholas Baudin cruised this area and bestowed Guichen Bay with its name. The town of Robe (pop. 740) was officially established in 1847, growing to be South Australia's third major port (before the downfall of shipping in 1864). It was used for exporting wool and horses and importing about 15,000 Chinese immigrants. The Chinese, on their way to Victoria's goldfields, had found an ingeniously simple way to avoid the £10-per-head poll tax charged by Victorian officials—they landed in South Australia and quietly made their way across the state line.

Sights

Robe is a peaceful and picturesque village with many historic buildings. The **National Trust Museum,** in the old Customs House (1863), will tell you of the town's early history. Hours are Tues.-Sat. 2-4 p.m. Admission is $1. For information, phone (087) 68-2419.

From **Beacon Hill,** you can get a great view of Robe, Guichen Bay, and the Southern Ocean. Or look out from the **obelisk,** right or left, to shimmering expanses of coastline.

Little Dip Conservation Park, four km south of Robe, comprises sand dunes, coastal strips, and salt lakes, through which waterbirds and wildlife roam, as can you—along the bushwalking tracks, that is. Rangers lead guided walks during the summer months.

Long Beach, a 17-km stretch of calm white sand along Guichen Bay, is noted for excellent swimming and windsurfing (the National Championships were held here in 1989). In the summer, you can drive along the beach and discover your own nook and cranny. Guichen Bay is also popular for sailing.

Anglers can get a bite just about anywhere. Crayfish lovers should visit Oct.-April, when the fleet brings in a fresh catch each day.

Events

The Sunday before 1 October is the annual **Blessing of the Fleet.** Afterwards, local fishermen invite tourists to join them for a jaunt around the bay.

Accommodations

You'll find all kinds of atmosphere-y accommodations in and around Robe. **Bushland Cabins,** Nora Criena Rd. (tel. 087-68-2386), has moderately priced units with kitchen facilities. The **Caledonian Inn,** Victoria St. (tel. 087-68-2029), built in 1858, offers newer cottages (moderate) and inexpensive rooms in the restored original section. **Flinders Rest Cottages,** Powell Ave. (tel. 087-25-2086), in the Long Beach area, rents fully equipped two-bedroom cottages with open fires; also moderately priced.

Or, choose from three caravan parks in the area. **Lakeside Select Caravan Park,** Main Rd. (tel. 087-68-2193), is on a safe swimming lake. **Long Beach Tourist Park,** the Esplanade (tel. 087-68-2237), is just 200 meters from the Long Beach water sporting area. **Sea-Vu Caravan Park,** Squire Dr. (tel. 087-68-2273), is near beaches and attractions. All have campsites, on-site vans, and cabins.

Information

Robe Historical Interpretation Centre, in the library building on Mundy Terrace (tel. 087-68-2465), can provide additional tourist information. Hours are Tues.-Fri. 10 a.m.-5 p.m., Saturday 8:30 a.m.-12:30 p.m.

BEACHPORT

Beachport (pop. 410) is another seaside lobster, crayfish, and one-time hustle-bustle port. Set at the northern edge of Rivoli Bay, this former whaling station, established by the Henty brothers in the 1830s, became a township in 1878, the same year a Beachport-Mt. Gambier railway line was built, instantly turning the town into a train-trip-away holiday resort. And, though the trains no longer run, Beachport is still a desirable destination for family excursions.

Sights

If you're coming from Robe, follow the detour to impressive **Woakwine Cutting,** a drainage project constructed by one farmer and his helper in less than three years. You can *ooh* and *aah* from the specially built viewing platform.

See fishing, farming, and whaling displays, as well as local relics, at the **National Trust Museum,** inside the old wool and grain store on Railway Terrace. Hours are Sunday 2-4 p.m. Admission is $2. For information, phone (087) 35-8013.

Bowman's Scenic Drive, from Foster St. to Wooleys Rocks, takes in terrific views of the town and Lake George on one side, the ocean on the other. You'll find lookout points at Backlers Lookout and Salmon Hole.

If you've got a 4WD vehicle you can drive past Wooleys Rocks, along sand dunes, and into **Beachport Conservation Park;** otherwise access is from Railway Terrace North. The park includes tracks through sand dunes and coastal vegetation, and around Wooleys Lake. The eight km drift, accessible only by four-wheelers or two feet, offers safe sailing and windsurfing.

Swimmers will do well around the jetty, scuba divers enjoy the **Back Beach** reef areas, and surfers like a spot known as the **Blowhole**. The **Pool of Siloam,** a very salty (six times more than the sea) lake near Beachport, is thought to be therapeutic.

Accommodations
Beachport Hotel (tel. 087-35-8003) and **Bompas Hotel** (tel. 087-35-8333), both on Railway Terrace, have inexpensive pub accommodations. **Beachport Motor Inn,** Railway Terrace (tel. 087-35-8070), is in the moderate range. Try the Beachport **YHA Hostel,** Beach Rd. (tel. 087-35-8197), for dorm beds at $8 per night.

Beachport Caravan Park, Beach Rd. (tel. 087-35-8128), with cabins and on-site vans, is situated on the foreshore with a jetty. **Southern Ocean Tourist Park,** Somerville St. (tel. 087-35-8153), is close to the beach. It has open fireplaces, cabins, and campsites. This park is also the local tourist information center.

MILLICENT

Bordered on the north and southeast by thick, fragrant pine forests, Millicent (pop. 5,075) is big timber country. From Kingston to Millicent, coastal travel is along Alternate Highway 1; it reconnects with the main highway here.

This mini-city, begun in 1870 as a rural community, shifted to a timber center after pines were cultivated in nearby ranges. Sawmills and paper mills soon moved in, and were followed by a steady stream of workers (including a large European population).

Sights
Millicent Museum, 1 Mt. Gambier Rd. (tel. 087-33-3205), is one of the region's most extensive facilities, with natural history and Aboriginal displays, restored horse-drawn vehicles, farm implements, tools, machinery, and a coin-operated waterwheel. The museum also houses **Admella Gallery,** which exhibits and sells local arts and crafts, and which also serves as the tourist information office. Hours are Mon.-Sat. 10 a.m.-4 p.m., Sunday 1-4 p.m. Museum admission is $2.50.

Tantanoola Caves, on Princes Hwy., 21 km from Millicent, are inside a dolomite marine cliff beside the highway. Take one of the hourly guided tours of the single chamber ($4), or sign up for a "wild cave tour" that explores the underground system (by appointment). At the nearby town of Tantanoola, you can view the stuffed carcass of *the* Tantanoola tiger, at—where else?—the **Tantanoola Tiger Hotel.** Load up on brew to go along with all the bull you'll hear about this legendary beast.

If you'd rather climb than cave, coastal **Canunda National Park,** beginning at Southend, 27 km west of Millicent, has a system of huge, wondrous sand dunes for you to sink your feet into. You can also camp here and, in the summer, take informative ranger-guided walks.

Accommodations
Sportsmans Hotel, 72 George St. (tel. 087-33-2017), has inexpensive rooms, but the facilities are shared. Other motels, all in the inexpensive to low-moderate range, are **Diplomat Motel,** 51 Mt. Gambier Rd. (tel. 087-33-2211), **Millicent Motel,** 82 Mt. Gambier Rd. (tel. 087-33-2655), and **Somerset Hotel Motel,** 2 George St. (tel. 087-33-2888).

Hillview Caravan Park, Dalton St. (tel. 087-33-2806), with campsites and cabins, is less than two km from the town center. **Millicent Lakeside Caravan Park,** Park Terrace (tel. 087-33-3947), also has on-site vans and is adjacent to a swimming lake.

Information
Millicent Tourist Information Centre is at the Millicent Museum. For information on Canunda National Park, contact the **Department of Environment and Natural Resources** at Southend (tel. 087-35-6053). To sign up for cave walks at **Tantanoola Caves Conservation Park,** phone the park office at (087) 34-4153.

MOUNT GAMBIER

The volcano has been extinct for 5,000 years, but the city of Mt. Gambier (pop. 20,815), built upon the volcano's slopes and situated about halfway between Adelaide and Melbourne, is a busy commercial center, regarded as the capital of the southeast. The city's big attractions are the many crater lakes. Of these, mysterious

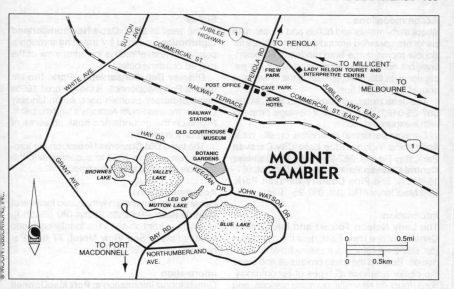

Blue Lake is the largest, with a circumference of five kilometers. It's so famous that Mt. Gambier is often called the "Blue Lake City." The lake, which is actually gray, mysteriously changes, almost overnight, into an extraordinary blue each and every November, staying that color until late March when it gradually reverts to gray. Long believed to be "bottomless," recently echo-sounding equipment dispelled that myth by measuring an 80-meter maximum depth. Blue Lake also supplies Mt. Gambier with its domestic water.

In 1800, Lieutenant James Grant, in the HMS *Lady Nelson,* was sailing along the coast when he sighted two peaks. He named them Mt. Schank (after Admiral Schank, who had invented the *Lady Nelson*'s centerboard keel) and Mt. Gambier (for Lord Gambier of the Royal Navy). Mount Gambier developed as an agricultural township in 1841, when Stephen Henty and his companions, enticed by the rich volcanic soil and appreciable annual rainfalls, built their cottages between Valley and Brownes Lakes and brought their stock to graze on the fertile farmlands. Though agriculture is still important, now the city's major source of employment is the forest industry and the area's six large sawmills.

Sights

Besides Blue Lake, Mt. Gambier's other unique feature is **Cave Park,** an open cave in the city center, surrounded by lovely rose gardens. In complete defiance of Mt. Gambier's southern latitude, two banana trees rise from the cave and stretch toward the light. Other caves are **Umpherston Cave,** with terraced gardens and picnic grounds, and water-filled **Engelbrecht Cave,** a popular diving spot. Other diving locations are **Little Blue Lake, Ewens Ponds, Picaninnie Ponds, Three Sisters,** and **Hell Hole.**

Historic buildings near Cave Park are the **post office, town hall,** and **Jens Hotel. Old Courthouse Museum,** Bay Rd., operated by the National Trust, displays the original courthouse furnishings and other local historic items. Hours are Mon.-Fri. noon-4 p.m., Sat.-Sun. 10 a.m.-4 p.m. Admission is $2.50. For information, phone (087) 24-1730.

Lewis' Museum, Pick Ave. (across from the showgrounds), is jam-packed with more than 30,000 Aboriginal, mechanical, industrial, and historical artifacts. Hours are daily 8 a.m.-4 p.m. Admission is $4. For information, phone (087) 25-1381.

Accommodations

About thirty motels and hotels and six caravan parks are sprawled around the town. Prices for double rooms range from moderate to expensive, but none of the accommodations are exceptional. In this town, a room at the cheap end should do you just fine.

The **Jens Hotel,** 40 Commercial St. East (tel. 087-25-0188), is a beautiful heritage property with inexpensive rooms.

Caravan parks with campsites, on-site vans, and cabins, include: **Blue Lake City Caravan Park,** Bay Rd. (tel. 087-25-9856); **Mt. Gambier Central Caravan Park,** 6 Krummel St. (tel. 087-15-4427); and **Pine Country Caravan Park,** Port MacDonnell Rd. (tel. 087-25-1988).

Information

The **Lady Nelson Tourist and Interpretive Centre,** Jubilee Hwy. East, near the city center (tel. 087-24-1730), is a treasure trove of information. Besides the usual brochures and such, the center arranges all types of accommodations, tours (to sawmills, pumping stations, and dairies), and provides everything you want to know about the lakes area (including issuing diving permits). It will even prepare a customized itinerary. While there, you can view a full-size replica of HMS *Lady Nelson,* hear Lieutenant Grant (another replica, and *no* competition for Madame Tussaud!) give his spiel, and watch the volcano erupt in a blaze of neon! The center is open daily 9 a.m.-5 p.m., closed Christmas Day.

For emergencies, contact **police** (tel. 087-25-9333), **Mt. Gambier Hospital** (tel. 087-24-2211), and, for road mishaps or info, the **Royal Automobile Association** (tel. 087-25-4101).

PORT MacDONNELL

South Australia's southernmost port and crayfish center is Port MacDonnell, 28 km south of Mt. Gambier. Once a bustling shipping center for freight being hauled between Adelaide and Melbourne, Port MacDonnell (pop. 650) these days is a quaint fishing village. On the way to Port MacDonnell, climb Mount Schank. Follow walking tracks both inside and outside the crater or just sit back and check out the grandiose view.

Sights

To the west of town, **Cape Northumberland Lighthouse,** reached by traveling through a petrified forest, affords a towering view of the rugged coastline below.

Dingley Dell Conservation Park, two km west of Port MacDonnell, is the restored 1860s home of horsey Scottish poet, Adam Lindsay Gordon (he was South Australia's big-time bard). Picnic on the grounds and soak up some of Gordon's inspiration.

The large **Old Customs House,** on the foreshore, was built in 1860 to accommodate the sizeable freight loads of the time.

Accommodations

Get an inexpensive room with shared facilities at **Victoria Hotel,** 40 Meylin St. (tel. 087-38-2213), or anything from on-site vans to fully equipped holiday flats at **Sea View Motel,** 77 Sea Parade (tel. 087-38-2243).

Information

Gather tourist information at **Port MacDonnell District Council,** Charles St. (tel. 087-38-2437).

For emergencies, phone the **police** (tel. 087-38-2216) or the **Royal Automobile Association** (tel. 087-38-2238).

PENOLA

North of Mt. Gambier, venture through the pine-forested communities of Tarpeena and Nangwarry to this tiny heritage town noted for its beautiful buildings and churches. Penola is also the gateway to the southeastern wine region.

Sights

Many 1850s cottages, built by the town's first settlers, still stand today. The **Penola Heritage Walk,** which departs from the tourist information center, takes in nearly 30 historic sites around Penola. **Petticoat Lane,** a sort of open-air museum of Penola's early architecture, features a number of traditional buildings, including the former Anglican rectory. Arts and crafts hounds will find galleries and gift shops inside many of the historic sites.

John Riddoch Interpretive Centre, Arthur St., in the former Penola Library and Mechanics

Institute, pays tribute to the town's heritage and its most prominent citizens (including John Riddoch). Hours are daily 10 a.m.-4 p.m. For information, phone (087) 37-2855.

Yallum Park, Old Millicent Rd., Riddoch's personal mansion, built in 1880, depicts the grand style of the upper crust. Hours are by appointment. Admission is $3. For information, phone (087) 37-2435.

Penola Conservation Park, 10 km west of town, features a signposted interpretive trail into this swampy wildlife sanctuary.

Accommodations
Haywards Royal Oak Hotel, 31 Church St. (tel. 087-37-2322), offers inexpensive pub rooms with shared facilities. Book a variety of heritage accommodations, at moderate-expensive prices, through **Australian Country Cottages,** 33 Riddoch St. (tel. 087-37-2250).

Information
Penola Tourist Information Centre, inside the John Riddoch Interpretive Centre, provides maps for scenic drives and heritage walks, and other local information. Hours are daily 10 a.m.-4 p.m., closed Christmas Day and Good Friday.

In emergencies, contact the **police** (tel. 087-37-2315), **hospital** (tel. 087-37-2311), and **Royal Automobile Association** (tel. 087-37-2367).

COONAWARRA

It was John Riddoch, Penola mogul, who liked the looks of the grape vines in his Coonawarra Fruit Colony and, subsequently, established the district's first winery. Though the vines of Riddoch's winery, built in 1893, thrived, demand was low. It wasn't until the 1960s that the industry really took off. Today, about 15 wineries in the district, which runs for 16 km north of Penola, are famous for the bold reds produced from the rich *terra rossa* soil.

Accommodations
Coonawarra offers nothing in the inexpensive category. The most moderately priced cottage accommodations are **Skinner, Redman,** and

The Pickers Hut (tel. 087-36-3304 or 36-3220, for all three).

Chardonnay Lodge, Penola Rd. (tel. 087-36-3309), is an expensive luxury motel with an art gallery, swimming pool, good restaurant, and complimentary continental breakfast.

Information
For tourist info, see the Penola Tourist Information Centre, above.

NARACOORTE

Proclaimed a town in 1870 (though the first hotel and store were erected in the 1840s), Naracoorte (pop. 4,640) functions mainly as a regional service and commercial center, with lovely old dwellings scattered all about.

Sights
The **Sheeps Back Museum** (tel. 087-62-1518), in the old flour mill on MacDonnell St. and run by the National Trust, traces the history of the wool industry. Hours are daily 10 a.m.-4 p.m. Admission is $2.

More interesting is the **Naracoorte Museum and Snake Pit,** Smith St. (tel. 087-62-2059), where more than 100 collections of gemstones, clocks, weapons, butterflies, and other artifacts commingle with venomous snakes and other reptiles lounging about rocks and cacti. Hours are Mon.-Thurs. 10 a.m.-5 p.m., Sat.-Sun. 2-5 p.m., closed mid-July through August and on Christmas Day. Admission is $5.

Take a look at **Padthaway Estate,** about 41 km north of Naracoorte, a gracious country mansion built in 1882. **Padthaway Conservation Park** boasts stringy bark and red gum forests where you can bushwalk or picnic.

Naracoorte Caves Conservation Park, 12 km southeast of town, features about 69 caves along a 25-km expanse of range. Daily tours explore Alexandra, Blanche, and Victoria Fossil caves, and during holiday periods, you can sign up for special wild-caving tours into undeveloped areas (be prepared to climb and crawl). For information and tour bookings, phone (087) 62-2340.

Bool Lagoon, a bit farther south, is a vast and diverse wetland where you can see about

75 species of birds and other wildlife. Self-guided and organized walking tracks are available. A bird blind and boardwalks, built over the lagoon, allow for excellent birdwatching. For information, phone (087) 64-7541.

Mary Seymour Conservation Park, near Bool Lagoon, is another sanctuary for breeding birds.

Accommodations
Naracoorte Hotel Motel, 73 Ormerod St. (tel. 087-62-2400), has inexpensive rooms with shared facilities in the older hotel; or, for $20 more, you can stay in the updated motel section. **Country Roads Motor Inn,** 28 Smith St. (tel. 087-62-3900), is more posh, with rooms in the moderate range. Big splurgers can spring for elegant accommodations at the historic **Padthaway Estate** (tel. 987-65-5039), where doubles run about $130, including breakfast.

Naracoorte Caravan Park, 81 Park Terrace (tel. 087-62-2128), is close to the town center and has campsites, on-site vans, and cabins. Camping is permitted at both **Naracoorte Caves** (tel. 087-62-2340) and **Bool Lagoon** (tel. 087-64-7541).

Information
The **tourist information office** is at Sheeps Back Museum. In an emergency, call **police** (tel. 087-62-2066), the **hospital** (tel. 087-62-2222), or the trusty **Royal Automobile Association** (tel. 087-62-2247).

BORDERTOWN

Situated 42 km northeast of Padthaway, along the Dukes Highway, Bordertown (pop. 2,320) isn't on but is near the Victorian border, 20 km away. Settled in 1852, along the route of the gold escort from Victoria to Adelaide, the area's rich farmlands produce wine grapes, small seeds, cereals, wool, meat, and vegetable crops. Also the former Australian Prime Minister Bob Hawke spent his early childhood here. His home has been renovated, and his bust has been bronzed.

Adjacent to Dukes Highway, **Bordertown Wildlife Park** is home to, besides the usual native birds and animals, four specially bred pure white kangaroos.

Accommodations
Several good motels with inexpensive to low-moderate prices line Dukes Highway. **Bordertown Caravan Park,** Penny Terrace (tel. 087-52-1752), near the town center, is another place to rest your head.

Events
The annual **Camel Racing Festival,** held each November, features camel and donkey races, parachute jumping, various other antics, and camels from every state and territory in Australia.

Information
For tourist information, contact **Bordertown Council Office,** 43 Woolshed St. (tel. 087-52-1044). For emergency assistance, contact **police** (tel. 087-52-1355), the **hospital** (tel. 087-52-1166), or the **Royal Automobile Association** (tel. 087-52-1270).

KEITH

Keith (pop. 1,190), 46 km northwest of Bordertown, was proclaimed a township in 1889. At one time the region was part of a 90-mile desert, but after zinc and copper were added to the soil, it became profitable grazing and farm land. Most of the old buildings sit along Heritage St., facing the Dukes Highway.

Sights
Peek into the foyer of the **Congregational Church,** on Heritage Street. The 1910 building features four interesting stained-glass windows, made by locals, depicting the pioneering era. Hours are daily 9 a.m.-5 p.m.

Mount Monster Conservation Park, 10 km south of Keith, has spectacular views from the lookout (a signposted walk will guide you) and a variety of vegetation, birds, and wildlife. Mount Monster, and others in a chain of granite outcrops, were islands about 40 million years ago.

Ngarkat Conservation Park, northeast of Keith, is perfect for bushwalks. The 5,000-hectare park is full of native animals and abundant in flora. **Warning:** there are a large number of beehives in this park.

Situated in the southwest corner 20 km north of Keith, **Mount Rescue Conservation Park** has 28,385 hectares of sand plains and dunes containing rare species of birds and plants.

Accommodations
Keith's only **hotel/motel** and **motor inn** both charge about $50 for a double. **Keith Caravan Park,** Naracoorte Rd. (tel. 087- 55-1957), has campsites and on-site vans.

Information
The **tourist information center** is inside the old Congregational Church, on Heritage Street. Hours are daily 9 a.m.-5 p.m. For information, phone (087) 55-1584.

In emergencies, contact **police** (tel. 087-55-1211), the **hospital** (tel. 087-55-1757), or **Royal Automobile Association** (tel. 087-55-1331).

BACK TO TAILEM BEND

Heading back to Tailem Bend, you'll pass through more grazing land. Stop by **Tintara,** 38 km northwest of Keith, which has a nice old post office and homestead (10 km west of town on Woods Well Rd.).

Mount Boothby Conservation Park, 20 km northwest of Tintara, features 4,045 hectares of heath, mallee, pink gum forest, and granite outcrops, where you can picnic or stretch your legs, between farmland scenes.

Watch for **Coonalpyn,** the last dot on the map before Tailem Bend.

TRANSPORT

Kendell Airlines (tel. 069-22-0100, or book through Ansett) makes the 50-minute flight from Adelaide to Mt. Gambier, and on to Melbourne, several days a week. Fare is $150 one-way from either capital city to Mt. Gambier. The standby fare runs about $25 less. **O'Connor Airlines** (tel. 087-25-6666, or book through Qantas) makes daily flights from Mt. Gambier to either Adelaide or Melbourne.

Catch **Mt. Gambier Motor Services** (tel. 08-8296-0111) from Adelaide's central bus station to Kingston ($30), Robe ($27), Millicent ($34), or Mt. Gambier ($35), or travel **Greyhound Pioneer Australia** (tel. 08-8233-2797, or 13-2030 toll-free) along Princes Highway to Mt. Gambier ($42).

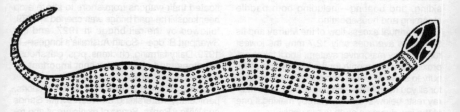

THE MURRAY RIVER

In these parts it's called the "Mighty Murray," and it conjures up all the romantic images a mighty river should—paddle steamers plying their trade, floating casinos and riverboat gamblers, dashing gents and bawdy women, a host of rascals, scoundrels, ne'er-do-wells, and free spirits, runaways aboard makeshift rafts, and secret trysts along the banks.

Beginning in the Snowy Mountains, traveling along the border between New South Wales and Victoria, the river gains momentum as it reaches South Australia, makes a sharp turn seaward at Northwest Bend, and eventually empties into Lake Alexandrina where its mighty mouth meets the great Southern Ocean. And, though the Murray has often been called the "Mississippi of Australia," and the flavor is much the same, this river—at 2,575 km from source to mouth—is less than half the length of its American counterpart.

Within South Australia's 640-km section, the Murray is divided into two districts—the Riverland and the Lower Murray. The Riverland includes the Murray's six locks, bountiful citrus groves, 17,000 hectares of vineyards, and the towns from Renmark to Blanchetown. This, in fact, is Australia's biggest wine-producing region (yes, *more* than the Barossa, Clare, and Coonawarra, and even the Hunter Valley, in New South Wales), noted for high-quality table wines and a variety of other products. The Lower Murray spans from below Blanchetown to Murray Bridge, where you'll encounter more orchards, large granite outcrops, waterfalls, lagoons, and phenomenal birdlife. Throughout the entire Murray area, you'll enjoy abundant sunshine with good fishing, swimming, waterskiing, and boating—including both paddle steaming and houseboating.

The annual excess flow of the Murray and its tributaries averages only 12.7 mm, the lowest runoff of any major river system, and it takes approximately one month for the Murray flow at Albury to arrive at South Australia. Furthermore—for all you riverphiles—the bed of the Lower Murray rests below sea level, thereby making it one of the few rivers on earth to run uphill!

History

In 1824, explorers Hume and Hovell were the first white men to sight the Murray. Six years later, Captain Charles Sturt steered a whale boat—while a group of soldiers and convicts rowed—some 2,735 km, from the Murrumbidgee and Murray Rivers to the sea and back again. Sturt named the river after Colonial Secretary Sir George Murray and, eventually, the Sturt Highway, which runs through the Riverland, was named for the brave captain himself.

Lady Augusta and *Mary Ann* were the first paddle steamers to navigate the river, making the journey in 1853, from Goolwa to Swan Hill in Victoria. Until the railway lines were built, river life was a-bustle, with trade being carted to and fro and river towns popping up along the banks (and with them a few rabble-rousers and river rats).

Then, in 1887, up in the Riverland, a fellow named Alfred Deakin, who'd been keeping tabs on irrigation in the California deserts, persuaded Canadians George and William Chaffey (experts in the field) to come to Renmark and set up Australia's first irrigation settlement. This project's success led to the high-grade citrus crops and wines produced in the region today.

MURRAY BRIDGE

Situated approximately 80 km from Adelaide, Murray Bridge (pop. 16,250) is the state's largest river town. This city should really be called Murray *Bridges*, since three of them cross the river here. Originally named "Edwards Crossing," the calm waters made this a favored spot for early settlers crossing the river—though at first they floated their wagons from shore to shore atop beer kegs! The road bridge was opened in 1879, followed by the rail bridge in 1927, and the Swanport Bridge—South Australia's longest—in 1979. Dairy farming, chickens, pigs, glasshouse tomatoes, and cereal represent important industries in this region.

Murray Bridge is an ideal spot for water sports, particularly waterskiing between White Sands and Willow Banks. Scads of picnic areas and re-

THE MURRAY RIVER

serves dot the riverfront, affording kick-back-and-relax opportunities for the road-weary. Or catch the Murray spirit and jump aboard the stern-wheeler *Proud Mary* for two- to five-day jaunts.

Sights

Re-live local history and heritage at **Captain's Cottage Museum,** Thomas St. (tel. 085-31-0049). Displays of engines, machinery, dolls, model riverboats, and photos, should enlighten you. Hours are Sat.-Sun. and public holidays 10 a.m.-4 p.m. Admission is $2.

Puzzle Park, Jervois Rd. (tel. 085-32-3709), is a fun park with an aquarium, miniature golf

course, and a 4.5-km maze in which to lose yourself (or perhaps an irritating travel companion). Hours are daily 10 a.m.-5:30 p.m., closed Christmas Day. Admission is $9.

Butterfly House, next door (tel. 085-32-3666), is the state's only place to prance with live tropical species. Hours are daily 10 a.m.-5 p.m. Admission is $4.

Accommodations and Food

If you're staying the night, the bare-bones **Balcony Private Hotel,** 12 Sixth Ave. (tel. 085-32-3830), is inexpensive and includes breakfast. Also inexpensive, **Motel Greenacres,** Princes

RULES FOR THE MURRAYLANDS

As part of a "Don't Muck up the Murray" campaign, aimed at preserving the river environment, the South Australia Department of Environment and Planning asks that visitors adhere to the following rules:

Protect Water Supplies
Do not bury excrement within 50 meters of the Murray.

Do not use pollutants, like soap, anywhere near the water.

Do not wash plates or utensils within 50 meters of the river.

Camp away from the river bank. Avoid blocking the access of stock or wildlife to the water; they need their water to live.

Respect Farmers, Their Property, and Stock
Leave machinery alone. Windmills, pumps, tractors, and generators are important for a farm's survival. Your interference could cause costly or ruinous breakdowns.

Do not frighten or disturb stock. Farm animals are valuable and easily disturbed, and some can injure you. They could be lambing or calving, so

give them a go and keep right away.

Camp away from windmills and pumps and don't interfere with farm water supplies, except in an emergency.

Report vandalism. If you see any acts of vandalism, notify the landowner.

Respect and Keep To Roads and Tracks
Fences, gates, roads, and tracks represent important investments to farmers and property owners, so while you're a guest on their land, be considerate of your responsibilities.

Leave gates as you found them.

Avoid damaging fences; use gates and stiles where they are provided.

Keep to existing roads and tracks and do not widen them.

Contact the landowner if you propose to drive off a track or travel across his property.

Avoid vehicle travel when roads are wet.

If you see persons violating or polluting the river, you are asked to phone **River Watch,** the Murray's 24-hour watchdog, at (085) 82-2700.

Hwy. East (tel. 085-32-1090), is a family-owned establishment five km southeast of the city center. Some rooms have kitchenettes.

Oval Caravan Park, 4 LeMessurier St. (tel. 085-32-2588), near the river, has cabins and on-site vans. **Avoca Dell Caravan Park,** Loddon Rd. (tel. 085-32-2095), on the Murray, has cabins and on-site vans, too, but also campsites.

Many **houseboats** are available for weekly rentals; inquire at the tourist information center.

Pick up natural foods, vitamins, herbal teas, and grains at **Murray Bridge Health Foods,** corner of Seventh and Fourth Streets. (tel. 085-32-4383). You can get handmade pickled preserves at **Cottage Harvest,** Rock Gully Rd. (tel. 085-31-1165), and handmade chocolates at **Cottage Box Chocolates,** Wharf Rd. (tel. 085-32-5055). Both are open daily 10 a.m.-5 p.m.

Information
The **tourist information center** is on Swanport Rd., between South and Mary Terraces (tel. 085-32-6660). Hours are Mon.-Fri. 8:30 a.m.-4 p.m., Saturday 10 a.m.-3:30 p.m., Sunday and public holidays 10 a.m.-2 p.m., closed Christmas Day.

For emergencies, contact the **police** (tel. 085-32-1888), **fire brigade** (tel. 085-32-1000), or **ambulance** (tel. 32-1122). The local branch of the **Royal Automobile Association** is on Railway Terrace (tel. 085-32-1935), and the **hospital** (tel. 085-32-1333) is at the corner of Swanport Rd. and Monash Terrace.

Transport
A local bus service operates Mon.-Saturday. For information, phone **Murray Bridge Passenger Service** (tel. 085-32-2633). There's a **taxi** stand off Bridge Street.

MANNUM

On your way to Mannum, stop at Mypolonga, eight km north of Murray Bridge on Mannum Road. It's a small farming community comprising both highlands and swamplands. Noted for its well-irrigated orange, apricot, peach, and pear orchards, Mypolonga is another water sport and houseboat haven.

Mannum (pop. 2,000), a wide spot in the river 21 km north of Murray Bridge, is the birthplace of Australia's paddle steamers. In 1853, Captain W.R. Randell (who had settled in the district some 10 years earlier) constructed *Mary Ann,* the first steamboat, and the following year sailed it up to Swan Hill in Victoria. In 1854, the busy captain also built Mannum's first house, which, over time, was bought, sold, and transformed into the Mannum Hotel. Subsequent to the *Mary Ann*'s inaugural voyage, Mannum became a busy shipbuilding center. Today Mannum is a peaceful community, known for its scenic beauty, rich heritage, and water activities, as well as its designation as new home port for the *Murray Princess.*

Sights
Recreation Reserve (called the "Rec" by locals) lines the banks of the Murray with 350 meters of grassy picnic and barbecue areas, a boat ramp, and scenic lookouts to town, river, and valley.

The National Trust operates **Mannum Museum** (tel. 085-69-1303) inside the restored 1896 paddle steamer *Marion.* Moored at Randell's original wharf at Arnold Park, the floating museum contains river relics and other memorabilia. The museum is open daily 9 a.m.-4 p.m., closed Christmas Day. Admission is $2.50.

The **Bird Sanctuary,** on Halidon Rd., is home to ducks, swans, pelicans, and other beautiful water birds. Have a look.

Mannum Waterfalls Reserve, 20 km south of town, offers picnic spots and walking tracks, but if you want to see the falls be aware that they flow mainly in the winter.

Accommodations and Food
Stay at Captain Randell's inexpensive homestead-turned-**Mannum Hotel,** 15 Randell St.

(tel. 085-69-1008), with shared facilities. **Leonaville,** 69 River Lane (tel. 085-69-2073), offers inexpensive bed and breakfast accommodations in an 1883 homestead. **Mannum Motel,** 76 Cliff St. (085-69-1808), is the expensive choice for standard motel amenities.

Mannum Caravan Park, Purnong Rd. (tel. 085-69-1402), adjacent to the Bird Sanctuary, has campsites and cabins.

Stroll over to **Kia Marina,** on Younghusband Rd., to check out weekly deals on the many **houseboats** for rent. (P.S. "Younghusband," in a piece of tourist lit, was misprinted "Hunghusband." A boat, perhaps, docked at the Freudian slip.) Anyway, young and/or hung, the boats are over at the marina.

Riverfront Coffee Spot, 67 Randell St. (tel. 085-69-1711), is open daily for cappuccino, croissants, cakes, and light meals.

THE MID MURRAYLANDS

The Mid Murraylands comprise the area from Bow Hill in the south (32 km from Mannum) to Swan Reach in the north, from Nildottie in the east to Sedan in the west. Just a 90-minute drive from Adelaide, this district offers lovely scenery and not-so-touristy river action where you can fish and boat in peace or just sit on the banks and float twigs downstream.

There's a stunning **scenic drive** along Younghusband Rd., on the way to Purnong, that takes in lagoons, lakes, stone quarries, and stupendous bird life. **Bow Hill,** before Purnong, is a popular waterskiing spot. **Purnong** is a slow-going holiday village but a barrage of river craft float past just the same. Great views can be enjoyed at **Caurnamont Landing,** a base for houseboat rentals. **Walker Flat,** sheltered by tall cliffs, is another location sought out by both waterskiers and water birds. Small, rural **Nildottie,** once an old paddle steamer landing, now bears citrus fruit and vegetable crops. **Big Bend** boasts big river red gums and sandstone cliffs that draw vast numbers of cockatoos to nest.

Surveyed in 1839, **Swan Reach** (pop. 200) is the Mid Murraylands' largest town and halfway point between the Barossa Valley and the Riverland. It's another holiday and water sport mecca. **Punuelroo,** seven km south, is a long-time holiday hot spot, and *not* the place to hit if you want peace and quiet. **Ridley Conservation Park,** five km south of Swan Reach, is where you might glimpse hairy-nosed wombats and the rare striped honeyeater bird. **Swan Reach Conservation Park,** 11 km northwest of Swan Reach, is 1,900 hectares of grasslands, thick mallee, false sandalwood, open woodland, and roaming wildlife, including emus and western gray kangaroos.

Sedan, about 16 km west from Swan Reach Conservation Park, provides facilities for the surrounding farm community. Established in the late 1890s, the town has preserved many of its old buildings. From Sedan, you can take a number of scenic drives. Best is the route that winds from Cambrai through the Marne River Valley—taking in huge river red gums, a granite quarry, a pinnacle of fossils, and a myriad of wildlife—then swings north to Ridley Conservation Park and back to Swan Reach.

Accommodations

Pub-style rooms are inexpensive at **Swan Reach Hotel** (tel. 085-70-2003). **Yookamurra Sanctuary,** Pipeline Rd. (tel. 085-62-5011), offers moderately priced bunkhouse accommodations within its delicate woodlands. All meals are included in the rates.

Punyelroo Caravan Park, on the riverbanks (tel. 085-70-2021), has campsites and on-site vans.

BLANCHETOWN

This popular holiday resort—which begins the Riverland—sits 28 km north of Swan Reach and 134 km northeast of Adelaide, along the Sturt Highway. Governor R.G. MacDonnell named this town for his wife, Lady Blanche. There were high hopes for Blanchetown, begun in 1855 as an important commercial center and established as a port in 1863, but they fizzled after northerly neighbor Morgan won the much-sought-after railway line. In 1922, construction began here on the complex system of locks and weirs created to control fluctuations of the river's water level. If you stand atop Blanchetown Bridge, you might see a houseboat passing through Lock Number One.

Sights

Brookfield Conservation Park, 11 km west of Blanchetown, features 6,332 hectares of open scrub mallee, mallee box, and yorrell, through which wander red kangaroos, hairy-nosed wombats, fat-tailed dunnarts, and a variety of birds. Don't veer off marked walking trails without checking with the ranger station (three km inside the entrance); some areas are closed due to scientific research on the hairy-nosed wombat.

Trenetas, Old Ferry Landing (tel. 085-40-5071), a floating sand gallery overlooking the river, exhibits and sells arts and crafts with a sand motif, and also houses a coffeeshop. Hours are Tues.-Sat. and public holidays 10 a.m.-8 p.m.

Accommodations

Riverside Caravan and Camping Park (tel. 085-40-5070) is a quiet riverfront park with a beach, offering campsites, on-site vans, cabins, and canoe-hire.

For **houseboats,** inquire at **Blanchetown** or **Kayandee Moorings.**

Information

In an emergency, contact the **police** (tel. 085-40-5013), **ambulance** (tel. 085-41-2444), or local **Royal Automobile Club** (tel. 085-41-2600).

MORGAN

At one time Morgan (pop. 1,265) was South Australia's second busiest port (Port Adelaide ranked first). Originally known as "Northwest Bend," "Great Bend," and the "Great Elbow" (this is where the Murray makes its sharp turn), Morgan was officially named for Sir William Morgan by Governor Musgrave in 1878, the same year a railway line was opened. In the good old days Morgan used to have a veritable traffic jam of steamers and barges unloading cargo, which was then transferred by rail to Port Adelaide.

Sights

Reminders of the town's formidable history include the huge wharf, built in 1878, and the heritage buildings along Railway Terrace. **Port of Morgan Historic Museum,** on Railway Terrace, displays original river charts and trading-days artifacts. The 1940s **Pumping Station and Walter Filtration Plant**, on Renmark Rd., can be toured on Tuesday 1-3 p.m.

Cross the river by ferry to **White Dam Conservation Park**, in the northwest bend, to view water birds in the wetlands or picnic under towering red gums.

Accommodations

Both the **Commercial Hotel** (tel. 085-40-2107) and **Terminus Hotel Motel** (tel. 085-40-2006), on historic Railway Terrace, have simple inexpensive accommodations. **Morgan Riverside Caravan Park** (tel. 085-40-2207) has on-site vans and cabins, with air-conditioning and telly.

Look for **houseboat rentals** along the riverfront.

WAIKERIE

Waikerie (pop. 1,700), reached from Blanchetown along the Sturt Highway, or from Morgan (passing Lock Number Two), is the "citrus center of Australia." Founded in 1880 by the Shepherd Brothers, the name "Waikerie" is a derivative of an Aboriginal word meaning "many wings or birds," no doubt because of the abundant colorful birds (and, nowadays, the gliders) hanging around the district's lagoons and riverbanks.

Mild sunny winters and hot temperate summers, combined with modern irrigation, have turned this former desert into a citrus-fruit oasis of more than one million bountiful trees, planted on over 5,000 acres (try to visit in Sept.-Oct. when they're in bloom).

Sights

In the center of town is **Waikerie Producers Packing House**, the largest of its kind in Australia. You can arrange for a tour there or at the nearby **Cresta Fruit Juice Factory**, on Virgo Rd. in Cresta.

Pooginook Conservation Park, 12 km northeast of Waikerie, is home to a variety of animal and bird life, in environs ranging from open to dense mallee. **Terrigal Fauna Park** (tel. 085-41-3414) and **Waikerie Fauna Park** (tel. 085-41-2077) also afford peeks at local critters. Or, catch your view from atop **Clifftop**

Lookout, a short walk from the town center, along Goodchild Street.

Accommodations and Food

The centrally located **Waikerie Hotel Motel**, McCoy St. (tel. 085-41-2999), has inexpensive to low-moderate rates, depending on which section you stay in. The restaurant offers both counter meals and a la carte dining. Air-conditioned on-site vans and cabins are available at **Waikerie Caravan Park**, Ramco Rd. (tel. 085-41-2651).

Purchase local citrus, dried, and glacé fruits, honey, juices, and nonalcoholic wines at **The Orange Tree**, on Sturt Hwy. (tel. 085-41-2332). A viewing platform looks out over the river and town. Hours are daily 9 a.m.-5 p.m.

Sports and Recreation

Waikerie, sight of the 1974 World Gliding Championships, is the perfect place to soar and spiral the skies. **Waikerie Gliding Club** (tel. 085-41-2644) offers glider joy flights, as well as instruction.

Information

The **tourist information center**, 20 McCoy St. (tel. 085-41-2183), can help with juice-queries and other needs. Hours are Mon.-Fri. 8:30 a.m.-5:30 p.m., Saturday 8:30-11:30 a.m., closed public holidays.

In emergencies call the **police** (tel. 085-41-2888) or an **ambulance** (tel. 085-41-2444). For road service, phone the **Royal Automobile Association** (tel. 085-41-2900).

BARMERA

Traveling 48 km east of Waikerie, past rural Kingston-on-Murray and the bird refuge at Wachtel Lagoon (part of the Moorook Game Reserve), the Sturt Highway enters Barmera (pop. 1,900), dubbed the Murray's "aquatic playground." Set on the shores of freshwater Lake Bonney, this town draws like flies those who take to the water like fish. Joseph Hawdon discovered the lake while hauling stock overland from New South Wales to Adelaide and named it after his pal Charles Bonney, who was with him. Originally called Barmera by local Aboriginals, the lake's title was transferred to the new township. Besides being a holiday resort, Barmera grows citrus and stone fruits, grapes, and vegetables.

Lake Bonney offers all types of water sports—swimming, fishing, windsurfing, yachting, waterskiing, and speed boating. (In 1964, Englishman Donald Campbell tried to break the world water speed record here.) Or you can picnic, barbecue, and laze around on one of the sandy beaches (Pelican Point, on the western shore, is a nude beach).

Sights

Built in 1859, the **Overland Corner Hotel Museum**, 19 km from Barmera on Morgan Road, was one of the Riverland's first stone buildings. This was where the weary overlanders and cattle drovers rested themselves and their bullock teams. Restored and run by the National Trust, the museum features pioneer exhibits and area artifacts. Hours are sporadic at the museum, but the pub sticks to its normal schedule. For information, phone (085) 88-7021.

Country-music fans can view memorabilia at **Rocky's Country Music Hall of Fame**, Monash Bypass Rd. (tel. 085-88-3035). Hours are daily 9-11 a.m. and 2-4 p.m. Admission is $2.

At **Cobdogla**, five km west of town, you can see the world's only operating Humphrey Pump and other historical displays at **Cobdogla Irrigation Museum**, Trussel Avenue. Admission is $4. For information, phone (085) 88-2289.

On the other side of Lake Bonney's Nappers Bridge, **Loch Luna Game Reserve**, set on 1,905 hectares, is another favorite fishing, canoeing, and waterfowl-breeding haunt. There's a picnic area at Lock Number Three, a few kilometers west of the reserve, where you can watch the action.

Accommodations

For lakeshore accommodations, **Lake Bonney Caravan Reserve** (tel. 085-88-2234) has everything from on-site vans to holiday flats, all at inexpensive prices. This is a huge family-oriented complex, complete with a gym, sauna, and squash courts. For more resortlike and expensive lodging, head to **Barmera Country Club**, Hawdon St. (tel. 085-88-2888), or **The Lake Resort**, Lakeside Dr. (tel. 085-88-2555).

Camping is permitted at the Pelican Point nude bathing beach, but there are no facilities. To reach the beach, go three km along Morgan Road, turn right onto Ireland Road.

Recreation and Events

Lake Bonney Aquatic Centre (tel. 085-88-2679) rents paddleboats, canoes, windsurfers, catamarans, and single and tandem bicycles. The center is open during school holidays, and weekends from Sept.-May.

Catch the **South Australian Country Music Awards**, each June on the Queen's birthday weekend, at the old Bonney Theatre.

Information

For tourist information, drop by **Barmera Travel Centre**, Barwell Ave. (tel. 085-88-2289). Hours are Mon.-Fri. 8:30 a.m.-5:30 p.m., Saturday 9-11:30 a.m., Sunday 9 a.m.-4:30 p.m., closed Good Friday.

For emergencies, contact **police** (tel. 085-88-2122), **fire brigade** (tel. 085-88-2000), **ambulance** (tel. 085-88-2501), or **Royal Automobile Association** (tel. 085-82-1644). **Barmera Hospital** (tel. 085-88-2006) is on Eyre Street.

BERRI

The name is certainly appropriate for this wine and citrus growing district; however, it does not stem from "berry," but from *"berri berri,"* Aboriginal for "wide bend in the river." Established about 1870 as a riverboat refueling stop, Berri (pop. 3,500) is *still* a refueling stop—for wines and juices. The town also sports the customary riverfront parks and water activities. Get your bearings at the lookout tower on Fiedler Street. And, if you're into bronco bulls, pay a visit on Easter Monday for the annual **Berri Rodeo.**

Sights

Berri Estates is reputedly the largest single winery-distillery in Australia—if not the entire Southern Hemisphere; anyway, it's big enough to produce annually seven million liters of premium varietals, bulk, cask, and fortified wines, as well as brandies. The winery is open for tastings Mon.-Fri. 9 a.m.-5:30 p.m., Saturday 9 a.m.-5 p.m. For information, phone (085) 83-2303.

RESPECT THE RIVER AND ALL OTHER USERS

The Department of Environment and Planning has issued the following warnings to Murray River users:

On the Murray it's important to have consideration for other river users, so please observe all boating and fishing regulations. This includes bag limits and closures, because these are in force to prevent the depletion of fish.

Before boating or swimming, check out the Murray. Get to know its waters. And watch out for snags.

When Swimming

Wear a buoyancy vest. It might look funny but it could save your life.

Don't even think about swimming the width of the Murray. With currents, snags, and power boats you might not make it.

Dive as shallowly as possible, especially if you're not certain of the depth. Steep dives have resulted in back or neck injuries.

Keep clear of busy boating areas. There's a chance the skippers might not see you.

When Boating

Carry all the required safety equipment on board.

Give a wide berth to other boats when overtaking.

Take care when turning and don't turn across the bow of another vessel.

Don't drink and drive. Swimming or driving a motorboat, when drunk, is setting a sure course for disaster. Alcohol, petrol, and water do not mix.

MARK MORRIS

When you're finished with the hard stuff, **Berrivale Orchards,** on McKay Rd., sells fruit juices, canned fruits, almonds, and gherkins, and presents a 10-minute video about the canning and juicing business. Hours are Mon.-Fri. 8:30 a.m.-4:30 p.m., Saturday 9 a.m.-noon, closed on major holidays. For information, phone (085) 82-1455.

Grant's Super Playground, in the nearby community of Monash, houses more than 180 amusements for kids of all ages. Equipment includes roller coasters, flying foxes, earthmovers, multiple slides, and rotary cones. The park is

always open and *free,* though donations are accepted.

The Riverland Big Orange, corner of Sturt Hwy. and the Monash bypass, is billed—in the spirit of Larry the Kingston Lobster—as the "largest (fake) orange in the world." You can pick up a bag of oranges and get your juices freshly squeezed. There's a small admission fee to the panoramic lookout. Hours are daily 9 a.m.-5 p.m. For information, phone (085) 82-2999.

Riverland Display Centre, adjacent to the Big Orange, houses a collection of vintage and classic cars, large-scale model airplanes, antique toys and dolls, as well as gem, mineral, and Aboriginal culture displays. Its hours are the same as the orange's. For information, phone (085) 82-2325.

A Special Place for Jimmy James is a commemorative riverfront walking trail and engraved granite slab dedicated to the esteemed Aborigine. The polished slab contains images of Jimmy's spirit world, and nearby are bronze plaques with statements from admirers.

Accommodations and Food

Rooms at the **Berri Hotel Motel,** Riverview Dr. (tel. 085-82-1411), are inexpensive to low-moderate, and the pub serves cheap counter meals. **Winkie Holiday Cottages,** Lower Winkie Rd. (tel. 085-83-2324), run inexpensive to moderate. You can get a campsite, or on-site vans and cabins with air-conditioning and television, at **Berri Riverside Caravan Park,** Riverview Dr. (tel. 085-82-3723).

If you enjoy fruit, you won't go hungry in these parts. **Berri Fruit Tree** (tel. 085-82-1666), on Sturt Hwy. toward Glossop, sells fresh and dried fruits, nuts, jams, and honey. Hours are Mon.-Fri. 8 a.m.-5 p.m., Saturday 9-11:30 a.m., Sunday 10 a.m.-2 p.m.

Information

Berri Tourist and Travel Centre, Vaughan Terrace (tel. 085-82-1655), can arrange accommodations, provide winery maps and general information. Hours are Mon.-Fri. 9 a.m.-5 p.m., Saturday 9-11:30 a.m., closed Christmas Day and Good Friday.

Emergency contacts are: **police** (tel. 085-82-2488), **ambulance** (tel. 085-82-2555), **fire brigade** (tel. 085-82-1000), and the **Royal Automobile Association** (tel. 085-82-2744).

LOXTON

Berri's twin ferries, the main link to Loxton, will whisk you across the river in one and a half minutes; from there you pass around Lock Number Four and Katarapko Island and head into town. Settled in the 1890s and established in 1907, Loxton (pop. 7,288) is a picture-postcard township overlooking both the Murray and a game reserve. Named for William Charles Loxton, a boundary rider who worked on the original station property, irrigation methods turned the area into the same rich grounds as the rest of the Riverland.

Sights

Loxton's most famous attraction is the **Historical Village,** a riverfront collection of 25 fully furnished early buildings, including a replica of William Charles Loxton's pine and pug hut. Early farm equipment and machinery are also on exhibit. Hours are Mon.-Fri. 10 a.m.-4 p.m., Sat.-Sun. 10 a.m.-5 p.m. For information, phone (085) 84-7194.

Penfold's Winery, Berri Rd. (tel. 085-84-7236), one of South Australia's largest bulk wineries, specializes in dealcoholized wines. Hours for sales and tastings are Mon.-Sat. 10 a.m.-5 p.m.

For easeful entertainment you can check flood levels on the trunk of **The Tree of Knowledge,** in Lions Park, on the riverfront.

Murray River National Park is home to almost 150 species of birds. You can camp, fish, or bushwalk through red gum floodplain, explore horseshoe lagoons and gentle backwaters. **Kai Kai Nature Trail,** beginning at campsite 20, is a 40-minute walk encompassing a wide variety of Katarapko Creek birdlife and natural habitat.

Alawoona, 35 km south of Loxton, is the entry point for mallee country. The 36,815-hectare **Billiatt Conservation Park** is home to the western grey kangaroo, hopping mouse, pygmy possum, and many mallee birds, including the endangered mallee fowl and red-lored whistler.

Accommodations and Food

Loxton Hotel Motel, East Terrace (tel. 085-84-7266), has both old pub rooms ($35) and newer, moderately priced riverview motel suites. The restaurant serves counter meals and offers an a la carte menu. **Loxton Riverfront Caravan Park** (tel. 085-84-7862), on the Murray, has campsites and on-site vans, plus bicycle and canoe rentals. A 48-bed hostel is also available. At **Nadia Host Farm** (tel. 085-87-4362), 20 minutes from Loxton, you can experience life on a wheat and sheep farm. Its moderate rates include breakfast.

East Terrace has a variety of decent cafes, as well as a Chinese restaurant. **Medea Cottage Fruit Train,** Bookpurnong Rd. (tel. 085-84-6837), is the place to buy homemade jams, nuts, and both fresh and dried fruits. Hours are daily 10:30 a.m.-5:30 p.m.

Information

Loxton Tourist and Travel, 45 East Terrace (tel. 085-84-7919), will assist you with accommodations and tours, as well as canoe, bicycle, or houseboat rentals. Hours are Mon.-Fri. 9 a.m.-5 p.m., Saturday during school holidays 9-11:30 a.m.

For emergency services, contact: **police** (tel. 085-84-7283), **ambulance** (tel. 085-84-7565), or **Royal Automobile Association** (tel. 085-84-7393).

Getting Around

Rent **trail bikes** from Loxton Motorcycle Hire Centre, 10 Bookpurnong Terrace (tel. 085-84-7698).

RENMARK

Renmark (pop. 4,256) sits on a willow-lined Murray River bend, 255 km northeast of Adelaide and very near the Victoria border. Founded in 1887, Renmark is Australia's oldest irrigation district—thanks to Alfred Deakin's idea and the Canadian Chaffey brothers' expertise, the system spurred the Riverland's thriving citrus and wine industry. Ironically, the Chaffey brothers inserted a prohibition clause in their plans for the town's development. In 1897, the British Commonwealth erected the Renmark Hotel, the first hotel to challenge the clause. And we know who won!

Today Renmark is a busy commercial and holiday center, with plenty of wine to taste, houseboats to rent, and arts and crafts galleries to browse.

Paringa, four km east from Renmark, is the location of **Lock Number Five,** and nearby lie the quite wonderful **Headings Cliffs Lookout Tower,** the quite interesting **Lyrup Village** communal growing settlement (dating from 1894), and the quite dumb **Big Tyre.**

Sights

The PS *Industry,* built in 1911, serves as historical museum. Through a coin-in-the-slot operation, you can see how paddle wheels and other engine parts function. Moored on the Murray, between 9th and 10th Streets, the museum is open daily 9 a.m.-5 p.m. Admission is $2. For information, phone (085) 86-6704.

Olivewood Homestead, Renmark Ave. and 21st St., the original home of Charles Chaffey, now operates as a National Trust museum. Hours are Thurs.-Mon. 10 a.m.-4 p.m., Tuesday 2-4 p.m. Admission is $2.50. For information, phone (085) 86-6175.

Bredl's Wonderworld of Wildlife, on the Sturt Hwy., five km from town, has pythons, taipans, cobras, boa constrictors, rare yellow anacondas, lizards, alligators, crocs, and other reptiles. Hours are daily 8 a.m.-6 p.m. in summer, 9 a.m.-5:30 p.m. in winter, and there are special snake feedings Sunday 2-3 p.m. Admission is $7. For information, phone (085) 95-1431.

Accommodations and Food

The historic **Renmark Hotel,** Murray Ave. (tel. 085-86-6755), has moderately priced rooms and motel units. The hotel features both a bistro and dining room. Prices are high-moderate at **Renmark Country Club,** Sturt Hwy. (tel. 085-95-1401), and include use of tennis court, swim-

ming pool, spa, and 18-hole grass golf course.

Riverbend Caravan Park, Sturt Hwy. (tel. 085-95-5131), and **Renmark Caravan Park,** Patey Dr. (tel. 085-86-6315), are situated on the riverfront. Both have campsites, on-site vans, and cabins for rent.

Rivergrowers Ark Kiosk, Renmark Ave. (tel. 085-86-6705), sells a variety of juices, nuts, honey, jams, chocolates, and fresh and dried fruits—most processed in the factory next door. Hours are Mon.-Fri. 10 a.m.-4 p.m., Saturday 9 a.m.-noon.

Sports and Recreation

Facilities at **Renmark Community Recreation Centre** include indoor tennis, indoor swimming pool, squash courts, weight-training equipment, spa and sauna, a suntan unit, and large multipurpose stadium for cricket, soccer, netball, badminton, volleyball, basketball, and roller skating. For information, phone (085) 86-6072.

Shopping

Most of the arts and crafts galleries are situated on or near Renmark Avenue. **Frank Harding's Folklore Gallery,** 117 16th St., features a huge ceiling mural that depicts Australian bushrangers.

Pick up surplus and camping equipment at **Riverland Army Disposals,** Renmark Ave. (tel. 085-86-6767).

Information

The **tourist information center,** Murray Ave. (tel. 085-86-6704), distributes info and rents tandem or single bicycles (there's a good cycling track to Paringa). Hours are Mon.-Fri. 9 a.m.-5 p.m., Saturday 9 a.m.-4 p.m., Sunday and public holidays 10 a.m.-4 p.m., closed Christmas Day.

TRANSPORT

Getting There

Sunstate Airlines flies daily from Adelaide to Renmark and on to Mildura. Book through Ansett.

Murray Bridge Passenger Service (tel. 085-32-2633) operates daily coaches between Murray Bridge and Adelaide's Franklin Street depot for about $14 one-way. **Stateliner** (tel. 08-8415-5544, or 085-86-6468 in Renmark) has daily coaches from Adelaide to Blanchetown ($16), Waikerie ($19), Barmera ($21), Berri ($23), Loxton ($26), and Renmark ($26). Many interstate coaches also serve the Lower Murray and Riverland.

River Cruising

Why not feel the river rush through your veins by traveling *on* the Murray, instead of along it? In the Lower Murray, you can rent **houseboats** at Murray Bridge, Mannum, Younghusband, and Purnong; in the Riverland, houseboats are based at Morgan, Waikerie, Loxton, Berri, Paringa, and Renmark. Houseboats are completely self-contained, accommodate four to 10 people, and are capable of traveling six to eight knots. Rental prices depend upon the size of boat, length of rental, and the season you rent it in—typically about $900 per week (you can get them as low as $600). However, keep in mind that this takes care of both transport and accommodations, as well as cooking facilities—and, if you share the cost with others, it even be-

comes cheap. At any rate, it will be a delightful and memorable experience, floating along the Murray, in comfort, and at will. Use a little imagination and you may run into Tom Sawyer, Matthew Flinders, or Mr. Lucky.

Book houseboats (*well* in advance) at any South Australian Tourism Commission Travel Centre, or through local tourist information centers. You won't need a boat operator's license, but a driver's license is required.

Or, leave the navigating to someone else. The 18-cabin *Proud Mary* luxury boat departs Murray Bridge for two- to five-day cruises. Cost is $325-700 per person. For information, phone (08) 231-9472. The 60-cabin paddle steamer *Murray Princess* departs Mannum for six-night Riverland cruises, at $850 per person. For information, phone (085) 69-1438. All of the above prices include accommodations and meals.

Get a quick taste of the Murray on a lunch, dinner, or other short sail. Operators offering a wide range of tours (at a wide range of fares) include *Lady Mannum* (tel. 085-69-1438) from Mannum and MV *Barrangul* (tel. 018-80-4256) from Murray Bridge.

MARK MORRIS

THE MID NORTH

South Australia's Mid North lies north of the Barossa Valley, west of the Riverland, east of Yorke Peninsula, and just south of the Flinders Ranges. And it is special—touristed, but not *touristy*.

Actually, the Mid North is my favorite part of the state. Burra, the historic copper mining town, was so awesome I dropped my camera, shattering it on the same cobblestone path once used by Cornish miners. Busted Olympus notwithstanding, I instamatically decided to live there for at least six months. And then there's Mintaro, a truly gorgeous heritage town. Down the road is Martindale Hall, a very chic B&B where *Picnic at Hanging Rock* was filmed.

Farther north is Peterborough, a railway junction, where buffs like me—with hearts that chug instead of beat—can all-aboard a narrow-gauge steam train through the Mid North countryside. Port Pirie, along the Spencer Gulf, is a mixture of heritage town, busy seaport, and commercial center.

You have a variety of options for exploring the Mid North. The Clare Valley is a 135-km zip north of Adelaide, along Main North Road.

From Adelaide, the Barrier Highway will lead you (with a couple of detours) to Burra and Peterborough. From Peterborough you turn westward to Jamestown, Gladstone, and Port Pirie, or continue north to the Flinders Ranges. At the junction of the Barrier and Sturt Highways, be sure to take the Kapunda turnoff. The back road, through Hamilton, Marrabel, and Saddleworth—where you'll reconnect with the Barrier Highway—is one of my favorite day-in-the-country drives.

Highway 1, also from Adelaide, travels to Port Wakefield (where you can cut over to Balaklava), up to Snowtown, Crystal Brook, and Port Pirie, then on to Port Augusta and the Eyre Peninsula, or across the Nullarbor to Western Australia.

Whichever road you follow, every once in a while veer off the beaten path—this territory is full of little surprises, marked by hand-lettered signposts, European-style back roads, an ornery cow, a stubborn mule, and unusual gusto in the breeze.

KAPUNDA

Located at the northern edge of the Barossa Valley, 75 km from Adelaide, Kapunda (pop. 1,620) was the location of South Australia's first significant copper find. An accidental discovery of green copper ore prompted the opening of one of the world's richest copper mines on 32 hectares owned by the Dutton and Bagott families. The mine operated 1844-1912, turning out approximately 14,000 tons of copper, and Kapunda soon grew into the state's largest country town. Though the community now lives off agri-

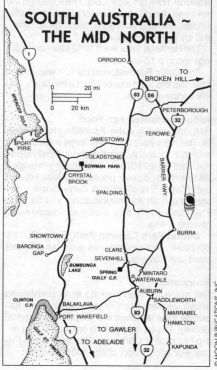

cultural rather than mining products, many historic buildings, cottages, and churches still stand, and the town retains a lot of its original charm. Particularly stunning is the decorative iron lacework, known as "Kapunda lace," made locally at the turn of the century.

Sights and Events

Kapunda Historical Museum (tel. 085-66-2657) is in the former Baptist church on Hill Street. Historical exhibits include colonial artifacts, memorabilia, and archival recordings. Hours are Sat.-Thurs. Sept.-May, and weekends June-Aug. 1-4 p.m.

The eight-meter-tall bronze sculpture of *Map Kernow* (Cornish for "Son of Cornwall"), at the south end of town, pays tribute to early Cornish miners.

Take the **Old Kapunda Copper Mine and Walking Trail,** an easy 1.5-km hike through the old mine, for close-up investigation of shafts, tunnels, the open cut area, the mine chimney, and an early miner's cottage.

The **Heritage Trail** leads to 42 historical buildings along a 10-km route.

The **Celtic Festival,** held the first weekend in April, fills the town's pubs with Celtic, bush, and folk bands and fans.

Accommodations and Food

Refurbished **Sir John Franklin Hotel,** Main St. (tel. 085-66-2106), has large inexpensive pub-style rooms. Across the street, **Ford House** (tel. 085-66-2280) is a beautifully renovated B&B with expensive prices ($10 less without breakfast). Excellent a la carte dinners are served at both accommodations, and Sir John Franklin's lively pub also has inexpensive counter meals.

Dutton Park Caravan Park, Baker St. (tel. 66-2094), rents campsites and has a tennis court and playground.

Information

Get maps for both walking trails mentioned above, as well as other information, from **Kapunda Tourist Centre** or Kapunda Historical Society. The tourist center is open daily 10 a.m.-1 p.m., closed Christmas Day and Good Friday. For information, phone (085) 66-2902.

MINTARO

The entire tiny township of Mintaro (pop. 80) is on the heritage list. Of course, you'll find only a handful of streets, but they're lined with 1850s slate, stone, and wooden colonial structures—influenced by Italian, English, and German hands—constructed of such diverse materials as Baltic pine and Indian cedar. Most buildings incorporate the locally produced fine slate—a specialty of this district—in walls, floors, or fences, and many of the old cottages have been converted into accommodation houses. The town is thought to have been named by Uruguayan mule drivers who stopped there while carting copper ore between Port Wakefield and Burra.

Mintaro sits 130 km from Adelaide and about 14 km from Clare, burrowed amongst gentle hills and rolling pastures. It is a gorgeous, quiet, country village. Go there!

Sights

Robinson's Cottage (tel. 08-8843-9029), a museum inside an original 1851 settler's cottage, features fire engine displays, fire appliances and memorabilia, classic and vintage cars, and other early equipment. Hours are daily 9 a.m.-4:30 p.m., closed Christmas Day.

Reilly's Cottage Gallery (tel. 08-8843-9013) exhibits local and national arts and crafts in a cottage over 120 years old. Hours are Wed.-Sun. 10 a.m.-5 p.m.

Martindale Hall, on the outskirts of Mintaro, is the positively splendid Georgian mansion portrayed as "Appleyard College" in the film *Picnic at Hanging Rock.* A bachelor named Edmund Bowen had the house built in 1879 as an attempt to win the hand of a spoiled rich girl, who promised to marry him if he built her a house as nice as her father's. Martindale Hall (which, in those days, cost the dear sum of £36,000) apparently wasn't up to snuff, for Edmund built the house but then lost the girl! The mansion is open for inspection daily 1-4 p.m., closed Christmas Day. It costs $7 admission, but you can visit the grounds for free.

Accommodations

All Mintaro accommodations are in converted historic digs going for prices that probably have the original inhabitants rolling over in their historic graves. **Pay Office Cottage,** Hill St. (tel. 08-8843-9026), once the cheapest, is now way up there. **Mintaro Hideaway** (tel. 08-8843-9011) and **The Teapot Inn** (tel. 08-8843-9037), both also expensive, include breakfast. **Mintaro Mews** (tel. 08-8843-9011) offers two (yes, expensive) deluxe cottages with breakfast included. And, if you're a romantic or film-crazy, you'll want to stay at the house Edmund built; **Martindale Hall** (tel. 08-8843-9011) will give you a scrumptious room, pamper you with attention, and feed you delectable candlelight dinners. Oddly, this once really expensive spot is now one of the cheapest if you just want a room with breakfast—toss in dinner and the rates double.

THE CLARE VALLEY

The Clare Valley, famous for winemaking since 1851, is a 30-km stretch, 135 km north of Adelaide, nestled within the northern Mount Lofty Ranges. Comprising the surrounding communities of Auburn, Watervale, Sevenhill, and Penwortham, more than 20 wineries—ranging from small boutiques to nationally known brands—take advantage of the district's high rainfall and rich soil to create premium products.

Edward Burton Gleeson founded Clare in 1840, naming the settlement for his native County Clare, Ireland. Only one year later the Hawker brothers set up Bungaree Station, one of Australia's best-known sheep stud farms. The winemaking didn't get going until 1848 when the Jesuits planted vines to produce altar wine, which Sevenhill Cellars still turns out, along with other fine vintages.

You'll find historic buildings, serene roadways, and picturesque scenery throughout the Clare Valley towns, all dating back to the early 1800s—and it's a lot less touristy than the Barossa.

Sights

Historic buildings in **Auburn** include: Miss Mabel Cottage Living (1859), Mechanics Institute (1859), Police Station and Courtroom (1860), St. John's Anglican Church (1862), post office (1862), Stonehurst Gallery and Library (1866), and Council Chambers (1879).

Stanley Grammar School, Uniting Church of Australia, Watervale Primary School, and the Methodist Church are National Trust buildings in **Watervale.**

Run by the National Trust, the **Old Police Station Museum** (1850), corner Victoria Rd. and West Terrace in Clare (tel. 08-8842-2374), was the valley's first courthouse and police station. Hours are Saturday 10 a.m.-noon, 2-4 p.m., Sunday 2-4 p.m. Admission is $2.

Take a tour of **Bungaree Station,** dating from 1841 when the Hawkers established the famous merino stud farm, and still run by their grandsons! The self-sufficient community has a church, council chambers, school, blacksmith shop, as well as wool shed, stable yard, and shearers quarters, that are still in use. One- to two-hour conducted tours are arranged by appointment only, as the station is still going full-stud. Original knitting patterns and woolen yarns are sold on the premises. For information, phone (08) 8842-2677.

Saint Aloysius Church and Sevenhill Cellars, College Rd., Sevenhill (tel. 08-8843-4222), is where the valley's first vines were planted. Father Aloysius Kranewitter, a young Jesuit priest, chose the site (patterned after the seven hills of Rome) as a cellar for his altar wines. Saint Aloysius Church was begun in 1856 and consecrated in 1875. Besides altar wines, Sevenhill specializes in dry red and white wines, and liqueur Tokay. Hours are Mon.-Fri. 8:30 a.m.-4:30 p.m., Saturday and holidays 9 a.m.-4 p.m., closed Sunday, Christmas Day, New Year's Day, and Good Friday (you know where you can get their wine on *those* days).

Wolta Wolta Homestead (tel. 08-8842-3656) was one of the earliest settler's cottages. Unfortunately, it burned down in 1983's devastating Ash Wednesday fire. The homestead, now restored, features antiques, artworks, history, and memorabilia relating to the Hope family, owners of the property for four generations. Tours are conducted Sat.-Sun. 10 a.m.-4:30 p.m. Admission is $3.

Accommodations and Food

You can stay inexpensively in the shearers' bunkhouse at **Bungaree Station** (tel. 08-8842-2677). Facilities include a large dining hall and modern kitchen. **Clare Valley Cabins** (tel. 08-8842-3917) offers seven two-bedroom self-contained cottages on a large property five km north of Clare. Rates are inexpensive to low-moderate. **Bentley's Hotel Motel,** 191 Main North Rd. (tel. 08-8842-2815), rents moderately priced rooms in both units. **Clare Central Motel,** 325 Main North Rd. (tel. 08-8842-2277), is down the street and runs about $20 more than Bentley's. **Stringy Brae Cottage** (tel. 08-8843-4313) and **Trestrail Cottage (tel. 08-8842-3794), in Sevenhill, both range high-moderate to expensive and include breakfast ingredients.**

Christison Park Caravan Park, Main North Rd. (tel. 08-8842-2724), near Clare, has campsites and on-site vans.

Cheap eats on the main drag are **Clare Valley Café, Salad Bowl,** and **Pantry Plus Coffee Shop. Bentley's Hotel** serves country-style meals at moderate prices. And more country cookin' is dished up at **Sevenhill Hotel** (tel. 08-8843-4217), for Mon.-Sat. lunch and dinner. **Clare Dragon Restaurant,** 308 Main North Rd. (tel. 08-8842-3644), is both a moderately priced licensed restaurant and an inexpensive takeaway.

Jones Bakery, 269 Main North Rd. (tel. 08-8842-2473), bakes up buns and cakes, pies and pasties. Choose from more than 24 types of breads, as well as pastries and cakes at **Maurie's Patisserie and Hot Bread Bakery,** 292 Main North Rd. (tel. 08-8842-3523).

Events

Similar to the Barossa event, Clare Valley's **Vintage Festival** happens during Easter of even-numbered years. The **Gourmet Weekend,** held every May, is when connoisseurs sip and sample, and the hungry pig out on a progressive lunch at area wineries.

Recreation

Lakota Ranch (tel. 08-8842-3875) organizes fully escorted horseback rides along the Clare Valley back roads and hills, as well as one-day cattle drives for begining to advanced riders.

There're good picnicking and leisurely walks at **Pioneer, Christison,** and **Spring Gully** parks.

Information

Clare Valley Tourist Centre, 229 Main North Rd., Clare (tel. 08-8842-2131), has maps of the Clare Valley wineries and other local information. Hours are daily 10 a.m.-4 p.m., closed Christmas Day.

You can get tourist information in Auburn at **Miss Mabel Cottage Living,** St. Vincent St. (tel. 08-8849-2208), Thurs.-Sun. and public holidays 10 a.m.-5 p.m.

BURRA

With the feel and flavor of a Down Under Bisbee, Arizona, Burra (pop. 2,225) is one of South Australia's most enchanting towns.

Originally, the community was a sheep-grazing area on the brink of bankruptcy. But in 1845, after shepherd William Streair discovered copper, followed by Thomas Pickett's find, the "Monster Mine" was created and Burra blossomed with prosperity. Named "Burra Burra" (Hindi for "Great Great") by Indian coolie shepherds, the district was collectively called "The Burra," and embraced several townships, all named according to their inhabitants' origins—thus Kooringa (Aboriginal), Redruth (Cornish), Ab-

bridge over Burra Creek

erdeen (Scottish), Hampton (English), and Lly-
wchrr (Welsh).

Though the mine was one rich mother lode,
operations ceased in 1877, when it dried up.
Agriculture (Burra was declared "Merino Capital
of the World" in 1988) and tourism are the local
revenue-takers these days. A leisurely 156-km
drive from Adelaide, Burra draws visitors to its
fascinating streets and dwellings to follow its
historic footsteps along the copper trail.

Sights

Just about the whole town can be classified a
sight, but you'll need a passport to cross many
thresholds. The **Burra Passport** is a rental key,
available from the tourist office, that allows you
entrance to **Burra Creek Miner's Dugouts,
Burra Open Air Museum, Redruth Gaol, Police Lock-up and Stables,** and **Unicorn Brewery Stables.** Cost of the passport is $15 per
family or vehicle, plus a $5 deposit.

Also included in the passport's attractions is
Morphett's Enginehouse. Built in 1858 and
reconstructed in 1986, it helped to pump water
from the mine. A 30-meter entry tunnel enables
visitors to walk into the shaft to view original
pump pipes.

Bon Accord Museum, on the site of the
original Bon Accord Mine, serves as an interpretive center, with a working forge, five- by six-
meter model of the Monster Mine, and tours of
the old mine shaft. Hours are Mon.-Fri. 12:30-
2:30 p.m., Sat.-Sun. and public holidays 12:30-
3:30 p.m. Admission is $3. For information,
phone (08) 8892-2056.

Paxton Square Cottages is three rows of
1850s miners' cottages overlooking Burra Creek.
The cottages are now visitor accommodations,
but **Malowen Lowarth,** furnished as a mine
captain's cottage, is open for inspection Saturday 1-3 p.m., Sunday 10:30 a.m.-12:30 p.m.
Admission is $3.

If you're into cemeteries, old **Burra Cemetery** is especially nice. If you're into diseases, it
will be of interest that most causes of death at
the time were typhoid, diphtheria, measles, and
consumption.

Market Square Museum consists of a general store, post office, and private home, built
1870-1915. Nearby is the 13-meter ironbark
and blue gum **Jinker,** which toted the huge

Schneider's engine-house cylinder from Port
Adelaide to Burra Mine in 1852. Hours are Saturday 2-4 p.m., Sunday 1-3 p.m., or by arrangement. For information, phone (08) 8892-2154.

Burra Gorge, 18 km east of town, has good
walking trails through river gum forests and other
scenic bushland.

Accommodations and Food

You can check into a pub for the night, but it's certainly more fun to stay in one of Burra's seep-
ing-with-history heritage dwellings. The tourist
center has all the info on these accommodations.
The exquisite **Paxton Square Cottages** (tel. 08-
8892-2622), with fully equipped kitchens, are a
very reasonable $40-50 double. **Bon Accord
Cottage** (tel. 08-8892-2615), the preserved mine-
manager's residence, is also available for $75.
Burra View House, 7 Mount Pleasant Rd. (tel.
08-8892-2648), is a B&B with excellent views
and moderate rates. Book all accommodations
(especially Paxton Cottages) well in advance.

Reasonably priced places to fill your belly
are **Polly's Tearooms** (tel. 08-8892-2544),
Pickett's Pantry (tel. 08-8892-2530), and the
counters at **Burra Hotel** (tel. 08-8892-2389)
and **Kooringa Hotel** (tel. 08-8892-2013).
Price's Bakery, in Market Square, is your stop
for homemade soups and fabulous wienies.

Information

Apply for cottage "passports" and load up on
brochures at **Burra Tourist Centre,** Market
Square (tel. 08-8892-2154). Hours are daily 10
a.m.-4 p.m., closed Christmas Day.

A number of historical books on the area are
also sold here (*Discovering Burra* is included
with your passport).

TEROWIE

Continuing up the Barrier Highway (be careful of
kangaroos) for 63 km north of Burra brings you
to Terowie, another historic town and a prominent part of the 1880s railway network. Horse
and bullock teams from the surrounding country
stations kept up a steady rush hour while loading or unloading produce, supplies, and stock.
And, history buffs, get this: Terowie, site of a
World War II army bivouac camp, was where

General Douglas MacArthur, fresh from his Philippines escape, made his famous "I came out of Bataan and I shall return" statement.

It's a good wander down Main Street, where the original century-old shopfronts reflect times past. **Arid Lands Botanic Garden,** also on Main St., features a large assortment of Australian arid-zone plants and is open daily.

Accommodations and Food
Terowie Hotel (tel. 086-59-1012) and **Imperial Hotel** (tel. 086-59-1011), both on Main St., offer inexpensive pub rooms with breakfast included. **Terowie Motel,** Barrier Hwy. (tel. 086-59-1082), also inexpensive, is air conditioned. **Dusty Kitchen,** Main St. (tel. 086-59-1073), serves meals, snacks, and cakes, daily.

Information
Terowie Information and Souvenir Shop, Main St. (tel. 086-59-1087), will organize visits to the Terowie Pioneer Gallery and Museum, as well as conducted tours of the town and buildings. Hours are daily 9:30 a.m.-5:30 p.m.

PETERBOROUGH

Turn off the Barrier Highway at Terowie for the 23-km ride into Peterborough—frontier town, historic railway depot, and gateway to the Flinders Ranges. Railway aficionados will thrill to find that Peterborough is one of the world's two known towns where three different rail gauges converge. This is still an important rail center on the Port Pirie-Broken Hill-Sydney main line. Get a good peek at the town (and the tracks) from **Tank Hill Lookout,** at the end of Government Road.

Sights
Don't miss a ride on the steam passenger train, along the narrow-gauge line, from Peterborough to Orroroo (about 38 km). The tourist center has schedules.

Round House Exchange, a unique railway turntable used for rerouting rolling stock, displays historic rail equipment.

Saint Cecelia, the former bishop's residence, is palatially furnished with paintings, antique pianos, polished mahogany, and stained-glass windows within its parlors, ballroom, 10 bed-

rooms, and library. The coach house now functions as an art center. Moderately priced accommodations are available in the main house, converted stables, coachman's room, or attached artist's studio, and include breakfast. Daily tours 1-4 p.m. are arranged through the tourist center. For information, phone (086) 51-2849.

The **Gold Battery** once extracted gold from locally mined crushed ore. Guided tours can be arranged. For information, phone (086) 52-3708.

Information
You can't miss the **Peterborough Tourist Centre** (tel. 086-51-2708)—it's in a railway carriage along Main Street. Get your steam train tickets here and, if you're headed to the Flinders Ranges, inquire about roads and routes. Hours are daily 9 a.m.-4 p.m., closed Christmas Day, New Year's Day, and Good Friday.

TO PORT PIRIE

Traveling coastward, the back road southwest of Peterborough hooks up with Route 83. At Jamestown, it starts east leaving Route 83, drops a bit southward at Gladstone, then curves northward, merging with Highway 1, heading to Port Pirie and beyond.

Jamestown
This wool-, wheat-, and barley-producing agricultural community, 44 km from Peterborough, originated back in the 1870s. Its **National Trust Museum** (tel. 086-65-2036) houses a collection of early memorabilia and historical relics. Hours are Mon.-Sat. 10 a.m.-5 p.m., Sunday 2-4 p.m. Admission is $2.

South Australia's first government forest plantation, **Bundaleer Forest Reserve,** nine km south of Jamestown, affords refreshing walks and picnics. Climb up to the lookout tower and you'll see Mt. Remarkable in the distance.

Gladstone
This pastoral and grazing community, 28 km southwest of Jamestown and adjacent to the Rocky River, also dates back to the 1870s. In 1877, after the railway connected Gladstone to Port Pirie, the community became an important grain collection center. Eventually it became

home to South Australia's largest inland silo (which now contains 82,500 tons of grain). At the Gladstone railway yards, you can view one of the world's few places where narrow, standard, and broad gauges are interlaid in one siding.

Experience conditions withstood by "inebriates, debtors and other prisoners" at century-old **Gladstone Gaol** (tel. 086-62-2068). (Some of the "other prisoners" included Italians and Germans interned there during WW II.) Hours are Monday, Tuesday, and Friday 1-4 p.m., Sat.-Sun. and school holidays 10 a.m.-4 p.m. Admission is $3.50.

PORT PIRIE

Port Pirie (pop. 15,114), 210 km from Adelaide, is well-positioned on the eastern side and northern end of Spencer Gulf, shadowed by the Flinders Ranges. As the Mid North's largest center, Port Pirie (named after the colonial workhorse windjammer *John Pirie*) is notable for its enormous lead smeltery, capable of producing 280,000 kilograms of silver, 250,000 tons of refined lead, 90,000 tons of sulphuric acid, 45,000 tons of electrolytic zinc, as well as gold, cadmium, copper matte, and antimonial lead alloys—the annual turnout from rich Broken Hill mines.

As the closest port to Broken Hill, the precious metal is railed in and treated at the smeltery or exported internationally. Other products shipped from the port are large quantities of wheat and barley.

Obviously industry and shipping get top billing at Port Pirie, yet you'll also discover intriguing old buildings, excellent sports facilities, and a surprising variety of entertainment.

Sights
Port Pirie National Trust Museum, Old Ellen St. (tel. 086-32-1080), is comprised of the railway station, customs house, and police station. Displays include historical exhibits, a scale model of the smelters, railway and shipping exhibits, 10,000- to 20,000-year-old diprotodon bones, and a former shunting engine. Hours are Mon.-Sat. 10 a.m.-4 p.m., Sunday 1-4 p.m., closed Christmas Day. Admission is $2.

The historical home **Carn Brae,** 32 Florence St. (tel. 086-32-1314), belonged to the pioneering Moyles, soft-drink moguls. Aside from fine architecture, collections include turn-of-the-century furnishings, paintings, glassware, and porcelain, as well as more than 2,500 antique and contemporary dolls. Hours are daily 10 a.m.-4 p.m., closed Christmas Day. Admission is $5.

Fishermen's Jetty, with fishing and boat-launching ramps, is either busy or tranquil, depending on the tide. **Solomontown Jetty** provides a safe swimming beach, children's playground along the reserve, and sunbathing area. **Port Davis,** 15 km south of Port Pirie off Port Broughton Rd., has both jetty fishing and a boat launch.

Accommodations and Food
Rooms are inexpensive at **International Hotel Motel,** 40 Ellen St. (tel. 086-32-2422). Moderately priced **Flinders Range Motor Inn,** 151 Main Rd. (tel. 086-32-3555), offers videos, room service, beer garden, swimming pool, tennis court, and a Saturday night dinner dance. **John Pirie Motor Inn,** Main Rd. (tel. 086-32-4200), features a swimming pool and room service, with moderate to expensive rates. Both **Port Pirie Caravan Park,** Beach Rd. (tel. 086-32-4275), and **Range View Caravan Park,** Highway 1 (tel. 086-34-4221), have campsites and on-site vans.

Hungry? Hope you like Chinese food and fish 'n' chips!

Entertainment and Events
Northern Festival Centre, at Memorial Park, is patterned after the Adelaide Centre. Theater, films, exhibitions, and performances by both visiting and local entertainers are scheduled regularly.

Information
Local details are provided by **Port Pirie Information and Tourism Centre,** 3 Mary Elie St. (tel. 086-33-0439). Hours are Mon.-Fri. 9 a.m.-5 p.m., Sat.-Sun. 1-4 p.m.

ALONG HIGHWAY ONE

Up Highway 1, beyond Gawler, the coastal road passes picturesque parklands, old copper ports, salty lakes, and sculptural rock formations.

Balaklava

A short 26-km detour east from Port Wakefield, Balaklava (pop. 1,365) was once a rest stop for bullock teams hauling copper ore from Burra to Port Wakefield. Nearby **Rocks Reserve,** with interesting rock formations, is a good picnic spot.

Port Wakefield

Port Wakefield, top of the Gulf St. Vincent, is a one-time copper and wool port with a lovely old wharf. Go bush at **Clinton Conservation Park,** just north of town. Back on Highway 1 and another 30 km north is **Bumbunga Lake,** a huge salt pan covering 3,530 acres. The lake changes color according to the weather—the weather's good if it's blue and unsettled if it's pink. You can tour the processing plant. The scenic drive along Lochiel-Ninnes Road affords a superb view of the inland lakes and countryside.

Snowtown

This primo sheep- and cattle-breeding township, 49 km north of Port Wakefield, was established in the 1840s by early settlers seeking greener pastures. These days Snowtown provides services for surrounding rural communities.

See what's left of **Burunga Gap Township,** 10 km west of Snowtown, established in 1873.

Crystal Brook

Scenic Crystal Brook (pop. 2,100), 52 km north of Snowtown, was declared a township in 1873, though it was named in 1839 by early explorer Edward John Eyre. It's a lovely town with tall river gums, picnic parks, water ponds, and, of course, the crystal brook, which runs from the lower Flinders Ranges to the River Broughton.

Bowman Park, five km east of Crystal Brook, is a peaceful parkland for picnics and play, as well as a Mid North point for the Heysen Trail. The Native Fauna Zone houses crocodiles, koalas, kangaroos, waterfowl, goannas, pythons, eagles, and other critters. Hours are daily 10 a.m.-4 p.m. Admission is $4.50. For information, phone (086) 36-2116.

Make camp at either **Crystal Brook Caravan Park** (tel. 086-36-2640) or the 22-bed lodge and tent sites for Heysen Trail trekkers (contact park manager at 086-36-2116).

TRANSPORT

Contact the **Country Passenger Depot** in Adelaide for coaches to Kapunda, Burra, Peterborough, and Port Pirie. For information, phone (08) 8231-4144.

The major transcontinental rail lines stop at Port Pirie and Peterborough on journeys between Adelaide and Perth, Alice Springs and Sydney. For information, phone (08) 8231-7699, or 13-2232 toll-free.

Or *walk!* **The Heysen Trail** passes from Tanunda (in the Barossa), through Burra, Mt. Bryan, Spalding, and Crystal Brook, in the Mid North.

YORKE PENINSULA

Rich fields of golden wheat and barley, moody beaches and sandy coves, wildlife peeking from the bush, fluttering birds, cotton-puff skies, sparkling blue seas, spring wildflower blankets, and Cornish mining settlements, combined with close proximity to Adelaide, make the Yorke Peninsula an attractive holiday getaway. (Either that or travelers miss it altogether, ending up on the Eyre Highway and headed for Western Australia, having lost the whole Yorke in one blink!)

Set between Spencer Gulf and the Gulf St. Vincent, most of the peninsula's parks, beaches, and towns are not more than a two- or three-hour drive from Adelaide. The two sealed highways follow the east coast and midsection of the peninsula, converge at Warooka, and end at Stenhouse Bay in Innes National Park (near the Park Headquarters). Gravel roads and dirt tracks spur off from the main highways, leading to hideaway beaches, rural communities, and patchwork farmlands. Yet, even on the inland route, you're never more than 25 km from the coast, with beaches to please anglers, divers, surfers, and sunners. So, if you're seeking a destination that lacks in the typical tourist trappings, is user friendly rather than hard-sell, the Yorke offers a laid-back environment where you can set your own sights. The fishing is good year-round, but it's the spring months (Sept.-Nov.)—when the wildflowers serve up a visual feast of daisies, wattles, orchids, and red flame bush—that are exceptional.

Detour off Highway 1, north of Port Wakefield (about 100 km from Adelaide), along the eastern coast, through the ports of Androssan and Edithburgh, down to Innes National Park, where the emus and kangaroos play. Take the scenic drive around Corny Point, meet the sealed highway at Warooka, pass through the "inland" communities of Minlaton and Maitland, up to the historic Copper Triangle towns of Moonta, Kadina, and Wallaroo, to Port Broughton, the seaside resort at the Yorke's northern tip.

History

Captain Matthew Flinders first sighted the Yorke Peninsula in 1802, the year he was exploring South Australia's coastline. Sheep farmers, looking for greener pastures for their stock, settled the region in the 1830s, but it was the 1859 discovery of copper at Kadina that made the Yorke prosper, plus provided a much-needed boost to South Australia's precarious economy. By 1861, extensive deposits were uncovered at Wallaroo and Moonta, and the copper rush was on. Cornish (and some Welsh) miners flocked to the Yorke, bringing their picks and shovels and leaving their heritage and pasties behind. Thus, the Copper Triangle towns of Kadina, Wallaroo, and Moonta also became known as "Little Cornwall." A bienniel festival pays tribute to the area's rich Cornish heritage.

The Yorke's copper mines operated up until the 1920s, when declining prices, combined with increased labor expenses and international competition, prompted closure (Poona Mine, at Moonta, reopened in 1988). Mines closed or not, the Yorke was hardly dried up. The flat plains of Australia's granary are considered one of the world's richest wheat and barley regions.

Information

For more information on the Yorke Peninsula, contact **Yorke Peninsula Tourist Information Centre,** Victoria Square, Kadina 5554 (tel. 08-8821-2093), or any South Australian Tourism Commission Travel Centre.

THE COPPER TRIANGLE

The historic Cornish townships of Kadina, Wallaroo, and Moonta are easily reached via the Kadina turnoff from Highway 1, three km north of Port Wakefield. Otherwise, if you're exploring the entire Yorke Peninsula, you'll catch these towns on your way up the west coast. Most of the artsy-craftsy galleries are in that "tri-city" area, so if you're dying for a locally painted landscape, you'll probably find it there.

Kadina

This is the Yorke Peninsula's largest town. As one-time center of the copper action, Kadina (pop. 3,500) has a distinctively Cornish atmosphere, reflected in many of the old buildings.

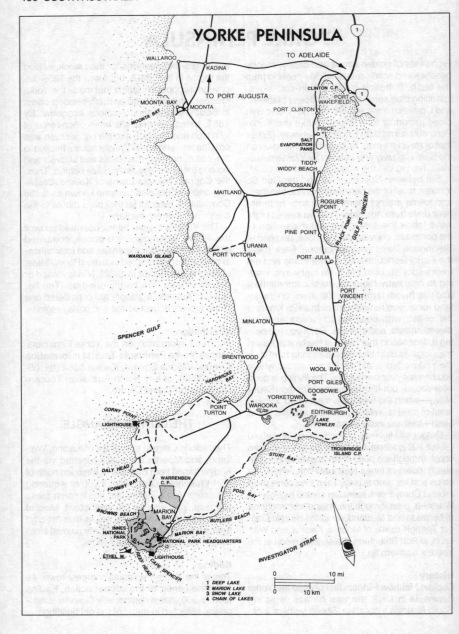

YORKE PENINSULA

TO ADELAIDE

WALLAROO
KADINA
TO PORT AUGUSTA

MOONTA BAY
MOONTA

MOONTA BAY

CLINTON C.P.
PORT WAKEFIELD
PORT CLINTON

PRICE

SALT
EVAPORATION
PANS

TIDDY
WIDDY BEACH

ARDROSSAN

MAITLAND

ROGUES
POINT

PINE POINT

GULF ST. VINCENT

BLACK POINT

WARDANG ISLAND

URANIA
PORT VICTORIA

PORT JULIA

PORT
VINCENT

SPENCER GULF

MINLATON

BRENTWOOD

STANSBURY

HARDWICKE
BAY

WOOL BAY
PORT GILES
COOBOWIE

CORNY POINT

POINT
TURTON

YORKETOWN
WAROOKA

EDITHBURGH

LAKE
FOWLER

LIGHTHOUSE

DALY HEAD

WARRENBEN
C.P.

STURT BAY

TROUBRIDGE
ISLAND C.P.

FORMBY BAY

FOUL BAY

BROWNS BEACH

MARION
BAY

BUTLERS BEACH

INNES
NATIONAL PARK

MARION BAY
NATIONAL PARK HEADQUARTERS

ETHEL M.

LIGHTHOUSE

LIFE HEAD SPENCER

INVESTIGATOR STRAIT

1 DEEP LAKE
2 MARION LAKE
3 SNOW LAKE
4 CHAIN OF LAKES

0   10 mi

0   10 km

THE CORNISH PASTY

The pasty was a traditional meal for the miners. Sometimes meat and veggies were placed at one end, fruit at the other. In all cases, there was crimping along the top. The crimping acted as a handle, so the men—hands filthy from work—could eat their meal and toss away the "handle." These days the crimped edge is devoured along with the contents.

The Original Cornish Pasty Recipe

Pasty rolled out like a plate, filled with turmut, tates an' mait. Doubled up an' baked like fate. Tha's a Pasty.

Matta House Museum, 1.5 km south of Kadina off Moonta Rd., contains many relics and exhibits pertaining to the good old Matta Matta mining days, housed in the former mine manager's home. Hours are Wednesday, Saturday, Sunday, and holidays 2-4:30 p.m. Admission is $2.

The **Banking and Currency Museum,** 3 Graves St. (tel. 08-8821-2906), displays every type of Australian currency ever issued, as well as other banking exhibits. The museum also buys and sells coins, notes, and medals. Hours are Fri.-Wed. 10 a.m.-5 p.m.; closed Good Friday, Christmas Day, and the month of June. Admission is $2.

A heritage drive leads to **Wallaroo Mines,** one km west of Kadina, on Wallaroo Road. Signposts lead you on a walking tour of the old site, where you'll see ruins of the two-story-high engine building and visit places named Jericho and Jerusalem.

Wombat Hotel, 19 Taylor St. (tel. 08-8821-1108), has inexpensive pub-style accommodations. **Kadina Village Motel,** 28 Port Rd. (tel. 08-8821-1920), has slightly higher rates, but includes breakfast. **Kadina Caravan and Camping Park,** Lindsay Terrace (tel. 08-8821-2259), has campsites and on-site vans and is close to all facilities.

Food? This is Cornish pasty country—they'll stick to your ribs but won't shrink your pocketbook. Buy 'em anywhere! Try **Cross's Cornish Bakeshop,** 20 Graves St., or **Wallis's Kadina Bakery,** 42 Graves Street. **Dynasty Room,** 4 Goyder St. (tel. 08-8821-2829), offers Chinese, Thai, and Australian cuisine at moderate prices.

For local info, contact the **tourist information center,** Victoria Square (tel. 08-8821-2093). Hours are Mon.-Fri. 10 a.m.-2 p.m., Sat.-Sun. 9:30 a.m.-1:30 p.m.

In emergencies, contact: **police** (tel. 08-8821-1200), **ambulance** (tel. 08-8821-1029), the local hospital (tel. 08-8821-1544), or **Royal Automobile Association** (tel. 08-8821-1111).

Wallaroo

Wheat and barley are shipped from this busy port (pop. 2,225), but it still doesn't equal the millions of tons of copper ore once trafficked over the jetty to destinations overseas.

Situated 10 km west of Kadina, Wallaroo was originally settled by the Welsh. The **Welsh Chimney Stack,** a Wallaroo landmark, contains 300,000 bricks in its huge square structure. For some reason Welsh masons built square chimney stacks and the Cornish masons made theirs round.

See an extensive pictorial display of sailing ships, exhibits related to the smelting industry, and postal and sporting relics at **Wallaroo Nautical Museum,** Jetty Rd., in the old post office (tel. 08-8823-2366). Hours are Wednesday, Saturday, Sunday, and public and school holidays 2-4 p.m. Admission is $2.

Other heritage buildings include **Harvey's Pumping Station,** the **Institute, General Store,** old **Methodist Church,** and original **Wesleyan Chapel.**

You can safely swim at Wallaroo's sandy beaches. The boating and jetty angling are excellent as well.

Wallaroo Hotel, 26 Alexander St. (tel. 08-8823-2444), is pretty basic, but rooms are only about $25 per double. **Sonbern Lodge Motel,** 18 John Terrace (tel. 08-8823-2291), has moderately priced heritage accommodations, with rooms in the motel section costing $10 more. **Kohler Village,** Heritage Dr. (tel. 08-8823-2531), offers moderate-expensive two-bedroom holiday units with cooking facilities.

Campsites and on-site vans are available at both **Wallaroo North Beach Caravan Park,** North Beach (tel. 08-8823-2531), and **Office Beach Holiday Flats and Caravan Park,** Office Beach (tel. 08-8823-2722).

Dine on moderately priced local seafood at **The Seafood Corner,** corner Charles Terrace and Irwin St. (tel. 08-8823-2288). For takeaway fresh and smoked fish, crayfish, and prawns, try **G & KF Studt,** 35 Owen Terrace (tel. 08-8823-3222).

Moonta

The third point in the Copper Triangle, Moonta (pop. 2,200) lies 10 km south of Wallaroo. Moonta is the nicest of the three mining towns—maybe because it was the richest. The dignified architecture, from tiny miners' cottages to the Gothic-esque Uniting Church, is a splendid reminder of times past.

After you've explored around town, head for the nearby mine site to investigate the old buildings and relics. The former schoolhouse, now **Moonta Mines Museum,** is a living history exhibit where you can experience what conditions were like for the miners, many of whom worked the 767-meter-deep Taylor Shaft. The museum will provide a self-guiding map. **Miner's Cottage,** adjacent to the museum, is a restored Cornish dwelling, open for public viewing. On weekends you can ride a narrow-gauge tourist railway around the mine's complex. Hours are Wednesday, Sat.-Sun., public and school holidays 1:30-4 p.m. Admission is $1. For information, phone (08) 8825-3422.

Both the **Royal Hotel,** 2 Ryan St. (tel. 08-8825-2108), and the **Cornwall Hotel,** 20 Ryan St. (tel. 08-8825-2304), have inexpensive pub accommodations. **Moonta Bay Caravan Park,** Tossell St. (tel. 08-8825-2406), on the foreshore, offers campsites and cabins.

For your Cornish pasty fix, go to **Wither's**

Moonta Bakery, 8 George St., or **The Cornish Kitchen,** 14 Ellen St. (tel. 08-8825-3030). The historic **Cornwall Hotel** serves homestyle Australian meals, and the **Shaft Steak House,** Ellen St. (tel. 08-8825-2981), specializes, obviously, in slabs of beef.

Events

Kerneweck Lowender, held in May of every odd-numbered year, is a festival commemorating the Copper Triangle's Cornish heritage. Activities include "A Golya," a Cornish feast with dancing and drinking, "A Fer Tref," all the fun of a village green fair, "A Fer Kernewek," a Cornish fair with traditional sports and the crowning of "Cousin Jack" and "Cousin Jenny," and the Gorseth ceremony, a gathering of bands from Cornwall and Australia. Aside from Cornish pasties, revelers can sip on Swanky, a specially brewed ale.

THE EAST COAST

A sealed thoroughfare follows the coast to Edithburgh, where you either cut inland to Yorketown, Warooka, and Innes National Park, or continue along the coast on mix-or-match gravel and dirt roads.

Port Clinton to Ardrossan

Port Clinton, the east coast's northernmost seaside resort, has good crabbing beaches and is a seashell's throw from Clinton Conservation Park. **Port Clinton Caravan Park,** on the foreshore (tel. 08-8837-7003), has campsites and on-site vans.

The Yorke Peninsula offers secluded beaches and secret fishing holes.

Tiddy Widdy Beach is a good spot for sunning and swimming. **Price Beach** is near a large salt refinery, harvesting from a vast area of pans pumped full of Gulf St. Vincent seawater.

Ardrossan, about 150 km from Adelaide, is not just the largest east coast port, with bulk grain handling facilities; it's also home of the stump-jump plough, the particular tool, invented by Clarence Smith in 1876, that enabled mallee scrubland to be turned into golden wheatfields all across the country. The folks over at the **Ardrossan District Historical Museum,** on Fifth St., will be delighted to fill you in on more of the town's history. Hours are Sunday 2:30-4:30 p.m. Admission is $1. For information, phone (08) 8837-3213.

You can catch a scenic view of Gulf St. Vincent from the **BHP lookout** or trap some crabs at the jetty.

Royal House Hotel Motel, 1 Fifth St. (tel. 08-8837-3007), charges inexpensive rates in the hotel, $20 more for motel rooms. **Ardrossan Caravan Park,** Park Terrace (tel. 08-8837-3262), offers campsites, cabins, and on-site vans.

For emergencies, contact: **police** (tel. 08-8837-3017), **ambulance** (tel. 08-8837-3295), or the local **hospital** (tel. 08-8837-3021).

TO EDITHBURGH AND BEYOND

Continuing south, along the coast, you'll pass the fishing "villagettes" of **Rogues Point, Pine Point, Black Point,** and **Port Julia.** Divers will want to check out the shipwrecked *Zanoni,* about 15 km southeast of Ardrossan.

Port Vincent, set on a sweeping bay 46 km south of Ardrossan, is an old ketch-landing place, and a popular swimming, yachting, and waterskiing resort. The **Port Vincent Fisherman's Retreat,** corner Parsons Rd. and Kemp St. (tel. 08-8853-7057), offers moderately priced holiday flats. **Seaside Flats and Caravan Park,** Minlacowie Rd. (tel. 08-8853-7011), rents inexpensive flats as well as campsites and cabins.

Stansbury, 16 km away, is another sought-after holiday resort. Originally known as "Oyster Bay," it still offers some of the state's best oyster beds. Jetty fishing is also excellent here, and you'll find a decent selection of tourist facilities.

The units at **Stansbury Villas,** Adelaide Rd. (tel. 08-8852-4282), are moderately priced self-contained holiday flats. **Stansbury Holiday Motel,** Adelaide Rd. (tel. 08-8852-4455), is on the deluxe side with moderate to expensive rates (every room has a sea view). Campsites, cabins, and on-site vans are available at **Stansbury Caravan Park,** on the foreshore (tel. 08-8852-4171).

Past **Wool Bay, Port Giles,** and **Coobowie** lies picturesque **Edithburgh.** A former salt-producing township (and the first proclaimed settlement on southern Yorke Peninsula), Edithburgh is celebrated by divers drawn to the many shipwrecks along its coastline. If you take the scenic drive up to **Troubridge Hill,** you'll be able to see part of the shipwreck *Clan Ronald.*

Swimmers will find a rock pool set into a small cove, while the jetty provides ideal conditions for anglers. The small **Edithburgh Museum** features maritime displays and artifacts. Hours are Sunday and public and school holidays 2-4 p.m. Admission is $1.

Take a guided day-tour over to **Troubridge Island,** to view fairy penguins and other birds contained within the 14-hectare conservation park. For **Troubridge Island Tours,** contact Chris Johnson, Blanche St., Edithburgh 5583 (tel. 08-8852-6290).

Motel accommodations in Edithburgh are moderately priced. If you plan to stay awhile, you can get a self-contained unit for $160-245 per week at **Ocean View Holiday Flats,** O'Halloran Parade (tel. 08-8852-6029). **Edithburgh House,** Edith St. (tel. 08-8852-6373), offers old-fashioned seaside guesthouse rooms for high-moderate to expensive rates, but they include dinner and breakfast. **Edithburgh Caravan Park,** corner South Terrace and O'Halloran Parade (tel. 08-8852-6056), situated on the foreshore, offers campsites, on-site vans, and cabins.

Venture inland from Edithburgh 16 km to **Yorketown,** one of the peninsula's earliest pastoral settlements. Surrounded by salt lakes where crystal formations decorate the shores, several of the lakes are pink and worth watching at sunset. You'll find inexpensive accommodations at **Melville Hotel Motel,** 1 Minlaton Rd. (tel. 08-8852-1019), or at **Yorke Hotel,** 1 Warooka Rd. (tel. 08-8852-1221), but neither place is really comfy. The motel section at the Melville is probably your best bet. Camping and on-site vans are available at **Yorketown Caravan Park,** Memorial Dr. (tel. 08-8852-1563).

Beyond Edithburgh, the coast road turns to gravel (and occasionally to dirt) as it travels a sparsely populated route along scenic beaches and secluded bays, merging with the sealed highway about 10 km north of Innes National Park.

Hillocks Drive, 16 km east of Marion Bay, is a scenic road leading to **Butlers Beach,** set on a seven-km sea frontage. Privately run by the Butler family, the property has two surf beaches, a number of fishing spots, camping facilities, and a small general store. The property is closed mid-June through mid-August. For information, phone (08) 8854-4002.

INNES NATIONAL PARK

The main entrance to Innes National Park is four km southwest of Marion Bay. Situated at the southernmost tip of the Yorke Peninsula, this spectacular coastal park's 9,141 hectares stretch from Stenhouse Bay on the east coast, around Cape Spencer, to Browns Beach on the west coast. Just a three-hour drive from Adelaide, the park is a favorite with city dwellers who come to surf, fish, dive, and bushwalk.

Big sightseeing attractions are the shipwreck *Ethel M,* run aground in 1904 and now disintegrating near an isolated cove called The Gap, and the old ghost town at **Inneston** (follow the historical markers past the Cape Spencer turnoff).

Clean beaches, crystal-clear water, and colorful marinelife create a delightful environment for aquatic activities. There's good fishing at Chinaman's Beach, Salmon Hole, Pondalowie Bay, Browns Beach (terrific for year-round salmon fishing), Little Browns Beach, Cape Spencer, and a host of rock fishing spots between Pondalowie and Stenhouse Bays (be careful of those wet rocks!).

Bushwalkers can choose from a variety of tracks leading through such diverse terrain as low scrub, salt lake flats, coastal dunes, and rugged cliffs—with a good probability of running into a friendly emu or kangaroo!

Camping is permitted within the park at several different areas. The main camping area is at Pondalowie Bay, where facilities were recently upgraded.

During Christmas holidays, park rangers conduct guided activities for children and young adults.

For camping permits and other information, contact **Park Headquarters,** Stenhouse Bay (tel. 08-8854-4044), or the **Warooka District Council Office,** Warooka (tel. 08-8854-5055). Admission is $3 per vehicle.

UP THE PENINSULA

Going northward from Innes National Park, the sealed road brushes by **Warrenben Conservation Park,** 4,061 hectares of dense mallee, dryland tea-tree vegetation, and native pines. The gravel road from Marion Bay sort of winds around the coast, with other gravel or dirt paths branching out to the beaches. **Daly Head** is yet another special fishing hole, as is **Corny Point** at the northwestern tip. Corny Point also has a lighthouse and camping facilities.

At Point Turton, you can either continue zigzagging the beachy back roads to the top of the peninsula or turn onto the seven-km sealed stretch that leads back to the main highway at Warooka.

In the tiny township of **Brentwood,** 17 km north of Warooka, visit **Brentwood Pottery** (tel. 08-8853-4255) in the old general store/post office. Rent a **gypsy wagon,** pulled by a gentle Clydesdale, for overnight camping by the sea or for a longer and leisurely ride around southern Yorke Peninsula. Rates run about $100 per day, with a three-day minimum. For information, contact Stansbury Holiday Motel (tel. 08-8852-4455) or Anthony Honner, Brentwood via Minlaton, SA 5575 (tel. 08-8853-4201). The same people also arrange farm holidays in moderately priced self-contained stone cottages.

Minlaton (pop. 900), about 14 km north of Yorketown, is referred to as the "Barley Capital of the World." It's also the home of Captain Harry Butler's *Red Devil,* a 1916 monoplane flown by the pioneering aviator during World War I. Ostensibly, this is the world's only remaining Bristol fighter plane, and lucky you can see it at the glass-fronted **Harry Butler Hangar/Museum,** near the town center. Nearby, on Main St., the **National Trust Museum** (tel. 08-8853-2127) exhibits photos, memorabilia, and farming implements, and, at the corner of Bluff and Maitland roads, **Jolly's Museum** (tel. 08-8853-2364) features restored tractors and other machinery. **Gum Flat Homestead Gallery,** Stansbury Rd. (tel. 08-8853-2287), two km east of Minlaton, is an arts-and-crafts center with locally made wares for sale.

Rooms are moderately priced at **Minlaton Hotel Motel,** 26 Main Rd. (tel. 08-8853-2014). Rent campsites or on-site vans at **Minlaton Caravan Park,** corner Bluff and Maitland Roads (tel. 08-8853-2435).

For Minlaton emergencies, contact: **police** (tel. 08-8853-2100), **ambulance** or local **hospital** (tel. 08-8853-2200), and **Royal Automobile Association** (tel. 08-8853-2243).

Turn off at Urania for **Port Victoria,** "last of the windjammer ports" and now a busy little fishing resort. Sailing and waterskiing are popular around Wardang Island. See relics and curios of the nautical past at **Port Victoria Maritime Museum** (tel. 08-8834-2057). Hours are Sunday and school holidays 2-4 p.m. Admission is $1.

Bayview Holiday Flats, 29 Davies Terrace (tel. 08-8834-2082), offers fully self-contained units at inexpensive to moderate rates, depending on season. Beachfront **Port Victoria Caravan Park** (tel. 08-8834-2001) has campsites and on-site vans.

Maitland, the heart of Yorke Peninsula, is Colonel Light's vision at work again—a modern agricultural center well laid out and surrounded by parklands. View agricultural artifacts and brush up on local history at **Maitland Museum,** corner Gardiner and Kikerran Streets (tel. 08-8832-2220). Hours are Sunday and public holidays 2-4 p.m. Admission is $1.

Maitland Hotel, 33 Robert St. (tel. 08-8832-2431), "where the beer is cold and the welcome warm," has inexpensive rooms. The pub serves good, home-cooked meals. **Eothen Farmhouse** (tel. 08-8836-3210), near beaches and bush, is a fully equipped separate home, with kitchen, lounge, open fires, and high-moderate rates.

Emergency numbers for Maitland are: **police** (tel. 08-8832-2621), **ambulance** and local **hospital** (tel. 08-8832-2626).

A 20-km jaunt westward from Maitland brings you to **Balgowan,** a century-old landing place for ketches making pick-ups and deliveries for local farmers. Today it serves as a serene retreat for fishermen.

Back on the main highway, it's a 35-km drive to Moonta, lower edge of the Copper Triangle, then about 60 km more through Kadina to **Port Broughton,** a seaside resort at the tippy-top of the peninsula, where there's a safe swimming beach for children and a good fishing jetty for anglers.

Spend the night at **Port Broughton Hotel,** on the foreshore (tel. 086-35-2004). Built in 1888, this family-style establishment has inexpensive rooms, with breakfast included. Other facilities include a main bar, saloon bar, beer garden, large dining room, a la carte dining room, and bottle shop. **Main Park,** 2 Broughton St. (tel. 086-35-2188), has campsites, on-site vans, and cabins.

Port Broughton Charter Boats, 19 Harvey St. (tel. 086-35-2466), offers fishing trips ($30-80) or pleasure cruises ($10, for one hour) in the Spencer Gulf.

For Port Broughton emergencies, contact: **police** (tel. 086-35-2255), **ambulance** (tel. 086-35-2544), the local **hospital** (tel. 086-35-2282), or **Royal Automobile Association** (tel. 086-35-2522).

TRANSPORT

Premier Roadlines (tel. 08-8415-5544) operates daily service from Adelaide to Kadina, Wallaroo, Moonta, Port Hughes, and Moonta Bay. One-way fare for the three-hour trip to Moonta is $21.

Yorke Peninsula Bus Service (tel. 08-8391-2977) travels daily from Adelaide to Ardrossan ($16), Port Vincent ($20), Edithburgh ($22), and Yorketown ($22).

All coaches depart Adelaide's **Country Passenger Depot,** 101 Franklin St. (tel. 08-8231-4144).

There is no public transport south of Warooka and, if you're hitching, road traffic is pretty minimal.

EYRE PENINSULA

Wild coastlines with stupendous surf and isolated beaches, round-the-clock steel mills and busy grain terminals, phenomenal rock formations and ancient ranges, gentle sea lion colonies and great white shark breeding grounds are some of the Eyre Peninsula attractions that keep travelers coming (and going).

The peninsula is *wide,* stretching 469 km from Port Augusta in the east, across the Eyre Highway, past the Gawler Ranges, to Ceduna, the last ample outpost before the Nullarbor Plain. Alternate Route 1 (called Lincoln Highway from Port Augusta to Port Lincoln, and Flinders Highway from Port Lincoln to Ceduna) traverses the peninsula, hugging the coast—and its bays, beaches, ports, and parks—along sheltered Spencer Gulf on the east, round the pounding Southern Ocean and the Great Australian Bight. The distance from Port Augusta back up to Ceduna is 668 km. Another option that enables you to see a sizeable chunk of this region is to follow the Eyre Highway. If you take this route you can journey into the Gawler Ranges to the north and explore famed Mt. Wudinna Rock along the way, and cut through the center of the peninsula along the Tod Highway (258 km of sheep and cereal scenery) down to Port Lincoln, the adjacent national parks, and the offshore islands. From there, depending on which way you're headed, you can either follow the east coast up to Whyalla (and back to Adelaide or onward to the Northern Territory) or take the west side, skirting round the sea-lion colony, passing through Streaky Bay to Ceduna and the great beyond.

History

By now you've surely guessed that super-sailor Captain Matthew Flinders charted the Eyre Peninsula during his 1802 mega-voyage aboard the *Investigator.* He was not using his own charts, however, but those of Dutch explorer Peter Nuyts who, in 1627, sailed his *Gulden Zeepaard* ("Golden Seahorse") as far as Streaky Bay. Nuyts, more inclined toward trade than homesteading, turned back when he got to the offshore islands now named Nuyts Archipelago.

By the time Flinders arrived, Abel Tasman and Captain Cook had already been there, Tasman circling the country and Cook glimpsing the peninsula's east coast. Flinders did a more thorough examination of the coastline, naming the majority of features after crew and family members, as well as locales around his hometown of Lincolnshire. The peninsula itself was named by Governor Gawler for Edward John Eyre, the explorer who in 1839-40 made a series of frustrating obstacle-fraught overland expeditions, culminating in the first east-west crossing of Australia.

Bountiful golden-grain harvests, iron ore deposits, a thriving steel industry, and an ocean bounty that makes this one of the country's largest commercial fisheries are the region's moneymakers. Port Lincoln and Thevenard, the two biggest seaports—both with road and railway connections—ship a steady flow of cargo worldwide.

Apropos of fish, the white pointer shark breeds around Dangerous Reef, off Port Lincoln's shores, and the underwater scenes in *Jaws* were filmed here.

PORT AUGUSTA

At the head of the Spencer Gulf, bustling Port Augusta (pop. 15,300) is the town at which Highway 1, the Eyre Highway (actually Highway 1 with a change of name and direction), and the Stuart Highway all converge. From this crossroads, travelers scurry and scamper north to the Flinders Ranges, south to Adelaide, east to Sydney, and west across the Nullarbor, or slightly southwest to the Lincoln Highway and the Eyre Peninsula coast. Besides that, it's on the main railway line used by the Ghan, Trans Australian, and Indian Pacific.

Established in 1852, Port Augusta served as a wool port for nearly a century. Today its major functions are transporting goods to and from the isolated Outback and generating electricity for much of South Australia.

Sights

Wadlata Outback Centre, 41 Flinders Terrace (tel. 086-42-4511), features displays, videos, and models depicting Aboriginal Dreamtime (including a big fiberglass serpent storyteller). Other exhibits highlight the early explorers and the history of electricity and communications. Hours are Mon.-Fri. 9 a.m.-5:30 p.m., Sat.-Sun. 10 a.m.-4 p.m. Admission is $6.

Homestead Park Pioneer Museum, Elsie St. (tel. 086-42-2035), displays pioneer artifacts and machinery. Hours are daily 10 a.m.-5 p.m., closed Christmas Day.

ETSA (Electricity Trust of South Australia) Northern Power Station (tel. 086-42-0521)

conducts one-hour behind-the-scenes tours of its $500 million coal-fired power plant Mon.-Fri. 11 a.m. and 1 p.m. (Strong footwear is advised.) Turn off Highway 1 at Andy's Truck Stop, 2.5 km east of Port Augusta.

Royal Flying Doctor Service, 4 Vincent St. (tel. 086-42-2044), provides medical care to Outback residents. The center is open for tours Mon.-Fri. 10 a.m.-noon and 1-3 p.m.

School of the Air (tel. 086-42-2077) offers educational programs to children residing in the Outback. Facilities are at Central Primary School at the southern end of Commercial Rd., and tours are conducted Mon.-Fri. 10 a.m., except holidays. Admission is $2.

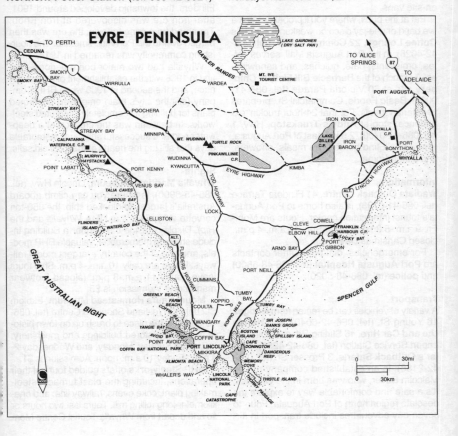

Accommodations and Food

Augusta Hotel, 1 Loudon Rd. (tel. 086-42-2701), has inexpensive pub rooms. **Myoora Motel,** 5 Hackett St. (tel. 086-42-3622), and **Port Augusta East Motel,** Hwy. 1 (tel. 086-42-2555), both offer comfy rooms at moderate rates. Also moderately priced is centrally located **Flinders Hotel Motel,** 39 Commercial Rd. (tel. 086-42-2544), with modern conveniences, family units, and good home cookin'.

Both **Shoreline Caravan Park,** Gardiner Ave. (tel. 086-42-2965), situated on the gulf, and **Big 4 Fauna Caravan Park,** corner of Hwy. 1 and Stokes Terrace (tel. 086-42-2974), set amidst peacocks and other birds, rent campsites and on-site vans.

Eat at the pubs, where you'll probably catch a live band or dee-jay disco on weekends. **Ozzie's Coffee Lounge,** 22 Commercial Rd. (tel. 086-42-4028), in the Port Augusta Mall, serves coffee, croissants, pâté, quiches, and sandwiches. A branch of the **Barnacle Bill Fish 'n' Chippery** sits at 60 Victoria Parade (tel. 086-41-0000). **Basic Foods,** Commercial St., prepares vegetarian meals. For that 24-hour truckin' experience, stop at **Andy's Truckstop,** Hwy. 1 (tel. 086-41-0700), 2.5 km east of Port Augusta, where you'll find home-style meals, showers, and a laundromat.

Information

Wadlata Outback Centre, 41 Flinders Terrace (tel. 086-41-0793), is also home to Port Augusta's tourist information center. Hours are Mon.-Fri. 9 a.m.-5:30 p.m., Sat.-Sun. 10 a.m.-4 p.m., closed Christmas Day.

For emergencies, dial 000. Other contacts are **Port Augusta Hospital** (tel. 086-48-5500) and **police** (tel. 086-48-5020).

Transport

A variety of vehicles can be rented from **Budget,** 16 Young St. (tel. 086-42-6040), and **Handy Ute and Car Hire,** 46 Stirling Rd. at Mobil Davenport Service Station (tel. 086-42-4255). **Butler's Outback Safaris,** 3 Prosser St. (tel. 086-42-2188), is an established company run by Malcolm Butler, who was born in the Outback. It's a safe and comfortable way to explore the desolate region north of Port Augusta. Four- to seven-day adventures include transport in air-conditioned 4WD vehicles, all meals, accommodations, and other necessary equipment.

WHYALLA

A big-time shipbuilding port until 1978, Whyalla (pop. 26,900) survives today on its round-the-clock steel production and shipments of ore from nearby Iron Knob and Iron Baron. As South Australia's largest provincial city—with a sunny, Mediterranean-style climate—facilities are good, and "pass-through" tourism gives yet another economic boost.

Originally called Hummock Hill by Captain Flinders, the township developed around 1901, after iron ore was discovered at Iron Knob. Trammed from mine to town, the ore was then barged over to the Port Pirie smelters. The flourishing community was renamed in 1914.

Whyalla had two major boom periods—the first in 1938 with the establishment of a blast furnace, and the second in 1958 when BHP Company (still the city's main employer) confirmed plans for building its completely integrated steelworks. In between was the creation of a deepwater port and successful shipyard, memorable days that still tug the hearts of the local old salts.

Sights

Whyalla Maritime Museum, Lincoln Hwy. (tel. 086-45-8900), is where you can climb aboard Australia's largest landlocked ship, the 650-ton corvette *Whyalla* (a.k.a. HMA *Whyalla* and the *Rip*). Displays inside the Tanderra Building include shipping memorabilia, valuable BHP models, and one of the country's largest model railways. Hours are daily 10 a.m.-4 p.m. Ship tours leave hourly 11 a.m.-3 p.m. (closed footwear mandatory). Admission is $5.

Mount Laura Homestead Museum, Ekblom St., behind Westland Shopping Centre (tel. 086-45-9319), is the place to brush up on town history and view restored buildings and machinery. Hours are Sunday, Monday, and Wednesday 2-4 p.m., Friday 10 a.m.-noon. Admission is $1.

BHP Steelworks offers guided tours of their operations, including the blast furnace, steelmaking plant, coke ovens, railway line, and one-kilometer-long rolling mill. Tours last two hours or so and depart from Whyalla Tourist Centre Monday, Wednesday, and Saturday 9:30 a.m. Be sure to wear closed footwear. Admission is $5. For information and bookings, phone (086) 45-7900.

Hummock Hill Lookout, site of a World War II gun battery, affords a dynamite view of Whyalla, the foreshore, upper Spencer Gulf, Port Bonython, Point Lowly, and the Middleback Ranges. Follow the brown and white "Route 61" (Whyalla Tourist Drive) signs.

Whyalla Wildlife and Reptile Sanctuary, Lincoln Hwy., across from the airport (tel. 086-45-7044), features koalas, wombats, dingoes, 'roos, emus, deadly snakes, and a walk-through aviary in natural bushland. Hours are daily 10 a.m.-6 p.m. (Nov.-April), 10 a.m.-4:30 p.m. (other months). Admission is $4.50.

Port Bonython, about 10 km north of Whyalla, off the Lincoln Hwy., is the site of the massive SANTOS plant, which distills liquid hydrocarbons that have passed from Moomba through a 659-km underground pipeline. Though you can't tour the facility, you can get a view of operations from along the roadway or shore.

Port Lowly, two km beyond SANTOS, offers beautiful gulf views, a popular summer beach, and the Port Lowly Lighthouse (over 110 years old), which looks out upon playful dolphins that often swim by.

The **Scenic Coastal Drive** is a 20-km combination sealed and gravel road along Spencer Gulf, from Fitzgerald Bay to Point Douglas. Take the marked turnoff before Port Bonython.

The **Whyalla Foreshore** redevelopment provides excellent facilities for swimming, jetty fishing, windsurfing, and picnicking. **Whyalla Marina** has a new four-lane launching ramp for all boating activities.

Murrippi Beach, off Eight Mile Creek Rd., 12 km south of Whyalla, is a legal nude beach (no facilities).

Accommodations and Food
As with most cities this size, you'll find pubs, motels, restaurants, and takeaways—all pretty standard. Most accommodations have their own dining facilities.

Pub rooms are inexpensive at either **Hotel Whyalla,** 9 Darling Terrace (tel. 086-45-7411), or **Lord Gowrie Hotel,** Gowrie Ave. (tel. 086-45-8955). **Airport Whyalla Motel,** Lincoln Hwy.

(tel. 086-45-2122), and **Sundowner Hotel Motel,** Lincoln Hwy. (tel. 086-45-7688), both offer comfortable rooms at low-moderate rates. Campsites, cabins, and on-site vans are available at **Whyalla Foreshore Caravan Park,** Broadbent Terrace (tel. 086-45-7474).

Entertainment and Recreation
Middleback Theatre, corner Nicolson Ave. and Racecourse Rd. (tel. 086-45-8022), presents live theater, musical performances and other stage presentations, as well as arts-and-crafts exhibitions. You can inspect the theater foyer, its mural, and stained-glass windows Mon.-Fri. 9 a.m-5 p.m.

Whyalla Recreation and Leisure Centre, off Racecourse Rd. near the junction of Nicolson Ave. (tel. 086-45-5488), welcomes visitors to use the heated indoor swimming pool, squash courts, gymnasium, weightlifting equipment, sweat track, and volleyball and tennis courts. Equipment is available for rental.

Information
Whyalla Tourist Centre (tel. 086-45-7900), next to BHP Steelworks on Lincoln Hwy., provides maps, tour bookings, and info on the local bus service (weekdays and Saturday mornings). Hours are Mon.-Fri. 9 a.m.-5 p.m, Saturday 9 a.m.-4 p.m., Sunday and public holidays 10 a.m.-4 p.m. Closed Christmas Day and Good Friday.

TO PORT LINCOLN

From Whyalla, the Lincoln Highway makes a slight inland jag, traveling for a short distance along the iron-ore-rich Middleback Ranges, angling back to the coast (in about 111 km) at Cowell.

Cowell
Set on scenic Franklin Harbour, a protected bay noted for calm waters and great fishing, Cowell (pop. 692) is also famous for its huge jade deposits, discovered in the nearby Minbrie Ranges in 1965, as well as some interesting marble uncovered along with the jade boulders. The area is thought to be the world's largest producer of green and black jade.

Several operators offer mine tours, or you can visit the factory and showroom of **Gemstone Corporation of Australia,** Second St. (tel. 086-29-2111).

Other attractions include the **Franklin Harbour Historical Museum,** in the old post office, and the **Agricultural Museum,** on Lincoln Highway. Both are open by appointment. For information, phone (086) 29-2032.

Lucky Bay, 16 km north of town, is a popular beach resort with safe swimming, good fishing, and a boat ramp. **Poverty Beach,** just south of town, has good surfing.

Rooms are inexpensive at the **Franklin Harbour Hotel,** 1 Main St. (tel. 086-29-2015). For moderate rates that include breakfast, **Shultz Farm,** Smith Rd. (tel. 086-29-2194), offers home-style accommodations on a sheep and grain property overlooking the coast. **Cowell Foreshore Caravan Park** (tel. 086-29-2307) has campsites, cabins, and on-site vans. Don't miss a taste of the delicious locally harvested oysters.

Obtain local **tourist information** at District Council of Franklin Harbour, 6 Main St. (tel. 086-29-2019).

Continuing Southward

From Cowell, you can cut inland 42 km to the rural community of Cleve. The scenic Cleve-

Cowell Hills drive provides great views of the countryside and Spencer Gulf. From Cleve, you can cut southeast 25 km back to the coast at Arno Bay. Or stick to the coastal road and pass along the wide, lovely beaches at **The Knob, Port Gibbon,** and **Point Price Sandhills.**

Arno Bay, halfway point between Whyalla and Port Lincoln, is a tranquil fishing village in winter and a tourist mecca in summer. **Redbanks,** six km north of town, is a designated geological monument of rock pools and just-as-rocky cliffs. **Arno Hotel** (tel. 086-28-0001), near the beach, has country-style rooms. Their low rates include breakfast.

Port Neill, 33 km south from Arno Bay and two km off the main highway, is another attractive, clean, safe water sports haven. Check out the blue water and the rolling hills from **Port Neill Lookout,** one km north of town. **Fauser's Museum,** opposite the caravan park (tel. 086-88-9041), is a private collection of steam and stationary engines, motorcycles, vintage autos, and other relics. Hours are daily 10 a.m.-4 p.m.

Port Neill Hotel, Peake Terrace (tel. 086-88-9006), has inexpensive rooms. **Henley's Holiday Flats,** Gill St. (tel. 086-88-9001), are fully self-contained units, also inexpensive. **Port Neill Caravan Park,** Peake Terrace (tel. 086-88-9067), rents campsites and on-site vans.

popular Redbanks Beach, near Arno Bay

BOB RACE

If you wait until low tide to visit **Lipson Cove,** another 20 km south, you can walk across to **Lipson Island,** a coastal bird sanctuary.

Tumby Bay shelters fishing and boating waters and is also service center for the surrounding rural townships. **C.L. Alexander National Trust Museum,** corner West Terrace and Lipson Rd. (tel. 086-88-2574), features local memorabilia in an original wooden schoolhouse. Hours are Friday and Sunday 2:30-4:30 p.m. Admission is $1.

Head to **Island Lookout** to catch a good view of town, bay, and the **Sir Joseph Banks Group of Islands,** 15 km offshore. Named by Captain Flinders for the renowned English botanist, the islands are bird sanctuaries for Cape Barren geese, pied cormorants, eastern reef egrets, crested terns, and many other species. If you don't have your own boat, sign on for a half- or full-day tour with **Sea Jade Charter,** 2 Pfitzner St. (tel. 086-88-2424).

Seabreeze Hotel, Tumby Terrace (tel. 086-88-2362), rents inexpensive rooms. **Tumby Bay Motel,** Berryman St. (tel. 086-88-2311), near the beach, has a swimming pool and is moderately priced. Campsites, cabins, and on-site vans are available at **Tumby Bay Caravan Park,** Tumby Terrace (tel. 086-88-2208), along the foreshore.

If you don't think you can live without another display of vintage implements, machinery, and artifacts (or if you just want to explore the hill country between Tumby Bay and Port Lincoln), take the 40-km detour to Koppio and the **Koppio Smithy Museum.** Try to get there for the annual Open Day, when all the machinery is turned on and huffs, puffs, toots, and honks in unison. Hours are Tues.-Sun. 10 a.m.-5 p.m. For information, phone (086) 84-4243.

Back on the coast, **North Shields,** just 11 km north of Port Lincoln, is home of the **Karlinda Collection,** an amazing amassment of more than 10,000 shells, rocks, minerals, fossils, and other marine curios. It's all housed in the building next to the post office. Hours are daily 9 a.m.-9 p.m. Admission is $1. For information, phone (086) 84-3500.

You can live cheaply and simply at the historic 1868 **Wheatsheaf Hotel,** Government Rd. (tel. 086-84-3531), where rates include continental breakfast. The Wheatsheaf serves counter meals in the pub and a la carte in the dining room overlooking Boston Bay.

Heading into Port Lincoln, you will pass through Australia's newest winegrowing region (vines planted in 1984, first harvest in 1987), and the cellars of **Boston Bay Wines.** Specializing in red and white table wines, the vineyard is open Sat.-Sun. and public holidays 11:30 a.m.-4:30 p.m., daily December and January. For information, phone (086) 84-3600.

PORT LINCOLN

At the Eyre Peninsula's southern edge, Port Lincoln (pop. 12,550) is often referred to as "blue water paradise." Paradise?—Not quite, but there *is* plenty of blue water. Boston Bay, stretching from Point Boston to the tip of Port Lincoln National Park, is three times larger than Sydney Harbour. Mild winters and comfortable summers, combined with ideal conditions for boating, fishing, skin diving, and windsurfing (and great white shark breeding!) keep the tourists coming.

Named by Captain Flinders after his home county of Lincolnshire, Port Lincoln was originally set to be South Australia's state capital. A lack of freshwater, along with Colonel Light's decided bent toward Adelaide, caused that plan to be withdrawn. The city didn't fare badly, though. Aside from a healthy tourist industry, Port Lincoln is home to Australia's largest commercial tuna fishing fleet and one of the country's busiest grain terminals.

Sights

Axel Stenross Maritime Museum, Lincoln Hwy. near Shaen St. (tel. 086-82-3889), features memorabilia from windjammer days, as well as early photos, a working slipway, and a blacksmith shop. Hours are Tuesday, Thursday, Sat.-Sun., and public holidays 1-5 p.m. Admission is $1.50.

A short distance from the maritime museum is the **First Landing Site.** See the freshwater spring that lured the early settlers—it's still bubbling and gurgling through the sand.

Mill Cottage and **Settler's Cottage** museums, located on the grounds of Flinders Park (at Lincoln and Flinders Highways), both display artifacts and historical exhibits of Port Lincoln's early beginnings. Hours for Mill Cottage are Tues.-Sun. 2-4:30 p.m. Admission is $1. Contact Port Lincoln Library to arrange entrance to Settler's Cottage.

Nearby, **Rose-Wal Memorial Shell Museum** (tel. 086-82-1868), on the grounds of the Old Folks' Home, displays a large and valuable collection of shells and sealife. Hours are daily 2-4:30 p.m. Admission is $1.

Apex Wheelhouse, Hindmarsh St. (tel. 086-82-2537) across from the caravan park, is a restored tuna boat wheelhouse and interpretive center. Photos, charts, and a color video will brief you on the fishing industry. Hours are daily 9 a.m.-5 p.m.

You'll find excellent **lookout points** at: **Winter's Hill,** five km northeast of town on Flinders Hwy.; **Puckridge Park,** on Angas St.; and the **Old Mill,** Dorset Pl., an 1846 flour mill (historic both because it's old and because it never operated).

A popular day-trip is the cruise to **Boston Island,** a working sheep station, discovered and named by Captain Flinders. Select either the Boston Island Safari (a trip to the island, sightseeing, and historical commentary) or Bay Island Cruise (usually run only if a landing on the island is not possible). Departures are from the jetty at Tasman Terrace. Tours are operated by **Investigator Cruises** and can be booked at the tourist office or Kirton Point Caravan Park.

More daring souls, who'd rather eyeball sharks instead of sheep, can journey to **Dangerous Reef,** "home of the great white shark" and locale for *Jaws'* underwater scenes. You can take a diving charter (good luck) or the *Dangerous Reef Explorer,* a high-speed commuter vessel (travel time about 40 minutes). A safer option for those who left their diving gear at home is a 30- by 12-meter underwater viewing platform with observatory and aquarium (and a dive cage). A large sea lion colony also lives on the reef. For info and bookings, contact the tourist office.

Accommodations and Food

If you plan to stay in a pub, I'm still partial to the old Wheatsheaf in North Shields (see above). Most of the motels are on Lincoln Highway or Tasman Terrace. **First Landing Motel,** 11 Shaen St. near the maritime museum (tel. 086-82-2919), has moderately priced rooms

with four-post beds. **Westward Ho Holiday Flats,** 112 London St. (tel. 086-82-2425), are fully self-contained units at moderate prices. **San Pan Windinna,** 34 Lincoln Hwy. (tel. 086-82-1513), is a fully equipped beachfront cottage in the expensive category. You can rent an inexpensive cabin or campsite at **Kirton Point Caravan Park,** Hindmarsh St. (tel. 086-82-2537). And, if you've got the bucks ($175 per week, per person, with a minimum of five people and maximum of 12), you can rent all of Boston Island. Tariff includes a six-bedroom home, fishing dinghies, tractor, and trailer. No linen, though—you must bring your own or pay an extra fee. For information, phone Peter Davis (tel. 086-82-1741) or contact the South Australian Tourism Commission Travel Centre.

Tasman Mall has the best cheap eats in town. Aside from that, look to the local pubs for meals and nightlife.

Information

Port Lincoln Tourist Office, Civic Centre, Tasman Terrace (tel. 086-82-6666), books tours and accommodations and provides info on bicycle rentals, boat charters, and local coach service. Hours are Mon.-Fri. 9 a.m.-5:30 p.m., Saturday 9 a.m.-noon, Sunday (during holidays) 10 a.m.-noon.

Events

Port Lincoln's big blowout is the annual **Tunarama Festival,** held each January. Festivities include parades, cavalcades, roving musicians, a variety of competitions, firework displays, rock concerts, dinner dances, and the crowning of Miss Tunarama.

TIP OF THE EYRE

The southernmost edge of the Eyre Peninsula stretches from Lincoln National Park, leaning on Spencer Gulf, to Coffin Bay National Park, jutting into the Great Australian Bight.

Lincoln National Park, 20 km south of Port Lincoln, covers 17,000 hectares with open spaces, rugged cliffs, and peaceful bays. Catch panoramic views of park and town from Stamford Hill. Conventional vehicles can access scenic spots like Surfleet Point, Spalding Cove,

Old Donington House, Cape Donington Lighthouse, and Taylor's Landing, but you'll need a 4WD to reach wilderness areas like Memory Cove and Cape Catastrophe. Check with the park ranger (tel. 086-88-3177) for camping information and road conditions.

You'll need a key and permit ($15 plus $3 deposit) to enter privately owned **Whaler's Way,** a dynamically scenic cliff-top drive at the very tip of the peninsula. Magnificent lookouts, blowholes, caves, sparkling beaches, and roaring surf—as well as a wildlife and bird sanctuary—are some of the features. Get yet another special permit to camp at the Redbanks area. On the road to Whaler's Way, you'll pass **Mikkira Station,** an 1840s sheep station. Pick up keys and permits at Port Lincoln Tourist Office or at service stations. Visits are limited to Sunday and school and public holidays.

Continuing along Flinders Highway, you'll pass **Port Lincoln Fauna Park, Little Swamp, Big Swamp,** and **Wanilla Forest.** Turn off toward Coffin Bay, through **Kellidie Bay Conservation Park** and the **Coffin Bay Lookout,** through the township, and straight into the national park.

Coffin Bay National Park, 46 km from Port Lincoln, is a massive 30,000 hectares of wilderness area, much of it accessible only to bushwalkers and those in four-wheel drives (there are some sealed roads for conventional vehicles). Hike the 25-km **Yangie Trail** to Almonta Beach, Avoid Bay, and Yangie Bay—be careful if swimming, **sharks are common.** The park is particularly spectacular early spring to early summer, when gorgeous wildflowers bloom. Inquire about road conditions and pick up camping permits at the ranger's headquarters, near the park's entrance.

The town of **Coffin Bay** is literally surrounded by parks and offers sheltered waters for fishing, boating, swimming, skin diving, and windsurfing. Normally a teeny township of 350 residents, the population leaps to nearly 10 times that in summer. Oysters cultivated here are renowned across Australia. Pay a visit to **Coffin Bay Oyster Farm,** where the motto is, "Eat fish and live longer, eat Coffin Bay Oysters and love longer."

Holiday flats, ranging from inexpensive to moderately priced, are lined up along the Esplanade. **Coffin Bay Caravan Park** (tel. 086-85-4170) has campsites, cabins, and on-site vans.

Pick up **tourist info,** bus tickets, postage stamps, fishing tackle, and hot roasted chicken at Beachcomber Agencies, the Esplanade (tel. 086-85-4057).

UP FLINDERS HIGHWAY

Climbing up the peninsula, the highway makes gentle jags inward to pastoral land and country townships, then teases you back to sparkling bays and beaches along the Great Australian Bight.

Turn off at Wangary, 29 km north of Coffin Bay, to **Farm Beach** and Anzac Cove (sometimes called Gallipoli Beach), where the movie *Gallipoli* was filmed. You'll pass Mt. Dutton on the way, a good climb, but get permission first, as the land is privately owned.

Back on Flinders Highway, it's mostly sheep and farm country. At **Coulta,** you can experience farm life for $28 at **Wepowie Farm,** Edilillie Rd. (tel. 086-87-2063). One- or two-day horseback trips and pack horse treks are offered, as well as customary farm activities. Close by are salty Lake Greenly, with hang gliding at Mt. Greenly, and good surfing at Greenly Beach.

Elliston, 100 km from Coulta, is a small fishing village on Waterloo Bay, where the scenic coastline jumps from rugged cliffs to sheltered inlets. Here you'll find "clogs," fossilized cocoons of the *Leptopius duponti* weevil thought to be nearly 100,000 years old. **Rocket Site Cottage,** on the Esplanade (tel. 086-87-9028), is a fully equipped cottage at inexpensive-moderate rates. Both **Elliston Caravan Park,** Flinders Hwy. (tel. 086-87-9061), and **Waterloo Bay Caravan Park,** Beach Terrace (tel. 086-87-9076), have campsites, cabins, and on-site vans.

Flinders Island, 35 km off the coast of Elliston, is a 3,700-hectare getaway with swimming beaches and picturesque views. Accommodations in either a renovated cottage or shearer's quarters cost about $280 double, with a four-night minimum stay. For bookings and air charters ($75 roundtrip), phone (086) 26-1132.

Talia Caves, 40 km north of Elliston, has wonderful limestone caves, gnarly rock formations, and bleached sand dunes to explore.

Venus Bay, another 22 km north, is a small township popular with small boat and jetty anglers and, increasingly, with surfers. **Needle Eye Lookout** gives a great view of the pounding sea, intriguing rocks and arches, and towering cliffs. Turn off at **Point Labatt,** a designated national park, to view Australia's only permanent mainland colony of sea lions.

Back on Flinders Highway, east of Point Labatt, you'll be able to glimpse **Murphy's Haystacks,** sculptured rock formations rising out of the wheatfields. These huge granite *inselbergs* are reputedly more than 1.5 billion years old.

Streaky Bay, 85 km north of Venus Bay (first sighted in 1627 by Dutch explorer Peter Nuyts), was named by Captain Flinders because of the seaweed streaks coloring the bay. This township (pop. 1,200), another of the myriad picturesque fishing villages, is also a service center for the local agricultural communities. Historical buildings of interest are the **School and Kelsh Pioneer Museum,** full of local artifacts, and **Hospital Cottage,** built in 1864. On Alfred Terrace, the **Restored Engine Centre** features a collection of 60-or-more engines, some dating back to the early 1900s. All of the museums are open Tuesday and Friday 2-4 p.m.

Koolangatta Farm, via Piednippie Rd. 25 km from town (tel. 086-26-1174), offers inexpensive country accommodations that include breakfast ingredients. Even cheaper is **Mulgunyah,** Poochera Rd. (tel. 086-26-1236), also a cottage on a farm. Breakfast not included but farm activities are. **Streaky Bay Motel,** 7 Alfred Terrace (tel. 086-26-1126), features moderately priced self-contained units with cooking facilities. Rent a campsite or a cabin at **Streaky Bay Foreshore Tourist Park,** Wells St. (tel. 086-26-1666).

Sheltered **Smoky Bay,** about midway between Streaky Bay and Ceduna, is a teeny villagette, best known for its annual Easter rodeo.

THE EYRE HIGHWAY

From Port Augusta to Ceduna, the Eyre Highway (Highway 1) spans 469 km of industrial sights, wheat belts, wilderness, and geological wonders.

Iron Knob, 68 km west of Port Augusta, is the birthplace of Australia's steel industry. Iron ore, discovered here in 1894, is quarried and shipped to the Whyalla Steelworks, along with supplies from the neighboring mines of Iron Monarch, Iron Baron, Iron Prince, Iron Queen, and Iron Duke (only Iron Knob is open to visitors). Tours are available Mon.-Fri. at 10 a.m. and 2 p.m., Saturday at 2 p.m. Cost is $3. For information, phone (086) 46-2129.

Iron Knob Mineral & Shell Display, 266 Gill St. (tel. 086-46-2130), features more than 2,000 crystals from all over the world and ore specimens from Iron Monarch mine. Hours are daily 10 a.m.-4 p.m. Admission is $1.

Rooms are inexpensive to low-moderate at either **Iron Knob Hotel,** Main St. (tel. 086-46-2013), or **Iron Knob Motel Roadhouse,** Eyre Highway (tel. 086-46-2058).

Kimba, 89 km from Iron Knob, is the "Gateway to the Gawler Ranges" and, really, not much else. If you need a rest, **Kimba Community Hotel Motel,** High St. (tel. 086-27-2007), has inexpensive rooms ($20 higher in the motel section) and a bar, bistro, beer garden, and dining room.

At Kimba, turn off onto the winding gravel road that leads through the Gawler Ranges, where you'll see gentle hills with unique rock formations, varied bird and animal life, and glorious spring wildflowers such as Sturt's desert pea, the state flower, which was first sighted here in 1839 by Eyre. You can camp at **Mt. Ive Station** (tel. 086-48-1817), near Lake Gairdner, in a range of very inexpensive facilities. A large part of the district is privately run, so visitors are asked to stick to the public roads, obtain permission before camping or hiking, leave all flora and fauna alone, and take all rubbish with them. Conventional vehicles can access much of the area, but, as in all wilderness and isolated regions, check the weather and road conditions regularly. **Gawler Ranges Wilderness Safaris,** P.O. Box 11, Wudinna, S.A. 5652 (tel. 086-80-2020), is an experienced operator offering two-to four-day 4WD safaris into the region.

Kyancutta, 89 km from Kimba, sits at the junction of the Eyre and Tod Highways. **Wudinna,** 13 km farther, is the service center for the surrounding rural community, and the airstrip is used for regular service to and from Adelaide. Travelers stop here en route to see Australia's econd largest granite outcrop, **Mt. Wudinna Rock** (261 meters high), 10 km northeast of own. Other weathered masses in this group re **Polda, Turtle,** and **Little Wudinna Rocks.**

If you need a place to stay in the area, **Gawler Ranges Motel,** Eyre Hwy. (tel. 086-0-2090), has both moderately priced modern ooms and a caravan park with campsites and n-site vans.

The **Minnipa** area, 38 km northwest of Wudina, has more granite outcrops. There you'll find he Minnipa-Yardea road, another route into the Gawler Ranges. As you head farther east on the Eyre Highway, you'll pass through plains-and-rains country, the townships of **Poochera** and **Virrulla,** and finally into Ceduna.

CEDUNA

On the shores of Murat Bay, and at the junction of the Eyre and Flinders Highways, Ceduna pop. 2,880) is the last full-service town before he vast reaches of the Nullarbor Plain. As such, ts name was quite aptly derived from *chedoona,* Aboriginal for "a resting place."

Established as a town in 1901, Ceduna is he business hub of the far west coast and an mportant regional cereal-growing center (with an airport and regular service to Adelaide). The community began originally at Denial Bay, about 2 km to the west, where cargo ships pulled up close to shore, waited until low tide, then loaded wagons with provisions for the settlers. You can still see the ruins at **McKenzie Landing,** on the oad to Davenport Creek. More recently, Thevenard (four km from Ceduna) serves as deep-sea port for the area, transporting grain, salt, and gypsum worldwide. (An interesting aside: According to map references in *Gulliver's Travels,* Gulliver encountered those little people of Liliput on St. Peter and St. Francis Islands, off he coast of Thevenard.)

Aside from being a supply and rest stop for travelers, Ceduna boasts a variety of local beaches for fishing, swimming, boating, and surfing.

Sights
The **Old Schoolhouse National Trust Museum,** Park Terrace (tel. 086-25-2210), displays

historic relics of Ceduna's early days. The **Telecommunication Earth Station** (OTC), 37 km northwest of town, is a global satellite system that channels approximately half of Australia's daily telecommunications with Asia, Africa, and Europe via Indian Ocean satellites. Guided tours of the facility are offered Mon.-Fri. 11 a.m. and 2 p.m. For information, phone (086) 25-2505.

Accommodations and Food
The hotel section in **Ceduna Community Hotel Motel,** O'Loughlin Terrace (tel. 086-25-2008), overlooking Murat Bay, is cheapest. Other motels, mostly along Eyre Highway, range from moderate to expensive. (There's not a lot of choice way out here.) Campsites, cabins, and on-site vans are available at **Ceduna Foreshore Caravan Park,** 5 South Terrace (tel. 086-25-2290).

Meals are at the pubs, motel dining rooms, coffee lounges, and takeaways, or make your own from the supermarket.

Information
Stop in at **Ceduna Gateway Tourist Centre,** 46 Poynton St. (tel. 086-25-2780), for local and Eyre Peninsula information. Hours are Mon.-Fri. 9 a.m.-5:30 p.m., Saturday 9 a.m.-2 p.m.

TRANSPORT

For air services operating to and about the Eyre Peninsula, contact: **Ansett Australia** (tel. 13-1300 toll-free); **Qantas Airways** (tel. 13-1313 toll-free); **Kendell Airlines** (tel. 069-22-0100); or **Lincoln Airlines** (tel. 1800-018-234).

Greyhound Pioneer Australia operates daily coach service along the Eyre Highway on the Adelaide-Perth route, with stop-offs at Iron Knob, Kimba, Wudinna, Minnipa, Ceduna, and the Nullarbor. Coaches depart Adelaide's central bus station. For information and bookings, phone 13-2030 toll-free. **Stateliner** coaches serve all west coast towns—on the peninsula and along the highway—from Adelaide. The trip to Port Lincoln (eight hours) costs about $50, and to Ceduna (10 hours), $59. For information and bookings, phone (08) 8415-5544.

CROSSING THE NULLARBOR

Now that the road is sealed, this isn't *quite* the adventure it used to be (we'll get to the authentic Outback later). But, sealed highway or not, it is still a long, lonesome (and, sometimes, loathsome) trek across the Nullarbor Plain into Western Australia—480 km from Ceduna to the state line, and another 725 km to Norseman, end of the Eyre Highway, where you either take the high road or the low road another 725 km to Perth.

Nullarbor is Latin for "No Trees," but you'll see some timber, a few saplings, and a bit of scrub along the coastal part of the highway, particularly if you travel after the winter rains. It's the transcontinental railway line, several hundred kilometers north, that traverses the really plain Plains, a span 692 km long and 402 km wide. (By the way, that 478-km chunk of single track is the world's longest stretch of straight railway.)

The usual Outback driving rules apply (review the tips in this book). Also, you'll encounter quarantine stations at Ceduna, in South Australia, and Norseman, in Western Australia. Either have a picnic before reaching those two checkpoints or be prepared to surrender plants, fruits, veggies, nuts, grains, wool, animal skins, honey, soil, and even used containers that held these products.

Another thing to remember (or discount altogether) is the time change between Balladonia and Nullarbor. Put your watch back 45 minutes at the border, unless it's daylight saving time—then it increases to three hours. But, all in all, three hours either way are pretty insignificant when you're smack in the middle of nowhere!

See "Transport" under "The Eyre Peninsula," above, for information on traversing the plain.

History

The Eyre Highway was named for Edward John Eyre who, in 1841, became the first fellow to cross the country from east to west—an agonizing five-month journey in which Eyre's buddy, John Baxter, bit the Nullarbor dust. Following

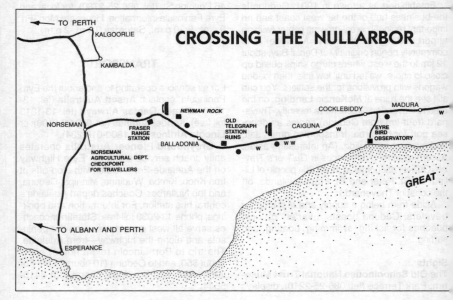

CROSSING THE NULLARBOR

TO PERTH
KALGOORLIE
KAMBALDA
NORSEMAN
FRASER RANGE STATION
NEWMAN ROCK
NORSEMAN AGRICULTURAL DEPT. CHECKPOINT FOR TRAVELLERS
BALLADONIA
OLD TELEGRAPH STATION RUINS
CAIGUNA
COCKLEBIDDY
MADURA
EYRE BIRD OBSERVATORY
TO ALBANY AND PERTH
ESPERANCE
GREAT

Eyre's dusty footsteps came John and Alexander Forrest, brothers who mapped out much of the overland telegraph route that would connect Perth with Adelaide. In 1877, the eastern and western sections of the telegraph line were linked up at Eucla, and in the 1890s those same bullock and camel tracks that helped build the line were followed by miners on their arduous trip to Western Australia's goldfields. After that, the Nullarbor was crossed by a succession of odd transport—camels, cycles, a 10-horsepower Brush car, a Citroen. In 1941, with the advent of World War II, army engineers commenced construction of the Eyre Highway. Cross-country traffic, at first a trickle in the 1950s, grew (thanks to the Commonwealth Games in Perth) to more than 30 vehicles a day in 1962. The Western Australia section of the highway was sealed in 1969, and the South Australia portion was surfaced seven years later.

Ceduna to Border Village

Penong, 73 km west from Ceduna, is the "Town of 100 Windmills" and a good place to stop for petrol and supplies. Rooms are inexpensive at **Penong Hotel** (tel. 086-25-1050).

Cactus Beach, 21 km south of Penong, is famous worldwide for its three perfect surfing breaks, "Castles," "Cactus," and "Caves," with both left and right breaks for serious surfers. Other nearby attractions are **Point Sinclair** and **Pink Lake. Fowlers Bay,** on the turnoff to **Nundroo,** is a great fishing hole. **Scott's Bay, Mexican Hat,** and **Cabot's Beach** are popular camel-trekking points. The **Nundroo Hotel Motel** (tel. 086-25-6120) features moderately priced rooms. You can buy locally made Aboriginal artifacts at **Yalata Roadhouse,** (tel. 086-25-6990), a tourist complex another 51 km along run by the Yalata Aboriginal Community. Accommodations there are inexpensive and campsites are also available.

From June through October **southern right whales** can be seen during their annual breeding migration along the coastline between Yalata and the border. In 1989, the largest group of these whales to visit the country's shores was spotted just off Yalata Reserve. Permits to enter the land can be obtained at Yalata Roadhouse.

From Nullarbor to the border, you'll pass along sheer coastal cliffs with plunging views of the rugged terrain and the Great Australian Bight.

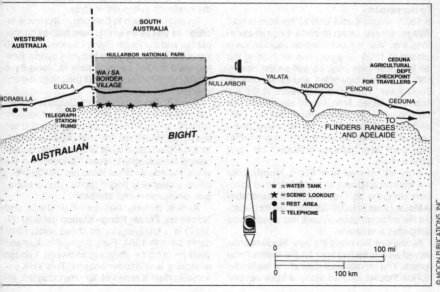

Nullarbor, 94 km from Yalata, is adjacent to the original **Nullarbor Homestead.** Rooms in **Nullarbor Hotel-Motel** (tel. 086-25-6271) are in the moderate price range. The Eyre Highway transects **Nullarbor National Park,** where signs point the way to spectacular lookouts over the Bunda Cliffs, a 200-km stretch from the Head of the Bight almost to the Western Australia border. The area around the Nullarbor is cave-land, but recommended for experienced cavers only. **Koonalda Cave** features a collection of Australia's earliest rock engravings. For information and camping permits, phone District Ranger, Department of Environment and Natural Resources, Streaky Bay (086) 25-3144. Permits to enter the area must be obtained from Yalata Roadhouse.

You'll know you've reached **WA/SA Border Village,** 184 km from Nullarbor, when you spot **Rooey II,** a hideous five-meter-tall fiberglass kangaroo. (Climb inside Rooey II's pouch if you're hard up for a photo op.) The signpost with distances to international locales like Paris, London, New York, etc., is another visited site. Rooms are moderate-expensive and campsites are cheap at **WA/SA Border Village** (tel. 090-39-3474).

To Norseman

In 1887, historic **Eucla,** only 13 km from Border Village, served as an important communications link. Visit the old telegraph station ruins (closed in 1924—the new line runs along the rail line), the town jetty, as well as the nearby cliffs, caves, and blowholes, and the sandhills at Eucla Pass. View gold rush relics at the old **School of Mines,** Mon.-Fri. 10 a.m.-4 p.m. Admission is $2. **Amber Motor Hotel** (tel. 090-39-3468) has moderately priced rooms (inexpensive in the old hotel section), plus a swimming pool, beer garden, restaurant, bar, and caravan park.

Sixty-six km west from Eucla, **Mundrabilla** is a tiny township with an animal and bird sanctuary along the highway. Rooms at **Mundrabilla Motor Hotel** (tel. 090-39-3465) are moderate, but the adjacent caravan park has inexpensive campsites and cabins.

Ninety-one km along the way, **Madura** once served as a breeding spot for the Indian Army horses. You can still view ruins of the old Madura Roadhouse, located along a track several

kilometers from the "new" roadhouse. Moderate-expensive rooms are available at **Madura Pass Oasis Inn** (tel. 090-39-3464), and the adjacent caravan park has campsites.

You can still see the stone ruins of an Aboriginal mission at **Cocklebiddy,** 66 km from Madura. In 1983, a team of French explorers set a world depth record at nearby Cocklebiddy Cave. If you have a four-wheeler, take the 32-km coastward detour before "town" to **Eyre Bird Observatory** (established in 1977), part of Nuytsland Nature Reserve. Housed inside the 1897 Eyre Telegraph Station, the observatory studies a variety of birds, flora, and other fauna. A small museum features old telegraph memorabilia. The observatory also houses a library donated by deceased American millionaire Harold Anderson, who believed a forthcoming nuclear disaster would spare this isolated spot. If you book in advance, you can overnight at the observatory for about $50 (cheaper if you stay longer or have a YHA card) including room and full board. Roundtrip transport from Cocklebiddy is about $25. For advance bookings (mandatory), phone (090) 39-3450. In Cocklebiddy, **Wedgetail Inn** (tel. 090-39-3462) has a lounge, pub, dining room, and takeaway. Accommodations are in the moderate to expensive range.

It's another 66 km to **Caiguna,** with service facilities as well as an airstrip used both by charter planes and the Royal Flying Doctors. About 10 km south is the memorial to Eyre's buddy, Baxter, killed in 1841 by angry natives. **John Eyre Motel** (tel. 090-39-3459) has moderate-expensive rates.

The 182-km distance from Caiguna to **Balladonia** is one of the world's longest straight stretches of road. Those rock-hole dams you see just before Balladonia are called **Afghan Rocks,** for the Afghan camel driver who was shot dead for having the audacity to wash his tootsies in the water. **Balladonia Hotel Motel** (tel. 090-39-3453) offers moderately priced rooms, plus a bistro, pub, dining room, and takeaway.

Almost midway between Balladonia and Norseman, **Fraser Range Station** (tel. 090-39-3457) is a family-operated sheep station that dates back to 1864. Pass through in July and you'll be in on the shearing; midwinter through midspring is wildflower season. This YHA associate offers a range of accommodations, in-

cluding dorm beds ($14 per night) and camp-
sites ($10 per night). If you're traveling by coach,
phone ahead for pick-up from the nearest Eyre
Highway drop-off.

You'll see mine shafts and tailings as you
near Norseman, where—depending on your
mood—you'll either drop south to the coast or
north to the goldfields.

THE FLINDERS RANGES

Photographers, painters, bushwalkers, and nature lovers travel to these desert range rock formations for hot shots, divine inspiration, colorful
adventure, and a breath of fresh air.

The Flinders Ranges—broken into southern,
central, and northern sections—begin to jut between Crystal Brook and Peterborough (about
250 km north of Adelaide), then sweep and arc
northward to a point 160 km east of Marree at
the edge of the Outback.

Thrust up from the sea about 1.6 billion or
so years ago, these bent, twisted, buckled, and
gorged ranges are best described as earth
sculptures. Minerals embedded in the ancient
plains and cliffs chameleon along with the sun or
moon, the time of year, a turn of your head into
delicate pink, salmon, mauve, purple, angry red,
and sunshine yellow. These ranges aren't high,
but they'll surely make you feel that way!

The scenery varies from woodsy slopes in
the temperate south to rugged peaks in the dry
north, with Wilpena Pound, the great natural
amphitheater in the central region, ranking as the
highlight of the Flinders Ranges. Wildflowers
(including South Australia's state flower, Sturt's
desert pea), wildlife, and birds can be seen
throughout the area. In fact, you're likely to spot
lots of interesting vegetation and pretty posies,
but please help preserve this fragile and beautiful
region by leaving your finds intact. As requested
by the Royal Automobile Asociation: "If you must
take something home—make it a photograph."

The most popular time to visit is April through
October. Summer months are usually very hot
and very cold. Rain, at any time of year, can
cause flash flooding and render roads impassable. Be sure to follow Outback driving regulations and inquire about road and weather conditions along your journey. It is imperative that
bushwalkers obtain detailed maps and information from park rangers or tourist information
centers before embarking on either a short trail
or lengthy trek. Those taking the Heysen Trail

should note that the Flinders section is closed 1
Nov.-30 April because of fire restrictions.

The easiest way to reach the Flinders Ranges
is via Highway 47 from Port Augusta. The road
is sealed to Wilpena Pound, and also up to Lyndhurst (junction of the Strzelecki Track). After
that it becomes gravel, dirt, and indescribable. A
popular "circle tour" is to start at Port Augusta,
pass through Quorn and Hawker to Wilpena,
continue northward through Flinders Ranges
National Park up to Blinman, swing west to
Parachilna, then south back to Hawker.

History
This region is older than the hills—literally.
Captain Matthew Flinders undoubtedly
thought he discovered the place when he visited
in 1802—after all it was later named after him.
Well, try telling that to the Aboriginals. Though
you won't find too many of them around anymore. You will find their paintings and rock carvings, some known to be 12,000 years old, scattered about the ranges. (*Please* do not tamper
with paintings, carvings, or relics.)

There are a number of historical sites in and
around the ranges, mostly old copper- and gold-
mining towns, homesteads that served as resting spots for overland teams. They're remnants
of the late-1800s wheat farming boom, nipped in
the sheaf by bad weather, plagues, and hunger.

SOUTHERN FLINDERS RANGES

You can travel any of several sealed roads from
the Mid North to tour the relatively gentler and
more accessible southern region.

Telowie Gorge
Located 25 km northeast of Port Pirie, with access off Highway 1, Telowie Gorge (1,946
hectares) is the southernmost park of the
Flinders Ranges. Steep red cliffs, open wood-

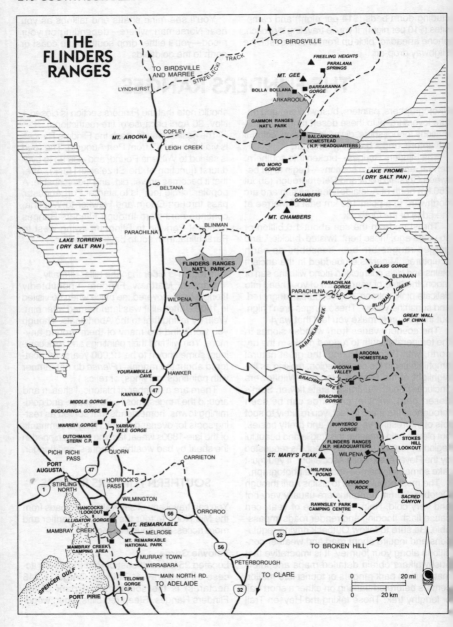

THE
FLINDERS
RANGES

(top) Aboriginal art at unmarked site on main gorge wall, Carnarvon National Park, Queensland
(bottom) large Aboriginal "sand painting" made of colored gravel, Tjilpa Valley, Northern Territory
(following page) get into the Pinnacles Desert, Nambung National Park, Western Australia

lands, spring wattle blossoms, yellow-footed rock wallabies, and prolific birdlife are the main features. There are no facilities and limited camping sites.

Melrose

This one-time copper town, situated at the foot of Mt. Remarkable, is the Flinders Ranges' oldest settlement. These days it's a grazing and wheat- and barley-growing community and a good base for exploring Mt. Remarkable National Park. In fact, a walking trail leads from town all the way to the top of Mt. Remarkable (956 meters). Good views can be had from either the **War Memorial** or **Lookout Hill.**

Historic buildings include the old **Police Station and Courthouse** (now a National Trust museum, open daily 2-5 p.m.), **post office, Jacka's Brewery,** and **Melrose Inn.** Two other oldies, built in the 1850s, are **North Star Hotel,** Nott St. (tel. 086-66-2110), and **Mt. Remarkable Hotel Motel,** Stuart St. (tel. 086-66-2119). Both offer inexpensive pub-type accommodations. **Melrose Caravan Park,** Joes Rd. (tel. 086-66-2060), rents campsites, cabins, and on-site vans.

Mt. Remarkable National Park

Wedged between the Melrose-Wilmington road and the Port Pirie-Port Augusta highway, Mt. Remarkable National Park (8,649 hectares) is known for its dramatic scenery and diverse plant and

animal life. The three best places to explore are the somewhat separate Mt. Remarkable (behind Melrose), the narrow Alligator Gorge (accessed one km south of Wilmington), and red-gum-lined Mambray Creek (accessed from a branch road about 45 km north of Port Pirie, off Highway 1). Walking trails with plenty of signposts lead to panoramic lookouts and isolated gorges from both Alligator Gorge and Mambrey Creek. Mambray Creek campground is open, except during fire-ban days; bush camping is permitted in some areas. Admission is $3 per vehicle. For information, phone (086) 34-7086.

Nearby points of interest are: **Hancock's Lookout,** north of the park, at the top of Horrocks Pass; the ghost towns of **Hammond** and **Bruce,** northeast of Wilmington; and, for all you rodeophiles, **Carrieton,** about 25 km northeast of the ghost towns, hosts a nationally known rodeo every October.

Quorn

From 1917 until 1937, Quorn (pop. 1,080) served as an important railway junction on both east-west and north-south transcontinental routes. Not so after a new standard gauge line was built to Marree in 1956, leaving the town to fend for itself. In 1974, after part of the old line was restored to accommodate a steam-powered tourist train, Quorn was back in business—not as the big-time rail depot it used to be but with travelers who want to putt-putt through Pichi Richi Pass.

Quorn's Pichi Richi Railway takes tourists on a sentimental journey.

Billed as the "Gateway to the Flinders Ranges," Quorn is about 40 km from Wilmington and a bit farther from Port Augusta.

The **Pichi Richi Railway** departs from old Quorn Railway Station for a picturesque two hour and 45 minute roundtrip journey (about $19) into Pichi Richi Pass, rolling over bridges, along the Pichi Richi River, and through the long-abandoned Pichi Richi township. The train only runs during school holidays and long weekends. Check at the tourist information office or phone (08) 8276-6232 (Adelaide) or (086) 48-6598 (Quorn) for schedules.

Quorn is full of historic buildings. Aside from the railway station, some of the best examples are the **public school, town hall, National Bank, Bank of Adelaide, courthouse, State Bank, Quorn Mill** (now the local museum), and the **Austral, Grand Junction,** and **Criterion Hotels.** Accommodations in any of the three hotels, all on Railway Terrace, are inexpensive-moderate. You can stay in the old **Quorn Mill,** also on Railway Terrace (tel. 086-48-6016), which is priced in the high-moderate range, including continental breakfast. **Quorn Caravan Park,** Silo Rd. (tel. 086-48-6206), offers campsites, on-site vans, and cabins.

Dutchman's Stern Conservation Park (3,532 hectares), five km west of Quorn, has sharp cliffs, steep gorges, and a wide range of plant and bird species (this is the northern limit for Adelaide rosellas, scarlet robins, kookaburras, and the yellow-faced honeyeater). The park has marked walking trails (only pro bushwalkers should attempt the climb to 800-meter Dutchman's Stern) and a picnic area. Camping is not permitted. For information, phone (086) 48-6571.

For Quorn emergencies, dial 000, or contact: **police** (tel. 086-48-6060), **fire brigade** (tel. 086-48-6000), **ambulance** (tel. 086-48-6366), **hospital** (tel. 086-48-6200), or **Royal Automobile Association (RAA)** (tel. 086-48-6012).

To Hawker
Take your pick: gorges, ruins, or caves. If you take the unsealed road, you'll pass through stunning **Yarrah Vale,** and the **Warren, Buckaringa,** and **Middle Gorges.** Traveling the highway will bring you to **Kanyaka,** remnants of a large sheep station dating back to 1851. Though the station once supported 70 families, all that's

left are bricks and pieces of the old stone buildings and graveyard. Farther along the road, behind a rise, is another group of ruins. Follow the track 1.5 km to **Death Rock Waterhole**—the road's end.

Other **historic ruins** in the area are Wilson, Gordon, Hammond, Saltia, Simmonston, and Willochra. Local information centers sell guidebooks to the sites.

About 10 km south of Hawker and a 30-minute walk from the road, **Yourambulla Cave** features Aboriginal rock drawings and paintings. (Remember—*don't touch!*)

CENTRAL FLINDERS RANGES

At Hawker, you enter the heart of the Flinders and junction of the "Circle Tour" that will take you through the best parts of these ranges.

Hawker
Hawker (pop. 300) is another old railway community, bypassed when the standard gauge was built. Billed as a "typical Outback town," Hawker provides tourist facilities for travelers to nearby Wilpena Pound.

Historical buildings worth checking out are the **railway station, Hawker Hotel, Sightseer's Café, post office, Institute Building,** and **Hawker Motors** (tel. 086-48-4014), formerly the Federal Boot Store, currently a small museum, fuel station, supply shop, and tourist information center.

Hawker Hotel Motel, corner Elder and Wonoka Terrace (tel. 086-48-4102), has pub and motel rooms ranging from inexpensive to moderate. **Outback Motel,** 1 Wilpena Rd. (tel. 086-48-4100), is a modern motel that costs about the same as the Hawker. **Yappala Station,** nine km northwest of Hawker, off Leigh Creek Rd. (tel. 086-48-4164), provides a variety of accommodations on its working sheep station. A two-night minimum stay is required. **Hawker Caravan Park,** 44 Chace View Terrace (tel. 086-48-4006), has campsites and on-site vans.

In case of an emergency, call 000. Other emergency numbers are: **police** (tel. 086-48-4028), **hospital** (tel. 086-48-4007), and **Royal Automobile Association** (tel. 086-48-4014).

Wilpena Pound

This natural amphitheater, 55 km north of Hawker, and encompassed by the 92,746-hectare Flinders Ranges National Park, is the most popular attraction of the ranges. Once a wheat-farming and sheep-grazing area, this is now a wildlife refuge for many species, particularly kangaroos and spectacular birds ranging from wedge-tailed eagles to colorful parrots. The basin is a grandiose 80 square km, surrounded by a circle of sheer, splintered, multicolored cliffs (the highest point is 1,190-meter **St. Mary's Peak**). Within the circle, however, gentle slopes lead into the vast central plain. Wilpena Pound is a bushwalker's heaven. Myriad trails guide you along everything from a casual one-hour stroll to a full-day's steep and stony climb. (Be sure to complete a log sheet at the park office, open 24 hours, before embarking on extended walks.) The only access into the pound is through the narrow gorge above **Sliding Rock,** near Wilpena Pound Motel.

The Pound is important in the Aboriginal mythology of the Flinders Ranges (*wilpena* means "a kangaroo skin curled up on its edges"). Tribal drawings, paintings, and carvings can be seen at **Arkaroo Rock,** near Moonarie Gap, and at **Sacred Canyon.** Both areas are about 19 km south of Wilpena (though on different roads).

Other points of interest within Flinders Ranges National Park are the **Bunyeroo** and **Brachina Gorges** and the **Aroona Valley,** where you can see ruins of the old homestead.

The only motel accommodations at the Pound are at expensive **Wilpena Pound Resort** (tel. 086-48-0004), with pool, bar, and dining room. Tent camping is permitted near the entrance to the Pound for about $10 per night. **Arkaba Station,** 35 km east of the Pound (tel. 08-232-5454), offers expensive (moderate if sharing) fully equipped cottage accommodations. **Rawnsley Park Camping Centre** (tel. 086-48-0008), 20 km south of Wilpena, offers campsites, on-site vans, and moderately priced holiday units. For camping within the park, see "Services and Information," below.

To and from Blinman

You'll be traveling on gravel once you leave the Pound. Engaging spots along the 59-km drive to Blinman are **Stokes Hill Lookout** and a long, ironstone-topped rock formation called the **Great Wall of China.**

Blinman (pop. 98), at the northern edge of Flinders Ranges National Park, was a hustle-bustle copper mining town from 1862 until 1890. Old mine machinery and relics are still in evidence, as are a few historic buildings. You can overnight at the 1869 **North Blinman Hotel** (tel. 086-48-4867), with a pool and inexpensive rates in either the hotel or motel sections. **The Captain's Cottage,** Mine Rd. (tel. 086-48-4894), is an expensive fully equipped three-bedroom cottage with fireplace. **Blinman Caravan Park,** Mine Rd. (tel. 086-48-4867), offers campsites.

Heading west to circle back to Hawker, two routes will get you to the highway junction at Parachilna: **Glass Gorge** is slightly out of the way along a dirt road, but the views are terrific, especially when the wild hops are in bloom; the gravel road goes through **Parachilna Gorge,** a tourist village at **Angorichina,** and the spring-fed **Blinman Pools** (near Angorichina, reached from the Parachilna and Blinman Creeks). **Angorichina Village Camping Area** (tel. 086-48-4842) rents campsites, cabins, and cottages.

Rejoin the main highway at **Parachilna,** and either go north 70 km to Leigh Creek or south 89 km to Hawker. **Prairie Hotel,** in Parachilna (tel. 086-48-4895), a "typical bush pub," has moderately priced rooms with or without breakfast included.

About 70 km east of Blinman, along one route to the Northern Flinders Ranges, **Chambers Gorge** features 100 meters of Aboriginal rock carvings on its left wall. **Mount Chambers** (409 meters) provides dynamic views of Lake Frome on one side, Wilpena on the other.

NORTHERN FLINDERS RANGES

Rugged, arid, remote, and exquisite, the northern ranges are reached from either Leigh Creek or the Chambers Gorge road.

Leigh Creek

Leigh Creek (pop. 1,635) used to be 13 km north of where it is now. That's right—the whole town just up and moved when the original site was needed for additional coal mining. Beat that for town spirit! Leigh Creek South reopened in 1981 and grass (the kind you mow) has been banned. Like it or not, this is your northern-ranges oasis, with shopping facilities, bank, post office, hospital, fuel, auto mechanic, as well as a regional office of the Department of Environment and Natural Resources. **Aroona Dam,** four km west of town, is a popular picnic area.

If you're a coal enthusiast, you'll enjoy looking down at some of the mine workings from the

THE HEYSEN TRAIL

visitor's viewing area, about three km from the turnoff to Leigh Creek Coalfields, on the Hawker-to-Marree highway. Free public tours are given March-Oct. and school holidays.

In emergencies, dial 000, the **police** (tel. 086-75-2004), or the **hospital** (tel. 086-75-2100).

Arkaroola
Despite the harsh, occasionally hostile environment, Arkaroola's 60,000-hectare sanctuary harbors a large variety of plants and wildlife. This former mining area was only established as a privately run reserve in 1968. Since then it's been the buzz of naturalists, adventurers, and travel guides.

At Arkaroola, see the art gallery, mineral and fossil museum, pioneer cottage, outdoor pastoral museum, and astronomical observatory (tel. 08-8212-1366); viewing is subject to light and weather conditions. Nearby points of interest are the Cornish smelters at **Bolla Bollana,** the dazzling view from **Mt. Painter** (790 meters), waterholes at **Barraranna** and **Nooldoonooldoona,** and **Sitting Bull, Spriggs Nob,** and **The Pinnacles** mountain tops. Radioactive **Paralana Hot Springs,** 27 km north of Arkaroola, is thought to be Australia's last site of volcanic activity, and is also an Aboriginal ceremonial spot.

Gammon Ranges National Park (128,228 hectares) is extremely rugged and isolated territory, accessed only by 4WD vehicles, except for the park headquarters area. Walking trails are not marked, and only very experienced and well-equipped bushwalkers should trek this area. Be sure to notify park rangers of your proposed route. For camping in the park, see "Services and Information" below.

Don't miss **Mt. Gee,** sitting between Mt. Painter and Freeling Heights. It's a crystal mountain, one gigantic mass of crystallized quartz.

Three different motels make up **Arkaroola Tourist Village.** Tariffs range from inexpensive to expensive, and camping sites cost about $15 per night. Book through Arkaroola Travel, 50 Pirie St., Adelaide, SA 5000 (tel. 08-8212-1366) or, on short notice, phone the village direct at (086) 48-4848.

Even if you're on a tight budget, spring $50 for the 4WD **Ridgetop Tour,** a four-hour adventure up, over, and around absolutely astounding scenery. Book through Arkaroola Tourist Village.

SERVICES AND INFORMATION

Fuel and **public telephones** are available at the following Flinders Ranges locations: Arkaroola, Beltana, Blinman, Carrieton, Copley, Hawker, Leigh Creek, Mambray Creek, Melrose, Morchard, Murray Town, Orroroo, Parachilna, Peterborough, Port Augusta, Port Germein, Quorn, Rawnsley Park, Wilmington, Wilpena, Wirrabara, and Yunta.

For comprehensive information, contact **Flinders Outback Tourism,** P.O. Box 41, Port Augusta, SA 5700 (tel. 086-42-2469). This agency also sells detailed maps of the Flinders Ranges and the Outback.

Other **regional information centers** are: Melrose Tourist Information Centre, Council Offices, Stuart St., Melrose (tel. 086-66-2014); Peterborough Tourist Centre, Main St., Peterborough (tel. 086-51-2708); Port Augusta Tourist Information Centre, 41 Flinders Terrace, Port Augusta (tel. 086-41-0793); and Quorn Tourist Information Centre, Council Office, Seventh St., Quorn (tel. 086-48-6031). Most motels, caravan parks, and roadhouses also carry tourist information.

Information and **camping permits** for the national and conservation parks within the Flinders Ranges can be obtained from the **Department of Environment and Land Management,** Far North Region, in Hawker (tel. 086-48-4244).

Contact **park rangers** at Flinders Ranges National Park (tel. 086-48-0048), Wilpena (tel. 086-48-0048), Oraparinna (tel. 086-48-0017), Balcanoona Homestead (tel. 086-48-4829), and Mambray Creek (tel. 086-34-7068).

Obtain detailed maps of the **Heysen Trail** from the Department of Recreation, Sport, and Racing, P.O. Box 1865, Adelaide, SA 5001, or at the department's shop at City Centre Arcade, Adelaide (tel. 08-8226-7374). Flinder's area shops, as well as map- and bookstores throughout Australia, sell a range of Ranges maps. Also collect maps and other motoring tips from RAA branches.

Northern Roads Condition Hotline (tel. 08-11-633) provides up-to-date info on Flinders and Outback road conditions.

TRANSPORT

Augusta Airways (tel. 086-42-3100) operates scheduled air service between Port Augusta, Adelaide, and Leigh Creek, as well as scenic and charter flights to Outback areas.

Stateliner (tel. 08-8415-5544, Adelaide, or 086-42-5055, Port Augusta) provides coach service to Arkaroola, Beltana, Booleroo Centre, Copley, Hawker, Leigh Creek, Melrose, Murray Town, Mambray Creek, Parachilna, Port Augusta, Port Germein, Peterborough, Quorn, Wilmington, Wilpena, Wirrabara, and Yunta. Sample fares are: Adelaide-Quorn, $40; Adelaide-Wilpena Pound, $50; Adelaide-Arkaroola, $68. **Greyhound Pioneer Australia** (tel. 086-42-5055, Port Augusta, or 13-2030 toll-free), offers a Port Augusta-Hawker-Leigh Creek service. The fare to Hawker is about $17, and to Leigh Creek $40.

Bushwalkers *must* carry detailed trail maps and adhere to all warnings. It is mandatory that you check in with park rangers before starting off. Heed rules for Outback travel and safety.

Organized Tours

For travelers who'd rather leave rules and regulations in the hands of experienced guides, a wide variety of Flinders Ranges tours are available. Sightsee by air, coach, four-wheeler, horse, or camel. Any tourist information center can provide a list of recommended operators. Also inquire locally—often a shopkeeper or motel manager has a tour-guide relative. **Wilpena Pound Resort** and **Rawnsley Park Camping Centre,** at Wilpena Pound, offer many different excursions.

Butler's Outback Safaris (tel. 086-42-2188) is a well-established company that operates a range of 4WD tours, as do **Flinders Ranges Safaris** (tel. 086-48-4031). **Arkaba Station** (tel. 086-48-4217) conducts 4WD tag-along tours, as well as nature walks and retreats. **Ecotrek** (tel. 08-383-7198) and **Exploranges** (tel. 08-294-6530) also offer eco-walks and tours.

Or ride a **camel** (Flinders Ranges Camel Farm, tel. 086-48-4874), a **horse** (Flinders Rides, tel. 085-28-2132), or a **motorcycle** (Flinders Ranges Bike Tours, tel. 086-42-4978).

INTO THE OUTBACK

This region may be as close as you'll ever get to feeling like you're on another planet—one reason being that it's not particularly well-suited to human life.

In 1845, explorer Charles Sturt described the Outback as "a country I firmly believe has no parallel on earth's surface" (then he died). And that is precisely why 99% of the state's population lives south of the 32nd parallel. Much of this area is no man's (or woman's) land. Peaceful, open space contrasts with harsh terrain, stony deserts, enormous salt pans, and eerie desolation. Then again, the challenge of surviving the elements is often what attracts travelers in the first place—that and thousands of native birds, fish jumpin' out of desert waterholes, the search for fiery opals, dry salt lakes, artesian springs, the odd spaceship, and a bunch of odd spaced-out characters.

Encompassing about 60 million hectares, the Outback presents a massive frontier to pioneering spirits, some pretty hazardous odds to those who gamble with nature, and breathing space galore for incurable claustrophobics. But pay attention to whose land you're on; vast areas are administered by the Department of Environment and Natural Resources, and others are Aboriginal reserves or part of the military's Woomera Prohibited Area. (Though *you* may feel free out here, the *land* is not!)

Choose from four Outback routes. **The Stuart Highway,** the sealed road connecting Port Augusta with Alice Springs, passes through the Woomera missile test site, Coober Pedy, and the opal-mining district. **Oodnadatta Track** is the old dirt road that follows the path of the old Ghan railway and overland telegraph lines, eventually meeting up with the Stuart Highway at Marla. Both the **Birdsville** and **Strzelecki Tracks** are long, hard treks through remote desert into remote Queensland. Whichever route you take, at some point you'll cross the dingo fence, a protective wire stretching more than 3,000 km across central Australia to keep those wild dogs from entering southern pastoral lands. Exceptionally adventurous souls—with a lot of time, money, and energy—might want to tackle the various "bomb roads" or the Canning Stock Route (see the special topics "Bomb Roads" and "Canning Stock Route").

The best time of year for Outback travel is April to September, when the weather is usually mild and dry, though early mornings can be frosty (camping from June through October can be very cold and uncomfortable). Summers, as you'd expect, are scorching infernos when you can indeed fry your eggs (and seated body parts) atop any rock in this hard place. Rains, though infrequent, should be taken quite seriously, particularly if you're off the sealed highway. Dirt tracks can be washed away suddenly, leaving you stranded for what could be a deadly long time. But the Outback is exquisite after a rainfall, carpeted with wildflowers and exotic plants.

Make certain both you and your vehicle are well prepared for your journey. Follow Outback driving rules, inquire about road conditions, carry detailed maps, keep your car full of petrol and your body full of water.

The first vehicle crossing from Adelaide to Darwin was made in 1908. Since then, historic journeys, in a wide assortment of transport, are still being made. Yours could be next!

ALONG THE STUART HIGHWAY

Woomera and Vicinity

Unless you're desperate for petrol or a quick snack, pass by the ugly little town of **Pimba,** 173 km northwest of Port Augusta. In the 1950s-'60s, Woomera, off the highway a few kilometers from Pimba, was a test site for British experimental rockets. The most famous launching was that of the *Europa,* 1964-70. About those same years NASA ran a deep-space tracking station at nearby Island Lagoon. The testing range and "Narrungar" (the communications station) are controlled by the Australian Defence Department. Woomera still serves as a military base, and U.S. personnel continue to be stationed here (and what *stories* people tell about what goes on at this place—spooky doings about spies, satellites, and alien spaceships!).

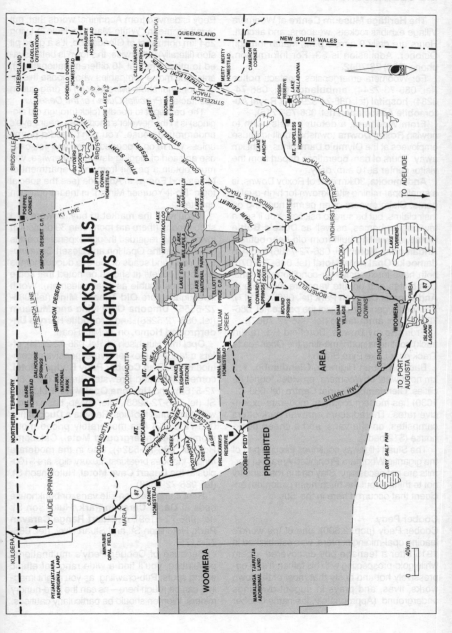

OUTBACK TRACKS, TRAILS, AND HIGHWAYS

The **Heritage Museum Centre** at Woomera Village exhibits rockets, weapons, and aircraft. Hours are daily 9 a.m.-5 p.m., March through October. Admission is $3. For information, phone (086) 73-7042.

For Woomera emergencies, contact: **police** (tel. 086-73-7244), **ambulance** (tel. 086-74-3234), **hospital** (tel. 086-74-3294), or **Royal Automobile Association** (tel. 086-73-7715).

From Woomera, a detour travels north to newish **Roxby Downs** township, built to house employees at the **Olympic Dam** mines, eight km away. Tours of dam operations depart from the visitor center at 10 a.m. daily.

Andamooka, 30 km east of Roxby Downs, is a small opal-mining site, known for high-quality gems. Claim owners often permit noodling on their claims, but be sure to ask first. You'll see a few dugout homes, as well as **Duke's Bottle Home,** a dwelling built from old beer bottles. **Andamooka Motel** (tel. 086-72-7186) and **Andamooka Opal Hotel Motel** (tel. 086-72-7078) both have inexpensive air-conditioned rooms. Campsites and on-site vans are available at **Andamooka Caravan Park** (tel. 086-72-7117).

For emergencies, contact the **police** (tel. 086-72-7072) or **ambulance** (tel. 086-72-7087).

From Roxby Downs, Borefield Rd. (a dirt track) continues north, meeting the Oodnadatta Track near Lake Eyre South.

Back on Stuart Highway, **Glendambo,** 113 km northwest of Woomera, provides tourist facilities. **Glendambo Tourist Centre** (tel. 086-72-1030) has modern rooms at moderate-expensive rates. The adjacent caravan park offers campsites, on-site vans, and a cheap bunkhouse ($12 beds).

The Stuart Highway continues through part of the gigantic Woomera Prohibited Area, but permits are not necessary. Stay on the road and try not to think about the hush-hush plutonium accident that occurred here in the '50s.

Coober Pedy

Coober Pedy (pop. 2,800), one of the world's leading opal-mining centers, was established in 1915 after a teenage boy discovered a gem while gold-prospecting with his father. It's so oppressively hot and dusty that most of the town works, lives, and prays in dugout dwellings underground. (Appropriately, the name Coober Pedy is derived from Aboriginal words that, put together, mean "White Man in a Hole.") Lying 254 km northwest of Glendambo, it's a good pit stop (literally); otherwise, this town is better suited to miners (about 40 different nationalities), ants, and movie companies who choose this locale for lunar shots *(Mad Max III)* or drag-queen spectacles *(Priscilla, Queen of the Desert).*

The best spot to noodle (pick through old diggings) is in the "jeweler's shop" area, near Faye's underground house. You don't need a permit unless you're on a pegged claim, and you can't use any sort of digging device—otherwise, you must obtain a permit from the Department of Mines and Energy in Adelaide (see the special topic "Do-It-Yourself Mining" in the Introduction chapter).

If you're in the market to buy, beware and shop around (there are more than 30 dealers in town). Highly regarded though expensive outlets are those at the Opal Inn and Desert Cave motels. You'll find scads of tours to dugout homes and opal outlets (it should be noted that some tour guides double as opal salesmen). Worth investigating are **Old Timer's Mine** (tel. 086-72-5555), **Umoona Opal Mine and Museum** (tel. 086-72-5288), and **Crocodile Harry's Underground Home,** on 17 Mile Road.

Opal Inn, Hutchison St. (tel. 086-72-2054), offers a range of inexpensive-expensive accommodations. Both **Coober Pedy Budget Motel,** corner Oliver and Brewster Streets (tel. 086-72-5163), and **Umoona Opal Mine,** Hutchison St. (tel. 086-72-5288), offer cheap, basic rooms with communal facilities. **Radeka's Dugout** (tel. 086-72-5223) has moderately priced motel rooms. The **Underground Motel,** Catacomb Rd. (tel. 086-72-5324), also in the moderate range, includes breakfast. Luxury digs are $100-plus at the **Desert Cave Motel,** Hutchison St. (tel. 086-72-5688).

Rent campsites, on-site vans, or bunkhouse beds at **Oasis Caravan Park,** Hutchison St. (tel. 086-72-5169), or **Stuart Range Caravan Park,** Hutchison St. and Stuart Hwy. (tel. 086-72-5179).

Because of Coober Pedy's multinational population, you'll find a wide range of ethnic eating spots. Pub-crawling, as you might imagine, can be rough here—as can the love-hungry miners. Women should be particularly cautious.

For emergencies, contact the **police** (tel. 086-72-5056), hospital (tel. 086-72-5000), or **Royal Automobile Association (RAA)** (tel. 086-72-5036).

Breakaways Reserve, 28 km north of Coober Pedy, is a 40-square-km block of low hills featuring a continually changing color landscape, unique flora and fauna, and walking trails.

Marla and Vicinity

The drive to **Cadney Homestead** (tel. 086-70-7994), 153 km north of Coober Pedy, is fairly dreary, but the place has expensive homestead accommodations, moderate bunkhouse beds, and cheap campsites. Refuel yourself and your vehicle and either cut east through Arckaringa Hills, Copper Hills, and the Painted Desert to Oodnadatta (160 km), or continue north on the Stuart Highway.

Another featureless 81-km drive brings you to Marla (pop. 240), established in 1978 as a tourist service center. This is also where the highway meets the Ghan railway line. Rooms at **Marla Travellers Rest** (tel. 086-70-7001) are moderate to expensive; campsites at the caravan park are cheap.

The opal fields at **Mintabie,** 50 km west of Marla (along a gravel road), have proved to be richer than those at Coober Pedy. It's another 165 km to the Northern Territory border, 185 km to teensy Kulgera township, and 464 km to Alice Springs.

ALONG THE OODNADATTA TRACK

Marree to William Creek

Marree (pop. 380), 379 km north of Port Augusta, is the beginning (and ending) point for both the Oodnadatta and Birdsville Tracks. During the 1880s this mini-town was a big depot for camel drivers transporting goods to the Outback. (You can still see a couple of leftover date palms and a few Afghani names, as reminders.) Between 1960 and 1980, it was the changing-gauge station for the old Ghan, choo-chooing to Alice Springs. **Marree Great Northern Hotel,** Main St. (tel. 086-75-8344), has inexpensive rooms. Campsites and on-site vans are available at **Marree Tourist Park** (tel. 086-75-8371).

It's 210 km from Marree to William Creek.

The track edges along **Lake Eyre South,** where two lookouts adjacent to the roadway afford views of this salt pan, which stretches 185 km north. (This is a baby compared with Lake Eyre North.) A rough piece of track leads to the lakeshore.

At **Stuart Creek** you can view a six-km piece of the original Ghan line, as well as a few preserved sheds, fettler's cottages, and a water tank. The oasis at **Coward Springs,** about 35 km farther north, includes railway ruins, an old plantation (now a bird refuge), some old date palms, and a warm, bubbling pond.

Bubbler and **Blanchecup** are mound springs, six km south of the track (you'll see fences around them), adjacent to Coward Springs. Bubbler is a bubbling pool of fine sand. Blanchecup is deceptively clear and clean-looking, but you have to dip in and out through a muddy, weedy stench. Either of the springs should open every pore in your body; stick your head in and you won't need a facial—or maybe even a shampoo—for years! (You'd pay a fortune for this in Europe!)

Other points of interest are the old **Beresford** railway siding and flowing bore (artesian well), 24 km north of Coward Springs, and, 11 km farther, **Strangways,** the old Overland Telegraph repeater, where there's also a flowing bore (a bare water pipe).

William Creek to Oodnadatta

William Creek, 45 km north of Strangways, is touted as South Australia's (some say the world's) smallest town that lies within one of the state's (if not the world's) largest cattle stations—30,027-square-km Anna Creek. The big thing to do here is hang around the pub, soaking up local color and lore, or gawking at other travelers, usually crowded around the pay phone. Basic accommodations at that same **William Creek Hotel** (tel. 086-70-7880) are inexpensive and campsites cost just $4 per person.

It's 206 km to Oodnadatta, a journey through gibber (Aboriginal for "stone") plains, ranging in color from sand to charcoal, and in size from pebbles to Frisbees. The gibbers also have a strange reflective quality. Sights along this section of track are **Edwards Creek** ruins and bore (you can take a shower here, but your hair will turn to Brillo), **Warrina Siding** ruin, a memorial to explorer Ernest Giles (in 1876 he crossed from Geraldton, Western Australia, to Peake Telegraph Station, east of the memorial), the **Algebuckina** siding ruin, one of the best old **Ghan railway bridges,** and **Mt. Dutton.**

Oodnadatta (pop. 230) sprang into being in 1891 with the arrival of the railway and then, in the 1980s, came close to disappearing when the rail line was moved and the Stuart Highway was sealed. This true Outback town (whose Aboriginal name translates to "flower of the mulga") has turned its old railway station into a museum, but the real attraction here is the **Pink Roadhouse,** which serves as social center, petrol stop, supermarket, "Oodnaburger" supplier, mechanic's garage, caravan park, info provider, tour organizer, and travelers' clearinghouse and meeting place. Both campsites and on-site vans are available. The roadhouse is open daily. For information, phone (086) 70-7822. Rooms at **Transcontinental Hotel** (tel. 086-70-7804) are inexpensive. **Oodnadatta Caravan Park** (tel. 086-70-7822) offers campsites, on-site vans, and a rather pricey bunkhaus.

For emergencies, contact the **police** (tel. 086-70-7805) or **ambulance** (tel. 086-70-7803).

The Oodnadatta Track continues northwest for 118 km, then turns west. From this junction, it's about 100 km to Marla and the Stuart Highway.

THE BIRDSVILLE TRACK

In the 1880s, the Birdsville Track was created so that stockmen could drive their cattle from the grazing grounds in southwest Queensland to the rail station at Marree, where they were loaded onto a train. This border community kept busy during the days when interstate customs were charged. In 1901, after free trade was instigated, they began to ship the cattle by truck along different routes.

The 517 km from Marree to Birdsville (in Queensland) pass by deserted homesteads and mission ruins, scalding bores and welcoming waterholes, not to mention phenomenal amounts of sandy dunes and rocky plains at the Tirari, Simpson, Sturt Stony, and Strzelecki Deserts. At **Clifton Hills Homestead** the road splits: the inside track, which crosses **Goyder Lagoon,** is closed; the Birdsville goes around it.

Seek advice before picking your fork—a wrong decision could be fatal. Also keep in mind that the lagoon is a breeding ground for snakes.

Birdsville, 12 km across the Queensland border, was established in 1882 to serve stockmen headed down the Birdsville Track. Today it caters to travelers following in the stockmen's tracks. Original buildings are the old pub and mission hospital. Even though this is a remote outpost town, after an arduous Outback trek Birdsville's simple tourist facilities seem like a limo ride down Rodeo Drive. (See "Birdsville" under "Channel Country" in the "Outback Queensland" section of the next chapter.)

This route is for very well-prepared vehicles and bodies. Check in with police at either Marree or Birdsville, and follow all Outback driving rules and local advice.

THE STRZELECKI TRACK

For those with more larceny than cow pie in their souls, who'd rather follow in the bootsteps of outlaws than stockmen, the background on this route has a bit more juice to it.

The Strzelecki Track came into being in 1871 when bushman Henry Radford (a.k.a. "Midnight") used it to drive his herds of stolen cattle from Queensland down to the Adelaide markets. (Strzelecki Creek had been named earlier by Charles Sturt, for his fellow explorer Count Strzelecki.) Other drovers, legitimate and otherwise, used the track also, alternating the route a bit around Cooper Creek where there were more watering holes. The track fell into disuse for many years until the Moomba gas fields southwest of Innamincka were established. The Moomba section of this track (from Strzelecki Crossing to Innamincka) is better kept, but the original bit will appeal more to wanna-be rustlers.

Lyndhurst to Innamincka

Starting at Lyndhurst, 193 km north of Hawker and 79 km south of Marree, the Strzelecki Track wends 459 km northeasterly to Innamincka, a tiny service town, then cuts north for 305 km, turning west in Queensland for the 110-km portion that leads into Birdsville. It's also possible to cross into Queensland from Innamincka and the Arrabury Homestead junction, and to travel

53 km east to Betoota and beyond, instead of going west to Birdsville (just keep in mind, you're still a long, long way from "civilization").

Pick up any necessary provisions at Lyndhurst; this is your last fuel stop until Innamincka (don't expect a petrol pump at the Moomba gas fields).

Following the northern edge of the Flinders Ranges, you'll pass ruins of several old homesteads, cruise through the Cobbler Desert between Lakes Blanche and Callabonna (incidentally, **Lake Callabonna** is the site of the fossilized diprotodon, the largest known marsupial), finally crossing Strzelecki Creek about 85 km north of Mt. Hopeless Homestead. From the creek crossing, you must choose either the track that passes the **Moomba gas fields** (no tourist facilities except a telephone at the security gate) or the old road that goes through **Merty Merty Homestead**, where if you're one of those people who likes to sprawl across different sides of borders at the same time (and have a photo taken!), you can drive 109 km southeast to **Cameron Corner,** a coming-together of South Australia, Queensland, and New South Wales.

Innamincka and Beyond
Innamincka, another outpost town a la Birdsville, is also the place where explorers Burke and Wills bit the dust (you can see their legendary **Dig Tree** along Cooper Creek, about 42 km east of the post office). Several historic spots are dotted about this bitsy service town, most of them memorials to the exploring dead—places where bodies were found, moved to, finally buried, where rescue parties set up camp, where the sole survivor was discovered by Aborigines, etc. On Cooper Creek, rock carvings by the Yantrwantas Aboriginal tribe can be seen at the eastern end of Cullyamurra waterhole. Fish can be found inside that very same waterhole as well as the waterholes along the northwest branch of Cooper Creek.

Find inexpensive accommodations at **Innamincka Trading Post** (tel. 086-75-9900). Barbecues, dances, and other raves with locals are usually held weekends at the "upmarket" **Innamincka Motel** (tel. 086-75-9901).

The **Coongie Lakes,** 112 km northeast of Innamincka, a bird and wildlife refuge, also offers excellent fishing opportunities. It's a long, rough drive from Innamincka to Birdsville, past Cordillo Downs and Arrabury Homesteads (no facilities) and the ruins of Cadelga Outstation, used in the 1930s by the Royal Geographic Society to observe the transit of Venus.

Again, this is not an out-for-a-Sunday-drive road. Make sure you are well prepared, and check in with police at Lyndhurst.

OUTBACK PARKS

Only the most well-equipped and preinformed travelers should explore the remote, arid Outback parks. Desert park passes must be obtained in advance from the Department of Environment and Natural Resources. The issuing office will provide you with all necessary rules and regulations.

Lake Eyre National Park
The 1,228,000 hectares of Lake Eyre National Park encompass Lake Eyre North (Australia's largest salt lake), adjacent Tirari Desert, and a desert wilderness conservation area. Lake Eyre, normally a huge dry salt pan, is where, in 1964, Sir Donald Campbell set a world land-speed record (640 km/h) in Bluebird, his jet-powered car; when I visited a few years ago, the lake was full of water! Reaching a depth of 16 meters below sea level (where the salt crust measures 230 mm thick), the lake has filled only a few times since European settlement. Smaller salt lakes lie within the duney desert section, and fossil deposits have been discovered at Lake Ngapakaldi, on the far eastern edge.

The park has no facilities. Access is via Muloorina Homestead, 90 km north of Marree or, alternately, travel six km east of William Creek, then 51 km east to Belt Bay, on the lake's southwest corner.

Elliot Price Conservation Park
Located 105 km northwest of Marree on the southern edge of Lake Eyre North, Elliot Price Conservation Park (64,570 hectares) was the first arid zone reserve. Red kangaroos, grass owls, and low sparse vegetation make the park their home. Hunt Peninsula, within the park, is a long limestone arm reaching into Lake Eyre North. The park has no facilities.

BOMB ROADS

Bomb roads—offspring of the 1950s, and brainchildren of surveyor Len Beadell—were constructed during the Woomera rocket- and Emu A-bomb tests era. Len and his "Gunbarrel Road Construction Party" went to work. The Gunbarrel Highway, Len's first and most well-known feat, was completed in 1958. More than 6,000 km of "road" (really desert tracks, *really* a rocket range) span western South Australia and a chunk of neighboring Western Australia, north of the intercontinental railway line. Some of the roads run east-west, joining up at points with various south-north stretches. Outback adventurers with 4WD vehicles love this desert grid. These are difficult roads. As with all remote Outback travel, make sure your body is healthy, your vehicle is in excellent condition, and that you are well-equipped for breakdowns and emergencies. You will need to carry quite a bit of extra petrol, and permits are required for many of the roads. (Also, be prepared to run into "radioactivity warning" signs!) Detailed information can be obtained from Royal Automobile Club offices.

Gunbarrel Highway: The original Gunbarrel is a very rough, rugged, and desolate stretch running from Victory Downs Homestead, near the junction of the Stuart Highway and Northern Territory and South Australia borders, to Carnegie Homestead (349 km east of Wiluna). Other than the turnoff beyond Giles Meteorological Station to Docker River Aborignial Community, the Gunbarrel leads to plenty of nowheresville. "Fake imitations," such as the Laverton-Warburton Road and a more "improved" version of the Gunbarrel, will get you from Uluru (Ayers Rock) to Wiluna or Leonora in Western Australia; obtain permits from Central Land Council, Alice Springs (for the Northern Territory section),

and Aboriginal Affairs Planning Authority, Perth (for the Western Australia section).

Anne Beadell Highway: Coober Pedy west to Emu (watch the radioactivity warning signs!), across South Australia/Western Australia border, crossing Connie Sue Highway, to Laverton; obtain permits from Defence Support Center (P.O. Box 157, Woomera, SA 5720, tel. 086-74-3370), Maralinga-Tjarutja Council, or Maralinga Land Council.

Connie Sue Highway: North from Rawlinna railway siding, past Anne Beadell Highway and the Laverton-Warburton Road, to Gunbarrel Highway; obtain permits from Aboriginal Affairs Planning Authority, Perth.

Gary Highway: North from the Gunbarrel Highway (known as Everard Junction) to Canning Stock Route at Well 35—from there heading west, on a mostly unused track, northwest to the Indian Ocean, north of Marble Bar; no permits necessary.

Sandy Blight Junction Road: Between the Gunbarrel Highway, west of Docker River Aboriginal Community, and Sandy Blight Junction, near Kintore Aboriginal Community; obtain permits from Central Land Council, Alice Springs.

Canning-Papunya Road: Alice Springs west, through Papunya, Sandy Blight and Gary junctions, to Canning Stock Route at Well 35; obtain permits from Central Land Council, Alice Springs.

Talawana Track-Windy Corner Road: West on Windy Corner Road at Gary Junction, crossing Canning Stock Route near Well 24, becoming Talawana Track, continuing into Pilbara Region (WA), south of Marble Bar; no permits necessary.

For more information, see the special topic "Canning Stock Route" in the Western Australia chapter.

Witjira National Park

Witjira National Park, 120 km north of Oodnadatta, comprises flat hills, salt pans, sandy dunes, desert and gibber plains, and numerous mound, thermal, and hot springs. Formerly Mount Dare Homestead, these 776,900 hectares just became a national park in the 1980s. The most popular attractions here are the 80 or so **Dalhousie Springs,** Australia's largest artesian baths, in which visitors soak and laze away in the bubbles of the tepid waters. This same mineralized bath

water originated as rainfall in north Queensland about four million years ago!

Near the springs are ruins and relics of early farming days. After a rain, wildflowers spurt up around the pools. Native birds include brolgas, darters, gibbers, thrush, and cinnamon quail.

A campground is available near the springs. **Mount Dare Homestead** (tel. 086-70-7835), 70 km northwest of the springs, has accommodations, camping, food, emergency repairs, fuel, and an airstrip.

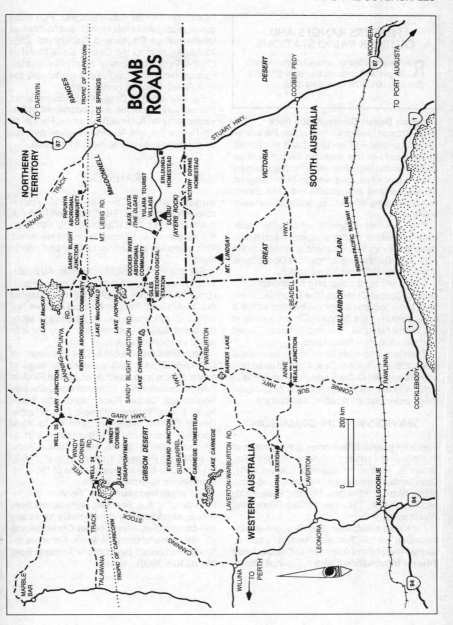

BOMB ROADS

TO DARWIN

NORTHERN TERRITORY

87

TROPIC OF CAPRICORN

RANGES

ALICE SPRINGS

MacDONNELL RANGES

MT. LIEBIG RD.

TANAMI TRACK

PAPUNYA ABORIGINAL COMMUNITY

SANDY BLIGHT JUNCTION

KINTORE ABORIGINAL COMMUNITY

MT. HOPKINS RD.

KATA TJUTA (THE OLGAS)

YULARA TOURIST VILLAGE

ULURU (AYERS ROCK)

DOCKER RIVER ABORIGINAL COMMUNITY

GILES METEOROLOGICAL STATION

MT. LINDSAY

ERLDUNDA HOMESTEAD

VICTORY DOWNS HOMESTEAD

STUART HWY.

SOUTH AUSTRALIA

VICTORIA

COOBER PEDY

DESERT

WOOMERA

87

TO PORT AUGUSTA

1

TO PERTH

94

KALGOORLIE

COCKLEBIDDY

RAWLINNA

INDIAN-PACIFIC RAILWAY LINE

GREAT VICTORIA DESERT

NULLARBOR PLAIN

1

BEADELL HWY.

ANNE BEADELL HWY.

CONNIE SUE HWY.

NEALE JUNCTION

WARBURTON

WARBURTON RD.

BARKER LAKE

LAKE CHRISTOPHER

SANDY BLIGHT JUNCTION RD.

CANNING-PAPUNYA RD.

GARY JUNCTION

GARY HWY.

WELL 35

WINDY CORNER RD.

WINDY CORNER

WELL 24

LAKE DISAPPOINTMENT

GIBSON DESERT

EVERARD JUNCTION

GUNBARREL HWY.

CARNEGIE HOMESTEAD

LAKE CARNEGIE

LAVERTON-WARBURTON RD.

YAMARNA STATION

LAVERTON

LEONORA

WILUNA

WESTERN AUSTRALIA

CANNING STOCK ROUTE

TALAWANA TRACK

TROPIC OF CAPRICORN

MARBLE BAR

LAKE MacKAY

LAKE MacDONALD

94

200 km

FLINDERS RANGES AND OUTBACK RADIO STATIONS

Radio stations that broadcast into the Flinders Ranges and Outback are: 5CK 639; 5CL 729; 5AN 891; 5CS 1044; 5AU 1242.

Simpson Desert Conservation Park

The Simpson Desert Conservation Park is an enormous (692,680 hectares) arid wilderness in the middle of the Simpson Desert. A large bird population, including zebra finches, budgerigars, black kites, and wedge-tailed eagles, shares the land with parallel red sand dunes, salt lakes, gidgi woodlands, and post-rain wildflowers.

The park has no facilities. More-than-adequate provisions, proper equipment, and a first-class 4WD vehicle are essential. Access to the park is via Dalhousie Springs from Oodnadatta, or via Poeppel Corner from Birdsville.

Large areas surrounding Innamincka, including Cooper Creek and the Coongie Lakes, have been declared a regional reserve, as has a huge portion of the Simpson Desert outside of the Witjira National Park and Simpson Desert Conservation Park boundaries.

Travelers who wish to make the hazardous trek across the Simpson Desert should do so only with experienced Outback drivers, in top-condition 4WD vehicles, with massive amounts of equipment, provisions, information, and stamina.

SERVICES AND INFORMATION

Fuel and **public telephones** are available at the following Outback locations: Andamooka, Birdsville, Cadney Homestead, Coober Pedy, Glendambo, Innamincka, Kulgera, Lyndhurst, Marla, Marree, Mintabie, Olympic Dam, Oodnadatta, Pimba, Tarcoola, William Creek, and Woomera.

For tourist information, see "Services and Information" in the "Flinders Ranges" section, above. Also obtain information at **Coober Pedy Tourist Information Centre,** Council Office,

Hutchison St. (tel. 086-72-5298). Purchase cards, maps, and local-interest publications at **Underground Books and Gallery** (tel. 086-72-5558), next to the Desert Cave Motel in Coober Pedy. Additionally, most pubs, motels, caravan parks, and roadhouses (particularly the Pink Roadhouse) carry information.

For information on **Desert Park Passes,** about $50 per vehicle, contact the **Department of Environment and Natural Resources,** Far Northern Region (tel. 086-48-4244). Passes can also be purchased at various shops in the area.

TRANSPORT

Augusta Airways (tel. 086-42-3100) operates a "Channel Mail Run" between Port Augusta and Mount Isa (Queensland), with stops in Innamincka and Birdsville on the weekend. This company also offers charter and scenic flights.

For commercial flights between Adelaide, Woomera, Olympic Dam, and Coober Pedy, contact **Ansett** (tel. 13-1300 toll-free), **Qantas** (tel. 13-1313, toll-free), or **Kendell Airlines** (tel. 069-22-0100). Fares run about $150 to Woomera and $250 to Coober Pedy. They are subject to frequent changes.

Stateliner (tel. 08-8415-5544, Adelaide, or 086-42-5055, Port Augusta) operates frequent coach service from Adelaide and some Flinders Ranges communities to Andamooka, Cadney Homestead, Coober Pedy, Glendambo, Lyndhurst, Marla, Marree, Olympic Dam, Pimba, Roxby Downs, Woomera, and on to Alice Springs. Fares are approximately $50 to Woomera, $65 to Marree, $85 to Coober Pedy. **Greyhound Pioneer Australia** (tel. 13-2030 toll-free) provides service to some of the communities via its express routes.

For **organized tours,** see "Services and Information" in the "Flinders Ranges" section, above. Arrangements can be made for fishing and cruising trips along **Cooper Creek,** as well as other Innamincka area tours. For more information, contact **Innamincka Trading Post** (tel. 086-75-9900).

OUTBACK NEW SOUTH WALES AND QUEENSLAND

Okay, okay, so you had to get those east coast cities out of your system—you flew in, saw the sights, choked some fumes, caught some waves; in short you've citied, gagged, and beached with multitudes of other Aussies and in-significant others. Ready to purge your binge with ancient history, secluded shores, and plenty of breathing space? Head out of town on whichever route that's closest, and come with me.

OUTBACK NEW SOUTH WALES

Although it is generally accepted that the "real" Outback lies west of the Darling River, which flows in a southwesterly direction from up near Lightning Ridge to the Murray River west of Mildura, the only official boundaries of Outback New South Wales are the borders of Queensland to the north and South Australia to the west. The area west of the Darling encompasses nearly a quarter of the state, but vast tracts of land on the Pacific Ocean side qualify as the Outback, if only for the vast, intimidating landscape, empty except for a few isolated communities and sprawling sheep stations.

The thriving rural center of Dubbo, 410 km northwest of Sydney, is the gateway to this part of the Outback. Famous for the world's greatest concentration of black opal is **Lightning Ridge,** north of Dubbo. To the northwest is **Bourke,** a classic Outback town that began as a wool transportation center. The Barrier Highway is the main route west. It passes through **Nyngan,** the town that disappeared under water during the floods of 1990; runs past the mining town of **Cobar;** and crosses the Darling River at the historic town of **Wilcannia.**

South of the Barrier Highway is **Menindee,** a

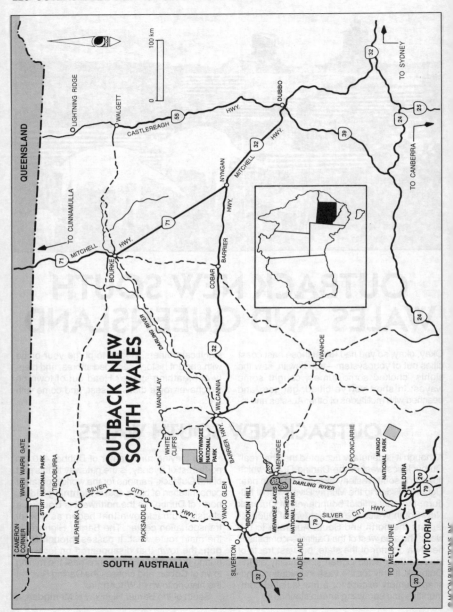

town with strong links to the legend of the hapless Burke and Wills and the gateway to the lush oasis of lakes that make up **Kinchega National Park.** South of Menindee is World Heritage-listed **Mungo National Park,** site of astonishing discoveries that have changed the way anthropologists see the evolution of culture in prehistoric peoples.

The Outback's largest center is **Broken Hill,** a cosmopolitan city of 25,000, closer to Adelaide and Melbourne than Sydney. The city has grown, literally, on top of the world's largest and richest lode of silver, lead, and zinc.

North of Broken Hill, Silver City Highway passes through **Corner Country,** millions of hectares of sheep country, with the land so harsh that the average holding supports only one sheep for every eight hectares. Northeast of Broken Hill is **Mootwingee National Park,** protecting hundreds of exceptionally well-preserved Koori rock art sites, scattered among gorges in the ancient Bynguano Range. The only settlements along the Silver City Highway north of Broken Hill are **Packsaddle, Milparinka,** and **Tibooburra,** which have a combined population of around 200. If you can drag yourself away from the shady verandas and cold beer of the classic hotels in these towns, chances are you'll end up in **Sturt National Park,** in the far northwest corner of the state. This park is a vast tract of red sandhills and mulga scrub, characterized by jump-ups (mesas) that cross the park.

To the government, the Outback of New South Wales is known by the rather uninspiring name **Western Division,** an area encompassing more than 40% of the state and with a population that hovers around 50,000 (half of which live in Broken Hill). When this area was first settled, farmers were given grazing rights to as much land as they liked. This law was replaced in 1864, with the government granting only smaller sections. After a disastrous drought at the end of last century, the government changed the rules again. This time small holdings were merged and large holdings split up, allowing family-run operations to control most of the stations and shutting out large pastoral companies. Early in 1991, the changing economy of the wool industry saw the lifting of many restrictions and land ownership has reverted mostly to companies.

Outback Tours

If you only have a few days to spare, the best way to cover the great distances of Outback New South Wales would be to fly into Broken Hill and take a tour. Many companies offer tours that take in all the best features of this part of the country. **Silver City Tours** (tel. 080-87-6956) operates day tours from Broken Hill out to Mootwingee and Kinchega national parks and White Cliffs. The six-day tour includes all the above, plus sights closer to Broken Hill. It also includes basic motel accommodations for $478 per person. **Broken Hill's Outback Tours** (tel. 080-87-7800) is another option. Their four-day Outback National Parks tour departs twice weekly and costs $615 per person. The most comprehensive tour is offered by **Centrek Safaris** (tel. 03-9775-2211), who include the dingo fence and Cameron Corner in a seven-day 4WD safari; $995 per person, includes airfare from Melbourne.

CASTLEREAGH HIGHWAY

The Castlereagh Highway starts at Dubbo, 410 km northwest of Sydney, and heads in a northerly direction before turning into a dusty track somewhere near the Queensland border north of Lightning Ridge.

Gilgandra is a good starting point for traveling up the Castlereagh Highway, as it's an easy day's drive from Sydney and is halfway between Sydney and Brisbane. The town's main attraction is **Gilgandra Observatory,** owned and operated by Jack Estens, a local resident whose zest for astronomy never seems to wane. The observatory is open for day viewing Thurs.-Mon. 2-4 p.m. and for night viewing Thurs.-Mon. dusk-10 p.m.

Walgett

Walgett is on the Barwon River, one of a dozen rivers that flow from the Darling Downs into the Darling River. The area was first settled in the mid-1800s by graziers, but with the closest rail line at Maitland and a difficult and long river trip to the Murray, links to the outside world were few. By the turn of the century, the rail line was in place and Walgett was on the map as the birthplace of the Wolseley Shearing Machine, which changed the face of the shearing industry.

Today, the population is a healthy 2,500, and the town is popular with fishers as a base for fishing the Barwon, Narran, Castlereagh, and Macquarie rivers.

The pubs in town can't really be recommended for a quiet night's sleep; instead, stay at the **Walgett Motel,** 14 Fox St. (tel. 068-28-1355), where the nightly room rate is about the same as a block of land—$50. **Two Rivers Caravan Park** is on Pitt St. (tel. 068-28-1381). Bistro and restaurant meals are available at the R.S.L. Club on Fox Street.

For town information, head to **Walgett Shire Council Chambers,** also on Fox St. (tel. 068-28-1399); open Mon.-Fri. 8:30 a.m.-4:30 p.m.

LIGHTNING RIDGE

Lightning Ridge, a dry, dusty frontier town of 3,000, near the end of the Castlereagh Highway, 760 km northwest of Sydney, is synonymous with opal. The many hundreds of small-scale mining operations around the area produce most of the world's black opal, Australia's national gemstone. Even so, don't believe every miner's story you hear in the pub. Opal is found in varying qualities in the United States, Mexico, and Brazil, but the black opal of Lightning Ridge, reflecting all colors of the spectrum through the dark body of the rock, has few equals in the world.

Opal had been discovered in the area as early as 1887, but it wasn't mined until 1902. With the miners came the buyers, and, as the population increased, the services improved; today "The Ridge" boasts all of the facilities of a small country town. Its name, Lightning Ridge, came about in the 1870s when a drover was killed by lightning while sheltering from a storm on a ridge.

Surrounding the town are an estimated 1,000 claims, each mined by small-time operators, hoping against hope for the same success that they had out at Nebea Hill in the 1970s when $3 million worth of opal was extracted in two years. You don't need a license to fossick on abandoned mullock heaps—they are strewn with chips of boulder opal, and there's always a chance of finding a good one. Stephen and Lesley Henley offer tours of their mine on Three

Mile Rd. and a demonstration of opal cutting daily at 10 a.m. (tel. 068-29-0247). The **Walk-in Mine,** at Bald Hill (tel. 068-29-0473), is a similar setup with tours departing at 9 a.m. and an audiovisual shown regularly. The **Spectrum Opal Mine,** Bald Hill Rd. (tel. 068-29-0581), has an underground showroom chock full of spectacular opals, including one worth over $80,000. They show a film here hourly, and aboveground is an area for fossicking and a picnic area with barbecues. Along Opal and Manilla Streets are a number of shops selling opals.

If you want to buy opals, this is the place to do it, as their prices often double by the time they reach the east coast. Often, cheaper pieces are from other parts of Australia, so, if that is important to you, ask before you buy. You can buy good chunks of "solids" for under $100. Top-quality black opals sell for about $3000 a carat.

The Ridge is also known for artesian bores, bubbling up at around 40° C. The therapeutic powers of the water have soothed the muscles of work-weary miners for a hundred years, but also attract visitors, whose arthritic conditions are claimed to improve in the water. The pools are open 24 hours; admission is free.

Accommodations and Food

Lightning Ridge Motor Village, west of town on Onyx St. (tel. 068-29-0304), is a four-hectare complex with accommodation styles to suit all budgets. Motel rooms with private facilities are $50-59 s, $65-69 d; unpowered sites are $9, powered sites $11. On site is a bistro, bar, and restaurant, and a small area is set aside for fossicking. The **Black Opal Motel,** Opal St. (tel. 068-29-0518), has basic rooms for $51 s, $59 d, each with a safe for those precious opals. Another inexpensive option is **Lightning Ridge Caravan Park,** Harlequin St. (tel. 068-29-0532), where basic on-site vans are $25, cabins are $42, and sites for tents and vans are $9-11.

Digger's Rest Hotel, Opal St. (tel. 068-29-0404), serves bistro meals noon-2 p.m. and 6-8 p.m., ranging $6-10. If you're after more than steak and mashed potato, go to the **bowling club** on Morilla St. (tel. 068-29-0408) or, for Chinese, **Miner's Mate Restaurant** on Opal St. (tel. 068-29-0215).

Services and Information

Apart from its remote location, Lightning Ridge is like any similar-sized town, with all the expected services including a doctor (tel. 068-29-0416), banks, butchers, a bakery, gas stations (80-90 cents a liter for fuel), a post office, and a supermarket.

The **tourist information center** is on Fred Reece Way (tel. 068-29-0565); open Mon.-Fri. 8:30 a.m.-4:30 p.m.

Transport

The **Log Cabin Opal Shoppe,** 47 Morilla St. (tel. 068-29-0277), is the agent for all public transportation, including Transcity, McCafferty's, Sid Foggs, and rail bookings. A Countrylink bus/rail ticket from Sydney to Lightning Ridge is $67. Flightseeing and air charters are available out at the airstrip, south of town off Fred Reece Way (tel. 068-29-0771). For a cab, call (068) 29-0833.

MITCHELL HIGHWAY

The Mitchell Highway begins at Dubbo and runs northwest to Nyngan and Bourke, then into Queensland to Cunnamulla. This highway is the most direct route between Sydney and the Northern Territory and is sealed all the way to Cunnamulla.

Nyngan

Nyngan is at the junction of the Mitchell and Barrier Highways, 167 km northwest of Dubbo. A helicopter in Vanges Park, on the main drag through town, is one of the few reminders of the disastrous floods in April 1990, when water from the usually dry **Bogan River** rose to such a height that the town all but disappeared and residents had to be airlifted by helicopter to Dubbo. During that time, an area larger than Great Britain was underwater north of Nyngan. A sandbag levee, constructed between the Bogan River and town, remains, but the town has pretty much returned to normal, servicing the surrounding wool, cattle, and wheat industries. A part of the railway station is a small museum, and the old stationmaster's cottage has been restored to its 1880s glory.

Places to stay include: **Canonba Hotel,** 129 Pangee St. (tel. 068-32-1559), where rooms

with shared facilities are $35 s, $45 d, including breakfast; **Country Manor Motor Inn,** 145 Pangee St. (tel. 068-32-1447), with a saltwater pool, $46 s, $56 d; and **Alamo Motor Inn,** Mitchell Hwy. (tel. 068-32-1660), which has clean, comfortable rooms for $45 s, $55 d. Meals are available at both the hotel and the R.S.L. Club, across from the Country Manor Motor Inn.

Information about the town and other Outback destinations is available from **Burn's Video and Gift Shop** at 105 Pangee St. (tel. 068-32-1155); open seven days.

Bourke

You only need look at a map of N.S.W. to understand how the saying "Back o' Bourke" has come to mean a long way from anywhere. This remote town of 3,500 is on the eastern bank of the **Darling River,** 780 km northwest of Sydney. In the 1890s, when famous bush-poet Henry Lawson lived in one of the town's 22 pubs, Bourke was a bleak frontier town, where wool was transported by camel train from outlying stations and loaded onto barges for the long trip down the Darling River to Echuca and then on to England. The town remains an important wool center, although flood, drought, and overstocking of the land have taken a toll on the industry.

Bourke has changed little since Lawson's days, and many buildings remain from that era, including an impressive stone courthouse, built in 1899. The main drag is Mitchell Street, but service and civic buildings are scattered for four blocks between here and the Mitchell Highway. Many of the area's attractions are a fair drive from Bourke. **Mount Gunderbooka,** on Mulgowan Station, has Aboriginal rock spread along a spectacular gorge, with three paintings in shallow caves directly across Mullareena Creek from the camping and picnic area. Up the gorge a couple of kilometers are a number of other paintings and from these it is possible to continue to the long ridge that forms the summit of the mountain. The mountain is signposted along the Bourke-Cobar road, but you'll need a mud map tours brochure (available at the information center) for details.

Rooms at the **Old Royal Hotel,** 32 Mitchell St. (tel. 068-72-2544), are $24 s, $30 d, with shared facilities, and $60 for the rooms with private facilities. **Darling River Motel,** 74 Mitchell St. (tel. 068-72-2288), has rooms of a reasonable standard and is only a short walk to the center of town; $38 s, $48 d. The flashiest place in town is **Major Mitchell Motel,** back out on the highway (tel. 068-72-2311). Facilities include a pool, laundry, and barbecue area; rates here start at $58 s, $66 d. **Mitchell Caravan Park** is one km east of town, along the road out to Brewarrina (tel. 068-72-2791). Sites are $10, those en suites are $15, and the on-site vans are $25 d. **Paddlewheel Caravan Park,** Mitchell St. (tel. 068-72-2277), is right in town and similarly priced.

All the hotels serve counter meals, with the atmosphere at the **Carrier Arms Hotel,** 71 Mitchell St. (tel. 068-72-2040), being the most authentic. The restaurant area looks much the same as the days when Henry Lawson lived upstairs. Service isn't that slick, but for $8-10 you won't go hungry. Other restaurants are in the bowling, golf, and R.S.L. clubs, while the **Darling River Cafe** on Mitchell St. is open for breakfast.

Buses run four times daily between Bourke and Dubbo; from there trains make the connection to Sydney ($70 one way). The local agent is Lachlan Travel at 35 Oxley St. (tel. 068-72-2092).

The **tourist information center** is in the railway station on Mitchell St. (tel. 068-72-2280) and is open daily.

North from Bourke

From Bourke to the Queensland border is 138 km, but the first full-service town is **Cunnamulla,** 119 km north of the border. The only community before the border is **Enngonia,** a small settlement with a pub and a petrol pump. The grave of bushranger Midnight, whose "gentlemanly" conduct and dashing attire were the inspiration for the character Captain Starlight of the book and movie *Robbery Under Arms,* is 35 km west of Enngonia.

BARRIER HIGHWAY

The Barrier Highway heads west from Nyngan through to Broken Hill and on to Adelaide and is sealed the entire way. The scenery is fairly mundane, featuring low undulating scrub-covered hills, until you cross the Darling River at Wilcannia, where red soils, typical of the Outback, dominate.

Cobar

Like Broken Hill, Cobar (population 6,000) thrives on its tremendous mineral wealth and, unlike other towns of Outback N.S.W., is away from any natural river source. Town water in Cobar is piped from the Macquarie River, east of Nyngan. This area's vegetation has changed dramatically in the last 100 years, with vast areas that were cleared for stock now dominated by woody shrubs such as mulga, turpentine, and hapbush. This has decimated native fauna populations, although large numbers of kangaroos remain.

The mineral outcrop around which the town was founded in 1871 is still being mined, with 920,000 tons of copper, lead, and zinc extracted annually. Tours of the mine are offered Friday at 2 p.m.; book ahead by calling (068) 36-2001.

Cobar Regional Museum has some excellent displays pertaining to the history of the area and the people who settled in this harsh part of the country. An Aboriginal display shows the various bush tucker to be found in the Outback, while upstairs is devoted to mining and the mineralogy of the land upon which Cobar was built. The museum is on a rise overlooking the town, on the Barrier Hwy., and is open daily 9 a.m.-5 p.m.

The **Great Western Hotel,** on the corner of Linsley and Marshall Streets (tel. 068-36-2503), built in 1898, has always been the grandest establishment in town. Rooms have shared facilities and are $25 s, $35 d, with breakfast $4-6 per person extra. **Cobar Hi-way Motel,** corner Morrison St. and Barrier Hwy. (tel. 068-36-2000), has large rooms with comfortable beds for $44 s, $54 d.

Longworth Restaurant and Bar, 55 Linsley St. (tel. 068-36-2611), is a formal eatery in a house built in 1899 for Thomas Longworth, one of the original directors of the Great Cobar Copper Mine. The setting is historically authentic, with pressed-metal ceilings and period furnishings. The menu features a wide variety of dishes ranging $13-21. Open daily at 7 p.m. The restaurant in the **Great Western Hotel** is the place to go for an inexpensive yet hearty meal, or head to one of the three cafes along Marshall Street.

Vicinity of Cobar

If you are passing through Cobar in early August, the detour to **Louth**, 132 km northwest of Cobar, is worthwhile. The first or second Saturday in August (call Louth Hotel at 068-74-7422 to check dates) is the annual Louth race meeting, which has grown in stature to boast over $30,000 in prize money and live television coverage across Australia. On the road out to Louth is the Elura Mine, where 1.3 million tons of ore are extracted annually.

West of Cobar, 40 km along the Barrier Hwy., a 35-km road spurs north to **Mt. Grenfell Historic Site,** where over 1,300 pieces of Koori rock art are scattered over rock walls and overhangs. Toilets and water are supplied for campers.

Wilcannia

Wilcannia, 265 km west of Cobar and 200 km east of Broken Hill, spreads out along the west bank of the Darling River, at the junction of the Barrier and Cobb Highways, the latter of which heads south to Ivanhoe and Echuca on the Murray River. The town grew as a staging point for wheat and wool transported from Outback stations and sent downriver on massive barges. Today's 1,000 inhabitants still rely heavily on the sheep and cattle industry, along with the passing-tourist trade, to make up the local economy. The wharf used by paddle steamers still stands, as does a historic jail, courthouse, and post office. The town has two motels and a couple of hotels that offer meals.

White Cliffs

White Cliffs is as famous for its housing as for its black opals. Most of the population lives underground, escaping the climatic extremes of unbearably hot summers and near-freezing nights during winter. The town is very remote, 100 km north of Wilcannia along a gravel road that leads up to the northwestern corner of New South Wales. The sign at the edge of town records the population at 300, but, besides during the searing heat of summer, it's many times this number as miners descend on the town to find their fortune. The surrounding landscape is dotted with hundreds of mullock heaps—the remains of small-scale opal mining operations that characterize the elusive nature of opal mining.

White Cliffs Underground Motel, one km south of town (tel. 080-91-6677), is just that—underground, where temperatures remain constant at 22° C, day and night, winter and summer. Rooms are small but adequate and have shared facilities; $34 per person. Aboveground is **White Cliffs Hotel** (tel. 080-91-6606), where rooms are $15 per person.

SOUTH OF THE BARRIER HIGHWAY

Menindee

Menindee is accessed by gravel road from Wilcannia (160 km) or by sealed road from Broken Hill (110 km). The town has lost much of its original charm, but one of its oldest features, **Maidens Menindee Hotel** (tel. 080-91-4208), stands proudly on the main street. When Charles Sturt passed through Menindee in 1844 it was a remote outpost on the newly discovered Darling River. In 1860 Burke and Wills arrived, resting in Maidens Menindee Hotel for a few nights before heading north on their ill-fated expedition across the continent. Apart from the hotel and coal-stained riverbanks, signs of the settlement's earlier days have all but disappeared—so there's nothing really to do except have a beer in the pub or a meal in the historic dining room.

Menindee lies in an area surrounded by shallow lakes, which act as an overflow when the Darling River floods. The flow of water is now controlled, creating a water supply for Broken Hill and an ideal spot for water sports. Campsites are spread out along the lakeshore north of town, or head south into Kinchega National Park.

Kinchega National Park

This 44,180-hectare park surrounds Menindee and Cawndilla Lakes, whose waters are regulated by a complex system of weirs. At one time, 140,000 sheep were run on the property that is now the park. The former woolshed and outbuildings are now a living museum. Apart from the lakes, the park's landscape consists of mostly sandy plains and black river soils, and, although the park's eastern boundary, the Darling River, is lined with impressive river red gums, the vegetation is generally prickly wattle, bluebush, and canegrass. A variety of waterfowl congregate around the lakes and, of course, 'roos are prevalent.

When you visit, take **River Drive,** a 16-km loop that follows the Darling River from west of Menindee; **Lake Drive** traverses sections of the two major lakes' shorelines. Campsites are spread along both roads and the historic woolshed houses a park information center (tel. 080-91-4214).

Mungo National Park

Little known outside the world of anthropology, the ancient landscape of this remote 27,840-hectare park seems, at first, uninspiring. But the geology and human history will fascinate even the most casual observer. Although the park is on the "wrong" side of the Darling River to be classed as the real Outback, a sense of isolation prevails. From all directions it is a long, dry, and dusty drive to the park—the closest town of more than a handful of people is Mildura, 110 km to the southwest, while Balranald, on the Sturt Hwy., is 150 km south, and Menindee is 210 km north.

Around 35,000 years ago the Lachlan River brought so much water off the Great Dividing Range that it spilled into the **Willandra Lakes,** a vast area of water and wetlands that remained for 15,000 years. The lakes, filled with fish and mollusks, attracted thousands of waterbirds, and provided a food source for giant marsupials, such as seven-meter-tall kangaroos. With dramatic climatic changes at the end of the last ice age, rainfall lessened, rivers changed course, and over a period of thousands of years, the lakes dried up. **Lake Mungo,** once 200 square km in area, has been dry for 15,000 years. During that time, prevailing southerly winds have blown sediments from the dry lakebed into crescent-shaped sand dunes, known as the **Walls of China,** extending for over 30 km along the eastern edge of dried-up Lake Mungo.

In 1968 a geologist found bones in the dunes, which led to some of the most important anthropological finds ever made. They included the burnt bones of a young woman, dated at 26,000 years. Proof of early habitation was a sensation in itself, but the fact that the bones

had been burnt and "buried" was of special significance, as it established the world's earliest evidence of cremation, establishing that Mungo Woman lived in a society that had cultural and spiritual practices. Since that find, over 100 others have been made, including a whole skeleton dated at 30,000 years.

At the park entrance is an unmanned park information center (open daily 9 a.m.-5 p.m.) with panels showing the park's natural and human history, including life-size replicas of the gigantic mammals that once inhabited the Willandra Lakes. Beside the center is a woolshed dating to 1869. From the main facility area, a road leads through the dry lakebed to the Walls of China. It's easy to spend a few hours in and around the dunes' bizarre landscape. A 60-km loop road leads over Lake Mungo and along and over the Walls of China.

The main camping area, near the park information center, is spread through a cleared area with drinking water and basic facilities. Another camping area is along the loop road. The modern **Mungo Lodge,** a privately owned operation three km from the visitor center, has rooms for $55 s, $65 d, and self-contained cottages for $75. Also at the lodge is a restaurant; for reservations call (050) 29-7297.

BROKEN HILL

The town of "Silver, Sin, and Six-penny Ale," as C.J. Dennis described it, may have changed over the years, but this legendary Outback city in the middle of nowhere typifies the hardships of life in Australia and, through a colorful past, boasts a distinctive Australian character. With a population of 25,000, Broken Hill is the largest Outback center and, in fact, in 1900 was Australia's sixth largest city. The Silver City, as it's best known, is in the state's far west and is closer to Adelaide (510 km) and Melbourne (830 km) than Sydney (1,160 km).

History

Broken Hill's extravagant civic buildings and tree-lined boulevards are often a surprise to first-time visitors, but they belie a tumultuous history of the classic struggle between a large mining company and miners.

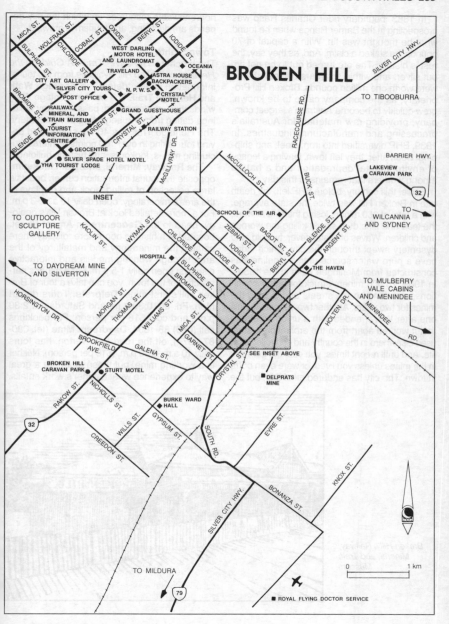

BROKEN HILL

INSET

MICA ST.
WOLFRAM ST.
CHLORIDE ST.
COBALT ST.
OXIDE ST.
BERYL ST.
IODIDE ST.
SULPHIDE ST.
WEST DARLING MOTOR HOTEL AND LAUNDROMAT
OCEANIA
TRAVELAND
CITY ART GALLERY
ASTRA HOUSE BACKPACKERS
SILVER CITY TOURS
N.P.W.S.
POST OFFICE
CRYSTAL MOTEL
BROMIDE ST.
RAILWAY, MINERAL, AND TRAIN MUSEUM
GRAND GUESTHOUSE
ARGENT ST.
TOURIST INFORMATION CENTRE
CRYSTAL ST.
RAILWAY STATION
BLENDE ST.
GEOCENTRE
McGILLVRAY DR.
SILVER SPADE HOTEL MOTEL
YHA TOURIST LODGE

SILVER CITY HWY.
TO TIBOOBURRA

RACECOURSE RD.

LAKEVIEW CARAVAN PARK

BARRIER HWY.

32

TO WILCANNIA AND SYDNEY

TO OUTDOOR SCULPTURE GALLERY

TO DAYDREAM MINE AND SILVERTON

KAOLIN ST.
WYMAN ST.
SCHOOL OF THE AIR
CHLORIDE ST.
ZEBINA ST.
IODIDE ST.
BAGOT ST.
BUCK ST.
BLENDE ST.
BERYL ST.
ARGENT ST.
McCULLOCH ST.

HOSPITAL
MORGAN ST.
THOMAS ST.
SULPHIDE ST.
OXIDE ST.
BROMIDE ST.
WILLIAMS ST.
MICA ST.
GARNET ST.
GALENA ST.
CRYSTAL ST.

HORSINGTON DR.

THE HAVEN

TO MULBERRY VALE CABINS AND MENINDEE

HOLTEN DR.

MENINDEE RD.

SEE INSET ABOVE

BROOKFIELD AVE.
BROKEN HILL CARAVAN PARK
STURT MOTEL
NICHOLLS ST.
RAKOW ST.
WILLS ST.
GYPSUM ST.
BURKE WARD HALL
SOUTH RD.

DELPRATS MINE

EYRE ST.

KNOX ST.

32

CREEDON ST.

SILVER CITY HWY.

BONANZA ST.

TO MILDURA

79

0   1 km

ROYAL FLYING DOCTOR SERVICE

MOON

In 1883, boundary rider Charles Rasp was prospecting in the Barrier Range when he found what he thought was tin. With a capital of 70 pounds, he staked a claim. And, as they say, the rest is history. The ore turned out to be not tin, but silver, and within six years original shares were worth one million pounds. Broken Hill Proprietary, as the company came to be known, grew quickly to become Australia's largest company, providing raw materials for Australia's processing and manufacturing industries. In 1939, BHP diversified into iron, steel, and shipping. Soon after, they left town, leaving a legacy of environmental depredation and a hatred among workers that remains to this day.

Earlier this century, before BHP left, the death rate in Broken Hill was twice the state average, with a total of 360 miners losing their life at work, the lead and zinc dust slowly killing the women and children. Waves of scarlet fever, typhoid, and dysentery swept through the city, which didn't have a pure water source until a pipeline was constructed from Menindee Lake in the 1950s. In 1909, 15,000 miners struck for better conditions, marching on the streets and closing the mines for two years. Another two-year strike, this one after WW I, ended with a union so strong that it worked apart from the arbitration system used elsewhere in the country and controlled civic life. And until recent times, you couldn't get work in the mines unless you lived, or were even born, in town. The city has endured all of this, but the

nonrenewable resources on which the city depends are declining, and tourism is growing.

Town Sights

The brochure *The Silver Trail—A Guide to the Heritage of Broken Hill,* available from the tourist information center, details the **Heritage Walk** and **Heritage Trail.** The two-km Heritage Walk winds through downtown, passing many buildings dating from the beginning of this century. The Heritage Trail is a 40-km self-guided driving tour taking in over 100 points of interest, including mines, lookouts, and historic buildings.

The **Railway, Mineral, and Train Museum,** opposite the tourist information center, boasts a large collection of rolling stock and displays of the area's mineralogy; open daily 10 a.m.-3 p.m. For a more detailed look at Broken Hill's geology, head to the **Geocentre** on Argent Street. Located in a historic bond store, displays here catalog the mineralogy and metallurgy of the area through working models and interactive displays; open daily 1-5 p.m. For a miner's perspective of the town, you can take a tour of Broken Hill's first mine, **Delprats.** Tours depart Mon.-Fri. at 10:30 a.m. and Saturday at 2:30 p.m., and cost $18 per person. For bookings call (080) 88-1604. **Daydream Mine** (tel. 080-87-6077), off the road to Silverton, has tours daily 10 a.m.-3:30 p.m. ($10 per person). Neither is a working mine, but these tours are a great way to experience what a miner's work entails.

Broken Hill's Railway, Mineral, and Train Museum

Out at the airport is a museum dedicated to the work of the **Royal Flying Doctor Service of Australia** (tel. 080-88-0777). Admission is $2, which includes a tour and audiovisual display. Book yourself for the tour at the tourist information center. Another Outback institution is **School of the Air,** a distance-education facility that broadcasts lessons to school-age children living in remote parts of the country. To sit in on "classes" contact the tourist information center.

Galleries

Some of Australia's most renowned contemporary artists call Broken Hill home. The most famous of these are Jack Absolum and Pro Hart, whose works command tens of thousands of dollars and are in demand around the world. The **Pro Hart Gallery** is at 108 Wyman St. (tel. 080-87-2441); open Mon.-Sat. 9 a.m.-5 p.m., Sunday 1:30-5 p.m. **Ant Hill Gallery,** 24 Bromide St. (tel. 080-87-2441), has works from the largest range of local artists. Includes interesting pottery; open Mon.-Sat. 9 a.m.-5 p.m., Sunday 1:30-5 p.m. The stunning Outback landscapes of Eric and Roxanne Minchin are displayed at **Minchin Gallery,** 105 Morgan St. (tel. 080-87-7446), open daily 9 a.m.-5 p.m. The only gallery with an admission charge is **Broken Hill City Art Gallery,** corner Blende and Chloride Streets (tel. 080-88-9252), but it's only $2. The gallery has a huge collection of works, all by local artists, spread through three galleries. Open Mon.-Fri. 9 a.m.-4 p.m., Saturday 9 a.m.-1 p.m.

Broken Hill Outdoor Sculpture Gallery, five km north of town, comprises 12 large sculptures scattered on a rocky outcrop. They were created by sculptors during a 1993 symposium.

Silverton

Through the Barrier Range, 26 km northwest of Broken Hill, is Silverton. It is promoted in all the tourist literature as a ghost town, when, in fact, there isn't an empty building in town. At its peak, in 1880, the town boasted a population in excess of 3,000, and hotels with names like Silver King and Nevada reflected the early dreams of entrepreneurs who came to make a fortune in this harsh country. The gold rush lasted less than a decade, with most miners moving back to Broken Hill. The only prospecting done around

town today is for tourists. You can still get a beer in the sandstone and brick **Silverton Hotel,** and many of the other original buildings remain—making this photogenic town the perfect setting for movies, including *Mad Max II, A Town Like Alice, Razorback, Hostage,* and, more recently, *Race the Sun* starring James Belushi. A small museum is housed in the jail, an information center is in the school building (tel. 080-88-5327), and three good art galleries are scattered along the main street.

Camel rides are offered by Bill Canard, who ties his beasts up by the hotel. A 15-minute ride is $5, a one-hour ride is $20, and overnight adventures are also offered; call Bill at (080) 91-4880 for details.

Accommodations

The **Grand Guesthouse,** 313 Argent St. (tel. 080-87-5305), has an excellent standard of pub-style rooms with shared facilities. Rates start at $42 s, $54 d, and rooms with private facilities are $80, including a continental breakfast. **West Darling Motor Hotel,** 400 Argent St.(tel. 080-87-2691), has rooms for $23 s, $36 d. The least expensive motel in town is the **Sturt Motel,** 153 Rakow St. (tel. 080-87-3558), but it's three km west of town; $41 s, $47 d. Within walking distance of downtown is **Silver Spade Hotel Motel,** 157 Argent St. (tel. 080-87-7021), where motel-style units are $52 s, $58 d. Facilities include a restaurant, laundry, barbecue area, and pool. **Crystal Motel,** 328 Crystal St. (tel. 080-88-2344), has the most comfortable rooms in town and a ton of facilities; rates of $69 s, $74 d include a cooked breakfast.

Mulberry Vale Cabins, Menindee Rd. (tel. 080-88-1597), is five km east of town. The cabins are set among native bush and each is self-contained with rates at $50-60 d including a cooked breakfast.

The **YHA Tourist Lodge,** 100 Argent St. (tel. 080-88-2086), is only 100 meters from the bus depot and tourist information center. Facilities include communal kitchen, lounge and recreation rooms, laundry, and shaded courtyard. Rates are $10 for members, $13 nonmembers. **Astra House Backpackers,** 393 Argent St. (tel. 080-87-7788), has facilities of a similar standard but is a little farther from town, and has bikes for hire; $10 per night.

Broken Hill Caravan Park is three km west of downtown on Rakow St. (tel. 080-87-3841); sites are $10 unpowered, $13 powered. Lakeview Caravan Park is a similar distance northeast of town on Mann St. (tel. 080-88-2250). It has similar facilities as well as a pool. Sites are $8-10, and cabins $30-40 d.

Food and Entertainment

The clubs are the best place for an inexpensive meal. The Musicians Club, 276 Crystal St. (tel. 080-88-1777), is open daily for lunch and dinner and most meals are under $10. The Barrier Social and Democratic Club, 218 Argent St. (tel. 080-88-4477), is another good option. Of the hotels, Black Lion Inn has counter meal lunches for $5 and dinners for $8-10. Oceania, 423 Argent St. (tel. 080-87-3695), is a Chinese joint open for lunch and dinner with specials starting at $6. The Haven, 577 Argent St. (tel. 080-88-2888), is a casual seafood and steak restaurant open seven nights a week.

Two-up is an Australian game where punters bet on the fall of two coins tossed in the air. It is legal only in casinos and on Anzac Day, but has recently been legalized at a two-up "school" in Burke Ward Hall on Wills St., operating on Friday and Saturday nights. The pubs and clubs are where Broken Hill's thirsty residents head for a drink, and so these are the best places to experience the city after dark. Theatre Royal Hotel, on Argent St., is the only one with a disco. Try the Barrier Social and Democratic Club, also on Argent St., or the Musicians Club, on Crystal St., for cheap beer and occasional live music.

Services and Information

Broken Hill Base Hospital is at 174 Thomas St. (tel. 080-88-0333). A laundromat, at 400 Argent St., is open daily 7 a.m.-10 p.m. For camping gear, head to Disposals of Broken Hill at 55-57 Oxide St. (tel. 080-88-5977). Outback Books, 309 Argent St. (tel. 080-88-1177), stocks a lot of local and general Outback literature. Charles Rasp Memorial Library is on Blende St. (tel. 080-88-9291).

The tourist information center is right downtown at the corner of Blende and Bromide Streets (tel. 080-87-6077). As well as all the usual literature, there's a historic display, a cafe,

and all long distance buses use the center as a depot. Open daily 9 a.m.-5 p.m. The National Parks and Wildlife Service has an office at 5 Oxide St. (tel. 080-88-5933); open Mon.-Fri. 8:30 a.m.-4:30 p.m.

Transport and Tours

Hazelton has daily flights from Sydney out to Broken Hill ($337 one way) and Kendell connects Broken Hill to Adelaide. Traveland, 350 Argent St. (tel. 080-87-1969), is the Broken Hill agent for both these airlines. The Indian Pacific, Australia's transcontinental train service, stops in town ($86 one way from Sydney) twice weekly, departing Sydney Monday and Thursday. The railway station is on Crystal St., tel. (080) 87-1400. All the major bus companies stop at Broken Hill on the Sydney-Adelaide run. To Sydney is $80 one-way and to Adelaide $40.

Silver City Tours, 328 Argent St. (tel. 080-87-6956), operates a dozen different tours around town, to Silverton, and out to the nearby national parks. The basic town tour is $20.

The various car rental agencies are: Avis (tel. 080-87-7532), Hertz (tel. 080-87-2719), and Thrifty (tel. 080-88-1928). As the name suggests, Broken Hill 4WD Hire (tel. 080-87-2927) rents 4WDs, with rates starting at $80 per day. For a taxi, call Yellow Radio Cabs at (080) 88-1144.

NORTHWEST CORNER

The northwest corner of New South Wales is the state's least visited and most remote region, an area larger than many European countries, yet with only a few towns where the population exceeds five. Only gravel roads lead into the area, and although the main ones are passable in 2WDs, travel after rain is impossible. From Broken Hill, the Silver City Highway is the main access with other 2WD roads leading north from Wilcannia and west from Bourke. Like all Outback areas, travel requires forward planning—spare tires, extra fuel, and water are the basic prerequisites for safe travel.

Mootwingee National Park

Dominated by the knobbed and broken Bynguano Range rising from the surrounding stark landscape, this large 68,912-hectare park is a mysterious place, dotted with Aboriginal rock art and intriguing geological formations. The Bynguano Range is a sloped layer of sedimentary rock, laid down in a seabed 400 million years ago. Over time, erosion has gouged out gullies and cliffs, forming contorted geological features and exposing conglomerate from which the Koori extracted smooth stones to use as tools. The Wilyakali people took shelter in the range, protecting themselves from the elements while feasting on the flora and fauna living around the rock pools that remained after other water sources had dried up.

Over 300 Koori sites are scattered through the range—but vandalism has taken its toll and two of the most concentrated areas are accessible only on a ranger-led tour. The tour takes in **Snake Cave,** featuring an eight-meter serpent. Hiking through the magical Bynguano Range is a highlight of Mootwingee. One of the most interesting, yet easiest, hikes is through **Homestead Gorge,** on a loop track following a dry creek bed up through crumbling cliffs. Watch overhangs anywhere along the route for rock art. Up near the entrance to the gorge is rock art from a more recent time—the initials of William Wright, who guided Burke and Wills through the range. This trail begins north of the campground. On the opposite side of the access road is the **Western Ridge Trail,** which climbs to a low summit from where sunrise and sunset can be seen in all their glory. The return trip takes three hours. Another interesting area to explore is **Old Mootwingee Gorge,** south of the campground. This narrow gorge, one km from the carpark, marks the end of the marked trail, but if you want to take to the water, swimming up the gorge is a unique experience.

The campground is well-equipped, with drinking water, showers (you'll need some Outback common sense to operate them), and a handful of gas barbecues. Fees are $10 per night, plus a park-use fee of $7.50.

Ask at the tourist information center in Broken Hill about tours out to the park—apart from these, you're by yourself. The park is 130 km northeast of Broken Hill; turn off Silver City Highway 55 km north of the city.

Near the park entrance is a covered area with information boards and camping registration slips. Also look for details on tours into restricted areas (usually Wednesday and Sat.) or call (080) 91-5937.

Milparinka

It is 296 km from Broken Hill to Milparinka along the Silver City Highway, with the only fuel, beer, and food available en route at Packsaddle, 180 km north of Broken Hill. Gold was found in the Milparinka area in 1880. Within a few years a minor gold rush had taken place and the township gained an air of permanence, with three hotels, a few stores, and a stone courthouse serving 3,000 miners. By the mid-1930s, the Albert Hotel was the only business still operating—and it has been open ever since. Rooms are $23 per person (tel. 080-91-3963), the beers are cold, and basic pub meals are inexpensive. If you'd like to have a look inside the courthouse, pick up the key at the hotel.

A worthwhile detour is northwest to **Depot Glen,** a waterhole where Captain Charles Sturt and his party rested for six months in the summer of 1844-45. The area is a small oasis surrounded by dry plains—it is easy to see why Sturt chose it. A couple of km east of Depot Glen is a grevillea tree with "J.P. 1845" carved into its trunk, marking the resting place of James Poole, who died during the ordeal.

Tibooburra

Meaning "Place of Granite" in the language of local Koori, Tibooburra is New South Wales' most remote town, being 340 km north of Broken Hill and 1,500 km northwest of Sydney. It is also the state's hottest place, with summer temperatures occasionally topping 50° C. Tibooburra is in an area known as Corner Country, over a million hectares of sandhills and mulga, of which Sturt National Park is most people's destination. Today, Tibooburra resembles a town of the U.S. Wild West, with a smattering of buildings along a small section of paved road.

Tibooburra grew from a gold rush in the 1890s, but the gold proved elusive, and after a couple of decades the population had dipped perilously low. The pastoral industry kept Tibooburra alive. Then, in the 1950s, the town served as a service center for natural gas exploration across the northeast part of South Australia.

Tibooburra's most famous buildings, and those that locals and tourists alike spend the most time in, are the two hotels. The **Family Hotel,** (tel. 080-91-3314), was the home of Outback artist Clifton Pugh for most of the 1960s. He spent his time decorating the walls with his distinctive style of art for free beer. In the end, he decided he liked the place so much, he bought it. Pugh died a few years back, and the pub is now run by his ex-wife. The veranda is the perfect place to view the town's goings-on. Across the road is the no-less-grand **Tibooburra Hotel** (tel. 080-91-3310), known locally as the "two-story."

Both pubs have accommodations for about $25 s, $30 d, or you can stay in **Granites Motel** (tel. 080-91-3305), which lacks atmosphere but has a pool; $36 s, $46 d. At the north end of town is **Dead Horse Gully Campground.** It is officially within the border of Sturt National Park (see below) and has toilets and a few broken tables in an area of unusual boulders.

Before leaving Tibooburra, visit Sturt National Park Visitor Centre (Briscoe St., tel. 080-91-3308) for road conditions, an excellent interpretive display, and park literature.

Sturt National Park

For many, the stark desert landscape of this 310,634-hectare park may be monotonous, but this is the Outback at its best, with desolate gibber plains extending seemingly forever. The park is a conglomeration of six sheep stations, stretching for 80 km along the Queensland border from Cameron Corner. Since the removal of stock, the park has regenerated quickly, with native grasses covering much of the park, attracting large numbers of red kangaroos, flocks of emus, a variety of lizards, and other birds such as wedge-tailed eagles and kestrels. The park is divided into two halves by its most domi-

nant geological feature, the **Grey Range,** bluffs of sandstone rising 150 meters above the red plains. For these rises, this area is known as "jump-up country," as the bluffs seem to jump up from the surrounding landscape.

The biggest attraction west of the jump-ups is the long dusty drive out to Cameron Corner, but in the east, the land is more varied and there are two interesting circuits to drive around. **Gorge Loop Road** begins in Tibooburra and heads west to Mt. Wood Homestead, where you'll find camping and a small **Pastoral Museum** featuring a *whim,* which is turned by horses to draw water from bores deep below. The road continues north to a spectacular gorge before rejoining Silver City Highway. From this junction, it's south to Tibooburra. But most people would want to drive the **Jump-up Loop Road,** along which there's a campground from where short interpretive trails start.

Access to the western portion of the park is from two km south of Tibooburra. It is 140 km from the Silver City Highway to Cameron Corner. **Fort Grey,** 30 km from the corner, is a camp set up by Charles Sturt in 1845 on his journey to find an inland sea. At this site is a seven-km trail and campground.

Cameron Corner

Cameron Corner, 140 km northwest of Tibooburra, is the spot where three states—New South Wales, Queensland, and South Australia—meet. It was surveyed by John Cameron in 1880. His unenviable task that year was to survey the entire border of N.S.W. and Queensland (when resurveyed in 1969, his pegs were found to be accurate within the meter). Until 1990, the corner boasted only a marker peg, but in that year the **Corner Store,** transported from South Australia, opened for road-weary travelers to quench their thirst.

OUTBACK QUEENSLAND

While most visitors to Queensland are diving on the reef and sunning themselves on the beaches, a few are venturing over the Great Dividing Range and across the tablelands to the Outback, an area of endless plains and red-soil desert, where towns are hundreds of kilometers apart, existing on water pumped from artesian bores, serving vast cattle stations and road weary travelers. Among this desolate landscape are many surprises—pleasant country towns where hospitality is second nature, and huge national parks protecting all the best natural features.

Outback Queensland is generally regarded as everything west of the **Matilda Highway,** a collection of highways 1,700 km long, passing through areas of historical importance, beginning on the New South Wales/Queensland border about 700 km inland and making a big long arc on the edge of the Outback to Mt. Isa and the Queensland/Northern Territory border. Travel is best May-October. The rest of the year is stifling hot and during the wet season roads can be underwater for weeks.

MITCHELL HIGHWAY

The Mitchell Highway enters Queensland in the south of the state, 138 km north of Bourke, and parallels the **Warrego River** to Cunnamulla. This highway, and those that continue through to the Gulf of Carpentaria, are promoted as the Matilda Highway.

Cunnamulla
First town north of the border, Cunnamulla is on the tree-lined banks of the Warrego River. This town of 1,500 is at the western terminus of the rail line used to transport sheep to eastern markets. The small **Bicentennial Museum,** on John St., is worth investigating, but little else is. To the west of the town is **Yowah Opal Field,** where opal nuts—opal in a shell of ironstone—are highly sought after.

Charleville
Charleville (population 3,500), surrounded by hundreds of thousands of hectares of sheep and cattle stations and 800 km from the coast, is the hub of southwest Queensland. Reminders of the town's earliest days abound, the most interesting being a Stiger Vortex rainmaker gun. During a terrible drought in 1902 Clement L. Wagge imported six of the guns from Germany, setting them at strategic locations around Charleville. Each was loaded with gunpowder and fired skyward in the hope of creating rain. Two guns imploded, a few horses stampeded, and Mr. Wagge rode out of town the following day—under a cloudless sky. You'll find the remaining gun in Centennial Park, just south of town.

The 1881 **Queensland National Bank,** on Alfred St., houses memorabilia from the town's past, and out back is a vintage fire engine and steam engine; open Mon.-Fri. 9 a.m.-4 p.m., Saturday 9 a.m.-noon.

On Old Cunnamulla Rd. is one of Queensland's three **Royal Flying Doctor Service** bases. Beside the base is a visitor center, where the importance of the service is put into perspective through a video and displays. Open Mon.-Fri. 8:30 a.m.-4:30 p.m. (tel. 076-54-1181).

Just east of Charleville, the Department of Environment and Heritage operates a **research station** (tel. 076-54-1255), where various species of kangaroos and wallabies can be seen grazing among three hectares of native bushland; open Mon.-Fri. 8:30 a.m.-4:30 p.m.

Charleville Waltzing Matilda Motor Inn, 125 Alfred St. (tel. 076-54-1720), has the least expensive rooms in town; those with shared facilities are $29 s, $40 d (the roof of this place was used as a helipad during flooding in April 1990 when the entire town was underwater). Of a higher standard is **Warrego Motel,** 75 Wills St. (tel. 076-54-1299), which has large air-conditioned rooms; $55 s, $65 d. Campers should head to **Bailey Bar Caravan Park,** 196 King St. (tel. 076-54-1744), with good facilities including a laundry, kiosk, and barbecues. Sites are $10-12, and on-site vans cost $28.

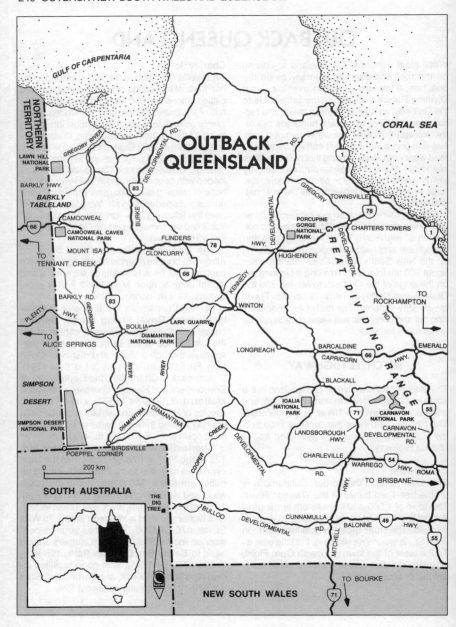

The **tourist information center** is on Wills St. (tel. 076-54-3057); open daily 9:30 a.m.-4:30 p.m.

CARNARVON NATIONAL PARK

A bone-shaking 100 km from the nearest sealed road, and 580 km northeast of Charleville, this park encompasses 251,000 hectares of a plateau rising high above the surrounding plains. Remarkable **Carnarvon Gorge** is the park's major attraction. Almost 30 km long, 250 meters deep, and with innumerable arms, the gorge area is a dramatic landscape of sheer-sided cliffs, natural bridges, and caves. The gorge has been created by **Carnarvon Creek,** little more than a babbling stream most of the year, but a raging torrent during the Wet. Thousands of years of water erosion have eaten into the multicolored sandstone layers deposited on the bottom of an ocean many millions of years ago.

The creek flows year-round, supporting an oasis of ferns and mosses that thrive in an otherwise desolate landscape and attracting a surprisingly large number of animals. Forests of dry eucalypt dominate higher elevations, while the lush vegetation of the gorge is mainly tree ferns, cabbage tree palms, orchids, and, along the creek bed, moss-covered boulders.

The gorge's first human visitors were Aboriginals, who used the many caves as ceremonial places, burying their dead among the rocky caves. Kenniff Cave is adorned with early rock art; stencil paintings depict animals and people with boomerangs and shields.

Hiking

The road into the park ends at the entrance to the gorge, leaving exploring on foot the only option. The main trail leads 9.3 km to **Cathedral Cave,** its lower walls covered in ancient art. Along the route sidetracks lead to the aptly named **Art Gallery** and the park's most magnificent feature, the **Amphitheatre,** five km from the Visitor Centre. The final approach is up a steel ladder and through a one-meter gap into a chasm surrounded in sheer sandstone walls towering over 100 meters above. An easy walk from the Visitor Centre leads to the **Moss Garden** in Violet Gorge. Here, lush palms, mosses, and ferns thrive on the small creek that tumbles down a long ravine.

Practicalities

The camping area by the Visitor Centre has toilets, drinking water, and cold showers; bookings are essential during holiday periods; tel. (079) 84-4505. Just outside the park entrance is **Oasis Lodge** (tel. 079-84-4503), consisting of individual cabins spread around native bushland. Each has a bathroom, refrigerator, tea and coffee-making facilities, and veranda. It also has a lounge, library, and a packed program of activities and guided walks (April-Nov. only). Rates, inclusive of all meals, are $150 per person per night, $399 per person for three nights. In the low season (Dec.-March) rates drop to $96 per person per night, $270 for three nights. Flight West (tel. 1800-77-7879) offers a package, including flights from Brisbane to Roma, a charter flight out to the lodge, and all-inclusive accommodations for three nights for $859 (high season).

Spectacular Aboriginal rock art can be found in all corners of the Outback.

CHANNEL COUNTRY

In the southwestern corner of the state is an area known as Channel Country, so named for the mosaic of watercourses that flow through it. It's either very wet or very dry out here. Summer rains to the north fill the many rivers and creeks, which flow southwest toward Lake Eyre. The watercourses divide, rejoin each other, and eventually dissipate into the soft soils in the far northeastern corner of South Australia. After exceptionally heavy rains, the whole basin floods, creating a massive system of temporary lakes that isolate remote stations and flood roads for months.

Diamantina Developmental Road
This 1,350-km road is the main route through Channel Country, heading west at Charleville and ending at Mt. Isa. It also provides access to the north end of the Birdsville Track.

Quilpie, 210 km west of Charleville, is a cattle transportation railhead surrounded by many productive opal mines. The next town en route to Mount Isa is Windorah, with a population under 100 but enough passing trade to justify a pub, petrol pump, and general store. Continuing west, the highway passes brilliantly colored red sandhills, which rise from the Channel Country like a mirage. Then it's 500 km of gravel to Boulia. It's a long trip, the arid landscape broken occasionally by an outcrop of sandstone and the town of Bedourie, consisting of just a pub and petrol pump. A track heading south from Bedourie leads to Birdsville. After crossing the Georgina River and passing the small town of Boulia, the land becomes rocky, changing subtly, as the road climbs the Isa Highlands to Mt. Isa.

Birdsville
Famous for its pub, this is Queensland's most remote town. It grew from a store established on the Diamantina River in 1872, the last stop for stockmen driving cattle southward through the Simpson Desert to Adelaide. Named by a settler's wife for the profusion of birdlife on the river, Birdsville boasted three hotels, a couple of shops, and dozens of houses in its heyday. Today, the population is under 100, but each September over 5,000 punters descend on the town for the annual Birdsville Races, a colorful celebration of everything that Outback Australia stands for. Needless to say, an amazing amount of beer is consumed over the weekend, much of it in and around the Birdsville Hotel (tel. 076-56-3244), right by the airport. This hotel has rooms for $42 s, $64 d.

Simpson Desert National Park
In the extreme west of the state, and accessible only by 4WD, is the enormous one-million-hectare Simpson Desert National Park. It encompasses just the northeast corner of a 20-million-hectare desert for which the park is named. The landscape is barren, featuring waves of sand dunes, gibber flats, and large areas of clay plains. The extensive dune system extends through much of the park, typified by dunes up to 25 meters high, spaced 300-400 meters apart, and extending for up to 70 km in an amazing parallel northwest-to-southeast direction. A surprisingly large number of lifeforms exist in the park—a few species of spinifex, wattle, grevilleas, snakes, lizards, marsupials, and birds of prey all thrive in this harsh, waterless environment.

Permits are required before entering the park (available from the Department of Environment and Heritage in Longreach, tel. 076-58-1761, or Charleville, tel. 076-54-1255), and you must also register with the police in Birdsville. The park has no established camping area, but as the only formed road leads from Birdsville to Poeppel Corner (150 km) most people camp somewhere en route.

CHARLEVILLE TO LONGREACH

Blackall
In 1892, gun-shearer Jack Howe set a new world record, shearing 321 sheep in less than eight hours. For blade shearing, the record stands to this day, and it took until 1950 for a machine shearer to equal it. A statue of the great man stands in the main street of Blackall, a pleasant Outback town 300 km north of Charleville.

Blackwall Woolscour, four km north of town (tel. 076-57-4637), was where wool was washed and dried, then sorted, pressed, and transported to eastern ports. Much of the plant remains

(top) riding camels on Cable Beach, Broome, Western Australia
(bottom) Manning Gorge, Mount Barnett Station, Western Australia
(following page) coastal sandstone, Gantheaume Point, Broome, Western Australia

as the day it closed, allowing an authentic glimpse at the industry upon which Outback Australia was built. The complex is open daily 8 a.m.-4 p.m.; admission is adult $5, child $2. Like many Outback towns, Blackall's drinking water is from artesian bores, and one is located at the woolscour.

The **Barcoo Hotel,** 95 Shamrock St. (tel. 076-57-4197), is right in the center of town and has rooms with shared facilities for $35 s, $50 d, which includes a cooked breakfast. Lunches at the bar are $4-6 and Friday and Saturday nights there's a barbecue in the beergarden. **Blackall Motel,** also on Shamrock St. (tel. 076-57-4611), has standard rooms for $40 s, $50 d. **Blackall Caravan Park,** 53 Garden St. (tel. 076-57-4816), has unpowered sites for $9, powered sites are $11.50, on-site vans $16-22, and cabins $28-40.

Avington Outback Holiday Station, (tel. 076-57-5952) allows guests to enjoy life on a working cattle station, horseback riding, rounding up sheep, and watching shearers at work, as well as cruising on the Barcoo River, golf on a unique nine-hole course, and tennis. Rooms, large and air-conditioned, cost $50 s, $90 d, and include meals. To get there, head north out of Blackall for 18 km, then take Avington Rd. for 57 km northwest to the homestead.

Idalia National Park
Located 100 km southwest of Blackall, deep in the Gowan Ranges, which form the eastern boundary of Channel Country, is this new 144,000-hectare park. It encompasses the headwaters of the Bulloo River, and although the river is dry for most of the year a variety of vegetation thrives, including stands of river red gums around low-lying areas. Access is by 4WD only and camping is permitted at Monk's Tank.

Barcaldine
The pleasant town of Barcaldine lies at the junction of the Capricorn and Landsborough Highways, 580 km west of Rockhampton. In 1891 over 1,000 striking shearers converged on the town, meeting under a big ghost gum outside the railway station to demand higher wages and better working conditions. The following year, union leaders endorsed a candidate for parliament, under the same tree, beginning the for-

mation of the Australian Labor Party. The tree stands today, in mute testimony to the shearers' resolve. The role ordinary working Australians, such as shearers, played in the development of the country is celebrated at the **Australian Workers Heritage Centre,** on Ash St. (tel. 076-51-1422), which opened in May 1991, on the centenary of the strike. The large complex features a museum, interactive displays, films, historic buildings transported to the site, a seven-story theater where *Celebration of a Nation,* a tribute to all Australians, is shown, and extensive landscaped gardens complete with a billabong. Open daily 9 a.m.-5 p.m.

Barcaldine Motel, on the main drag through town (tel. 076-51-1244), has basic rooms for $35 s, $45 d. With nicer rooms and a laundry and pool is **Landsborough Lodge,** also on the highway (tel. 076-51-1100); $55 s, $68 d. **Homestead Caravan Park,** Blackall Rd. (tel. 076-51-1308), has shady sites, a barbecue area where damper meals (with full bush tucker) are cooked nightly, and friendly hosts who organize tours to anywhere in the region. Sites are $10-12, on-site vans $28, and small cabins $32.

The **Barcaldine Tourist Information Centre** is on Oak St. (tel. 076-51-1724); open daily 9 a.m.-5 p.m.

LONGREACH

Home to the Australian Stockman's Hall of Fame, Longreach (population 4,000) is the largest town in the central west. It is located 1,232 km northwest of Brisbane—sealed highway the whole way—or 24 hours on Queensland Rail's Spirit of the Outback.

Longreach began life as a campground for shearers, receiving a boost when a rail line was completed from Rockhampton in 1892. **Qantas** (Queensland and Northern Territory Aerial Services) was born in Longreach. The airline's first flight was made in 1922, and for seven years its headquarters was centered in Longreach. You'll find the original Qantas hangar at the airport. Plans to build a museum dedicated to the history of the airline are well underway, with the **Qantas Founders Museum Preview Centre** in the tourist information center a taste of what's to come; open daily 9 a.m.-5 p.m.

The **Powerhouse Museum** is on the site of an old power station and remains as it was built in 1921 with many working exhibits. Power was produced by enormous generators, whose engines were cooled by artesian-bore water; open April-Oct. daily 2-5 p.m.

On the Landsborough Highway, east of town, is **Longreach School of Distance Education.** Pupils spread around central Queensland attend lessons broadcast over UHF radios, sending homework by mail and getting together a few times a year. Tours are offered weekdays at 9 a.m., 9:45 a.m., and 10:30 a.m.

Australian Stockman's Hall of Fame And Outback Heritage Centre

No one could begrudge the stockmen and others who developed the Outback a tribute to their pioneering spirit and never-say-die attitude. And this is it, a magnificent museum dedicated to everything the Outback stands for. It opened in 1988, amid much fanfare; even the Queen of England made it to town for the occasion. The architects have combined traditional Outback materials with modern design concepts to create a totally unique building. The complex comprises a series of corrugated iron half-pipes, overlapping to form one long roof. Exhibits include those dedicated to shearers, miners, traveling salesman, women of the Outback, and Aboriginals. One display provokes much comment—an 1860s settler's hut. The hut is the size of an average bedroom, but it provided a home for one woman and three children, with a stove crammed in one corner and beds taking up most of the rest of the dirt floor. Historical displays are only a part of the Hall of Fame; computers and audiovisual programs help bring the history of the Outback to life. The complex also has a gift shop and cafe. Open daily 9 a.m.-5 p.m. Admission is a worthwhile $15 adult, $7 child, family $35. For further information call (076) 58-2166. Allow at least half a day here.

Entertainment and Events

Most afternoons, the pioneering spirit of the Outback comes alive at **Banjo's Outback Theatre and Pioneer Shearing Shed,** at the end of Stork Rd. (tel. 076-58-2360). Demonstrations of wool shearing, pressing, classing, and spin-

ning take place, with everyone invited to try their hand. A whole lot of bush poetry is read, yarns spun, and light snacks served at the end of it all; $10 per person. Performances are Mon.-Thurs. and Saturday at 2:30 p.m.

The **Outback Muster and Drovers Reunion** brings together stockmen from throughout the Outback, and while the old-timers spend the weekend drinking, spinning yarns, bronco-branding, and rough-riding, a range of unique Outback sports keep the city slickers occupied. All the action takes place the last week of April. On the third weekend of July, **The Diamond Shears,** Australia's most prestigious shearing event, takes place.

Accommodations and Food

Welcome Home Hotel, 128 Eagle St. (tel. 076-58-1361), has air-conditioned rooms with shared bathrooms for $20 s, $35 d. Another inexpensive option is **Swaggies,** 81 Wompoo Rd. (tel. 076-58-3777), a backpacker place with communal kitchen, laundry facilities, and lounge. Beds are $12 per person. **Jumbuck Motel,** Landsborough Hwy.(tel. 076-58-1799), has a pool, air-conditioned rooms, and a good restaurant; $45 s, $55 d. The best place in town is **Albert Park Motel,** Landsborough Hwy. (tel. 076-58-2411), with a covered pool, sundeck area, and large modern rooms; $56 s, $66 d. Both of the above motels are within 500 meters of both the airport and Hall of Fame. **Gunnadoo Caravan Park,** 12 Thrush Rd., (tel. 076-58-1781), has a pool, barbecue area, and laundry facilities. Sites are $10-12, cabins $45 d.

Along Eagle St. is **Merino Bakery** and a number of cafes open breakfast through dinner. Try the **Star Coffee Shop,** where hearty breakfasts are $6-9. For lunch, all the hotels serve counter meals for under $7. The **R.S.L. Club,** on Duck St., is another option for an inexpensive meal. **Squatters,** Landsborough Hwy. (tel. 076-58-3215), is an Aussie-style restaurant with entrees ranging $11-16. The Jumbuck Motel also has a restaurant.

Services and Information

The **post office** is at 100 Eagle Street. For the hospital call (076) 58-1133.

The **tourist information center** is located in a replica of the first Qantas booking office in

Qantas Park (tel. 076-58-3555). Open daily 9 a.m.-5 p.m.

Transport and Tours

Flight West (tel. 1800-77-7879), serves 36 western Queensland towns, with Longreach the central-western hub. Flights depart Brisbane ($199 one-way) and Townsville daily for Longreach.

A favorite and traditional way to reach Longreach is aboard **Spirit of the Outback,** a twice-weekly rail service between Brisbane and Longreach via Rockhampton. The train departs Brisbane Tuesday and Friday 7 p.m., with the less-interesting scenery traversed at night and the climb through the Drummond Ranges west of Rockhampton taking place in daylight hours. The train has a themed dining car and bar, and seating to suit all budgets. (It is part of Australian folklore that in 1859, when Queensland was granted statehood, it could only afford three-foot, six-inch gauge rail line, the narrowest in Australia—and you'll come to realize its downside when eating and drinking.) The one-way economy class fare is $118, economy sleeper $148, and first-class sleeper $226. For bookings call **Queensland Rail,** toll-free tel. 13-2232 .

Greyhound Pioneer and **McCafferty's** have daily services to and from Brisbane (16 hours one-way, $77) and Mt. Isa (eight and a half hours, $53) with McCafferty's also running to Rockhampton thrice weekly (nine hours, $51). There's a 50% discount for booking 15 days in advance. All buses stop at Outback Travel Centre, 115 Eagle St. (tel. 076-58-1776).

The major car rental companies with offices in Longreach include **Avis** (tel. 076-58-1799) and **Hertz** (tel. 076-58-1155). For a taxi call **Carolyn's Cabs** at (076) 58-1083.

Outback Aussie Tours (tel. 076-58-3000 or 1800-81-0510) offers a great variety of day and overnight tours. The Outback Longreach Link tour takes in everything there is to do and see in town, including the Stockman's Hall of Fame, a visit to an outlying station, and an evening cruise on the Thompson River. All meals included; $99.

LONGREACH TO THE GULF

Winton

Winton may not have a Stockman's Hall of Fame to draw the tourists, but its close ties to the legendary Australian bush poet Banjo Patterson provide the basis for a thriving tourist industry. The town began its life as Pelican Waterhole, with one main street lined with pubs and

---

WALTZING MATILDA

Oh! There once was a swagman camped in a billabong,
Under the shade of a coolabah tree;
And he sang as he looked at his old billy boiling,
"Who'll come a-waltzing matilda with me?
Who'll come a-waltzing matilda, my darling,
Who'll come a-waltzing matilda with me?
Waltzing matilda and leading a water bag—
Who'll come a-waltzing matilda with me?"

Down came a jumbuck to drink at the waterhole,
Up jumped the swagman and grabbed him in glee;
And he sang as he stowed him away in his tucker-bag,
"You'll come a-waltzing matilda with me."

Down came the squatter a-riding his thoroughbred;
Down came policemen—one, two, three.
"Whose is the jumbuck you've got in the tucker-bag?
You'll come a-waltzing matilda with me."

But the swagman, he up and he jumped in the waterhole,
Drowning himself by the coolabah tree;
And his ghost may be heard as it sings in the billabong
"Who'll come a-waltzing matilda with me?"

the usual array of businesses associated with an Outback town. In 1895 Patterson wrote *Waltzing Matilda* after hearing stationhands' recollections of a swagman's suicide in a local billabong. The station owner's wife, Christina Macpherson, sang the words in the North Gregory Hotel on 6 April 1895. Its appeal was immediate, and it soon became Australia's favorite song, recited with pride around the country. The original North Gregory Hotel is long gone. Its replacement, a jewel of 1950s architecture, sits on the main street, and a statue of a not-so-jolly-looking Jolly Swagman stands opposite the pool. The terribly named **Qantilda Museum,** in Pioneer Place, exhibits early Qantas and Waltzing Matilda memorabilia. For those interested, Combo Waterhole, where the swagman took his fatal plunge, is 170 km northwest of Winton, then five km out of Kynuna. **Matilda Expo,** beside the Kynuna Hotel, catalogs the history of the song and Richard Magoffin, the bloke who runs the place, will sing the tune for anyone who so desires; open daily 9 a.m.-4 p.m.

  North Gregory Hotel, 67 Elderslie St. (tel. 076-57-1375), has rooms for $20 s, $40 d, or stay in **Matilda Motel,** 20 Oondooroo St. (tel. 076-57-1433), which has small but comfortable rooms for $42 s, $47 d. Campers should head to **Matilda Country Caravan Park,** on Chirnside St. (tel. 076-57-1607).

Lark Quarry

While Winton and Longreach provide tourists with a glimpse of the past 100 years, a dry rocky area 115 km southwest of Winton provides a look much further back in our history. It's Lark Quarry, site of a dinosaur stampede some 95 million years ago. Today's rocky outcrops and spinifex-studded gullies are much different than they were then, when the landscape was flat and high rainfall ensured that lush vegetation such as ferns and palms thrived. A carnosaur (flesh-eating lizard) walking along a riverbed disrupted a herd of around 200 much smaller animals drinking from a lake and, panic-stricken, they stampeded across an area of thick mud. Paleontologists are able to re-create the events of that day incredibly accurately, right down to the fact that the stampeding dinosaurs were moving at 15-30 kilometers per hour. Three areas have been excavated; the largest is about 20 meters long, and interpretive boards along its length reveal further details. The site is accessible by 2WD, except after rain. **Diamantina Outback Tours** (tel. 076-57-1514) departs Winton daily at 8 a.m. for the quarry, and other natural features en route; $75 per person includes lunch.

Diamantina National Park

The road from Winton out to Lark Quarry continues in a southerly direction for 270 km to Windorah, on the Diamantina Developmental Road. Beyond Lark Quarry 30 km, a rough 4WD track leads west to Diamantina National Park, encompassing 470,000 hectares of Channel Country on either side of the Diamantina River. Except during the Wet, the river is dry, with just billabongs (small pools of water) remaining along its bed. The only vegetation is spinifex and stunted eucalypts. The park has no facilities, and if planning a trip seek advice from the Department of Environment and Heritage in Longreach (tel. 076-58-1761).

McKinlay

Anyone who has seen the movie *Crocodile Dundee* will want to stop at this small town of 20, halfway between Winton and Cloncurry. The small pub here was featured as **Walkabout Creek Hotel** in the movie, and although you're unlikely to see anyone wrestling crocodiles, it's a pleasant place to stop for a beer and meal. The hotel has rooms for $30 s, $46 d, and a few campsites out back (tel. 077-46-8424).

Cloncurry

Large lodes of copper were discovered in the hills around Cloncurry in the 1860s and by WW I the town was Australia's largest copper producer. As the mineral-rich Isa Highlands to the west were developed, interest in Cloncurry waned. Today abandoned mining claims surround this town of 2,500. The town's main claim to fame is as the birthplace of the **Royal Flying Doctor Service.** The service was started by John Flynn (featured on the new twenty-dollar note) in 1927, when aircraft were still a novelty and wireless transmissions through the Outback were unheard of. Qantas built him an aircraft, and a Melbourne businessman helped fund the wireless transmission sets. **John Flynn Place** (tel. 077-42-1251) is a modern complex comprising a museum dedicated to Flynn, an art gallery, and theater; open Mon.-Fri. 7 a.m.-4 p.m., Sat.-Sun. 9 a.m.-3 p.m.

On the east side of town is **Mary Kathleen Memorial Park.** It's home to a couple of civic buildings transported from the uranium-mining town of Mary Kathleen, halfway between Cloncurry and Mt. Isa. The uranium mine was worked 1958-63, when atomic-hungry scientists searched the world for a reliable source of the mineral. After the mine closed, the town stood empty for many years and was then dismantled. The park's museum houses a mineral collection and other historic memorabilia; open Mon.-Fri. 7 a.m.-4 p.m., Sat.-Sun. 9 a.m.-3 p.m. (tel. 077-42-1361).

Cloncurry also holds the record for the highest temperature ever recorded in Australia. In 1889 the thermometer reached 53.1° C (127.8° F).

North from Cloncurry

Cloncurry marks the end of the Landsborough Highway and the beginning of the Burke Developmental Road, linking Cloncurry to the Gulf of Carpentaria (450 km one-way).

Quamby, the first settlement north of Cloncurry, consists of just a hotel, dominated by a large water tank painted as a can of Fosters.

Northwest of Cloncurry is the Selwyn Range, once home to the fierce Kalkadoon tribe, combatants in the bloodiest battle ever fought on Australian soil. During the 1880s, as Europeans settled on traditional hunting grounds, there were many clashes between the two groups. In 1884, a police cavalry charge saw most of the tribe's male population massacred on Battle Mountain. The hotel in Kajabbi (pop. 20), 26 km northwest of the Burke Developmental Rd., is named for the tribe. On Saturday night the publican puts on a barbecue, which is inevitably followed by a sing-along. The hotel also has rooms, or you can camp (tel. 077-42-5979).

From the Kajabbi turnoff, **Burke and Wills Roadhouse** (petrol, food, accommodations) is 136 km farther north and the historic gulf-town of **Normanton** is 331 km. Normanton began as a port for the gold rushes around Croydon in the 1890s. Many grand, old buildings remain from the era. Twice a week Normanton Railway Station comes alive when the Gulflander pulls out for a four-hour excursion to Croydon, passing classic gulf country of river flats, wetlands, and stands of ti trees.

Normanton isn't right on the gulf, but **Karumba,** a further 70 km north, is, right at the mouth of the Norman River. Karumba is a prawn and barramundi fishing port, with a variety of cruises leading through the wetlands to view crocodiles, brolgas, and cranes.

The other gulf community worthy of a detour is **Burketown,** 269 km northeast of the Burke and Wills Roadhouse. In the Wet Burketown can be isolated for weeks, as the surrounding saltpans and savannah grasslands become flooded from inland rainfall. The township has a pub on one side of the road and a few shops on the other.

TOWNSVILLE TO MOUNT ISA

For those wishing to combine the Great Barrier Reef with the Outback, the most direct route west is the **Flinders Highway** beginning in Townsville and ending in Mt. Isa (890 km one-way). The major town along this route is **Charters Towers,** in the Leichardt Range 130 km from the coast.

Porcupine Gorge National Park

The rolling hills around **Hughenden** seem never-ending, and the land is so harsh that graziers are only able to graze one sheep for every three hectares, but 45 km north of the highway is Porcupine Gorge, an oasis of lush vegetation supported by a creek flowing year-round. The gravel access road ends suddenly, right on the rim of the park's main feature, where sheer walls drop vertically 120 meters. Seeing the creek in the Dry, it's hard to comprehend the quantity of water that flows during the Wet and its power to carve the canyon in the soft sandstone. A couple of lookouts are along the gorge rim, but to get into the gorge continue north to **The Pyramid,** an isolated outcrop of rock, and descend into the valley from the parking area. This area is outside the park boundary. Camp here.

MOUNT ISA AND VICINITY

Best known as The Isa, this Outback city of 24,000 is one of the country's great mining towns. Although artesian bore water has allowed many gardens to thrive, the city is basi-

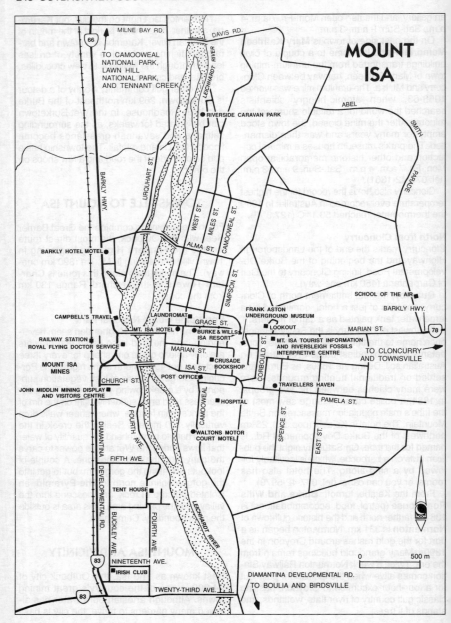

cally unappealing, its skyline dominated by the mine and a 270-meter lead-smelter stack. Mt. Isa does have one claim to fame: it's the world's largest city—in area, that is—with 40,978 square km; it's in the Guinness Book of Records to prove it. The city exists only because of the mine, but also plays a vital role in reducing the isolation of the Outback. It is the world's largest single-mine producer of lead and silver (150,000 tons of lead, 30 tons of silver annually) and the world's largest underground mine. It is also Australia's largest copper producer, yielding 155,000 tons annually. Over 200,000 tons of zinc are also produced here each year.

Mount Isa dates from 1923, when John Campbell Miles, an old-time prospector, found an ore outcrop in an area known as the Isa Highlands, the eastern end of a mineral-rich belt that rises over 400 meters above the surrounding landscape. The area may be desolate and uninviting, but it holds untold wealth. Many millions of years ago, as great forces pushed the land upward, molten intrusions impregnated the sedimentary rock, cooling to form the rich seams of minerals upon which the city grew.

Those who invested in the copper mines around Cloncurry had always banked on a port being established on the Gulf of Carpentaria. But one never eventuated, and by the 1920s, when a rail line was built from Townsville, interest in copper had waned. Up until this time, only small mines were operating farther west. But in 1924 Mount Isa Mines moved into the area, investing enormous sums of money to make mineral extraction viable.

Sights

Mount Isa Mines is across the Leichhardt River from downtown. Touring the mining operation is Mount Isa's main attraction. The three-hour **Underground Mine Tour** requires reservations well in advance. Before heading into the 500 km of tunnels, you are fitted out with hard hat, miner's light, overalls, and boots. These tours depart weekdays 8 a.m and 11:45 a.m.; $20. Book well ahead by calling (077) 44-2104. The two-hour **Surface Tour** departs daily April-Sept.; $12. **Campbell's Travel** (tel. 077-43-2006) takes bookings for this tour.

John Middlin Mining Display and Visitors Centre, on Church St., has an underground mine mock-up, mineral displays, and large pieces of mining equipment. Also displaying mining exhibits is **Frank Aston Underground Museum** on Shackleton Street. As well as mining equipment, there's a replica of a Kilkadoon camp. Open March-Nov. 10 a.m.-3 p.m.; $4 admission.

The **Mt. Isa Tourist Information and Riversleigh Fossils Interpretive Centre,** on Marian St. (tel. 077-44-4255), contains displays from Riversleigh, 300 km north of the city. Riversleigh, where limestone beds contain a variety of skeletons, is one of Australia's most important fossil sites. Open daily 9 a.m-5 p.m. Dating from the 1930s, **Tent House,** on Fourth Ave., is one of the few remaining examples of early mine-company housing; open April-Sept. Mon.-Fri. 9 a.m.-3 p.m. Other sights worth visiting are **School of the Air,** at Kalkadoon High School on Abel Smith Parade (tours schooldays at 10 a.m. and 11 a.m., tel. 077-43-0255) and the **Royal Flying Doctor Service** on the Barkly Hwy. (tel. 077-43-2800); open weekdays 9 a.m.-5 p.m., Sat.-Sun. 10 a.m.-2 p.m.

Accommodations and Food

Barkly Hotel/Motel, 55 Barkly Hwy. (tel. 077-43-2988), has a few air-conditioned rooms for $35 s, $45 d. Also central is **Waltons Motor Court Motel,** 23 Camooweal St. (tel. 077-43-2377), which has a laundry facility and pool; $40 s, $50 d. If you're willing to spend a few extra dollars, stay at **Burke & Wills Isa Resort,** corner Grace and Camooweal Streets (tel. 077-43-8000), a modern, two-story motel with a swimming pool, gym, spa, and restaurant; rooms here are $85 s, $90 d.

Travellers Haven, corner Spence and Pamela Streets (tel. 077-43-0313), has backpacker accommodations with a communal kitchen, pool, and air-conditioning. It's also only 500 meters from town. Dorm beds are $11, singles $22, doubles $26.

Riverside Caravan Park, 195 West St. (tel. 077-43-3904), is the best of four campgrounds in town and has a large pool, kitchen with barbecue and refrigerator, and laundry facilities. Unpowered sites $12, powered sites $16, on-site vans $29.

Many of the hotels and clubs serve excellent no-frills meals. The Barkly Hotel/Motel has counter lunches and dinners for $5-8, while **Mt. Isa Hotel,** 19 Miles St., is open for breakfast. Over 60 nationalities live in the Isa, many with their own-style clubs. The **Irish Club,** Buckley and 19th Streets (tel. 077-43-2577), is one such place, serving buffet lunches and dinners under $12.

Services and Information
The **post office** is on the corner of Isa and Camooweal Streets. **City Laundromat** is at 12 Miles Street. **Mt. Isa Base Hospital** is at 30 Camooweal St. (tel. 077-44-4444).

Crusade Bookshop, 11 Simpson St. (tel. 077-43-3880), has a good selection of Outback literature and a range of topographic maps. **Mt. Isa Tourist Information** is in a large complex on Marian St., between Corbould and Mullan Streets (tel. 077-43-7966). Open Mon.-Fri. 9 a.m.-5 p.m., Sat.-Sun. 10 a.m.-2 p.m.

Transport
Ansett Australia (tel.13-1300 toll-free), **Flight West** (tel. 1800-77-7879), and **Qantas** (tel. 13-1313 toll-free) fly into Mt. Isa from Brisbane, with Ansett Australia continuing to Alice Springs and Flight West to Townsville ($207 one-way) and Normanton ($231 one-way).

Queensland Rail's Inlander operates between Townsville and Mt. Isa, departing twice weekly (Sun. and Wednesday 6 p.m.); one-way, $95 economy, $125 economy sleeper, and $192 first-class sleeper. For bookings call 13-2232 toll-free.

Greyhound Pioneer and **McCafferty's** have a daily coach service between Townsville and Mt. Isa ($81 one-way), continuing to Tennant Creek ($68 one-way). Both companies operate a service from Brisbane via Longreach ($126 one-way), taking 24 hours.

The major car rental companies in town are: **Avis** (tel. 077-43-3733), **Hertz** (tel. 077-43-4142), and **Thrifty** (tel. 077-43-2911).

WEST FROM MOUNT ISA

From Mt. Isa, it's 200 km west to the Queensland/Northern Territory border, then 460 km far-ther to Tennant Creek, on the Stuart Highway. The only town to speak of is **Camooweal,** just east of the border.

Lawn Hill National Park
Aboriginals have been coming to Lawn Hill Gorge for at least 20,000 years, and little has changed in this time. It's a magical place, a lush oasis surrounded for hundreds of kilometers by a dry, harsh landscape. The gorge itself is only a small part of the 262,000-hectare park. Water from artesian springs to the west, on the Barkly Tableland, created the gorge, and tropical vegetation, such as palms, ferns, and figs, thrives. The creek is home to fresh-water crocodiles and turtles, and a variety of small mammals and marsupials come from afar to drink at the creek. The Riversleigh section, straddling the Gregory River in the south of the park and accessible only by 4WD, is the site of important fossil discoveries, some of which are displayed in Mt. Isa.

The park is 400 km from Mt. Isa. To get there, turn off the Barkly Highway 120 km west of Mt. Isa and follow the Burketown Road north for 180 km to **Gregory Downs** (rooms, petrol, food), then cross the Gregory River and head west for 100 km. A primitive camping area has been developed beside Lawn Hill Creek, and **Adel's Grove** (tel. 077-48-5502) at the park entrance, is a campground with hot showers, barbecues and basic supplies. For the park ranger call (077) 48-5572.

Camooweal Caves National Park
This 13,800-hectare park, north of Camooweal, protects sinkholes formed around 500 million years ago. Further water erosion has created an extensive cave system, with several caves over 200 meters long. With a torch and sturdy footwear anyone can explore the system. Aboveground are plains of Mitchell grass interspersed with stands of dry eucalypt extending to the horizon. At a small billabong, which attracts lots of birdlife, is a camping area with toilets. Check road access after rain by calling (077) 43-2055.

THE NORTHERN TERRITORY

INTRODUCTION

Ah, beware Australia's last frontier. Take just one look and it's likely to itch clear through your bones and sting your spirit, and not even those venerable Royal Flying Doctors will be able to cure you. Long after the red dust has settled and you've put Aboriginal myths to rest, your Dreamtime will be influenced forevermore by this superlative land with its big rocks, big crocs, and big thirst.

This barren-but-bewitching region, encompassing 1,346,200 square kilometers, is a veritable dynamo of contrasts—the tropical Top End and the arid Red Centre, sacred grounds and tourist meccas, Stone Age culture and Kmarts—inhabited by fewer than one percent of Australia's population (about 150,000), a quarter of them Aboriginal, and the remainder residing mainly in Darwin or Alice Springs.

Touring
Remote though the Territory is, you'll have no problem getting there on a number of scheduled flights into Darwin (which is closer to Indonesia and the Philippines than it is to Melbourne or Sydney), The Alice (Alice Springs), and yes, even the Rock with its nearby airstrip. The Ghan will rail you from Adelaide to Alice Springs, while coaches, cars, caravans, and trucks can take the straight-as-an-arrow, bitumen Stuart Highway, a.k.a. the Track, all the way to Darwin. From Darwin, it's easy to rent a car or sign up for an organized tour to Top End sites (almost mandatory for Aboriginal lands), and from The Alice you have the option of humping 'round the Red Heart on a friendly camel or riding through the desert on a horse with no name.

Don't come here expecting to find an Aboriginal guru to take you under his wing and impart Stone-Age-old knowledge while you're on holiday. But don't despair. Aboriginal-led tours and "experiences" are available at a variety of sites throughout the Territory.

And you can easily be your own guide—just find your way here, lose yourself immediately, and let your imagination run wild. You may find

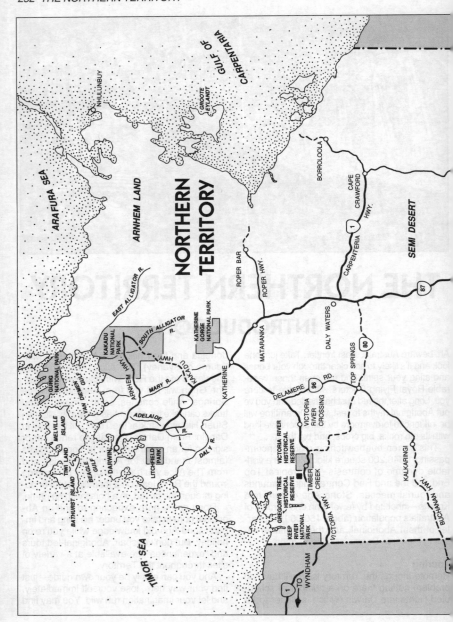

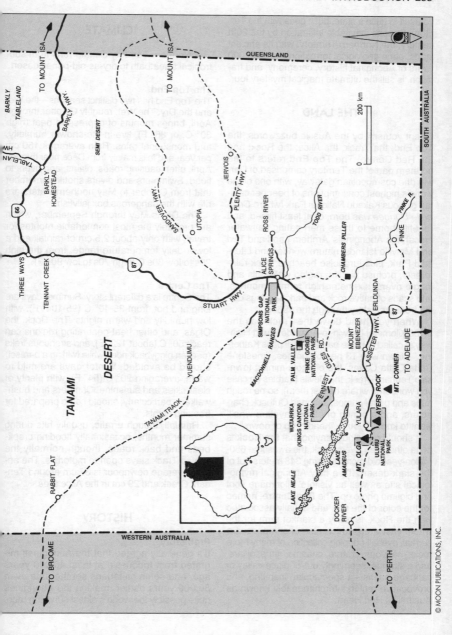

© MOON PUBLICATIONS, INC.

yourself in quite a state, but it goes with the Territory. Despite inevitable infiltration by the 20th century, the Northern Territory, with its ancient lands, eerie geological formations, and 40,000 years of Aboriginal history, ceremony, and tradition, is still the ultimate magical mystery tour.

THE LAND

Orient yourself by the Aussie buzzwords: the Top End; the Track; the Alice; the Rock; and the Red Centre. The **Top End** refers to the northern part of the Territory comprised of Darwin (the cosmopolitan gateway, with one of the world's highest consumptions of beer per capita), glorious Kakadu National Park (where *Crocodile Dundee* was born, or at least filmed, and real-life home to those man-eating saltwater crocs), the Aboriginals' Arnhem Land and Tiwi and Melville Islands, nature wonderland Litchfield Park, plus turquoise beaches, thick rainforests, profuse birdlife, raging waterfalls and jungle rivers, six-meter-high termite mounds, and scads of native rock and bark paintings dating from prehistory through the 1960s.

When you head down the Track—as the 3,188-kilometer Darwin-to-Adelaide Stuart Highway is called in these parts—you'll pass Katherine, a town with 13 nearby gorges, limestone Cutta Cutta Caves, the old gold-mining township Tennant Creek, the Devils Marbles (in case you wondered where he lost them), some rough pubs and petrol pumps, assorted Outback characters, and a bunch of other travelers who'll want to know if you're "headin' up or down."

It should go without saying that **the Rock** is none other than Ayers Rock, the awesome 650-million-year-old monolith rising 348 meters out of the stark desert. It's a holy Aboriginal mythological site as well as visitors' pilgrimage spot and bigtime photo op. The **Red Centre,** named for the color of the soil, and usually associated with the Rock, is really a blanket term for the whole vast area, which also encompasses a surreal, eyeball-popping collection of many more rocks, canyons, craters, chasms, gaps, pillars, and a strange, seemingly out-of-place valley of cabbage palms—a spectacular, inspiring, and provocative region interchangeably known as Australia's Red Heart.

CLIMATE

The Northern Territory climate runs from subtropical sweatbath to dry-as-old-bones desert.

The Top End
The Top End has two distinct seasons—the Wet and the Dry. The Wet, roughly October through April, brings months of oppressive heat (high 30° C, or 86° F), live-in-the-shower humidity, and monsoonal rains. Rain averages 150 cm per year and falls mainly from December through April, often causing roads, plains, and rivers to flood. Swimmers and divers should remember that from October to May northern waters are rife with the dangerous box jellyfish.

The Dry is May through September, which are probably the most comfortable months for travel, with only about 2.5 cm of rainfall and a lower daily temperature range, from the high 20s to low 30s C (high 70s to low 90s F).

The Centre
The Centre is a different story. Summer days are long and hot, from 35-40° C (95-104° F), with low humidity and warm nights. The Rock, the Olgas, and other heat-generating regions can reach 50° C (about 122° F), and strenuous treks (or even piggyback rides while twirling a parasol) should be avoided. Winter days are mild to warm, averaging 20° C (54° F), with plenty of clear skies and sunshine. Campers and bushwalkers, particularly, should come prepared for freezing nights.

Rainfall, though erratic, usually hits during summer months, occasionally flooding creekbeds and back roads, though normally the sealed Track stays open to motorists. The annual average downpour is 37 cm around Tennant Creek and 29 cm in the Alice area.

HISTORY

Prehistory
It's generally agreed that the Aborigines migrated from Indonesia at least 40,000 years ago, and some historians set the date even 80,000 years earlier, making the Aborigines quite possibly the world's oldest surviving race.

Any way you look at it, they've been in Australia a long time, with Arnhem Land in the Territory's northeast corner marking the spot of tropical Australia's first human settlement.

For several centuries the Aborigines enjoyed a sort of love-hate relationship with Macassarese fishermen from Indonesia who visited regularly in search of trepang (sea slugs) until the early 1900s, when the Australian government told them to scoot.

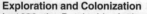

Exploration and Colonization

In 1623, the Dutch ship *Arnhem* became the first recorded European contact, followed by Abel Tasman's exploration of the northern coast in 1644. Aside from naming some of the features, the Dutch didn't seem terribly interested in the region. Additional charting of the coast was undertaken by Matthew Flinders in 1803, and then navigator Phillip King 14 years later.

The British began the old colonial ball rolling when, in 1824, Captain Gordon Bremer—in the name of King George IV—claimed the land as part of New South Wales. After settlement attempts failed at Melville Island, Raffles Bay, and Port Essington (lousy climate, no trade), the northern coast was left alone for about 15 years. In 1863, on the heels of John McDouall Stuart's ground-breaking south-north continental crossing, the Northern Territory became a vested interest of South Australia (called Northern Territory of South Australia). Another settlement was created by the territory's first government resident, Colonel Boyle Finniss, at Escape Cliffs near the Adelaide River mouth. Another failure.

Finally, in 1869, Surveyor-General George Goyder decided to try out Darwin as a prospective site. Bingo! Good choice, especially when shortly thereafter gold was discovered at nearby Pine Creek—bringing with it a railway line, followed by the Overland Telegraph Line and, subsequently, the predictable array of cattle ranchers, Chinese laborers, pastoralists, and signifi-

cant others. Additional mineral finds in the 1880s through the early 1900s cinched the area as "a go." The Track, lifeline between Alice Springs and Darwin, was not constructed until the 1930s and not sealed for about another 20 years.

Recent History

The Australian Commonwealth government took over control of the Territory in 1911, and though the Northern Territory became self-governing in 1978, it still remains economically dependent upon the commonwealth. Agriculture, cattle-raising, mining (gold, bauxite, uranium), and booming tourism are the region's major moneymakers.

The Aborigines

Wondering what happened to the Aborigines? Some tried to resist colonization of their land—in vain. The hunters and food gatherers who'd lived for so long in perfect harmony with the land were, by the early 1900s, herded onto government reserves, introduced to Christian charities, forced into hard labor for low pay, left to rot on the fringes of towns, and given a taste of alcohol. Only those few who lived in the most remote areas were left alone to practice their age-old traditions.

It took some time, but in the 1960s Northern Territory Aborigines began pressing for their rights—with various protests against mining, ranching, and other intrusions on their reserves—culminating with the passage of the 1976 Aboriginal Land (NT) Act, giving them control of their lands (i.e., designated reserves) and returning their sacred sites, including Kakadu and Uluru-Kata Tjuta (Ayers Rock and the Olgas). Currently the Aborigines comprise a majority of the management board of these heavily touristed areas, and word has it that by the year 2000 visitors will be banned from climbing the spiritual sites. Instead, they will just have to walk around them, gazing in wonder. Stay tuned.

The Act also allowed for the appointment of Aboriginal Land Commissioners and the creation of administrative Aboriginal Land Councils. Presently the Aborigines own about one-third of the Territory. Many have returned to their traditional ways and stay on the reserves, out of white reach; others live in squalid conditions around townships, ravaged by the effects of racism and alcohol; still others have turned militant or, worse, have become *capitalists*.

DARWIN

The Northern Territory's capital city was named for Charles Darwin, a shipmate of harbor discoverer John Lort Stokes, and the place has been in a state of evolution ever since.

Australians commonly joke about this Top End tropical city—with its difficult climate, transient population, and fabled thirst. Though true, those elements have also inspired a thriving frontier town, lively cosmopolitan center and, yes, lots of laughs as well as fisticuffs over that amazing intake of beer known worldwide as the Darwin Thirst. (Don't laugh—the Darwin stubby contains two liters of beer instead of the normal 375 milliliters; the average per person intake is 230 liters per year, and that's a *low* estimate.)

People don't stick around here long, that's a fact. The weather and the isolation take their toll. Heck, not even the city stays put! During WW II, more than 60 bomb attacks by the Japanese pretty much turned Darwin into a pile of rubble. Then, in 1974, Cyclone Tracy paid a surprise Christmas Day visit, leveling practically the entire city. With indomitable Territorian pull-together spirit (and no doubt *many* thirst-quenchers under their tool belts), Darwin was rebuilt into a durable, modern center, punctuated here and there by the few surviving historical structures, accented by flowering bougainvillea, frangipani blossoms, and swaying palms.

Today's Darwin, with a population of 68,000, is a conglomeration of 50 or so ethnic groups, including descendants of the Chinese miners, Japanese pearlers, Europeans who sought escape from postwar oppression, a relatively new onslaught of refugees from Southeast Asia, barramundi fishers, and a steady stream of travelers and backpackers headed to or from Asia, Top End attractions, or the rest of Australia. Most of the people who "do time" here work within some element of this Territorial administrative center's government, mining, or tourism sectors.

The city center, compactly situated on a peninsula looking toward Darwin Harbour, is easily explored on foot. The Stuart Highway becomes Daly Street as it enters the city, bisecting Smith Street. Head one km toward the harbor to Smith Street Mall, the main shopping district and location of the Darwin Regional Tourism Association Information Centre. The majority of central Darwin sites and services—including Darwin Transit Centre, the general post office, and the Automobile Association of the Northern Territory—fall within a few blocks' radius of the mall. Noteworthy suburban attractions are mostly located at Larrakeyah, Palmerston, Fannie Bay, and East Point, all within 10 kilometers to the north and east of city center. Head back away from the harbor and take a right turn off Smith St. onto Gilruth Ave. (which becomes East Point Rd.) to access most of these areas.

And, though you won't find the flair and sophistication of a highfalutin metropolis like Melbourne or Sydney, easygoing and eclectic Darwin can hold its own. And it can *certainly* hold its beer.

THE HISTORICAL TOUR

Yes, acts of war and God aside, a few dear structures—or pieces thereof—still stand. *A Walk Through Historical Darwin*, a booklet published by the National Trust, is a good source of information. This particular stroll may move your spirit as well as your feet. It starts off at the Tree of Knowledge, on the east side of downtown, continues in a loop around the Esplanade, heads down Smith Street Mall, and winds up at the Chinese Temple.

Tree of Knowledge
The ancient banyan behind the Civic Centre on Harry Chan Ave. is a longtime city landmark. Heralded as the Tree of Knowledge by Bud-

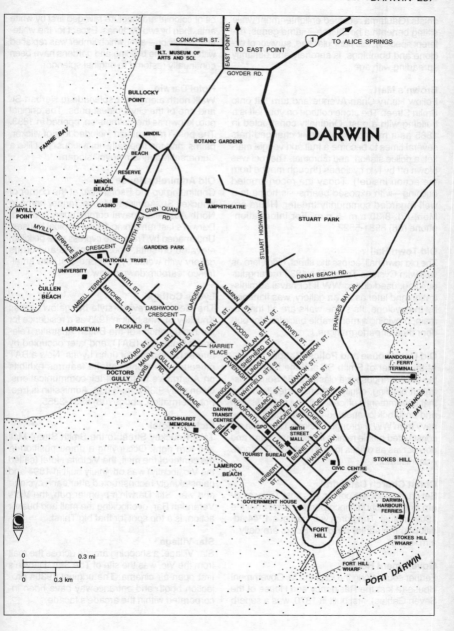

CONACHER ST.

TO EAST POINT

EAST POINT RD.

GOYDER RD.

TO ALICE SPRINGS

N.T. MUSEUM OF ARTS AND SCI.

BULLOCKY POINT

DARWIN

FANNIE BAY

MINDIL BEACH

RESERVE

BOTANIC GARDENS

MINDIL BEACH

CASINO

CHIN QUAN RD.

AMPHITHEATRE

MYILLY POINT

MYILLY TERRACE

GILRUTH AVE.

GARDENS PARK

STUART PARK

STUART HIGHWAY

TEMIRA CRESCENT

CRESCENT

NATIONAL TRUST

SMITH ST.

GARDENS RD.

DINAH BEACH RD.

FRANCES BAY DR.

UNIVERSITY

CULLEN BEACH

LAMBELL TERRACE

MITCHELL ST.

DASHWOOD CRESCENT

McMINN ST.

DALY ST.

WOODS ST.

DAY ST.

HARVEY ST.

BARNESON ST.

MANDORAH FERRY TERMINAL

LARRAKEYAH

PACKARD PL.

PACKARD ST.

MAUNA LOA ST.

GULLY

PEARY ST.

HARRIET PLACE

McLACHLAN ST.

SHEPHERD ST.

LINDSAY ST.

MANTON ST.

GARDINER ST.

FOELSCHE ST.

CAREY ST.

FRANCES BAY

DOCTORS GULLY

DOCTORS GULLY RD.

ESPLANADE

CAVENAGH ST.

WHITFIELD ST.

SEARCY ST.

EDMUNDS ST.

KNUCKEY ST.

LITCHFIELD ST.

LEICHHARDT MEMORIAL

BRIGGS ST.

SHADFORTH

DARWIN TRANSIT CENTRE

PEEL ST.

GPO

SMITH STREET MALL

STOKES HILL

LAMEROO BEACH

TOURIST BUREAU

LANE

BENNETT ST.

HARRY CHAN AVE.

HERBERT ST.

CIVIC CENTRE

DARWIN HARBOUR FERRIES

GOVERNMENT HOUSE

KITCHENER DR.

DARWIN HARBOUR FERRIES

FORT HILL

STOKES HILL WHARF

FORT HILL WHARF

PORT DARWIN

0   0.3 mi
0   0.3 km

dhists (Gautama received enlightenment while sitting beneath a bodhi tree—same genus, different species), this particular tree, survivor of cyclone and bombings, is serenely and defiantly spreading with age.

Brown's Mart
Follow Henry Chan Avenue and turn left onto Smith Street. The stone cottage on your left is a building with a past. Originally constructed in 1885 as a mining exchange, it changed hats several times to become a fruit and veggie market, a police station, and a brothel. The roof was blown off by two cyclones (though maybe from the action inside!). Today the reconstructed building—with exposed beams—is home to a well-regarded community theater. Hours are Mon.-Fri. 8:30 a.m.-5 p.m. For information, phone (08) 8981-5522.

Old Town Hall
The old town hall, across the street, didn't fare as well with Cyclone Tracy. The 1883 rectangular building, used during WW II for naval administration and later as an art gallery, was flattened by the cyclone. Its stone walls are all that remain, providing a memorable backdrop for outdoor theater performances.

Old Courthouse and Police Station
At the corner of Smith St. and the Esplanade, the old courthouse is a classic 1884 South Australian building, originally constructed to house that government's offices, with the police station and cellblock connected behind. Used by the navy from WW II through Cyclone Tracy, the reconstructed rubble retains its external charm and now serves as offices for the Northern Territory's Administrator.

Christ Church Cathedral
Set on the opposite corner, this post-Tracy modern Anglican church incorporates ruins from the 1902 original. The porch was part of a 1944 addition to the earlier building. Hours are daily 7 a.m.-6 p.m.

Government House
Farther south along the Esplanade, Government House (a.k.a. the Residency and House of the Seven Gables), first built in 1870, was a superb bit of colonial architecture ravaged first by white ants, then by two cyclones. Except for the white-ant demolition—after which timber was replaced with stone—the building and gardens have been continually restored to original splendor.

Hotel Darwin
Walk north along the Esplanade to Herbert St. and one of the city's oldest pubs. The original pub, known as the Palmerston, opened in 1883. The post-Tracy rebuild included lots of wicker, palms, and the tropically ubiquitious "just like a Somerset Maugham novel" slogan.

Old Admiralty House
Continuing up the Esplanade, at the corner of Knuckey St., Admiralty House, former home to North Australia's naval commander, is one of Darwin's last remaining 1920s tropical houses. Undamaged by Tracy, the cypress pine building, elevated on stilts, houses an arts-and-crafts gallery with works by Top End-ers, with an alfresco tearoom down below.

Lyons Cottage
The Georgian-revival-style bungalow across Knuckey St. was built in 1925 as a residence for the head honcho of the British Australia Telegraph Company (BAT), and later occupied by former Darwin mayor John Lyons. Now a BAT museum, the stone cottage features exhibits on Australia's history of telecommunications. Open daily 9:30 a.m.-3 p.m. Admission is free. For information, phone (08) 8981-3355.

Victoria Hotel
Take Knuckey Street to the Smith Street Mall and turn right. Occupying a prime position in the center of the mall, the Victoria Hotel (called the Vic, locally) was originally built in 1894 and painstakingly reconstructed after each cyclone and war. Still Darwin's premier pub, the Vic's Verandah Bar, overlooking the mall and busker action, is a top spot for that big Thirst.

Star Village
Star Village, a shopping arcade across the mall from the Vic, was the site of The Star, Darwin's first open-air cinema. The original 1930s projection booth and entranceway have been incorporated within the arcade's facade.

Commercial Bank
At the mall's Bennett St. corner, only the 1884 stone colonnade was saved and restored when the bank's 1981 counterpart was built.

Chinese Temple
Continue along Bennett St. to Woods St., site of the post-Tracy temple that serves Darwin's large Chinese community. The original 1887 structure couldn't weather the storm, and only the floor, altar masonry blocks, and stone lions were spared. The current temple, built in 1978, has taken care to blend the old ruins within its steel and concrete replacement. Open Mon.-Fri. 8 a.m.-4 p.m., Sat.-Sun. 8 a.m.-3 p.m. Admission is free. **Note:** Please do not take photos while people are praying. (Did I even have to tell you that?) For information, phone (08) 8981-3440.

OTHER CITY SIGHTS

Aquascene
Located on the Esplanade, at Doctors Gully, this is one of Darwin's best attractions. Almost every day at high tide, throngs of catfish, mullet, bream, milkfish, and others come along to nibble bread from the hands of knee-deep, wading tourists. This bizarre ritual began about 20 years ago when a local denizen tossed some scraps to passing mullet (who told their friends, who told *their* friends, who . . .). Anyway, talk about *wonder bread!* Open daily at high tide. Phone (08) 8981-7837 for each day's feeding time. Admission is $3.50.

Indo-Pacific Marine
This small aquarium, near the roundabout at Smith St. West and Gilruth Ave., is one of the few such facilities in the world with displays of isolated coral reef ecosystems. Other features include informative talks, a gift shop, and a small garden cafe. Open daily 10 a.m.-5 p.m. Admission is $10. For information, phone (08) 8981-1294.

National Trust
Consisting of four pre-WW II houses in the Myilly Point Heritage Precinct, just outside downtown, the National Trust buildings feature side-hung windows, louvres, feathered eaves, and other trappings of tropical architecture. Pick up booklets, brochures, good tips, and souvenirs at

the information center and gift shop within. Open Mon.-Fri. 8:30 a.m.-4:30 p.m. Admission is free. For information, phone (08) 8981-2848.

Botanic Gardens
Just outside the city center on Gardens Rd. (off Gilruth Ave.), Darwin's botanic gardens, wiped out by three cyclones and a fire since their creation in 1879, have returned to glory with collections of figs, palms (nearly 400 species), and other tropical flora. New additions include a rainforest and wetlands area, plus a greenhouse with ferns and orchids. The restored cottage of Dr. Maurice Holtze, the gardens' founder, houses a restaurant, and occasional live concerts are performed at the amphitheatre. Open daily 8 a.m.-sunset. Admission is free.

Aviation Museum
View more war paraphernalia such as wreckage of the Japanese Zero (first enemy aircraft ever shot down over Australia), a Boeing B-52 bomber (a loan from the U.S. Air Force), Mirage and Sabre jets, and a host of other aviation memorabilia. The museum is on Gardens Hill Crescent, Stuart Park (back near the botanic gardens). Open Mon.-Fri. 10 a.m.-2 p.m., Sat.-Sun. 10 a.m.-5 p.m. Admission is $4. For information, phone (08) 8981-7617.

Northern Territory Museum Of Arts and Sciences
The Territory's major museum, on Conacher St., Fannie Bay, features exceptional Aboriginal, Southeast Asian, and Oceanian galleries with arts and crafts, maps, photos, and artifacts (including a pearling lugger and Vietnamese refugee boat out front on the lawn). As a research and scientific institution responsible for cataloging plant and animal species, the museum also houses a comprehensive natural sciences section. One big attraction is Sweetheart, the five-meter, 780-kilogram saltwater crocodile that had terrorized trolling fishermen until its capture in the late 1970s.

The art gallery features works by important Australian artists such as Russell Drysdale, Sir Sidney Nolan, and Donald Friend, as well as touring exhibitions. The museum bookshop has a good selection of local lore as well as gift items. The Cornucopia Museum Café, set in tropical gardens, looking out at the Timor Sea, is a great spot for sunset-watching, contemporary cuisine, and good wines.

Open Mon.-Fri. 9 a.m.-5 p.m., Sat.-Sun. 10 a.m.-6 p.m. Closed Good Friday and Christmas Day. Admission is free. For information, phone (08) 8982-4211.

Fannie Bay Gaol

Farther along East Point Rd., Darwin's main prison from 1883 to 1979 is now a museum where visitors can reminisce about life in the cells and view the gallows where the last hanging took place in 1952. Comprehensive exhibitions devoted to Cyclone Tracy's devastation include newspaper clippings and videotaped news footage from that time. Open daily 10 a.m.-5 p.m. Admission is free. For information, phone (08) 8999-8211.

East Point

The north shore of Fannie Bay affords dramatic harbor, city, and sunset views. This peninsular reserve, with good bushwalking and cycling trails, is a popular spot at sunrise or twilight when wallabies frolic in the nearby field.

Check out heavy artillery, small arms, and other military memorabilia and relics of WW II at the **Royal Australian Military Museum,** a former coastal defense complex adjacent to the reserve. Open daily 9:30 a.m.-5 p.m., closed Christmas Day and Good Friday. Admission is $4. For information, phone (08) 8981-9702.

Wharf Precinct

Stokes Hill Wharf, transformed first by war, then by tourism, offers historic walking paths, a war-era tunnel and lookout, and tourist creations such as cheap restaurants, trendy bars, live entertainment, and sports, which include bungy jumping and parasailing.

BEACHES

Watch your tootsies October to May when it's the deadly box jellyfish season! Though you'll be tempted by Darwin's sparkling beaches (and the ever-present humidity)—*don't chance it.* Nightcliff Beach, off Casuarina Dr. in north Darwin, has a protective stinger net.

Nude bathing is allowed on a strip of beach at **Casuarina Coastal Reserve,** a 1,180-hectare area that also contains rainforests and WW II gun emplacements.

The first Sunday in May is the official opening of Darwin's beaches, and **Mindil Beach,** on Fannie Bay, is the place to be. Celebrations include rock bands, dancers, acrobats, foodstalls, fashion shows, and sandcastle-building contests. Mindil and nearby **Vesvey's** beaches stay crowded until the stingers return.

ACCOMMODATIONS

This gateway city with a frontier heart has accommodations to suit just about any lifestyle or pocketbook. The central city and surrounding suburbs feature a good selection of hostels, hotels, motels, and holiday flats, while most of the campgrounds and caravan parks are situated on the outskirts of town. If you're seeking a roommate, check out the downtown cafes or around the mall, where you're bound to meet other travelers.

Getting a room is usually not a problem, but advance bookings are a good idea if you plan to arrive during the more crowded Dry season and at festival times. Rates during the Wet are usually cheaper or at least up for bargaining. The Northern Territory levies a 2.5% Tourism Marketing Duty on all accommodations, with the exception of caravan and campsites (on-site vans and cabins are taxed). Revenues are supposedly used to promote tourism to the Territory.

City and Suburbs

Inexpensive (under $35): Darwin Transit Centre, 69 Mitchell St., inside the coach transit center (tel. 08-8981-9733), is one of the best deals in town. It's not gorgeous but it's certainly convenient—the bus is practically at your bedside. This former workers' residence has been revived with refurbished rooms, cooking facilities, a pool, sauna, gym, laundry, and game room. Bathroom facilities are shared. Nearby **Larrakeyah Lodge,** 50 Mitchell St. (tel. 08-8981-2933), is a long-established place with air-conditioned rooms, shared facilities, a pool, laundry room, and coffee shop.

Park Lodge, 42 Coronation Dr., Stuart Park, two km north of city center (tel. 08-8981-5692), is a friendly 20-room guesthouse with four shared bathrooms, communal kitchen, dining room, TV room, laundry, pool, and spa.

Moderate ($35-70): Coolibah Resort, 91 Aralia St., Nightcliff, about 12 km from city center (tel. 08-8985-4166), is in the moderate price range but has a cheap, air-condtioned, six-bed bunkroom with communal facilities and kitchen. **Air Raid City Lodge** (comforting name, eh?), 35 Cavenagh St., close to the GPO (tel. 08-8981-9214), has plain but clean rooms, private facilities, air conditioning, TVs, communal kitchen, and laundry room.

Hotel Darwin, 10 Herbert St. (tel. 08-8981-9211), near the post office, is the city's former grande dame. The colonial building is somewhat worn but still has some charm, as well as the requisite wicker and cane decor. Facilities include TVs, phones, pool, restaurant, pub, and laundry. **Asti Motel,** 7 Packard Pl. (tel. 08-8981-8200), with restaurant, pool, and spa, is large and comfortable.

Ponciana Inn, on the corner of Mitchell and McLachlan in the center of town (tel. 08-8981-8111), is a four-story motel with a pool. **Paravista,** 5 MacKillop St., Parap (tel. 08-8981-9200), near Fannie Bay attractions, also has a pool and barbecue area. Small and cozy **Palms Motel,** 100 McMinn St. (tel. 08-8981-4188), is about one km north of the post office.

Expensive ($70 and Way Up): All of Darwin's top-notch hotels provide the usual luxury range of restaurants, bars, recreational facilities, and business services. **The Beaufort,** the Esplanade (tel. 08-8982-9911), has colorful desert architecture. The **All Seasons Atrium,** Peel St. and the Esplanade (tel. 08-8941-0755), features—natch—a beautiful seven-story, glass-roofed atrium. **Diamond Beach Hotel Casino,** Gilruth Ave., Mindil Beach (tel. 08-8946-2666), features interesting geometric shapes, beachfront accommodations and an action-packed casino. The newer **Melia Darwin,** 32 Mitchell St. (tel. 08-8982-0000), the city's highest rise, is near the business district.

Hostels

Darwin's hostels are perfect places to meet travelers from everywhere and pick up tips—and maybe a companion. Dorm beds average $10 per night.

Darwin's **YHA Hostel** (tel. 08-8981-3995), next to the transit center on Mitchell St., features 182 beds in 90 rooms, shared bathroom and kitchen facilities, pool, courtyard, and friendly atmosphere. The convenient on-site travel office offers discounted tour and bus tickets. Make sure you have your YHA membership card in hand.

Fawlty Towers, 88 Mitchell St. (tel. 08-8981-5385), down the street from the YHA, is smallish, with air-conditioned dorm rooms, two communal kitchens, pool, barbecue, TV, video, and a helpful staff. Popular **Frogshollow Lodge,** 27 Lindsay St. (tel. 08-8941-2600), is largish, with spa and continental breakfast included.

The popular **YWCA,** 119 Mitchell St. (tel. 08-8981-8644), accepts both women and men at its 42-room facility with clean rooms, communal bathrooms and kitchens, and TV lounges. Dorm beds and single or double rooms are available. Other hostels that draw crowds are **Elke's Inner City Backpackers,** 112 Mitchell St. (tel. 08-8981-8399), and **Ivan's Backpackers Hostel,** 97 Mitchell St. (tel. 08-8981-5385).

The **CWA Hostel** (Country Women's Association), 3 Packard Pl. (tel. 08-8941-1536), offers two four-bed rooms for both men and women and four two-bed rooms for women only. Facilities include a communal kitchen, TV lounge, and large garden area.

Camping

Unfortunately all of Darwin's campsites are about 10-15 km outside the city. The following parks allow tents as well as caravans: **The Overlander Caravan Park,** McMillans Rd., Berrimah, 13 km east (tel. 08-8984-3025); **The Palms Caravan Park,** Stuart Hwy., Berrimah, 17 km east (tel. 08-8932-2891); **Shady Glen Caravan Park,** Stuart Hwy. and Farrell Crescent, Winnellie, 10 km east (tel. 08-8984-3330).

For additional camping opportunities in the Howard Springs area, 26 km from the city, see "Vicinity of Darwin" under "The Top End," below.

Camping gear can be rented from U-Rent, 50 Mitchell St. (tel. 08-8941-1280).

FOOD

What's your favorite nosh—buffalo, crocodile, camel, or kangaroo? You'll find such territorial specialties listed alongside fish 'n' chips in some restaurants. Tasty barramundi, fresh from local waters, is plentiful also. And, as might be expected in this multinational city, ethnic foods are widely offered, with Asian cuisine ranking supreme. Supermarkets, small groceries, and takeaways are easy to spot throughout city and suburbs, and the Smith Street Mall area is full of coffee shops and lunch counters. Darwin's best dining value—and the most fun—is at the Asian-style markets held several times weekly.

Inexpensive

Head to Smith Street Mall, though keep in mind that most of the coffee shops shut down when the shops do, meaning 5 p.m. on weekdays (except for Thursday), Saturday afternoon, and Sunday. **Central City Café** is a popular breakfast and gathering spot. **Cosmopolitan Café,** in Anthony Plaza, serves up good breakfasts and lunches. Next door, the **French Bakehouse** is open daily for coffee and light meals. The historic **Victoria Hotel,** opposite Anthony Plaza, features a relatively cheap lunchtime carvery upstairs, and good-value counter meals downstairs.

Toward the Knuckey St. end of the mall, **Darwin Plaza** houses a glut of Lebanese, Thai, Chinese, and health food counters. The **Taco House,** within that same plaza, is where you can sample croc, buffalo, and 'roo burgers, along with tacos, of course (watch that filling!). The **Sate House,** in Victoria Arcade, across from Anthony Plaza, has cheap Indonesian dishes.

Confetti's, 85 Mitchell St., is open late and serves homemade ice cream, cappuccino, pancakes, and a variety of smoothies, sundaes, and snacks. Open daily 11 a.m.-late. **The Pancake Palace,** Cavenagh St., is also open late every day to please pancake-heads.

The Barra Bar, 15 Knuckey St., is a good, cheap, fish 'n' chippery. **Fisherman's Eatery,** on Fisherman's Wharf, specializes in takeaway barramundi 'n' chips, and you'll find many other inexpensive choices in the Wharf Precinct.

Hana Sushi Bar, 31 Knuckey St., will feed you traditional Japanese tidbits.

Moderate

Jade Gardens, on the mall, serves Chinese banquets and business lunches. Open Mon.-Fri. lunch, daily dinner. **Rendezvous Café,** on Smith Street Mall, offers hot and spicy Malaysian meals. Open Mon.-Sat. lunch, daily dinner. The **Maharajah,** 37 Knuckey St., features an exten-

sive menu and excellent curries. Open Mon.-Sat. for lunch and dinner.

Lindsay Street Café, 2 Lindsay St., serves contemporary cuisine either inside its historical building or outside in the lush tropical gardens. Open Tues.-Fri. lunch, Tues.-Sat. dinner, and Sunday brunch.

Satisfy your pasta urge at **Guiseppe's,** Cavenagh St., with both regional and traditional Italian specialties. Open Mon.-Fri. lunch, Mon.-Sat. dinner. **Roma Bar Café,** 30 Cavenagh St., is a local favorite with an eclectic crowd, superb focaccias, pastas, and coffees. Open daily for breakfast and lunch. **Kafe Neon,** in the Wharf Precinct, is a casual eatery with superb Greek salads. Open daily for lunch and dinner.

Expensive

Christo's on the Wharf, in the Wharf Precinct (tel. 08-8981-8658), has fabulous seafood (try the garlic prawns) and is a splendid place to view the sunset. Open Tues-Fri. lunch, Tues.-Sun. dinner. **Hanuman Thai Restaurant,** 28 Mitchell St. (tel. 08-8941-3500), only opened in 1992 but has already been declared one of the country's finest dining establishments. Heavenly prepared Thai and Nonya delicacies are placed before you with grace and style. Open Mon.-Fri. lunch, nightly dinner.

Siggi's, at the Beaufort Hotel (tel. 08-8999-1179), is the city's classical-French star. Intimate settings and a changing menu keep the fat wallets coming back for more, more, and still *beaucoup plus.* Open Tues.-Sat. for dinner.

Markets

Darwin's thriving, colorful markets can be categorized equally under Food, Shopping, and Entertainment listings.

The foodaholics come early to set up folding tables and chairs beachside, watch the sunset, socialize, then tease their tastebuds at the **Mindil Beach Market.** Foodstalls serve up Thai, Indian, Malaysian, Chinese, Indonesian, South American, and other ethnic cuisine, as well as cakes, breads, fruits, and veggies at very reasonable prices. The market is held Thursday 6-10 p.m. during the Dry.

Other sniff-and-gobble markets are: **The Big Flea Market,** Darwin's oldest, held Sunday 8 a.m.-2 p.m. at Rapid Creek Shopping Centre;

The Parap Market, held Saturday 8 a.m.-2 p.m. at Parap; and **Palmerston Markets,** held Friday 5:30-9:30 p.m. at Frances Mall, Palmerston. Except for Mindil Beach, the markets are open year-round.

ENTERTAINMENT AND EVENTS

Don't expect big city culture, but there is a range of theaters, cinemas, pubs, clubs, and the casino for amusement. On the other hand, special events in this isolated region can be a whole lot of fun. The *Northern Territory News* provides listings of all the current doings. Again, if you're looking for companionship for a night on the town, scout around the Smith Street Mall, surrounding coffee shops, or the hostels. This is an easy town to meet people in.

Cinemas
You can catch the usual commercial showings (several months or so old) at **Cinema Darwin,** on Mitchell Street. **Darwin Film Society** (tel. 08-8981-2215) often hosts artier movies at the Museum Theatrette, Conacher St., Bullocky Point (tel. 08-8982-4211). Inquire at the tourist information center about **Deck Chair Cinema,** an open-air cinema with artsy films, which are sometimes upstaged by a showy night sky.

Pubs and Clubs
The oldies are goodies. The **Vic,** on the mall, features live bands in the upstairs veranda bar, Wed.-Saturday. The **Darwin Hotel,** on Mitchell St., hosts live bands on Friday night, piano in the lounge Wed.-Sat., and a poolside jazz barbecue on Sunday. On Sunday afternoons and Fri.-Sat. nights you can alternate between indoor and outdoor bands at the **Beachfront Hotel,** Rapid Creek. Or get down and grungy at the infamous **Nightcliff Hotel,** corner of Bagot and Trower, about 10 km north of the city center. Depending on which night you visit, entertainment consists of live bands, wrestling females covered in a variety of cooking sauces, very thirsty men, and wild women. The Nightcliff is what's referred to as a Darwin "experience."

Favorite discos, most open nightly, are: upmarket **Circles,** at the Beaufort Hotel; **Dix,** 21 Cavenagh St. in the Hot Gossip Complex; and **Beachcombers,** corner Daly and Mitchell Streets. Trendies should check out the array of nightclubs, piano lounges, and discos in the chichi hotels. Neat, casual dress is required.

Expect to pay a cover charge of about $5-7 in the pubs (when bands are on), $8-10 in the discos, and $12 or more at the five-star spots.

For those of you in the "Blowin' in the Wind" mood, the **Top End Folk Club** holds sessions at the East Point Gun Turret on the second Sunday of each month, from 8 p.m. Visitors and musicians are encouraged to join in the hoot. Admission is $6. For information, phone (08) 8988-1301 or 8941-1699.

The Casino
Depending on your inclination, wardrobe, luck, and budget (or *non*-budget), the **Diamond Beach Hotel Casino** might be the only entertainment you need. All the games are represented, including the Aussie "Two-up." The 350-seat Cabaret Room hosts a variety of theatrical entertainment, along with bar service and elaborate buffets; a coffee shop is open round-the-clock. During the Dry, the casino puts on a Sunday afternoon poolside barbecue with live jazz.

Dress regulations are strict: neat, clean, tidy clothing at all times; no shorts, thongs, running shoes, or denim wear of any kind (not even your best hole-in-the-knee Levi's); and, it should go without saying—keep your shirt on your back, even if you lose it in the casino.

Diamond Beach is on Gilruth Ave., Mindil Beach. Casino hours are daily noon-4 a.m. For information, phone (08) 8946-2666.

Corroborees
You're in your own Dreamtime if you're waiting for an invite to an authentic Aboriginal corroboree. These sacred spiritual ceremonies are off-limits to the general public. You *will* be able to join tours that feature a kind of pseudo event, with traditional dancing, singing, and didgeridoo-ing.

Theater, Dance, and Concerts
The **Darwin Performing Arts Centre,** 93 Mitchell St., next to the Beaufort Hotel (tel. 08-8981-1222), regularly stages theater, musical, and dance per-

BOB RACE

The old Brown's Mart mining exchange now houses a community theater.

formances. The playhouse (capacity 1,070) also houses a rehearsal room, exhibition gallery, and dance studio. Phone the center, or check the daily newspaper. The center can also provide details of upcoming events at the botanic gardens outdoor amphitheater.

Events

This isolated laid-back city takes every opportunity to come together for just about any occasion. **The Northern Territory Barra Classic,** a premier "tag-and-release" tournament held by the Darwin Game Fishing Club, is held about the first of May. The **Mindil Beach Carnival** in May (see "Beaches" above) celebrates the departure of the box jellyfish and the opening of the beaches. More than a decade old, the **Bougainvillea Festival** is held for 18 days in late May or early June, the flower's peak blossoming time. Numerous festivities include a Mardi Gras, grand parade, concerts, photography contest, art exhibitions, music and film festivals, a food and wine fair, picnics, ethnic events, and daily doings on the mall. A weekend Festival Fringe Club produces alternative music, dance, theater, and literature events.

Darwin's famous **Beer Can Regatta** tailgates the Bougainvillea Festival in early June, and is certainly an event to inspire the Darwin Thirst. Empty beer cans are used to construct rafts and boats, which then "race" in the local sea. Using full cans of beer to build the craft is strictly *verboten!*

Other big-turnout annual events—all falling in August—are the barefoot **Mud Crab Tying Competition,** the **Darwin Cup** horse racing meet, and the internationally known **Darwin Rodeo.**

The **Marratjila Festival** is a nine-day celebration of Aboriginal heritage that draws participants from both tribal communities and urban areas to join in dance and theater performances, contemporary and traditional music, and arts and crafts exhibitions.

SPORTS AND RECREATION

You'll find a wide range of sports and recreation opportunities in the city and suburbs, but bear the heat and humidity in mind if you're not fit or not used to the climate. Joggers and cyclists will find plenty of good, scenic tracks. Best bets are the waterfront area that follows the Esplanade, and the shoreline reserve from Fannie Bay to East Point.

Water sports and fishing are favorites here, but heed those box jellyfish and crocodile warnings! For information on any Darwin sport, phone the **Sports Hotline** (tel. 08-8981-4300).

Scuba Diving

Divers can explore the litter of WW II wrecks, as well as the large coral reef off Darwin's shores. Good dive shops are **Fannie Bay Dive Centre,** 2 Fannie Bay Pl. (tel. 08-8981-3049), and **Sand Pebbles Dive Shop,** De Latour St., Coconut Grove (tel. 08-8985-1906).

Fishing

Top End waters are jumping with sport fish, particularly Australia's famous **barramundi.** The best time to score a catch is from Easter through May. The prime spots near Darwin are around the harbor arms, Leader's Creek, Bynoes Harbour, and in the creeks and estuaries of Shoal Bay. Other common species are queenfish, Spanish mackerel, longtail tuna, giant trevally, threadfin salmon, and barracuda. **Mud crabbing** in the estuaries is another favorite local activity.

For information on **licenses, regulations,** and **fishing tours,** contact the Department of Primary Industry and Fisheries, Bennett St. (tel. 08-8999-4821). For **tidal charts,** contact the Port Authority, Henry Chan Ave. (tel. 08-8981-6701).

Swimming Pools

Practically every hostel, motel, and hotel has its own pool. In addition, you'll find public pools

DANGER !
BOX JELLYFISH CAN BE DEADLY

OCT. to MAY
DO NOT SWIM
JUNE to SEPT.
TAKE CARE SWIMMING

FIRST AID:
Resuscitation + Vinegar
(poured on affected area)
+Transport to Hospital = LIFE

NT DEPARTMENT OF HEALTH
AND COMMUNITY SERVICES

at Darwin, Casuarina, Nightcliff, and Winnellie. One of the better locations is on Ross Smith Ave., Fannie Bay (tel. 08-8981-2662).

Sporting Facilities
Tennis: Four courts are available for public use at the **Darwin Tennis Centre,** Gilruth Ave., The Gardens (tel. 08-89 85-2844). Courts are also available outside the casino, near Mindil Beach. For information, phone (08) 8981-2181.

Golf: Darwin Golf Club, Links Rd., Marrara (tel. 08-8927-1015), has the only 18-hole course in town. Nine-hole courses are available at **Gardens Park Golf Links,** opposite the casino (tel. 08-8981-6365), and at **Palmerston Golf Club,** Dwyer Crescent, Palmerston (tel. 08-8932-1324). Equipment can be rented on-site.

For information on other sporting facilities, phone the Sports Hotline, above.

Other Sports
Sailboards are available for rent in front of the Diamond Beach Hotel Casino at Mindil Beach. For **sailboat** hire, contact the Darwin Sailing Club (tel. 08-8981-1700). For information about weekend **hiking** expeditions, contact Darwin Bushwalking Club (tel. 08-8985-1484). **Darwin Gym,** 78 the Esplanade (tel. 08-8941-0020), features workout and fitness equipment.

The most prominent spectator sport in Darwin is **horse racing,** with greyhounds placing, and an occasional touch football game making quite a show.

SHOPPING

Darwin's major shopping areas are **Smith Street Mall, Darwin Plaza, The Galleria,** and **Casuarina Shopping Square,** in the northern sub-

urbs. Just about any creature comfort or service can be purchased at any of these places (and Casuarina has a Kmart, too). City shopping hours are Mon.-Fri. 9:30 a.m.-5:30 p.m., Saturday 8:30 a.m.-1 p.m., late-night trading Thursday until 9 p.m. Casuarina shopping hours are daily 9 a.m.-5:30 p.m., late-night trading Thursday and Friday until 9 p.m.

Markets
Darwin's markets have a lot more than just food-stalls. You can pick up crafts, books, plants, dolls, knicknacks, Indian and Balinese clothing, and other goodies (see "Markets" in the "Food" section above).

Crafts
Aboriginal art collectors will find a large variety of arts and crafts in Darwin. **Framed: the Darwin Gallery,** 55 Stuart Hwy., is the place to pick up fine Top End and central Australian bark paintings, sand paintings, weavings, didgeridoos, baskets, and hand-blown glass. Open Mon.-Sat. 8:30 a.m.-5:30 p.m., Sunday 11 a.m.-5 p.m. The **Raintree Gallery,** 29 Knuckey St., sells similar wares, specializing in items made by the Tiwi people from Bathurst and Melville Islands.

Purchase T-shirts printed with Aboriginal designs, as well as Tiwi printed fabrics, at **Riji Dij-Australian and Original,** 11 Knuckey Street.

Weavers Workshop, Parap Place, Parap, sells locally made handknits, pottery, natural soaps, and toiletries. **Shades of Ochre** (in the Old Admiralty House), 70 the Esplanade, displays and sells fine local arts and crafts.

Darwin Shipstores, Frances Bay Dr., sells flags from all over the world, including the Boxing Kangaroo and Northern Territory state flags.

Other Shops
Photo Supplies: You'll find camera houses at just about every turn in this photo-op territory. **Camera World,** in Darwin Plaza, Smith Street Mall, offers fast passport service, a good range of photo supplies, and one-hour film processing. **Palm Photographics Drive-in Transit Shop,** on Mitchell St., right next to the Transit Centre, provides film processing and sales daily 8:30 a.m.-10 p.m.

New Age: Center yourself at **Inner Dreams Book and Gift Shop,** Parap Shopping Village, with quartz crystals, incense, flower essences, oils, books, tapes, and videos.

Gear: Everything you need for going bush is stocked at the **Northern Territory General Store,** 42 Cavenagh St. (tel. 08-8981-8242). Inventory includes tents, boots, maps, compasses, knives, tarps, sleeping bags, mosquito nets, etc.

Surf Wear: Purchase top Australian brands at **Fannie Bay Beach Bums,** 2/5 Fannie Bay Pl., Fannie Bay. Open daily 10 a.m.-6 p.m.

Book Exchange: Nearly 20,000 books are stocked at **J.R. Book Exchange,** in Central Arcade, Smith St. Mall. You can also pick up good used clothing at this shop.

SERVICES

Branches of national and territorial banks are located on and around the Smith Street Mall. Many have suburban offices and automatic teller machines. Banking hours are Mon.-Thurs. 9:30 a.m.-4 p.m., Friday until 5 p.m. Be sure to take your passport or other identification.

Darwin's glossy newer **general post office,** 48 Cavenagh St., has instigated computerized postal services, including self-selection service, electronic counters, and digital readouts. Postal officers stand by to assist with any problems. Operating hours are Mon.-Fri. 8:30 a.m.-5 p.m.

For visa and work permit inquiries, call on the **Department of Immigration,** 40 Cavenagh St. (tel. 08-8946-3100).

Casual labor opportunities fluctuate. Check with the hostels or other travelers for up-to-date info.

INFORMATION

The **Darwin Regional Tourism Association Information Centre,** 33 Smith Street Mall (tel. 08-8981-4300), will quite likely be your one-stop shop for any information about the Territory. The bureau also provides free maps, informative booklets, and arranges accommodations, car rentals, and a variety of tours to fit all budgets. Hours are Mon.-Fri. 8 a.m.-6 p.m., Saturday 9 a.m.-2 p.m., Sunday 10 a.m.-5 p.m. In addition, there's a visitor office at Darwin's airport.

The **Australian Nature Conservation Agency,** Smith St., between Lindsay and Whitefield (tel. 08-8981-5299), provides information about the Territory's parks, regulations, and required permits. Alternately, the **Conservation Commission of the Northern Territory** (tel. 08-89-99-5511) is out in suburban Palmerston, about 20 km from the city center.

The **Disabled Persons Bureau,** Shop 7, Group floor, Casuarina Plaza, Casuarina (tel. 08-8922-7213), offers an information and referral service for disabled visitors.

Darwin Gay and Lesbian Society (tel. 08-8981-6812) offers info on social activities, counseling and health facilities, and other pertinent topics.

Maps, up-to-date road information, and camping and accommodation guides can be obtained from the **Automobile Association of the Northern Territory,** 79-81 Smith St. (tel. 08-8981-3837). The NTAA has reciprocal arrangements with both Australian and overseas automobile associations. Bring your membership card for free and discounted services.

Emergencies: Dial 000, or contact the **police** (tel. 08-8927-8888) or **ambulance** (tel. 08-8927-9000). **Royal Darwin Hospital,** Rocklands Dr., Casuarina (tel. 08-8920-7211), has a 24-hour accident and emergency center. **Central Darwin Dental Surgery,** 59 Smith St., CML Bldg. (tel. 08-8941-1899 or 8941-1717), also handles dental emergencies. For **Travel and Immunization Services,** phone 08-8981-7197.

More Information

The **State Reference Library of the Northern Territory,** 25 Cavenagh St. (tel. 08-8999-7177), has shelves full of books, photos, and other documents relating to the Territory. Interstate and international newspapers are available for browsing. Open Mon.-Sat. 10 a.m.-6 p.m. (come for free lunchtime entertainment Feb. to Nov.). The **city library** is in Paspalis Centrepoint arcade on Smith St. Mall.

Bookworld, 30 Smith St. Mall, is a good bookshop with regional literature, contemporary fiction, and an ample selection of everything else.

Darwin's local daily newspaper is the *Northern Territory News.*

TRANSPORT

Getting There by Air

Airlines serving Darwin from North America are **Qantas** (tel. 13-1313 toll-free), with a change of plane in Cairns, and **Garuda Indonesia** (tel. 08-8981-6149), with a change of plane in Bali. Other international carriers are **Merpati**, from Indonesia, and **Singapore, Qantas,** and **Royal Brunei** from Asia.

From other Australian states, Darwin is easily reached on **Ansett,** Shop 14, Smith St. Mall (tel. 08-8980-3333, or 13-1300 toll-free), and **Qantas,** 16 Bennett St. (tel. 08-8982-3333, or 13-1313 toll-free).

All international and domestic flights arrive and depart from **Darwin Airport,** just eight km north of the city center. Services include rental car desks, money exchange, and a visitor center. **Darwin Airport Bus Service** (tel. 08-8941-1656) will shuttle you to or from the city for $6. Taxis are ready and waiting; fare to the city is about $12.

Getting There by Bus

Greyhound Pioneer Australia (tel. 13-2030 toll-free) offers the most frequent service to Darwin from Australia's capital cities and Outback communities. The **three routes into the city** are: up the Track from Alice Springs, with stops at Tennant Creek and Katherine; the Barkly Highway from Townsville, Queensland, via Mt. Isa, joining the Track at Three Ways; the Victoria Highway from Western Australia through Broome, Derby, and Kununurra. One or more of the coach companies make daily runs along all routes. On Queensland routes it's sometimes necessary to change coaches at Tennant Creek or Three Ways.

McCafferty's Coaches (tel. 08-8941-0911) provides service along and from the east coast, and closes a Townsville/Darwin/Alice Springs/Adelaide loop.

Fares vary little among the coach lines and they all offer stopovers and money-saving passes (some need to be purchased outside the country).

All intercity coaches arrive and depart at **Darwin Transit Centre,** 69 Mitchell Street.

Getting There by Car

See the "By Bus" section above for routes into the city. The main highways are sealed with asphalt and have roadhouse facilities. But remember—it's a long way to the Territory Tipperary: 350 km from Katherine, 978 km from Tennant Creek, 1,482 km from Alice Springs, 3,215 km from Adelaide, 2,489 km from Townsville, and 4,430 km from Perth. Don't venture off the main roads without a good 4WD vehicle, emergency supplies, and a phone call to the nearest police facility.

Getting Around by Air

Due to airline deregulation, flying within the country has become much more affordable. Check with both the YHA and the visitor center, as well as with **Ansett** and **Qantas**—both airlines are booking agents for the small commuter carriers, which seem to change with the seasons.

Getting Around by Bus

Darwin Bus Service operates weekdays and Saturday morning, entering the city along Mitchell St. and departing by way of Cavenagh Street. Routes no. 4 (to Fannie Bay, Nightcliff, Rapid Creek, and Casuarina) and no. 6 (to Fannie Bay, Parap, and Stuart Park) will take you to most of Darwin's attractions and other points of interest. Fares, based on zones, range from 70 cents to $2. The city terminal is on Harry Chan Ave., near Cavenagh Street. For information, phone (08) 8999-7513.

Getting Around by Car

Taxis are available at the airport, or phone **Darwin Radio Taxis** (tel. 08-8981-8777).

Major **car rental** firms such as **Budget, Hertz,** and **Thrifty** have airport and city locations. Better deals might be had at **Territory-Rent-a-Car** (tel. 08-8981-8400), **Rent a Rocket** (tel. 08-8981-6977), or **Rent a Dent** (tel. 08-8981-1411). Rates start at about $35 per day with 150 free km—20 cents to 30 cents per km after that. Rates are higher if you take the car more than about 70 km outside Darwin—which is probably just about everywhere you want to go. Be sure to inquire about weekend specials or extended-rental deals. Check with **Territory Rent-A-Car** for 4WDs (starting at $75 per day, plus kilometer charges).

Getting Around by Bicycle

Check first with the backpackers hostels—either they'll have cheap deals or, if you're a guest, they might lend you one for free. Otherwise, try **U-Rent,** 50 Mitchell St. (tel. 08-8941-1280), or **Darwin Bike Rentals,** 57 Mitchell St. (tel. 08-89 41-0070). Rates are about $8 per half-day, $12 per 24 hours.

Getting Around by Boat

Take a ride across the harbor to Mandorah on **Darwin Harbour Ferries.** Service operates Mon.-Fri. year-round, from Stokes Hill Wharf. Fare is $18 roundtrip, and the journey takes 30-40 minutes each way. Two-hour sunset and harbor cruises are also available. For information and schedules, phone (08) 8978-5094.

Tours

The organized tour offerings in and around Darwin are numerous—Litchfield Park, Kakadu Park, Cobourg Peninsula, Arnhem Land, Bathurst and Melville Islands, crocodile farms, and other destinations and activities can be explored by plane, boat, jeep, chopper, canoe, or foot, for one day or longer. The visitor center has reams of info describing tours and operators, including prices and departure days. The **YHA** travel office also makes recommendations and bookings. Some tours operate infrequently, or not at all, during the Wet.

Also see the chart "Aboriginal Tours" in the On the Road chapter.

Getting Away

Due to its close proximity, Darwin is a popular gateway to Indonesia. **Garuda Indonesia** flies twice weekly between Darwin, Denpasar, and Jakarta (about $600 roundtrip to one or the other city). Garuda's city ticket office is at 9 Cavenagh St. (tel. 08-8981-6149).

Merpati, Indonesia's domestic carrier, flies twice weekly between Darwin and Denpasar and once a week between Darwin and Kupang, in Timor, with onward flights to many other Indonesian cities. Tickets can be purchased from the Indonesian government travel agency, **Natrabu,** 16 Westlane Arcade, beneath the Victoria Hotel on Smith St. Mall (tel. 08-8981-3694). Sample fares are $240 one-way from Darwin, with stops in Kupang, Maumere, Ruteng, Labuhanbajo, Bima, and Ampenan; $200 one-way from Darwin to Kupang, a bargain for island-hoppers headed toward Bali. Scour the newspaper listings and check with travel agents about the many APEX and excursion fares and package deals available to Indonesia.

Also check out special deals with **Singapore Airlines,** 48 Smith Street Mall (tel. 08-8941-1799).

Unless you're in the big bucks, cruises are not a practical option.

Hitching

It's not so easy (and it's illegal, remember?). Track traffic is sparse outside cities and towns. Many hitchhikers report long waits at Three Ways, junction of the Track and the road to Mt. Isa.

THE TOP END

Keep your hat on and knock your socks off. Ever since ad-rep Paul Hogan was reincarnated as Crocodile Dundee, the Northern Territory's tip-top has become one of Australia's most popular tourist destinations. Most of the moviedom believers head straight for Kakadu National Park and its realer-than-film-reel glories, with the spillover forging onward, upward, and backward to Arnhem Land, the Cobourg Peninsula, Litchfield Park, and Bathurst and Melville Islands. Most of these spots can be visited on day-trips from Darwin, but at some you'll no doubt want to stay longer. Make the most of your visit to this ancient and extraordinary region—there will be no sequel.

VICINITY OF DARWIN

Mandorah

Situated 10 km across the harbor from Darwin, this small resort on the northeast tip of Cox Peninsula is noted for its sandy beaches, superior fishing, and the tourist-oriented Aboriginal corroborees performed by the local Kenbi community and hosted by Mandorah Inn (tel. 08-8978-5044). Otherwise, hop on a Darwin Harbour ferry for an easy day-trip from the city. If you're driving up the Cox Peninsula road, you'll encounter magnetic anthills on the way into town. (By the way, they're called "magnetic" because they point north.)

Howard Springs

This nature park, 27 km southeast of Darwin along the Stuart Hwy., features a refreshing spring-fed pool set amid lush rainforest and is often crowded with city escapers. Additional features include a fish-viewing area, short bushwalking tracks, birds and wildlife, a kiosk, and barbecue facilities. The facilities are open daily 7 a.m.-5 p.m. For information, phone (08) 8983-1001.

Campsites are available at **Coolalinga Caravan Park,** Stuart Hwy. (tel. 08-8983-1026), and **Howard Springs Caravan Park,** 290 Whitewood Rd. (tel. 08-8983-1169). **Nook Van-**

O-Tel, Morgan Rd. (tel. 08-8983-1048), has campsites and on-site vans.

Darwin Crocodile Farm

I hate to tell you—many of the thousands of saltwater and freshwater crocs you see here are annually killed. But don't despair! You'll soon be able to admire them on someone's designer feet, slung over a fashion-setting arm, or inside tomorrow's burger. Come at feeding time when these beasts display their feelings about the future! Located 40 km from Darwin, on the Stuart Hwy., the farm is open daily 9 a.m.-5 p.m., with tours at 11 a.m. and 2 p.m. Feeding time is daily at 2 p.m., with an extra on Sunday at 11 a.m. For information, phone (08) 8988-1450.

Berry Springs

Two top attractions make this spot worth the 56-km journey (take the turnoff from Stuart Hwy.). **Berry Springs Nature Park** offers spring-fed, croc-free swimming sites with fewer people than Howard Springs, plus rainforest, picnic areas, and barbecue facilities. The springs are open daily 8 a.m.-7 p.m. year-round, except after extremely heavy rains. For information, phone (08) 8988-6030.

Territory Wildlife Park, next door, is a 400-hectare open-range sanctuary housing kangaroos, wallabies, water buffalo, dingoes, and other Northern Territory species, as well as a 20-meter-high walk-through aviary, an aquarium, natural lagoon with waterbirds and a viewing blind, and a nocturnal house. A motor train transports visitors along a four-km link road. Open daily 8:30 a.m.-6 p.m. (no admittance after 4 p.m.), except Christmas Day and Good Friday. Admission is $10. For information, phone (08) 8988-6000.

Litchfield Park

Long overshadowed by Kakadu, this becoming-more-and-more-developed 65,700-hectare reserve, just a two-hour drive from Darwin, is now basking in the tourist limelight.

Dominated by the vast sandstone Tabletop Range and escarpment, some of the notable

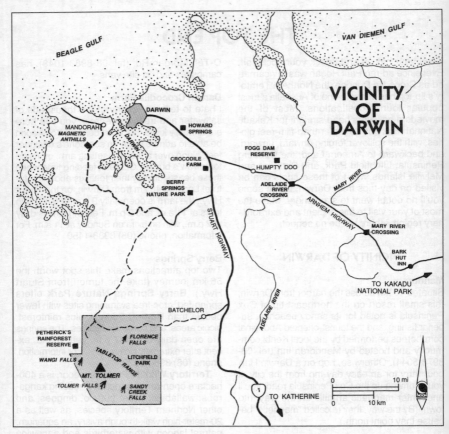

features of this awesome area region include four major waterfalls cascading over the plateau (each with its own swimming pools and rainforest), creeks, caves, abundant flora, birds, and other wildlife, gigantic magnetic termite mounds, and numerous excellent bushwalking trails.

The **Lost City,** about six km east of Tolmer Falls, is a mysterious area of gigantic sandstone outcrops that resemble buildings, pillars, and humans. Adding to the mystique is the fact that no Aboriginal settlement has been traced here. The "city" is accessible by foot or 4WD.

Swimming is safe in the falls area of the park (i.e., no crocs), but saltwater crocs *do* inhabit

Surprise Falls and the Finniss and Reynolds Rivers, so watch your tail there. **Camping** is permitted at Florence Falls, Buley Rockhole, and Tjaynera Falls; bush campsites are available at Walker and Bamboo Creeks.

Privately owned **Petherick's Rainforest Reserve,** 10 km north of Wangi, features thick monsoon rainforest, waterfalls, rock pools, and wildlife. A series of marked walking trails includes a special botanist trail where trees are identified. Entrance and camping fees total $5 per person. **The Drover's Rest,** just before Petherick's, offers a similar deal plus 15-minute helicopter rides ($55).

To reach Litchfield Park, take either the Cox Peninsula/Wangi Road (beyond Berry Springs) or the Stuart Hwy. to Batchelor and into the park. It's possible to make somewhat of a loop, entering at the northern boundary (which has a ranger station), continuing about 18 km to Wangi Falls, 10 km to Tolmer Falls, 20 km to Florence Falls on the eastern edge, and out through Batchelor to the Track. Conventional vehicles should have no problem on the ring road, but a 4WD is necessary for access to other areas.

For information, phone the **Conservation Commission** (tel. 08-8999-5511).

A plethora of tours operate out of Darwin to Litchfield Park.

BATHURST AND MELVILLE ISLANDS

These two flat islands (pop. 2,500), about 80 km north of Darwin and divided by narrow Apsley Strait, comprise an area of 8,000 square km. As with much of the Top End, the seasons produce dramatic changes in this region. In the Dry, grass withers, turns to straw, and burns; the Wet brings monsoon rains and lush greenery.

History

Strange as it seems, these islands and their Tiwi owners not only had little contact with Europeans but, until the late 1800s, had limited dealings with mainland Aborigines. The British attempted to establish their first settlement on Melville Island in 1824, but disease, isolation, and the animosity of the Tiwis sent the new residents quickly packing. Other visits were made by Macassarese fishermen, possibly the Portuguese, and a Japanese pilot who crashed onto Melville during WW II. Nguiu, a Catholic mission begun in 1911 in Bathurst's southeast, is the main settlement, followed by Milikapiti and Pularumpi, both on Melville.

Crafts

Tiwi culture is particularly rich and relatively unscathed. Locally produced arts and crafts include unique carved totems and burial poles, screen printing, bark painting, pottery, and interesting ethnic clothing.

Tours

Permits are not given to independent tourists, so the only way to visit these islands is through an all-inclusive organized tour that will fly you over from Darwin. Other than watching the Tiwis create their art (with, of course, an opportunity to make purchases), many tours allow visitors to experience traditional Aboriginal living, including the preparation and ingestion of typical bush tucker (*not* for the dietarily squeamish). A swim and lunch stop at **Turacumbie Falls** is another recreational feature.

Tiwi Tours (tel. 08-8981-5144), the largest local operator, has a wide range of half- or full-day "Tiwi experience" excursions, costing $175-240; two- to three-day tours, $450-600, include accommodations at **Putjamirra Safari Camp** on the northwest tip of Melville Island, where guests are given the opportunity to really share in the Aboriginal lifestyle. **Australian Kakadu Tours** (tel. 08-8981-5144) offers two-, three-, and five-day Putjamirra stays, costing $550-1100.

It's best to bring necessities with you from Darwin. Stores stocking incidentals are located at Nguiu and at Barra Lodge at Port Hurd. Except for the bar at Barra Lodge, no alcohol is permitted on the islands.

ALONG ARNHEM HIGHWAY

The Arnhem Highway joins the Stuart Highway 34 km southeast of Darwin, traveling 217 km to Jabiru in the heart of Kakadu National Park. City buses go out as far as Humpty Doo, but you'll have to rely on the Kakadu-bound coaches or a car for other sites.

Humpty Doo

You can't miss this little service town (pop. 3,000) 10 km into this stretch—a massive replica of a croc decked out with red bulb-eyes and boxing gloves signals your arrival.

Turn west four km to **Graeme Gows Reptile World,** where you can see one of Australia's largest collections of snakes and lizards. Of special interest are Goddess Marael and Psycho, two of the world's deadliest snakes, and *Crocodile Dundee* python-stars Hoges and Strop. Informative talks are given each day.

Open daily 9 a.m.-5 p.m. Admission is $5. For information, phone (08) 8988-1661.

Stop in at **Humpty Doo Hotel,** home of the annual Darwin Stubby Drinking Competition (31 July). Any time of year this pub is full of local color, serves counter meals, has an occasional live band, and is adorned with Territorial memorabilia.

Fogg Dam

Once an experimental rice farm, this 1,569-hectare conservation reserve, 11 km east of Humpty Doo, is an important refuge for waterbirds such as magpie geese, herons, ducks, egrets, brolgas, and rainbow pitta. Other wildlife includes jabirus, wallabies, frilled-neck lizards, file snakes, and pythons. Dawn and dusk during the Dry are the best viewing times. Camping is not allowed.

Adelaide River Crossing

Another eight km along the Arnhem Highway, the *Adelaide River Queen* (tel. 08-8988-8144) departs from the western bank for 90-minute upstream cruises to view crocs (who leap for morsels being dangled from poles), buffalo, pigs, and birds. The two-story vessel has an air-conditioned lower deck and snack bar. Cruises operate Tues.-Sun. Feb.-Oct., less frequently Nov.-January. Cost is $45 from Darwin, $20 at the jetty. Two-hour excursions are conducted by **Frontier Jumping Crocodile Cruises** (tel. 08-8941-0744). Cost is $50 from Darwin, $25 at the jetty.

Leaning Tree Lagoon

Off the highway, some 13 km from the river crossing, Leaning Tree Lagoon Nature Park (101 hectares) is another waterbird refuge during the Dry. The locals come here to picnic, canoe, and camp (no facilities).

Mary River Crossing

Continue another 25 km to this 2,590-hectare reserve, shelter to barramundi, saltwater crocs, waterbirds during the Dry, and wallabies who peek from the granite outcrops. Boating, fishing, and camping are permitted.

Bark Hut Inn

Built in the 1970s, this favorite roadside pub (two km beyond Mary River Crossing) is the replica of a 1918 Annaburroo Station homestead and is decorated with all the Territorial trappings. An on-site wildlife enclosure houses dingoes, donkeys, kangaroos, wallabies, emus, buffalo, and pigs. Accommodations are in the moderate range, but campsites are also available. For information, phone (08) 8976-0185.

The **YHA Annaburroo Lodge and Backpackers Hostel,** off the Arnhem Hwy., lies in the wetlands on Annaburroo Billabong. Tours are available to Kakadu and Mary River, as are bushwalks to Aboriginal sites and wildlife areas. With prior arrangment, Greyhound Pioneer will drop you off at the hostel. For information, phone (08) 8978-8971, or inquire at the Darwin YHA hostel.

KAKADU NATIONAL PARK

Hallelujah—you've arrived at one of Australia's most majestic, mystical natural wonderlands, a tropical wilderness encompassing 1,307,300 hectares and six major topographical regions stretching some 100 km to the western border of Aboriginal-controlled Arnhem Land. Listed as a World Heritage site for its important wetlands and cultural significance, Kakadu's spectacles include a fortress-like sandstone escarpment, thick-as-thieves woodlands and forests, magnificent rock formations, lowland savannah, wide floodplains, amazing birds and wildlife, gorges, waterfalls, caves, lagoons, mangrove-covered tidal flats, plentiful fish, flowers, and crocs, and an exquisite collection of Aboriginal rock art—some dating back 30,000 years or more.

It is recommended that, if possible, visitors experience the park during both the Wet and Dry seasons as features undergo drastic metamorphoses. During the oppressively humid Wet, rain falls in thunderous sheets over the weathered Arnhem Land escarpment, causing floodplains to swell, landscapes to green, posies to blossom, birds to breed, fish to jump, and all the beasties of the jungle to send out invites to fertility rites. In the height of the Dry, however, the searing sun cracks the earth, plants wither away, the fish die off, the abundant birds fight over the last bit of feed. (Secret: Shaded gorges and billabongs off the main roads are still green and filled with wildlife.)

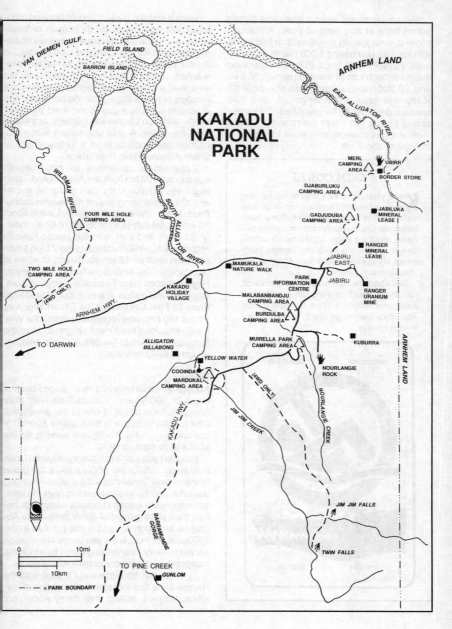

Nature lovers will have a hard time getting bored here at any time of year. Kakadu is home to a staggering variety of flora and fauna, with species numbering 1,000 plants, 50 mammals, 75 reptiles, 25 frogs, 275 birds (check out the massive flocks of magpie geese), 55 fish, and 10,000 insects (bring lots of repellent). Many are rare or endangered, and new species continue to be identified. One interesting fish is the silver barramundi, which makes a sex change from male to female at the age of about six.

CROCODILES

Know your crocs and take those warning signs seriously! There are two kinds: saltwater ("salties") and freshwater. The smaller freshwater croc is usually harmless unless provoked, while the larger saltie poses a definite danger. Worse, the saltie also inhabits freshwater! My opinion—don't trust either of 'em. They're smart and *fast.*

Aside from the obvious swimming hazards, you should avoid cleaning fish, leaving food waste, and hanging out near the water's edge. Also, crocs seem to get upset around dogs and teasing boaters.

Wanna-be croc hunters should have no problem spotting some of the thousands of freshwater and saltwater dinosaur cousins inhabiting the park. It's the saltwater croc ("saltie," in Aussie parlance) that's the big threat. **Be forewarned:** Salties do not live only in saltwater but wherever they damn well please, and they are masters of camouflage. Also, do not ignore any crocodile-warning signs (don't steal them, either!), and don't leave food scraps anywhere near the water. A safe way to see these prehistoric descendants is on a Yellow Water or South Alligator River boat cruise.

Approximate distances to and through Kakadu are 120 km from the Arnhem and Stuart Highways junction to the park entrance, another 100 km east along sealed roadway to Jabiru. From Jabiru: The Ranger Uranium Mine is about 10 km southeast; Ubirr is 38 km north on mostly dirt road; and turn onto the sealed Kakadu Highway just west of Jabiru, going 21 km south and then another 12 km southeast, to arrive in Nourlangie. The sealed portion of the Kakadu Highway ends near Mardukal camping area, Cooinda, and Yellow Water; it's unsealed from there to Pine Creek and the Stuart Highway (about 160 km), and impassable during the Wet. It's 20 km along the Kakadu Highway from the Nourlangie turnoff to the Jim Jim Falls detour—60 km of 4WD-only track.

History

Aboriginal settlement has been traced back at least 25,000 years. "Kakadu" derived from "Gagadju," the name of one of the area's first tribes; today the park is back under Aboriginal control, with many Aborigines serving on the staff and as park rangers.

Wouldn't you just know that the Kakadu lands hold about 10% of the whole world's top-grade uranium ore? Three major mine sites—Ranger, Jabiluka, and Koongarra—sitting near the eastern edge, were leased to outside companies before the establishment of either the park or Aboriginal land rights. Land rights granted in the 1970s did not include the yea or nay of mining on sacred territory, only leasing terms by which the independent mining companies would abide.

In 1978, the Aborigines cut a deal with the Ranger Mine that included a nice chunk of royalties. So nice, in fact, that many Aboriginal owners of Jabiluka and Koongarra now feel that a little uranium mining might well be worth the enormous royalties. Currently, only the Ranger Mine is in full swing, but future operations may still be in the offing.

A vast area of Kakadu, in what is known as "stage three," has been set aside as a protected conservation zone, with the exception of mineral rights—for now, that is. If no mining company comes forth with an acceptable plan in due course, then stage three will continue life as a national park. Naturally, environmentalists are extremely concerned over the destructive forces of the Ranger, as well as any additional pollution and defilement of the land and heritage sites. Who'll win? Protesting conservationists, powerful mining interests, kissy-assed politicians, sell-out Aborigines, or the almighty dollar? Care to lay odds?

Rock Art
The park's natural environment is of profound spiritual significance to Aborigines—just read the paintings on the walls. More than 5,000 archaeological sites within Kakadu's confines provide a rock-art record of Aboriginal culture and mythology, as well as a picture of changing environmental and historical conditions, spanning a period from 20,000 years ago up until the 1960s. Aborigines used their art forms and natural canvases to convey messages and myths, to link past centuries with the present day. And though you'll happen upon tours, pamphlets, and explanations galore, don't be surprised or disappointed if you feel like you're still missing something—many works communicate only to the Aboriginal heart.

Distinctive styles that evolved with the ages include hand and object imprints (the oldest), naturalistic outline drawings of stick-figure-like hunters and extinct animals (such as the Tasmanian tiger), dynamic "in motion"-type drawings with naked women and mythological beings, strange yam-shaped figures, and "X-ray" images showing skeletal structures and internal organs of mostly barramundi and crocs (the most recent at 1,000-9,000 years old).

More elaborate "X-ray" studies, produced within the last 1,000 years, convey the Aboriginal contact with Macassarese fishermen and European "discoverers." Yellow, red, and white powdered minerals, blended with water, are the predominant colors in all the works. Other artifacts include little odds and ends like 20,000-year-old edge-ground stone axes.

Though contemporary Aboriginal artists have pretty much abandoned rocks as a medium, opting to work on sand or bark commercial creations, the ancient sites are revered and carefully guarded. Visitors are allowed at three major locations: both Nangoloar and Anbangbang galleries at Nourlangie, and Ubirr. A number of sacred sites are kept private and off-limits to the public. Visitors are asked to stay on marked paths, follow signs, and to refrain from touching or interfering with any site.

Kakadu Holiday Village
Set amid rainforest and bushland, this tourist complex features inexpensive and moderately priced motel accommodations, shady campsites, dining facilities, rainforest walking tracks, tennis courts and swimming pool (for paying guests only), souvenir shops, and petrol stations. For information and booking, phone (08) 8979-0166.

South Alligator River cruises depart daily from the nearby crossing. Popular two-hour tours depart daily during the Dry. Cost is $25. For information and bookings, phone (08) 8941-0800.

Jabiru
Jabiru (pop. 1,300) was established in 1982 to provide housing and services for the miners working at nearby Ranger. With the onslaught of tourism, however, the township now offers visitor facilities as well, including shops, a lake with sandy beach, picnic areas, golf, tennis, and car-rental agencies.

One-hour tours of the **Ranger Uranium Mine** depart three times daily from the Jabiru East Airport, six km east. Cost is $10. For schedules and bookings, phone Kakadu Air at (08) 8979-2411.

Jabiru is also the location of **Gagudju Crocodile Hotel Kakadu,** Flinders St. (tel. 08-8979-2800). This is the crocodile-shaped *expensive* hotel where guests enter through the "jaws" then pay through the nose to sleep and eat inside the belly and brains. The croc "head" houses shops, restaurants, and bars. It's definitely worth a look just for the reptilian kitsch angle.

Kakadu Frontier Lodge and Caravan Park (tel. 08-8979-2422) offers camping.

For emergencies, contact: **police** (tel. 08-8979-2122) or **medical aid** (tel. 08-8979-2018 or 08-8979-2102).

Ubirr

Also known as Obiri Rock, this major rock-art site is home of some of the country's most important works, which are contained within six different sheltered areas. A one-km path leads visitors to all of the sites, but most impressive is the main gallery with its exquisitely preserved "X-ray" paintings that depict jungle and sea wildlife, as well as several haughty white boys in a 15-meter frieze. Another path leads to the top of the rock and magnificent views of Kakadu and Arnhem Land (some *Crocodile Dundee* scenes were shot up there).

Facilities include picnic grounds and a park headquarters with interpretive display and informative brochures. Park rangers lead guided tours during the Dry. Near Ubirr sit a border store and 20-bed **Hostel Kakadu,** closed during the Wet. Beds are $12, and on Thursday evenings park rangers host a slide show. For information and opening dates, phone (08) 8979-2333. Keep in mind that the gravel road to Ubirr is impassable for conventional vehicles—and often 4WDs—during the Wet.

Nourlangie Rock

The other major art site, reached via a short jog off the Kakadu Highway, is open year-round. The Aborigines call this rock Burrung-gui, and the surrounding area Nawulandja, both of which somehow were bastardized into Nourlangie.

Rising from the Arnhem Land escarpment, this massive weathered sandstone, sheer-cliffed outcrop features several formidable areas: **Anbangbang,** an Aboriginal shelter for at least 20,000 years, where mythological figures such as Namarrgon, "Lightning Man," are friezed in time; **Anbangbang Gallery,** behind the shelter, with works created by Najombolmi (a.k.a. Barramundi Charlie) as recently as the 1960s; and **Nangaloar Gallery,** reached by a three- to four-km walk, with styles including "X-ray" paintings, hand stencils, and stick figures with subjects ranging from mythical beings and fish to European ships.

On the way back to the highway, a turnoff to the left leads a short walk's way to **Nawulandja lookout,** where park rangers will guide you to the only known blue paintings.

Facilities include interpretive displays, guided walks, and a picnic area.

Jim Jim Falls

You'll take a 4WD-only road, then walk one kilometer across boulders to reach these dramatic falls, which plunge 200 meters over the Arnhem Land escarpment, thundering during the Wet and, in comparison, trickling during the Dry.

Visitors trek here for the majestic scenery, deep-plunge pool, freshwater crocs, sandy beach with shallow swimming area, breathtaking bushwalks, and good camping.

Twin Falls

It's not quite so easy to reach Twin Falls, 10 km south of Jim Jim Falls, where access is gained by fording Jim Jim Creek. Take your choice of two double-dare routes: make a few short swims and rock climbs up the gorge and hope you don't run into any freshwater crocs (no one said they were *safe,* just *safer*); or scramble, climb, and walk your way across Jim Jim Creek. On arrival you'll be rewarded by the glorious vision of the crystal falls (yes, two of them), lush ferns and greenery, and a sandy palm-lined beach.

Yellow Water

No worries—despite its name, this billabong derives its color from an algae that, when concentrated, produces a distinctive yellow tinge. These wetlands are a sanctuary for a large number and variety of waterbirds (whistling ducks, jabiru, egrets, pelicans, magpie geese, spoonbills, etc.), as well as crocs, and boat trips on the mangrove-lined billabong are one of the park's highlights.

Access to Yellow Water is through Cooinda, about four km off the Kakadu Hwy., 48 km from its junction with the Arnhem Highway. Accommodations at Cooinda are either at the expensive **Gagudju Lodge Cooinda** (tel. 08-8979-0145) or at the adjacent caravan park, which also has campsites and a bunkhouse section. Other facilities in the tourist complex include a restaurant, bistro, bar, takeaway, small supermarket, souvenir shop, petrol station, tourist information center, car rental agency, and airstrip.

Gagudju Lodge Cooinda Tours operates two-hour Yellow River cruises departing three times daily. Cost is $24. Twice-daily 90-minute tours are a few bucks less. If you can keep your eyes open early in the morning, shoot for the first trip (around 6:30 a.m.) when birdlife is most active (you know who catches the worm . . .). Advance bookings are essential for this popular outing. Phone the hotel for information, and don't forget to wear plenty of insect repellent.

To Pine Creek

Just past the Cooinda turnoff, the Kakadu Highway becomes mostly dirt for the 208-km, southwesterly "back way" to Pine Creek on the Stuart Highway. The road is often closed during the Wet; check with park rangers or police at either end for current status. **Barramundie Gorge**, about 35 km along the highway from Cooinda, then a 10-km turnoff on 4WD track, is lush with rainforest patches, gorge pools and beaches, freshwater crocs, and abundant birdlife. Camping is allowed.

Farther south and west, and often inaccessible during the Wet, **Waterfall Creek** (also known as Gunlom, and once known as Uranium Development Project Falls) is part of that iffy stage-three region, as well as another site locale for *Crocodile Dundee*. Features include a 100-meter waterfall, interesting flat rocks, a large pool bordered by paperbark and pandanus, freshwater crocs, aerobic bushwalks, camping, and picnic areas.

Camping

Aside from the privately run campgrounds mentioned above, Kakadu has a variety of campsites under jurisdiction of the Australian Nature Conservation Agency. Major sites with showers, flush toilets, hot water, and drinking water are at **Merl** (near the border store), **Muirella Park** (near Nourlangie Rock), and **Mardukal** (just south of the Cooinda turnoff). Other camping areas are Djaburluku, Gadjuduba, Melabanbandju, Burdulba, Jim Jim Falls, Barramundie Gorge, Gunlom (Waterfall Creek), Alligator Billabong, Black Jungle Spring, Two Mile Hole, and Four Mile Hole.

All of the campgrounds except Mardukal are subject to wet-season closures. Permits (get them at park headquarters) are required for bush camping outside of designated areas. Camping fees are $7 per person, per night, and are payable at the park information center. Bush camping is free.

Information

The **Kakadu National Park Information Centre** is a few kilometers south of Jabiru on the Kakadu Highway. The center provides extensive literature, guide maps, and tour info (particularly the ranger-led art and nature tours), as well as audiovisual displays ($3 admission) and video screenings. The center is open daily 8 a.m.-5 p.m. For information, phone park headquarters at (08) 8979-2101.

Tourist information is also available at Jabiru Airport and the hotels. In Darwin, contact the **Australian Nature Conservation Agency**, Smith St., Darwin, or write G.P.O. Box 1260, Darwin, NT 0801 (tel. 08-8981-5299).

Entry fee to the park is $10 and is good for two weeks' stay. Impromptu checkpoints are set up throughout the park, so do the right thing.

Transport

Kakadu Air (tel. 08-8979-2411) provides regular service between Darwin and Jabiru, as well as scenic flights over the park.

Greyhound Pioner Australia travels daily between Darwin and Kakadu, stopping variously at Humpty Doo ($15), Bark Hut ($24), Kakadu Holiday Village ($35), Jabiru ($48), and Nourlangie Rock and Cooinda ($52). Service may be delayed or suspended during the Wet.

Rental cars and 4WD vehicles can be procured in Darwin or within the park from Territory Rent-A-Car, Gagudju Crocodile Hotel Kakadu (tel. 08-8979-2800).

Bushwalkers can choose from marked trails or isolated terrain. Contact Darwin Bushwalking Club (tel. 08-8985-1484) for information on Kakadu walks. **Willis's Walkabouts** (tel. 08-8985-2134) organizes two-day to two-week bushwalks.

Tours

For visitors arriving by bus or conventional vehicle, there are a number of tour companies longing to take you around. Aboriginal-owned **Magela Tours** (tel. 08-8979-2227) conducts day tours around the park's lesser-traveled areas, but the price is a pretty hefty $200-plus (includes Jabiru pick-up). **Kakadu Gorge and Waterfall Tours** (tel. 08-8979-2025) offers 4WD jaunts from Jabiru or Cooinda to Jim Jim and Twin Falls for around $120 during the Dry.

Most tours depart Darwin, are of two-day duration (in the $180 range), and embrace the typical Nourlangie Rock, Jim Jim Falls, and Yellow River-cruise intinerary. Some respected companies include: **All Terrain** (tel. 08-8941-0070); **Hunter Safaris** (tel. 08-8981-2720); and **Saratoga** (tel. 08-8981-6473). **Australian Kakadu Tours** (tel. 08-8981-5144), for the less adventurous, does a one-day tour to Kakadu for about $90.

The **Darwin Regional Tourism Association Information Centre** in Darwin has an exhaustive listing of Kakadu tour operators. The park information center, Kakadu Holiday Village, Gagudju Lodge Cooinda, and Gagudju Crocodile Hotel Kakadu all book a number of excursions within the park.

For **boat trips**, see "Kakadu Holiday Village" and "Yellow Water" above.

ARNHEM LAND AND BEYOND

Within this huge region (pop. 5,000), comprising the entire eastern half of the Top End, scattered groups of Aborigines keep their traditional fires burning in a homeland filled with escarpments and plateaus, gorges and rivers, an abundance of rock-art sites and birdlife.

The district was named by Matthew Flinders in 1803 for one of the Dutch ships that "discovered" the coast in 1623—though earlier "discoverers" were most likely Malaccans, Indonesians, and Portuguese on a visit.

Don't even try to go onto these designated Aboriginal lands without the necessary permit— and don't count on getting one very easily either. Permits are seldom given to curious tourists, but several tour operators can take you up to the Cobourg Peninsula and to Bathurst and Melville Islands, and a couple of companies offer trips deep into Arnhem Land. (Stop in at the Darwin Regional Tourism Association Information Centre for tour info—also see the special topic "Permits for Outback Travel" and the chart "Aboriginal Tours" in the On the Road chapter.)

If flying in, you won't need a permit to visit Gove Peninsula, at the northeast tip.

Gurig National Park

Isolated on the Cobourg Peninsula, 200 kilometers northeast of Darwin, Gurig National Park (220,700 hectares) embraces exquisite virgin wilderness, important wetlands, protected coral reefs and marinelife, vast numbers of migratory birds, relics of the Macassarese trading days, and, of course, rich Aboriginal culture. The park is operated by the Conservation Commission

*Cape Arnhem—
really away from it all!*

in conjunction with traditional owners (the Gurig people, made up of about 40 clans), many of whom live near Black Point and work within the tourist sector.

The Cobourg Peninsula was the location for several of those pre-Darwin, failed European settlements. Ruins of **Victoria Settlement,** the 1838 British garrison community at Port Essington, include building foundations, walls, stone chimneys, and a half-buried powder magazine. An interpretive walking track incorporates many sights; pick up informative pamphlets at the **Visitors Centre and Museum** at Black Point.

The British left more than just their ruins—imported livestock still roaming the peninsula include Indian sambar deer, Timorese ponies, Balinese banteng cattle, and Javanese buffalo and pigs. Saltwater crocs, turtles, sea cows, and numerous tropical fish inhabit the coastal waters (though I won't credit the Brits for those). Along the sandy shores, beachcombers are apt to walk away with some primo shells for their collections. Fishing is idyllic year-round, but swimming is not recommended, unless you don't mind playing Russian roulette with the sharks, saltwater crocs, and box jellyfish.

A small **campground** near the shore at Smith Point has showers, toilets, a picnic and barbecue area, jetty, and nearby store with sporadic hours.

The peninsula is about a nine-hour drive from Darwin along the Arnhem Highway, turning northwest from Jabiru. It's 4WD only from East Alligator River to Gurig, and the road is closed during the Wet. Advance permits to enter Arnhem Land are mandatory. For information, contact the **Northern Territory Conservation Commission** (tel. 08-8999-5511). Be forewarned: Only 15 vehicles per week are allowed access, and bookings are now running one to two years behind (most of the permits are snatched up way in advance by fishers on their way to Smith Point).

If you have a fat wallet (or a gold card), indulge yourself at **Seven Spirit Bay,** a super-remote, super-luxurious eco-resort that's accessible by light aircraft or boat. Gourmet cuisine is part of the $400 per person double-deal, as are various eco-activities. This is a favorite hide-away for celebs and type-A's (who probably go nuts after half a day). For information and bookings, phone (08) 8979-0227.

An **organized tour,** all-inclusive of air or land transport, accommodations, and necessary permits, is really the easiest way to go. Again, check with the tourist center and YHA Travel Centre. "Mini-tours" into Arnhem Land from Kakadu are offered by **Kakadu Parklink** (tel. 08-8979-2411) and **Arnhemlander** (tel. 08-8979-2411).

Gove Peninsula

This remote region on Arnhem Land's very far away northeastern tip was first charted in 1803 by Matthew Flinders, but only settled at Nhulunbuy as late as 1969—when the bauxite mining began. The local Yirrkala Aborigines protested the intended rape of their traditional land and, though mining proceeded anyhow (surprise, surprise), a government inquiry and subsequent compensation award attracted national attention, planting a seed for the ongoing land-rights movement.

Visitors come to this balmy, tropical region expressly because it is so isolated and untouristy. White-sand beaches, wildlife, reef and big-game fishing, varied sports facilities, and saltwater croc and buffalo safaris are the big attractions. In addition, **Yirrkala,** a former mission, displays and sells art and artifacts produced by local Aborigines. Free half-day tours of the **Nabalco Mine** are given on Thursday mornings.

The only practical way to get up to Gove is by air. Ansett flies into Nhulunbuy, and no permit is necessary. The cheapest fares are in conjunction with land packages, which include accommodations and sightseeing. Driving up here is not practical because of the long distances (800 km of pretty lousy road from Katherine) and the number of complicated permits involved. Coastline explorers who fly in can rent cars in Nhulunbuy (see the special topic "Permits for Outback Travel" in the On the Road chapter).

For information on tour operators to the peninsula, contact the **Darwin Regional Tourism Association Information Centre** (tel. 08-8981-4300). Most tours depart from Darwin or Jabiru.

DOWN THE TRACK

It's about 1,500 km from Darwin to Alice Springs on the Stuart Highway (National Route 87). Closely paralleling explorer John McDouall Stuart's path (its namesake) and the 1872 Overland Telegraph Line, the Track has grown from a pre-WW II dirt stretch to a two-lane, sealed, all-weather highway. Sights on or near the road add interest to the long drive.

DARWIN TO KATHERINE

See "Vicinity of Darwin" above for towns and attractions on the Track within about 50 kilometers south of Darwin.

Manton Dam
This huge reservoir, 42 km down the Track from Darwin and another few kilometers along the turnoff, was originally built for WW II military personnel stationed in the Territory. The 440-hectare recreation area features sailing, swimming, waterskiing, and barbecue facilities. Open Mon.-Fri. 9 a.m.-5 p.m., Sat.-Sun. 8 a.m.-7 p.m. For information, phone (08) 8999-5511.

Lake Bennett
Situated 80 km down the Track and then seven km east, this 404-hectare human-made lake provides a large range of water activities, including windsurfing, swimming, sailing, canoeing, and fishing. Other features include prolific birdlife, tropical wilderness areas, bushwalks, and barbecue facilities. Accommodations at **Lake Bennett Holiday Park** (tel. 08-8976-0960) consist of campsites or camp-o-tels (a combination tent and motel).

Batchelor
This Litchfield Park gateway (pop. 600) and former service town to the defunct Rum Jungle uranium and copper mine lies 84 km from Darwin and another 13 km to the west, in a lush forest setting with colorful birdlife. Nearby is an old airstrip, used from time to time by General Douglas MacArthur during WW II, as well as other wartime memorabilia. **Karlstein Castle,** a

miniature replica of a Bohemian castle, sits oddly out of place across from the police station. **Rum Jungle Lake,** six km from town, is a popular center for sailing, swimming, and canoeing. This town is also the site of an **Aboriginal Teacher Training College** and base for the **Top End Aerial Sports Association**'s parachuting and gliding activities.

Moderate to expensive accommodations are available at **Rum Jungle Motor Inn,** Rum Jungle

SECRET RECIPE FOR BILLY TEA

Brew your own "cuppa," just like the original Outback pioneers. It's an easy picker-upper from the land Down Under. Here's how:

Equipment: one Billy can (a small metal bucket), a campfire, cups, one hand with a limber wrist.

Ingredients: water, loose black tea, milk, sugar.

La méthode: Fill the Billy can with cold water, allowing it to boil on the campfire; add a big old handful of tea (three to four heaping tablespoons); grab the Billy by its handle and swing that baby around and around to blend tea; place Billy back on campfire, allowing the tea leaves to settle and steep; pour tea into cups, adding lots of milk and sugar. Ah, you'll be ready to conquer the Outback.

Rd. (tel. 08-8976-0123). **Batchelor Caravillage,** Rum Jungle Rd. (tel. 08-8976-0166), offers on-site vans and campsites, and also arranges tours of the Rum Jungle Mine.

Adelaide River

Located on the Adelaide River (but not the crossing on Arnhem Hwy.), 110 km south of Darwin, this tiny township (pop. 200) was a hub of WW II military activity, undoubtedly due to its railway depot and prime position. Relics and armaments still in evidence include the **Snake Creek Arsenal,** a major armaments depot and wartime military camp; **Adelaide River War Cemetery,** Australia's largest such graveyard where most of the Darwin dead have been laid to rest; and a host of old airstrips smattered around the Track. The restored **Railway Station** (built 1888-89) is a designated National Trust property, housing a **tourist information center** (tel. 08-8976-7010), open Wed.-Sun. 8:30 a.m.-5 p.m. The **Railway Bridge,** built the same year as the station, occasionally doubled as a road bridge during the Wet.

Adelaide River Inn, Stuart Hwy. (tel. 08-8976-7047), offers inexpensive rooms, and **Shady River View Caravan Park,** War Memorial Dr. (same phone), has campsites.

For emergencies, contact the **police** (tel. 08-8976-7042) or an **ambulance** (tel. 08-8927-9000).

The Scenic Route

From Adelaide River you can continue on the Track or take the scenic Old Stuart Highway, an extra 14-km jog slightly to the west, for a variety of interesting attractions—though during the Wet, access is sometimes impossible.

First stop is **Robin Falls,** 17 km southwest of Adelaide River and a short walk from the road. Aside from the 12-meter-high falls (which are but a few drips and trickles during the Dry), this spot features a monsoon-forested gorge, good swimming, and, for those up to the climb, excellent views from the top.

The **Daly River** area is a bit of a detour (109 km southwest of the highway at Adelaide River), but it's worth the drive for several attractions. The town of Daly River (pop. 250), an 1880s copper mine, was the scene of a bloody race riot between Aborigines, who opposed the mine, and white miners. Though the mine did not stick around for long, the Jesuit mission, established around the time of the conflict, did—today it is run by the local Aboriginal council. The town has a variety of services, including a supermarket, Aboriginal art center, roadside inn, takeaway food, and petrol and camping gas.

Nearby attractions are: **Daly River Nature Park** (tel. 08-8978-2347), a 60-hectare reserve with barramundi fishing, boating, picnic and camping facilities; **Bamboo Creek Rainforest Park** (tel. 08-8975-3410), 13 km from Daly River on Woolianna Track, featuring fishing, canoeing, guided motorbike and boat tours, camping, and moderately priced cottage accommodations; and **Daly River Mango Farm** (tel. 08-8978-2464), five km south of Daly River and another seven km from the turnoff, offering a variety of scenic, wildlife, croc-spotting, fishing, and hunting tours, plus safari tents, campsites, and moderately priced cabins. Be sure to inquire at the Aboriginal council office in Daly River as to travel on local tribal lands.

Travel back to the old highway and turn another 35 km southwest (just before the junction with the Track) to reach **Douglas Hot Springs Nature Park** (tel. 08-8973-8770). The top attraction of this 3,107-hectare park is the thermal pools, particularly **Hot Springs Lagoon,** with 40° C (104° F) bathtub water. Swimming, bushwalks, and camping are also popular here. **Butterfly Gorge Nature Park** (tel. 08-8989-

5511), 17 km farther along a 4WD track, is a 104-hectare tranquil woodland reserve with swarming butterflies, deep rock pools, and a high-cliffed gorge ideal for bushwalking, fishing, and swimming. As crocs may be present, check first with the **ranger station,** located about five km from the park's turnoff. Next to the ranger station, **Corn Patch Riverside Holiday Park** (tel. 08-8975-3479) offers a variety of facilities including general store, petrol, bar, restaurant, takeaway, camping gas, and campsites.

Back on the Track, keep your eyes peeled for one of Australia's largest **termite mounds** (6.7 meters tall and 7.35 meters around the base) set in the bush near **Hayes Creek.**

Pine Creek

This historic township (pop. 500) 230 km south of Darwin was the site of a massive gold rush during the 1870s. Discovery of the precious metal during the building of the Overland Telegraph Line brought not merely an influx of gold diggers but the accoutrements that follow—Chinese coolies to do the hard labor, and lots of Chinese-run stores and butcheries. At one point the Chinese so outnumbered the Europeans that a law was passed in 1888 forbidding Chinese admittance to the Northern Territory. Originally named Playford in 1888, the town was renamed Pine Creek for—obviously—the pines that used to grow by the creek. Though Pine Creek was hardly even noticed during the world wars, the 1960s and '70s' uranium and iron ore mining brought renewed activity, followed by present gold-mining ventures and increased tourism.

Your first stop should be **Pine Creek Museum** in the old repeater station on Railway Terrace, the oldest surviving prefab building in the Territory. The National Trust, located within the museum, has identified approximately 140 historic sites in and around the town and provides visitor guides and heritage trail maps. Hours are daily April-Sept. 11 a.m.-1 p.m., closed Oct.-March. Admission is $2. For information, phone (08) 8976-1279.

Opened in 1889, **Playford Club Hotel** is the Territory's oldest surviving pub, now a private residence. Also located on Main Terrace is the 1888-89 **Railway Precinct,** including the station, weigh bridge, crane, water tank, sheds, and employee housing. **Miners Park,** next door, features assorted mining relics.

Pine Creek Hotel/Motel, Moule St. (tel. 08-8976-1288), has moderately priced rooms. **Pine Creek Caravan Park,** Moule St. (tel. 08-8976-1217), features campsites as well as a fully equipped bunkhouse.

In case you forgot—or haven't read that part yet—Pine Creek is also the "back road" gateway to Kakadu Highway and Kakadu National Park. Pine Creekers fish for barramundi, black bream, and catfish at Mary River, at the park's edge.

KATHERINE

This third-largest Northern Territory center, 350 km south of Darwin, has practically doubled in population, from 6,200 to about 10,000, with the 1988 opening of RAAF Tindal, Australia's largest air base. Other than military activities, Katherine is a booming tourist town renowned for nearby Katherine Gorge and Cutta Cutta Caves as well as being a service town and turnoff point for the Kimberley region in Western Australia.

Set amidst tropical woodland and along the Katherine River banks, the town grew up in conjunction with the installation of the Overland Telegraph Line and railway. World War II brought a number of airstrips to the area and, more recently, regional administration, agriculture, cattle stations, and service facilities have added prosperity to this middle-of-nowhere tourist center.

Katherine Museum and Historical Park, on Gorge Rd., opposite the hospital, features a variety of local history displays and architectural relics, in a former airport terminal building. Hours are Mon.-Fri. 10 a.m.-4 p.m., Saturday 10 a.m.-2 p.m., Sunday 2-5 p.m. Admission is $3. For information, phone (08) 8972-3945.

Katherine Railway Station, on Railway Terrace, houses railroad memorabilia and the local branch of the National Trust. Pick up a self-guided tour brochure to 10 heritage sites. Hours are Mon.-Fri. 1-3 p.m. late April-Sept., closed public holidays. For information, phone (08) 8972-3956.

Watch teachers in action with their Outback students at **School of the Air,** Giles Street.

Guided tours are available Mon.-Fri. 9 a.m.-5 p.m. Admission is $2. The **O'Keefe Residence,** on Riverbank Dr. across from Campbell Terrace, is an exceptional example of Territorial architecture, built of bush poles, corrugated iron, and asbestos(!). Hours are Mon.-Fri. 1-3 p.m. late April-Sept. Admission is $2. For information, phone (08) 8972-2204.

Katherine Low Level Nature Park, a 104-hectare section of the Katherine River, is a local favorite for fishing, swimming (safe mainly during the Dry), and picnicking. Check locally about the possibility of freshwater crocs.

Knotts Crossing marks the site of Katherine's beginnings. Accessed via a turnoff past the hospital, the original settlement included a pub, store, telegraph, and police station. The old pub, located at the top of the riverbank, is now a private residence.

Springvale Homestead

Located eight km southwest of Katherine, on Shadforth Rd., Springvale, established in 1878, is reputedly the Territory's oldest original station homestead. Now a tourist facility, the homestead's features include period-costumed staff, walking tours, canoeing, croc-spotting, swimming (in the Dry), fishing, and Aboriginal corroborees (in the evening). Free tours of the homestead are given daily during the Dry at 9 a.m. and 3 p.m. (historical reenactments coincide with the afternoon tour). Croc cruises and corroboree nights cost $35. Canoe hire is $5 per hour or $20 for the day. For information, phone (08) 8972-1044.

Lazy L Stables, at the homestead's entrance, offers trail rides and pony rides. For information, phone (08) 8972-2618.

Katherine Gorge National Park

This glorious park (180,352 hectares), 32 km northeast of Katherine township, ranks third—after Ayers Rock and Kakadu National Park—among the Territory's most visited attractions. Now returned to the Jawoyn Aborigines, its traditional owners, the park is administered jointly by the Conservation Commission and the Jawoyn people.

A total of 13 gorges, carved by the Katherine River through Arnhem Plateau sandstone merely 25 million years ago (though the base material is some 2.3 billion years old), are geological

marvels with sheer rock faces rising 75 meters high, exquisitely patterned stone floors, and weathered canyon walls adorned with Aboriginal paintings and engravings. Aside from the magnificent gorges, the landscape encompasses rugged escarpments and plateaus, and a superb variety of flora and fauna, especially birds and aquatic life. This is an area of mosses and ferns, pandanus and paperbark, freshwater crocs and long-necked tortoises, red-winged parrots and blue-winged kookaburras—and bat caves. Ten **bushwalks,** taking from two hours to several days, cover approximately 100 km of always scenic, sometimes rugged, track. The longest walk is the 76-km trek to **Edith Falls,** a series of low falls and cool rock pools at the extreme western edge of the park. In case you're contemplating a swim, be forewarned: freshwater crocs inhabit these waters. Katherine Gorge is another place that changes markedly with the seasons, becoming thunderous during the Wet, drying into deep pools as the rains subside.

The **visitor center,** near the park entrance, provides area and bushwalking maps, informative displays, and literature, and also issues the required permits for long-distance or wilderness hikes.

Cutta Cutta Caves

Situated west of the Track, 27 km south of Katherine, this series of limestone caverns dates back 500 million years, give or take a year or so. Classic stalactite and stalagmite formations and tower karsts are the primary characteristics of this protected nature park (1,499 hectares). Rare and strange cave dwellers include blind shrimp and the golden horseshoe bat. Though Katherine tour operators often include these caves in their excursions, if you come on your own you can sign up for an informative ranger-led tour (you can only enter the caves while on a guided tour). Ninety-minute ranger-led tours operate daily at 10:30 a.m., noon, and 1:30 p.m., except during the Wet, when caves are closed. Cost is $6. For information, phone (08) 8973-8770.

Accommodations

Springvale Homestead, Shadforth Rd. (tel. 08-8972-1355), offers inexpensive rooms in historic surroundings. For moderately priced ac-

remnants of Never Never Land

commodations, try **Kuringgai Motel,** Giles St. (tel. 08-8971-0266), or **Beagle Motor Inn,** corner Fourth and Lindsay St. (tel. 08-8972-3998). The **Palm Court Backpackers Lodge,** corner Giles and Third (tel. 08-8972-2722), charges $12 per person for shared rooms. **Kookaburra Lodge,** corner Lindsay and Third (tel. 08-8971-0257), features $12-per-night dorm rooms.

Campsites are available at **Katherine Gorge Caravan Park,** Katherine Gorge National Park (tel. 08-8972-1253), **Katherine Low Level Caravan Park,** Shadforth Rd. (tel. 08-8972-3962), and **Riverview Caravan Park,** 440 Victoria Hwy. (tel. 08-8972-1011).

Events
Though Aboriginal lands are normally off-limits to the public, everyone is invited to the big **Barunga Festival** at Beswick Aboriginal Land Trust, 130 km south of Katherine and an additional 29 km off the highway. Held over the Queen's Birthday weekend in June, it draws Aborigines from throughout the Territory for a four-day celebration of dancing, sports, arts and crafts, plus bush-tucker stalls. Sunday is the best day, with fire lighting as well as a boomerang- and spear-throwing competitions.

Information
Pick up heaps of local info and maps at the **Katherine Region Tourist Association,** Stuart Hwy. (tel. 08-8972-2650). Hours are Mon.-Fri. 9 a.m.-5 p.m.

For emergencies, contact the **police** (tel. 08-8972-0211) or **hospital** (tel. 08-8972-9211).

Transport
Regularly scheduled flights operate between Katherine, Alice Springs, and Darwin. Check with **Ansett** (tel. 13-1300, toll-free) or **Qantas** (tel. 13-1313 toll-free).

Greyhound Pioneer Australia (tel. 13-2030 toll-free) and **McCafferty's** (tel. 08-212-5066) stop in Katherine on their Port Augusta-Darwin runs. Fare from Darwin is about $48 one-way; from Alice Springs, $125 one-way.

Rental cars are available from **Avis,** Hobbitt's Auto Electrical, 47 Victoria Hwy. (tel. 08-8972-1482), or **Freedom Hire,** Happy Corner Complex, Third St. (tel. 08-8971-1411).

Inquire at the tourist bureau for best local tours. **Travel North** (tel. 08-8972-1253) and **Frontier** (tel. 08-8971-1381) operate a variety of Katherine Gorge excursions, including river cruises ($20-60); Frontier also runs 15-minute helicopter flights. Canoes can be rented from **Kookaburra Canoe Hire** (tel. 08-8972-3604).

Bill Harney's Jankangyina Tours (tel. 08-8972-2650) are excellent two-day, one-night Aboriginal adventures including rock-art sites, bush foods, and campfire stories. Prices range $225-270.

TO WESTERN AUSTRALIA

It's 513 km southwest from Katherine to the Western Australia border along the **Victoria Highway.** Though the road is bitumen all the way, it's extremely narrow and impassable during the Wet, when torrential rain causes rivers to flood bridges and roadways.

Note: Exercise caution when driving this route—if another vehicle approaches, so does an impending barrage of stones; slow down and pull as far off the road as possible.

It's 125 km along the Victoria Highway to the **Delamere Road** turnoff. **Top Springs** (pop. 15), 164 km south at the Buchanan Highway junction, features a popular beer-guzzler (an average of nine tons per week!) roadhouse, pools for swimming, moderately priced accommodations, campsites, and the usual range of services. For information, phone (08) 8975-0767. The Buchanan continues 170 km southwest to **Kalkaringi** (pop. 250), a service town for the Daguragu Aboriginal Land Trust, and another 222 km to the Western Australia border. Four-wheel-drives are recommended for this highway, which is often flooded during the Wet.

Back on Victoria Highway, **Victoria River Wayside Inn** (tel. 08-8975-0744), 196 km southwest of Katherine, sits at Victoria River Crossing, backed by smooth ranges and rugged cliffs. Known as the "friendliest pub in the scrub," facilities include a general store, supermarket, restaurant, pub, takeaway, petrol station, tourist information center, mechanic and towing service, campsites, and moderately priced motel rooms. **Red Valley boat tours** depart from here or Timber Creek three times daily (April-Oct.) on cruises of the scenic river and gorges. Cost is $10-20. Barramundi and bream fishing are good in these parts, but both freshwater crocs and salties live in the water as well, so stave off your temptation to swim.

Surrounding the Wayside Inn and Victoria River and stretching all the way to Timber Creek is more recently established **Gregory National Park** (10,000 square km), which encompasses much of the surrounding scenery, plus traces of Aboriginal and European presence, several historic homesteads, a few excellent camping spots (with no facilities), rare flora and fauna, abundant birdlife, and bushwalking trails. **Kuwang Lookout** offers spectacular views of Stokes Range. Access, at present, is mainly by 4WD. Park headquarters is in Timber Creek. For information, phone (08) 8975-0888.

Historic **Timber Creek** (pop. 100), 91 km from the Wayside Inn, was noteworthy for its Victoria River Depot and massive cattle stations. The old port, established in 1891, is now a historical reserve, located about eight km from town. The **Police Station Museum** presents displays, artifacts, and an occasional informal talk relating to police action and racial turmoil in the 1880s (tip: don't ask about those subjects *today!*). **Gregory's Tree Historical Reserve,** west of town, features a baobab tree carved with early explorers' initials.

Campsites and moderately priced accommodations are available at **Circle F Motel and Caravan Park,** Victoria Hwy. (tel. 08-8975-0722). A 16-bed **youth hostel** is located behind the police station.

Most basic services are available at Timber Creek. For emergencies, contact the **police** (tel. 08-8975-0733).

Keep River National Park (59,700 hectares) is 190 km from Timber Creek, at the Western Australia border. The park, known for its extraordinary land formations and distinctive geology, also is characterized by tropical savannah, dramatic escarpments and plateaus, enormous baobab trees, Aboriginal art sites, volcanic rocks, and profuse plantlife, birds, and reptiles. Before embarking on bushwalks, make sure you are prepared for the searing heat and have plenty of water on hand. Check in with the park ranger located near the park entrance at Waters of Cockatoo Lagoon. **Camping areas,** with marked interpretive walking tracks, are located at **Gurrandalng** (15 km from Victoria Hwy.) and **Jarrnarm** (28 km within the park). Conventional vehicles can access the park, though roads may be closed during the Wet. For information, phone (091) 67-8827.

TO TENNANT CREEK

Mataranka

Heading south on the Track, Mataranka (pop. 150) is 109 km from Katherine. Tropical bushland, crystal-clear thermal pools, a *very* colorful pub, and a chunk of literary history are the celebrated characteristics of this small cattle and service community.

Historic **Mataranka Homestead,** nine km east of town, is a wooded tourist resort bordering Waterhouse River. Adjacent is **Mataranka Pool Nature Park,** a four-hectare reserve with relaxing thermal pools, plentiful birdlife, as well as palm, paperbark, pandanus, and passion fruit forest—and growing crowds of tourists.

Near the homestead stands a replica of **Elsey Station Homestead,** a set for the 1981 film *We of the Never Never,* based on the well-known Outback novel of the same name in which author Jeannie Gunn relates the life and times at the remote station she managed for a brief time. **Elsey Cemetery,** 13 km south of Mataranka and eight km east of the Track, is the ashes-to-ashes, dust-to-dust home of *Never Never* characters including Jeannie and Aeneas Gunn, Fizzer the mailman, and Muluka.

Old Elsey Roadside Inn, the colorful pub on the Track (tel. 08-75-4512), features inexpensive accommodations and counter meals. **Mataranka Homestead** (tel. 08-8975-4544) offers moderately priced motel rooms, a **YHA Hostel,** and campsites. Another choice in the moderate range is **Territory Manor,** Martin Rd. (tel. 08-8975-4516), with both motel rooms and campsites, and a pool.

Canoes can be rented ($6 per hour) at Waterhouse River jetty. Historic **homestead walking tours** are available daily at 11 a.m. **Brolga Tours** (tel. 08-8975-4538) offers a highly recommended four-hour tour of the Roper River, historic Elsey Station (the real one is at McMinns Bar on the Roper River), and Red Lily Lagoon ($60).

In emergencies, contact the **police** (tel. 08-8975-4511) or **ambulance** (tel. 08-8972-1200).

Roper Highway

The Roper Highway intersects the Track seven km south of Mataranka. Another 185 km east—on mostly sealed road—is Roper Bar, a small tropical outpost (pop. six), popular for boating and barramundi fishing (not swimming, though—both salties and freshwater crocs call this place home). Facilities at "The Roper" include general store, takeaway, picnic and barbecue area, visitor information, boat ramp, airstrip, petrol station, Aboriginal art tours, moderately priced rooms, and campsites. For information, phone (08) 8981-9455.

Private Aboriginal lands begin just past Roper Bar.

Larrimah

Lots of WW II activity took place in this former railhead township (pop. 25), 68 km south of Mataranka. Apart from being a supply base, a top-secret airfield was located here, from where General Douglas MacArthur made some heavy-duty decisions. The original settlement was actually five km away at Birdum but, except for the 1920s Birdum Hotel which was moved to Larrimah, the rest of the town was abandoned after the war. The railway closed down in 1976, due to lack of funding and Cyclone Tracy's devastation, but its remains, as well as those of the Overland Telegraph Station and old post office,

KATHERINE
WATERHOUSE RIVER
TO DARWIN
ROPER BAR
MATARANKA HOMESTEAD
MATARANKA
ROPER HWY.
ELSEY STATION HOMESTEAD
WE OF THE NEVER NEVER GRAVES
LARRIMAH
DALY WATERS
CARPENTARIA HWY.
DALY WATERS JUNCTION
BUCHANAN HWY.
DUNMARRA
TO TENNANT CREEK
ELLIOTT
STUART HWY.
RENNER SPRINGS
BARKLY HWY.
JOHN FLYNN MEMORIAL
THREE WAYS
66
OLD TELEGRAPH STATION
DEVILS PEBBLES
TENNANT CREEK
TO ALICE SPRINGS
87
NOBLES NOB MINE

0   50 mi
0   50 km

© MOON PUBLICATIONS, INC.

are near the hotel. **Larrimah Hotel,** another old bush pub, is not to be missed for its dining specialties—how do boar's tits on toast tickle your taste buds?

Campsites and cheap rooms are available at **Larrimah Wayside Inn,** Stuart Hwy. (tel. 08-8975-9931). **Green Park Tourist Complex,** Stuart Hwy. (tel. 08-8975-9937), offers campsites and is also a good clearing house for local information.

Daly Waters

First stop is **Daly Waters Pub,** 89 km from Larrimah and another three km off the highway. Known as one of the Territory's best and oldest Outback pubs, visitors are certain to soak up any color they desire amid a setting of Australian bush and traditional architecture, surrounded by tropical forest. The front bar "museum" displays pioneer and Aboriginal artifacts. A sign above the bar offers free credit to any 80-year-old woman who is with her mother. Inexpensive rooms and campsites are available. For information, phone (08) 8975-9927.

Daly Waters (pop. 20), two km beyond the pub, is a former campsite for Overland Telegraph Line workers and cattle drovers, as well as a refueling stop for Qantas Airways' first international route between Brisbane and Singapore in the 1930s.

Carpentaria Highway

Often mistaken for the real Daly Waters, **Daly Waters Junction** is another four km south,

where the Stuart and Carpentaria Highways meet. The **Hi-Way Inn** roadhouse only dates back to 1974—thus many of us can well imagine both its history and the origins of its name. All the usual Outback roadside facilities are offered, including inexpensive accommodations, campsites, restaurant, shop, pub, beer garden, and petrol station. For information, phone (08) 8975-9925.

From the junction, the bitumen Carpentaria Highway travels 391 km east to Borroloola within the Narwinbi Aboriginal Land Trust, passing **Cape Crawford** (and the Heartbreak Hotel) 275 km along the way. The **Heartbreak** (tel. 08-8975-9928) offers moderately priced rooms, campsites, restaurant, takeaway, shop, bar, picnic area, camping gas, and petrol station. From Cape Crawford, you can either turn south on the **Tablelands Highway** (also sealed) 378 km to Barkly Homestead on the Barkly Highway, or continue on the Carpentaria Highway, 116 km northeast to Borroloola.

Once a booming, colorful 1880s frontier town, today's **Borroloola,** set along the MacArthur River, is a famous barramundi fishing hole and site of the Easter **Barra Classic** barramundi fishing competition. Some of the old building ruins, including the former police station, can still be seen. Inexpensive bunkhouse accommodations are available at **Borroloola Holiday Village** (tel. 08-8975-8742), and **McArthur River Caravan Park** (tel. 08-8975-8734) offers on-site vans and campsites. Camping along the riverbanks is not advisable due to croc danger.

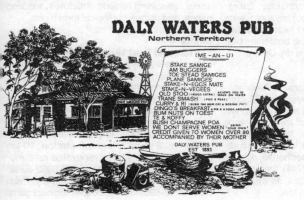

DALY WATERS PUB
Northern Territory

(ME – AN – U)

STAKE SAMIGE
AM BUGGERS
TOE STEAD SAMIGES
PLANE SAMIGES
STAKE–N–EGGS MATE
STAKE–N–VEGEES
OLD STOO (FROGS EXTRA) ALLOWS YOU TO WALK ON WATER
TRANE SMASH (PIES & PEAS)
CURRY & RI (BURN THE BUM OFF A BOEING 747)
DINGO'S BREAKFAST A PEE & A LOOK AROUND
BUM NUTS ON TOAST
TE & KOFFY
BUSH CHAMPAGNE POA
WE DONT SERVE WOMEN — BRING YOUR OWN
CREDIT GIVEN TO WOMEN OVER 80
ACCOMPANIED BY THEIR MOTHER

DALY WATERS PUB
EST 1893

some daily fare at the Daly Waters Pub

Dunmarra

It's 36 km along the Track from Daly Waters Junction to the Buchanan Highway turnoff (another route to Top Springs), and another eight km to Dunmarra, a WW II staging camp for southbound convoys from Larrimah. **Shell Wayside Inn** (tel. 08-8975-9922) offers moderately priced accommodations, campsites, travelers' services, and facilities.

Elliott

The landscape gets drier as you near this Darwin-Alice Springs near-halfway point, 120 km south of Dunmarra and 23 km beyond **Newcastle Waters** historic cattle station. Also a former WW II staging camp, Elliott (pop. 600) is a low-key regional service center for the surrounding cattle-raising community. **Elliott Hotel** (tel. 08-8969-2069) has moderately priced rooms. **Halfway Caravan Park** (tel. 08-8969-2025) offers campsites, and **Midland Caravan Park** (tel. 08-8969-2037) has campsites and an inexpensive bunkhouse.

For emergencies, contact the **police** (tel. 08-8969-2010) or **ambulance** (tel. 08-8969-2060).

Renner Springs

The pub building is a typical example of postwar roadhouse architecture, and the pub interior is a prime example of wayside ambience—a few growls and a few giggles. Moderately priced rooms, campsites, dining, takeaway, petrol, and mechanical services are offered. For information, phone (08) 8964-4505.

According to Aboriginal mythology, Lubra Lookout, a flat-topped mesa four km south, was the place where local women kept watch for visitors. It is also considered the borderline between the wet Top End and the dry Centre.

Three Ways

Marked by a large stone memorial to Reverend John Flynn, founder of the Royal Flying Doctor Service, Three Ways, 134 km south of Renner Springs, sits at the junction of the Track and the Barkly Highway. A fabled "getting stuck" place, this little hole in the Track is also known as hitchhiker hell. **Three Ways Roadhouse**, right at the crossroads (tel. 08-8962-2744), features inexpensive rooms and campsites, as well as a sign warning hitchhikers not to loiter.

Barkly Highway

From Three Ways, the Barkly Highway travels 643 east to Mt. Isa, in Queensland. **Barkly Homestead,** 185 km along the way, is a modern roadhouse that provides basic facilities, including moderately priced accommodations, a caravan park, campsites, and petrol. For information, phone (08) 8964-4549.

TENNANT CREEK

Other than Katherine, Tennant Creek (pop. 3,400) is the biggest town between Alice Springs and Darwin. Situated 675 km south of Katherine and 507 km north of Alice Springs, Tennant Creek is a modern Outback cattle and tourist town as well as an important past and present gold-mining center.

According to legend, the town's location is attributed to the breakdown of a beer cart—instead of crating the beer and building materials back to the intended site, the camp was moved to where the beer had fallen! Another tribute to laziness is that the shops and pub were supposedly built closest to the creek because the miners didn't want to walk any farther than necessary.

After gold was discovered here in 1932, 100 mines sprang up before WW II (though most were small producers), followed by copper mining in the 1950s, which continues to the present day along with that of gold and silver. The Tennant Creek area, home to Warumungu Aborigines, who call the place Jurnkurakurr, features some interesting historic structures, working mines, and unique geological formations.

Sights

The **National Trust Museum,** Schmidt St., originally a WW II army hospital, features early memorabilia and historical displays. Open Mon.-Fri. 4-6 p.m. during the Dry.

Church of Christ the King, Windley St., a classified historic corrugated-iron and wood structure, was originally built in Pine Creek in 1904 and eventually moved to its present location.

The 1872 stone **telegraph station,** 10 km north of town, has been renovated as a museum. For information, phone (08) 8962-3388.

Artworks Gem and Mineral Display, Peko Rd. (tel. 08-8962-3388), exhibits regional gems and minerals, as well as locally produced art. Hours are daily 9 a.m.-4 p.m.

Watch the ongoing action of gold-bearing ore being crushed and flushed at **Battery Hill,** about two km along Peko Road. Erected in 1939, it is one of Australia's few 10-head batteries still in operation. You can take a guided tour and nose around the museum, which features historical displays and other artifacts. Tours are daily at 8 a.m., 9:30 a.m., and 4 p.m. Admission is $5. For information, phone (08) 8962-3388.

The **Dot Mine,** Warrego Rd., is one of Tennant Creek's oldest mines. Originally leased in 1936 to German-born Otto Wohnert, the mine was signed away to friends after war broke out and Otto was interned. While Otto was tucked away, malicious rumors spread that he had poisoned the local waterholes. It's no surprise that after the war Otto returned to a burnt-out mine and home and a lot of missing machinery. It is still possible to glimpse gold extraction by the old gravitation method. Tours are Mon.-Fri. at 9 a.m., 11 a.m., 2 p.m., 4 p.m. For information, phone (08) 8962-2168.

One of Tennant Creek's best views is at **One Tank Hill Lookout,** two km east along Peko Road. Eleven significant local sites are depicted on plaques embedded in a semicircular wall. **Purkiss Reserve,** corner of Ambrose and Peko Roads, has a shady barbecue and playground area, and a swimming pool. A better recreation spot is at **Mary Ann Dam,** six km north of town, with a lake perfect for swimming and boating. Bicycle and bushwalking tracks plus boat and sailboard rentals are also offered.

Devils Pebbles, 11 km north on the Track and another six km left on a dirt road, are rounded boulders—weathered from a 1.7-billion-year-old granite mass—heaped across the landscape. Come at sunset when the combination of minerals and evening sun produces exquisite colors. Camping is permitted, but there are no facilities.

Accommodations and Food
Moderate to expensive accommodations are available at **Eldorado Motor Lodge,** Paterson St. (tel. 08-8962-2402); **Goldfields Motor Hotel,** Paterson St. (tel. 08-8962-2030); **Bluestone Motor Inn,** Paterson St. (tel. 08-896-2617); and **Safari Lodge,** Davidson St. (tel. 08-8962-2207). Safari Lodge has cheap bunkhouse beds.

Campsites and on-site vans can be rented at **Outback Caravan Park,** Peko Rd. (tel. 08-8962-2459), and **Tennant Creek Caravan Park,** Paterson St. (tel. 08-8962-2325).

A 26-bed **YHA Hostel** is on Leichhardt St. (tel. 08-8962-2719).

Most restaurants and takeaways are on or around Paterson Street. **The Dolly Pot Inn,** Davidson St., a combination squash court/ restaurant, is supposed to have the best food in town ($8-16). The **Coffee Place** and **Gallery Restaurant,** 53 Paterson St. (in the Tavern), are the town's artsy/trendy attempts.

Tennant Creek's pubs beckon a heavy-duty drinking and fighting clientele. Unless you're game for that kind of action, stick to the tamer bars at the **Tavern, Swan,** and **Goldfields** Hotels, all on Paterson Street.

Services and Information
The **Tennant Creek Visitor Information Centre,** Paterson St., in the transit center, provides literature and information and books tours and accommodations. Hours are Mon.-Fri. 9 a.m.-5 p.m. For information, phone (08) 8962-3388.

In emergencies, contact the **police** (tel. 08-8962-1211) or **hospital** (tel. 08-8962-4399).

Transport
Ansett (tel. 13-1300 toll-free) operates regular flights into Tennant Creek.

Greyhound Pioneer Australia (tel. 13-2030 toll-free) and McCafferty's (tel. 08-212-5066) stop in Tennant Creek on daily services between Darwin and Alice Springs.

Rent cars from **Outback Caravan Park,** Peko Rd. (tel. 08-8962-2459), or **Ten Ant Tours,** 104 Paterson St. (tel. 08-89 62-2358).

Ten Ant Tours offers various local excursions, including a popular two-hour fossicker and plant-lover expedition to Kraut Downs. Cost is $22.

Allow plenty of room to pass!

TO ALICE

Devils Marbles Conservation Reserve (1,828
hectares), 104 km south of Tennant Creek, is
situated on both sides of the Track. These magnificent, precariously balanced granite boulders,
spread across a wide shallow valley, were created from a single granite mass (similar to the
Devils Pebbles). The Warumungu Aborigines
believe the marbles are eggs that were laid by the
Rainbow Serpent. Sunrise and sunset are the
optimal visiting times to this Stonehenge-esque
region. A short walking trail has signposts ex-
plaining the marbles' origins. Camping is allowed.
For information, phone (08) 8951-8211.

Wauchope, 113 km south of Tennant Creek,
is a 1938 characteristic bush pub, full of tall
tales and imaginative stories. A one-time post office and store, Wauchope offers inexpensive
rooms, campsites, and roadhouse facilities. For
information, phone (08) 8964-1963.

Wycliffe Well (tel. 08-8964-1966), 18 km
south of Wauchope, is another roadhouse rest,
boasting one of Australia's largest selections of
foreign beers.

The oldest roadhouse on the Track is **Barrow
Creek** (tel. 08-8956-9753), another 88 km south.
Its widely known "bush bank" is a wall covered
with all types of notes and currency, signed by
patrons to ensure they'll never go broke. (No
withdrawal has ever made it beyond the bar.)
This combination pub, art gallery, museum, and
community center is definitely one spot where
you'll meet some "real locals."

Barrow Creek was not always the site of jovial
goings-on: in 1874 the old telegraph repeater
station was attacked by local Aborigines, resulting in the deaths of the stationmaster and
linesman (graves nearby the pub), as well as
a number of Aborigines. Inexpensive accommodations, campsites, a restaurant, takeaway,
tourist information, six-hole golf course, petrol,
camping gas, and other necessary services are
provided.

Ti Tree, 76 km from Barrow Creek, serves
both the tourist sector and the surrounding Aboriginal community with a range of facilities including **Ti Tree Roadhouse** (tel. 08-8956-9741)
and the adjacent **Aaki Gallery,** which sells locally produced arts and crafts.

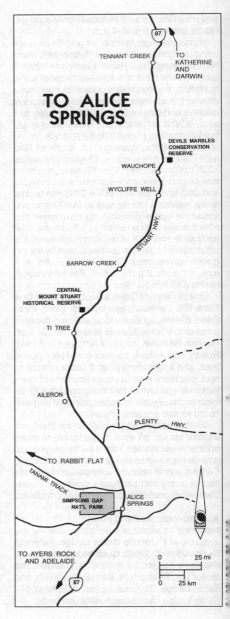

Last roadhouse stop before Alice Springs is **Aileron** (tel. 08-8956-9703), which provides the necessary services.

Another 65 km farther, the Track meets the **Plenty Highway,** a part sealed, part gravel, and part dirt track to the Queensland border and Mt. Isa. The first portion of the Plenty is a popular fossicking area. The **Sandover Highway** links up to the Plenty 27 km off the Track, heading farther north through Aboriginal land to a dirt track that eventually connects to the Barkly Highway.

The **Tanami Track** turnoff, 48 km past the Plenty Highway junction, travels 604 km northwest to Rabbit Flat in the Tanami Desert, near the Western Australia border. Fascinating plant and wildlife inhabit this region, but most of it sits on Aboriginal lands. Check with the Central Australian Tourism Industry Association in Alice Springs regarding necessary permits and other preparation, including good maps. The Tanami Track, with only about the first 100 km sealed, is suitable only for 4WD vehicles.

ALICE SPRINGS

Welcome to Alice (the Alice, as it's also known), the Red Centre of Australia. The thought can send chills up the straightest spine even in the most brain-meltdown heat. But, if you're thinking of the frontiersy Outback depicted in Neville Shute's slap-on-the-back novel *A Town Like Alice,* you'll be disappointed. However, the Alice isn't so bad, and, enclosed as it is within the MacDonnell Ranges, the surrounding area is downright astonishing. Just keep in mind that this is no longer an Outback town but a convenient tourist center for exploring the real Outback.

History

Originally "a town called Stuart" (after explorer John Stuart) and site of an important 1871 telegraph station built alongside normally dry Todd River (after telegraph superintendent Charles Todd) and its permanent spring (named Alice, after Todd's wife). When the repeater station was shifted into town in 1933, Stuart was renamed "Alice Springs." The town's growth was slow-going, particularly as supplies were delivered only once yearly by Afghan camel teams. Though the railway arrived in 1929, the European population was only about 250. Cattle and mining industries, as well as establishment of a government seat from 1926-31, still barely doubled Alice's population.

It was war and the WW II Darwin bombing that created a comparable population explosion. As a major military base, postwar rumors about the area's attributes were leaked, creating tourist interest and subsequent development. Presently the Alice Springs area is home to ap-

proximately 20,000 inhabitants. Besides being a service center to the neighboring Aboriginal and pastoral communities, and its obvious importance as a tourist base, nearby Pine Gap is home to a major (and controversial) hush-hush U.S. communications base.

A WALKING TOUR

Alice proper is easily explored on foot. The city center (including most accommodations and restaurants) is bordered by the Track (Stuart Highway) on one side, the Todd River (creekbed) on the other, Anzac Hill on the north, and Stuart Terrace on the south—about a five-square-block grid. Todd Street and its pedestrian mall between Wills and Gregory terraces is the main shopping street and site of the general post office. The bus terminal and Central Australian Tourism Industry Association are nearby.

Old Telegraph Station

The original settlement site is now a 570-hectare historical reserve, featuring *the* Alice spring (you can swim in it), a small museum, several restored buildings, a walking trail to Trig Hill Lookout, picnic areas, and a wildlife enclosure. The reserve is an easy walk from town center along the path on the western edge of the Todd River bank. Hours are daily 8 a.m.-9 p.m. Oct.-April, 8 a.m.-7 p.m. May-September. Free ranger-guided tours are given Sunday 10 a.m., but book ahead. Admission is $2.50. For information, phone (08) 8950-8211.

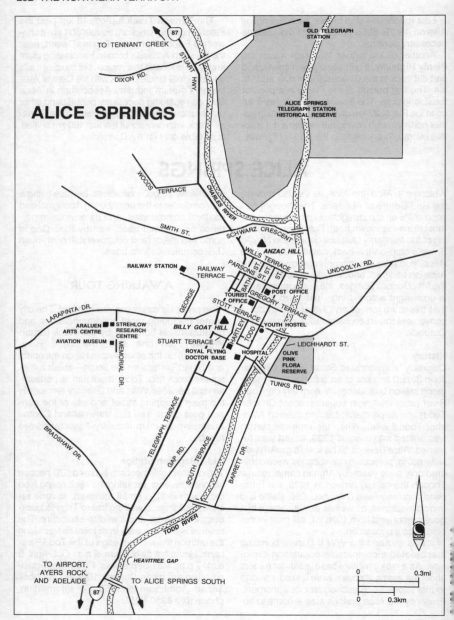

ALICE SPRINGS

TO TENNANT CREEK

STUART HWY.

DIXON RD.

OLD TELEGRAPH STATION

ALICE SPRINGS TELEGRAPH STATION HISTORICAL RESERVE

WOODS TERRACE

CHARLES RIVER

SMITH ST.

SCHWARZ CRESCENT

ANZAC HILL

WILLS TERRACE

UNDOOLYA RD.

RAILWAY STATION

RAILWAY TERRACE

PARSONS ST.

BATH ST.

TODD ST.

HARTLEY ST.

POST OFFICE

TOURIST OFFICE

GREGORY TERRACE

LARAPINTA DR.

GEORGE

STOTT TERRACE

BILLY GOAT HILL

YOUTH HOSTEL

ARALUEN ARTS CENTRE

STREHLOW RESEARCH CENTRE

AVIATION MUSEUM

MEMORIAL DR.

STUART TERRACE

LEICHHARDT ST.

ROYAL FLYING DOCTOR BASE

HARTLEY

TODD

HOSPITAL

OLIVE PINK FLORA RESERVE

TUNKS RD.

BRADSHAW DR.

TELEGRAPH TERRACE

GAP RD.

SOUTH TERRACE

BARRETT DR.

TODD RIVER

TO AIRPORT, AYERS ROCK, AND ADELAIDE

HEAVITREE GAP

TO ALICE SPRINGS SOUTH

87

0   0.3mi

0   0.3km

MOON

Anzac Hill

Just north of the town center, Anzac Hill provides superb views of Alice and the surrounding ranges. Sunset and sunrise are the best viewing times. Walk up via "Lions" walk opposite the Catholic church on Wills Terrace.

Spencer and Gillen Museum

On Todd Mall, at the corner of Parsons St., this museum of central Australia features natural history, Aboriginal culture, and early pioneering displays relating to the local region. Hours are Mon.-Fri. 9 a.m.-5 p.m., Sat.-Sun. 10 a.m.-5 p.m. Admission is $2. For information, phone (08) 8951-5335.

Adelaide House

On the mall, across Parsons St., Adelaide House operated 1920-26 as the first Alice Springs Hospital, later became a convalescent home, and in 1980 was declared a museum. Established by Reverend John Flynn (founder of the Royal Flying Doctor Service) and his Australian Inland Mission, the stone radio hut behind the building marks the spot where Traeger and Flynn sent their first field transmission in 1926, prompting the invention of Traeger's Pedal Radio, which Flynn used for Outback communication in his Flying Doctor service. The **Flynn Memorial Church,** next door, was built to honor the good doctor. Hours are Mon.-Fri. 10 a.m.-4 p.m., Sat.-Sun. 10 a.m.-noon, March-November. Admission $2.50. For information, phone (08) 8952-1856.

Old Government Homes

On Hartley St., between Stott and Stuart Terraces, these dwellings built for government officers in the 1930s were constructed of concrete blocks, timber, fly-wire verandas, and other architectural details indicative of that period. Hours are Mon.-Fri. 10 a.m.-4 p.m. For information, phone (08) 8952-6955.

Royal Flying Doctor Base

Straight ahead, across Stuart Terrace, this medical facility and lifeline to Outback residents offers educational tours including an informative film, displays, memorabilia, and a gift shop. Hours are Mon.-Sat. 9 a.m.-4 p.m., Sunday 1-4 p.m. Tours are given every half hour. Admission $2.50. For information, phone (08) 8952-1129.

Olive Pink Flora Reserve

Behind the Flying Doctor Base, near the hospital, follow Tunks Rd. across the Todd River causeway to see this excellent collection of central Australian native plants. Founded by Olive Pink, who lived with the local Aborigines, this arid-zone botanical reserve also features a visitor center and several short walking trails. Hours are daily 10 a.m.-6 p.m. For information, phone (08) 8952-2154.

Billy Goat Hill

Back across Stuart Terrace (and the other side of the Royal Flying Doctor Base), Billy Goat Hill was an early goatherding location with goat yards built around its base and Aboriginal shepherds leading their flocks to wells near the present expanse of lawns.

Panorama Guth

Heading back toward town, on Hartley, Panorama Guth is a 360-degree realistic landscape painting of the Centre created by Dutch artist Henk Guth. Viewers can check out the scene from an elevated platform. But wouldn't you rather see the real thing? An art gallery exhibits a range of works by Hermannsburg School watercolorists. Hours are Mon.-Sat. 9 a.m.-5 p.m., Sunday 2-5 p.m., closed Sunday and public holidays Dec.-February. Admission $3. For information, phone (08) 8952-2013.

Hartley Street School

Farther up the street, across Gregory Terrace, the first government school opened in 1929. Architectural contrasts between the original building and later octagonal addition depict typical Alice Springs '20s and '40s styles. The building houses the National Trust office. Hours are Mon.-Fri. 10:30 a.m.-1 p.m., closed public holidays. For information, phone (08) 8952-4516.

The Residency

On the other side of the post office, this 1927 stone structure, built for John Charles Cawood, Alice's first government resident, now serves as a museum with Territory history, Aboriginal art, and meteorite exhibits. Hours are Mon.-Fri. 9 a.m.-4 p.m., Sat.-Sun. 10 a.m.-4 p.m. For information, phone (08) 8951-5335.

Old Stuart Gaol

Across Hartley St., on Parsons St., the old gaol was built in 1907-08 and is the oldest building in Alice, having housed offenders from horse thieves to railway stowaways until its closure in 1938. Hours are Tuesday and Thursday 10 a.m.-12:30 p.m., Saturday 9:30 a.m.-noon. Admission is $2.

Old Court House

Across Parsons St. diagonally from the jail, this courthouse served as Administrator's Council Rooms 1926-31, and operated as Alice Spring's primary court until 1980, when a new facility was constructed. Viewing is from the outside only.

Railway Terrace

Continue along Parsons St. to Railway Terrace. Toward your right, three 1920s concrete-brick **railway cottages** can be seen. Turn to the left to see the **Wild Dog** (Gnoilya Tmerga) sacred site, which depicts an Aboriginal legend about a great white Dog Man.

LARAPINTA DRIVE SIGHTS

Across the railway tracks from Billy Goat Hill, Stott Terrace becomes Larapinta Drive, a winding road with several additional attractions.

Pay your respects to some of the early pioneers at **Pioneer Cemetery,** the original Stuart Town graveyard on George Crescent, off Larapinta Drive.

The **Aviation Museum,** on Memorial Dr., just off Larapinta, is housed inside the former Connellan Hanger, site of Alice's first airport. Besides the predictable early aviation memorabilia, exhibits include a couple of (previously) missing aircraft and a road train. Open Mon.-Fri. 9 a.m.-4 p.m., Sat.-Sun. 10 a.m.-2 p.m. Free admission.

Next to the Aviation Museum, also on Memorial Dr., **Memorial Cemetery** contains a few more interesting graves—most notably those of Aboriginal artist Albert Namatjira and Harold Bell Lasseter. (Lasseter was the fellow who claimed to have found a gold reef near Docker River on the Northern Territory/Western Australia border. The resulting hoopla was astounding and has continued from the 1930s to the present day, with the gold reef being lost, found, and lost

again, many times over. Lasseter's reef may be folly, but his grave is well marked.)

Back on Larapinta Drive, you'll find the multi-million-dollar **Strehlow Research Centre,** opened in 1992 to commemorate the work of anthropolgist Theodor Strehlow. Professor Strehlow devoted much of his life to studying the Aranda traditional people, ultimately being honored with the designation *ingkata,* or ceremonial chief. Much of the hands-on collection is hands-off due to its religious significance, but the public exhibits are still quite informative, giving a unique glimpse into the Aranda people's lifestyle and belief system. Hours are daily 10 a.m.-5 p.m. Admission is $4. For information, phone (08) 8952-8000.

Next door, **Araluen Arts Centre** houses two art galleries (one with paintings by noted Aboriginal artist Albert Namatjira), a craft center, restaurant, and bar, and presents a variety of performances. Hours are Mon.-Fri. 9 a.m.-4 p.m., Sat.-Sun. 10-4 p.m. Admission is $2.50. For information, phone (08) 8952-5022.

Beyond the arts center, **Diorama Village** features gaudy displays of Aboriginal Dreamtime legends. Hours are daily 10 a.m.-5 p.m. Admission is $2. For information, phone (08) 8952-1884.

SOUTH ALICE SIGHTS

Yet another group of sights is clustered around the Stuart Highway, on Old South and Emily Gap Roads, south of the town center.

Pitchi Ritchi Aboriginal Experience

This open-air museum, south of the Heavitree Gap causeway, showcases a large collection of vintage machinery and other early relics, as well as Aboriginal sculptures by noted Victorian artist William Ricketts (most of Ricketts's work is in his sanctuary, outside Melbourne). A kiosk on the premises sells souvenirs. Hours are daily 9 a.m.-2 p.m., and guided tours by local Aborigines are available. Admission $8. For information, phone (08) 8952-1931.

Stuart Auto Museum

See restored vintage cars and motorcycles, as well as old phonographs, telephones, steam engines, and exhibits relating to Territorial motoring history (including the saga of the first car to cross the Territory back in 1907). A restaurant serves light meals and refreshments. Hours are daily 9 a.m.-5 p.m. Admission $3.

Mecca Date Gardens

Australia's only commercial date farm features more than 20 different varieties of this ancient tree crop, introduced to the area by the Afghan camel drivers. Dates are available for purchase, and tours are given regularly. Hours are Mon.-Sat. 9 a.m.-5 p.m., Sunday 10 a.m.-4 p.m. April-October. For information, phone (08) 8952-2425.

Frontier Camel Farm

This strange site includes a camel museum, camel rides and tours, and a big reptile house filled with goannas, lizards, and desert snakes. The staff offers informal talks. Hours are daily 9 a.m.-5 p.m., camel rides at 10:30 a.m. and 2 p.m., closed Christmas Day to New Year's Day. Admission is $8, $5 without the camel ride. For information, phone (08) 8953-0444.

Old Timer's Folk Museum

If you haven't had enough pioneering-day reminders, then stop in, pay a buck, and get another fix. Hours are daily 2-4 p.m., except summer months. For information, phone (08) 8952-2844.

Ghan Preservation/MacDonnell Siding

Okay, now we're talking *my* fix—trains. Come join other railway aficionados at this MacDonnell Siding site (built to original design specs), with restored and preserved classic 1929 Ghan locomotives and carriages along a 26-km stretch of the old train track. The Old Ghan, named for the Afghan camel drivers, operated between Alice and Adelaide for 51 years, until it was replaced by the New Ghan in 1980. Open daily 9 a.m.-5 p.m. April-Oct., 10 a.m.-4 p.m. Nov.-March. Admission is $3. Guided train journeys are $15; in July, night tours, including dinner, cost $50. Daily one-way journeys are also offered, with return by coach. For information, phone (08) 8955-5047.

Chateau Hornsby Winery

Take the Colonel Rose Dr. turnoff from Stuart Highway, then hang a left at Petrick Rd., to visit central Australia's only winery, where you can sip and taste shiraz, cabernet sauvignon, riesling, semillon, and chardonnay. A restaurant is open for lunch (with wine, of course). Hours are daily 9 a.m.-5 p.m., closed Christmas Day. For information, phone (08) 8955-5133.

Next to the winery, a commercial carnation farm offers sales and tours on weekdays.

ACCOMMODATIONS

Most Alice accommodations are conveniently located smack-dab in the center of town, while campsites and caravan parks are scattered around the fringes. If possible, book ahead—especially at the most and least expensive places. Rates are usually somewhat lower during the hotter-than-hell summer months.

Inexpensive (Under $35)

The **Todd Tavern,** on Todd Mall (tel. 08-8952-1255), features simple accommodations with shared facilities and continental breakfast, but beware the noise from live bands playing in the pub most weekends. **Desert Rose Inn,** 15 Railway Terrace (tel. 08-8952-1411), has an inexpensive hotel section and a pricier motel with pool and spa. **Alice Lodge,** 4 Mueller St. (tel. 08-8953-1975), is a small seven-room establishment with weekly rates and a four-bed dorm. Facilities include a communal kitchen and laundry, plus pool and barbecue area.

Moderate ($35-70)

Alice Sundown Motel, 39 Gap Rd. (tel. 08-8952-8422), features modern rooms with TVs, pool, barbecue area, and courtesy coach. One of Alice's best values is **Desert Palms Resort,** Barrett Dr. (tel. 08-8952-5977), with large rooms, cooking facilities, pool, and half-court tennis. For longer stays, **Alice Tourist Apartments,** corner Gap Rd. and Gnoilya St. (tel. 08-8952-2788), is also a good value, with a variety of rooms particularly well suited to groups of travelers who pool their resources. Pool, laundry, cooking, and barbecue facilities are available.

Outback Motor Lodge, South Terrace (tel. 08-8952-3888), offers clean, simple rooms with kitchen facilities as well as a pool and barbecue area. A pool and fully equipped, self-contained units with TVs are available at **The Swagmans Rest,** 67 Gap Rd. (tel. 08-8953-1333). A good choice near Alice South attractions is **Sienna Apartments,** corner Palm Circuit and Ross Hwy. (tel. 08-8952-7655). TVs, pool, and cooking facilities are included.

Expensive ($70 and Up)

The top choice for big budgets is **Plaza Hotel,** Barrett Dr., about 1.5 km from town (tel. 08-8952-8000). This 243-room property with pastel decor and manicured grounds offers all the luxury comforts including TVs, videos, room service, pool, spa, sauna, tennis court, health club, restaurants, bars, live entertainment, and boutiques. **Vista Alice Springs,** Stephens Rd. (tel. 08-8952-6100), is about twice as far from town as the Plaza Hotel, half the size, but not quite half the price. Amenities include a pool, tennis court, rental bicycles, gift shop, restaurant, and bar. **Lasseter's Hotel Casino,** 93 Barrett Dr. (tel. 08-8952-5066), reopened after a long hiatus, offers well-appointed rooms, tennis, pool, nightclub, and, of course, the casino.

Hostels

Backpackers will find plenty of options in Alice. Dorm beds average $10-14 per night and should be booked ahead during peak holiday periods. The **Pioneer YHA Hostel,** corner Parsons St. and Leichhardt Terrace (tel. 08-8952-8855), is a busy, centrally located operation, housed inside an old outdoor movie theater. Facilities include air-conditioned rooms, communal kitchen, recreation room, a laundry and small food store. Travelers here will pick up all sorts of helpful information on the local scene.

Melanka Lodge, 94 Todd St. (tel. 1800-81-5066 toll-free), is another popular choice, offering a variety of accommodations from backpackers' and dorm beds to guesthouse and motel rooms. **Toddy's Resort,** 41 Gap Rd. (tel. 08-8952-1322), also has a wide range of accommodations consisting of dorms, a bunkhouse, cabins, and double rooms with or without private baths.

The **YWCA Stuart Lodge,** Stuart Terrace (tel. 08-8952-1894), accepts both men and women, though many of the 31 rooms are occupied by permanent guests.

Dorm and bunkhouse beds are also available at **Gapview Resort Hotel,** corner Gap Rd.

and South Terrace (tel. 08-8952-6611), with a pool, tennis courts, bar, and restaurant.

Camping

All of the following parks allow caravan and tent camping, and many rent on-site vans as well: **G'day Mate Tourist Park,** Palm Circuit (tel. 08-8952-9589), near South Alice sights; **Greenleaves Tourist Park,** Burke St. (tel. 08-8952-8645), two km northwest of Todd River causeway; **Stuart Caravan Park,** Larapinta Dr. (tel. 08-8952-2547), near the arts center; **Wintersun Gardens Caravan Park,** Stuart Hwy. (tel. 08-8952-4080), two km north of the post office; **Carmichael Tourist Park,** Tmara Mara St., off Larapinta Dr. (tel 08-8952-1200); **Heavitree Gap Caravan Park,** Emily Gap Rd. (tel. 08-8952-2370), adjacent to the Todd River; **MacDonnell Range Tourist Park,** Palm Pl., off Ross Hwy. (tel. 08-8952-6111), also near Alice South attractions; and **Ross River Homestead,** (tel. 08-8956-9711), at the end of Ross Highway.

FOOD

Foodies who'll die without nouvelle cuisine better steer clear of Alice—'cause steer is exactly what you'll find on most menus, and well-done, shoe leather steer at that. Along with the frozen barramundi and other occasional fish, it's good old meat and taters in mid-Oz—just like it is in middle America. (By the way, that Kentucky Fried Chicken place is at the corner of Todd St. and Stott Terrace.)

Inexpensive

Todd Street Mall is lined with coffee shops and takeaways and most are open seven days a week. **Jolly Swagman,** opposite Flynn Church, is open daily from 5:30 a.m. for breakfast, homemade cakes and dampers, and vegetarian and Asian-style meals. **Thai Kitchen,** off the mall, offers decent Asian food.

The **Fish and Chips** shop, on Lindsay Ave., near the corner of Undoolya Rd., is highly recommended by locals. **Eranova Cafeteria,** 72 Todd St., offers continental-style dining, a diverse selection, and good value. Open Mon.-Sat. for breakfast, lunch, and dinner.

Alice Plaza lunch spots consist of **Fawlty's, Red Centre Chinese,** and **Doctor Lunch;** all cheap and casual. For pub meals, try **Stuart Arms Bistro,** upstairs in the Alice Plaza on Todd Street Mall.

Moderate
Lilli's, at Heavitree Gap Motel, Ross Hwy. (tel. 08-8952-2370), specializes in Australian delicacies (watch out for that witchetty grub sauce). **La Casalinga,** 105 Gregory Terrace, is an Alice favorite for pizza and Italian specialties. Open daily for dinner. **Camel's Crossing,** in Fan Arcade, off Todd Mall (tel. 08-8952-5522), features Mexican and vegetarian dishes. **Swinger's Café,** 71 Gregory Terrace, is a show-off place, but with good pasta and curry.

For Chinese meals, try **Chopsticks,** in Yeperenye Shopping Centre on Hartley St. (tel. 08-8952-3873), **Oriental Gourmet,** 80 Hartley St. (tel. 08-8953-0888), or **Golden Inn,** 9 Undoolya Road. All are open daily.

Expensive
The **Overlanders Steakhouse,** 72 Hartley St. (tel. 08-8952-2159), serves up genuine Aussie tucker, including buffalo, camel, and kangaroo steaks, accompanied by live Australian folk entertainment.

Puccini's, corner Todd Mall and Parsons St. (tel. 08-8953-0935), offers fine Italian cuisine—surprisingly fine, in fact, for the Territory.

Rossini's, in the Diplomat Hotel (tel. 08-8952-8977), is another unique find with its continental cuisine and formal settings.

El Patio, in the Plaza Hotel (tel. 08-8952-8000), and **Kings,** in Lasseter's Hotel Casino (tel. 08-8952-5066), are other good choices.

ENTERTAINMENT AND EVENTS

Cinemas
Films screen regularly at **Araluen Arts Centre,** Larapinta Road. The **Alice Springs Film Society** presents cinema programs at Totem Theatre, Anzac Oval, on the second and fourth Tuesday of each month. For information, phone (08) 8950-2383.

Pubs and Clubs
The pub scene is somewhat limited. The **Todd Tavern,** corner Todd St. and Wills Terrace, features live piano-bar entertainment Thurs.-Sat., disco Thurs.-Sat., Monday night jam sessions, and Sunday night folk concerts. **Stuart Arms Bistro,** Todd Mall, occasionally presents cabarets and live weekend entertainment.

Simpsons Gap Bar, in the Plaza Hotel, a popular hangout for travelers, offers live entertainment every night and a DJ Thurs.-Saturday. Hipper-than-hip **Uncles,** corner of Hartley St. and Gregory Terrace, buzzes every night, but Friday is the big scene. **Alice Junction Tavern** (AJ's), at Heavitree Gap Tourist Resort, off Ross Highway, features disco Fri.-Sat., and **Bojangles Restaurant and Nightclub,** Todd St., also has occasional late-night disco.

Bush Entertainment
Chateau Hornsby Winery presents the long-running **Ted Egan Outback Show,** with tall tales, bush lore, and Outback songs. Performances are three times a week. Cost is $15, about twice that with dinner included. For bookings, phone (08) 8955-5133.

The **Overlanders Steakhouse,** 72 Harley St., features local entertainers nightly, including sing-alongs and bush bands.

Often the big hotels will host a **Bust Tucker Night,** which typically includes campfire meals and storytelling.

Theater and Music
Araluen Arts Centre, Larapinta Dr., is Alice's venue for cinema, musical and theatrical performances, and visual arts. For schedules and ticket information, phone (08) 8952-5022.

Events
Alice hosts a variety of strange and colorful events, usually during the cooler winter months.

The end of April or early May brings the **Camel Cup,** a series of camel roundups and races on the Todd River bed, commemorating the old Afghan camel train days. A **Food and Wine Festival** takes place the day after Camel Cup on the lawns of Verdi Club, Undoolya Road. The **Alice Springs Cup** annual horse race runs practically neck-in-neck with the camels.

The **Bangtail Muster,** held the first Monday in May, once glorified the cutting of horses' tails before they were shipped out, but today it's an excuse for a colorful and satirical parade.

In June, the **Finke Desert Race, Taps, Tubs and Tiles** is a 500-km, two-day endurance race for trail bikes and off-road vehicles.

Rodeo lovers will revel in August's weeklong **Alice Springs Rodeo,** with heaps of events, and cowboys and wanna-bes parading around town in full drag.

The **Henley-on-Todd Regatta,** in late September, is Alice's most famous event: competitors "race" along the dry riverbed in an amazing variety of bottomless boats, racers' legs poking out as they pick up their craft and speed along on foot. The series of peculiar events is followed the next day by the **Annual Beer Festival,** featuring live entertainment, children's activities, food, and many beer stalls.

SPORTS AND RECREATION

Swimming Pools
Almost every hotel and motel has its own pool. Alice Springs Swimming Centre, Speed St. (tel. 08-8952-3757), also has a water slide, trampoline, and aquarobics classes. Open daily, mid-Sept.-April.

Sporting Facilities
Squash: Guests are welcome at Alice Springs Squash Centre, 13 Gap Rd. (tel. 08-8952-1179). Equipment is available for rent.

Tennis: Public courts and private coaching can be hired at Traeger Park, off Traeger Ave. (tel. 08-8952-4320).

Golf: Alice Springs Golf Club, Cromwell Dr. (tel. 08-8952-5440), welcomes visitors.

Gambling: Lasseter's Hotel Casino is the venue for gaming tables and pokeys. A dress code is enforced (decent, not dressy).

Spectator Sports
Australian Rules **football** and **baseball** are played at Traeger Park, Gap Road. **Rugby League** meets at Anzac Oval, and Larapinta Oval, Memorial Dr., is the **softball** venue. The season for most sports is April-September.

Bond Springs Airstrip, North Stuart Hwy. (tel. 08-8952-1417), is the site of weekend **gliding.**

SHOPPING

You've got a humongous Kmart, Woolworth, and a mall—those will take care of most immediate shopping needs. But Alice's big consumer draw, of course, is Aboriginal art. Alice is the place to pick up a didgeridoo or boomerang for that special someone. Distinctive works include Papunya sand paintings, batiks from the local Utopia settlement, as well as a good selection of weavings, carvings, and bark paintings.

Highly recommended outlets are **Jukurrpa Gallery and Artists,** 35 Gap Rd., both a gallery and working studio, and the **Original Dreamtime Gallery,** 63 Todd Mall, with an impressive range of Aboriginal arts and crafts. Other good shops are the **Papunya Tula Artists** shop, Todd St., south of the mall; **Gondwana Gallery,** on the mall; and the **Central Australian Aboriginal Media Association** shop, on Hartley Street.

Opal buyers might enjoy the gems and jewelry at the **Gem Cave,** 85 Todd Street Mall.

Camping supplies can be purchased or rented from **Alice Springs Disposals,** off the mall, on Reg Harris Lane (tel. 08-8952-5701). **Centre Canvas,** 9 Smith St. (tel. 08-8952-2453), manufactures quality swags (bed rolls).

SERVICES

Branches of national **banks** and automatic teller machines are located on Todd Mall, Todd Street, and Parsons Street. Almost all banks will change overseas traveler's checks, usually for $2-3 per transaction.

The **general post office,** Hartley St., is open Mon.-Fri. 9 a.m.-5 p.m. For information, phone (08) 8952-1020.

The **Wash-house Launderette,** corner Stuart Hwy., Parsons St., and Railway Terrace, provides coin-op machines for do-it-yourself washing and ironing, daily 8 a.m.-8 p.m. Almost every hotel, motel, or hostel has laundry facilities.

INFORMATION

The **Central Australian Tourism Industry Association,** corner Hartley St. and Gregory Terrace (tel. 08-8952-5199), dispenses information, maps, and literature, and books tours and accommodations. Hours are Mon.-Fri. 9 a.m.-5 p.m., Sat.-Sun. and public holidays 10 a.m.-3 p.m. For information, phone (08) 8952-5199.

Pick up maps, books, and information on ranger-led tours at the **Conservation Commission of Northern Territory,** either at the desk in the tourism office or at the main office, off the Stuart Hwy., several km south of town. For information, phone (08) 8951-8211.

In emergencies, dial 000, or contact the **police** (tel. 08-8951-8888) or **Alice Springs Hospital,** Gap Rd. (tel. 08-8951-7777). The hospital provides 24-hour emergency service, plus an outpatient walk-in clinic Mon.-Friday.

For details about local driving conditions (including those rough, unpaved "roads"), contact **Road Conditions Information** (tel. 08-8952-3833).

The **public library,** near the corner of Leichhardt and Gregory Terraces, is open Mon.-Fri. 9 a.m.-5:30 p.m., Saturday 9 a.m.-3:30 p.m.

A branch of the **Angus and Robertson** bookshop chain is in the Yeperenye Centre. Other good shops are the **Arunta Gallery,** Todd St., south of the mall, and **Dymocks** in the Alice Plaza.

Stock up on even more maps at the **Automobile Association of the Northern Territory,** Gregory Terrace (tel. 08-8953-1322), or at the **Department of Lands, Housing and Local Government,** also on Gregory Terrace (tel. 08-8951-5743).

Almost every newsagent stocks *The Central Advocate,* Alice's local paper, which comes out on Wednesday and Friday, and many carry a large selection of air-freighted national dailies and mags.

TRANSPORT

Getting There by Air
Alice Springs Airport, 14 km southeast of town center, is served by **Ansett** (tel. 13-1300 toll-free) and **Qantas** (tel. 13-1313 toll-free) with daily scheduled flights from all capital cities. Offices are opposite each other at Todd and Parson Streets. In case you'd like to skip Alice and fly directly to the Rock, direct flights are available from both Sydney and Adelaide.

Alice Springs Airport Shuttle Service (tel. 08-8953-0310) meets all flights and provides transport to the city center for $9. Book ahead for service to the airport. **Taxis** into the city cost about two bucks more. Taxi ranks are located at the airport, or phone **Alice Springs Taxis** (tel. 08-8952-1877).

Left luggage lockers are available at the airport.

Getting There by Bus
Interstate coaches arrive and depart from the terminal on Hartley St., near Wills Terrace. Daily services between Alice, Darwin, and Adelaide are operated by **Greyhound Pioneer Australia** (tel. 13-2030 toll-free) and McCafferty's (tel. 08-212-5066 Adelaide, 08-8952-3952 Alice Springs. You can also pick up a daily connection to the Rock and the Olgas. Fares are approximately $175 from Darwin or Adelaide. Buses change at Three Ways Roadhouse for connections to Queensland, and at Katherine for the route to Western Australia.

Getting There by Train
The **Ghan** does not have quite the same flair and sense of adventure as its famous predecessor, but it's a terrific ride all the same. Half the fun of the original train was the dreadful track, frequent flooding, and the good chance of being stuck in the middle of nowhere and having emergency supplies parachuted in!

These days, darn it, the new track is fairly flood-proof, the train carries twice as many passengers in half the time (20 hours from Adelaide, instead of 50), and probably nothing exciting will happen along the trip. The scenery, however, and the ability to take a shower while choo-chooing through the central Australian desert, make this one of the country's great rail journeys.

Trains depart Adelaide on Monday and Thursday, returning to Adelaide on Tuesday and Fri.; one additional service runs April-January. If you purchase a rail pass, the Ghan journey is included. Otherwise, one-way fares run about $145 economy sitting, $249 holiday-class berth, or $456 first-class berth, with meals included. For information and bookings, phone **Rail Australia** (tel. 13-2232 toll-free).

Getting There by Car, Thumb, Hook, or Crook

Basically it's the straight and narrow Track all the way from Adelaide or Darwin. Be careful hitching; traffic is light. Many hitchikers report long waits at Three Ways. Women should not hitch around the Outback without a male companion. Check the Alice YHA notice board for possible rides.

Getting Around

Other than taxis, Alice has no public transportation. **Alice Springs Taxis** (tel. 08-8952-1877) offers local transport.

Rental cars will cost $30-70 per day, plus insurance and per-km charges; a 4WD will run $85-160 per day, typically including 100 free km per day. Many vehicles cannot be taken outside a 50-km radius of town or on dirt roads without written permission—and extra fees. Read all fine print regarding insurance, as some coverages don't apply when vehicles leave paved roads (why else would you rent a 4WD in the Outback?)

Rental companies include **Avis** (tel. 08-8952-8899), **Brits Rentals** (tel. 08-8952-8814), **Budget** (tel. 08-8952-8899), **Centre Car Rentals** (tel. 08-8952-1405), **Territory Rent-a-Car** (tel. 08-8952-9999), and **Thrifty** (tel. 08-8952-2400).

Most of the above offices are located on or near Todd Mall, and some have airport counters. Also inquire regarding moped, campervan, and motorhome rentals.

Rent **bicycles** (about $12 per day) from just about any of the backpacker hostels.

Tours

As with Darwin, you can choose from a seemingly endless array of organized tours to the

Rock and other Red Centre sites, traveling by air-conditioned coach, 4WD, camel, balloon, or airplane. Call into the Central Australian Tourism Industry Association for advice and bookings, according to your specific interests. The Pioneer YHA also arranges tours.

Rod Steinert offers a variety of outings, including his ever-popular **Dreamtime Tour and Bushtucker Tour,** a half-day excursion that'll give you a taste of Aboriginal culture including bush food preparation, boomerang- and spear-throwing, and a "quickie" Dreamtime explanation. Cost is $45. For information, phone (08) 8955-5000.

Tourists also flock to Alice for camel treks—everything from a quick ride to breakfast and dinner outings (yes, *on* the camel), to treks of several days. The tourist bureau will provide details and bookings, or contact **Frontier Camel Farm** (tel. 08-8953-0444). Or saddle up on a horse with **Trail Rides** (tel. 08-8952-2308). *Or,* saddle up on a Harley with **Harley Davidson Scenic Tours** (tel. 08-8953-4755).

Other good all-around companies include **Trek About** (tel. 08-8953-0714) and **Tracks Outback Expeditions** (tel. 08-8995-30244).

Sunrise **hot-air balloon** rides are particularly mesmerizing over the Red Centre. Costs range $100-150 (including silver service breakfast) and are offered by **Outback Ballooning** (tel. 1800-80-9790 toll-free) and **Ballooning Downunder** (tel. 08-8952-8816).

The **Alice Wanderer** (tel. 08-8953-0310) operates daily, on hourly rounds to most tourist sites in town. For $18, passengers can get on and off the bus at whim. A running commentary explains each point of interest.

Also see the chart "Aboriginal Tours" in the On the Road chapter.

VICINITY OF ALICE

Weathered gorges, rocky walls, and sheer cliffs of the ancient MacDonnell Ranges run east and west of Alice, with many of these scenic and mysterious spots an easy day-trip or overnight away from the town center.

About the same age as Ayers Rock (650 million years old, give or take a few years), the mostly sandstone MacDonnells reach 400 km east to west and 160 km north to south. As babies, the ranges stood more than 3,000 meters above sea level, eroding over the millennia to an average height today of under 500 meters. The rocky crags, crevices, and chasms are variegated with ferrous red, olive, and forest green—made even

more evident by sparse vegetation. In spring, wildflowers provide an even more spectacular sight, while shy wildlife, such as the black-flanked rock wallaby, is a bit more difficult to spot (try early morning or late afternoon). Whichever direction you travel in this majestic and meditative region, you'll end up gorged and centered.

TO THE EAST

Emily and Jessie Gaps
These two gaps, just east of Alice on the Ross Highway, form a 695-hectare nature park noted

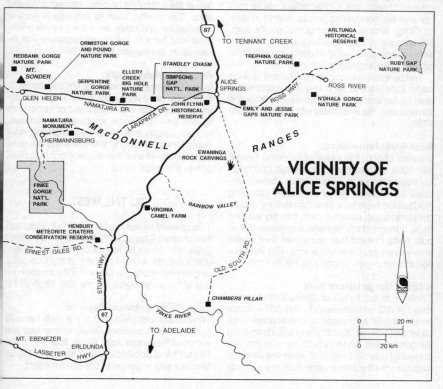

for its scenic river red gums and waterholes. The area was also significant to Aborigines, who have left rock paintings along the eastern face of Emily Gap. The area is popular with picnickers. For information, phone (08) 8952-1013.

Corroboree Rock

Local Aborigines used this limestone rock outcrop, located 46 km east of Alice on the Ross Highway, for both manhood rituals and as a storage area for sacred stones used in Dreamtime storytelling. The seven-hectare conservation reserve features a short walking trail and picnic and barbecue facilities. Camping is allowed. For information, phone (08) 8956-9765.

Trephina Gorge Nature Park

A few km north of the Ross Highway, and 80 km east of Alice, this 1,770-hectare nature park features two contrasting gorges: scenic Trephina Gorge with its tall river gums, gentle pool, and wide sandy creekbed, and, a few kilometers west, shady and secluded John Hayes Rockhole, an area especially rich in birdlife.

The park offers grand campsites and walking tracks (one leads to John Hayes Rockhole); access for conventional vehicles may be limited in some areas. For information, phone (08) 8956-9765.

Ross River Homestead

Situated about 12 km east of Trephina Gorge, this 1898 whitewashed homestead (the original headquarters of Loves Creek Station) features a variety of tourist pleasures including moderate to expensive accommodations, a budget bunkhouse, caravan park, country walking trails, horse and camel rides, a restaurant, and pub. Keep in mind that tour buses love it here also—even so, it's worth a stop. For information and bookings, phone (08) 8956-9711.

N'Dhala Gorge Nature Park

Continue about 10 km southeast of the homestead (4WD is necessary) to this 501-hectare park noted for its thousands of prehistoric rock carvings (at least 35,000 years old) decorating the gorge walls. Mystery fact: Present-day Aborigines have no inkling of what the designs mean or who the artists were! A short trail leads to the engravings. Picnic and barbecue facilities are available and camping is allowed, but you have to bring your own water. For information, phone (08) 8956-9765.

Arltunga Historical Reserve

Set along the eastern edge of the MacDonnells, 44 km northeast of Ross River Homestead, Arltunga preserves the remains of this particularly isolated gold-mining town that was in operation 1887-1912 and held a population only of about 75 people during that period. Ruins within the 5,506-hectare reserve include mine offices, miners' graves, a police station, jail, assayer's residence, the old stamp batter and cyanide works, and many other sites. Walking tracks and picnic facilities are provided within the park. **Arltunga Tourist Park,** referred to as the "loneliest pub in the scrub," has a small campground and shop. The graded track to Arltunga is recommended for 4WD only, as is the 111-km northwest loop back to the Stuart Highway. For information, phone (08) 8956-9770.

Ruby Gap Nature Park

If you're in a 4WD, head 39 km southeast to Ruby Gap (also known as Ruby Gorge), an unusual geological site composed of ribbon-like quartz and limestone strata along glorious, rugged gorges that parallel the winding Hale River. Bush camping is allowed along the river, but take care of your own waste. For information, phone (08) 8956-9770.

TO THE WEST

Two different routes lead to sights in the western MacDonnell Ranges. You start off on Larapinta Drive and, about 54 km out of Alice (past Standley Chasm), either continue along Larapinta or turn onto Namatjira Drive. For information on any of the parks below, phone (08) 8950-8211.

John Flynn Historical Reserve

What historical reserve? It's a half-hectare gravesite on Larapinta Drive, where rest the ashes of Reverend John Flynn, founder of the Royal Flying Doctor Service. One of the Devils Marbles was imported to the site for effect.

Simpsons Gap National Park

Conveniently located only 18 km west of Alice, this is a great spot to get your gap-and-gorge fill if you're short on time, money, or energy. Comprised of purple-tinged mountains, steep ridges, huge white ghost gums, wooded creekbeds, and colonies of rock wallabies, Simpsons Gap (30,950 hectares) is a favorite with tourists. A variety of good walking tracks begin at the excellent visitor center (pick up maps and other literature) and include 20-km unmarked climbing treks, 18-km roundabout bushwalks, and short, easy trails to lookout points. The park has picnic facilities but camping is not allowed.

Standley Chasm

Photographers love to shoot this steep rusty-walled crevice, 50 km west of Alice, especially when the sun provides natural overhead lighting that turns the chasm fireball red. As you can probably imagine, it's not likely you'll be the only one clicking away. A kiosk sells snacks, refreshments, and souvenirs, and picnic facilities are available.

Namatjira Drive

Ellery Creek Big Hole Nature Park (1,766 hectares), 43 km beyond Standley Chasm, is another exquisite gorge with steep red cliffs and a large river-red-gum-shaded waterhole. This is an especially popular location for picnickers and energetic bushwalkers who climb to the ridge tops for majestic views.

Another 11 km west will bring you to narrow, winding **Serpentine Gorge Nature Park** (518 hectares), which is actually two gorges with high rock walls, waterholes, and palmlike cycad vegetation. Picnicking and camping are allowed.

Next stop, 28 km down the road, is **Ormiston Gorge and Pound Nature Park** (4,655 hectares). The dominant two-km-long red cliff, rugged wilderness, permanent waterhole, and towering ghost gum and cypress pine forests have earned Ormiston its reputation as one of the most scenic and colorful gorges in the western MacDonnells. Features include wonderful walking tracks (the seven-km trail through the pound area is reputedly one of the country's finest wilderness treks), a visitor center, and small campground.

Glen Helen Gorge, just one km farther, is a 386-hectare nature park where the Finke River (supposedly the world's oldest, having run this same course for 350 million years) begins its journey through the MacDonnells to the Simpson Desert. An interesting walking track follows along the riverbed. **Glen Helen Lodge,** a restored 1930s homestead, provides a range of accommodations including modern motel-style rooms, campsites, and a YHA-affiliated hostel. Other lodge facilities are a restaurant, bar, bistro, occasional live entertainment, takeaway, and petrol station. For bookings, phone (08) 8956-7489.

Redbank Gorge Nature Park (1,295 hectares) is situated 30 km west of Glen Helen; recommended for 4WD vehicles. Steep slopes with those mighty ghost gums hovering above this remote site provide the scenic beauty. If you intend to jump into one of the deep pools, be forewarned that the walls are slippery and the water is icy cold. Redbank also makes a good base for experienced climbers who wish to scale nearby **Mt. Sonder** (1,380 meters). Picnicking and camping are allowed.

Continuing along Larapinta Drive

The first sight you'll come to, about 100 km from Standley Chasm, is **Namatjira Monument,** which honors Albert Namatjira, one of Australia's most noted Aboriginal artists, famous for his central Australian landscape paintings.

Hermannsburg, another 30-40 km along, is the site of an 1880s mission brought to the Aranda people by Lutheran pastors. Though the Aranda own the mission now, this township still retains links with the Lutheran church. Historic buildings include the original church, Bethlehem church, schoolhouse, and smithy. A museum and tearooms are housed within two of the old residences, and a variety of local Aboriginal art and souvenirs can be purchased. The town also has a petrol station, garage, supermarket, and hardware store.

Finke Gorge National Park (36,000 hectares), 12 km south of Hermannsburg, can be reached only via 4WD vehicle. Within its protected wilderness, the park straddles the southward-bound Finke River and contains large waterholes, bird refuges, sculpted rock formations, more sandstone gorge, and a very comprehensive collection of central Australian plants. The park's most famous attraction, however, is **Palm Valley,** a strange and bizarre

Huh? What are these palms doing in the middle of the Red Centre?

tropical area encompassing approximately 400 plant species, including the red cabbage palm *(Livistona mariae),* found nowhere else in the world. The valley is thought to be a remnant from the days (about 10,000 years ago) when the Centre supported a moister climate. An information and ranger station is near the entrance to Palm Creek. Picnicking and camping are allowed. For information, phone (08) 8951-8211.

TO THE ROCK

Back on the Track and aiming toward Ayers Rock, more fascinating sights await travelers willing to steer off the very well-beaten path. One route will take you along the Old South Road, which parallels the Old Ghan line shortly past the Ross Highway junction; the other is the Kings Canyon turnoff (Ernest Giles Road), a gravel road that cuts into the Track about 145 km south of Alice. (Be careful if driving this road during or after rains—it gets very slippery.) Or you can just keep on the Track all the way to Lasseter Highway (200 km south of Alice) and turn west 241 km to the Rock.

Along Old South Road
Ewaninga Rock Carvings are located within a six-hectare conservation reserve 39 km south of Alice. As with the N'Dhala Gorge site, these prehistoric engravings contain symbols so ancient that not even today's Aborigines can figure them out. Other features here include abundant plants, birds, and wildlife. Visitors are asked to not climb on the boulders.

With a 4WD you can access **Chambers Pillar Historical Reserve,** 104 km south of the carvings. This impressive sandstone pillar rises 58 meters out of the surrounding flat plain, casting a phenomenal glow at sunrise and sunset. Used as a landmark by early explorers, the pillar still bears the evidence of pioneers who scratched their names onto the surface. (Don't *you* do this!)

Still on Track
Virginia Camel Farm, 93 km south of Alice along the Stuart Hwy., is run by breeder Noel Fullerton, founder—and ofttimes winner—of the Camel Cup. Noel runs the outfit that can take you humping through the center on short rides or long safaris. He even arranges packages in which you can take your camel to breakfast, lunch, or dinner. Longer expeditions tour nearby **Rainbow Valley Nature Park** (2,483 hectares), a sublime region of richly colored, broken sandstone gorge. You can camp here on your own, but you'll need to bring a 4WD and your own water. For information about the camel farm and Rainbow Valley tours, check with the tourist bureau or phone (08) 8956-0925. Virginia Camel Farm is open daily 7 a.m.-5 p.m.

Along Ernest Giles Road
About 13 km from the Track (144 km southwest of Alice), follow the signpost to **Henbury Meteorite Craters,** a 16-hectare conservation reserve encompassing 12 separate craters, thought to have been created by a meteor shower 5,000 years ago. The craters range in size from two to 180 meters across, and one is a

whopping 15 meters deep! An easy walking track offers explanatory signs. This is another "look but don't touch" site.

Next stop along this road—and probably a welcome one—is **Wallara Ranch,** about 85 km west of the meteor craters and about halfway to Kings Canyon. This rambling local pub is a winner with tourists who stop to soak up the local atmosphere and stock up on supplies. Facilities include moderately priced motel accommodations, a bunkhouse, campsites, a dining room, takeaway, a swimming pool, petrol station, and day tours of the canyon. For information, phone (08) 8956-2901. From Wallara Ranch, you can take an alternate route 70 km south to the Lasseter Highway or keep going to the canyon, at road's end.

Kings Canyon, often called Australia's Grand Canyon, is a dramatic gorge and escarpment situated 100 km past Wallara Ranch. Now called **Watarrka National Park,** some of the more unusual natural features of this 106,000-hectare area include the **Garden of Eden** palm shelter and the **Lost City,** a strange grouping of weathered outcrops that look like domed houses. A somewhat strenuous walking trail leads to most of the sights, or try the steep climb to the plateau for terrific canyon views. Park facilities include a ranger station and visitor center, plus picnic and camping areas. For information, phone (08) 8956-7460.

Lasseter Highway
You're almost there! **Erldunda Desert Oaks Resort,** at the junction of the Track and Lasseter Highway, offers roadhouse facilities including a range of motel accommodations, a caravan park, campsites, dining room, pub, takeaway, souvenirs, pool, tennis court, petrol station, and tourist information. For information, phone (08) 8956-0984.

Mt. Ebenezer is another roadhouse, 55 km west, owned by the neighboring Imanpa Aboriginal people. Aside from the normal roadhouse features, Mt. Ebenezer also houses a gift shop that displays and sells local artifacts and paintings. For information, phone (08) 8956-2904.

Another 100 km will bring you to the **Curtin Springs** roadhouse, which is also a working cattle station. Founded in 1943, this inn exudes local atmosphere while providing necessary services. For information, phone (08) 8956-2906.

Travel 82 more kilometers west to Yulara, gateway to Ayers Rock and the Olgas.

AYERS ROCK AND THE OLGAS

Uluru National Park (132,566 hectares), by encompassing Ayers Rock and the Olgas, contains one of the world's great natural wonders and one of Australia's top tourist destinations. It is also the heart of Australia—the big red heart.

Uluru National Park encompasses more than 400 plant species, 150 types of birds, and about 25 mammal varieties in a sensitive geological landscape that contrasts drastically from sandy flat plains to those big old rocks. Though Uluru has been returned to its Aboriginal owners, the park was leased to the Australian Nature Conservation Agency and is presently comanaged by that office and the Anangu people.

Blissfully, all the "civilized" trappings are located in **Yulara,** a tourist village built in 1984 specifically to accommodate the hundreds-of-thousands of annual visitors from all over the world. Situated 20 km from the Rock, this complex—a joint government-private sector scheme—features all the comforts any modern-day traveler to a Stone Age site could desire.

Uluru (Ayers Rock)
I would like to be able to spew fluffy prose at you—to say that this incredible rock, of deep spiritual and cultural significance to the Aborigines (who have lived here for at least 10,000 years), is a sacred shrine quite unlike any other. Though that is certainly no lie, it's not the complete truth either; this spectacular monolith is also the site of resorts, facilities, tourist buses, and tourists themselves, decked out in straw sunhats or beer-ad visors and printed T-shirts as they huff and puff their way up the Rock (supporting themselves on the specially installed safety chain). The traditional owners have been pushing, however, to get visitors off their rock and to, perhaps, admire it from a more reverent distance at or around its base.

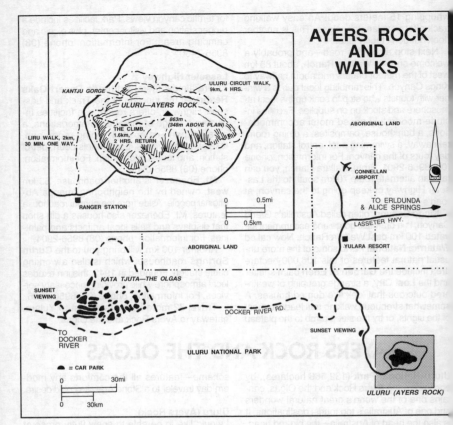

AYERS ROCK AND WALKS

KANTJU GORGE

ULURU—AYERS ROCK

ULURU CIRCUIT WALK, 9km, 4 HRS.

THE CLIMB, 1.6km, 2 HRS. RETURN

863m (348m ABOVE PLAIN)

LIRU WALK, 2km, 30 MIN. ONE WAY.

RANGER STATION

ABORIGINAL LAND

0   0.5mi

0   0.5km

CONNELLAN AIRPORT

TO ERLDUNDA & ALICE SPRINGS

LASSETER HWY.

YULARA RESORT

ABORIGINAL LAND

KATA TJUTA—THE OLGAS

SUNSET VIEWING

DOCKER RIVER RD.

TO DOCKER RIVER

SUNSET VIEWING

ULURU NATIONAL PARK

= CAR PARK

0   30mi

0   30km

ULURU (AYERS ROCK)

Ayers Rock (Uluru, to the Aborigines), no matter who's crawling around it, is a pretty breathtaking sight—a 650-million-year-old sandstone behemoth, rising 348 meters above the pancakelike surrounding plain (and it's supposed to be about twice as big *beneath* the surface!). Its dimensions are indeed impressive—8.8 km around the base, 3.6 km long, and 2.4 km wide—but Uluru's most awe-inspiring feature is the ecstatic glow and haunting colors it exudes at different times of the day (sunrise and sunset are best).

The Rock also features weathered gullies, eerie caves, and Aboriginal carvings and paintings (some 10,000 years old). The public is not permitted access to some declared sacred sites.

If you want to climb The Rock, you are supposed to be in excellent physical condition (a real chuckle once you check out some of the climbers). Also be aware that the higher slopes are often hit by gale-force winds (climbers have died while trying to retrieve a Foster's visor). Check with the park rangers for necessary equipment. Another option is the three- to four-hour walk around the base, which is fringed with caves, waterholes, and a variety of desert vegetation. Admission is $10.

Ayers Rock Observatory, Napala Dr., in Yulara village, is a perfect place to gaze into the clear and astounding Outback skies. Optical telescopes and binoculars allow viewing of the

mystical Ayers Rock

southern skies and the Aboriginal legends with which they're associated. Hours are nightly 8:30-11:30 p.m. Admission is $15. For information, phone (08) 8921-8170.

The Olgas

The Olgas (Kata Tjuta, or "Many Heads," to the Aborigines) lie about 27 km to the west and are also part of the protected Uluru National Park. These huge rocks, just as old and once much larger than Ayers Rock, are a jumble of more rounded monoliths, separated by gorges, valleys, and chasms. Many visitors enjoy exploring the Olgas more than the Rock because they have more hidden areas to discover and are a bit less intimidating and less touristed.

A favorite attraction is deep, narrow **Olga Gorge,** which runs between 546-meter-high Mt. Olga and slightly shorter Mt. Wulpa. The Olgas' three main **walking trails** are the two-km track from the carpark to Olga Gorge, the four-km route up to **Kata Tjuta Lookout,** and a four-km circular track around the mysterious **Valley of the Winds,** on the north side. Another option for very fit walkers is the two-km track that joins up with the Valley of the Winds track from

Kata Tjuta Lookout. Make sure you carry plenty of water for these excursions. It's also recommended that you check in with the ranger station before exploring the Olgas on your own. Rangers will advise you on accessible areas and necessary equipment.

PRACTICALITIES

Accommodations and Food

The cheapest place you'll find out here is the bunkhouse at **Outback Pioneer Lodge** (tel. 08-8956-2170). Two dorms, each with 40 beds, run

---

CLIMBING THE ROCK AND THE OLGAS

Uluru is extremely steep and the climb should not be attempted by any person with a heart condition, high blood pressure, angina, asthma, fear of heights, vertigo, or dizziness. Additionally, strong winds at the top can send both hikers and their possessions aflight. The top of the Rock can be very dangerous, with surfaces prone to sudden collapse into deep ravines. Hikers should be absolutely certain to carry adequate drinking water at all times. A hat, sunblock, and good walking shoes or boots are essential. Don't attempt a climb whenever the temperature is above 38° C. The best month is July, the worst is January.

For the Olgas (Kata Tjuta), most of the above rules apply, plus be sure to check in with a park ranger before starting out—particularly on that Olga Gorge Track.

$18 per person. "Budget" cabins are already in the expensive range, as are rooms with small kitchenettes—and shared facilities—at **Spinifex Lodge** (tel. 08-8956-2131). If you're not bothered by room rates almost as high as the Rock, your choices are **Sails in the Desert** (tel. 08-8956-2200) or the **Desert Gardens Hotel** (tel. 08-8956-2100). All the luxuries come with the price tag (in the $200-250 bracket).

Ayers Rock Campground (tel. 08-8956-2055) has campsites and on-site vans, plus a pool. Camping is not allowed anywhere within Uluru National Park.

Both the Sails in the Desert and Desert Gardens offer dining options from snack bars to upscale restaurants. **Ernest Giles Tavern** features both counter and bistro meals. **Outback Pioneer Hotel** has simple fare and takeaways. A **kiosk** at the campground sells a variety of foodstuffs, but there's a better selection at the **supermarket** in the shopping square. **Yulara Coffee Shop** is open daily for snacks, light meals, and takeaways.

Shopping
The **shopping square complex** has a newsagent, supermarket, T-shirt shop, travel agency, and photo processor. Pick up Aboriginal handicrafts and paintings at the **Maruka Arts and Crafts Centre** (owned by the Anangu people), and souvenirs at the **Ininti Store, Ranger Station,** or at the hotel gift shop/galleries. **Mulgara Gallery,** in Sails in the Desert Hotel, features high-quality (and high-priced) arts, crafts, and jewelry.

Services and Information
A **bank, post office, police,** and **fire station** are located in Yulara Village.

The **Visitors Centre,** on Yulara Drive, features informative displays on the area's history, geography, flora, and fauna, and also presents regular slide shows. A variety of literature is available, including walking maps, visitor's guides, and *The Yulara Experience* newsletter. Open daily 8 a.m.-9 p.m. For information, phone (08) 8956-2240.

The **ranger station,** at the Rock, also dispenses maps, information, and helpful advice. For information, phone (08) 8956-2299.

A **medical clinic** at the Royal Flying Doctor base, near the police station (tel. 08-8956-2286), is open Mon.-Fri. 9 a.m.-noon and 2-5 p.m., Sat.-Sun. 10-11 a.m.

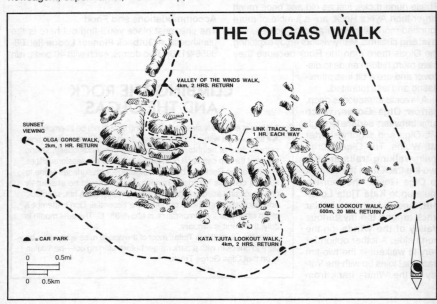

THE OLGAS WALK

VALLEY OF THE WINDS WALK,
4km, 2 HRS. RETURN

SUNSET VIEWING

OLGA GORGE WALK,
2km, 1 HR. RETURN

LINK TRACK, 2km,
1 HR. EACH WAY

DOME LOOKOUT WALK,
600m, 20 MIN. RETURN

= CAR PARK

KATA TJUTA LOOKOUT WALK,
4km, 2 HRS. RETURN

0   0.5mi

0   0.5km

In emergencies, dial 000, or contact the **police** (tel. 08-8956-2166) or **ambulance** (tel. 08-8956-2286). An emergency alarm is located at the base of the Rock.

TRANSPORT

Getting There
Yulara's Connellan Airport, six km north of the village, is served by **Ansett** (tel. 13-1300 toll-free), **Qantas** (tel. 13-1313), and **Kendell Airlines** (tel. 069-22-0100). Direct flights are available from Adelaide, Alice Springs, Cairns, Sydney, and Perth.

AAT Kings (tel. 08-8956-2171) operates shuttle coaches between the airport and the village for $9. Taxi service, at about the same fare, is available from **Sunworth Taxi Service** (tel. 08-8956-2152).

Greyhound Pioneer Australia (tel. 13-2030 toll-free) operates daily service between Alice Springs and Ayers Rock (450 km). Roundtrip day tours cost about $150, and a one-way bus ticket costs around half that. Many agencies offer all-inclusive packages, which include transportation, lodging, and sightseeing.

Holders of bus passes should book ahead as coaches fill up quickly.

Getting Around
It can cost big bucks to rent a car in Yulara—maybe $75-100 per day, including the "remote surcharge." Rental companies include **Avis** (tel. 08-8956-2266), **Budget** (tel. 08-8956-2121), and **Territory Rent-a-Car** (tel. 08-8956-2030). **Sunworth Taxi Service** (tel. 08-8956-2152) also provides service to the Rock.

Spinifex Lodge (tel. 08-8956-2131) rents bicycles (including safety helmet) for $18 per day and mopeds for $30 per half-day. Current identification and a $50-100 deposit are required.

If you're planning to head out to the Olgas, the road is *miserable!*

Organized Tours
Zillions are available but some of the best are the **ranger-conducted** tours, organized by both the Australian Nature Conservation Agency and the Conservation Commission—and some of these are free. The two-hour **Liru Walk** led by Aboriginal rangers offers a traditional perspective of the land (Tuesday, Thursday, and Saturday 8:30 a.m. summer, 9:30 a.m. winter). See and learn about local flowers and plants with a knowledgeable botanist on the 90-minute **Botanical Tour** (Sunday, Wednesday, and Friday, 3 p.m.), or take a 90-minute **Mala Walk,** starting from the climb's base, for an introduction to Arangu culture (daily 10 a.m.). Book all of these tours well in advance. For information, contact the Visitors Centre (tel. 08-8956-2240).

Uluru Experience (tel. 1800-80-3174 toll-free) offers interesting and informative tours led by geologists, biologists, and other knowledgeable guides. The **Aboriginal Desert Culture Tour** focuses on bush foods and medicines ($45); the **Uluru Walk** emphasizes the environment, geology, cave paintings, as well as Aboriginal culture ($55, including breakfast).

Flightseeing over the Rock and the Olgas is organized by **Skyport** (tel. 08-8995-62093) and **RockAyer** (tel. 08-8956-2345). Cost is $75-120 per person for the almost-two-hour flight. **Helicopter rides** cost about the same but only last 15 minutes.

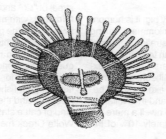

WESTERN AUSTRALIA

INTRODUCTION

Western Australia is the country's "sexy" state—a land of rising pinnacles and deep cuts that come in all shapes and sizes; the fabulous sea with its ebb and flow of wave upon endless wave; the veritable orgy of this state's famous wildflowers, blossoming from well-pollinated pouches of fertile seeds. Fact is, W.A. (as the Aussies call it) is not mere organic lust, but the makings for some down-and-dirty wanderlust.

THE LAND

Western Australia is not merely big, it is humongous. Its 2.5 million square kilometers, taking up about one-third of the Australian continent and boasting an area more than triple the size of little ol' Texas, comprise the harsh, desolate expanses of the Great Sandy, Gibson, and Great Victoria Deserts, sandwiched like dry toast between the Kimberley Plateau and the Nullarbor Plain. Yet within all this space dwell a mere 1.5 million inhabitants (approximately 10% of the

country's total population), most of them in or around Perth, the relaxed and youthful state capital, or along the southwest coastal sections.

Western Australia is divided into eight regions: the **South Coast,** famed for its wineries, beach resorts, and surfer and sailor havens; the **Southwest** (or Great Southern), boasting more swimming, surfing, and wave-pounded coastlines, as well as forests, wildflowers, coves, and capes; the **Wheatlands,** notable not only for the obvious grain and wheat fields, but for its unusual rock formations; the **Goldfields,** with its street of "sin" and "pound their chest" miners; the **Midwest,** with more wildflowers, coastal hideaways, and the port city of Geraldton; the **Gascoyne,** with sights ranging from tame dolphins at Monkey Mia to relatively unknown Mount Augustus, the world's largest monocline; the **Pilbara,** famed for rich iron ore mines, stunning landscapes, fishing villages, and big-ship Port Hedland; and the remote **Kimberley,** a rugged land of cattle stations, eyeball-popping gorges, Wolfe Creek meteorite crater, the beehive-ish

Bungle Bungle Ranges, and the old pearling port of Broome with its mini-Chinatown and maxi-dinosaur footprints.

It probably goes without saying that distances between Western Australia's sights and cities are vast and not always easily accessible, so plan your itinerary and your timetable carefully. However, it is this very remoteness and the consequent self-reliance of which Western Australians—particularly the residents of Perth—are so proud. Chances are, unless you are a surfer or a sailor, you didn't even know Western Australia existed until the Americans won back the America's Cup at Fremantle in 1987. The U.S. recaptured the cup, but W.A. managed to keep luring visitors not just to the site of the "victory" in Fremantle but also up the coast, down the coast, into the interior, and especially to the Kimberley, where adventurous and pioneering spirits can explore deserts, fertile plains, beehive mounds, and lots of gorges and chasms.

Wildflowers

An astounding 8,000 species of wildflowers burst from Western Australia's soil, many of them in and around Perth, from Kalbarri on the Midwest coast to Albany in the Southwest, and interspersed throughout the Wheatlands. The "season" runs from early August into early November, following the rainy months of May, June, and July. Some of the more extraordinary flora include 150 types of ground orchids (including a fully underground orchid), the largest known mistletoe, grass trees ("blackboys"), several black-flower plants, trigger plants that have neuromuscular-type reflexes, and 80 different types of carnivorous plants.

CLIMATE

Perth reputedly has the best climate of any Australian city—"best" meaning sunny with mild temperatures and low humidity. Summer months (Dec.-Feb.) range from a low 17° C (63° F) to a high of 29° C (84° F). Winter (June-Aug.) sees lows of 9° C (48° F), highs of 18° C (65° F), and about 16.6 cm of rainfall per month.

The northern part of the state is similar in climate to the Northern Territory's Top End, ex-periencing both wet and dry seasons as well as intense heat and humidity. You will be more comfortable traveling this region in the winter months; besides, many areas are closed during the Wet due to impassable roads and other weather-provoked conditions. Winter is also the best time to traverse the state's desert areas. Though nights can be freezing, it still beats the summertime average of 40° C (104° F).

Make sure when you're on those roads less traveled that you check with local police or the Automobile Association for the latest road and weather conditions, and that you and your vehicle are prepared for breakdowns and other emergencies. There will *not* be a McDonald's around the next bend.

HISTORY

In 1616 Dutchman Dirk Hartog and his fellow sailors rowed ashore from their vessel the *Eendracht,* making them the first acknowledged Europeans to land on Western Australia's coast. Between then and 1699 so many Dutchmen, traveling around South Africa on their way to Indonesia, sighted or alighted upon the shores that the region was dubbed "New Holland."

Buccaneer William Dampier landed near Broome in 1688, then again in 1699, but his findings went ignored by the British, who were none too impressed with his description of the area. Though Sydney was settled in 1788, the British showed little interest in extending their boundaries for another 38 years, when two important events took place: Matthew Flinders sailing 'round Australia in 1801 concluded that the east coast and New Holland were one and the same continent; and Britain got wind that the French, who'd been stirring about the local waters, might be planning to colonize. The usual barrage of dispatches, reports, and proposals were bandied about until, in 1826, Major Edmund Lockyer arrived from Sydney with a band of convicts and soldiers to settle a small penal colony at King George Sound (now Albany).

Shortly afterward, Captain James Stirling was dispatched by the governor of New South Wales to check out the Swan River region, already partially surveyed by the French, leading to the settlement of both Perth and Fremantle in 1829.

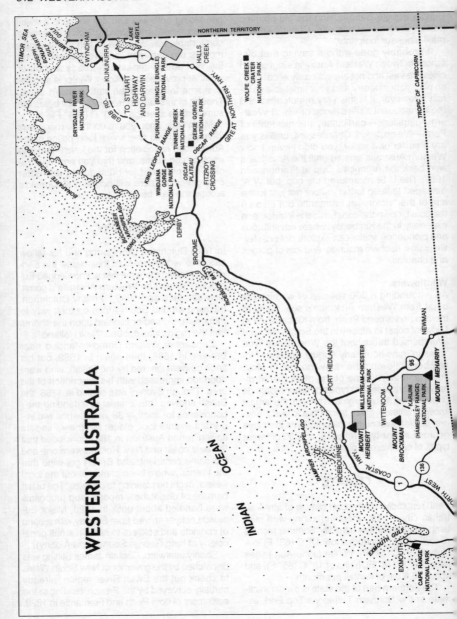

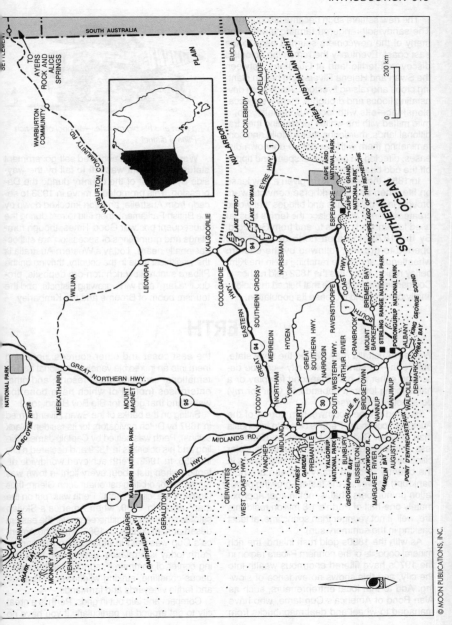

© MOON PUBLICATIONS, INC.

The new settlers soon became discouraged. The sandy soil rendered farming terrible and many of the newcomers scurried back to the east coast. Eventually the remaining colonists discovered fertile land at Guildford, between the Swan and Helena Rivers, and began planting crops and raising livestock. Aside from devastating floods and droughts, there were occasional face-offs with local Aborginals who, a mite miffed with the whites for stealing their traditional lands, murdering their kinfolk, and contaminating them with heretofore unknown diseases, directed an occasional spear and ripped off the odd beast.

In 1850, the settlers were given a new lease on life when those workhorse convicts were brought in to build roads and bridges that would create vital links and replace the ferries thus far used to transport goods to and from Guildford. By the 1870s the area north of Perth was opened to grazing, followed by the eastern wheatlands, and cattle ranching up in the Kimberley region, but it was the 1892 gold rushes at Coolgardie and Kalgoorlie that helped the colony finally prosper and increase its population.

a man and his big monster—symbol of the rich Pilbara district

Western Australia achieved self-government status in 1890 but was left to fall by the wayside by the rest of the country during the Depression. This prompted a move in 1933 to secede from Australia, an effort knocked down by the British Parliament, then laid to rest during the subsequent postwar Good Times, though rumblings and grumblings of secession are still occasionally heard. Today's Western Australia is the wealthiest state in the country, thriving on the Pilbara's incredibly rich iron-ore deposits, productive farm and wine-growing districts, and the tourism boom of Broome and the Kimberley.

PERTH

Western Australia may well be the sexy state, but Perth—its sunny capital city—can be described either as pant-a-second foreplay or a half-snoring lover. It depends on your (or *my*) perspective, of course.

Isolated on the southwestern corner of the Australian continent, Perth is closer to Indonesia than to either Sydney or Melbourne. Nonetheless, this laid-back metropolis outdid its sister cities by once boasting the most millionaires in the country (though many of these are now bankrupt) as well as the fastest-growing population (in numbers, that is, not in age; approximately one-half of Perth's 1.8 million residents are, well, if not younger than springtime, at least basking in the summery sun).

As with the 1890s gold rush inland, the rich mineral deposits of the northern Pilbara region in the 1970s have filtered enormous wealth into the city, and this shows no evidence of slowing. Add to that local entrepreneurs, such as Alan Bond of America's Cup fame, who have managed to wheel and deal megabucks from

the east coast and other sources, parlaying them into an incredible variety of national and international conglomerates, resorts, and other enterprises (not all of which have done too well—and that goes for Big Boy Bond, too.)

Sitting on the banks of the Swan River (named in 1697 by Dutch navigators for its resident black swans), Perth was settled by Captain James Stirling and his colonists in 1829 and declared a city in 1856. In 1962, Perth achieved worldwide attention when just about every light in town was turned on for orbiting astronaut John Glenn, thus tagging it the "city of lights." Perth was "put on the map" again in 1980, when America's Skylab satellite smashed to smithereens over the eastern desert and, of course, in 1987, when the America's Cup was held in neighboring Fremantle. Perth today is a relaxed, beach- and boat-loving center of commerce, surrounded by a gorgeous coastline, striking wildflower meadows, and fertile vineyards and farmlands.

Compact and laid out in grids, Perth is a great city to get around in, particularly if you have no car—it's easy to walk just about anywhere. Both the bus and metropolitan railway stations are on Wellington St. just a few blocks from the city center, as are the general post office and tourist information center. Parallel to Wellington St., heading south, are Murray and Hay Streets, the main shopping district; then comes St. George's Terrace, the major business street. Beyond St. George's Terrace is the Swan River and Barrack Street Jetty (with many of the big high-rise hotels sandwiched in between), and Kings Park sits at the west edge of town. North of the railway tracks is the suburb of Northbridge, home to many of the backpacker hostels, inexpensive ethnic eateries, chic cafes, and the Perth Cultural Centre.

Many books and brochures liken this city to California's San Diego or some place on the Mediterranean—the perfect blend of pant-a-second and half-a-snore.

ST. GEORGE'S TERRACE

This tour of the city's main business thoroughfare—a mix of glitzy modern banks and office buildings interspersed with historic structures—begins on the west side of Victoria Avenue and continues westward to Barracks Archway, then covers the north side of the street returning back to the government buildings.

Perth Concert Hall
Adjacent to Government House, this elaborate space with four foyers and two exhibition halls is the city's premier venue for folk music, orchestra recitals, and other year-round musical performances by both national and international artists. For information, phone (09) 325-9944.

Government House
This Gothic-revival-style residence complete with turrets and arches (a la the Tower of London), built between 1859 and 1864 at a cost of $30,000, still serves as the official home to the governor of Western Australia, as well as to visiting royalty. The public is welcome to visit the surrounding expansive gardens during special celebrations.

Council House
On the other side of Government House, Perth's civic administration center, opened by HRH

Queen Elizabeth in 1963, houses five levels of offices, a circular council chamber, councillors' dining room, a large reception area, and a free public library. Hours are Mon.-Fri. 9 a.m.-4 p.m. (ground floor only). Guided tours are available Mon.-Fri. at 10:30 a.m. and 2:30 p.m. Admission is free. For information, phone (09) 425-3333.

The Supreme Court
Just below Government House, the Supreme Court complex (Francis Burt Law Centre) includes the **Old Court House,** one of the city's oldest surviving colonial buildings (erected in 1836 with a few rear additions made in 1905), with many original details still intact. Presently serving as a legal history museum, the Old Court House includes a replica of an early legal office and related objects. An audiovisual presentation depicts the history of the law and the W.A. legal profession. The surrounding **Supreme Court Gardens,** sheltered by Norfolk Island pines, are a popular brown bag lunch spot for city workers. The **Barrack Street Jetty,** ferry and riverboat departure point, is just beyond the gardens.

The Old Court House hours are Tuesday and Thursday 10 a.m.-2 p.m. Admission is free. For information, phone (09) 325-4787.

Alan Green Conservatory
Continuing west across Barrack St. along the green lawns of the Esplanade, you'll see this pyramid-shaped conservatory, which houses a wide range of exotic tropical and semitropical plants within its controlled environment. Hours are Mon.-Sat. 10 a.m.-4 p.m., Sunday and public holidays noon-4 p.m. Admission is free. For information, phone (09) 425-3333.

R and I Tower
Head north on William St. back to St. George's Terrace. The R and I Tower, at the corner, is home to both the beautifully restored, ornate old **Palace Hotel** (currently used as banking chambers) and Alan Bond's astounding collection of impressionist paintings (which may have been confiscated or sold off by the time you get there). For information, phone (09) 320-6206.

Old Perth Boys' School
Pointing west again, and situated along St. George's Terrace between William and Mill

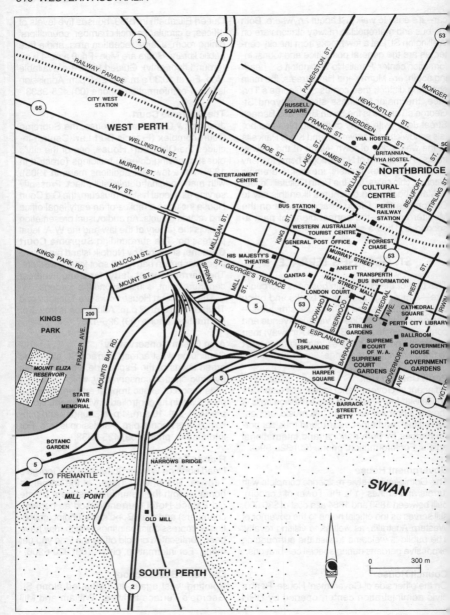

PERTH

(53)

(51)

BULWER ST.

WEST PARADE

TO GUILDFORD ROAD

SUMMERS ST.

EAST PERTH
TERMINAL

EDWARD ST.

LORD ST.

RY ST.

HA HOSTEL

ORT ST.

EAST PERTH

CLAISEBROOK
STATION

McIVER STATION

MOORE ST.

ROYAL PERTH
HOSPITAL

WELLINGTON
SQUARE

HAIG PARK

YMCA JEWELL
HOUSE

PLAIN ST.

PERTH MINT

GODERICH ST.

WATERLOO CRESCENT

ROYAL
AUTOMOBILE
CLUB

HILL ST.

BENNETT ST.

(65)

GLOUCESTER PARK
TROTTING GROUND

NELSON AVE.

ADELAIDE TERRACE

QUEENS
GARDENS

W.A.C.A.
OVAL

NGLEY

PARK

TERRACE RD.

(65)

RIVERSIDE DR.

TRANSPERTH
DEPOT

(5)

RIVER

CAUSEWAY

(5)

ISLAND

HEIRISSON

TO THE GREAT
EASTERN
HIGHWAY

TO
ALBANY HIGHWAY

© MOON PUBLICATIONS, INC.

Streets, this former government school (built in 1854) resembles a medieval church with its quarried limestone, steeply pitched gable roof, and Gothic windows. Several additions were constructed in 1860, 1865, and 1876. The building presently serves as headquarters for the National Trust of Western Australia. Hours are Mon.-Fri. 9 a.m.-5 p.m. Admission is free. For information, phone (09) 321-6088.

Barracks Archway
At the western end of St. George's Terrace (where it branches off and becomes Malcolm Street), the three-story Tudor-style archway, built in 1863-66 of Flemish bond brickwork, stands as a memorial to W.A.'s early pioneers and is all that remains of the old Pensioners Barracks, which were demolished in 1966. The archway fronts **Parliament House,** which is open for conducted tours on weekdays. For information, phone (09) 222-7222.

The Cloisters
Between King and Milligan Streets on the north side of St. George's Terrace, the snappy brick Cloisters, established in 1858, was W.A.'s first boys' secondary school.

His Majesty's Theatre
Turn north on King St. to see this restored Edwardian building—frequently referred to as "gracious"—a venue for ballet, opera, and theater performances. For information, phone (09) 322-2929.

London Court
Back on St. George's Terrace, beyond William St., the London Court Arcade, built in 1937, is a great bit of Aussie kitsch. Running all the way to Hay Street Mall, the *very* mock-Tudor laneway, the brainchild of hit-it-rich gold miner Claude de Bernales, features sublimely silly details like medieval clocks with mechanical jousting knights. The clock at the Hay Street end is a mini-Big Ben.

Town Hall
Walk a short distance along the Mall to Barrack Street. Perth Town Hall, on the southeast corner, was constructed by convicts to resemble an English market. Check out the tower—still visible is a piece of hangman's rope carved in the stone. Another interesting feature are some of the tower

windows built in the shape of reversed broad arrowheads—a symbol meaning "convict-built."

St. George's Cathedral
Reached from Cathedral Ave., off St. George's Terrace, this was the site of Perth's first church, constructed of timber and rush in 1829, then replaced by a stone building that served worshippers until 1841. The foundation stone for the present cathedral was laid in 1880.

The Deanery
At the corner of St. George's Terrace and Pier St., the Deanery, which currently functions as Anglican church offices, was built in the late 1850s as a residence for the first Anglican dean of Perth and ranks among W.A.'s few remaining houses from that period.

OTHER CITY SIGHTS

Perth Cultural Centre
Cross the railway tracks at Horseshoe Bridge to reach Northbridge, site of the Perth Cultural Centre, a "mall" comprised of several buildings, including the Art Gallery of Western Australia and the Western Australian Museum.

Closest to Horseshoe Bridge, the **Art Gallery of Western Australia** exhibits contemporary and traditional Australian and European paintings and sculpture, including a collection of Aboriginal paintings and crafts (with informative pamphlets). Hours are daily 10 a.m.-5 p.m., closed Good Friday and Christmas Day. Admission is free. Free guided tours are offered Tues.-Fri. at noon. For information, phone (09) 328-7233.

On the corner of the Mall and Beaufort St., the **Western Australian Museum** is centered on the **Old Gaol**, a restored, convict-built Georgian stone courthouse and jail that served its purpose from 1856 to 1889 (the grounds were used for a number of public executions). Now serving as a museum, exhibitions feature W.A. historical and cultural memorabilia, including household items, political records, early mementos, a collection of meteorites (one weighs 11 tons!), a 25-meter blue whale skeleton, plus an outstanding Aboriginal gallery. Hours are Mon.-Fri. 10:30 a.m.-5 p.m., Sat.-Sun. 1-5 p.m., closed Christmas Day and Good Friday. Admission is free. For information, phone (09) 328-4411.

More Museums

The **Mineral Museum of Western Australia,** 100 Plain St. East (in Mineral House), features rocks, minerals, and special displays related to mining and geology. Hours are Mon.-Fri. 8 a.m.-5 p.m. Admission is free. For information, phone (09) 222-3333.

Perth's oldest **fire station,** corner Irwin and Murray Streets, serves as a museum which depicts W.A.'s firefighting techniques and machinery from 1901 to the present day. Hours are Mon.-Thurs. 10 a.m.-3 p.m. Admission is free. For information, phone (09) 323-9468.

At the northeast edge of the city, at the junction of Lord and Bulwer Streets, the **Army Museum of Western Australia** houses uniforms, badges, medals, and other military items ranging from the colonial period to the present. Hours are Sunday and Thursday 1-4:30 p.m. A donation is requested. For information, phone (09) 227-9269.

Scitech Discovery Centre

At the corner of Railway Parade and Sutherland St., Scitech features entertaining hands-on experiments (for kids of all ages) on a variety of high-tech equipment. Hours are Mon.-Fri. 10 a.m.-5 p.m., Saturday 10 a.m.-9 p.m., Sunday 10 a.m.-6 p.m. Admission is $10. For information, phone (09) 481-6295.

It's a Small World

See a huge museum collection of little things—miniature cars, rooms, trains, et cetera, located at 12 Parliament Place, West Perth. Hours are Sun.-Fri. 10 a.m.-5 p.m., Saturday 2-5 p.m. Admission is $4. For information, phone (09) 322-2020.

Old Mill

Perth's first flour mill, built in 1835, is at the southern end of the Narrows Bridge and displays many pioneering relics. Hours are Monday, Wednesday, and Thursday 1-5 p.m., Sat.-Sun. noon-4 p.m. A donation is requested. For information, phone (09) 382-4144.

Perth Mint

Dating from 1899, the mint still produces gold, silver, and platinum bullion coins. Displays include various coins, including a one-kg nugget coin. Located at 310 Hay Street. Hours are Mon.-Fri. 9 a.m.-4 p.m., Saturday 9 a.m.-1 p.m. Admission is free (no place to put any more coins?). For information, phone (09) 421-7277.

Perth Zoo

Across the Swan River (and beyond the Old Mill), at 20 Labouchere Rd., South Perth, the zoo is easily reached by bus or ferry from the city center. Noteworthy attractions include the great ape complex, nocturnal house, wallaby park, great cat enclosure, gibbon lake, walk-through aviary, and the Conservation Discovery Centre. Hours are daily 10 a.m.-5 p.m. Admission is $6. For information, phone (09) 367-7988.

Parks and Gardens

Kings Park, at the west edge of the city, is Perth's park supreme—even though bushfires in 1989 burned nearly half of it. A short drive or easy walk from city center, its nearly 400 hectares consist mostly of natural bushland as well as a five-hectare **botanic garden** (noted for its spring wildflowers), natural trails, picnic areas, and paths for walking, jogging, and cycling. You'll catch some terrific views of the city, river, and surrounding countryside from a variety of perches and lookouts—especially from **Mount Eliza,** the park's most prominent knoll. Free guided tours are available. For information, phone (09) 321-4801.

On the eastern edge of the city, **Queens Garden,** corner Hay and Plain Streets, is a quiet English-style park with a water garden. **Hyde Park,** corner William and Vincent Streets, North Perth, caters to families with its adventure playground and to birdwatchers with its ornamental lake. **Lake Monger,** in the close-by suburb of Wembley, is a popular spot for watching those seductive black swans, as well as wild ducks and other birdlife.

Beaches

Pick and choose from any of Perth's well-known beaches. For calm, Swan River swimming beaches, try **Crawley, Peppermint Grove,** and **Como.** If you'd rather tackle the surf, head for the beaches along the Indian Ocean—best bets are **Cottesloe, City Beach** (site of many national surfing contests), **Scarborough,** and **Trigg Island.** If you're looking for surf *and* you forgot your bathers, **Swanbourne** (north of Cottesloe) is a popular nude beach. Almost all beaches can be easily reached by bus.

SUBURBAN SIGHTS

Claremont Museum
Housed within one of W.A.'s oldest buildings (constructed by convicts in 1861-62), the museum's displays depict early settlement, convict and farming life, as well as replicas of bootmaker and barber shops. Located at 66 Victoria Ave., Claremont. Hours are Tues.-Thurs. and Sunday 1-4 p.m., daily 2-5 p.m. during school holidays. Admission is $2. For information, phone (09) 386-3352.

Museum of W.A. Sport
Inside the Superdrome, trophies and other memorabilia recall the good and not-so-good moments of Western Australian sports figures. It's on Stephenson Ave. in Mt. Claremont. Hours are daily 8 a.m.-8 p.m. Admission is free. For information, phone (09) 387-8542.

Museum of Childhood
Two buildings contain dolls (wax, wooden, and bisque), toys, photographs, literature, clothing, furniture, and other curios and playthings (almost 20,000 items) associated with W.A.'s pioneer children. Located at 160 Hamersley Rd., Subiaco. Hours are Mon.-Fri. 10 a.m.-3 p.m., Sunday 2-5 p.m. Admission is $2.50. For information, phone (09) 381-1103.

Aviation Museum
Exhibits depicting the history of civil and military aviation from the origins up to the present (with an emphasis on W.A.) feature historic aircraft (such as the Lancaster heavy bomber and the Spitfire fighter), uniforms, medals, models, photos, and other aero-memorabilia. The museum is on Bull Creek Dr. in Bull Creek. Hours are daily 11 a.m.-4 p.m., closed Christmas Day and Good Friday. Admission is $4.50. For information, phone (09) 332-7205.

Swan Brewery
Tour W.A.'s famed brewery and guzzle or sip some of the "homegrown" brews such as Swan Lager, Swan Draught, and Emu. Located at 25 Vaile Rd., Canning Vale. Tours last 90 minutes to two hours and are available Mon.-Thursday. Advance reservations are necessary. For information, phone (09) 350-0222.

Cohunu Wildlife Park
Visit the Southern Hemisphere's largest aviary (on Mills Rd. in Gosnells) and see native animals in a "natural" environment. This is also the spot to have your photo taken with a koala (400 tame kangaroos and photo-loving koalas are "natural?"). Hours are daily 10 a.m.-5 p.m. Admission is $7.50. For information, phone (09) 390-6090.

Elizabethan Village
Full-size re-creations of Shakespeare's birthplace and Anne Hathaway's cottage are furnished with 500-year-old antiques. The village is on Canns Rd. in Armadale. Hours are Mon.-Fri. 10 a.m.-4 p.m., Sat.-Sun. 10 a.m.-5 p.m. Admission is $5. For information, phone (09) 399-3166.

Pioneer World
This working model of a 19th-century gold miners' village allows visitors to pan for their own gold nuggets, filings, and dust (30-minute limit). Other attractions include working craftsmen, sing-alongs, silent movies, vaudeville shows, and other entertainment. Located at junction of South West and Albany Highways, Armadale. Hours are daily 10 a.m.-5 p.m. Admission is $8.50. For information, phone (09) 399-5322.

ACCOMMODATIONS

Perth's varied accommodations are as conveniently located as everything else in town. Older, cheaper hotels and some hostels are clustered in and around the city center, while others are just across the railway tracks in Northbridge. South Perth and several of the closer suburbs also provide motel and holiday-flat units. Big spenders will find no shortage of luxury hotels, most of which are between St. George's Terrace and the Swan River.

Optimism over Perth's tourism boom in conjunction with the America's Cup—and its accompanying groupies—saw upmarket accommodations increase by several thousand rooms. Many of these hotels have since experienced low occupancy, so it may be possible to strike a good deal on rates. Campgrounds and caravan parks are scattered 10-20 km from town.

As with all Australian cities and tourist centers, it's advisable to book rooms in advance. If you

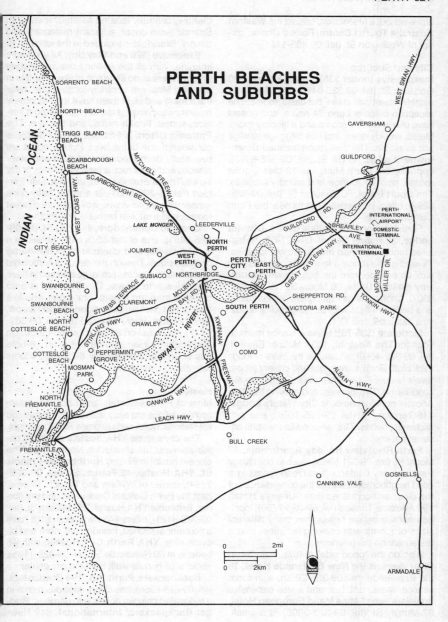

PERTH BEACHES AND SUBURBS

arrive without a reservation, contact the **Western Australia Tourist Centre,** Forrest Chase, corner of Wellington St. (tel. 09-483-1111).

City and Suburbs

Inexpensive (under $35): **Jewell House,** 180 Goderich St. (tel. 09-325-8488), is a YMCA-run establishment with clean, but basic, rooms. The reception office is open 24 hours, and guests have use of two TV rooms and a laundry room. Meals, weekly rates, and free baggage storage are available. The well-recommended **Downtowner Lodge,** 63 Hill St. (tel. 09-325-6973), opposite the Perth Mint, has 12 clean, quiet rooms, plus TV lounge and laundry facilities. The **Court Hotel,** 50 Beaufort St. (tel. 09-328-5292), offers inexpensive rooms near the Perth Cultural Centre.

Farther beyond the Cultural Centre, **Cheviot Lodge,** 30 Bulwer St. (tel. 09-227-6817), features modern kitchen and bathroom facilities, TV and game room, a laundry room, and free pick-up service from the bus station. **Mountway Holiday Units,** 36 Mount St. (tel. 09-321-8307), close to Kings Park, offers self-contained one-bedroom flats with cooking facilities, full-size bathtubs, and TVs.

Moderate ($35-70): Make advance reservations for **The Adelphi,** 130A Mounts Bay Rd. (tel. 09-322-4666), situated at the base of Kings Park bluff. Rooms are bright and cheery (upper levels feature Swan River views) and have air-conditioning, TVs, phones, and cooking facilities. Another popular choice is **City Waters Lodge,** 118 Terrace Rd. (tel. 09-325-1566), also with kitchens, phones, TVs, air-conditioning, and off-street parking.

Perth Riverview Holiday Apartments, 42 Mount St. (tel. 09-321-8963), close to both Kings Park and city center, offers clean rooms in a good neighborhood, with all the conveniences of the other self-contained flats. **Airways Hotel,** 195 Adelaide Terrace (tel. 09-323-7799), located near the deluxe hotels, has many different sizes of rooms with cooking facilities, plus a restaurant on the premises.

Also on the "good side" of town, with Swan River views, is the **New Esplanade Hotel,** 18 the Esplanade (tel. 09-325-2000), with room service, restaurant, bar, and a less-expensive "travelers' wing." **Miss Maud European Hotel,** 97 Murray St. (tel. 09-325-3900), is a small,

friendly, centrally located establishment with Scandinavian decor, adjacent restaurant and bakery. Breakfast is included in the rates.

Expensive ($70 and Way Up): As you might imagine, with all the millionaires and money around, there is no shortage of luxury hotels in this city. Most are centrally located (i.e., near the banks) and all of them have the customary amenities such as restaurants, bars, room service, shops, health clubs, and the like. The **Parmelia Hilton,** Mill St. (tel. 09-322-3622), is considered one of the best. Public rooms are beautifully decorated with antiques and other artwork, and guest rooms have either river or city views. The **Sheraton Perth,** 207 Adelaide Terrace (tel. 09-325-0501), is another hefty-price winner with terrific views, well-decorated guest rooms, and a superb formal dining room.

Chateau Commodore, 417 Hay St. (tel.09-325-0461), one of the city's older hotels, is a local favorite, and cheaper than the name brands above. Though the decor is somewhat . . . robust, the rooms are large and some have balconies with views. The Chateau is also cheaper than the others. For those who like their action packed, **Burswood Island Resort,** Great Eastern Hwy., Victoria Park (tel. 09-362-7777), has a full-on 24-hour casino (largest in the Southern Hemisphere), plus an 18-hole golf course and beautifully decorated rooms with city or river views.

Hostels

Most of Perth's hostels and backpacker accommodations are easy walks from the bus and rail stations. Dorm beds average $9-14 per night.

The city's three **YHA hostels** are busy establishments, all situated in Northbridge. The closest hostel is 87-bed **Northbridge-Francis St. YHA Hostel,** 42 Francis St. (tel. 09-328-7794), corner of William and Francis Streets, past the Perth Cultural Centre. Around the corner, **Britannia YHA Hostel,** 253 William St. (tel. 09-328-6121), offers 145 beds. Both sites have a communal kitchen, laundry, rec room and bicycle hire. **YHA Perth City Hostel,** with 48 beds, is at 60 Newcastle St. (tel. 09-328-1135), about a 15-minute walk from the city center.

Backpackers Perth Inn, 194 Brisbane St. (tel. 09-328-9958), has clean, spacious rooms in a renovated colonial house with gardens. **Budget Backpackers' International,** 342 Newcastle St. (tel. 09-328-9468), and **North Lodge,** 225 Beaufort St. (tel. 09-227-7588), are other choices with communal lounges and kitchens.

Males and females are segregated in the two-houser **Perth Travellers Lodge,** 156 Aberdeen St. (tel. 09-328-6667). Other possibilities on the same street are: **Aberdeen Lodge,** 79 Aberdeen St. (tel. 09-227-6137), with four-bed dorms; **12.01 Central,** corner of Aberdeen and Fitzgerald Streets (tel. 09-227-1201), with a deli and cafe below; and **Backpackers International,** corner of Aberdeen and Lake Streets (tel. 09-227-9977).

Travelers of both sexes are welcome to mix and mingle with residents and retirees at the main **YMCA** facility in the city center at 119 Murray St. (tel. 09-325-7627). They're pretty basic accommodations, but the weekly rates are a good deal. The renovated **Grand YWCA Central,** 379 Wellington St. (tel. 09-221-2682), offers varied accommodations and $15 bunk beds, along with a restaurant and cafe.

Camping

The following campgrounds and caravan parks fall within 20 km of the city and offer both on-site vans and campsites: **Central Caravan Park,** 38 Central Ave., Redcliffe (tel. 09-277-5696); **Kenlorn Caravan Park,** 229 Welshpool Rd., Queens Park (tel. 09-458-2604); **Caversham Caravan Park,** Benara Rd., Caversham (tel. 09-279-6700); **Careniup Caravan Park,** 467 North Beach Rd., Gwelup (tel. 09-447-6665); **Starhaven Caravan Park,** 18 Pearl Parade, Scarborough (tel. 09-341-1770); **Kingsway Caravan Park,** corner Kingsway and Wanneroo Rd., Landsdale (tel. 09-409-9267); **Perth Tourist Caravan Park,** 319 Hale Rd., Forrestfield (tel. 09-453-6677); **Forrestfield Caravan Park,** 351 Hawtin Rd., Forrestfield (tel. 09-453-6378); **Guildford Caravan Park,** 372 West Swan Rd., Guildford (tel. 09-274-2828); and **Orange Grove Caravan Park,** 19 Kelvin Rd., Orange Grove (tel. 09-453-6226).

FOOD

Perth is hardly a culinary tour de force like Melbourne, but those millionaires do like to eat. About 700 restaurants dot the city, including many ethnic establishments along William Street in North-

bridge, coffee shops and cafes in the city center, and high-priced gourmet dining rooms in hotels or spattered about the inner suburbs. Fresh, local seafood tops many of the menus.

Inexpensive

The cheapest—and perhaps tastiest—places to eat at are the foodstalls and halls, where you can do a budget-type graze of many different types of food for less than a greasy spoon takeaway. One of the best choices is **Down Under Food Hall,** near William St., downstairs in the Hay Street Mall. Select from a variety of ethnic goodies such as Indian, Indonesian, Chinese, and Mexican. Hours are Mon.-Wed. 8 a.m.-7 p.m., Thurs.-Sat. 8 a.m.-9 p.m. Nearby, but a bit more expensive, is **Carillon Food Hall,** in Carillon Arcade, also on Hay Street Mall. Hours are Mon.-Sat. 8 a.m.-9 p.m. In Northbridge, try **Northbridge Pavilion,** corner Lake and James Streets, **Victoria Gardens,** on Aberdeen St. overlooking Russell Square, or the two Asian halls on James Street.

Fast Eddy's, corner Hay and Milligan Streets, is a 24-hour burger joint. **Magic Apple,** 445 Hay St., features healthy salads, smoothies, and sandwiches. Another health-style lunch spot is **Granary Wholefoods,** 37 Barrack St. (downstairs), with a good range of vegetarian selections. Down the way, **Mr. Samurai,** 83 Barrack St., is a top choice for cheap Japanese specialties.

Northbridge is packed with ethnic restaurants, many of them inexpensive. Take your tummy for a walk along William Street and you'll never go hungry—**Hare Krishna Food for Life** is just one of your options.

A local favorite for beachside breakfast is **North Cott Café,** 149 Marine Parade, Cottlesloe.

Moderate

Kings Park Garden Restaurant, with city and river views, is a delightful spot for lunch and morning or afternoon teas. Dinner, with live music, is in the expensive range. For those not-to-be-missed yuppie lunches, infiltrate **Moon and Sixpence Bar,** 300 Murray St., or **44 King Street,** around the corner. And don't miss the oh-so-cool **Frostbites Bar and Grill,** 397 Murray Street.

Super Italian fare is served at **Mamma Maria's,** 105 Aberdeen Street. Other pasta feasts line Aberdeen St., including **Café Navona, La Luna Café,** and **Aberdino's.**

In Subiaco, **Bar Bzar,** corner of Railway Rd. and Rokeby St., is rife with wanna-be-but-never-will Bohemians. The **Witch's Cauldron,** 89 Rokeby St., casts its spell with killer garlic prawns and other potent concoctions.

Suburban Leederville is becoming another see-and-be-seen haunt. Cruise Oxford St., between Aberdeen and Vincent Streets, for everything from rock 'n' roll pizza to postwar Vietnamese.

Expensive
Inquire about dress codes and reserve tables well ahead, especially for weekends and holiday periods. **Fraser's,** in Kings Park (tel. 09-481-7100), is a two-level, river-and-city view establishment, with fresh, flavorful contemporary cuisine. Open daily for lunch and dinner.

Searching for a top-notch, noisy, crowded, chic, imaginative, 24-hour brasserie with great cakes and a wonderful wine list? Choose from a cast of one: **Oriel,** 480 Hay St., Subiaco (tel. 09-382-1886).

Perugino, 77 Outram St., West Perth (tel. 09-321-5420), is considered Perth's best Italian restaurant. Regional specialities are prepared with fresh ingredients and fresh imagination. Recently renovated, the garden setting lures locals involved in romantic encounters, important business, or pure self-indulgence. Open Mon.-Fri. lunch, Mon.-Sat. dinner.

And, for one of the best French restaurants, the prizewinner is **Pierre's,** 8 Outram St., West Perth (tel. 09-322-7648). Pierre's is elegant, formal, and very expensive. This magnificently restored colonial residence offers scrumptious cuisine and—naturally—a fabulous wine list. Open Mon.-Fri. lunch, nightly dinner.

In Northbridge, **Choi's Inn,** 68 Roe St. (tel. 09-328-6350), is a friendly, casual Chinese establishment that serves traditional Cantonese and fiery Sichuan meals. Advance orders are necessary for the beggar's chicken and Peking duck. Open daily for lunch and dinner.

ENTERTAINMENT AND EVENTS

Much of Perth's entertainment scene is geared toward its vibrant, young (or young at heart) residents, with Northbridge being the major gathering spot. Check local newspapers, particularly the lift-out entertainment guide in Thursday's

West Australian newspaper for current listings of arts and cultural events. For gig info, pick up a copy of *X-Press,* the free weekly music mag, at any record shop and many other locations. The *Westside Observer,* free at Arcane Bookshop (212 William St.), has lists of gay and Lesbian entertainment venues.

Cinemas
Perth has the usual round of commercial cinema complexes, with most of the flicks appearing months after their U.S. debut. Movie houses that show more arty and/or cerebral films are: the **Lumiere,** in the Perth Entertainment Centre; **Cinema Paradiso,** 164 James St., Northbridge; and the **Astor,** corner of Beaufort and Walcott Streets, Mt. Lawley.

There's a two-level wraparound **Omni Theater** at the corner of Railway Parade and Sutherland St., West Perth (tel. 09-481-6481).

Pubs and Clubs
Plentiful clubs, pubs, and discos feature live music most nights of the week. Northbridge is the prime area for contemporary and casual venues ($4-8), while discos and nightclubs in the big hotels cater to the yup-and-coming ($10-15).

Catch live music in Northbridge at: **Brass Monkey Tavern,** 209 William St.; **Aberdeen Hotel,** 84 Aberdeen St.; and **The Lone Star,** corner of Beaufort and Newcastle Streets (travelers' night is Wednesday). **Aqua,** 232 William St., is a favorite late-night spot (Thursday is Latin American night), popular with the hip set. For pure dance, **St. James' Nightclub,** 139 James St., is a huge club with four bars, playing retro and mainstream tunes to a bebopping young crowd.

Exit Nightclub, 187 Stirling St., has split-levels and split-styles (techno, rap, and hip-hop), appealing to sophisticates who like to pretend they're not.

In Leederville, **Hip-E Club,** corner of Newcastle and Oxford Streets, spins the tunes of the '60s and '70s to the never-were hippie set (Tuesday is backpackers' night).

Perth has the usual round of hot discos with cold meat inspectors. Fashion victims might try: **Brannigan's,** Irwin St., in the Perth International Hotel; **Geremiah's,** Milligan St., in the Orchard Hotel; **The Loft,** 237 Hay St.; or **Club Rumours,** 418 Murray Street.

For good old drinkin' pubs, try **Sherwood's Tavern,** 77 St. George's Terrace; **Milligan's,** 205 James St.; and the **Northbridge Hotel,** 198 Brisbane Street.

The Casino
Burswood Island Resort, W.A.'s first casino, features more than 140 gaming tables, including roulette, baccarat, blackjack, craps, and Australia's own two-up. Restaurants, bars, and a cabaret are also part of this luxury resort complex on the banks of the Swan River, near the city. Open 24 hours a day except Christmas Day and Good Friday. For information, phone (09) 362-7777.

Theater, Dance, and Concerts
The stunning **His Majesty's Theatre,** 825 Hay St. (tel. 09-322-2929), is home not just to many of Perth's theatrical productions but also to the **West Australian Ballet Company** and the **West Australian Opera Company.** Modern and traditional ballets are performed in February, May, June, and October, while the operatic season (April, August, and November) features classical works and operettas.

The **Playhouse Theatre,** 3 Pier St. (tel. 09-325-3500), is headquarters of the **Western Australian Theatre Company,** which presents a number of classical and contemporary plays throughout the year. Other good local theaters include: **Dolphin Theatre,** University of Western Australia, Crawley (tel. 09-380-2432); **Regal Theatre,** 474 Hay St., Subiaco (tel. 09-381-1557); **Subiaco** and **Hole in the Wall,** 180 Hamersley Rd., Subiaco (tel. 09-381-2733).

Perth Entertainment Centre, on Wellington near Milligan St., is where the big-name rock concerts and other major events are held. You can't miss the **Betts & Betts Walk of Fame** out front—a walkway of celebrities' autographed footprints. For information, phone (09) 322-4766.

Folk music, orchestra recitals, and more "mellow" concerts are performed at **Perth Concert Hall,** 5 St. George's Terrace (tel. 09-325-9944). In summer, the band shell in the **Supreme Court Gardens** presents a variety of live music.

Schedules for almost every entertainment event are advertised in the lift-out entertainment guide in Thursday's *West Australian.*

BOCS is the state's major ticket booking agency for everything from concerts and ballet to theater and sporting events. For information, phone (09) 484-1133, or stop by the outlet at the Western Australia Tourist Centre, on Forrest Place.

Theme Parks
Adventure World, 179 Progress Dr., Bibra Lake, is a family-oriented entertainment complex with an amusement park, native animals, waterways, and parklands. Hours are daily, Sept.-May and school holidays, 10 a.m.-5 p.m. Admission is $18, children $15. For information, phone (09) 417-9666.

Travel through an underground acrylic tunnel to view approximately 5,000 species of underwater life (such as starfish, crustaceans, and a small Port Jackson shark) at **Underwater World,** Hillary's Boat Harbour, West Coast Highway. Other attractions include Microworld, where you can watch seahorses, shellfish, and anemones through a video camera, and Touch Pool, where you can feel the creatures. There's also a gift shop, and an underwater cafe that looks out on the Indian Ocean. Hours are daily 9 a.m.-5 p.m. Admission is $14. For information, phone (09) 447-7500.

Events
The city's big extravaganza is the annual **Festival of Perth** held in February and March. The festival showcases international and national big-name talents, as well as local joes, with a program roster that includes music, theater, dance, film, visual and literary arts, and a host of outdoor activities. For information, contact the University of Western Australia, Mounts Bay Rd., Crawley (tel. 09-386-7977).

SPORTS AND RECREATION

Great weather, great beaches, great park—it means Perth offers all types of land and water sports and year-round recreational opportunities. Call or drop by the **Western Australia Tourist Centre** on Forrest Place. for information on spectator and participant sports throughout the state.

Diving
A few scattered, centuries-old shipwrecks offshore should make things interesting for divers.

Contact **Perth Diving Academy,** 281 Wanneroo Rd., Nollamara (tel. 09-344-1562), or the **Australasian Diving Centre,** 259 Stirling Hwy., Claremont (tel. 09-384-3966).

Fishing
You'll luck out on the catch of the day at many coastal ports, particularly Fremantle, as well as along the Swan River banks. The prized fish in these parts is the blue marlin. Charter boats are available (check the yellow pages).

Swimming Pools
Not happy with the ocean or the river? A freshwater swimming pool is located at the **Superdrome,** Stephenson Ave., Mt. Claremont (tel. 09-441-8222).

Sporting Facilities
Tennis: Fees are reasonable at public tennis courts within metropolitan and suburban parks. For sites and details, contact **Tennis West** (tel. 09-472-1195).

Golf: Select from one of the city's many public golf courses after consulting with the **Western Australia Golf Association** (tel. 09-474-1005) or the tourist office. Some of Perth's country clubs are on the snooty side (but what else is new?).

Other Participant Sports
Yachties should head straight for the tourism office. **Catamarans** and **windsurfers** are available for hire at the Coode Street Jetty, South Perth (tel. 09-367-2988). They are popular on weekends and holidays, so book ahead. Depending on weather conditions, you can **parasail** on weekends at the South Perth foreshore. For information, contact **Flying High Parasailing** (tel. 09-446-1835).

Bushwalkers, cyclists, and **joggers** will find excellent trails throughout Kings Park and along the Swan River. The tourist office has maps and brochures, or contact the **Ministry of Sport and Recreation** (tel. 09-387-9700).

Spectator Sports
Aussie-rules football is the prime winter spectator sport, with games played every Saturday afternoon March through September, at various league grounds throughout the city. For information, phone the **Western Australia Football League** (tel. 09-381-5599). In summer

months, **cricket** is the buzz, with Sheffield Shield, Test, and one-day cricket played at the W.A.C.A. (Western Australia Cricket Association) grounds in Nelson Crescent, East Perth. For information, phone the **W.A.C.A.** (tel. 09-325-9800).

Other spectator sports include **rugby, soccer, basketball, baseball,** and **hockey.** Watch for details of all matches and sporting events in the Sports section of the Friday and Saturday newspapers.

Racing is a big-time favorite of Western Australians. For schedules and locales of **horse, trotting,** and **greyhound** racing, watch the Sports section of the morning newspapers. For **motor racing,** contact the W.A. Sporting Car Club (tel. 09-381-4432). For **motorcycle racing,** phone the Motorcycle Racing Club of W.A. (tel. 09-409-1002). On Friday nights throughout spring and summer months, the **RAS Showground** in Claremont hosts thriller speedcar and motorcycle races. Look for details in Thursday's *West Australian.*

SHOPPING

Perth's main shopping district is the pedestrians-only Hay Street Mall and Murray Street Mall, both running parallel between William and Barrack Streets, and the many arcades that branch off to St. George's Terrace and Wellington Street. Major department stores are located here, as are Woolworth, Coles, scads of boutiques, specialty shops, bookshops, schlock and dime stores, cinemas, coffee lounges, and all kinds of general merchandise. King Street, a few blocks away, within the past few years has nosed its way into the shopping mecca with some choice galleries and funky shops. Customary shopping hours are Mon.-Fri. 9 a.m.-5:30 p.m., Thursday until 9 p.m., and Saturday 9 a.m.-noon.

Markets
Colorful, bargain-filled markets offering a wide range of merchandise are: **Subiaco Market,** near Subiaco Railway Station, at Roberts and Rokeby Roads (Thurs.-Sun. 8 a.m.-6 p.m.); **Canning Vale Market,** corner of Bannister and Ranford Roads (Sunday 7 a.m.-4 p.m.); and **Midland Sunday Market,** 284 Great Eastern Hwy. (Sunday 8 a.m.-4 p.m.).

Crafts

For **Aboriginal handicrafts,** don't miss the **Creative Native,** 32 King St. (tel. 09-322-3398), with its excellent range of traditional and contemporary handmade Aboriginal art, including carved emu eggs and boomerangs.

Crafts Council Gallery, Wellington St., at the railway station (tel. 09-325-2799), exhibits crafts by leading Western Australians and provides listings of other craft shops and outlets.

For items constructed from native jarrah and grass tree wood, visit **Contempo Gallery,** 329 Murray St. (tel. 09-322-2306).

Other Shops

How about gems and money? See gems before they're turned into rings, pendants, and key chains at **Perth Lapidary Centre,** 58 Pier St. (tel. 09-325-2954). Purchase proof-issue coins, commemoratives and bank notes, coin jewelry, and books related to coin collecting and Western Australia's pioneering prospectors at **The Perth Mint,** 310 Hay St. (tel. 09-421-7277).

Record collectors and purveyors of the local *muso* scene will groove at **78 Records,** 884 Hay Street. On the way to or from, you'll be faced with enough retro and grunge wear for all your nights on this town.

SERVICES

Branches of all the major national **banks** are on or about St. George's Terrace, along with the ubiquitous automatic teller machines. You'll find **Bank of America Australia** at 28 the Esplanade (tel. 09-322-7555). Banking hours are Mon.-Thurs. 9:30 a.m.-4 p.m., Friday 9:30 a.m.-5 p.m.

The **general post office,** 3 Forrest Place (tel. 09-326-5211), between the railway station and Hay Street Mall, is open for all postal services Mon.-Fri. 8 a.m.-6 p.m., Saturday 9 a.m.-noon.

For migrant information (employment, permits, etc.), see the **Immigration Office,** 12 St. George's Terrace (tel. 09-220-2311).

Some countries with Perth-based consulates are: **United States,** 16 St. George's Terrace (tel. 09-221-1177); **Canada,** 44 St. George's Terrace (tel. 09-322-7930); **United Kingdom,** 95 St. George's Terrace (tel. 09-322-3200); **New Zealand,** 16 St. George's Terrace (tel. 09-325-7877); and **Germany,** 16 St. George's Terrace (tel. 09-325-8851). Don't ask about **France.**

INFORMATION

As with all of Australia's capital cities, the state tourist office is chockablock with information, accommodations, and tour bookings. The **Western Australia Tourist Centre** (also known as WATC) is on Forrest Place, at the corner of Wellington Street and across from the railway station. Hours are Mon.-Fri. 8:30 a.m.-5:30 p.m., Saturday 9-1 p.m. For information, phone (09) 483-1111. A **Perth City Tourist Booth** is located along Hay Street Mall.

The **ACROD Access Committee,** 189 Royal St., East Perth (tel. 09-222-2961), provides **disabled visitors** with helpful brochures and information on accommodations, restaurants, theaters, and recreational areas within the state. **Paraquad** (tel. 09-381-0173) has info on accessible accommodations.

To obtain maps and touring advice, call in at the **Royal Automobile Club of W.A.,** 228 Adelaide Terrace (tel. 09-421-4444). The bookshop has a good section of travel books, literature, and maps (many are free if you have proof of membership with a reciprocal club in another country). For an even broader range of maps, call into **The Perth Map Centre,** 891 Hay St. (tel. 09-322-5733).

The **library** is at the Perth Cultural Centre, James St. (tel. 09-427-3111).

In an emergency, dial 000 to summon **fire, police,** and **ambulance** services. **Royal Perth Hospital,** Victoria Square (tel. 09-224-2244), maintains a 24-hour emergency room. For relief from killer toothaches, go to **Perth Dental Hospital,** 196 Goderich St. (tel. 09-325-3452).

Other Information

Angus and Robertson, 199 Murray St. and 625 Hay St., is the large commercial reading outlet. Another good shop is **Down to Earth Books,** 874 Hay Street. *We* love **Arcane Bookshop,** 212 William St., Northbridge (big selection of alternative literature, gay and Lesbian sections, and poetry), and ditto for **New Editions,** South Terrace, Fremantle (with a cafe for real bookshop lovers).

The *West Australian* is the Monday through Saturday paper, while the *Sunday Times* finishes the weekend. **Plaza Newsagency,** in the Plaza Arcade off Hay Street Mall, sells national and international newspapers, as do some of the large hotels.

TRANSPORT

Getting There by Air

If you're coming from Europe, Africa, or Southeast Asia, Perth will most likely be your Australian gateway city. **International carriers** include Qantas, Air New Zealand, United Airlines, British Airways, South African Airways, Garuda Indonesia, Malaysian Airlines, Thai Airways, Singapore Airlines, and Japan Airlines.

Domestic carriers that serve Perth from other Australian states are Ansett (tel. 13-1300, toll-free) and **Qantas** (tel. 13-1313 toll-free). For up-to-date prices and cheapest deals, consult the **Britannia YHA,** 253 William St., Northbridge (tel. 09-328-6121), or **STA,** 100 James St., Northbridge (tel. 09-227-7569). Inquire into moneysaving **passes** before you leave home (or enter the country).

Perth International Airport is about 16 km northeast of the city center and the separate **domestic terminal** is about 10 km closer. Moneychanging and other customary big-city facilities are available.

The **Perth Airport Bus** (tel. 09-250-2838), a private shuttle, meets all incoming flights and drops passengers off at city airline offices and major hotels. Fare is $7 international, $6 domestic. Several **Transperth** city buses operate between the domestic airport and city center. Services run daily, every 40-50 minutes 6 a.m.-10 p.m., less frequently on Saturday, not at all on Sunday. William St., between St. George's Terrace and the Esplanade, is the main pick-up and drop-off spot. Fare is $2. **Taxis** are readily available and the 25-minute ride to city center should cost $15-20.

Getting There by Train

Interstate trains arrive into and depart from the **East Perth Railway Terminal,** West Parade.

The fabled **Indian-Pacific** runs between Perth and Sydney. The 64-hour, three-night journey passes through Broken Hill and Adelaide and crosses the Nullarbor Plain on the world's longest straight stretch of railway line. Trains depart Sydney on Monday and Thursday, and Perth on Monday and Friday. One-way fares are: $932,

first-class berth with meals; $598, economy berth with meals; and $290, economy seat. The Indian-Pacific is included in the **Austrailpass** (except the eight-day Austrail Flexi-Pass), which must be purchased outside the country.

For information and bookings, phone **Rail Australia** (tel. 13-2232 toll-free) or **Westrail** (tel. 09-326-2813 or 13-2232).

Contact Westrail for bookings on the Prospector (six times weekly Perth-Kalgoorlie, $58) and the Australind (daily Perth-Bunbury, $35). The Australind departs from the Central Railway Station, Wellington St., next to the bus station.

Getting There by Bus

Greyhound Pioneer Australia (tel. 13-2030 toll-free) serves Perth daily from other Australian states. Routes from the east coast usually travel via Adelaide, while the Darwin-to-Perth coaches journey across the Top End and down the west coast. Sample fares are: Sydney-Adelaide-Perth (61 hours), $310; Adelaide-Perth (37 hours), $189; Darwin-Perth (59 hours), $347. Inquire about stopover privileges and special passes for overseas visitors.

Getting There by Car

Western Australia is long, far, and wide. Sealed roads, suitable for conventional vehicles, are: Eyre and Great Eastern Highways from Adelaide (2,697 km); Eyre, South Coast, and South Western Highways from Adelaide (3,212 km); Stuart, Victoria, Great Northern, North West Coastal, and Brand Highways from Darwin (4,379 km); and Stuart, Victoria, and Great Northern Highways from Darwin (4,253 km). Make sure your vehicle and body are prepared for the arduous trek.

Though roadhouse facilities are available along the major byways, distances between them can be vast. The road from Ayers Rock is unsealed all the way to the Goldfields region, where it connects with the big highways. Carry plenty of spare everything, even passengers to share the *very* long—and often boring—drive and expensive petrol costs. Also see "Crossing the Nullarbor" in the South Australia chapter.

Hitching

It's fairly cheap—and a lot less exhausting—to take the bus or share a ride (check the YHA bulletin boards). Waits of several days are not uncommon, plus who knows where you'll be waiting. There are some creepy stories about hitchhiking out there! Some friends once picked up a haggard old guy—who looked as if he hadn't eaten for a year—from the edge of the Nullarbor and the middle of nowhere. He drove with them about 100 km even deeper into nowhere, said, "This is where I get out," and wandered off into the proverbial sunset. I'm sure that story has one of the better endings!

If you're dead set on thumbing it, hop a train to Midland if you're headed north or east, or Armadale if your direction is south. Women should be especially careful, and preferably travel with a male companion (or a pit bull).

Getting Around on Buses and Trains
Transperth, the metropolitan transit district, operates five free City Clipper buses approximately every 20 minutes, Mon.-Fri. 7 a.m.-6 p.m. Routes are color-coded and circle the city center, covering most tourist attractions. The Yellow Clipper, around the central city, also runs on Saturday morning. Other buses connect the business center with suburban areas, and though not free, they're still good deals. Tickets, good for two hours from the time of issue, range $1.50-2.50, depending on the number of zones you travel. Going to Fremantle, for example, you'll go through only two zones and it's about 20 km away! Even sweeter, tickets are interchangeable on all Transperth buses, trains, and ferries.

If you're sticking around for a while, you might want to consider a **multirider ticket,** which gives you 10 trips for the price of nine. Buses operate Mon.-Fri. 6 a.m.-11:30 p.m., less frequently on weekends and public holidays.

Obtain maps, schedules, tickets, and other information from Transperth Information Services, Perth Central Bus Station, Wellington St. (tel. 13-1213 toll-free), or at the City Bus Port, Mounts Bay Rd., at the bottom of William Street. Even more convenient is the Transperth information office in the Plaza Arcade, off the Hay Street Mall. Hours are Mon.-Fri. 6:30 a.m.-8 p.m., Saturday 8 a.m.-5 p.m.

Taxis
Meter-operated taxis can be hailed on city streets, plucked from taxi ranks around the central business district and Fremantle, or hired

by phoning **Swan Taxis** (tel. 09-322-0111) or **Black and White Taxis** (tel. 09-333-3333). Taxis for **disabled passengers** are available Mon.-Fri. 8 a.m.-4:30 p.m. For information, phone (09) 333-3377. Cab fare begins at $2.20 plus 70 cents per km, rising to a base charge of $3.70 6 p.m.-6 a.m.

Car Rentals
The big-name rental car companies are located at both the domestic and international airports and in the city center. Charges range $50-90, depending on size—some include unlimited kilometers while others give only the first 100-150 km for a free allowance. For information, contact **Avis** (tel. 09-325-7677), **Hertz** (tel. 09-321-7777), or **Budget** (tel. 09-322-1100).

Rent heartier vehicles for Outback travel from **South Perth Four Wheel Drive Rentals,** 80 Canning Hwy., Victoria Park (tel. 09-362-5444).

Plenty of other companies are listed in the phone book, but be cautious: sometimes the bigger companies can afford to give the better deals, particularly if you book your car from outside Australia. Get tips from the YHA hostels or STA office in Northbridge.

Bicycles
Excellent trails and climate make Perth an ideal city for cycling. Rent bicycles for $10 per day from the YHA on Francis St. or from **Rideway Cycle Hire,** on the western side of the causeway (tel. 09-354-2393). A guaranteed buy-back scheme is offered at **WA Bicycle Disposal Centre,** 47 Bennett St., East Perth (tel. 09-325-1176).

Ferries
Transperth ferries depart from the Barrack Street Jetty to Mends Street Jetty, across the Swan River in South Perth, daily 6:45 a.m.-7:15 p.m. One-way fare is under $1. Contact Transperth Information Services, Perth Central Bus Station, Wellington St. (tel. 13-1213 toll-free), for details. (Don't forget—your two-hour bus ticket is good on this ferry.)

For **Rottnest Island** ferries, contact **Boat Torque** (tel. 09-221-5844) or **Oceanic Cruises** (tel. 09-430-5127).

Tours
The Western Australia Tourist Centre can help you plan and book organized tours within the city

and state. Prices vary $20-120 and include such destinations as wildflower-viewing sites (Aug.-Nov.), Swan Valley, the Darling Ranges, Wave Rock, Monkey Mia, Mt. Augustus, and Yanchep National Park. Longer three- to four-day treks up and down the coast average $400-550. Again, first check with YHA and STA for the best deals with, possibly, more simpatico companions.

City Sights coach tours run about $18 for a half day, $10 for the **Perth Tram** (actually a bus in drag), which makes 90-minute commentator-assisted trips around the city sights. The tram operates daily 9:30 a.m.-6:30 p.m. Pick-up point is at 124 Murray St. (near Barrack St.).

Free guided **walking tours** of Kings Park are available April-October. For information, phone (09) 321-4801. A three-hour **Perth and Beyond** tour takes in the city as well as the park. For information, phone (09) 483-2601.

All **boat cruises** leave from Barrack Street Jetty. The bargain of the lot is Transperth's MV *Countess II*, which departs at 2 p.m. daily except Saturday, on a three-hour upstream Swan River cruise. Fare is $12. For information, phone (09) 425-2651. Both **Boat Torque** (tel. 09-221-5844) and **Captain Cook Cruises** (tel. 09-325-3341) operate a number of scenic cruises including Swan River journeys, winery visits, and lunch and dinner extravaganzas.

Whalewatching cruises are offered by various operators, including **Boat Torque** (tel. 09-246-1039), **Oceanic Cruises** (tel. 09-430-5127), and **Mills Charters** (tel. 09-401-0833). **Rocking-ham Dolphins** (tel. 09-527-1803) departs Magles Bay for two-hour dolphin sightings.

Westrail offers a variety of rail excursions lasting from one day to one week, covering everything from coastal resorts and timber forests to wildflowers and goldfields. For information and bookings, contact the Western Australia Tourist Centre, or Westrail (tel. 09-326-2222).

And, who would want to miss the free 90-minute tour of **Swan Brewery**? Tours depart Mon.-Wed. 10 a.m. and 2:30 p.m., Thursday 2:30 p.m. only. For bookings, phone (09) 350-0650.

Getting Away

Ansett (tel. 13-1300 toll-free) schedules regular services between Perth and many W.A. communities including Broome, Derby, Kununurra, Port Hedland, Newman, Exmouth, Carnarvon, Geraldton, and Kalgoorlie.

Skywest (tel. 09-334-2288, or book through Ansett) flies from Perth to Albany, Esperance, Kalgoorlie, Geraldton, Cue, Meekatharra, Wiluna, and other communities. **Western Airlines** (tel. 09-277-4022) links Perth with Geraldton, Kalbarri, Useless Loop, and Monkey Mia.

For Rottnest Island Service, contact **Rottnest Airlines** (tel. 09-277-4198).

Transperth (tel. 13-1213 toll-free) operates frequent rail service between the city center and Fremantle, Midland, Armadale, and points in between. Trains run less often on weekends and public holidays.

VICINITY OF PERTH

Even though this mega-state spans a third of the continent, you can still manage to get to some pretty interesting places in the course of a day or two.

FREMANTLE

You've heard of Fremantle—site of the 1987 America's Cup race where Kevin Parry lost the yachties' prized petunia to San Diego's Dennis Connor. Believe it or not, Fremantle actually existed *before* then—and has continued since.

Perth's port district (pop. 25,000), called "Freo" by the locals, sits 19 km southwest of Perth, where the Swan River kisses the Indian Ocean. Founded along with Perth in 1829, the city was named for Captain Charles Howe Fremantle, who claimed Australia's west coast for the British Crown. The settlement was practically dormant until those hardworking convicts were brought in to construct many of the town's buildings—including their own jail.

"Freo" hosted the 1987 America's Cup.

Though Fremantle is a modern port, much of the old district with its 19th-century buildings and shop fronts has been preserved and—thanks to the Cup race—spruced up and painted, at least within the last decade. It's an easy stroll, a popular tourist town of historical sites, art galleries, and sidewalk cafes. The place is—dare I say it—"picturesque, charming, and quaint."

Historical Sights

If you arrive by train, you'll begin your tour at **Fremantle Railway Station,** Victoria Quay, opened in 1907 to serve the harbor. Check out the cluster of black swans on the building's facade, as well as the **memorial water trough** in the park out front which commemorates the death of two Outback explorers (who died of thirst).

The **Round House** (1831) at Arthur Head, west end of High St., actually has 12 sides and is W.A.'s oldest remaining public building. Now roofless and empty, this was originally the colony's first jail, site of its first hanging, and later a "holding tank" for Aborigines being shipped to Rottnest Island. Hours are daily 10 a.m.-5 p.m. Admission is free.

The convict-built **Western Australian Maritime Museum** (1850), corner of Cliff St. and Marine Terrace, was once a commissariat store. Exhibits include relics from a number of 17th-century Dutch ships wrecked off the coastline. One highlight is the ongoing reconstruction of the 1629 *Batavia* hull, a process that visitors can view as conservationists work. Hours are Mon.-Thurs. 10:30 a.m.-5 p.m., Fri.-Sun. 1-5 p.m. Admission is by donation.

Following Marine Terrace back toward town, you'll pass the **Old Court House** on your left, and a statue of **C.Y. O'Connor** (he's the bloke who built the artificial harbor here in the 1860s) off to the right. Continue on Marine Terrace, turning left at Essex Street, which, as you cross South Terrace, becomes Henderson Street.

Fremantle Markets, on the corner, date from 1897. Reactivated in the mid-'70s (wasn't everything?), this is still the area's most lively weekly market. Approximately 170 stalls offer fruit, veggies, arts, crafts, and other market kitsch, bargains, and buskers. Shopping hours are Friday 9 a.m.-9 p.m., Saturday 9 a.m.-5 p.m., Sunday and public holidays 10 a.m.-5 p.m.

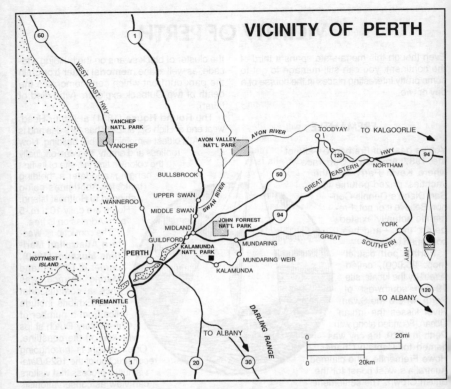

VICINITY OF PERTH

The **Sail and Anchor** pub, across Henderson St., is a restored 1903 building that served as "command post" during the America's Cup trials and also houses a brewery (sheer coincidence, no doubt). This one-time site of the old Freemason's Hotel has housed pubs since the 1850s. Next to the markets, on South Terrace, **Scots Presbyterian Church** also dates from the 19th century.

The **Warders' Quarters** (1851), near the corner of William St., are stone terraces built by convicts to house their keepers at Fremantle Prison. The grim **Fremantle Prison,** on The Terrace off Fairburn St., was also constructed by convicts between 1851-59 and was used as a lock-up until 1991, and a tourist attraction ever since. A museum next to the prison gates depicts prison history and features prison memorabilia and other articles of bondage. Hours are

daily 10 a.m.-6 p.m., closed Christmas Day and Good Friday. Admission is $10—and you're free to leave whenever you like.

Going left at William St., it's a two-block walk to St. John's Square. **Fremantle Town Hall** (1887), past the information center, is an elegant structure opened in conjunction with Queen Victoria's Jubilee. Opposite the Town Hall, on William St., the **Federal Hotel** is another atmospheric pub that dates from 1887. **St. John's Anglican Church** (1881), next door, is a stone structure that took three years to complete.

Old **St. Patrick's Church** sits at the corner of Adelaide and Quarry Streets. **Proclamation Tree,** across Quarry St., is a Moreton Bay fig tree planted around the turn of the century. On the opposite side of Adelaide St., the **Old Fremantle Boys' School** used to be guess what.

Fremantle Museum and Arts Centre, corner of Ord and Finnerty Streets in Fremantle Park, served as the local lunatic asylum between 1861-65, a women's home (i.e., old ladies) in the early 1900s, and the 1942 headquarters for American Forces stationed in Western Australia. After a 13-year restoration, the Gothicesque sandstone building reopened in 1972 as a museum and art center featuring changing exhibitions (with an emphasis on Western Australian artists), a museum wing with displays and mementos of Fremantle's history, a lecture room, and cloistered courtyard used for music and theatrical performances and crafts fairs. Museum hours are Thurs.-Sun. 1-5 p.m. Arts center hours are daily 10 a.m.-5 p.m., Wednesday 7-9 p.m. Admission to both wings is free. For information, phone (09) 335-8211, museum, or (09) 335-8244, arts center.

One block south, at the corner of Ord and Ellen Streets, **Samson House** (1888) was and still is associated with a prominent Fremantle family (name of Samson). Contained within are historic photographs, antique furnishings, and a 20-meter-deep, in-house well. Hours are Sunday and Thursday 1-5 p.m. Guided tours are available.

Other Sights
Down in the B Shed, at Victoria Quay, **Historic Boat Shed Museum** features a wide range of vessels, including the America's Cup winner *Australia II* and a full-size replica of the *Endeavour*, the ship in which Captain James Cook discovered Australia. Hours are daily 1-5 p.m. Admission is free.

Fremantle Wharves and Passenger Terminal, accessible by car, is usually filled with assorted ships from all over the world—free entertainment for boat lovers of all ages.

Up Mews Road toward the Esplanade, **Fremantle Crocodile Park** is home to more than 200 fresh- and saltwater crocs, living as they might in their Kimberley homeland. Viewing is from the safety of a raised metal walkway, enclosed with a tall chainlink fence. Education tours and a film document crocodile history and explain how the Aussie crocs were saved from extinction. Hours are daily 10 a.m.-5 p.m. Admission is $8. For information, phone (09) 430-5388.

Eyeball the terrific view of Fremantle Harbour from the **Observation Tower** of Fremantle Port Authority, 1 Cliff Street. Tours, departing the foyer, are available Mon.-Fri. at 2:30 p.m.

If you're into gas and electricity, you can study its local history at the **Energy Museum,** 12 Parry Street. Hours are Mon.-Fri. 12:30-4:30 p.m., Sat.-Sun. 1-4:30 p.m. Admission is free.

Arts and Crafts
Fremantle is filled with artisans, and their wares are on display and for sale in converted boat sheds, warehouses, and historic buildings and markets throughout town.

Bannister Street Craftworks, 8 Bannister St., is a converted warehouse that houses a variety of studios representing pottery, stained glass, fabric printing, leatherwork, woodwork, weaving, and gold- and silversmithing. Hours are Tues.-Sat. 10 a.m.-5 p.m., Sunday and public holidays 12:30-5:30 p.m.

Bather's Beach Gallery and Potters Workshop, Mews Rd., Bather's Beach, features the work of 20-or-so Western Australian artists, including renowned potter Joan Campbell. Hours are Mon.-Fri. 10 a.m.-5 p.m., Sat.-Sun. 11 a.m.-5 p.m.

A Shed Cafe and Gallery, Victoria Quay (next to B Shed, of course), has been transformed into an arts and crafts venue and atmospheric cafe. Hours are daily 10 a.m.-5 p.m.

Accommodations
Inexpensive pub accommodations are available at the **Newport Hotel,** 2 South Terrace (tel. 09-335-2428). The **Norfolk Hotel,** 47 South Terrace (tel. 335-5405), and the **Fremantle Hotel,** 6 High St. (tel. 09-430-4300), both historic beauties, are moderately priced pub offerings.

The huge 200-room **Ocean View Lodge,** 100 Hampton Rd. (tel. 09-336-2962), features a variety of inexpensive rooms, good weekly deals, and a pool, gym, sauna, and billiard room.

Studios and one-bedroom apartments are costly at the river-view **Tradewinds Hotel,** 66 Canning Hwy., East Fremantle (tel. 09-339-2266). The **Fremantle Esplanade,** 46 Marine Terrace (tel. 430-4000), represents the big splurge ($150-290 per night), with all the goodies that come with big bucks.

Dorm beds are available at **Bundi Kudja Homestead,** 96 Hampton Rd. (tel. 09-335-3467). This former nurse's quarters also has cheap rooms, plus kitchens, a video lounge, and game room.

Fremantle Village Caravan Park, corner of Cockburn and Rockingham Roads (tel. 09-430-4866), a couple kilometers from town, has campsites and cabins.

Homestays can be arranged, at a variety of rates, through **Fremantle Homestays** (tel. 09-319-1256).

Food
You'll find plenty of reasonably priced pub meals and ethnic eateries in Fremantle, but fresh fish and seafood are the local specialties.

Lombardo's, Mews Rd., Fishing Boat Harbour, is a waterfront complex with everything from takeaway fish and chips stalls and outdoor cafes to bistros and fine restaurants.

South Terrace is another popular area lined with cappuccino bars and sidewalk cafes. One of Fremantle's ranking favorites is **Old Papa's,** 33 South Terrace, which serves coffee, cakes, and pasta dishes on a terrace overlooking the street. If there's a long wait, try the **Mexican Kitchen** next door, or—if you have your heart set on Italian—**Pizza Bella Roma** across the street. If you have your heart set on being *seen* eating Italian, **Gino's,** 1 South Terrace, is a good bet. And, at 64 South Terrace, the historic **Sail and Anchor Hotel** has an enjoyable brasserie and an ever more enjoyable brewery (this was the first Australian on-site brewery, hopping the way for the boutique-beer industry).

The best breakfasts are at **Pisa Café,** 1 High St., and the **Round House Café,** also on High Street. **Vung Tau,** 19 High St., serves up Vietnamese and vegetarian dishes.

The **Upmarket Food Centre,** Henderson St., across from the market, is full of mostly Asian chow-down stalls. Hours are Thurs.-Sun. noon-9 p.m. Be prepared for long lines on market days.

The Left Bank, 15 Riverside Rd., East Fremantle, in a colonial mansion on the Swan Riverbank, is *the* trendy, upmarket, hip, cool spot in town. Runner-up is the **Surf Club,** on the beachfront, at North Fremantle. Both places house expensive restaurants and cheap-ish cafes.

Entertainment
High Street and South Terrace are where you'll find most of the live bands and a disco or two.

Try **West End Hotel** and the **Orient,** both on High Street, both with bands at high volume. **Seaview Tavern** and **Newport Arms** are two frontrunner band venues on South Terrace.

Catch techno, house, rap, and dance music into the wee hours at **Metropolis,** 58 South Terrace. **Fly By Night Musicians Club,** Parry St., draws the reggae, blues, and folk crowd. **Harbourside Tavern,** 4 Beach St., features local bands most weekends.

Information
Pick up info, brochures, and walking tour maps at the **Fremantle Information Centre,** Kings Square, in the Town Hall. Hours are Mon.-Fri. 9 a.m.-5 p.m., Saturday 9 a.m.-1 p.m., Sunday 10 a.m.-3 p.m. For information, phone (09) 430-2346.

Transport
Frequent bus and train service connect Perth with Fremantle. **Transperth buses** (tel. 13-2213 toll-free), traveling various routes, depart from St. George's Terrace, while trains (traveling only one route) leave from Perth Central Station.

Captain Cook Cruises (tel. 09-325-3341) provides daily ferry service from Perth ($12). In addition, some Rottnest Island ferries make a stop at Fremantle. For information, phone **Oceanic Cruises** (tel. 09-430-5127) or **Boat Torque Cruises** (tel. 09-430-7644).

For bicycle rentals, contact **Captain Munchies,** 2 Beach St. (tel. 09-339-6633), or **Fleet Cycles** (tel. 09-430-5414). The **Fremantle Tram,** like the Perth Tram, makes frequent tours (with accompanying commentary) around the local sights. Cost is $7. A harbor tour ($7) and Top of the Port tour ($10) are also available. For information, phone (09) 339-8719.

ROTTNEST ISLAND

This sandy island resort—affectionately known as "Rotto"—lies just 19 km off the Fremantle coast and is a favorite day excursion and holiday destination for Perth residents drawn to its bleached beaches, turquoise waters, and activities (or inactivity).

Rottnest translates to "Rat's Nest," a name bestowed upon it by Dutch mariner Willem de

Vlamingh. Landing there in 1696, Willem mistook the native quokkas—a type of small marsupial—for a bunch of big, old rats. These days the quokkas are a protected species and one of the island's big tourist attractions.

Originally used as a prison settlement for mainland Aborigines back in 1838, the prison was vacated in 1903, and 14 years later it became a getaway spot for white society—and still is today. Thomson Bay is the main resort area of this tiny 11-km-long, five-km-wide island, and is one of the few shady spots. The rest of the landscape consists of sparse vegetation, a few low hills, some shallow salt lakes, plenty of white-sand beaches, and secluded rocky bays. Add to that the surrounding reef, protected lagoons, and some 12 shipwrecks to explore.

Sights

Get your bearings at **Rottnest Museum,** located at the main settlement. Exhibits and memorabilia cover convict history, wildlife, and shipwrecks. Walking-tour leaflets, including info and directions around the remaining convict-built buildings, are available. Hours are daily 10 a.m.-1:30 p.m. and 2:30-4:30 p.m. Dec.-Feb., daily 11 a.m.-1:30 p.m. and 2:30-4 p.m. other months. For information, phone (09) 372-9752.

Vlamingh Lookout, via Digby Dr., offers panoramic views of the island, surrounding ocean, and Gordon Lake. **Oliver Hill,** via Digby Dr., offers yet another dynamic island view and a leftover artillery battery.

Constructed of locally quarried limestone, **Rottnest Lighthouse,** Wadjemup Hill, in the center of the island, dates back to the mid-1800s. **Bathurst Lighthouse,** Gem Rd., Bathurst Point, the second of Rotto's lighthouses, was built in 1900.

Located in the island center east and northeast of the jetty are the small **salt lakes**—Government House, Serpentine, Herschell, Baghdad, Pink, and Garden Lakes. You'll see those quokkas (relatives of the wallaby) at the **Quokka Colony,** between Government House and Herschell Lakes. This lot—used to having their faces stuffed by tourists—is quite tame.

Best **swimming beaches** include **Parakeet Bay,** at the northernmost tip of the island, and **The Basin,** north of the main settlement. **West End,** the westernmost point on the island, is popular (and crowded) with hopeful **fishers. Shipwreck** sights are signposted along a marked trail around the island; however, snorkelers will need a boat to reach most of them. (Boats, and snorkeling and fishing gear, can be hired on the island.)

Accommodations and Food

If you want to make Rotto more than a day-trip, keep in mind that accommodations must be booked way in advance, particularly during holidays and summer months when the Perthos descend en masse. For information on rates and bookings, phone **Rottnest Island Authority** (tel. 09-372-9729).

Accommodations are concentrated around the Thomson Bay settlement and comprise cabins, hotel and motel rooms, a hostel, and campground. Due to a water shortage, showers at Rotto accommodations are saltwater; bring saltwater shampoo and soap with you as it's more expensive on the island.

Moderately priced **Rottnest Hotel** (tel. 09-292-5011) overlooks the main beach and is Rotto's gathering spot. Built in 1864 as the summer residence of Western Australian governors, it was reopened as a hotel in 1953. **Rottnest Island Authority Cottages** (tel. 09-372-9729) sleep four to eight people, at a cost of $175-675 per week.

Kingston Barracks Youth Hostel (tel. 09-372-9780), about one km from the ferry terminal, is in a former 1936 barracks and still looks the part. Facilities include a lounge and kitchen, but hot water is scarce. Beds cost $13-16.

Campsites, tents, and cabins are available at **Thomson Camping Areas** (tel. 09-372-9737).

Food is relatively expensive, as on most tourist-type islands—even at the general store and fast-food center. **Rottnest Hotel** serves moderately priced steaks and salads in a casual environment, while another section offers fine dining. The **Rottnest Island Lodge** has a similar setup: the restaurant is a la carte and expensive; the bar section features inexpensive all-you-can-eat midweek meals. Buy fresh bread and yummy baked goodies at the **Rottnest Island Bakery.**

Information

Tourist information and walking and cycling maps are available at the **tourist information center,** at the end of the main jetty (tel. 09-372-9729). Hours are daily 9 a.m.-4 p.m.

Dial 000 to request **emergency assistance** or contact **Rottnest Medical Centre** (tel. 09-372-9727).

Transport

Rottnest Airlines (tel. 09-277-4198) flies daily from Perth for about $45 roundtrip. A shuttle bus takes you from Rottnest Airport to the main wharf area.

Boat Torque Cruises operates a daily ferry service to the island aboard its *Star Flyte*, departing from Perth's Barrack Street Jetty and from Fremantle. Fare is $42 roundtrip from Perth, $25 roundtrip from Fremantle. *Sea Raider III* departs daily from Hillarys Boat Harbour, north of Perth. For information and bookings, phone (09) 430-7644.

White Dolphin Cruises, operated by Boat Torque, and **Oceanic Cruises** (tel. 09-430-5127), travel between Fremantle and Rottnest Island. Fare is $12-15, extended stay fares are $20-25 (Oceanic Cruises is cheapest for now anyway—watch for continuing price wars).

No cars are allowed on the island. Most visitors rely on bicycles—a round-the-island bike path covers 26 kilometers. Bring your own cycle on the ferry (an extra $5) or rent one from **Rottnest Bike Hire,** behind the Rottnest Hotel (tel. 09-372-9722). Rates run $10 per day.

Bus service is available during summer months, and bus tours around the island are available most months. Check with the tourist information office for schedules and bookings. *Underwater Explorer* takes passengers on 45-minute boat tours over primitive corals, marinelife, and shipwrecks. Departures are from the main jetty. Fare is $12. For information, phone (09) 221-5844.

YANCHEP NATIONAL PARK

Only 51 km north of Perth, Yanchep National Park is a 2,799-hectare, family-oriented coastal wonderland with bushland, caves, walking trails, a wildlife sanctuary, boating lake, swimming pool, golf course, footie ovals (football fields), limestone gorges, fauna exhibits, aviaries, a beer garden, and a museum. Despite all these attractions, 90% of the park has been maintained in its natural state.

Of the numerous caves set in the limestone hills, **Crystal Cave,** open to the public, features an underground stream in the main grotto, good examples of stalactites and stalagmites, and "fantasy lighting." Guided tours are offered several times daily.

Another favorite activity is the **Yanjidi Trail,** a 28-km walk through the Loch McNess wetlands, a refuge for waterfowl and other birds (and the Loch McNess monster?). Signs along the path—which follows the tracks used by the local Yaberoo Aborigines—explain the wetland ecology.

To reach Yanchep, follow the West Coast Highway north out of town, or catch a daily Transperth bus from Perth Central Bus Station. Admission is $5 per vehicle, or $2 per bus passenger.

Other Sights

Traveling the West Coast Highway from Perth, you'll pass through **Wanneroo,** another popular wine-producing area and a fast-growing artsy-craftsy-touristy center. The **Gumnut Factory,** 30 Prindiville Dr., Wangara Centre (tel. 09-409-6699), manufactures all types of gumnut creations and *you,* folks, can watch it happen. Don't miss Gumnutland, a model village with more than 30 handcrafted buildings, working railways, roads, and mini gumnut people—all crafted from timber, flowers, and gumnuts. Hours are daily 9 a.m.-5 p.m. Admission is $1.

If you're passing through Wanneroo on the weekend, stop at the **market** in the carpark at the corner of Prindiville Dr. and Ismail St., where 200 stalls offer a wide range of goods for sale.

Wineries offering tastings are **Bonannella Wines,** 96 Pinjar Rd. (tel. 09-405-1084), and **Paul Conti Wines,** 529 Wanneroo Rd. (tel. 09-409-9160).

And then there's **Wild Kingdom Wildlife Park,** also on Two Rocks Rd. (tel. 09-561-1399), with wombats, dingoes, foxes, and other animals, as well as birdlife. Hours are daily 9:30 a.m.-5 p.m., closed Christmas Day. Admission is $3.

Accommodations

The **Yanchep Lagoon Lodge,** 11 Nautical Court (tel. 09-561-1033), at Yanchep Lagoon, has moderately priced guesthouse accommodations. **Club Capricorn,** Two Rocks Rd. (tel. 09-561-1106), is an expensive beachfront resort with lodge and chalet accommodations, plus restaurant, swimming pools, and tennis courts.

Information

For info on **Yanchep National Park,** phone (09) 561-1661. In **Wanneroo,** the tourist information center is at 935 Wanneroo Rd. (tel. 09-405-4678).

THE DARLING RANGE

This range, full of wooded hills, valleys, and dams, runs east of Perth and parallel to the coastline. It's a popular picnic, bushwalking, and weekend-away place for Perth dwellers, particularly from September to November when an astounding assortment of more than 4,000 wildflower species are in bloom. You can take a number of different roads as far and flung as you like; one easy, close-to-Perth route is to catch Kalamunda Rd. from South Guildford, to Kalamunda sights, then pick up Mundaring Weir Rd., meeting the Great Eastern Highway back into Perth. Transperth buses journey to the range on a variety of routes.

Sights

For some great coastal plain and city lights views, negotiate three kilometers of sharp hairpin and hair-raising turns on the one-way **Zig Zag Road** (formerly a railway line). Signs are posted off Kalamunda Road, Gooseberry Hill. You can also reach steep, 33-hectare Gooseberry Hill via Gooseberry Hill Rd., Williams Rd., or Lascelles Parade.

Stirk Park and Cottage, 9A Headingly Rd., Kalamunda, is a restored 1881 cottage surrounded by a public reserve with scenic walks and waterways, an ornamental lake, model boat pond, and bowling greens. Hours are daily 9 a.m.-9 p.m. The cottage is open Sunday 1:30-4:30 p.m.

History Village, corner Railway and Williams Roads, Kalamunda, is a museum on the site of

the old railway station, plus the original state school building, post office, and a settler's cottage, transported to the site. Memorabilia and displays illustrate the area's early history. Hours are Thurs.-Sat. 9 a.m.-noon, Sunday 2-4:30 p.m. Admission is $1.

Kalamunda National Park, via Kalamunda Rd., offers 375 hectares of forest scenery, granite boulder outcrops, seasonal wildflowers, wildlife, and birdlife. Visitors must carry their own water in hot weather.

Mundaring Weir, Mundaring Weir Rd., Mundaring, is the reservoir that provides water for the goldfields towns more than 500 km away. The **C.Y. O'Connor Museum,** named for the engineer who devised this system, features displays and exhibits relating to the complicated water system. Museum hours are Monday, Wednesday, Thursday, Friday, and public holidays 10:30 a.m.-3 p.m., Saturday 1-4 p.m., Sunday noon-5 p.m.

John Forrest National Park, reached via the Great Eastern Highway, consists of 1,577 hectares of open forest and woodland, spring wildflowers, city and coastal views, and scenic walking trails. Western Australia's first national park was declared in 1895 and named for Lord John Forrest, the state's premier 1890-1901.

Accommodations

Travellers Rest, 885 Great Eastern Hwy. (tel. 09-295-2950), offers moderately priced holiday units with cooking facilities, a pool, and continental breakfast included. Expensive **Mundaring Weir Hotel,** Mundaring Weir Rd. (tel. 09-295-1106), is a popular getaway for Perth runaways.

The YHA operates a **hostel** at Mundaring, on Mundaring Weir Rd. (tel. 09-295-1809), offering dorm beds for $10 per night.

Campsites are available at Mundaring Caravan Park, Great Eastern Hwy. (tel. 09-295-1125).

SWAN VALLEY

The good news is that the scenic, fertile Swan Valley and its 20 or so wineries are a mere 20 km northeast of Perth—an easy car ride or river cruise away. The bad news is that the area is so close to the city and the city is expanding so rapidly that many of the rural communities are blending into urban-ity. The Swan River meanders the wide valley set at the foot of the Darling Range—a patchwork mix of small farms and award-winning wineries, stretching from Perth through historic Guildford to the Upper Swan, passing a number of interesting sights along the way.

Sights

The 1830 **Tranby House**, Johnson Rd., Maylands, is Western Australia's oldest inhabited property. Hours are Mon.-Sat. 2-5 p.m., Sunday 11 a.m.-1 p.m. and 2-5 p.m. Admission is $2.50. View nearly 30 locomotives (including steam, diesel, and electric), antique carriages, and other railway memorabilia, photos, and artifacts at the **Rail Transport Museum,** 136 Railway Parade, Bassendean (300 meters east of Ashfield Railway Station). Steam train tours are available May-October. Hours are Sunday and public holidays 1-5 p.m., Wednesday 1-4 p.m. during school holidays. Admission is $3. For information, phone (09) 279-7189.

In Guildford, situated at the rear of the historic 1840 Rose and Crown Hotel, 105 Swan St., the private **Hall Collection** consists of 40,000 antique and nostalgic artifacts, including porcelain, paintings, glass, copper work, cameras, musical instruments, toys, and kitchen items. Hours are Tues.-Sun. 10 a.m.-4:30 p.m. Admission is $3. For information, phone (09) 279-6542.

Woodbridge House, Third Ave., Guildford, is the National Trust-restored 1885 residence of Perth personality extraordinaire Charles Harper. Hours are daily except Wednesday 1-4 p.m., Sunday 11 a.m.-1 p.m. and 2-5 p.m. Admission is $2. For information, phone (09) 274-2432.

The **Historic Gaol and Settlers Cottage,** Meadow St., Guildford, exhibits period furnishings and clothing, blacksmithing tools and equipment, and bric-a-brac. Hours are 2-5 p.m. March to mid-December. Admission is $1. For information, phone (09) 279-1248.

Other 19th-century Guildford buildings are **St. Matthew's Church,** in Stirling Square, and the jail, corner of Swan and Meadow Streets. See local pottery at **Guildford Potters,** 105 Swan Street. Hours are daily 10 a.m.-3 p.m.

Caversham Wildlife Park and Zoo, corner of Arthur Rd. and Cranleigh St., West Swan, is a wildlife park featuring Australian and imported animals and birds. Hours are daily 10 a.m.-5 p.m. Admission is $4.50. For information, phone (09) 274-2202.

Gomboc Gallery, James Rd., Middle Swan, displays paintings, sculptures, and graphics by Western Australian artists. Hours are Wed.-Sun. and public holidays 10 a.m.-5 p.m.

Wineries

Swan Valley vineyards are sprinkled along the river, from the Guildford area to Upper Swan. Though vines were first planted in the 1830s, it's the Middle Swan district (with its more recent plantings) that is responsible for much of the high production. Most of the wineries welcome visitors for divine tastings.

Olive Farm Winery, 77 Great Eastern Hwy., South Guildford (tel. 09-277-2989), named for the olive trees planted along with the vines, is the region's oldest winery. Hours are Mon.-Fri. 10 a.m.-5:30 p.m., Saturday and public holidays 9 a.m.-3 p.m.

Some of the valley's renowned wineries include: **Houghton Wines,** Dale Rd., Middle Swan (tel. 09-274-5100); **Jane Brook Estate Wines,** Toodyay Rd. (tel. 09-274-1432); **Sandalford Wines,** corner West Swan and Middle Swan Roads, Caversham (tel. 09-274-5922); **Twin Hill Wines,** Great Northern Hwy., Baskerville (tel. 09-296-4272); and **Westfield Wines,** Memorial Ave., Baskerville (tel. 09-269-4356).

For maps and information about all of the wineries plus other Swan Valley attractions, stop into the Western Australia Tourist Centre in Perth or the **Swan Valley Tourism Association,** Great Eastern Hwy., Midland (under the Town Hall clocktower), or phone (09) 274-1522.

Transport

Transperth buses and trains depart regularly for the Swan Valley. Trains stop at Guildford, then go on to the valley's gateway town of Midland. Buses travel all the way to Upper Swan along Middle Swan Road. For information, phone Transperth (tel. 13-2213 toll-free).

If you're traveling by car (30-40 minutes' drive), take Guildford Road or the Great Eastern Highway to Midland, then turn onto the Great Northern Highway through the valley's center.

AVON VALLEY

Homesick English settlers fell in love with this lush, hilly valley, which reminded them of their very own Avon—hence the name. Rainfall-green in winter and parched-sun brown in summer, this rural land, settled only one year after Perth, follows the course of the Avon River (an east- and southward branch of the Swan), running through the historic towns of Toodyay, Northam, and York.

Toodyay

Say "Two Jay," otherwise you'll be ignored—or worse. Toodyay (pop. 560) sits at the bend where the Avon River turns from east to south, and is the smallest of the river towns. There was an earlier Toodyay settled in the 1830s, some eight km downstream; today's Toodyay—established in 1860 as Newcastle—was rechristened in 1910. The National Trust declared the town "historic" in 1980, and some 13 buildings have been classified as worthy of preservation.

Connors Mill, corner of Stirling Terrace and Piessa St., contains a steam engine, 1941 generator, and the **Moondyne Gallery,** which recounts the story of infamous bushranger Joseph Bolitho Jones (a.k.a. Moondyne Joe). Hours are Mon.-Sat. 9 a.m.-5 p.m., Sunday and public holidays 10 a.m.-5 p.m. Admission is $1.

Trace the lives (and deaths) of 1800s pioneers and convicts at the **Old Gaol Museum and Police Station,** Clinton Street. The Old

Gaol, an early stone and shingle-roofed structure, includes original cells. Hours are Mon.-Fri. 11 a.m.-3 p.m., Saturday 1-4 p.m., Sunday and public holidays 11 a.m.-4 p.m. Admission is $2.

White Gum Flower Farm, Sandplain Rd., features commercially grown wildflowers amid 283 hectares of white gum timberland. Hours are Wed.-Sun. 10 a.m.-4 p.m. Closed Christmas Day through March.

Avon Valley National Park, via Toodyay Rd. (make a left at Morangyup Rd. and follow posted signs), is a beautifully scenic 4,377-hectare park with valleys, slopes, woodlands, and open forest.

Northam

Believe it or not, Northam (pop. 6,800) is not only the largest Avon Valley town, but W.A.'s second-largest inland center (it's on the railway line to Kalgoorlie), notable for its black swans, white swans, and the whitewater Avon Descent Race.

See the **Avon Valley Arts Society,** 33 Wellington St., which comprises two historic structures—the Old Post Office (1892) and the Old Girls School (1877). The art center sells locally made arts and crafts. Hours are Tues.-Fri. 9 a.m.-4 p.m., Sat.-Mon. 10 a.m.-4 p.m.

The **Old Railway Station,** Fitzgerald St. West, contains early 1900s appliances and railway relics, plus renovated carriages and an old steam train. Hours are Sunday 10 a.m.-4 p.m. Admission is $2.

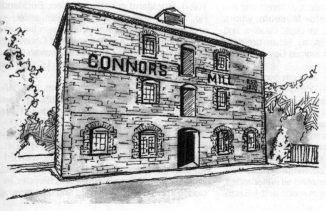

Built in 1870, this information center was originally a flour mill.

Other historic sights are: **Pioneer Graves,** Goomalling Rd.; **Morby Cottage** (1836), Avon Dr.; the **police station** (1866) and **courthouse** (1896), both on Wellington St.; **St. John's Church** (1890), Wellington St.; **St. Saviour's Church** (1862), Toodyay Road; and **Presbyterian Church** (1908), Duke Street (present home of the Link Theatre).

Near Northam, at Irishtown, **Buckland House** (1874) is one of the state's most stately homes. The restoration, and collections of antique furnishings, paintings, and silver, are worth a peek. Hours are Mon.-Wed. and Sat.-Sun. 10 a.m.-5 p.m. Closed Christmas Day through February. Admission is $4. For information, phone (096) 22-1130.

York

Settled in 1830, this one-time commercial center for the Avon Valley declined when the railway passed it by in 1894, and it reverted to an agricultural community. In the 1970s, York (pop. 1,140) was rediscovered for its architectural delights and reputedly has more original buildings than any other town in Western Australia.

Avon Terrace, the main street, features buildings reflecting architectural styles ranging from the 1860s to the turn of the century. The **Old Police Station** complex comprises the old courthouse, troopers' cottage, stables, and cell blocks. Hours are Mon.-Fri. 11 a.m.-3 p.m., Sat.-Sun. and public holidays 10 a.m.-4 p.m. The **Post Office Museum** illustrates York's postal history beginning from 1840. Phone (096) 41-1301 to arrange admittance. Car lovers can rev their engines at the **Motor Museum,** where more than 100 veteran, vintage, classic, and racing vehicles are on display. Hours are daily 10 a.m.-5 p.m., closed Christmas Day and Good Friday. Admission is $6.

Trace printing history through commentary and demonstrations on a century-old letter press at **Sandalwood Press.** Hours are Tues.-Thurs. and Sat.-Sun. 1-3 p.m.

The **Art Gallery,** Avon Terrace, exhibits locally crafted jarrah furniture, paintings, and stained glass. Hours are Sun-Fri. 10 a.m.-4 p.m., Saturday 10 a.m.-1 p.m. The **Doll Museum,** also on Avon Terrace, features more than 1,000 doll babies representing all nationalities. Hours are Sat.-Sun. 10 a.m.-noon and 1-3 p.m.

One of York's oldest buildings is the **Residency Museum,** Brook Street. In a structure dating back to 1842, the museum displays photographs and artifacts of the town's early days. Hours are Tues.-Thurs. and school and public holidays 1-3 p.m., Sat.-Sun. 1-5 p.m.

Balladong Farm, 5 Parker Rd., outside York on the way to Beverley, has been restored by the National Trust to show visitors what farm life was like in the 19th century. Displays include original breeds of stock and farm machinery, plus demonstrations of blacksmithing, milking, and wool spinning. Hours are Tues.-Sun. 10 a.m.-5 p.m. Guided tours can be arranged. For information, phone (096) 41-1279. Admission is $5.

Accommodations

Toodyay: Avondown Inn, 44 Stirling Terrace (tel. 09-574-2995), a one-time convent, offers inexpensive rooms. For inexpensive pub rooms, try either the **Victoria Hotel** (tel. 09-574-2206) or the **Freemasons Hotel** (tel. 09-574-2201). Both are on Stirling Terrace. **Appleton House,** Julimar Rd. (tel. 09-574-2622), is a moderately priced, colonial-style B&B nestled in the hills. Campsites and on-site vans are available at both **Toodyay Caravan Park,** Railway Rd. (tel. 09-574-2612), and **Broadgrounds Park,** Stirlingia Dr. (tel. 09-574-2534). **Avon Valley National Park** (tel. 09-574-2540), 35 km west of Toodyay, has campsites with limited facilities.

Northam: Find basic pub rooms at **Avon Bridge Hotel,** Fitzgerald St. (tel. 096-22-1023), or the **Grand Hotel,** Fitzgerald St. (tel. 096-22-1024). **Buckland** country mansion, Buckland Rd., Irishtown (tel. 096-22-1130), offers stately—and expensive—accommodations in two upstairs rooms. The mansion is closed Christmas Day through February. **Mortlock Caravan Park,** Great Eastern Hwy. (tel. 096-22-1620), has campsites and on-site vans.

York: Opposite the railway station, the **YHA Hostel,** 3 Brook St. (tel. 096 41-1372), features dorm beds in a converted hospital for $11 per night. The **Castle Hotel,** Avon Terrace (tel. 096-41-1007), is the recommended pub. Moderately priced **Hillside Homestead,** Forrest Rd. (tel. 096-41-1065), a classified historic site, is an Edwardian residence with B&B accommodations, swimming pool, tennis court, and bicycles included in the price. Campsites and on-site vans can be rented at **Mt. Bakewell Resort and Caravan Gardens,** Eighth Rd. (tel. 096-41-1421).

Events

Avon Valley has about a dozen noteworthy events. Toodyay's **Moondyne Festival,** held annually in April, is a celebration of the colonial past including mock shoot-em-up holdups, jail breaks, coppers and convicts, plus an array of other fun sports and games.

The **Avon Descent Race,** begun at Northam each year on the first August weekend (when the river is full), features 800 or so canoeists in a fast-paced and furiously paddled whitewater race to Perth—a distance of 133 kilometers. The cheering crowds partying on the banks are just as much fun to watch—and join.

Other popular draws are October's **Jazz Festival** and the **Vintage and Veteran Car Race** in August.

Information

In Toodyay, the **tourist bureau** is on Stirling Terrace, in Connors Mill. Hours are Mon.-Sat. 9 a.m.-5 p.m., Sunday and public holidays 10 a.m.-5 p.m. For information, phone (09) 574-2435.

The **Northam Tourist Bureau,** 138 Fitzgerald St., is open Mon.-Fri. 9 a.m.-5 p.m., Sat.-Sun. and public holidays 10 a.m.-4 p.m. For information, phone (096) 22-2100. **York Tourist Bureau,** 105 Avon Terrace, is open Mon.-Fri. 9 a.m.-5 p.m., Sat.-Sun. 9 a.m.-4 p.m. For information, phone (096) 41-1301.

Transport

Westrail operates buses to Northam and York, departing Perth every morning. Fare is about $12 one-way.

The Prospector rail service, also operated by Westrail, calls at Toodyay and Northam on its daily run to Kalgoorlie. Fares are a buck or two more than the bus. For information, schedules, and bookings, phone (09) 326-2222.

It's about an hour-and-some's drive from Perth to any of the Avon Valley towns, and the distance between each of them averages 30 kilometers. The two main valley roads branch from Midland. Choose either the Great Eastern Highway to Northam and York or the Toodyay Road to Toodyay. If you're returning to Perth, take one route going and the other coming back.

THE SOUTH COAST

Below Fremantle the coastal road to Augusta, down in the southwest corner, passes nickel smelters, seaside resorts, industrial towns, established vineyards, and superb beaches (including W.A.'s best surfing spot). The inland route takes in some good bushwalking trails, dams, waterfalls, and a historic structure or two.

TO BUNBURY

Rockingham

Facing the Indian Ocean, Warnbo Sound, and Shoalwater Bay, Rockingham (pop. 25,000), 47 km south of Perth, once a major seaport (1872-1908—before Fremantle grabbed the honors), is now a favored holiday resort.

Rockingham Museum, corner Flinders Lane and Kent St., is a social history museum with memorabilia related to the district's early set-

tlers. Hours are Tues.-Thurs. and Saturday 1-4:30 p.m., Sunday 10 a.m.-4:30 p.m. Admission is $1.

Safe **swimming beaches** are at the Foreshore Reserve, Rockingham Rd., and Point Peron, at the southern end of Cockburn Sound. (Point Peron is favored by photographers who click with the superb sunsets.) Daily ferry service will transport you to **Penguin Island,** a colony of fairy penguins, and to **Seal Island,** with a colony of guess what.

A good Sunday **market** is held on Flinders Lane, 9 a.m.-4 p.m.

Good-value **accommodations** are offered at **CWA Rockingham,** 108 Parkin St. (tel. 09-527-9560). Two units house six to eight people. **Rockingham Ocean Clipper,** Patterson Rd. (tel. 09-527-8000), is a moderately priced hotel with room service, pool, and TVs. Campsites and on-site vans are available at **Lakeside Caravan Park,** Mandurah Rd. (tel. 09-524-

1182), and **Rockingham Palm Beach Holiday Village,** 37 Fisher St. (tel. 09-527-1515).

Yachties should note that the annual **Cockburn Sound Regatta,** W.A.'s largest, takes place here between Christmas and New Year's.

For local info (including ferry schedules), see the **Tourist Bureau,** 43 Kent St. (tel. 09-592-3464). Hours are Mon.-Fri. 9 a.m.-4:30 p.m., Sat.-Sun. 10 a.m.-4 p.m.

Transperth buses will get you there from Perth or Fremantle. For information, phone 13-2213 toll-free.

Mandurah

Another 29 km south will bring you to Mandurah (pop. 11,000), one more beat-the-heat spot, situated at the entrance of Peel Inlet and at the mouth of Harvey Estuary (where dolphins are occasionally sighted).

Hall's Cottage, on Leighton Rd., built in the early 1830s, is the local history museum. Hours are Sunday 1-4 p.m. Admission is $1.

Other historic structures are: **Christ Church** (1871), Scholl St. and Pinjarra Rd.; **Cooper's Cottage** (1845), Mandurah Terrace, near the bridge; **Eacott Cottage** (1842), Gibla St.; **Allandale** (1913), Estuary Rd., Dawesville (south of town); and **Hardy's Cottage** (built from local materials), Estuary Rd., Dawesville.

Kerryelle's Unique Collectors Museum, Gordon Rd. (tel. 09-581-7615), exhibits collections of gemstones, seashells, coins, banknotes, stamps, old bottles, dolls, and model cars. Hours are Tues.-Fri. 10 a.m.-4 p.m., Sat.-Sun. 10 a.m.-5 p.m. **House of Dunnies,** Henry Rd., Melrose Beach (15 km south), features a series of handcrafted, folk dunnies (that means outhouses—a real Australian art form). **Threlfall Galleries,** Old Coast Rd. (tel. 09-534-2704), houses a collection of paintings and sketches depicting the local history. Hours are daily May-Aug. 9:30 a.m.-4 p.m.

Estuary Drive, a detour from the Old Coast Road, is the scenic route to Peel Inlet and Harvey Estuary, weaving through bushland and picnic spots. The **Foreshore Reserve,** in central Mandurah, is home to Slim Jim, Australia's tallest cotton palm. About 60 years old, Jim stands 39-plus meters high.

Marapana Wildlife World, Paganoni Rd. (tel. 09-537-1404), is W.A.'s first drive-through deer park and kangaroo sanctuary. Other wild things

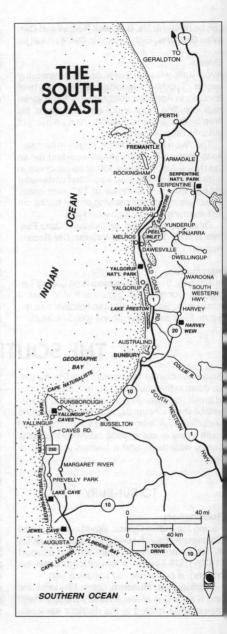

include donkeys, emus, and cockatoos. Visitors can feed the animals (food provided). Hours are daily 10 a.m.-5 p.m. Admission is $5.

See a large variety of Australian birds in natural bushland and water settings at **Western Rosella Bird Park,** Old Pinjarra Rd. (tel. 09-535-2104). Hours are daily 9:30 a.m.-5 p.m., closed Good Friday and Christmas Day. Admission is $4.

Brighton Hotel, Mandurah Terrace (tel. 09-535-1242), has inexpensive pub rooms and counter meals. Also centrally located, the **Crabshell,** Gibson St. (tel. 09-535-5577), has motel rooms in the low-moderate range, plus air-conditioning, TVs, and a saltwater pool. The **Albatross Guesthouse,** 26 Hall St. (tel. 09-581-5597), offers moderately priced B&B accommodations.

Some of the many camping and on-site van facilities are: **Peninsula Caravan Park,** Ormsby Terrace, at the entrance to Peel Inlet (tel. 09-535-2792); **Belvedere Caravan Park,** 153 Mandurah Terrace (tel. 535-1213); **Dawesville Caravan Park,** Old Coast Rd., Dawesville (tel. 09-582-1417); and **Timbertop Caravan Park,** Peel St. (tel. 09-535-1292).

For tourist info, contact **Mandurah Tourist Bureau,** 5 Pinjarra Rd. (tel. 09-535-1155). Hours are Mon.-Sat. 9 a.m.-5 p.m., Sunday 9 a.m.-4 p.m.

Transperth (tel. 13-2213 toll-free) and **Westrail** (tel. 09-326-2222) provide bus service from Perth and Fremantle to Mandurah.

Yalgorup National Park

About halfway between Mandurah and Bunbury, on a narrow coastal strip that includes Lake Clifton and Lake Preston, Yalgorup contains 11,545 hectares of heath, woodland, smaller lakes, interesting geological formations, and diverse bird- and wildlife (some birds migrate, visa-free, each year from the Soviet Union). Preston Beach, accessed through the park, offers good swimming and fishing. For information, phone (097) 39-1067.

Warning: Tiger snakes are known to inhabit the paperbark swamps and sedge lands; additionally, the lakes are salty—be sure to carry freshwater on long bushwalks during summer.

Australind

The name is a contraction of Australia-India, derived from an 1840s plan to colonize the area

and breed horses for the Indian army. The ambitious venture never got off the ground, but the name sure stuck.

Located on the eastern bank of Leschenault Inlet, Australind (pop. 2,900), along with neighboring Bunbury, is famed for blue manna crabs—thousands of which are caught in the inlet each season.

The **Gemstone and Rock Museum,** 267 Old Coast Rd. (tel. 097-97-1241), contains displays of Bunbury agates and other Australian gemstones, natural crystals, as well as Aboriginal, Native American, and English stone artifacts, *and* a cactus garden. Hours are Tues.-Thurs. and Sat.-Sun. 10 a.m.-5 p.m. Admission is $1.

St. Nicholas' Church (1860), Paris Rd., is supposedly the smallest church (four by seven meters) in Western Australia—though the expanding congregation necessitated building a large adjacent edifice (circa 1987). **Henton Cottage** (1840), also on Paris Rd., once the Prince of Wales Hotel, is now an arts and crafts center.

The **scenic drive,** skirting the estuary, leads to crabbing and picnicking sites, while the **Collie River** offers recreational swimming, boating, and fishing.

Leschenault, 14 Old Coast Rd. (tel. 097-97-1352), on the estuary, is a moderately priced B&B with two guest rooms, TV lounge, and a pool. Campsites and on-site vans are available at **Leschenault Inlet Caravan Park,** Scenic Dr. (tel. 097-97-1095).

Most Bunbury-bound coaches from Perth call in at Australind.

The Inland Route

The South Western Highway runs from Perth, some 20 km inland, until it merges with the Old Coast Road at Bunbury. Various roads crisscross between the two highways, allowing travelers to venture inland through pine and jarrah forests or coastward en route.

Serpentine National Park (635 hectares), 52 km south of Perth on the western edge of Darling Scarp, consists of lots of hills with steep gullies, granite outcrops and slopes, and the Serpentine River flowing through the middle. The park's most popular facility is its natural rock pool, ideal for swimming. Steep trails make bushwalking difficult, and rockclimbing is not recommended. Admission is $4 per vehicle, $2 per bus passenger. For information, phone (09) 525-2128.

Pinjarra (pop. 1,340), 86 km south of Perth, was settled by farmers in 1830, making it one of W.A.'s oldest towns. Located on the estuary, this agricultural and timber-producing township features a number of historic structures. **Hotham Valley Tourist Railway** operates steam train journeys, August to October, on the preserved 1913 railway line between Pinjarra and the timber community of **Dwellingup**. Fares are $25-30. For information, phone (09) 221-4444.

Waroona, 25 km south of Dwellingup, is the turnoff for Yalgorup National Park and Preston Beach. **Waroona Dam**, on Scarp Rd., is a power-boating, waterskiing, and fishing area.

In 1916, the state's first controlled irrigation scheme was built at **Harvey** (pop. 2,480), 28 km beyond Waroona. If you drive out to **Harvey Weir**, three km east off Weir Rd., you can still see some of the workers' campsites. The 20-meter-tall **Big Orange** houses a small zoo, a miniature train, arts and crafts, and fruit and veggies.

BUNBURY

Located 180 km south of Perth, on Koombana Bay, Bunbury (pop. 22,000) wears many hats—port, resort, industrial town, gateway to the Southwest, and blue-manna-crab-lovers' paradise.

Sights

King Cottage Museum, 77 Forrest Ave., was built in the 1880s with bricks made from clay dug on the property. Examine pioneer memorabilia Sat.-Sun. 2-4 p.m. Admission is $2.

Other early structures are **St. Mark's Church** (1842), corner Flynn Rd. and Charterhouse St., and **St. Patrick's Cathedral** (1921), Parkfield Street—that spire however is a 1960s contribution. The **Cathedral Church of St. Boniface**, corner Parkfield and Cross Streets, though only about 25 years old, is impressive for its interior built from native blackbutt wood.

The **Old Convent of Mercy** (1860s), Wittenoom St., has been turned into city and regional art galleries and a community arts complex. Hours are daily 10 a.m.-5 p.m.

The **Boyanup Transport Museum**, South Western Hwy., Coombana Bay (20 minutes from Bunbury), houses the *Leschenault Lady* and *Koombana Queen*, two of Australia's oldest steam trains. Hours are daily 10 a.m.-4 p.m. For information, phone (097) 31-5250.

Catch some great views from: **Boulter Heights**, Withers Crescent; the **Lighthouse**, Apex Dr. off Malcom St.; **Marleston Hill Lookout Tower**, Apex Dr.; and along **Ocean Drive**, which follows the coastline for eight kilometers.

Big Swamp Bird Park, Prince Phillip Dr. (tel. 097-21-8380), has a walk-in aviary with 2,000 birds, a wildlife and waterfowl wetland, and a penguin pool and cave. Hours are Wed.-Fri. 1-5 p.m., Sat.-Sun. and holidays 10 a.m.-5 p.m.

On Koombana Beach, the **Bunbury Dolphin Trust** is a mini-Monkey Mia, where visitors can interact with playful bottlenose dolphins. Established in 1989, the dolphins "went public" shortly thereafter, and regularly come for feedings in the Inner Harbour—a flag signals their (and the tourists') arrival.

Accommodations and Food

Prince of Wales, Stephen St. (tel. 097-21-2016), has inexpensive pub rooms. **Clifton Beach Motel**, 2 Molloy St. (tel. 097-21-4300), and **Admiral Motor Inn**, 56 Spencer St. (tel. 097-21-7322), offer moderate rates and modern facilities. The **Lord Forrest**, Symmons St. (tel. 097-21-9966), is Bunbury's big and expensive luxury hotel.

YHA operates **The Residency Retreat Hostel**, corner of Stirling and Moore Streets (tel. 097-91-2621). This lovely restored 1895 building offers $13 dorm beds. **Bunbury Backpackers**, 22 Wittenoom St. (tel. 097-21-3359), offers hostel accommodations for $12 per night—free transport to the dolphin site is included.

Grab campsites and on-site vans at: **Bunbury Village Caravan Park**, corner Bussell Hwy. and Washington Ave. (tel. 097-95-7100); **Waterloo**, South Western Hwy. (tel. 097-25-4434); or **Punchbowl Caravan Park**, Ocean Dr. (tel. 097-21-4761).

For **food**, check out the numerous cafes around the town center, as well as the **International Food Hall**, on Symmons St., and the **Centrepoint** shopping center.

Memories of the Bond Store, on Victoria St., is a good local haunt, as is nearby **Drooly's,** for pizza. Also on Victoria St., for Chinese food, choose from the **Golden Flower** and the **Friendship.**

Try the counter meals—and the many beers on tap—at the **Rose Hotel** on Wellington Street. Meatheads can pig out at **Lump of Rump,** 119 Beach Rd., and foodies can do their nouvelle number at **Louisa's,** 15 Clifton Street.

Information

Tourist info can be obtained at the **Bunbury Tourist Bureau,** Carmody Place, in the old railway station (tel. 097-21-7922). Hours are Mon.-Fri. 8:30 a.m.-5 p.m., Saturday 9 a.m.-4 p.m., Sunday 9:30 a.m.-4:30 p.m., public holidays 10 a.m.-3 p.m.

Transport

South West Coachlines (tel. 09-324-2333) operates a daily Perth-Bunbury service, continuing to Busselton. **Westrail** (tel. 09-326-2222) also provides daily service. Cost is $17.

Westrail's train Australind makes the trip twice a day for about the same fare as the bus. **Westrail Coaches** meet the train at Bunbury and go on to Busselton and Margaret River. Augusta is its last stop.

Bunbury City Transit (tel. 097-91-1955) covers the area from Australind to the north and south down to Gelorup.

FARTHER SOUTH

Busselton and Vicinity

Sheltered by Geographe Bay, Busselton (pop. 6,470) is a peaceful seaside resort not unlike Bunbury, 49 km to the north—a lazy place to fish, crab, and have beachy fun. It's also close to **Yallingup,** which some say is Australia's very best surfing beach.

The **jetty,** two km long, used to be the longest wooden jetty in the Southern Hemisphere until 1978, when Cyclone Alby shortened its act. At the corner of Queen and Albert Streets, see the Ballarat, a timber-hauling locomotive and W.A.'s first engine. Other historic sights are: **Wonnerup House and Old School** (1859), Layman Rd., Wonnerup; **Newtown House** (1851), Bussell

Hwy., Vasse; and **St. Mary's Church of England** (1843), Queen St., the oldest stone church in the state.

The **Old Court House,** 4 Queen St., now completely restored, houses an art gallery, information center, book and craft shops, coffee shop, and artists' studios. Hours are Tues.-Sat. 10 a.m.-4 p.m. The **Old Butter Factory** (it's not "Ye Olde," but it has the same flavor), Peel Terrace, features 16 rooms of early pioneer furnishings, clothing, and artifacts, plus machinery and working models. Hours are Wed.-Mon. 2-5 p.m. Admission is $2. **Bunyip Craft Centre,** Bunyip Rd., Wonnerup, exhibits the wares of more than 150 craftspeople. Hours are Wed.-Mon. 10 a.m.-4 p.m.

The **Oceanarium,** Geographe Bay Rd. near the jetty, displays local fish, including a white pointer shark and stingrays. Hours are daily 9 a.m.-9 p.m. Dec.-March, 9 a.m.-3 p.m. April-November. Admission is $2.

Slightly north of Busselton, **State Tuart Forest,** Bussell Hwy. between Capel and the Sabina River, is the world's only natural tuart forest. Some trees are estimated to be 300-400 years old.

Dunsborough, 24 km west of Busselton, is a pretty holiday town. For an impressive view of the Indian Ocean, continue another 13 km to **Cape Naturaliste Lighthouse** at the tip of Geographe Bay.

Yallingup Beach, eight km southwest of Dunsborough, is surf heaven according to national and international sources. Each November, the **Margaret River Surfing Classic** draws champions from around the world. Pick up a copy of the *Down Under Surf Guide* at the Dunsborough tourist office. It's full of information on wave and swell sizes and wind direction—and it's free.

Follow Caves Road. **Yallingup Cave,** off Caves Rd. north of Yallingup, a limestone cave discovered in 1899, is highlighted with stalactites, stalagmites, pillars, columns, flowstone, cave crystals, helictites, and straws. Hours are daily 9:30 a.m.-3:30 p.m. For information, phone (097) 55-2152.

Accommodations: In Busselton, the **Geographe,** 28 West St. (tel. 097-52-1451), and **Villa Carlotta,** 110 Adelaide St. (tel. 097-54-2026), are inexpensive B&B guesthouses. **Motel**

Busselton, 90 Bussell Hwy. (tel. 097-52-1908), offers inexpensive motel rooms but is often heavily booked.

Broadwater Resort, corner of Bussell Hwy. and Holgate Rd. (tel. 097-54-1633), offers one- or two-bedroom apartments in the expensive range.

This area has many caravan parks offering campsites and on-site vans. Some suggestions are: **Mandalay Caravan Park,** Bussell Hwy. (tel. 097-52-1328); **Acacia Caravan Park,** Bussell Hwy. (tel. 097-55-4034); and **Busselton Caravan Park,** 163 Bussell Hwy. (tel. 097-52-1175).

Hostel accommodations in the Dunsborough area are available at **YHA,** 285 Geographe Bay Rd., Quindalup, two km south of Dunsborough (tel. 097-55-3107). Canoes, sailboards, and bicycles can be hired. Beds are $14. Campsites and on-site vans are offered at **Yallingup Beach Caravan Park,** Valley Rd. (tel. 097-55-2164), and **Caves Caravan Park,** corner of Caves and Yallingup Beach Roads (tel. 097-55-2196).

Information: For information about the Busselton area, contact the **Busselton Tourist Bureau,** Southern Dr. (in the civic center), Busselton (tel. 097-52-1350), or the **Dunsborough Tourist Centre,** Naturaliste Terrace, Dunsborough (tel. 097-55-3517). Both are open Mon.-Fri. 9 a.m.-5 p.m., Sat.-Sun. 10 a.m.-4 p.m.

Margaret River

Midway between Yallingup and Margaret River, along Caves Road, is a cluster of wineries, with several more sprinkled around the Margaret River valley. Indeed, Margaret River (pop. 800), tiny though it may be, has come into its own as a wine-growing district that's giving the Swan Valley a run for the grapestakes. **Leeuwin Estate, Cape Mentelle,** and **Sandalford** wineries are just a few of the delectable labels, now numbering about 35 in this region.

A tourist-oriented township, 47 km south of Busselton, situated on its eponym, Margaret River is enticingly close to pounding surf beaches and calm swimming bays.

The **Old Settlement Craft Village,** on the banks of the Margaret River, depicts 1920s settlement life with period farm buildings and machinery, along with crafts studios with gift items for sale. Hours are daily 9 a.m.-5 p.m., closed Christmas Day. For information, phone (097) 57-2775.

View displays of seashells at **Bellview Shell Museum,** Bussell Highway. Hours are daily 8 a.m.-6 p.m. Interesting buildings include **St. Thomas More Catholic Church,** Mitchell St., and the **Greek Chapel,** Wallcliffe Road.

Set in bushland, **Eagle's Heritage,** Boodjidup Rd. (tel. 097-57-2960), boasts the largest collection of Australia's birds of prey. Hours are daily 10 a.m.-5 p.m. Admission is $4.50.

The **Marron Farm,** Wickham Rd. (tel. 097-57-6279), 11 km south of town, produces thousands of the chestnut-like marron, which can be seen in their various stages of development. Swimming and picnic facilities are provided. Hours are daily 10 a.m.-4 p.m. Guided tours are available several times each day.

Popular **Prevally Park,** south of the rivermouth, 10 km west of town, is known to have powerful surf. Follow Caves Rd. south through the lovely **Boranup Karri Forest.**

Mammoth Cave, 21 km south of Margaret River off Caves Rd., is noted for its fossil remains (including skeletons of Tasmanian tigers) and huge stalactites. **Lake Cave,** a few kilometers farther south, reached via a natural winding staircase down into a vast crater, contains an underground lake. The big bonanza, however, is **Jewel Cave,** eight km before Augusta, on Caves Road. Western Australia's largest tourist cave features one of the world's longest straws (5.9 meters long and more than 3,000 years old), as well as gigantic pillars, grotesque formations, and a mysterious underground river. All caves are open daily except Christmas, with guided tours available several times a day.

Accommodations and Food: As with most wine regions, B&Bs are staked almost as often as the grapes. Some of the many choices are: **Margaret River B&B,** 28 Fearn St. (tel. 097-57-2118); **Margaret House,** Devon Dr. (tel. 097-57-2692); and **Croft Guesthouse,** 54 Wallcliffe Rd. (tel. 097-57-2845).

The YHA **Margaret River Lodge,** 220 Railway Terrace (tel. 097-57-2532), offers dorm and bunkhouse accommodations for $11 per night, plus use of a swimming pool and TV lounge with open fireplace.

For campsites and on-site vans, contact **Margaret River Caravan Park,** 36 Station Rd. (tel. 097-57-2180), or **Riverview Caravan Park,** 8 Willmott Ave. (tel. 097-57-2270).

For cheap pub food, try the **Settler's Tavern,** Bussell Highway. The **1885 Inn,** on Farrelly St., has continental cuisine, superb regional wines, and expensive prices. For everything in between, you'll find a host of diners and cafes along Bussell Highway.

Or pick your own strawberries (Oct.-April), raspberries, boysenberries (Dec.-Jan.), and kiwi fruit (May-Aug.) at **Berry Farm Cottage,** Bessell Rd. (tel. 097-575-5054). Jams and wine are available for purchase. Hours are daily 10 a.m.-4:30 p.m.

Information: Winery maps and other tourist information are available at **Margaret River Tourist Bureau,** corner Tunbridge Rd. and Bussell Hwy., Margaret River (tel. 097-57-2911). Hours are daily 9 a.m.-5 p.m.

Augusta

Situated near Australia's southwestern tip, Augusta (pop. 470) sits 320 km from Perth and is W.A.'s third-oldest settlement. Blue waters and white beaches, surfing and swimming sites keep holidaymakers happy.

The **Augusta Historical Museum,** Blackwood Ave., displays early shipping relics and historical exhibits. Hours are daily 10 a.m.-noon and 2-4 p.m. summer, 10 a.m.-noon winter. Admission is $1.

Hillview Lookout, Golf Links Rd. off Caves Rd., affords panoramic views and a directional plate to help you pick out nearby landmarks. **Cape Leeuwin Lighthouse,** at the end of Cape Leeuwin Rd., marks the junction of the Indian and Southern Oceans and functions as an important meteorological station. Open to visitors daily 9:30 a.m.-3:30 p.m. Admision is $3.

Nearby, see the waterwheel, built in 1895 to provide water for lighthouse builders, now encrusted in salt deposits.

Accommodations: Inexpensive holiday flats with kitchen facilities are offered at **Calypso,** Ellis St. (tel. 097-58-1944). **Augusta Hotel Motel,** Blackwood Ave. (tel. 097-58-1944), has moderately priced hotel rooms but expensive motel units.

The **YHA,** corner Bussell Hwy. and Blackwood Ave. (tel. 097-58-1433), has one cottage, which accommodates 11 warm bodies. Beds run $10 per night.

Doonbanks Caravan Park, Blackwood Ave. (tel. 097-58-1517), features a riverfront location with campsites and on-site vans.

The **Augusta Hotel,** Blackwood Ave., offers an a la carte food-service area, as well as the usual counter-meal setup. **Squirrels,** next door, has a good selection of sandwiches and burgers. And, for sheer romance (or more tourist kitsch), head over to the **Last Café Before Antartica,** on Albany Terrace, and gawk at the intercourse between Flinders Bay and the Blackwood River.

Information: Augusta Information Centre, 70 Blackwood Ave., Augusta (tel. 097-58-1695), assists with local inquiries. Hours are Mon.-Fri. 8:30 a.m.-5 p.m., Sat.-Sun. 8:30 a.m.-1 p.m. (open weekends only in winter months).

Transport

Daily buses operate between Perth and the Busselton/Margaret River/Augusta region. For information and bookings, contact **South West Coachlines** (tel. 09-324-2333) or **Westrail** (tel. 09-326-2222).

THE SOUTHWEST

A few different routes will take you through Western Australia's Southwest to the coastal region, known as the "Great Southern," with glorious beaches, rugged ranges, capes and parks, holiday resorts, and historic settlements. The South Western Highway travels inland from Bunbury, meeting the coast (and the South Coast Highway) at Walpole. The Albany Highway runs *way* inland in a southeasterly direction from Perth, connecting with the coastal highway at Albany. Other itineraries include the Great Southern Highway from Perth, Vasse Highway (from Busselton), the Brockman Highway (north of Augusta), and the Muirs Highway (between Manjimup and Mount Barker).

THE SOUTH WESTERN HIGHWAY

Leaving Bunbury, you'll journey into **Donnybrook,** the center of Western Australia's oldest apple-growing region, where Granny Smith is queen of the crop (try to make this trip in late October when it's apple blossom time). Many artsy-craftsy shops and studios permeate this area. Farther along the landscape gives way to rolling hills, pine plantations, jarrah and karri forests, and—eventually—the big, blue sea.

One particularly scenic detour is the stretch from Balingup, 29 km beyond Donnybrook, to **Nannup,** an old timber town on the Vasse High-

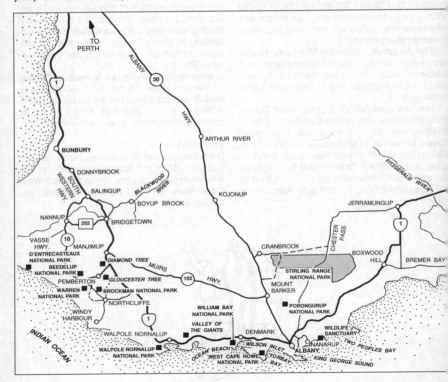

way. The narrow, winding, 45-km drive crosses, then follows, the Blackwood River.

Westrail buses serve South Western Highway towns and most Vasse Highway communities several times each week. **South West Coachlines** also travels into some areas.

Bridgetown

Settled in 1857, Bridgetown (pop. 1,520) is a peaceful little community 95 km south of Bunbury in the heart of jarrah land. Visit **Bridgedale,** 1 Hampton St., the town's oldest house, built in the 1860s and restored by the National Trust. Hours are Wed.-Sat. and Monday 2-5 p.m., Sunday 11 a.m.-1 p.m. and 2-5 p.m.

The **Brierly Jigsaw Gallery,** Hampton St., is supposedly the country's only public jigsaw gallery. The collection includes puzzles from all over the world and visitors are invited to go to

pieces over unfinished works. Hours are Thurs.-Mon. 10 a.m.-4 p.m. Admission is $2.

Good bushwalking and picnic spots are at **Bridgetown Jarrah Park** on Brockman Highway and **Blackwood River Park** at the southern edge of town.

Carnaby Butterflies and Beetles, Bridge St., is 31 km northeast in Boyup Brook. The collection contains many rare specimens and is reputed to be the largest outside of the British Natural History Museum. Hours are daily 10 a.m.-4 p.m.

The **Bridgetown Hotel,** 38 Hampton St. (tel. 097-61-1030), offers inexpensive pub rooms with breakfast included. **Riverwood House,** South Western Hwy. (tel. 097-61-1862), is a moderately priced, no-smoking-allowed B&B. Campsites and on-site vans are available at **Bridgetown Caravan Park,** South Western Hwy. (tel. 097-61-1053).

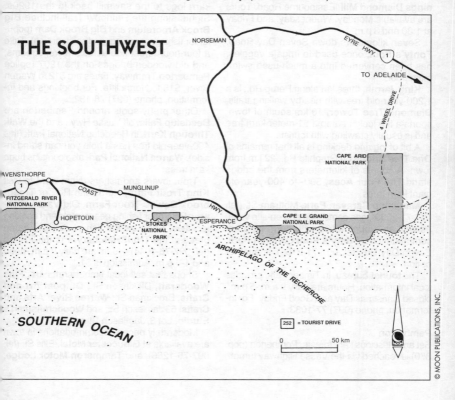

THE SOUTHWEST

Pick up tourist info at the **Bridgetown Tourist Bureau,** Hampton St. (tel. 097-61-1740). Hours are daily 9 a.m.-5 p.m.

Manjimup

You can't miss that fact the Manjimup (pop. 4,150), 37 km from Bridgetown, is the gateway to the Tall Timber Country—timber arches signal your arrival at both edges of town. Karri trees, more than a century old, are abundant here.

Bone up on the local timber industry at **Timber Park,** corner Rose and Edwards Streets. The complex houses Timber Park Gallery, Bunnings' Age of Steam Museum (W.A.'s only timber museum), displays of vintage machinery and implements, and a variety of other attractions. For a close-up look at the industry, put on a pair of sturdy shoes and visit the **Bunnings Diamond Mill,** Eastbourne Road. Tours are available Monday, Wednesday, and Friday at 1:30 and 3 p.m.

Seven kilometers down Seven Day Road, **Fonty's Pool,** once used to irrigate veggies, has been converted into a much-used swimming pool.

King Jarrah, three km along Perup Rd., is a 1,200-year-old tree with nearby walking trails. **Diamond Tree Tower,** 10 km south of town, sports a fire lookout atop a 51-meter karri tree and is usually crawling with tourists.

A bit of log and decking is all that remains of **One Tree Bridge** on Graphite Rd., 22 km from town. A couple of kilometers from the bridge stand **The Four Aces,** 300- to 400-year-old giant karri trees.

Manjimup Caravan Park, Mottram St. (tel. 097-71-2093), has campsites and on-site vans, as well as a bunkhouse with dorm-type accommodations. **Fonty's Pool Caravan Park,** Seven Day Rd. (tel. 097-71-2105), is another option.

The **tourist bureau,** in Timber Park, provides local information. Hours are daily 9 a.m.-5 p.m., closed Christmas Day and Good Friday. For information, phone (097) 77-1083.

Pemberton

Set amid luscious karri forests, Pemberton (pop. 870) is reached via the Vasse Highway turnoff,

15 km south of Manjimup, or along the Vasse Highway from Nannup (76 km).

The **Pioneer Museum,** Brockman St., houses records, photos, and machinery from the early forestry settlement. Hours are daily 9 a.m.-5 p.m. Admission is $1.

Restored **Brockman Saw Pit,** on the Pemberton-Northcliffe road, depicts lumber-cutting methods of bygone days. The **Pemberton Sawmill,** conversely, is highly automated and one of the largest in the Southern Hemisphere. The tourist bureau can arrange tours.

Follow the signs to **Gloucester Tree** off Brockman St., the world's highest fire lookout tree. The view from up top is great, but don't attempt the dizzying 60-meter climb unless you're in good shape and vertigo-free!

The **Rainbow and Tramway Trails** were the original 91-mm gauge railways that transported karri logs to the sawmill back in the 1920s. Sights along the Rainbow Trail include **Big Brook Arboretum** and **Big Brook Dam** (popular for fishing, canoeing, and sailboarding). Take a four-hour forest ride across rivers, streams, and old wooden bridges on the 1907 replica **Pemberton Tramway.** Fares are $12 to Warren River, $18 to Northcliffe. For bookings and information, phone (097) 76-1322.

Other pretty spots around Pemberton are **Beedelup Falls,** off Vasse Hwy., and the **Walk Through Karri,** in Beedelup National Park (this 400-year-old tree has a hole you can stand inside). **Warren National Park** also contains huge karri trees.

Trout lovers and fishers might want to visit **King Trout Farm,** Northcliffe Rd., or **Treenbrook Downs Trout Farm,** Old Vasse Highway. Both offer fishing gear rentals and cooking facilities. See how the fish you've just eaten breed at the **Trout Hatchery,** Pumphill Road (tel. 097-76-1044). Hours are daily 9 a.m.-noon and 1-4 p.m. Admission is $1.

Shops that sell local timber crafts are: **Fine Woodcraft,** Dickinson St.; **Outpost Art and Crafts,** Brockman St.; **Warren River Arts and Crafts,** 63 Jamieson St.; and **Woodcraftsman's Studio,** Lot 6, Jamieson Street.

Moderately priced accommodations in town are available at **Gloucester Motel,** Ellis St. (tel. 097-76-1266), and **Tammeron Motor Lodge,**

Widdeson St. (tel. 097-76-1019). **Pump Hill Farm,** Pump Hill Rd. (tel. 097-76-1379), offers mudbrick cottages, with fireplaces and cooking facilities, in the expensive range.

The **YHA Hostel,** Pimelea Rd. (tel. 097-76-1153), sits in the middle of the state forest, about 10 km northwest of town. Dorm beds run $10 per night.

Campsites with limited facilities are offered at **Pemberton Forest Camp** and **Warren National Park.** For information, phone (097) 76-1200.

Tourist information is available at **Pemberton Tourist Centre,** Brockman St. (tel. 097-76-1133). Hours are daily 9 a.m.-5 p.m.

Beyond Pemberton

Northcliffe, 28 km southeast of Pemberton, features more virgin karri forests. **Northcliffe Forest Park,** adjacent to town, is an ideal place to bushwalk, especially when the wildflowers are in bloom (Sept.-Nov.). The park is also home to the twin and hollow-butt karri trees. The **Pioneer Museum,** Wheatley Coast Rd., displays early settlement artifacts. Hours are daily May-Aug. 10 a.m.-2 p.m. Admission is $1.

Keep going another 27 km to reach **Windy Harbour,** a relatively deserted coastal beach popular with rock climbers for its huge D'Entrecasteaux Cliffs. Limited **camping** facilities (summer only, with a three-day maximum) are available at Windy Harbour Camping Area (tel. 097-76-7056).

Walpole/Nornalup

This coastal region with luscious bays, coves, and forests is reached via the South Western Highway, 119 km southeast of Manjimup. It marks the beginning of the South Coast Highway and the Rainbow Coast.

Walpole and Nornalup are two townships at either edge of **Walpole Nornalup National Park,** 18,116 hectares of bushwalking trails, eucalyptus forests, desolate beaches, and diverse bird- and wildlife. **Valley of the Giants** is a scenic drive through tingle and karri tree forests, three km east of Nornalup. Check out the view or stop for a picnic along **Knoll Drive,** also three km east of Nornalup in the park.

There's good fishing at **Walpole/Nornalup inlets, Mandalay Beach,** and on the **Frank-**

land River. Deep River, 36 km northwest of Walpole, is favored by canoeing enthusiasts.

Tinglewood Homestead, Walpole (tel. 098-40-1035), has moderately priced B&B accommodations. Book ahead for dorm beds at the **Dingo Flat YHA Hostel,** Dingo Flat Rd. off Valley of the Giants Rd. (tel. 098-40-8073). Beds are $6 per night (the property is on a cattle and sheep station). Campsites, on-site vans, cottages, and cabins are available at **Rest Point Tourist Centre,** Walpole Inlet (tel. 098-40-1032).

For tourist information, contact **Walpole Tourist Bureau,** Pioneer Cottage, Pioneer Park (tel. 098-40-1111).

Denmark

No, this is not a Danish settlement. Denmark (pop. 985), 66 km east of Nornalup, was named for Dr. Alexandra Denmark, an 1800s naval physician. It's a favorite of surfers and hippies. Located on the Denmark River, recreational opportunities include surfing, swimming, fishing, waterskiing, bushwalking, and a couple of wineries.

In town, the **Denmark Gallery,** 27 Strickland St., sells and exhibits local arts and crafts. **Groundrey Wines,** 11 North St. (tel. 098-48-1525), housed within a converted 1928 butter factory, features local crafts as well as wine sales and tasting. Hours are Mon.-Sat. 10 a.m.-4:30 p.m., Sunday 11 a.m.-4:30 p.m.

Wilson Inlet is the local windsurfing, fishing, boating, and waterskiing haven, while **Ocean Beach** is favored by surfers.

The **Fauna Sanctuary,** Ocean Beach Rd. adjacent to the caravan park, shelters a variety of marsupials, including endangered—and unexplainable—species such as the tammar, woillie, darma, agile, and bettong. Hours are Tues.-Thurs. and Sat.-Sun. 2:30-4:30 p.m.

Best ocean and countryside views are from **Mount Shadford Scenic Drive** off South Coast Hwy., along North St. to Mount Shadford Road. **William Bay National Park,** 15 km west of town, eight km off South Coast Hwy., offers close-up views of rocks and reefs.

Denmark sports a wide range of holiday accommodations. **Denmark Guesthouse,** 31 South Coast Hwy. (tel. 098-48-1477), offers inexpensive rooms with shared facilities. **Gum Grove Chalets,** Ocean Beach Rd. (tel. 48-

Elephant Cove, William Bay National Park

1378), and **Riverbend Chalets,** E. River Rd. (tel. 098-48-1107), have moderately priced, self-contained accommodations.

The **YHA Hostel** is at **Wilson Inlet Holiday Park,** Ocean Beach Rd. (tel. 098-48-1267). Beds cost $10 and facilities include a tennis court and boat hire. Book ahead.

Campsites and on-site vans are available at **Rivermouth Caravan Park,** Inlet Dr. (tel. 098-48-1262), and **Rudgyard Beach Holiday Park,** Rudgyard Rd. (tel. 098-48-1169).

The **Tiger and Snake,** beneath Denmark Guesthouse, serves Indian and Chinese dishes (judging by the name, you might want to check on ingredients when ordering). **Blue Wren Café,** on South Coast Hwy., and **Mary Rose,** on North St., are other possibilities, along with **Scoundrel's Brasserie,** along the river.

If you visit in December, January, or on Easter Saturday, drop by the annual **Arts and Crafts Market Days,** along the Denmark River, where all kinds of goodies are for sale.

For tourist information, contact **Denmark Tourist Bureau,** Strickland St. (tel. 098-48-1265). Hours are daily 9 a.m.-5 p.m.

ALONG THE ALBANY HIGHWAY

From Perth, the Albany Highway passes through a hodgepodge of timber, sheep-farming, and mixed agricultural districts and small service towns. En route, **Williams, Arthur River,** and **Kojonup** are smattered with assorted historic buildings, crafts galleries, picnic areas, and simple accommodations. **Cranbrook** is an access

point for Stirling Range National Park. Turn off at **Kendenup** to see the site of W.A.'s very first gold find.

Mount Barker

Though the local industries are mainly sheep and cattle grazing, Mount Barker (pop. 1,520), some 359 km southeast of Perth, is also known for its wine production. Eyeball panoramic views of the area from atop the 168-meter-high TV tower on **Mount Barker Hill.**

The **Old Police Station,** Albany Hwy., built by convicts in 1867, has been preserved as a museum with period furnishings and pioneer artifacts.

Mount Barker Tourist Bureau, 57 Lowood Rd. (tel. 098-51-1163), provides local information and maps to the wineries. Hours are Mon.-Fri. 9 a.m.-5 p.m., Saturday 9 a.m.-2 p.m., Sunday 10 a.m.-2 p.m., closed Christmas Day.

The Stirlings and the Porongurups

Sounds like the guest list for an amusing country weekend, doesn't it? Nope—these are two mountain ranges (and national parks) that rise dramatically from the surrounding flat, agricultural plains. Both parks are close enough to Albany for a day outing.

Stirling Range National Park (115,671 hectares)—about 66 km long and 18 km wide—is filled with mountains, valleys, cliffs, delicate wildflowers, eucalyptus forests, rare plants, profuse bird- and wildlife, and moody mountain views. **Bluff Knoll** (1,073 meters) is W.A.'s third highest peak, and the park's most popular climb, followed by **Toolbrunup** (1,052 meters) and

Ellen Peak (1,012 meters and a *hard* trek). You must obtain permission from the ranger on duty before embarking on any climb. If you don't feel like walking, a scenic drive will take you through the center of the park. For more information, phone (098) 27-9230.

Closer to Albany, **Porongurup National Park** (2,401 hectares) features karri forests, excellent birdwatching, panoramic views, easy walking tracks, and some of the world's oldest rock. The best bushwalks are to **Castle Rock** (570 meters), **Hayward's Peak** (610 meters), **Devil's Slide** (671 meters), **Nancy Peak** (662 meters), and **Morgan's View** (662 meters). For information, phone (098) 53-1095.

Campsites with limited facilities are available at Stirling Range National Park (tel. 098-27-9278). The **YHA**, Bluff Knoll turnoff (tel. 098-27-9229), has $12-per-night dorm beds in eight chalets. Campsites and on-site vans are also available at **Stirling Range Caravan Park,** Chester Pass Rd., South Borden (tel. 098-27-9229).

At Porongurup, **Karribank Guest House,** Main St. (tel. 098-53-1022), offers inexpensive rooms plus swimming pool, tennis court, and golf course. Adjacent to Karribank, **Porongurup Caravan Park,** Main St. (tel. 098-53-1057), rents campsites and on-site vans.

ALBANY

Albany (pop. 16,320) is Western Australia's oldest settlement and, because of its superb Princess Royal Harbour, it remained the state's principal port for years. Since its creation in 1826 as a military outpost to ward off French colonists, Albany (called Frederickstown until 1832) has served as both a whaling port and coaling station. Situated 409 km southeast of Perth, this town is presently known as the Great Southern's commercial center as well as a tourist resort.

Historical Sights

Albany has preserved a number of its colonial buildings; most are on or around York St., Stirling Terrace, and the harbor foreshores.

The **Residency Museum,** Residency Rd., sits on the exact site where Major Edmund

Lockyer and his merry band of convicts landed in 1826. Built in 1850, the museum was formerly the local magistrate's home and a naval training facility. Exhibits concern regional history, geography, and environment. Hours are daily 10 a.m.-5 p.m., For information, phone (098) 41-4844.

Explore a full-scale replica of Lockyer's brig *Amity,* Port Rd., near the museum. You can go below deck and imagine how some 45 men and accompanying livestock survived in the cramped quarters. Hours are daily 9 a.m.-5 p.m., closed Christmas Day. For information, phone (098) 41-6885.

The one-time convict-hiring depot and **Old Gaol** (1851) in Stirling Terrace now serves as a museum with WW I and II relics, pioneer tools and equipment, and Aboriginal artifacts. Hours are daily 10 a.m.-4:15 p.m., closed Christmas Day and Good Friday. For information, phone (098) 41-1401.

The restored **post office** (1870), Stirling Terrace, once housed the customs and bond store, court, holding cells, magistrate's and jury rooms. These days it comprises an Inter-Colonial Communications Museum and a restaurant. Hours are daily 10 a.m.-5 p.m.

Constructed of wattle and daub, **Patrick Taylor Cottage** (1832), Duke St., is thought to be Albany's oldest building. The cottage contains thousands of items, including early costumes, old clocks, and kitchenware. Hours are daily 2-4:15 p.m. Admission is $2. For information, phone (098) 41-6174.

Strawberry Hill Farmhouse, Middleton Beach Rd., built in 1836, is W.A.'s oldest farm. Originally the private home for the government resident, the two-story stone house has been restored by the National Trust. You can take tea in the adjoining miner's cottage. Hours are daily 10 a.m.-5 p.m., closed during June. Admission is $2.50. For information, phone (098) 41-3735.

Other historic structures include: **St. John's Church of England** (1848), York St., the first church consecrated in Western Australia; **Albany Town Hall** (1888), refurbished in 1983 and converted into the Albany Town Theatre; **Vancouver Arts Centre** (1880s), used for regular arts and crafts exhibitions; and **Princess Royal Fortress** (1893).

Other Sights

Dog Rock, a huge granite outcrop near the corner of Middleton Road and Young Street, resembles the head of a big dog.

Emu Point, where Oyster Harbour enters the sea, is a favorite place for boating, swimming, and windsurfing. Other good swimming sites are **Middleton Beach, Ellen Cove,** and **Jimmy Newell's Harbour,** south of town.

Mount Clarence offers the best views plus a recast of the original Desert Mounted Corps memorial erected at Suez in 1932 (Gallipoli, remember?). You can see bullet marks in the granite blocks, transported from Suez. **Mount Melville** and **Marine Drive Lookout** offer other wide-eye panoramas.

On the coast, 21 km south of Albany, **Torndirrup National Park** affords a number of spectacular sights including the blowholes, Natural Bridge, and The Gap. To reach the park, follow Frenchman Bay Road.

At the end of Frenchman Bay Rd., **Whaleworld,** the former whaling station responsible for taking up to 850 whales each season (until operations ceased in 1978), now serves as a museum. Have a whale of a time learning the history of Albany's oldest industry. Hours are daily 9 a.m.-5 p.m. Admission is $4.50. For information, phone (098) 44-4021.

Two Peoples Bay, 24 km east of Albany along Two Peoples Bay Rd., features more pretty beaches and a nature reserve that protects a small colony of noisy scrub birds. Believed to be

Dog Rock, Albany's bow wow landmark

MARK MORRIS

extinct, the birds were rediscovered in 1961. Other nearby attractions are **Two Peoples Marron Farm,** Two Peoples Bay Rd., and **Valley Ponds Trout Farm,** Gull Rock Road.

Accommodations and Food

Colonial Guesthouse, 136 Brunswick Rd. (tel. 098-41-3704), and **Middleton Beach Guesthouse,** 18 Adelaide Crescent (tel. 098-41-1295), are inexpensive B&Bs.

Moderately priced motels are: **Travel Inn,** 191 Albany Hwy. (tel. 098-41-4144); **Friendly Motel,** 234 Albany Hwy. (tel. 098-41-2200); and the **Albany International Motel,** 270 Albany Hwy. (tel. 098-41-7399). Heaps of others are scattered around town and along Albany Highway. The best and most expensive ($160-230) hotel is **The Esplanade,** Middleton Beach (tel. 098-42-1711), with views to everywhere and the usual mega-plethora of amenities.

The **Albany YHA Hostel,** 49 Duke St. (tel. 098-41-3949), offers communal facilities and dorm beds for $11 per night, but fills up quickly.

You'll find many caravan parks to choose from. Some offering both campsites and on-site vans are: **Mount Melville Caravan Park,** 22 Wellington St. (tel. 098-41-4616); **Middleton Beach Caravan Park,** Flinders Parade, Middleton Beach (tel. 098-41-3593); **Panorama Caravan Park,** Frenchman Bay Rd. (tel. 098-44-4031); and **Emu Beach Caravan Park,** Medcalfe Parade, Emu Point (tel. 098-44-1147).

Looking for food? Stirling Terrace is filled with fill-you-up eateries. For burgers, pancakes, and other light meals, try **Dylan's on the Terrace,** 82 Stirling Terrace. **Kooka's,** at 204 Stirling Terrace (tel. 098-41-5889), offers excellent fresh and nouvelle-ish cuisine in a colonial cottage with a kookaburra theme. Meals are in the expensive range and reservations are advised. The **Post Restaurant,** 33 Stirling Terrace, in the old post office, features moderately priced seafood specialties and cook-your-own steaks in a colonial atmosphere.

For Asian fare try **Lemon Grass Thai,** 370 Middleton Rd.; **Three Plenties** Chinese restaurant, York St.; or **The Melting Pot,** 338 Middleton Road.

Information

For a free copy of *Albany Experience,* a local mini-guide, or for other info, contact the **Albany**

Tourist Bureau, corner York St. and Peels Pl. (tel. 098-41-1088). Hours are Mon.-Fri. 8:30 a.m.-5:30 p.m. Sat.-Sun.; public holidays 9 a.m.-5 p.m.

Pick up street maps and other road info at the **Royal Automobile Club,** 110 Albany Hwy. (tel. 098-42-1210).

Transport

Ansett (tel. 13-1300 toll-free) and **Skywest** (book through Ansett) operate daily flights from Perth Airport to Albany (about $150).

Westrail (tel. 09-326-2222) provides daily coach service from Perth ($35) and travels to Denmark four times each week ($45).

If you're driving, the Albany Highway from Perth (409 km) should get you here in under five hours. The South Western and South Coast Highways from Bunbury (402 km, not counting detours) will take about the same time.

Love's Bus Service, the local transport company, travels weekdays and Saturday mornings to points along the Albany Highway, as well as to Middleton Beach, Spencer Park, and Emu Point.

Rental cars are available from **Avis** (tel. 098-42-2833), **Budget** (tel. 098-41-2299), and **Albany Car Rentals** (tel. 098-41-7077). Rates are about $50 per day with unlimited kilometers.

Contact the **Albany YHA Hostel** for bicycle hire outfits (about $10 per day) and cheap tours into the Stirling Ranges or up and down the coast ($15-30). The **tourist bureau** can also arrange local tours.

THE WESTERN BIGHT

From Albany to Esperance, the South Coast Highway teases its way along the western end of the Great Australian Bight—a 480-km odyssey through capes and parks, bays and beaches.

Out of Albany

Turn off at Boxwood Hill, 117 km northeast of Albany, and veer coastward another 63 km to **Bremer Bay,** a popular location for fishing, boating, waterskiing, and scuba diving.

Back on South Coast Highway, **Jerramungup** is about 60 km north of Boxwood Hill. The **Military Museum,** on the highway (tel. 098-35-1119), features a large privately owned collection of fighting memorabilia, including vehi-cles, badges, medals, guns, and swords. Hours are Mon.-Fri. 10 a.m.-3 p.m., Sat.-Sun. 10 a.m.-1 p.m. Admission is $2.

Ravensthorpe

A former gold and copper mining town, Ravensthorpe (pop. 330) is 114 km northeast of Jerramungup.

Cocanarup Homestead, classified as a historical site by the National Trust, is made up of several century-old stone buildings. The early 1900s **Dance Cottage Museum** is home to the local historical society's memorabilia collection. The old smelter sits three km from town, while ruins of a baked-out bakery and a played-out gold mine can be explored at **Kundip,** some 20 km farther. If you want to check out the **Ravensthorpe Range** at the northern end of Foater Road, beware of the old mine shafts in that area!

Ravensthorpe Motel, junction Hopetoun and Esperance Roads (tel. 098-38-1053), and **Palace Motor Hotel** (tel. 098-38-1005) both offer inexpensive to moderate accommodations. Campsites are available at **Ravensthorpe Caravan Park,** Morgan St. (tel. 098-38-1050).

Local info can be obtained at the **Ravensthorpe Tourist Information Centre,** Morgan St. (tel. 098-38-1001). Hours are Mon.-Fri. 8:30 a.m.-5 p.m.

Below and Beyond Ravensthorpe

Hopetoun, situated on the coast 50 km south of Ravensthorpe, offers more secluded bays, beaches, inlets, and fishing holes. Whales can often be seen near these shores in August and September.

Fitzgerald River National Park, accessed either from Hopetoun, Jerramungup, or Bremer Bay, features 240,000 hectares of sand plain, river valleys, narrow gorges, rugged ranges, coastal cliffs, sandy beaches, visible wildlife, and approximately 1,350 species of wildflowers and native plants. Check in with a ranger before you go bushwalking, and be sure to carry plenty of water. Swimmers should be aware of dangerous coastal rips. Some park areas are restricted at certain times of the year. For information, phone (098) 35-5043.

Stokes National Park (10,667 hectares), reached via gravel roads off the South Coast Highway east of Young River, is a coastal region for bushwalking, ocean fishing, inlet swimming, and birdwatching (seals have been sighted, too). Facilities are limited and you must carry your own water. For information, phone (098) 76-8541.

ESPERANCE

Beautifully situated across from the Archipelago of the Recherche, 730 km southeast of Perth, versatile Esperance (pop. 6,375) wears three hats—seaport, seaside resort, and agricultural center.

Named for the French frigate *L'Esperance* in 1772, the town was settled in 1863 when the Dempster brothers arrived with their families after an overland trek. Some 30 years later, with the advent of gold exploration, Esperance boomed as a port, then faltered again when the gold rush rushed out. Then, shortly after World War II *and* after a lot of research, it was discovered that trace elements were missing from the surrounding soil, which prohibited agriculture. The situation was remedied and voila—a rich agro-center and grain-loading port.

Sights

Esperance Municipal Museum, James St., features early machinery, tools, furnishings, and—best of all—a big Skylab display (Esperance was the lucky spot where Skylab decided to fall to earth in 1979). The museum park also

houses **Craft Village,** where you can buy locally produced arts and crafts. Hours are daily 1:30-4:30 p.m. Admission is $2. For information, phone (090) 71-1579.

Local crustaceans, fish, other marinelife, and shells are on view at **George's Oceanarium,** the Esplanade. Hours are Tues.-Sun. 10 a.m.-4 p.m., Sept.-May. For information, phone (090) 71-2940.

The original **Dempster Homestead,** Dempster and Emily Streets, is privately owned and can be admired only from the road.

The **Australian Parrot Farm,** Fisheries Rd., Yarrumun, exhibits a large number of parrots, pheasants, guinea fowl, and peafowl, plus a collection of more than 2,000 vintage bottles. Hours are daily 9 a.m.-5 p.m. For information, phone (090) 76-1284.

Salt-tolerant algae and saline are what makes **Pink Lake** pink—and sometimes purple. Some years, as much as 500,000 tons of salt are dredged from the lake, which is three km out of town along Pink Lake Road.

Twilight Beach Scenic Drive leads from town up to Observatory Point and Lookout, then to Pink Lake. **Rotary Lookout,** on Wireless Hill, affords yet another town-and-bay vista.

Twilight Cove, near the town center, is a good, safe swimming and fishing beach.

Islands and Parks

The **Archipelago of the Recherche,** also known as the Bay of Isles, is comprised of ap-

Look out over the astounding, pounding southern coast.

proximately 100 islands with sandy beaches, turquoise waters, plentiful water birds, and seal and penguin colonies. The MV *Cape Le Grand II* makes scenic two-hour cruises of the archipelago, or the MV *Sea Lion* will take you over to Woody Island—a wildlife sanctuary—for a five-hour picnic trip (January, February, and major holidays). For information, phone (090) 71-1772.

Cape Le Grand National Park (31,390 hectares), 48 km southeast of Esperance, has some dynamite coastal scenery. Sand plains, freshwater pools, swamps, and massive granite outcrops (Mt. Le Grand, 353 meters, is the highest) make up the remaining terrain—home to birds, reptiles, grey kangaroos, possums, and bandicoots. A marked 15-km walking trail will lead you along the coast from Cape Le Grand to Rossiter Bay. Come September through November, when the wildflowers are in bloom. For information, phone (090) 71-3733.

Cape Arid National Park (279,415 hectares), 125 km east of Esperance, can be reached by conventional vehicle, but tracks within the park are suitable only for four-wheel-drive (weather permitting). Cape Arid also features splendid coastal scenery, granite outcrops, and excellent lookouts as well as diverse fauna. You must obtain permission from a park ranger before rockclimbing; swimmers should be wary of rips. *Cape Arid* also translates as *bring your own water*. For information, phone (090) 75-0055.

Accommodations and Food

Pink Lake Lodge, 85 Pink Lake Rd. (tel. 090-71-2075), offers inexpensive rooms.

Moderately priced, self-contained holiday flats are available at: **Captain Huon,** 5 the Esplanade (tel. 090-71-2383); **Esperance All Seasons,** 73 the Esplanade (tel. 090-71-2257); and **Esperance Beachfront Resort,** 19 the Esplanade (tel. 090-71-2513).

The **Watersedge YHA Hostel,** Goldfields Rd. (tel. 090-71-1040), is two km east of the town center. Eight dorm and two twin rooms accommodate 110 happy hostelers. Dorm beds cost $11 per night. **Wirraway House Esperance Backpackers,** 14 Emily St. (tel. 090-71-

4724), is a new hostel with dorm beds for $12 per night and inexpensive double rooms.

Rent a campsite or on-site van at **Bather's Paradise Caravan Park,** corner Westmacott and Chaplin Streets, (tel. 090-71-1014); **Bushlands Holiday Village,** Collier Rd. (tel. 090-71-1346); **Esperance Bay Caravan Park,** corner the Esplanade and Harbour Rd. (tel. 090-71-2237); or **Pink Lake Caravan Park,** Pink Lake Rd. (tel. 090-71-2424). Campsites with limited facilities are offered at both Cape Le Grand and Cape Arid National Parks.

Numerous coffee shops, cafes, and fish-and-chip shops provide belly stuffers. **Spice of Life,** Andrew St., leans toward the vegetarian appetite. **Ollie's on the Esplanade** is open daily, early morning to late night, and offers a variety of choices.

Information

For tourist and tour information, contact the **Esperance Tourist Bureau,** Dempster Street, in Museum Village (tel. 090-71-2330). Hours are daily 9 a.m.-5 p.m.

Transport

Ansett (tel. 13-1300 toll-free) and Skywest (phone Ansett for bookings) fly daily from Perth to Esperance ($190), and **Goldfields Air Services** (tel. 090-93-2116) makes a once-a-week trip from Kalgoorlie via Norseman ($140).

Three times each week the Prospector Perth-Kalgoorlie train connects with a Westrail coach to Esperance. If you'd rather take the bus all the way, Westrail coaches also depart Perth for Esperance three times a week. For information, phone (09) 326-2813.

The YHA hostel rents **bicycles** for $10 per day.

If you're heading up to the Goldfields region, take the Coolgardie-Esperance Highway north out of town, straight up to Coolgardie (375 km north of Esperance and 39 km southwest of Kalgoorlie), or turn onto the Eyre Highway at Norseman (207 km) for the eastward trek across the Nullarbor Plain (see "Crossing the Nullarbor" in the South Australia chapter).

THE WHEATLANDS

Don't be put off by the boring name—this agricultural heartland, stretching from Perth to Coolgardie and north of Albany to the Great Eastern Highway, has some wild rock formations, Aboriginal rock carvings, and worth-a-stop historical sights.

YORK TO HYDEN

Beginning at the Avon Valley, weave and wind your way through side-ways and byways to various Wheatlands attractions, ending at the simply *awesome* Wave Rock.

The Yoting-Kellerberrin Road, beyond the small wheaty township of Quairading (166 km east of Perth), accesses both **Kokerbin Rock,** with caves, a lookout, and a scenic drive, and **Mount Stirling,** a huge granite outcrop often climbed for the view.

Bruce Rock, 77 km east of Quairading, is another noteworthy outcrop. **Bruce Rock Museum,** 24 Johnson St., contains pioneering items. Hours are daily 10 a.m.-4 p.m. Admission is $2.

Situated 68 km southwest of Bruce Rock, **Corrigin** (pop. 840) dates back to the 1880s. The **Pioneer Museum,** corner of Kunjin Rd. and Kirkwood St., displays early machinery and pioneering memorabilia. Hours are daily 10 a.m.-4 p.m. Admission is $2.

Locally produced handicrafts can be purchased at the **Craft Cottage,** Walton Street. Hours are Mon.-Fri. 10 a.m.-5 p.m., Saturday 9:30-11:30 a.m.

Gorge Rock, 23 km southeast of Corrigin, is a swimming area created from a dammed gorge. **Jilakin Rock,** 50 km southeast, through Kulin, is a gray granite monolith overlooking a 1,214-hectare lake surrounded by bushland.

Wave Rock, three km outside Hyden and 108 km southeast of Corrigin, is the destination of most Wheatland travelers. This enormous 50-meter-high granite rock formation—shaped by wind and rain—is estimated to be 2.7 billion years old. It resembles a huge curling wave made even more distinctive by vertical bands of color on its sloping face. A marked track will lead you around the base of Wave Rock over to **Hippo's Yawn,** another unique outcrop. **Bates Cave,** 21 km northwest of Hyden, features Aboriginal hand paintings.

Inexpensive accommodations in Hyden are offered at **Dieps B&B,** 17 Clayton St. (tel. 098-80-5179). **Hyden Hotel,** 2 Lynch St. (tel. 098-80-5052), is in the moderate range. Campsites are available at **Wave Rock Caravan Park,** Wave Rock (tel. 098-80-5022).

The **Hyden Tourist Information Centre** is on Lynch St. (tel. 098-80-5182). Hours are daily 10 a.m.-4 p.m.

WESTERN AUSTRALIA TOURISM BUREAU

Don't try riding this wave!

THE GREAT SOUTHERN HIGHWAY

Situated on the Avon River, 66 km south of York, **Beverley** is known for its **Aeronautical Museum,** Vincent St., with displays of aviation equipment, model airplanes, and the *Silver Centenary,* W.A.'s first privately made airplane. Hours are daily 10 a.m-4 p.m. For information, phone (096) 46-1555.

Historical buildings include **St. Paul's Church** (1862), Avon Dr., **St. John's in the Wilderness** (1895), Dale-Beverley Rd., and Beverley's oldest surviving building (now a museum), **Dead Finish** (1872), 138 Vincent Street.

Narrogin (pop. 5,000), 137 km south of Beverley, is the commercial hub of this district. The **Court House Museum,** Norseman Rd., gives insight into early industry and society. Hours are Tuesday, Friday, and Sunday 2-4:30 p.m.

Albert Facey's Homestead, on the road between Wickepin and Nomans Lake, was built

by the colorful character of the same name. Facey's autobiography, *A Fortunate Life,* later became a TV miniseries. The homestead is open Mon.-Fri. 9 a.m.-5 p.m. Admission is $2.50.

Attractions around **Wagin,** 50 km down the highway, include the **Giant Ram Tourist Park** (the ram is 15 meters long and seven meters high and called the "largest (fake) ram in the Southern Hemisphere"), **Wagin Historical Village,** and nearby **Mount Latham,** for rock-climbing and bushwalking. **Puntapin Rock** is another large, intriguing rock formation. **Lake Dumbleyung,** 39 km kilometers east of Wagin, is the spot where Donald Campbell broke the world water speed record in 1964. Around a portion of the lake is a nature reserve with varied birdlife, a scenic drive, and a lookout point.

Settled in the 1840s, **Katanning** (pop. 4,415) mixes a bit of history with modern services. The **Old Mill** (1889), Main St., houses early machinery, equipment, and a crafts shop. Hours

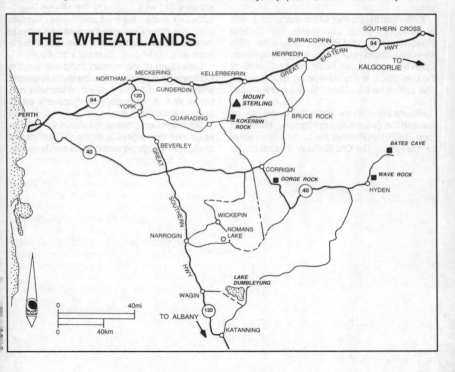

THE WHEATLANDS

are Mon.-Fri. 10 a.m.-4 p.m., Saturday 10 a.m.-noon. Admission is $1.

The Great Southern Highway joins the Albany Highway 85 km south of Katanning.

THE GREAT EASTERN HIGHWAY

The 500-km stretch from Northam to Kalgoorlie is also known as the Goldfields Heritage Trail and follows the original 1860s route established by surveyor Charles Hunt.

Meckering, a little rural town 133 km east of Perth, was severely damaged in a 1968 earthquake. Though the town was immediately rebuilt, you can see mementos of the destruction at the tourist center gazebo.

The Municipal Museum at **Cunderdin,** 24 km east, displays assorted vintage farm machinery, tractors, photos, and other relics. Hours are daily 10 a.m.-4 p.m. Admission is $2. Cunderin Hill itself puts on a good spring wildflower show.

Kellerberrin, another 47 km eastward, is one of the route's oldest settlements. The **District Museum,** Leake and Bedford Streets (tel. 090-45-4006), displays yet more early implements. Open by appointment. Kellerberrin Hill, north of the post office, is a good viewing spot. You can also turn off here for Mount Stirling and Kokerbin Rock.

Situated on both the Perth-Kalgoorlie railway line and the Great Eastern Highway, **Merredin** (pop. 3,520) represents the commercial center for this region. The **Old Railway Station** on the highway is a group of four 1920s buildings that now serve as a museum and arts center. Hours are Mon.-Fri. 9 a.m.-3 p.m., Sat.-Sun. and school holidays 10 a.m.-4 p.m. Admission is $2. Two walks that start off from the railway station are **Merredin Peak Heritage Trail,** an easy jaunt around the town's historic buildings, and a longer (six km) hike around the peak. **Burracoppin Rock,** 24 km east of Merredin, is a large rock outcrop popular with picknickers.

Merredin Oasis Hotel, 8 Great Eastern Hwy. (tel. 090-41-1133), has moderately priced, air-conditioned rooms with TVs, as well as a swimming pool. Campsites and on-site vans are available at **Merredin Caravan Park,** Great Eastern Hwy. (tel. 090-41-1535).

Western Australia's gold rush began in 1887 at **Southern Cross,** 109 km east of Merredin. Though the fever quickly moved east to Coolgardie and Kalgoorlie, Southern Cross (pop. 800) still retains its wide streets and historic buildings. **Yilgarn History Museum** (1892), Antares St., was originally the Mining Registrar's Office, then the town courthouse. Exhibits trace the town's early settlement and include mineral displays. Hours are Mon.-Sat. 9 a.m.-noon and 1:30-4 p.m., Sunday 1:30-4 p.m.

Other turn-of-the-century buildings are the **Forrester's Resource Centre** and **Lisignolis Shop,** both on Antares Street. **Wimmera Hill,** site of W.A.'s first major gold discovery, offers good views of the area.

Southern Cross marks the end of the Wheatlands and the beginning of the 188-km desert stretch to Coolgardie and the Goldfields region.

THE GOLDFIELDS

Western Australia's goldfields are hot, flat, and extremely arid, punctuated with deserted outposts, preserved ghost towns, and its semi-thriving hub, Kalgoorlie. The streets are wide, shoot-'em-out affairs (made that way so camel trains could turn around easily), and many of the buildings exude the wealth and opulence associated with gold frenzy. Try to ignore the cranes, conveyers, and tailings dumps and envision the Golden Mile's hundred mines all flourishing simultaneously.

History

Until that 1887 gold strike in Southern Cross, Western Australia received merely poor-relative status from the eastern colonies. But what brings relatives flocking faster than gold? Though the Southern Cross find quickly ran dry, in 1892 prospector Arthur Bayley (acting on a hot tip given by a man he'd saved from death) staked a claim at Bayley's Reward, a huge gold reef about three kilometres east of Coolgardie. By 1900, the town's population soared to 15,000, dropping considerably by 1905 when the rush rushed elsewhere. Bayley's Reward, however, continued to produce gold until 1963.

In 1893, Irish prospectors Paddy Hannan, Tom Flannigan, and Dan Shea found gold near the site of the present Mount Charlotte Mine. Though surface gold soon ran out, a bigger and deeper find was discovered along the Golden Mile (reputedly the world's richest square mile of gold-bearing earth), prompting companies and diggers to go underground. At one time, the Golden Mile boasted more than 100 working mines.

One enormous problem was the lack of water, or the pollution of what water there was: miners were dropping like flies from thirst and disease. Engineer C.Y. O'Connor came up with the perfect invention—a 563-km wood and pitch water pipe from Mundaring Weir, near Perth, to Kalgoorlie. Mocked and taunted by ignorant disbelievers, O'Connor nonetheless persevered with his pipeline. Unfortunately, three days after the water pumps were started and there was still nary a trickle, the despondent O'Connor shot himself to death—not realizing the water

would take two weeks to travel such a distance. Dead or not, he'd solved the problem. By 1903 water began filling Kalgoorlie's new reservoir.

KALGOORLIE

"Queen of the Golden Mile," Kalgoorlie (pop. 20,000) sits 596 km east of Perth at the end of the Goldfields Heritage Trail. Kalgoorlie goldfields continued to produce during the lean 1920s, ebbing and falling during depression and war. Just as the mines were faltering economically (Mount Charlotte Mine is the only big operation), the 1960s nickel boom brought renewed prosperity—and tourism—to town.

Sights

Kalgoorlie's biggest tourist attraction is **Hannan's North Tourist Mine,** Boulder Block Rd., Fimiston (on the Golden Mile). See mining memorabilia and the inner (or under) workings. Visitors can take a 30-minute surface tour, 90-minute underground tour, or both. Tours depart several times daily and cost about $14 each, though you can explore the surface displays on your own, for free. For information, phone (090) 91-4074.

Learn the history and development of W.A.'s eastern goldfields at the **Museum of the Goldfields,** 22 Outridge Terrace—look for the Ivanhoe mine headframe. Check out the exhibits and the underground gold vault, then ride the elevator to a viewing platform on the headframe for a miner's-eye view. The museum encompasses the teensy **British Arms Hotel,** supposedly the narrowest pub in Australia. Hours are daily 10 a.m.-4:30 p.m., closed Good Friday and Christmas Day. Admission is free. For information, phone (090) 21-8533.

The **W.A. School of Mines and Mineral Museum,** Egan St., features displays of minerals, meteorites, gold nuggets, and gemstones. Hours are Mon.-Fri. 9 a.m.-4 p.m. For information, phone (09) 22-0109.

The 1903 **Town Hall,** Hannan St., houses historical memorabilia and an art gallery. Outside the building, a bronze statue of Paddy Hannan holding his waterbag doubles as a drinking fountain. Hours are Mon.-Fri. 9 a.m.-5 p.m. For information, phone (090) 21-2544.

Other architectural delights on Hannan St. are the **post office** and the **Exchange Hotel.**

Paddy Hannan's Tree, Outridge Terrace, near the head of Hannan St., marks the spot where Paddy found Kalgoorlie's first gold back in 1893.

Mount Charlotte Reservoir off Park St., near the end of Hannan St., is where C.Y. O'Connor ended his pipeline. The lookout gives a good town view.

Hammond Park, Lyall St., Lamington, is a flora and fauna reserve with tame emus and kangaroos and a detailed model of a Bavarian castle. Hours are daily 9 a.m.-5 p.m.

The **Arboretum,** adjacent to Hammond Park, features a marked walking trail to individual trees and a variety of birdlife.

Illegal and Legal

Amsterdam it ain't, but Hay Street is lined with brothels, a la Dutch treat, where costumed ladies of the night beckon the menfolk passing by. Though officialdom turns its eagle eye from this

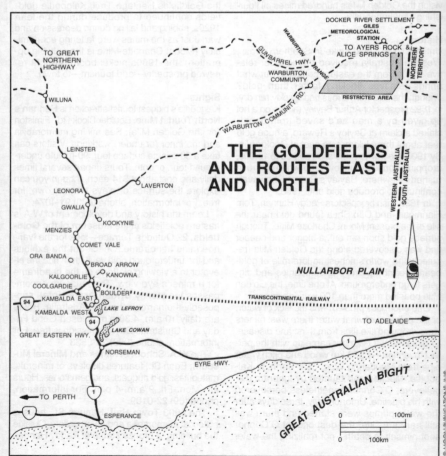

THE GOLDFIELDS
AND ROUTES EAST
AND NORTH

long-practiced local activity, it is not actually legal.

The **Two Up School,** Broad Arrow Rd., six km north of Kalgoorlie, is Australia's only legalized bush two-up school. This famous Aussie gambling game has been played in Kalgoorlie since the beginning of the gold rush. Hours are Mon.-Sat. 1:30 p.m.-dark, Sunday 11 a.m.-dark. Closed on race days and the mine's payday. Don't bring alcohol and don't come if you're under 18 years old. For information, phone (090) 21-1413.

Accommodations

Would you want to stay anywhere but one of the classic old pubs? Find inexpensive to moderate rooms at the: **Exchange Hotel,** Hannan St. (tel. 090-21-2833); **York Hotel,** Hannan St. (tel. 090-21-2337); **Palace Hotel,** Hannan St. (tel. 090-21-2788); and **Surrey House,** 9 Boulder Rd. (tel. 090-21-1340). The **Star and Garter,** 497 Hannan St. (tel. 090-21-3004), has motel rooms in the expensive range, TVs, and a swimming pool.

Campsites and on-site vans are available at: **Golden Village Caravan Park,** Hay St. (tel. 090-21-4162); **Goldminer Tourist Caravan Park,** Great Eastern Hwy. (tel. 090-21-3713); and **Prospector Tourist Park,** Great Eastern Hwy. (tel. 090-21-2524).

Food

All of the pubs serve filling counter meals at reasonable prices. Hannan St. is lined with taverns and eateries. The **Palace, Exchange,** and **York** Hotels are especially recommended. **Matteo's,** 113 Hannan St., makes up good pizzas, and the **Victoria Café** is a popular local breakfast spot. The **Broccoli Forest Health Food Store and Kitchen,** at the top end of Hannan St., serves eat-in or takeaway vegetarian meals and stocks bulk nuts, fruits, grains, and other natural foods.

If you've just hit gold, reserve a table at the very expensive **Amalfi,** 409 Hannan St. (tel. 090-21-3088). This long-established Italian restaurant is famous for its scaloppine.

Kalgoorlie brews its own beer, aptly named **Hannan's.**

Shopping

Got that gold fever? You can buy prospecting supplies and metal detectors at **International Lapidary,** 67 Hannan St. (tel. 090-21-3017), or rent equipment through the tourist office.

Information

For local information and tour bookings, contact **Kalgoorlie-Boulder Tourist Centre,** 250 Hannan St., Kalgoorlie (tel. 090-21-1966). Hours are Mon.-Fri. 8:30 a.m.-5 p.m., Sat.-Sun. 9 a.m.-5 p.m.

A branch of the **Royal Automobile Club** is at the corner of Hannan and Porter Streets. For information, phone (090) 21-1511.

For **emergencies,** phone 000 or the **Kalgoorlie Regional Hospital** (tel. 090-21-2222).

Transport

Both **Ansett** (tel. 13-1300 toll free) and **Skywest** (book through Ansett) fly to Kalgoorlie daily from Perth ($225). **Goldfields Air Services** (tel. 090-93-2116) does the Esperance-Norseman-Kalgoorlie route every Tuesday ($135).

Greyhound Pioneer Australia (tel. 13-2030 toll-free) stops in Kal en route to the capital cities ($75 from Perth); **Westrail** (tel. 090-21-2023) operates three times weekly between Kal and Esperance ($32); and **Kalgoorlie Express** (tel. 09-328-9199) does a twice-a-week run between Kalgoorlie and Perth, venturing into northern towns.

The Indian-Pacific and Trans-Australian trains both stop at Kalgoorlie on their way to and from Perth several times each week. The Prospector leaves East Perth Rail Terminal every day for the eight-hour trip ($60, including a meal). For information and bookings, phone Westrail (tel. 090-326-2222)—book this one ahead.

The local **bus** operates regular runs between Kalgoorlie and Boulder for $1 each way. The tourist center has timetables.

Taxis are available 24 hours a day; a ride between the town and the airport is about $10. For bookings, phone (090) 21-2177.

All of the major car rental firms are at Kalgoorlie Airport.

Bicycles can be hired for $12 per day from **Johnston Cycles,** 76 Boulder St. (tel. 090-21-1157).

Goldrush Tours, Palace Chambers, Maritana St. (tel. 090-21-2954), offers a variety of guided tours and excursions including town tours, gold detector tours, ghost towns, and in-season wildflowers.

Tour the local **Royal Flying Doctor** base, 56 Piccadilly St., Mon.-Fri. at 2:30 p.m. For information, phone (090) 21-2899.

VICINITY OF KALGOORLIE

Looking for gold? It's still out there. Grab a metal detector and join other weekend prospectors, but be sure you're well prepared—carry water, spare parts, and good maps. Check in with the tourist center and Royal Automobile Club before venturing out into this rugged, remote region. Both Boulder and Coolgardie are popular pit stops. Good luck.

Boulder

Boulder (pop. 5,600) is actually a satellite town of Kalgoorlie, built during the boom to service the Golden Mile. Boulder Block pubs used to see nonstop action, but, alas, the town is much quieter these days.

The **Boulder Town Hall,** on Burt St., features an ornate clocktower and an exhibition of works by local artists. Next door, the **Goldfields War Museum** houses military artifacts and vehicles but—as of press time—was closed for renovations. For information, phone (090) 93-1083.

The 1897 Boulder City Railway Station is home to the **Eastern Goldfields Historical Society** and its historical and pioneering exhibits. Hours are daily 9-11:30 a.m.

The **Cornwall Hotel,** on Hopkins St., is another gorgeous old grand dame.

The **Rattler** tourist train departs daily from Boulder City Railway Station for a one-hour, commentary-accompanied journey of the entire Golden Mile. This is the train that originally linked Kalgoorlie with Boulder. Fare is $10. Departures are daily 10 a.m., Sunday and holidays 10 a.m. and noon. For information and bookings, phone (090) 21-7077.

Coolgardie

You won't find the frenzied boom town of 1892. Settled into ghost-town retirement, Coolgardie (pop. 900), 40 km southwest of Kalgoorlie, is still a popular stopping place for gold-era aficionados. You'll easily get a sense of what this town was like in its glory just by the size of the streets and structures.

Details of Coolgardie's history can be gleaned from the 150 markers placed about town, which recount the original use of each building. An index to the markers is posted near the **Goldfields Exhibition** on Bayley Street. The exhibition relives Coolgardie's not-so-humble beginnings and includes goldfields memorabilia and a 35-minute video. Hours are daily 10 a.m.-5 p.m., closed Christmas Day. Admission is $2.50. For information, phone (090) 26-6090.

The **Old Railway Station,** Woodward St., serves as a transport museum and features a display of Modesto Varischetti's rescue. The name doesn't ring a bell? In 1907, Modesto became trapped by floodwaters while 300 meters underground and was rescued by divers some 10 days later. Hours are daily 9 a.m.-5 p.m., closed Thursday afternoon and Christmas Day. **Ben Prior's Open Air Museum,** Bailey St., is an amazing assortment of gold-boom junque sitting by the edge of the road. Open daily.

Warden Finnerty's House, Hunt St., belonged to the gold rush rule maker. Hours are Tuesday 1-4 p.m. and Sunday 10 a.m.-noon. Admission is $2.

Before jails were built, prisoners were chained to the old **Gaol Tree,** on Hunt St., over the old railway bridge. The attached leg irons are replicas. **Bayley's Reward,** Kalgoorlie Rd., is the site of Coolgardie's first gold find. **Coolgardie Cemetery,** Great Eastern Hwy., west of town, has some interesting old graves and headstones, including those of a few Afghan camel drivers.

Learn the history of camels in the goldfields and take a ride yourself at the **Camel Farm,** Great Eastern Highway. Hours are daily 9 a.m.-5 p.m. Admission is $2 (rides are $2.50). For information, phone (090) 26-6159.

Queen Victoria Rock Nature Reserve, Queen Victoria Rock Rd., is a huge rock surrounded by woodlands, with a walking trail across the rock and up to the summit. You might be able to sight the "freckled duck," one of the world's rarest waterfowl, at **Rowles Lagoon,** Bonnie Vale Road. Rockclimbing is popular at **Cave Hill Nature Reserve,** Sunday Soak Track. **Burra Rock Nature Reserve,** Burra Rock Rd., offers rock exploration, swimming, and wide views.

Pick up tourist info at the **Coolgardie Tourist Bureau,** 62 Bayley St. (tel. 090-26-6090). Hours are daily 9 a.m.-5 p.m.

The **Denver City Hotel,** Bayley St. (tel. 090-26-6031), and the **Railway Lodge,** Bayley St. (tel. 090-26-6166), two of the beautiful original hotels, offer inexpensive pub rooms. The **Coolgardie Motor Inn,** Great Eastern Hwy. (tel. 090-26-6002), has moderate prices and a swimming pool.

The **YHA Hostel,** 56 Gnarlbine Rd. (tel. 090-26-6051), has dorm beds for $11 per night.

Campsites and on-site vans are available at **Coolgardie Caravan Park,** Bayley St. (tel. 090-26-6009).

The **Coolgardie Motel** has a passable restaurant, but the **Premier Café,** Bayley St., is a step higher. For counter lunches, try the **Denver City Hotel.**

All of the interstate coaches stop in Coolgardie on the way to and from Kalgoorlie. **Bonnie Vale Station,** 12 km away, is a stop for Kalgoorlie-bound trains.

Kambalda

Kambalda, 55 km south of Kalgoorlie, was originally a gold-mining town called Red Hill (1897-1906). Regaining new importance—and a new name—when nickel was discovered in 1966, Kambalda continues to exist as a major mining center of the region. Situated on the shores of saltwater Lake Lefroy, Kambalda is a popular spot for weekend land yachting.

Red Hill Lookout offers vantage points of the town, lake, and surrounding countryside. **John Hill View Point** will give you a vantage point of the mine and slime dump.

Pick up permits to visit the mines at **Kambalda Tourist Bureau,** Irish Mulga Dr., Kambalda West (tel. 090-21-1446). Hours are Mon.-Fri. 9 a.m.-5 p.m.

Norseman

Often called the "eastern gate to the western state," Norseman (pop. 1,900) sits at the western end of the Eyre Highway and is a major junction for travelers heading east across the Nullarbor Plain, south to Esperance (207 km) or the Rainbow Coast, or north to Coolgardie (also 207 km) and on to Perth. Since 1892, the Dundas Goldfields have been yielding gold from their super-rich quartz reef.

A collection of gold-rush tools and other items is on display at the **Historical and Geological**

Museum, Battery Road. Hours are Mon.-Fri. 10 a.m.-4 p.m. Admission is $2. For information, phone (090) 39-1593.

Mount Jimberlana, seven km east of town, is an estimated 550 million years old—one of the oldest geological areas in the world. A walking trail to the summit takes about 30 minutes each way and affords great views of the hills, salt lakes, and mine operations. The **Heritage Trail**—dating from the turn-of-the-century—leads through bushland to **Dundas Rocks,** a popular picnic and bushwalk site 24 km south of Norseman.

If you want to try your luck fossicking in the **Western Gemstone Area,** first pick up a permit ($10) at the tourist bureau. The main gemstones to be found are moss agate, moss opalite, chrysophase, and jasper. Or, if you're more inclined toward panning for gold, get a permit for the **Gold Lease.**

Norseman Tourist Bureau is on Roberts St. (tel. 090-39-1071). Hours are daily 9 a.m.-5 p.m. Free conducted tours of the mine workings depart the tourist bureau Mon.-Fri. at 10 a.m. and 1 p.m. Cost is $5.

On Robert St., the **Norseman Hotel** (tel. 090-39-1023) and **Railway Hotel** (tel. 090-39-1115) both offer inexpensive rooms. The **Norseman Eyre Motel,** Robert St. (tel. 090-39-1130), is in the expensive range. Campsites and on-site vans are available at **Gateway Caravan Park** (tel. 090-39-1500), on Prinsep Street.

Goldfields Air Services (tel. 090-93-2116) can put down in Norseman on its Kalgoorlie-to-Esperance service. All of the interstate coaches stop in Norseman on the way to and from Kalgoorlie.

NORTH OF KALGOORLIE

Be prepared for long, lonely stretches with no services or facilities. The road is sealed only up to Leonora, 237 km north of Kalgoorlie, and from Leonora to Leinster (131 km north) and Laverton (124 km northeast). This region of once-bustling gold towns harbors few reminders of the glory days (and far fewer residents).

Kanowna, 22 km along a dirt road northeast of Kalgoorlie, used to be filled with hotels, churches, and about 12,000 residents, but all that remains is the old railway station.

CANNING STOCK ROUTE

This old stock route, spanning 1,750 km from Wiluna to Halls Creek in Western Australia, is the harshest, lengthiest, most difficult (and probably most expensive) 4WD journey in Australia.

In the early 1900s pastoralists in the Kimberley region had become desperate for an overland route by which to move their livestock down south to the monied meat-eaters in the goldfields. An outbreak of cattle tick had banned all ship transport around the coast—the southern graziers were taking no chances that it would spread to their land. Another discovery was that the nasty little ticks would simply and conveniently die during a trip through the sizzling desert.

In 1906, after the Kimberley boys pressured the government and put up some of the bucks, Alfred Canning, surveyor extraordinaire, was hired to make a preliminary exploration. His report was favorable—he could sink 54 wells approximately 20 km apart. Canning and his construction party went to work, completing the route between March 1908 and April 1910. The first stock trod by in 1911. In 1958 the route was abandoned with the introduction of road trains. As of 1995, the four-wheelers are still trying to keep on track.

In 1929, a team led by William Albert Snell refurbished the wells up to No. 35 and Alfred Canning (retired by then) finished the job. Fear of a Japanese invasion of Australia's north spurred another refurbishment in 1942—just in case citizens and livestock had to flee the area.

In their prime, the wells each possessed a hand-operated windlass, two buckets, a whip-pole for water-hauling, and a galvanized steel trough for cattle-watering. Unfortunately, since 1958 the wells have been desecrated by termites, rust, and fires; some retain only a bit of wood, ironwork, and the odd bucket.

Warning: This is an extremely arduous journey, requiring major preparations, a top-notch 4WD vehicle, permits from pastoralists, two-way radio transceivors, a *lot* of fuel, and other provisions. There is no help along the way. Travelers—increasingly—die on this journey. It should only be undertaken late April until early October, with June through August being the best months.

The Royal Automobile Club puts out an excellent map and can provide you with information, but even their literature carries red-ink warnings.

On the sealed road, **Broad Arrow** has held onto one turn-of-the-century hotel. The 1911 Ora Banda Hotel, along the dirt road west of Broad Arrow, has been restored since its 1960s movie debut in *The Nickel Queen*. Stone ruins are all that's left of **Comet Vale**, on the highway beyond Lake Goongarrie. **Menzies,** 132

the vintage Grand Hotel, in Kookynie, north of Kalgoorlie

km north of Kalgoorlie, managed to keep a number of buildings, including the Town Hall and Old Railway Station. The **Grand Hotel,** with its large rooms and wide verandas, lives on at **Kookynie,** 25 km along a dirt stretch east of the main road.

Forging northward another 105 km will bring you to **Leonora** (pop. 525) and its twin town **Gwalia.** After gold was discovered in 1896, the Sons of Gwalia Mine claimed its fame as the largest underground mine outside the Golden Mile. And who do you suppose the mine's first manager was? Herbert Hoover—future president of the United States. Small world. Though the mine closed in 1963, much of it remains intact, as do many of the original structures. To get a feel for the place, see a historical display at the Gwalia Mine office, or walk the one-kilometer-long **Gwalia Heritage Trail.** Present-day Leonora serves as an administrative center for renewed gold, copper, and nickel mining operations.

Turn-of-the-century, gold-boom life was *wild* at **Laverton** (pop. 875), 124 km northeast of

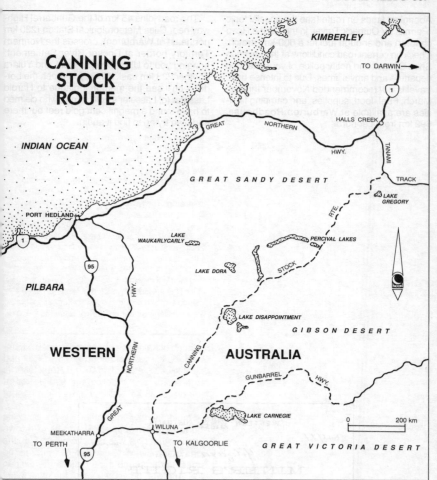

CANNING STOCK ROUTE

KIMBERLEY

TO DARWIN →

INDIAN OCEAN

HALLS CREEK

GREAT NORTHERN HWY.

TANAMI TRACK

GREAT SANDY DESERT

LAKE GREGORY

PORT HEDLAND

RTE.

LAKE WAUKARLYCARLY

PERCIVAL LAKES

STOCK

LAKE DORA

PILBARA

HWY.

LAKE DISAPPOINTMENT

GIBSON DESERT

NORTHERN

WESTERN

CANNING

AUSTRALIA

GUNBARREL HWY.

GREAT

LAKE CARNEGIE

0   200 km

MEEKATHARRA

WILUNA

TO PERTH

TO KALGOORLIE

GREAT VICTORIA DESERT

Leonora, until the gold (and the town) died out in the early 1900s. The 1970s Poseidon nickel boom—and the huge Windarra Mine—have considerably revived Laverton, often used by visitors as a base from which to explore surrounding ghost towns and gold mines.

North of Leonora, the sealed road ends 131 km away at Leinster, another nickel-producing town. Following the unsurfaced road 166 km northwest will take you to **Wiluna** (a has-been

1930s arsenic-mining community), and then to **Meekatharra** (183 km west), on the Great Northern Highway between Port Hedland and Perth.

The sealed portion of the **Warburton Community Road** to Ayers Rock (1,033 km northeast) ends at Laverton. If you intend to travel this route, make sure you have a well-equipped 4WD or conventional vehicle with good ground clearance (the road is not suitable for caravans or trailers). You will also need permits to enter

Aboriginal lands en route (see the special topic "Permits for Outback Travel" in the On the Road chapter) and enough fuel for a 600-km stretch. Check on current road conditions at the Laverton Shire Council and notify police of your intended departure and arrival times. Due to intense heat, travel is *not* recommended November through March. Fuel, food, supplies, and camping facilities are available at **Warburton Roadhouse,** 692 km from Leonora.

The road joins 45 km of the Gunbarrel Highway near Giles Meteorological Station (230 km northeast of Warburton), crosses the Northern Territory border at Docker River Settlement, bringing you to Uluru (Ayers Rock) and Yulara another 233 km east. When you reach the border, you'll see the memorial plaque to Harold Lasseter (of Lasseter's Folly fame), who claimed to have found a magnificent gold reef out there and died trying to find it again.

THE NORTH COAST

The northern part of Western Australia has undergone so much expansion that, in 1976, the Brand Highway was opened to smooth the way for travelers who had previously relied on the Midlands Road up to Dongara (80 km longer and with many more stops). Above Geraldton the Brand becomes the North West Coastal Highway, linking with the Great Northern Highway from Port Hedland to Broome and through the Kimberley. Collectively, all of these roadways are still Highway 1, the sealed route that circles Australia.

It's a 1,780-km journey from Perth to Port Hedland, passing through the state's Midwest, Gascoyne, and Pilbara regions. The coastal road only really becomes coastal as it nears the Midlands Road junction; until then it runs about 40 km inland. Both the inland and coastal highways are *hot* during summer months.

PERTH TO GERALDTON

The Brand Highway cuts into the Great Northern Highway 55 km northeast of Perth. It's 150 km to the turnoff for Cervantes (pop. 240), a fishing town established in 1962, and the closest town to **Nambung National Park.** A spectacular site within the park is The Pinnacles, calcified spires of widely varying shades, sizes, and shapes, scattered eerily amid 400 hectares of yellow and ochre sand. Some of the long-eroded formations are thought to be 30,000 years old. Several lookouts over the desert and coast can be accessed via a 500-meter walking trail. The best time for Pinnacle viewing is sundown. Day tours depart Cervantes Service Station daily at 1 p.m. For information, phone (096) 52-7041. For park and Pinnacle information, contact the **Department of Conservation and Land Management** (tel. 096-52-7043).

Warning: Bushwalkers should be wary of **kangaroo ticks**—use the appropriate repellent.

To reach **Jurien,** a tiny rock lobster port on a sheltered bay, follow the side track 50 km north of Cervantes. **Drovers Cave National Park,** six km east of Jurien, has some good bush-

walks, but all of the numerous caves have been locked up.

Greenhead, 56 km north of Jurien via the gravel Jurien Road or the sealed Brand Highway, features safe swimming, skin diving, and all kinds of fishing. **Leeman,** a short distance away, is also a relaxed fishing village.

Dongara (pop. 1,155) and neighboring **Port Denison** are holiday resorts and crayfish ports that touch the coast 359 km north of Perth. **Royal Steam Roller Flour Mill,** Walldeck St., is part of a restored village that includes the 1870 Old Dongara Police Station and tourist information center. Hours are Mon.-Fri. 9 a.m.-5 p.m., Sat.-Sun. 10 a.m.-2 p.m. The 1870 **Russ Cottage,** Port Leander Dr., is furnished with period items. Hours are Sunday and public holidays 2-4 p.m. Admission is $1.

The National Trust has classified a number of stone buildings at **Greenough,** an 1850s wheat-farming hamlet 41 km north of Dongara. The **Pioneer Museum,** Wonga Park, will fill you in on local folklore. Hours are Sat.-Thurs. 10 a.m.-4 p.m.

Midlands Road

The old Midlands Road begins 30 km farther up the Great Northern Highway, past the Brand Highway turnoff. This is well worth the drive in spring when the wildflowers put on a stupendous show.

At **Coorow,** you can detour 12 km west along Greenough Road to Perth Basin, one of the world's deepest sedimentary basins. **Yarra Yarra Lakes,** between Carnamah and Three Springs, is a salty lake system with some wild color variations (red, green, and blue), plus prolific birdlife. Climb to the top of **Mingenew Hill** for excellent east and west views of the Irwin Valley.

Wildflower Way

One more alternate route to Geraldton is Wildflower Way, which runs parallel to the Midlands Road beginning at Wubin, off the Great Northern Highway, and continuing 222 km to Mullewa, where you hook up to Highway 123 west. **Mullewa** (pop. 918), a sheep and wheat farming town-

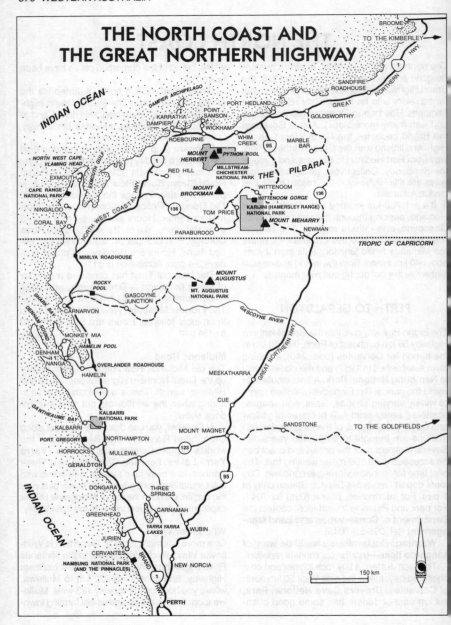

THE NORTH COAST AND THE GREAT NORTHERN HIGHWAY

BROOME

TO THE KIMBERLEY

SANDFIRE ROADHOUSE

INDIAN OCEAN

DAMPIER ARCHIPELAGO

KARRATHA

POINT SAMSON

PORT HEDLAND

GREAT

GOLDSWORTHY

DAMPIER

WICKHAM

MARBLE BAR

ROEBOURNE

WHIM CREEK

NORTH WEST CAPE
VLAMING HEAD

MOUNT HERBERT

PYTHON POOL

95

THE PILBARA

EXMOUTH

RED HILL

MILLSTREAM-CHICHESTER NATIONAL PARK

CAPE RANGE NATIONAL PARK

EXMOUTH GULF

MOUNT BROCKMAN

WITTENOOM

WITTENOOM GORGE

138

NINGALOO

136

KARIJINI (HAMERSLEY RANGE) NATIONAL PARK

TOM PRICE

CORAL BAY

MOUNT MEHARRY

PARABURDOO

NEWMAN

TROPIC OF CAPRICORN

MINILYA ROADHOUSE

MOUNT AUGUSTUS

ROCKY POOL

MT. AUGUSTUS NATIONAL PARK

GASCOYNE JUNCTION

CARNARVON

GASCOYNE RIVER

SHARK BAY

MONKEY MIA

DENHAM SOUND

HAMELIN POOL

MEEKATHARRA

DENHAM

NANGA

OVERLANDER ROADHOUSE

HAMELIN

CUE

1

KALBARRI NATIONAL PARK

GANTHEAUME BAY

MOUNT MAGNET

SANDSTONE

TO THE GOLDFIELDS

KALBARRI

PORT GREGORY

NORTHAMPTON

HORROCKS

MULLEWA

123

GERALDTON

INDIAN OCEAN

DONGARA

THREE SPRINGS

CARNAMAH

95

GREENHEAD

WUBIN

JURIEN

YARRA YARRA LAKES

CERVANTES

NAMBUNG NATIONAL PARK
(AND THE PINNACLES)

BRAND HWY

NEW NORCIA

PERTH

0   150 km

ship, features a number of historical and natural sights. It should go without saying that Wildflower Way is a springtime bloom-a-thon that will knock your petals off.

GERALDTON

Established in 1849 as a major seaport for the Murchison lead mines (and later the Murchison Goldfields), Geraldton (pop. 20,895) is the major town of W.A.'s Midwest region. Situated 424 km north of Perth, it is a leading winter holiday resort and renowned for its crayfish and rock lobster industry.

Sights

View 17th- and 18th-century Dutch shipwreck artifacts at **Geraldton Museum,** Marine Terrace. Other displays relate to the district's cultural and natural heritage. Hours are Mon.-Sat. 10 a.m.-5 p.m., Sunday 1-5 p.m., closed Christmas Day and Good Friday. For information, phone (099) 21-5080.

Monsignor John Hawes, both a priest and architect, was responsible for the California-mission-style **St. Francis Xavier Cathedral,** Cathedral Avenue. Building commenced in 1916 but was not completed until 1938.

The Hermitage, Cathedral Ave., was built to be Monsignor John Hawes's retirement home. Hours are by appointment only. For information, phone (099) 21-3999.

The Geraldton Historical Society headquarters is at the **Lighthouse Keeper's Cottage,** Point Moore Road. In continuous operation since 1878, the 35-meter-high lighthouse is banded in red and white stripes. Hours are Thursday 10 a.m.-4 p.m. For information, phone (099) 21-3999.

Geraldton Art Gallery, corner Durlacher St. and Chapman Rd., exhibits work by regional artists. Hours are Mon.-Sat. 10 a.m.-5 p.m., Sunday 1:30-4:30 p.m., closed Christmas Day and Good Friday. For information, phone (099) 21-3999.

Mount Tarcoola, Sydney St., and **Separation Point Lookout,** Willcock Dr., both offer expansive views.

Most of the local beaches offer safe swimming. Lifeguards patrol **Mahomets Beach** on summer weekends.

Accommodations

Marine Terrace is the main drag for oldie-but-goodie seaside guesthouses with inexpensive lodging. Suggestions: **Sun City Guesthouse,** 184 Marine Terrace (tel. 099-21-2205), and **Grantown Guesthouse,** 172 Marine Terrace (tel. 099-21-3275).

The **Mariner Motor Hotel,** 298 Chapman Rd. (tel. 099-21-2544), offers inexpensive rooms. **Geraldton's Ocean West,** corner Hadda Way and Willcock Dr., Mahomets Beach (tel. 099-21-1047), has moderately priced, self-contained cottages with TVs and cooking facilities. Motels in the same price range include **Hacienda Motel,** Durlacher St. (tel. 099-21-2155), and **Club Sun City Resort,** 137 Cathedral Ave. (tel. 099-21-6111). **Hospitality Inn,** 169 Cathedral Ave. (tel. 099-21-1422), and **Quality Inn,** Brand Hwy. (tel. 099-21-2455), are the two chain representatives with the representative high rates.

The **YHA Peninsula Backpackers Hostel,** 311 Marine Terrace (tel. 099-21-4770), has eight rooms for 50 people. Dorm beds run $12 per night. More $12 beds are available at **Batavia Backpackers,** corner of Chapman Rd. and Bayly St. (tel. 099-64-3001).

Campsites and on-site vans are available at: **Separation Point Caravan Park,** corner Portway and Separation Way (tel. 099-21-2763); **Sun City Caravan Park,** Bosley St., Sunset Beach (tel. 099-38-1655); and **Belair Gardens Caravan Park,** Willcock Dr., Point Moore (tel. 099-21-1997).

Food

Marine Terrace is also the location for takeaways, cafes, pubs, cake shops, pizza places, and Chinese restaurants. Geraldton, in fact, ranks high on the list of fast-food heavens. Put together a good international meal at the **Cuisine Connection** food hall, on Durlacher Street—Australia, Thailand, Italy, China, and India are all well-represented. The **Boatshed,** on Marine Terrace, has excellent seafood, albeit at higher prices.

Information

The **Geraldton Tourist Bureau,** Chapman Rd. (in the Bill Sewell Community Recreation Centre), provides local and statewide information, as well as coach, tour, and accommodations bookings. Hours are daily 9 a.m.-5 p.m., closed Christmas Day and Good Friday. For information, phone (099) 21-3999.

Transport
Both **Ansett** (tel. 13-1300 toll-free) and **Skywest** (book through Ansett) fly between Perth and Geraldton ($160). **Western Airlines** (tel. 09-277-4022) wings a Perth-Geraldton-Kalbarri-Useless Loop-Denham route three times a week ($140).

    Westrail (tel. 09-326-2222) and **Greyhound Pioneer Australia** (tel. 13-2030 toll-free) both provide regular coach service to and from Perth. Fare is in the $50 range. Northbound buses travel Highway 1 en route to Broome and Darwin. The coach terminal is in the same building as the tourist bureau.

    A **local bus** provides service to neighboring communities. For information, phone (099) 21-1034.

    Avis, Budget, and Hertz have Geraldton agencies, but the best rates (from $35 per day) are at **Batavia Coast Hire Cars,** 25 Marine Terrace (tel. 099-21-2767). Hire bicycles for $10 per day from **Wheel Nuts Bicycle Hire,** Chapman Rd. (tel. 099-21-6600).

    Batavia Tours (tel. 099-23-1006) operates a number of day trips to Monkey Mia and other nearby areas.

FARTHER NORTH

Beyond Geraldton
Leaving Geraldton, the Brand Highway metamorphoses into the North West Coastal Highway. **Northampton** (pop. 750), 50 km north, was a favorite Aboriginal site until lead and copper mines were established in the 1840s. Today the community prospers from the surrounding farmlands. Constructed of local sandstone, **Chiverton House Folk Museum** (1868-75), North West Coastal Hwy., houses a collection of early machinery and memorabilia. Hours are Thurs.-Sun. 10 a.m.-noon and 2-4 p.m. For information, phone (099) 34-1215.

    Horrocks Beach, 22 km west of Northampton, features a reef surrounding its five-km swimming beach, as well as good fishing (kingfish, whiting, herring, skippy, tailor, and rock lobster).

The **Bowes River** turnoff, four km south of Horrocks, is the location for a number of ancient Aboriginal cave paintings. Bowes River is another jumpin' fishing spot.

    Port Gregory, 43 km northwest of Northampton, is the Midwest coast's oldest port, and nearby **Lynton** is a former convict-labor hiring depot. Though the town is defunct, many of the old ruins can still be seen.

    From Lynton, follow Yerina Springs Rd. north, then turn east on Ogilvie West Rd. to **Hutt River Province,** where self-appointed "Prince Leonard" is ruler. Having seceded from the Australian Commonwealth in 1970, Prince Leonard's kingdom rakes in revenue off special stamps, money, souvenir items, tearooms, a swimming pool, and other tourist snares.

Kalbarri
Situated where the Murchison River meets the Indian Ocean, Kalbarri (pop. 820) is a holiday resort famous for its gorgeous gorges and terrific fishing. This is also the area where the Dutch ship *Zuytdorp* was wrecked, *and* the long-ago home of a 400-million-year-old, two-meter-long scorpion known as the eurypterid.

    Kalbarri National Park (186,096 hectares) features awesome sandstone cliffs and banded-in-red gorge walls (formed 400-500 million years ago). The fossil tracks of prevertebrate marine creatures have been located in the sandstone. The park also harbors a wide variety of wildlife and flora; try to come during the spring wildflower season. **Ross Graham** and **Hawk's Head** lookouts provide dynamic gorge views. A 35-km scenic drive leads to **The Loop** and **Z Bend,** two other spectacular viewing perches. Park facilities include short and long walking trails as well as picnic sites. Carry your own drinking water. For information, phone (099) 37-1140.

    Jake's Corner, a few kilometers south of Kalbarri, has some of W.A.'s best surfing breaks. **Red Bluff,** just south, is where you can see tracks left by the ancient eurypterid (possibly the first creature to have walked on land) and explore frozen, tearlike threads of rock and other intriguing formations (also thought to be 400 million years old).

    Rainbow Jungle, Red Bluff Rd., is lush with palms, ferns, tropical plants, rare and tropical birds, and fish. Open Tues.-Sun. 10 a.m.-5 p.m.

Admission is $4. For information, phone (099) 37-1248. **Fantasyland,** Grey St., combines collections of dolls, marinelife, fossils, and gemstones. Every morning at 8:45 a.m., the proprietor feeds pelicans on the foreshore opposite. Hours are Sun.-Fri. 9 a.m.-noon and 1:30-5 p.m., Saturday 9 a.m.-noon. Admission is $3.50. For information, phone (099) 37-1062.

Sailboats, canoes, surf cats, and pedal boats can be hired at **Kalbarri Boat Hire** (tel. 099-37-1245), on the foreshore across from Murchison Caravan Park. **Kalbarri Sports and Dive,** Grey St. (tel. 099-37-1126), hires diving equipment and offers instruction.

Av-er-est, Mortimer St. (tel. 099-37-1101), offers inexpensive weekly rates on self-contained holiday units with TVs and cooking facilities. Holiday units in the moderate range include **Kalbarri Reef Villas,** Coles St. (tel. 099-37-1165), and **Sunsea Villas,** Grey St. (tel. 099-37-1187). Campsites and on-site vans are rented at **Kalbarri Tudor Caravan Park,** Porter St. (tel. 099-37-1077); **Murchison Caravan Park,** Grey St. (tel. 099-37-1005); and **Red Bluff Caravan Park,** Red Bluff (tel. 099-37-1080).

Western Airlines (tel. 09-277-4022) provides service between Kalbarri and Perth three times a week ($155). **Westrail** (tel. 09-326-2222) operates bus service three times a week, in each direction ($60). A shuttle connects with **Greyhound Pioneer Australia** (tel. 13-2030 toll-free) on its thrice-weekly runs along the North West Coastal Highway.

Rent bicycles at **Murchison Cycle Hire,** Porter St. (tel. 099-37-1105), for about $10 per day. For local tours (including a cruise up the Murchison River on the *River Queen*) contact **Kalbarri Travel Service,** Grey St. (tel. 099-37-1104).

AROUND SHARK BAY

The Overlander Roadhouse (179 km north of Kalbarri) marks the turnoff from the North West Coastal Highway to Shark Bay, site of the first European landing on Australian soil (Dutchman Dirk Hartog in 1616).

Stromatolites, among the world's oldest living fossils, can be seen in **Hamelin Bay's** clear, shallow waters. **Shell Beach,** near Nanga via Denham Rd., is created from billions of minute shells packed about 20 meters deep. Actual shell "blocks" (compacted by nature) have been constructed by locals along the Shark Bay foreshore. **Freshwater Camp,** Nanga's pioneer homestead, features the usual relics.

One-time pearling port **Denham,** 48 km northwest of Nanga, sits on the west side of Peron Peninsula (just above the 26th parallel) and is Australia's westernmost town. Sightseeing

DOLPHIN ETIQUETTE

Please—Monkey Mia is *not* a dolphin Disneyland. These babies are not trained for your pleasure. When you're wading with the dolphins observe the following rules:

• wade about knee-deep
• wait until the dolphins approach you
• never touch, or put anything into, the blowhole
• don't touch the head, dorsal fin, or tail (pat gently along the side of the body)
• do not scare the dolphins with loud noises
• don't try to swim with the dolphins, and don't reach over them for any reason
• check with rangers before feeding—the dolphins are fussy about their food

• If a dolphin gives you a fish, don't give it back. Accept it and say "thank you."

one of the untrained dolphins at Monkey Mia

MARK MORRIS

cruises and fishing trips depart Denham Jetty. For cruise bookings and information on other local tours, contact **Shark Bay Tourist Information Centre,** 83 Knight St. (tel. 099-48-1253). Hire **bicycles** ($10 per day) at **Shark Bay Recreation Centre** (tel. 099-48-1218).

Well-posted signs lead to **Monkey Mia,** one of the country's—and the world's—most unusual natural attractions, 25 km northeast of Denham. Since 1964, when a woman from one of the area's fishing camps began the practice, dolphins have regularly come up to these shores to be hand-fed by rangers and throngs of visitors. These sweet mammals will only accept whole fish, not any that have been gutted or gilled. Obey rangers' instructions on feeding and petting. There is no set feeding time—the dolphins are free to come and go as they please. An information center provides educational exhibits and videos on dolphin behavior. Fresh fish are sold for your feeding pleasure. Hours are daily 8:30 a.m.-4:30 p.m. Admission is $3. For information, phone (099) 48-1366.

Bay Lodge, 109 Knight Terrace, Denham (tel. 099-48-1278), is a YHA associate. Backpackers' accommodations run $12 per night, while self-contained holiday units are in the moderate range. Other moderately priced, self-contained units are **Denham Villas,** 4 Durlacher St. (tel. 099-48-1264), and **Hartog Holiday Villas,** Denham-Hamelin Rd. (tel. 099-48-1323). **Heritage Resort Hotel,** Knight Terrace (tel. 099-48-1133), with deluxe facilities, is the expensive choice. **Shark Bay Accommodation Service** (tel. 099-48-1323) manages a variety of holiday flats and cottages.

Campsites and on-site vans are available at: **Denham Seaside Caravan Park,** Knight Terrace (tel. 099-48-1242); **Shark Bay Caravan Park,** Spaven Way, off Durlacher St. (tel. 099-48-1387); **Blue Dolphin Caravan Park,** Hamelin Rd. (tel. 099-48-1385); and **Monkey Mia Dolphin Resort** (tel. 099-48-1320).

Local restaurants offer the usual counter meal and takeaway fare. The **Old Pearler Restaurant,** Knight Terrace, Denham (tel. 099-48-1373), is built out of shell blocks. Food is on the upmarket side and reservations are recommended. The **Shark Bay Hotel** is your counter-meal stop.

Western Airlines (tel. 09-277-4022) operates a Perth-Denham service three times a week. Fare is $190 one way.

Greyhound Pioneer Australia (tel. 13-2030 toll-free) will drop you at the Overlander three times a week ($125); from there, a Denham Tourist Centre shuttle will transport you to to Denham and Shark Bay ($25).

Hired cars cost about $80 per day from **Budget** (tel 099-48-1247) and **Shark Bay Hire Cars** (tel. 099-48-1203), both in Denham.

A local bus departs Denham for daily forays to Monkey Mia. Check with the tourist office for fares and schedules.

Dolphin Express Hovercraft (tel. 099-41-1146) will whisk you from Carnarvon to Monkey Mia—$90 roundtrip for the 90-minute journey and you're almost sure to see dolphins en route.

CARNARVON

Positioned at the mouth of the Gascoyne River, Carnarvon (pop. 5,050) is known as the tropical gateway to the north. This seaside commercial center is famed for its tropical fruit plantations (particularly bananas) and its mile-long jetty, beloved by fishers. This was also the spot about which Captain Dirk Hartog and various other explorers said such lousy things, but post-jetty, big-banana Carnarvon has redeemed itself. After all, the place can't be all bad if the fish come up to the foreshore to be hand-fed.

Carnarvon Museum, Robinson St., features historic displays and a shell collection. Hours are Mon.-Fri. 9 a.m.-5 p.m., Sat.-Sun. 9 a.m.-noon and 2-5 p.m. For information, phone (099) 41-1146. Other local relics—including a whale bone arch—can be seen at **Pioneer Park,** Olivia Terrace.

Ponder trial plantings of tropical fruits and winter veggies at **Gascoyne Research Station,** South River Rd., North Carnarvon. Hours are Mon.-Fri. 8 a.m.-5 p.m. For information, phone (099) 41-8103.

Check with the tourist office for directions to the former **NASA Tracking Station** (closed in 1975).

Pelican Point is a good swimming and fishing site, just five kilometers from town. Other top fishing spots include **Dwyer's Leap** and **Prawn Jetty Beach.**

Practicalities

Old-ish, cheap pub-hotels are: **Gascoyne Hotel,** Olivia Terrace (tel. 099-41-1412); **Port Hotel,**

Robinson St. (tel. 099-41-1704); and the **Carnarvon Hotel,** Olivia Terrace (tel. 099-41-1181). **The Outcamp,** 16 Olivia Terrace (tel. 099-41-2421), is a wonderful B&B that doesn't cost much more than the old pubs.

Both **Carnarvon Close,** 96 Robinson St. (tel. 099-41-1317), and **Carnarvon Beach Holiday Resort,** Pelican Point Rd. (tel. 099-41-2226), offer moderately priced, self-contained holiday units.

The YHA **Backpackers Paradise,** Robinson St. (tel. 099-41-2966), has beds for $12 per night—and only two beds per room! Weekly rates are an even bigger bargain. **Carnarvon Backpacker's,** 46 Olivia Terrace (tel. 099-41-1095), has communal facilities, is centrally located, and also charges $12 per night.

Among the numerous caravan parks offering campsites and on-site vans are: **Plantation Caravan Park,** Robinson St. (tel. 099-41-8100); **Carnarvon Caravan Park,** Robinson St. (tel. 099-41-8101); and **Startrek Caravan Park,** North West Coastal Hwy. (tel. 099-41-8153).

The Gascoyne, Port, and Carnarvon Hotels all have similar counter meals at reasonable prices. Robinson Street is the food strip: fish and chips, pizza, and the ubiquitous coffee lounge.

Tel-O-Mac, 280 Robinson St. (tel. 090-41-1873), sells fishing, camping, and diving gear. **Rosco's Sports Shop,** 11 Robinson St. (tel. 090-41-1385), rents diving equipment.

For local information, including tours and fishing charters, contact **Carnarvon District Tourist Bureau,** 6 Robinson St. (tel. 099-41-1146). Hours are daily 9 a.m.-5 p.m.

Daily Perth-Carnarvon flights are operated by **Ansett** (tel. 13-1300 toll free)—about $250 oneway from Perth, but many special deals are available. Carnarvon is a regular stop on the north-south **Greyhound Pioneer Australia** route (tel. 13-2030 toll-free), and is also served by **Westliner** (tel. 09-250-3318). Fare is around $100.

Rent bicycles from **Rosco's Sports Shop** for about $9 per day.

VICINITY OF CARNARVON

Oyster-picking and crayfishing are specialties at the **Blowholes,** 70 km north of Carnarvon, via Pt. Quobba Road. Salt headed for Japan is loaded at **Cave Cuvier,** a deep natural port some 30 km north of the Blowholes.

Rocky Pool is a deep, freshwater swimming pool, on Gascoyne Junction Rd., 55 km inland. **Gascoyne Junction,** another 122 km east, is a gateway to the rugged Kennedy Range, full of wildlife, Aboriginal caves, rock paintings, and semiprecious gemstones. Gascoyne Junction Hotel, constructed of corrugated iron, is a famous old bush pub.

Mount Augustus, a 289-km gravel drive from Gascoyne Junction, is the world's largest monocline, measuring 717 meters above the surrounding plain (1,105 meters above sea level), and it remains one of Australia's best-kept secrets. Mount Augustus National Park, only just proclaimed in 1989, is also noted for Aboriginal rock paintings and unusual flora and fauna. Coach tours and scenic flights operate out of Carnarvon. **Mount Augustus Station Tourist Resort** (tel. 099-43-0527), at the foot of the rock, offers campsites and moderately priced units.

CONTINUING NORTH

The Ningaloo Reef
You'll be able to view everything from humpback whales to egg-laying turtles around this mini-Great Barrier Reef, one of the world's major reef systems. Running 260 kilometers along the North West Cape from Exmouth to Amherst Point, Ningaloo Reef—far more accessible than Queensland's Great Barrier—is fast becoming a snorkeling, scuba diving, fishing, and boat-trip mecca. Get there before the developers do!

Also, environmentalists are concerned about this region, now that the North West Cape region is heavy into offshore drilling. State legislation in 1994 decreed drilling in the fragile marine park to be off-limits, but since when does local government usurp the power of oil interests?

The turnoff from North West Coastal Highway is just past the Minilya Roadhouse, 142 km north of Carnarvon.

Coral Bay, 78 km from the roadhouse (you'll cross the Tropic of Capricorn about midway), is the main entry point to **Ningaloo Marine Park,** just meters offshore. The reef covers more than 5,000 square kilometers of the Indian Ocean, is made up of almost 200 types of coral, and shelters incredibly diverse marinelife—from teensy tropical fish to scary-looking whale sharks—in its crystal waters. Five shipwrecks around Ningaloo Station provide additional fun for divers. Sign up for a tour aboard the *Sub-Sea Explorer Coral Viewer* (tel. 099-42-5955), a semi-submersible viewing craft, or contact **Bay View Caravan Park** (tel. 099-42-5932) for a glass-bottom boat cruise. **Coral Dive** (tel. 099-42-5940) runs a full program of diving courses and rents necessary equipment. For game and deep-sea fishing charters, contact **Coral Cruiser** (tel. 099-42-5900) or **Norstar** (tel. 099-42-5940).

At Coral Bay, **Bayview Holiday Village Caravan Park** (tel. 099-42-5932) offers campsites, cabins, chalets, and on-site vans. Rates run from inexpensive to moderate. Self-contained holiday units are in the expensive bracket at **Coral Bay Lodge** (tel. 099-42-5932), but facilities include tennis courts and hired boats.

You'll need a 4WD to access most of **Cape Range National Park** and its 50,831 hectares of coastal scenery, limestone rocks, and gorges. Marked bushwalking trails lead to some of the gorges and lookout points. **Lightfoot Heritage Trail** is a seven-km walk through rugged limestone formations. First-come, first-served campsites are available at selected locations. Come April through October for best weather. For information, phone (099) 49-1676.

Exmouth

Exmouth (pop. 2,590), at the tip of the peninsula and 155 km north of Coral Bay, is also popular for fishing, diving, and other beach activities. The town was founded, however, as late as the 1960s to service and house personnel at the joint U.S./Australian naval base at the top of the North West Cape. Used as an Allied base known as "Potshot" during WW II, the facility has ostensibly been used to maintain international contact with U.S. Navy vessels (including submarines) via 13 very low frequency radio transmitters. If the oil tycoons have their way, proceeding with offshore drilling around Ningaloo Marine Park, Exmouth may soon become their "company town."

Take steep **Lighthouse Drive** for panoramic views of the reef, cape, and communication towers.

Norcape Lodge Resort, Truscott Crescent (tel. 099-49-1334), offers lodge accommnodations, family apartments, motel rooms, and campsites in every price range. For other campsites and on-site vans, contact: **Exmouth Cape Tourist Village,** corner Truscott Crescent and Murat Rd. (tel. 099-49-1101); **Lighthouse Caravan Park,** Vlaming Head (tel. 099-49-1478); or **Exmouth Accommodation and Caravan Park,** Yardie Creek Homestead (tel. 099-49-1389).

For reef dives and equipment hire, contact **Q Dive Exmouth Sales Hire and Service** (tel. 099-49-1662) or **Neilsen Diving** (tel. 099-49-1201).

Collect tourist information and book reef or fishing tours at **Exmouth Tourist Bureau,** Thew St. (tel. 099-49-1176). Hours are daily 9 a.m.-5 p.m.

Ansett (tel. 13-1300 toll-free) flies every day except Saturday between Perth and Exmouth ($325).

Several-times-weekly Perth-Exmouth bus service is provided by **Greyhound Pioneer Australia** (tel. 13-2030 toll-free) and **Westliner** (tel. 09-250-3318). Fare is around $150.

Avis (tel. 099-49-1014) and **Budget** (tel. 099-49-1052) rent cars for about $65 per day. Hire **bicycles** at Norcape Lodge (tel. 099-49-1334) or Exmouth Squash Centre (tel. 099-49-1149). Rates are $9 per day.

THE PILBARA COAST

The coastal portion of the Pilbara region is a cluster of early pioneering towns that are getting fat off their own natural resources and the rich inland mines. The Burup Peninsula area harbors some 10,000 ancient Aboriginal petroglyphs, most depicting the wildlife of the time.

Karratha (pop. 8,400), on Nickol Bay about 530 km northeast of Minilya Roadhouse, was established mainly because of the Hamersley Iron Project. Additional growth can be attributed to the Woodside Petroleum Project, which has developed a gigantic natural gas reserve on the North West Shelf. The **Woodside LNG Visitors' Centre** (tel. 091-83-8100) will acquaint you with the project—at least one side of it. Hours are Mon.-Fri. 9 a.m.-4:30 p.m. during winter months.

The 3.5-km **Jaburara Heritage Trail,** beginning at the water tanks, will lead you to Aboriginal carvings, grinding stones, shellfish middens, and taboo spiritual sites.

Up the road, **Dampier** (pop. 2,500) was built in the 1960s to serve as port facility for Hammersley Iron. The **Dampier Archipelago,** which the town faces, has a more exciting history of shipwrecks, whaling, and pearling. Boating and fishing these waters (with reefs containing more than 200 species of living coral) are primary pastimes.

Roebourne (pop. 1,700), 32 km southeast of Karratha, is known as "Gateway to the Pilbara." Established in 1864 along with the gold and copper mines, Roebourne is the oldest town in the northwest, as evidenced by its many remaining early stone buildings.

Aiming toward Cape Lambert, **Cossack,** the northwest's first port, once known as Tien Tsin Harbour, also has preserved its beautiful stone buildings. Nearby, **Wickham** is another iron ore company town. **Point Samson,** though modernized, is still a lovely little fishing village.

Accommodations in this area are on the expensive side. **King Bay Holiday Village,** the Esplanade, Dampier (tel. 091-83-1440), a YHA associate, is still in the moderate-expensive range. **Victoria Hotel,** Roe St., Roebourne (tel. 091-82-1001), has moderately priced pub rooms, and the least expensive motel is **Samson Accommodation,** Samson Rd., Point Samson (tel. 091-87-1052). Campsites and on-site vans, probably your best bet, are available at: **Karratha Caravan Park,** Mooligum Rd., Karratha (tel. 091-85-1012); **Harding River Caravan Park,** De Grey St., Roebourne (tel. 091-82-1063); and **Solveig Caravan Park,** Samson Rd., Point Samson (tel. 091-87-1414).

Forget the shopping center food and go to Point Samson for fresh fish 'n' chips and other seafood. **Moby's Kitchen** specializes in fresh local seafood in a garden setting overlooking the ocean, plus offers takeaways.

For Roebourne area tourist information, contact: **Karratha and Districts Tourist Office,** Karratha Rd., (tel. 091-44-4600); **Dampier Community Association,** the Esplanade, in King Bay Holiday Village (tel. 091-83-1440); or **Roebourne Tourist Bureau,** Roe St., Roebourne (tel. 091-82-1060).

Ansett (tel. 13-1300 toll-free) flies daily to Karratha from Perth. For bus info, contact **Greyhound Pioneer Australia (tel. 13-2030 toll-free) or** Westliner (tel. 09-250-3318). Fare is about $120 from Perth.

Vicinity of Roebourne

Traveling 60 km inland on the Wittenoom Road will bring you to **Python Pool,** a former oasis for Afghan camel drivers *and* for the area's many pythons.

Millstream-Chichester National Park (199,710 hectares), 60 km farther, is an odd contrast to its semiarid surroundings, with natural springs, permanent river pools, lily ponds, and groves of date palms (thought to have been brought by the camel drivers). Carry your own food and water, and be prepared for heavy rain and rough roads. Camping is allowed in designated facilities. For information, phone (091) 84-5144.

Back on the North West Coastal Highway, 78 km east of Roebourne, the 1887 **Whim Creek Hotel** was a rowdy Outback pub, built to serve the Whim Well Copper Mine. Historic photos are on display and today's brew is on tap.

Port Hedland

Established originally as a service center for the surrounding cattle stations, Port Hedland (pop. 11,200), 1,762 km from Perth, is now the major deepwater port for the megabuck Pilbara iron ore industry—visited by some of the world's biggest ships. By tonnage, it is Australia's biggest port. The entire town and **South Hedland,** its satellite, live and breathe for those rich inland mines. And, as if those miners aren't salty enough, the real stuff is produced a few kilometers away where huge salt dunes encrust the landscape.

Pretty Pool, behind Cooke Point Caravan Park, is a favorite spot for fishing and shell collecting. Wear sturdy shoes if you want to walk on the reef at low tide—these waters are full of venomous stonefish.

For the most part, Port Hedland accommodations are comparatively high in price. **Pier Hotel,** the Esplanade (tel. 091-73-1488), in the upper-moderate range, is the best deal, and next best is **The Esplanade,** corner of Anderson St. (tel. 091-73-1798).

Port Hedland Backpackers Hostel, 20 Richardson St. (tel. 091-73-2198), offers dorm beds for $12 per night.

Campsites and on-site vans are available at: **South Hedland Caravan Park,** Hamilton Rd., South Hedland (tel. 091-72-1197); **Dixon's Port Hedland Caravan Park,** opposite the airport (tel. 091-72-2525); and **Cooke Point Ocean Beach Caravan Park,** Athol St. (tel. 091-73-1271).

Food is the usual coffee lounge, pub, and supermarket put-togethers. The **Hedland Hotel,** corner Lukis and McGregor, does the best counter meals. The **Coral Trout** has excellent fish in both its restaurant and takeaway section.

For local information and tour bookings, contact **Port Hedland Tourist Centre,** 13 Wedge St. (tel. 091-73-1711). Hours are daily 9 a.m.-5 p.m.

Port Hedland Airport is an international gateway. **Garuda** provides service between Port Hedland and Bali.

Ansett (tel. 13-1300 toll-free) operates daily flights to Port Hedland from Perth ($375). Frequent flights serve Broome, Derby, and Darwin. **Greyhound Pioneer Australia** (tel. 13-2030 toll-free) and **Westliner** (tel. 09-250-3318) make regular runs between Perth and Port Hedland ($125); to Broome ($58); and to Darwin ($185).

Avis, Budget, and **Hertz** have agencies at Port Hedland Airport, and a taxi into town runs about $15. **Hedland Bus Lines** (tel. 091-72-1394) operates Mon.-Sat. between Port Hedland and South Hedland.

The Backpackers Hostel has **bicycles** for hire.

THE GREAT NORTHERN HIGHWAY

Though the coastal route to Port Hedland is more interesting, the inland Great Northern Highway is actually more direct. From Perth, the highway travels northeast through the Midwest and Pilbara regions, veers coastward at Newman, meeting up with the North West Coastal Highway 42 km south of Port Hedland.

Perth to the Pilbara

Up the highway, 132 km northeast of Perth, **New Norcia** is a strange contrast to other country towns. Founded in 1846 by Benedictine monks who came to inflict their gospel on the Aborig-

ines, the Spanish village-esque monastic community consists of the monastery, church, old mill, jail, hotel, and the original boarding schools (now used as a Catholic college). The Benedictine monks still live and work there, much as they used to. The **Museum and Art Gallery** relates the town's history and also houses a **tourist information center.** Hours are daily 10 a.m.-4:30 p.m., closed Christmas Day and Good Friday. For information, phone (096) 54-8056.

Mount Magnet, Cue, and **Meekatharra**—560, 640, and 760 kilometers respectively from Perth—are old Murchison River goldfields. Gold is still being mined at Mount Magnet. Nearby **ghost towns** include Austin (20 km south of Cue), Cuddingwarra (10 km west), Pinnacles (24 km east), Reedys (60 km northeast), and Tuckanarra (40 km north).

Prospecting for gold is still popular at **Sandstone,** 158 km east of Mount Magnet, which is also surrounded by a myriad of abandoned mining settlements. From Meekatharra, it's 183 km of unsealed road to Wiluna where the road turns south to Kalgoorlie, 534 km away (with the 166-km Wiluna-Leinster portion unsealed).

The Pilbara

This region encompasses 510,335 square km of isolated territory, rugged ranges, deep gorges, gigantic mining operations, company towns, and enormous wealth. Come see men and their ultra-big monsters rip the earth apart and extract its riches, then cart it off to Port Hedland for worldwide shipment.

More than 100,000 tons of iron ore are produced daily at **Newman,** 422 km north of Meekatharra, then shipped via private railway to Port Hedland and the big blue yonder. **Mount Newman Mining Company** operates free tours of its Mount Whaleback Mine (the world's largest open-cut mine). Tours depart Mon.-Fri., except public holidays, at 8:30 a.m. and 1:30 p.m. For information and bookings, phone (091) 75-1511.

Karijini National Park (formerly Hamersley Range National Park) is reached via unsealed road off the Great Northern Highway, 180 km west of Newman. The 617,606-hectare park encompasses a variety of spectacular gorges, stony watercourses, and permanent pools, as well as Mount Meharry (1,245 meters), Western Australia's highest mountain. Campsites with limited facilities are available. For information, phone (091) 89-8157.

I'll tell you the truth: I have not been to Wittenoom and I am *not* going—ever. And I'm not going to advise anyone else to go, either. Yes, I *know* it is the heart of the Pilbara, and that it sits at the mouth of the breathtaking Wittenoom Gorge. However, in this instance, the word "breathtaking" is given a whole new meaning: asbestos. Wittenoom mined blue asbestos 1937-66, when the mine closed and the population dropped from 1,500 down to 60. The fact is, microscopic asbestos fibers are still present in the Wittenoom tailings dumps and in the landfill used in and about town, and the place continues to be a health risk. (An aside: A friend of mine who previously was unable to conceive immediately hatched twins after a visit to Wittenoom—and she was traveling *alone*.)

Tom Price, W.A.'s highest town, at 747 meters, and **Paraburdoo,** on the edge of the Hamersley Range, are two other company towns south of Wittenoom that rail their ore production over to Dampier. Continuing along the Wittenoom Road (Highway 136) will take you to the North West Coastal Highway.

Another off-the-beaten path from Newman is along unsealed Highway 138. **Marble Bar** (pop. 357), 306 km north, is reputedly Australia's hottest place. It was hot gold-wise, too, with more than two million ounces produced since an 1891 discovery. The town was named for the Marble Bar, Australia's only jasper bar, easiest seen where it crosses the Coongan River, 10 km west of town. You're not allowed to chip at it, but you can get a sample at the jasper deposit on the road to Comet Mine. The **Comet Mine,** 10 km south of town, is still operating and features a souvenir shop with beautiful rocks, including the regional Pilbara jade. This whole area offers superb fossicking.

Goldsworthy, almost at the coast, was the Pilbara's first iron ore town, and it thrived until mining shifted eastward to **Shay Gap.** Both towns took the brunt of Cyclone Enid when it hit in 1980.

As the Great Northern Highway merges with the North West Coastal Highway, south of Port Hedland, it remains the Great Northern Highway throughout the Kimberley region and almost to the Northern Territory border. It's 610 km from Port Hedland up to Broome. **Eighty Mile Beach** and several roadhouses are the diversions along the way.

THE KIMBERLEY

This is it, my nouveau-pioneer readers—the last outpost, the frontier for which Daniel Boone would give the coonskin off his cap for the chance to explore. Even with phones, faxes, and the sealed highway, this 350,000-square-km region is remote and rugged, and *was* sparsely traveled until it hit the cover of *National Geographic* and prime-timed its way onto the "must-be-seen" travel circuit.

Though an 1885 gold find at Hall's Gap provided the first lure to this isolated area, it was soon supplanted by cattle ranching, and—thanks to the successful Ord River Irrigation Scheme—tropical fruit production for both domestic and worldwide markets.

The Kimberley is a magical haven of desert ranges, Outback stations, tropical forests, raging rivers, national parks, and more, more, more. The weather is a big drawback, however. It's best to travel here April to September, during the Dry. At other times of the year, not only do temperatures swelter above 40° C, but the very wet Wet swells rivers, floods roads, leaves settlements stranded, blackens tempers, and renders attractions inaccessible. Also common are bone-biting cold nights, May to July. You'll need a well-equipped 4WD for off-highway exploration.

BROOME

As the "gateway to the Kimberley," Broome (pop. 3,670) is one of the hottest (in both temperature and popularity) destinations in the country. Situated 2,353 km northeast of Perth, this dusty, cosmopolitan town is filled with boab trees, red dust, and oodles of character (and characters).

Pearls before swine—or at least cattle—certainly held true here. Beginning in the 1880s, the gung-ho pearling industry provided work for about 400 luggers (boats) and 3,000 men, contributing 80% of the world's mother-of-pearl until the advent of plastics. Now only a few luggers remain, in conjunction with newly established cultured pearl farming. But there's beef—and *plenty* of it as Broome's modern meatpacking industry is capable of processing some 40,000 head of cattle each season.

Though the Japanese targeted Broome during WW II, evidence of damage by both sides can be seen in the wrecked carcasses of Allied flying boats in Roebuck Bay and the Japanese plane engines mounted near the Continental Hotel.

The Asian pearlers contributed to Broome's rich cultural mix, mini-Chinatown, and atmos-

pheric appeal for a new breed of travelers—backpackers, frontrunners, and high-lifers.

Chinatown

Bounded by Carnarvon St. and Dampier Terrace, Short St. and Napier Terrace, "Chinatown" basically refers to Broome's older section—once alive with saloons, billiard parlors, boardinghouses, and pearling sheds—now lined with restaurants, souvenir shops, and ubiquitous pearl purveyors.

The **Roebuck Bay Hotel** is *rowdy* most nights and weekends. Live bands play in the beer garden most Saturday afternoons, and you won't want to miss those arm wrestling and wet T-shirt contests!

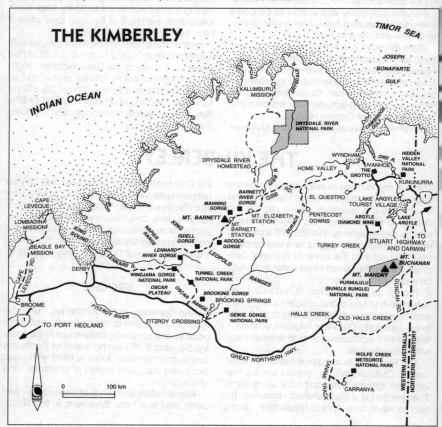

THE KIMBERLEY

Dating from 1916, **Sun Pictures,** near the corner of Short and Carnarvon Streets, is one of Australia's few remaining open-air cinemas. Regular screenings of not-terribly-old releases are shown nightly. For program information, phone (091) 92-1677.

The glass-encased model of a **Chinese temple** sits on Dampier Terrace, near Short Street.

Other Sights
The **Broome Historical Society Museum,** Saville St. (in the old customs house), presents pearling-era items, historical displays, and a shell collection. Hours are Mon.-Fri. 10 a.m.-4 p.m., Sat.-Sun. 10 a.m.-1 p.m. Admission is $2. For information, phone (091) 92-2075.

The **Courthouse,** Frederick St., offers another sweep at Broome's past. Hours are Mon.-Fri. 9 a.m.-noon and 1-4 p.m.

Horrie Miller (founder of Ansett WA) displays his Wackett aircraft outside the **Library and Art Gallery,** corner Mary and Hammersley Streets.

The marble headstones with Japanese inscriptions and a commemorative column are the most interesting at the **cemetery** on Ann Street.

Buccaneer Rock, at the entrance to Dampier Creek, commemorates the visit by Captain William Dampier and the *Roebuck.*

The **Golden Staircase to the Moon** is an effect created by the full moon's reflection off the ocean bed during low tides. Check with the tourist bureau for dates and best vantage points.

Sights near Broome
Popular **Cable Beach,** six km from town on Gantheaume Bay, is a white-sand and turquoise stretch for surfing, swimming, and sunning (nude, beyond the rock at the northern edge). Stingers invade these shores during summer months.

See some 500 crocs, ranging from babies to six-meter-long adults, at **Broome Crocodile Park,** Cable Beach Rd., Cable Beach. Primarily a research center, the farm also presents tours and video screenings. Hours are daily 10 a.m.-5 p.m. Admission is $9. For information, phone (091) 92-1489.

Dinosaur footprints, 130 million years old, are visible at low tide at Gantheaume Point, seven km south of Broome, at the end of Cable Beach. If you're not able to see the real thing, cement casts are displayed near the beacon on the cliff. **Anastasia's Pool,** a humanmade rock pool north of Gantheaume Point, fills up at high tide for those who want to take a dip.

Pearl Coast Aquarium, Port Dr., eight km from town at the deepwater port, supplies aquariums worldwide with local tropical fish. A pearling display explains modern farming techniques. Hours are daily 10 a.m.-5 p.m. For information, phone (091) 92-2443.

Birdwatchers can view more than 200 species of their feathered friends at the **Broome Bird Observatory,** 18 km east of town on Roebuck Bay. Hours are Tues.-Sun. 8 a.m.-noon and 2-5 p.m. For information, phone (091) 93-5600.

Cape Leveque Road, from Broome to Cape Leveque Lighthouse, spans a distance of around 200 km. Sights along the way include the Beagle Bay and Lombadina Aboriginal communities and their beautiful churches, plus another at One Arm Point, beyond Cape Leveque Lighthouse. Only the churches and souvenir shops welcome travelers.

Accommodations
The tourist influx has, unfortunately, driven accommodation rates way up. It's best to book ahead, especially during Australian school holidays.

Forrest House, 59 Forrest St. (tel. 091-93-5067), is a moderately priced guesthouse with breakfast included in the tariff. **Kimberley Holiday Home,** Herbert St. (tel. 091-92-1134), offers self-contained holiday units with cooking facilities in the upper-moderate range.

Both the **Continental Hotel,** Weld St. (tel. 091-92-1002), and **Roebuck Bay Hotel/Motel,** Carnarvon St. (tel. 091-92-1221), have air-conditioning, TVs, and swimming pools, and are expensive. **Cable Beach Club,** Cable Beach Rd. (tel. 091-92-0400), with bungalows, suites, and studio units, is super-posh and super-expensive.

The YHA operates two **hostels: The Last Resort,** 2 Bagot St. (tel. 091-93-5000), and the more sedate **Ocean Lodge,** Cable Beach Rd. (tel. 091-93-7700).

Campsites are located at: **Broome Vacation Village,** Port Dr. (tel. 091-92-1057); **Cable Beach Caravan Park,** Millington Rd. (tel. 091-

92-2066); **Roebuck Bay Caravan Park,** Walcott St. (tel. 091-92-1366); and **Broome Caravan Park,** Great Northern Hwy., (tel. 091-92-1776).

Food

The sometimes-too-lively **Roebuck Bay Hotel** in Chinatown serves a good range of counter meals for lunch and dinner, and higher-brow fare in its restaurant section.

For Chinese in Chinatown, try **Wing's** on Napier Terrace and **Murray's Asian Affair** on Dampier Terrace. **Chin's Chinese Restaurant,** Hamersley St., offers Asian specialties at moderate prices, plus takeaways.

The **Tea House,** Saville St., serves a good variety of Thai-style seafood. **Charters,** in the Mangrove Hotel, has a wonderful reputation for its seafood specialties.

Weld Street Bistro in the Continental Hotel offers daily changing menus, with emphasis on seafood, in the moderate-and-up price range.

For your splurge in fine dining, Broome's best is the **Club Restaurant** at Cable Beach Club, where only fresh ingredients are used. For reservations (required), phone (091) 92-2505. **Lord Mac's** is a more casual spot to watch the hot sun slip away over a cold beer.

Shopping

Absolutely scads of shops will be happy to sell you **pearl jewelry** at expensive prices. Some high-quality (and high-priced) outlets are: Paspaley Pearling, Short St.; Linney's, Dampier Terrace; and the Pearl Emporium, Dampier Terrace.

Information and Services

For tourist information and local tour bookings, contact **Broome Tourist Bureau,** corner Great Northern Hwy. and Bagot St. (tel. 091-92-2222). Hours are daily April-Nov. 9 a.m.-5 p.m., and in other months, Mon.-Fri. 9 a.m.-5 p.m., Sat.-Sun. 9 a.m.-1 p.m.

Broome Hospital, Anne St. (tel. 091-92-1401), has a casualty department.

Transport

Ansett (tel. 13-1300 toll-free) offers scheduled service from Perth ($470) and Darwin ($350). The local Ansett office is on the corner of Barker and Weld Streets (tel. 091-93-5444).

Greyhound Pioneer Australia (tel. 13-2030 toll-free) operates regular bus service to Broome from Perth ($190) and Darwin ($170). The local office is at **Broome Travel,** Hamersley St. (tel. 091-92-1561).

Broome Coachlines runs buses between Broome and Cable Beach. For schedules and information, phone (091) 92-1068.

Major car rental firms are represented at the airport, with prices beginning at about $60 per day. You might get a better deal at **Topless Rentals,** Hunter St. (tel. 091-93-5017), or **Woody's,** Napier Terrace (tel. 091-92-1791).

Broome is an easy town for cycling. **Broome Cycle Centre,** at Checkpoint Service Station, corner of Hamersley St. and Napier Terrace (tel. 091-92-1702), rents bicycles for $8 per day, with a break for weekly rentals.

Tours

Many local and extended tours depart Broome. For example, you can take a glorious twilight cruise aboard a yacht, a pseudo-lugger, or on *The Dampier*—an authentic pearl lugger. Cost is around $50, including beer or wine. Book this and other tours through the tourist office.

Kimberley Hovercraft will take you for a one-hour glide over Roebuck Bay for $50. For information, phone (091) 93-5025.

Inquire at the tourist office for the latest on bushwalks, 4WD safaris, and Harley rides.

DERBY

Broome may be the "gateway to the Kimberley," but Derby (pop. 3,000)—at the heart of many scenic attractions—has been dubbed "gateway to the gorges." Situated on the King Sound shore 220 km northeast of Broome, this port town was lively during the 1880s gold boom, until it, too, went the cattle route. More recently oil, diamonds, and, of course, tourism have played an important role in the town's development as both an administrative center and a base for travel to some of W.A.'s most stunning gorges.

Sights

The **Derby Cultural Centre,** Clarendon St., exhibits Aboriginal artifacts, local arts and crafts, Jowlaenga sandstone, and a palm tree botanic garden. Hours are Mon.-Wed. and Friday 10 a.m.-4 p.m., Thursday 1-7 p.m., Saturday 8 a.m.-noon. For information, phone (091) 91-1733.

At the corner of Loch and Elder Streets, the 1920s **Wharfinger's House,** built for the harbormaster, typifies tropical architecture.

The original **Old Derby Gaol,** dating from the 1880s, is situated next to the modern-day Derby Police Station.

The present **jetty,** constructed in 1963-64 to replace the original 1885 wooden structure, is used mainly for fishing or observing the tidal movements (tides up to 11 meters give this the highest tidal range of any wharf in the Southern Hemisphere).

Visitors are welcome to see Outback medical care in action (or about-to-be action) at the Kimberley headquarters of the **Royal Flying Doctor Service,** 60 Clarendon Street. For information, phone 091-91-1211.

Estimated to be 1,000 years old, the hollow **Boab Prison Tree,** seven km south of town, was used as an overnight "holding cell" for prisoners on their way to Derby.

Pigeon Heritage Trail details the adventures of an Aboriginal outlaw and folk hero named Pigeon who was shot and killed in 1887, following a three-year standoff with police and white settlers. The self-guiding tour is presented in two stages—one from Derby, the other from Windjana Gorge. The tourist bureau provides brochures.

Events

The annual two-week **Boab Festival** in late June and early July presents a rodeo, mardi gras, street parties, arts and crafts exhibits, and mud football.

Accommodations and Food

West Kimberley Lodge, corner Sutherland and Stanwell (tel. 091-91-1031), and **Spinifex Hotel,** Clarendon St. (tel. 091-91-1233), offer inexpensive guesthouse lodging. On the moderate side is **Derby Boab Inn,** Loch St. (tel. 091-91-1044). **King Sound Tourist Hotel,** Delewarr St. (tel. 091-93-1044) is the expensive choice.

Aboriginal Hostels Ltd., 233 Villiers St. (tel. 091-91-1867), has $10 beds and cheap meals.

Derby Caravan Park, Rowan St. (tel. 091-91-1022), has campsites and on-site vans.

The **Spinifex Hotel,** Clarendon St., and the **Derby Boab Inn** both serve moderately priced counter meals. **Lwoy's,** on Loch St., offers a Chinese fix, and **Wharf's Restaurant,** on the jetty, specializes in seafood.

Information

Walking maps, tourist literature, and tour bookings are available at **Derby Tourist Bureau,** Clarendon St. (tel. 091-91-1426). Hours are Mon.-Fri. 8:30 a.m.-4:30 p.m., Saturday 8:30-11:30 a.m.

For emergencies, dial 000, the **police** (tel. 091-91-1444), **hospital** (tel. 091-93-3333), or **Royal Automobile Club** agency (tel. 091-91-1256).

Transport

Daily flights from Perth ($450) or Darwin ($300) are operated by **Ansett** (tel. 13-1300 toll-free). The local Ansett office is at 14 Loch St. (tel. 091-91-1266).

Greyhound Pioneer Australia (tel. 13-2030 toll-free) and **Westliner** (tel. 09-250-3318) run buses to Derby from Broome ($25), Port Hedland ($80), Perth ($200), and Darwin ($150).

Cars can be rented through Avis or Hertz, and begin at $70 per day.

The tourist bureau can arrange scenic flights to Koolan and Cockatoo Islands, as well as to some of the other Buccaneer Archipelago islands, but they start from $100 per person, with a four-person minimum. **Buccaneer Sea Safaris** (tel. 091-91-1991) will cruise you along the Kimberley coast.

GIBB ROAD

This 705-km back road is used primarily to transport beef from the Kimberley's huge cattle stations to ports at Derby and Wyndham. It's also the most direct route over to Wyndham with convenient, if not always easy, access to the majestic gorge country and—for the well-prepared adventurer—to places where no one else has ever set foot! Although it's possible for conventional vehicles in excellent condition to negotiate this harsh road (a combination of bitumen, gravel, and natural earth, marked with some very large pits and pocks), a 4WD is advisable. Make this trip only April through November, and carry plenty of extra supplies. Petrol is available approximately midway at Mount Barnett Station.

The road to Windjana and Tunnel Creek Gorges shoots off Gibb Rd. 120 km east of Derby. **Windjana Gorge** features awesome multicolored cliffs that rise 90 meters above the Lennard River (which rages during the Wet, trickling down to a few pools during the Dry). **Windjana Gorge National Park** (2,134 hectares), part of the Napier Ranges, is home to a variety of native fauna—including crocodiles. Campsites with limited facilities are available May to October. For information, phone (091) 91-5121.

Pigeon's first victim, Constable Richardson, was killed at **Lillmooloora Police Station,** a couple of kilometers beyond Windjana Gorge.

Aptly-named **Tunnel Creek,** about 35 km south, has cut a 750-meter-long tunnel through the Oscar Range. A central shaft exposes natural light. During the Dry, the tunnel can be explored, but bring a torch or lantern, be ready for a short wade through cold water, and watch out for flying foxes. Aboriginal cave paintings can be seen near the tunnel's north end. From Tunnel Creek, it's 68 km to the Great Northern Highway and another 37 km to the roadhouse services at Fitzroy Crossing.

Back on Gibb Road, you'll mosey along the foothills of the King Leopold Ranges, a rugged area of tall granite outcrops, then you'll pass through Ingliss Gap to the top of the range before dipping down to the Broome Valley. Along the way are sidetracks to **Lennard River Gorge, Isdell Gorge,** and **Adcock Gorge.**

Replenish petrol (no LPG) and other supplies at **Mount Barnett Station,** 308 km east of Derby, on the banks of the Barnett River. Campsites with limited facilities are available. For information, phone (091) 91-7007. **Manning Gorge,** on Mount Barnett Station, offers swimming, fishing, and a two-km walking trail to a waterfall.

Forging onward, the turnoff to **Barnett River Gorge** is another 22 km. Moderately priced accommodations and cheap campsites are available at **Mount Elizabeth Station** (tel. 091-91-4644), 30 km off Gibb Road. The station also operates 4WD tours and scenic flights.

You must know where you are going, what you are doing, and—probably not a bad idea—

who you are doing it with before adventuring onto **Kalumburu Road.** This extremely isolated, rough, and rocky road is often closed. **Drysdale River Homestead,** 66 km from the Gibb-Kalumburu Road junction, is the last information center and service point. From there on out, you're on your own—*really* on your own. Many of the attractions, such as Mitchell Plateau and Drysdale River National Park, can only be reached by foot. And, if you do make it to **Kalumburu,** at the end of the 276-km haul, you'll discover that Kalumburu Mission is an Aboriginal reserve, requiring an entry permit (see the special topic "Permits for Outback Travel" in the On the Road chapter).

The next pit stop along Gibb Rd. is **Jack's** (or, sometimes, Joe's) **Waterhole** on the Durack River, a popular swimming, fishing, and camping stop. **Durack River Homestead** (tel. 091-61-4324) has moderately priced accommodations with all meals included. Four-wheel-drive tours of the region depart from here daily.

Home Valley Homestead (tel. 091-61-4322) is 56 km beyond Jack's (or Joe's). Accommodations, camping, and local tours are available here also. **El Questro Homestead** (tel. 091-61-4320), on the Pentecost River, has a fully self-contained stone cottage that accommodates six people, and a riverside camping area—it has been pushing for the yuppie/trendy clientele. This is the last facility on Gibb Road. It's 33 km to the junction of the Great Northern and Victoria Highways, where you go north to Wyndham or continue east to Kununurra.

THE GREAT NORTHERN HIGHWAY

Fitzroy Crossing and Vicinity

From Derby, it's 214 km to the gravel road north to Windjana Gorge and Tunnel Creek National Parks, and another 42 km to **Fitzroy Crossing** (pop. 430) on the Fitzroy River. Basically a cattle town, this little township is enjoying the fruits of Kimberley's popularity, providing services to travelers, either about to cross the river or stranded because of the Wet's floods, and giving access to **Geikie Gorge National Park** (3,136 hectares), 21 km northeast. The 14-km-long gorge cuts through a fossilized "barrier reef" dating from the Devonian period some 350 million years ago, and fossil deposits can be seen in the limestone cliffs. The park is filled with interesting vegetation and abundant wildlife including sawfish and stingers (usually found only near the sea), freshwater crocodiles, kangaroos, and wallabies. The park is open April to November (depending on the river's level). Boat tours of the gorge depart daily at 9:30 a.m. and 2 p.m.

The historic 1890s **Crossing Inn** (oldest pub in the Kimberley), near Brooking Creek (tel. 091-91-5080), offers moderately priced B&B rooms and plenty of local color.

Darlngunaya Backpackers, in the old post office on Geikie Gorge Rd. (tel. 091-91-5140), is four km from town, but has $10 dorm beds.

During the Dry, campsites with limited facilities are available within the park; in Fitzroy Crossing, try the **Fitzroy River Lodge Caravan Park** (tel. 091-91-5141), **Fitzroy Crossing Caravan Park** (tel. 091-91-5080), or **Tarunda Caravan Park** (tel. 091-91-5004).

Brooking Gorge is also close to Fitzroy Crossing, but inquire first at Brooking Springs Station both for directions and permission to cross the privately owned land.

Fitzroy Crossing Information Centre is at Fitzroy River Lodge, Great Northern Hwy. (tel. 091-91-5141).

Halls Creek and Vicinity

The turnoff to Tanami Track is 272 km beyond Fitzroy Crossing and 16 km before Halls Creek—then it's another 114 km of unsealed road south to **Wolfe Creek Meteorite Crater National Park** (1,460 hectares). Discovered in 1947 (but probably dating back a couple million years), the crater measures 835 meters wide and 50 meters deep and is the second-largest meteorite crater in the world. The road is usually accessible from May to November, but check at Halls Creek for current conditions. **Carranya Station** (tel. 091-68-8927), seven km south of the crater, provides limited supplies and camping facilities.

Western Australia's first gold rush took place in 1885 at **Halls Creek** (pop. 1,000), although the gold dried up just a few years later. Now the center of the vast East Kimberley beef lands, you can still see crumbling reminders of the old gold days at the town's original site, 15 km away along Duncan Road. **Mount Bradley Mine** off Duncan Rd. is one of the region's original mines (some shafts are still open—and deep—so take care when walking around). You can still see the rusting machinery left behind at the **Ruby Queen Mine,** abandoned in the 1970s.

Good local swimming and picnic spots are at **Caroline Pool, Sawpit Gorge,** and **Palm Springs. China Wall,** on the way to old Halls Creek, is a natural white-quartz formation that resembles a mini-Great Wall of China.

Moderately priced, basic cabin accommodations with air-conditioning are available at **Shell Roadhouse,** 31 McDonald St. (tel. 091-68-6060). Lodging in the expensive range is offered at the **Kimberley Hotel,** Roberta Ave. (tel. 091-68-6101)—though there's a cheap backpacker section—and **Halls Creek Motel,** Great Northern Hwy. (tel. 091-68-6001). **Halls Creek Caravan Park,** Robert Ave. (tel. 091-68-6169), has campsites and on-site vans.

Fresh bread is baked Mon.-Sat. at **Halls Creek Bakery,** Great Northern Highway. The **Kimberley Hotel** has the usual counter meals and a higher-quality bistro (the bar here has a readily apparent black/white border).

Halls Creek Information Centre, Great Northern Hwy. (tel. 091-68-6262), is open from May to September; info is also available at the shire office, Thomas St. (tel. 091-68-6007). In emergencies, dial 000, or the **police** (tel. 091-68-6002) and **hospital** (tel. 091-68-6002).

One of Australia's greatest natural wonders is the 208,000-hectare **Purnululu National Park** (formerly Bungle Bungle National Park), with its amazing tiger-striped rock formations banded with black lichen and orange silica, plus thousands of low, domed, beehive-appearing peaks. Though Purnululu was only "discovered" in 1983, the place was no secret to the Kidja Aboriginals—and now no secret to tourists who may well turn this area into the next Uluru (Ayers Rock). Vegetation is composed of everything from the Bungle Bungle fan palm to spiniflex and eucalpyts. Access to the park (a *very* rough 55 km from the Great Northern Hwy., 108 km from Halls Creek) is difficult, limited only to 4WDs with good clearance, and only during April to October. Check on road and weather conditions beforehand. Daytime temperatures can be extreme and water must be carried.

Hikes can be taken to **Echidna Chasm** in the north, **Cathedral Gorge** in the south, and **Piccaninny Gorge,** an intense 18-km roundtrip. Entrance fee is $20 per vehicle. Because of the fragile ecology and travel difficulty, many visitors choose to take a scenic flight (departing from either Halls Creek or Kununurra) over the park—inquire at both tourist offices. **Camping** is permitted at Belburn Creek. For information, phone the **Department of Conservation and Land Management,** P.O. Box 242, Kununurra, WA 6743 (tel. 091-68-0200).

The Great Northern Highway calls into **Turkey Creek Roadhouse** (tel. 091-68-7882), 53 km north of the Purnululu turnoff. The roadhouse offers petrol, overnight accommodations, and 4WD Bungle Bungle tours.

Sorry, folks, they won't let you into the **Argyle Diamond Mine** up the road from Turkey Creek unless you fly in on an air tour from Kununurra (about the same cost as a small diamond). Discovered in 1979, this is supposedly the world's largest diamond deposit. Its annual production of 30 million carats includes white, champagne, and cognac diamonds, as well as rare and valuable pink diamonds.

From Turkey Creek, it's 151 km to the Great Northern and Victoria Highways junction, from where you proceed north to Wyndham or east to Kununurra.

WYNDHAM

Western Australia's northernmost port welcomes you with a 20-meter-long concrete "Big Croc" sculpture at the town's entrance—a replica of the salties that inhabit its waters. Situated on Cambridge Gulf, at the end of the Great Northern Highway, Wyndham (pop. 1,500) is nicknamed the "top town in the West." During the Halls Creek gold rush days the town prospered, then declined, made a comeback in 1919 when the Meatworks was established, then fizzled again after a 1985 fire closed the plant down. Today it survives mostly on tourism and as a service center for surrounding pastoral and Aboriginal communities.

Sights

What do you think about a spot called **Blood Drain Crocodile Lookout?** Located on the gulf side of the Meatworks complex, the adjacent creek once was used as a blood drain. Well, guess who came for dinner? And about 20 of them at a time! Since the Meatworks closed and the blood stopped flowing, fewer crocs dropped by until feeding began in 1987. Inquire at the tourist information center for feeding times and tide charts (they eat an hour before the full tide).

Five Rivers Lookout, at the top of the Bastion Range, offers magnificent views of the Forrest, Pentecost, Durack, King, and Ord Rivers, as well as the port, Meatworks, surrounding gulf, and mudflats. Sunrise and sunset are the best viewing times.

Three Mile Valley, a miniature East Kimberley Range, is reached via Five Rivers Road. Rough gorges, splintered rocks, clear pools, and colorful vegetation closely duplicate the larger range. Walking trails lead to a variety of good sites.

Aboriginal rock paintings depicting spiritual figures and animals are located on the road to Moochalabra Dam. Built to provide the town's water supply, the dam is also a good picnic spot and fishing hole.

The **Grotto,** a rockbound waterhole off the Wyndham-Kununurra Road, is a favorite swimming spot. **Prison Tree,** King River Rd., is a huge boab tree lockup dating back to the 1890s.

Pay your respects to the historic dead at the **Gully, Bend,** or **Afghan** cemeteries.

Accommodations

It's sparse pickings up here. Least expensive motel units are at **Wyndham Roadhouse,** Great Northern Hwy. (tel. 091-61-1290). Accommodations in the moderate-expensive bracket are **Wyndham Town Hotel,** 19 O'Donnell St. (tel. 091-61-1003), and **Wyndham Community Club,** Great Northern Hwy. (tel. 091-61-1130). **Three Mile Caravan Park,** Baker St. (tel. 091-61-1064), offers campsites and on-site vans.

Information

Wyndham Tourist Information Centre, O'Donnell St. (in the Old Port Post Office), provides tourist literature, including a brochure detailing the heritage trail. For information, phone (091) 61-1054. Hours are daily 8 a.m.-5 p.m.

For emergencies, dial 000, the **police** (tel. 091-61-1055), **hospital** (tel. 091-61-1104), or local **Royal Automobile Club** (tel. 091-61-1305).

Transport
Ansett (tel. 13-1300 toll-free) has a daily Perth-Kununurra flight ($570 one-way), or from Darwin ($200).

From Kununurra, **I.J. and S.A. Thorley** (tel. 091-61-1201) provide daily coach transport to Wyndham. Fare is $25 one-way.

Rental cars begin at about $70 per day and are available at Branko BP Motors, Great Northern Hwy. (tel. 091-61-1305).

KUNUNURRA

Where were *you* in the sixties? Kununurra (pop. 2,100) was just being born as center of the Ord River Scheme, the Kimberley region's successful irrigation project. Then, in 1979, it was a double whammy when the world's largest diamond deposit was discovered south of town at Smoke Creek. Surrounded by water, natural attractions, birds, and wildlife, Kununurra is a travelers' stopover en route west to Broome (1,057 km) or east to Darwin (825 km).

Sights
Pandanun Palms Wildlife Park, Packsaddle Plains Rd., is a still-developing wildlife park with a range of native animals and birds. Hours are daily 8 a.m.-6 p.m. Admission is $2. For information, phone (091) 68-1114.

The **Zebra Rock Gallery** features displays of this unusual striped rock found only near Kununurra. Hours are daily 8 a.m.-6 p.m. For information, phone (091) 68-1114.

Collections of Aboriginal artifacts are displayed and sold at **Waringarri Aboriginal Arts,** Speargrass Road. This Aboriginal-run outlet offers boomerangs, didgeridoos, paintings, spears, fighting sticks, and many more crafts. Postcards, books, and music are also for sale. Hours are Mon.-Fri. 9 a.m.-5 p.m. For information, phone (091) 68-2212.

Kelly's Knob, near the town center, is a 191-meter-high viewpoint over the town, Ord River, and surrounding farmlands.

Adjacent to town, artificial **Lake Kununurra** has a wealth of wildlife and vegetation both on the lake and in the wetlands. Boat cruises are available.

The town fishing hole is **Ivanhoe Crossing,** a permanent waterfall on the Ord River near the Ivanhoe Station Homestead.

Hidden Valley National Park (1,817 hectares) near town is termed a "mini-Bungle Bungle." Features of this 300 million-year-old region include scenic gorges, rugged sandstone hills, Aboriginal rock art, abundant birdlife, and short walking trails.

Created by the Ord River dam, **Lake Argyle,** 72 km south of Kununurra along Parker Rd., contains nine times the water of Sydney Harbour. Rugged islands—which used to be mountain peaks—support a large number of birds and wildlife. Watch for Aboriginal rock paintings during the drive in. Boat cruises on Lake Argyle depart daily.

Moved from its original Lake Argyle site, the reconstructed **Argyle Homestead Museum,** Parker Rd., provides the history of early settlers' lives. Hours are daily 9 a.m.-4 p.m.

Accommodations
Seasons up here mean as much to travelers as to Aborigines when it comes to accommodations rates—there can be a wide variation. If you come during low (inferno-hot) season, you might well get an inexpensive deal at a "better" place.

Ranging moderate-expensive are **Country Club Hotel,** Coolibah Dr. (tel. 091-68-1024), **Kimberly Court,** corner of River Fig Ave. and Erythrina St. (tel. 091-68-1411), and **Hotel Kununurra,** Messmate Way (tel. 091-68-1344). And that shining beacon—the **Quality Inn**—is located on Duncan Hwy. (tel. 091-64-2622). **Lake Argyle Inn and Tourist Village,** Parker Rd. (tel. 091-68-7360), offers expensive rooms and cheap campsites.

Choose from three **hostels: Desert Inn Backpackers** (most popular), Tristania St. (tel. 091-68-2702); **Kununurra Backpackers,** 112 Nutwood Crescent (tel. 091-68-1711); and the YHA associate **Raintree Lodge,** Coolibah Dr., at the Uniting Church (tel. 091-68-1372). Dorm beds range $10-12.

LOOKALIKES

The vicinity of Kununurra is inundated with lookalike rock formations:

- **Shark Fin Tree,** on Parker Road, looks like . . .
- **City of Ruins,** Weaber Plains Road, looks like . . .
- **Zebra rocks,** in the East Kimberleys, near Kununurra, look like . . .
- **Sleeping Buddha,** along the Ord River on Victoria Highway, looks like . . .
- **Elephant Rock,** an end-on view of the Sleeping Buddha, looks like . . .
- **Sleeping Mummy** looks like **Sleeping Buddha** looks like **Elephant Rock** looks like . . . *you?*

Campsites are available at: **Hidden Valley Caravan Park,** Weaber Plains Rd. (tel. 091-68-1790); **Kimberleyland Holiday Park,** Duncan Hwy. (tel. 091-68-1280); **Town Caravan Park** (on-site vans, too), Bloodwood Dr. (tel. 091-68-1763); and **Kona Lakeside Caravan Park,** (tel. 091-68-1031), a bit out of town, but worth it for its lakeside location and prolific bird population.

Food
Gulliver's Tavern, corner of Konkerberry Dr. and Cotton Tree Ave., is a local drinking hole that also serves counter meals as well as more upmarket dinners in the dining room.

The **Kununurra Hotel** is another counter-meal establishment. A decent Chinese restaurant is housed inside the **Country Club Hotel** on Coolibah Drive.

Snackers might try **Three Star Café,** Banksia St., the **Salad Bowl,** Coolibah Dr., or **Valentines Pizza,** on Cottontree Avenue.

Information and Services
For information on local attractions and tours, contact **Kununurra Visitors' Centre,** Coolibah Dr. (tel. 091-68-1177). Hours are daily 8 a.m.-5 p.m.

For emergencies, dial 000, the **police** (tel. 091-69-1122), **hospital** (tel. 091-68-1522), or **Royal Automobile Club** (tel. 091-68-2236).

Transport
Ansett (tel. 13-1300 toll-free) has a daily Perth-Kununurra flight ($570 one-way), as well as flights from Broome ($250) or from Darwin ($200). Ansett's local office is in the Charlie Carter shopping mall (tel. 091-68-1444).

Greyhound Pioneer Australia (tel. 13-2030 toll-free) stops through on the Darwin-Perth route.

For **bicycle rentals** ($10 per day), inquire at any of the hostels or at the visitor center.

Rental cars start at $70 per day and are available from **Avis,** Bandicoot Dr. (tel. 091-68-1258), and **Hertz,** Poinciana St. (tel. 091-68-1257).

A full range of **tours** depart from Kununurra to surrounding sights. Book with the visitor center or the YHA Hostel (you'll get a discount if you're staying there). Just a few choices include the increasingly popular Purnululu scenic flights, horseback treks through the Kimberley Ranges, Ord River cruises, Lake Argyle cruises, and an extensive range of 4WD safaris and coach excursions.

From Kununurra, it's 513 km along the Victoria Highway to Katherine, junction of the Victoria and Stuart Highways. Proceeding 321 km north on the Stuart Highway (also called the Track) will bring you into Darwin—a kangaroo hop from Indonesia.

GLOSSARY

You only *think* they speak English down here. They don't—they speak "Strine" (Australian). Also, they do *not* parlez français. Here is one linguistic idiosyncracy that will make beaucoup de fou: "ballet" is pronounced "bal-ette," "filet" is "fill-ette," "gourmet" is "gor-mette," and picturesque" is "picture-skew." Another point to remember: Many words are shortened by adding "y" or "ie" to them (e.g., brekkie for breakfast, telly for television), and an "o" is often attached to the end of someone's name (as in "Johno" or "Bozo").

abo—derogatory term for "Aborigine," best avoided

amber fluid—beer

Anzac—Australia and New Zealand Army Corps

arvo—afternoon

avago—have a go, give it a try (also, **avagoyermug**)

back o'Bourke—in the middle of nowhere (also **back of beyond**)

banana bender—a Queenslander

banker—a nearly overflowing river

barbie—put another shrimp on the . . .

barra—barramundi

barrack—to cheer on or root for a team

bathers—bathing suit (also **cozzie**)

battler—one who struggles

beaut or beauty—great, wonderful

bikies—motorcyclists

billabong—pond or waterhole in an otherwise dry riverbed

billy—a tin can with a wire handle used for fixing "billy tea" over a campfire

bitumen—a sealed or surfaced road

black stump—the back o'Bourke begins at the black stump

bloke—a man

blowies—blow flies

bludger—a nonworking person who parasites off another's resources

bluey—swag

bonnet—the hood of a car

bonzer—terrific

boomer—huge

boomerang—curved flat wood used as an Aboriginal hunting tool

boot—the trunk of a car

booze bus—the Breathalyzer police van

bottle shop—liquor store

brolly—umbrella

bruss—Central Oz Aboriginal for mate or brother

Buckley's—no chance

bull bar—extra-large front bumper protection from road animals

bungarra—a large goanna, especially Gould's goanna—an Aboriginal food source

bunyip—mythical swampland bush spirit

bush—the country, forest, or Outback (almost anyplace outside the city)

bushrangers—Wild West-type outlaws (though some were good guys)

bush tucker—Outback grub au naturel

bushwhackers—hicks

BYO—bring your own (booze); a restaurant that permits patrons to bring their own liquor

camp draft—rodeo, Australian-style

carn—rallying cry at football games (e.g., "carn the Magpies")

cheeky—sarcastic, insolent, rude (e.g., your irreverent author, Ms. Marael)

chook—chicken

chunder—vomit

cobber—old-timer's term for "mate"

cocky—a farmer

come good—turn out okay

compo—compensation, such as worker's compo

cooee—originally an Aboriginal shouting-distance greeting, i.e. "you hoo"

corroboree—an Aboriginal meeting, usually with song, dance, and ceremonies

counter meal—pub food

cozzies—swimming garb

crook—sick

crow eater—a South Australian
cut lunch—sandwiches

dag, daggy—a nerd, or nerdlike (actually the dirty wool lump on a sheep's bottom)
damper—bush bread cooked in a camp pot
dekko—to take a look at
dero—derelict
didgeridoo—Aboriginal mens' wind instrument
digger—several meanings: a miner; soldier or veteran; old timer
dill—idiot
dilly bag—Aboriginal woven-grass carrying bag
dingo—a wild yellow dog
dinkum—honest, true (also **fair dinkum**)
dinky-di—genuine
Dog Fence—the world's longest, installed to protect southeastern Australia from dingoes
donk—automobile engine
don't come the raw prawn—don't fool me!
drongo—a stupid or worthless person
duco—automobile paint
duffing—cattle-stealing
dunny—an outhouse

earbash—nonstop chatter
Esky—popular brand of portable ice chest

fair go—an equal opportunity
fall pregnant—to get pregnant
financial—to be in good monetary condition
flat out—busy
footy—football
footpath—sidewalk
fossicking—gem- or rockhounding

galah—a fool or idiot (also a noisy parrot)
garbo—trash collector
g'day—good day
gibber—stony desert
good on ya—good for you, well done
good oil—good information or ideas
grazier—big-time sheep or cattle farmer
The Green—The Wet, in the Kimberley

homestead—station owner or manager's residence
hoon—a jerk or noisy rabble-rouser

Hughie—sometimes God, sometimes just surf and rain God
hump—to carry something
humpy—temporary bark hut used by Aborigines

icy pole—popsicle or ice cream on a stick

jackeroo—male ranch hand
jillaroo—female ranch hand
joey—pouch-riding baby kangaroo or wallaby
journo—a journalist
jumbuck—sheep
jumper—a sweater

Kiwi—a New Zealander
knackered—extremely tired
knock—to criticize
knockers—those who knock others (down)
Koori—Aborigine from southeastern Australia

lay by—lay away (to hold something in a store or shop)
lollies—candy
loo—toilet

mad as a cut snake—*really* crazy or crazy mad
manchester—household linen items
mate—friend or casual aquaintance
Matilda—swag
milk bar—the corner shop or convenience store
milko—milkman
mozzies—mosquitoes
mud map—rough hand-drawn map
mulga—the bush
Murri—Aborigine (usually Queensland)
muster—round up sheep or cattle

never never—way out in the Outback
new Australians—newer immigrants (usually non-British descendants)
no worries—no problem
nought—zero
nulla-nulla—Aborigines' wooden club

ocker—a brash, rude Aussie
offsider—an assistant
on the piss—out drinking
O-S—overseas

Outback—Australia's—and one of the world's—most remote regions
OYO—Own Your Own (flat, condo, apartment)
Oz—Australia

paddock—a fenced-in area for livestock
pastoralist—bigger big-time than a grazier
perve—to lust after
piss—beer
pissed—drunk
pissed off—irritated
plonk—rot-gut wine
pokies—poker or slot machines
pom—an English person
postie—a mail person

randy—horny
rapt—*really* pleased or enraptured
ratbag—mild rebuke for an eccentric or trouble-stirrer
ratshit—lousy
reckon—"I reckon that randy, ratshit ocker will push the milko down the loo."
rego—car registration
ridji didge—the genuine article (also "ridgy didge")
right—okay ("She'll be right, mate.")
ripper—good, great, terrific
road train—a semi with several trailers
rollies—roll-your-own ciggies
ropable—intensely angry or fiery-tempered
rubbish—garbage (also, to tease)
rug rat—toddler

sandgroper—a Western Australian
sandshoes—sneakers
see ya later—maybe you will, maybe you won't
shanty—typically, an unlicensed pub in goldmining enclaves
sheila—archaic term for "girl"
she'll be right—no problem
shoot through—leave *fast*
shout—to treat or buy a round of drinks ("It's your shout.")
sickie—a day off work (often not having anything to do with sickness)
singlet—sleeveless T-shirt
smoko—tea break

snag—sausage
spunk, spunky—good-looking ("He's a spunk")
station—a large ranch or farm
stickybeak—nosy or curious person
stinger—box jellyfish
stuffed—exhausted, beat
sunbake—sunbathe
super—superannuation, pension
surfies—surfers
swag—bedroll containing your possessions (often carried over your shoulder)
swagman—a swag-toting itinerant worker
sweets—dessert

ta—thank you
tacker—toddler
takeaway—takeout, fast food
tall poppies—successful people, often cut down
taxi rank—taxi stand
tea—dinner, supper, evening meal
terra nullius—the outrageously racist claim of the Australian government that no one had lived on the continent before 1788
thingo—you know, a *thing* (a-ma-bobby)
true blue—honest, real, dinkum
tucker—food, grub
Two-up—Aussie gambling game

uni—university
ute—pickup truck

waddy—Aborigines' wooden club
wag—to cut school
walkabout—a long walk away from civilization
waltzing Matilda—old term for a swagman
watch house—police station holding cell
weatherboard—wooden dwelling
whinge—whine or complain
willy-willy—dust storm
wobbly—shaky behavior
wowser—a tightass, prude

yabber—jabber, chat, yak yak
yahoo—loud, ill-mannered person
Yank—an American
yarn—a story or tale
yobbo—an unmannered, brash person

BOOKLIST

The majority of books listed can be purchased at either chain or independent bookshops in Australia, and many are available in the United States. Australian embassies and consulates often house libraries with a wide range of reference and reading matter. The most comprehensive collections are found at the Australian High Commission (London), the Australian Embassy (Washington, D.C.), and the Australian Consulate (New York). International Specialized Book Services (5602 N.E. Hassalo St., Portland, OR 97213; tel. 800-547-7734 or 503-287-3093) stocks many Australian titles, including university press publications and maps.

ABORIGINAL CULTURE, HISTORY, AND STUDIES

Berndt, Ronald, and Catherine Berndt. *The Speaking Land: Myth and Story in Aboriginal Australia.* Penguin, 1989. Nearly 200 myths from a variety of Aboriginal societies and cultures are compiled in this first-of-a-kind anthology.

Broome, Richard. *Aboriginal Australians.* Allen and Unwin, 1982. A black response to the white invasion spanning 1788-1980.

Dixon, R.M.W. and Martin Duwell, eds. *The Honey-Ant Men's Love Song & Other Aboriginal Song Poems.* University of Queensland Press.

Edwards, W.H. *An Introduction to Aboriginal Societies.* Social Science Press, 1988. Though mainly a college text, this volume is an excellent introduction to Aboriginal economic, social, religious, and political organization and values.

ABORIGINAL WRITINGS

Davis, Jack, Stephen Muecke, Mudrooroo Narogin, and Adam Shoemaker, eds. *Paperbark: A Collection of Black Australian Writing.* University of Queensland Press, 1989. More than 40 black authors have contributed oral literature, poetry, drama, novella, and other literary forms.

Gilbert, Kevin, ed. *Inside Black Australia: An Anthology of Aboriginal Poetry.* Penguin, 1988. Diverse voices from riverbanks, universities, jail cells, urban ghettoes, campfires, and reserves.

Headon, David, ed. *North of the Ten Commandments.* This anthology of Northern Territory writings is filled with insights and discoveries from a wide range of contributors.

Morgan, Sally. *My Place.* Fremantle Arts Centre Press, 1987. A powerful and poignant autobiography that traces three generations of Aborigines.

Narogin, Mudrooroo. *Master of the Ghost Dreaming.* HarperCollins, 1993. In this book by the first Aboriginal novelist, Jangamuttuk, the custodian of the Ghost Dreaming, uses his shamanist powers to will his tribal people to their land.

Narogin, Mudrooroo. *Wild Cat Falling.* HarperCollins, 1993 (orig. 1964). The first novel ever published by an Aboriginal writer, this is the study of an Aboriginal youth who is convicted of petty theft, jailed, and then plunked back out into society.

Narogin, Mudrooroo. *Wildcat Screaming.* Harper Collins, 1993. This satirical sequel to *Wild Cat Falling,* written 27 years later by Australia's most prolific Aboriginal author, sees our fellow back in jail.

Neidjie, Bill, Stephen Davis, and Allan Fox. *Australia's Kakadu Man.* Bill Neidjie, one of the last of the Kakadu tribe, passes along some of his people's ancient wisdom through text and color photos.

Nunukul, Oodgeroo. *My People.* Jacaranda-Wiley, 1981. Formerly known as Kath Walker, Oodgeroo's provocative book of poems is now in its third edition.

Nunukul, Oodgeroo. *Stradbroke Dreamtime.* HarperCollins, 1993. The Aboriginal author has penned a two-part book: the first half is a childhood memoir, the second contains Aboriginal folklore tales.

ART AND PHOTOGRAPHY

Bachman, Bill. *Local Colour.* Odyssey, 1994. A hardback coffee table edition with 354 exquisite and unique photographs. Bachman, king of Outback photography, supplies his own insightful and humorous text, supplemented by that of award-winning Western Australian author Tim Winton.

Bachman, Bill. *Off the Road Again.* Lothian, 1989. A terrific compendium of both quirky and mystical Outback photos.

Coleman, Peter. *Bruce Beresford: Instincts of the Heart.* Angus and Robertson, 1993. An in-depth study of the Aussie director with film credits such as *Driving Miss Daisy, Tender Mercies,* and *Breaker Morant.*

Granville, James. *Australia the Beautiful.* Weldons, 1983. This glossy volume of photography and text will take you on a pictorial journey of the continent and its inhabitants.

Isaacs, Jennifer, ed. *Aboriginality: Contemporary Aboriginal Paintings and Prints.* University of Queensland Press, 1992. This lavish, revised edition showcases 25 contemporary artists committed to expressing their cultural heritage in a variety of vibrant works.

Isaacs, Jennifer. *Australian Aboriginal Paintings.* Weldons, 1989. A selection of traditional canvas and bark paintings from tribes of Arnhem Land and the western desert regions, including translated information from the artists.

Spencer, Sir Walter Baldwin. *The Aboriginal Photographs of Baldwin Spencer.* Viking, 1987. A coffee-table edition of the widely acclaimed Aboriginal photos, taken by Sir Walter 1894-1927, on expedition in northern and central Australia.

AUSTRALIAN CLASSICS

Baynton, Barbara. *Bush Studies.* Angus and Robertson. A female view of bush life told through a collection of stories.

Clarke, Marcus. *For the Term of his Natural Life.* HarperCollins/Angus and Robertson. An Australian literary classic depicting the gruesome life inside a penal colony.

Clark, Manning. *A Short History of Australia.* Penguin, 1987. The acclaimed historian's abridged and accessible version of his five-volume *A History of Australia.*

Franklin, Miles. *My Brilliant Career.* HarperCollins/Angus and Robertson. The novel-turned-film of a smarty-pants young woman coming of age in turn-of-the-century Outback Australia.

Herbert, Xavier. *Capricornia.* HarperCollins/Angus and Robertson, 1977. Originally published in 1938, this elaborate saga portrays the mistreatment of half-castes in Australia's north.

Stowe, Randolph. *The Merry-Go-Round in the Sea.* Penguin. A classic story, against a World War II backdrop, of a young bloke coming of age in Outback Western Australia.

BUSH BALLADS AND YARNS

Edwards, Ron. *The Wealthy Dog.* Rams Skull Press. Classic Australian yarn-spinning—a genre of its own, akin to the "tall tale."

Lawson, Henry. *The Best of Henry Lawson.* Angus and Robertson. Bush ballads and poems from one of the country's most famous balladeers and poets.

Paterson, A.B. "Banjo." *Collected Verse.* HarperCollins. A selection of bush ballads and poems from the country's *most* famous balladeer and poet.

Semmler, Clement, ed. *Banjo Paterson.* University of Queensland Press. A collection of classic works—many depicting Outback characters—by Andrew Barton "Banjo" Paterson of *Man from Snowy River* fame.

FICTION, LITERATURE, AND SOME HYPE

Bryson, John. *Evil Angels.* Bantam. Saga of the 1980s Lindy Chamberlain trial and media event, in which she swore her baby was carried off by a dingo from an Uluru (Ayers Rock) campground. Ultimately tried, convicted, then released, Lindy's story is *still* being bandied about. (Besides, she was played by Meryl Streep in the movie version.)

Facey, A.B. *A Fortunate Life.* Penguin, 1988. An Australian best-seller, written by Bert Facey (published when he was 87 years old), describing the "ordinary" life of this extraordinary man.

Flood, Tom. *Oceana Fine.* Allen and Unwin, 1989. An award-winning fantasy/thriller/whodunit novel set in Marvel Loch, Western Australia—a place of myth and mystery.

Keneally, Thomas. *The Chant of Jimmy Blacksmith.* Penguin. A very disturbing and brutal account of the inner psyche and outer workings of an Aboriginal criminal.

McCullough, Colleen. *The Thorn Birds.* Avon Books. Be-still-my-heart saga (and miniseries), set in Western Australia, of lusty forbidden love between priest and parishioner.

Morgan, Marlo. *Mutant Message Down Under.* HarperCollins, 1994. The unlikely tale of a middle-aged Missouri woman "chosen" by a small Aboriginal tribe to become privy to their culture, dreams, and way of life—all in the span of four months. Oh *pleeease!* Originally, this self-published book was sold as fact but the HarperCollins edition sensibly carries an ass-covering disclaimer and catalogues the work as fiction.

Pritchard, Katharine Susannah. *Coonardoo.* HarperCollins/Angus and Robertson, 1975. This story of interracial love between a white station owner and his Aboriginal housekeeper was hot stuff in 1929 when it was first published.

Shute, Nevil. *A Town Like Alice.* Published in 1950, *Alice* was the first widely read Outback-themed novel. *In the West* (1953) and *Beyond the Black Stump* (1956) were other Outback-based Shute follow-ups.

White, Patrick. *The Aunt's Story,* Penguin, 1948.

White, Patrick. *The Tree of Man.* Penguin, 1955.

White, Patrick. *Voss.* Penguin, 1957. Australia's Nobel prize-winner portrays Outback life, hardships, and characters in his heavy epic works

Winton, Tim. *Cloudstreet.* Graywolf. The superb Mr. Winton spins an engaging tale of two families sharing a household in postwar Perth.

Wongar, B. *The Last Pack of Dingoes.* Angus and Robertson, 1993. Aboriginal and non-Aboriginal cultural differences exposed through clever short stories which combine an intriguing blend of political critique with mythological beliefs.

Wongar, B. *The Track to Bralgu.* HarperCollins, 1993. An enlightening though hardly upbeat short-story collection depicting the Aborigines' trials and tribulations.

GENERAL INTEREST

Antipodes. American Association of Australian Literary Studies (190 Sixth Ave., Brooklyn, NY 11217). A twice-yearly Australian literary journal featuring Aussie poetry, fiction, essays, book reviews, and literary scene updates.

BP Touring Atlas of Australia. Viking O'Neil, 1990. This large-format, fully indexed road atlas contains easy-to-read maps, including key maps and capital city maps.

Dunstan, Keith. *The Amber Nectar.* Viking O'Neil, 1987. A book celebrating the brewing and imbibing of Australian beer.

Goodwin, Ken, and Alan Lawson, eds. *The MacMillan Anthology of Australian Literature.* MacMillan, 1990. Thematically organized sketches, narratives, speeches, poems, and historical and biographical material.

Hirst, Robin. *Pocket Guide to the Southern Skies.* Dynamo Press, 1985. Get your bearings on the Southern Cross, Magellan's Clouds, and other phenomena of the southern skies.

Johansen, Lenie. *The Dinkum Dictionary: A Ripper Guide to Aussie English*. Viking O'Neil, 1988. More than 16,000 entries of slang, usage, and Aussie vernacular.

Mayo, Oliver. *The Wines of Australia*. Faber and Faber. Tipple over Aussie-made vintages and their vintners.

Saunders, R. *Prehistoric Aussiegami: Paperfolding Dinosaurs*. Lothian Publishing, 1992. Lots of diagrams and illustrations guide you through your creation of dinkum Aussie origami dinosaurs.

Warren, Mark. *Atlas of Australian Surfing*. HarperCollins. Good guide to riding Australia's famous waves.

You Can Draw a Kangaroo. Australian Government Publishing Service. A step-by-step how-to paperback—fun for kids as well as adults tempted by those "try-to-draw" matchbook advertisements.

HISTORY

Aitchison, Ray. *The Americans in Australia*. AE-Press, 1986. Americans have exerted considerable influence in Australia.

Cannon, Michael. *Who Killed the Koories?* Heinemann Australia. A no-bedtime-lullaby of the violent clash between inland-bound settlers and Aborigines in 1840s New South Wales.

Grant, Joan, ed. *The Australopedia*. McPhee Gribble/Penguin Books, 1988. Informative descriptions for young readers about the workings of Australia after 200 years of civilization.

Gunn, Aeneas. *We of the Never Never*. Random Century Australia, 1987. This turn-of-the-century account of Outback pioneer life and Aboriginal encounters is an Australian classic.

Hawke, Stephen. *Noonkabah*. Fremantle Arts Press. A former Premier's son relates the early 1980s headlock between Aborigines and the Labor Party over oil exploration near Fitzroy Crossing.

Hughes, Robert. *The Fatal Shore*. Collins, 1986. The best-seller that traces the country's convict origins, beginning with the 1788 arrival of the First Fleet.

Isaacs, Jennifer. *Pioneer Women of the Bush and Outback*. Weldons, 1990. Learn how ordinary bush and country women coped with daily life and hardships beginning from the last century onward.

Pilger, John. *A Secret Country*. Knopf. Read all about Aboriginal maltreatment, racism, British nuclear experiments, and other political and social dirt—spewed forth by a genuine-born Aussie bloke.

Rajkowski, Pamela. *In the Tracks of the Camelmen*. Angus and Robertson, 1987. The lowdown on some of Outback Australia's most intriguing pioneers.

Rosser, Bill. *Up Rode the Troopers: The Black Police in Queensland and Dreamtime Nightmares*. University of Queensland Press. Nineteenth-century Queensland's dispersion methods for ridding the land of Aborigines, along with reasons why the indigenous people had little chance of resistance.

Sherington, Geoffrey. *Australia's Immigrants, 1788-1988*. Allen and Unwin, 1990. This recently revised volume explores the role migration has played in Australian society.

Webby, Elizabeth. *Colonial Voices*. University of Queensland Press, 1989. An anthology with glimpses of 19th-century historical events as well as daily life.

Whitlock, Gillian and David Carter, eds. *Images of Australia*. University of Queensland Press. This introductory guide to Australian studies includes historical development, Aboriginal culture, muliculturism, bush legends and suburban lifestyles.

NATURAL HISTORY

Bush Dwellers of Australia. Australian Government Publishing Service. A second edition with color shots of critters you're apt to encounter out bush.

Cogger, Harold G. *Reptiles and Amphibians of Australia.* More than 800 species are featured in photos and line drawings.

Dangerous Australians: The Complete Guide to Australia's Most Deadly Creatures. Bay Books, 1986. Read up on venomous and dangerous wildlife, creepies, and crawlies.

Ellis, G., and S. Cohen. *Outdoor Traveler's Guide: Australia.* HarperCollins/Angus and Robertson, 1988. This descriptive guide—containing many color photos and maps—embraces Australia's geography, vegetation, wildlife, parks, and natural areas.

Flood, Josephine. *The Riches of Ancient Australia.* University of Queensland Press Australia. Follow the continent's prehistoric heritage in this book complete with maps, photos, and drawings.

Longhurst, Peter. *Bush Strokes.* Bay Books, 1987. A full-color portfolio of 20 native Outback animals, combined with informative text.

MacKness, Brian. *Prehistoric Australia.* Golden Press, 1987. Catch up on four billion years of the continent's evolution.

Phillips, Bill. *Koalas: The Little Australians We'd all Hate to Lose.* Australian Government Publishing Service. Learn more about the koala and its fragile existence.

Slater, Peter. *The Birdwatcher's Notebook.* Weldons, 1989. A field notebook with useful sighting charts, birdwatching techniques, bird characteristics, and much more birding info.

Triggs, Barbara. *The Wombat: Common Wombats in Australia.* The New South Wales University Press. Wombats, wombats, and more wombats: One-third of this book is photographs.

Webb, G. and C. Manolis. *Australian Freshwater Crocodiles.*

Webb. G. and C. Manolis. *Australian Saltwater Crocodiles.* G. Webb Pty. Ltd. Both 33-page texts feature color photos of fascinating and terrifying crocs.

TRAVEL INSPIRATIONS

Chatwin, Bruce. *The Songlines.* Viking, 1987. In this superb account, the author chronicles his life with central Australian Aborigines and helps to demystify some of the cultural complexities.

Davidson, Robyn. *Tracks.* Allen and Unwin, 1982. An interesting tale of a determined woman who walks alone with her camels from Alice Springs to the Western Australia coast.

Hawthorne, Susan and Klein, Renate, eds. *Australia for Women: Travel and Culture.* Spinifex Press, 1994. Rural and urban Aboriginal and Australian women share their culture and experiences in this unique compendium specifically for women travelers.

Stewart, D., ed. *Burnum Burnum's Aboriginal Australia, a Traveler's Guide.* Angus and Robertson, 1988. A large hardback volume that sets you exploring the country from an Aboriginal viewpoint.

INDEX

Italicized page numbers indicate information in captions, charts, illustrations, maps, or special topics.

ABOUT THE AUTHOR

Marael Johnson has been exploring and writing about Australia since 1983. She has freelanced as an area editor, researcher, and writer for a number of publications and worked extensively on many Fodor's Travel Guides, specifically in the Australia, New Zealand, and South Pacific regions. She has also reviewed Australia's hotels and resorts for Star Service Worldwide Hotel Guide. Recent publications include *Fielding's San Diego Agenda* (Fielding Worldwide, Inc., 1995) and *Why Stop? A Guide to California Roadside Historical Markers* (Gulf Publishing Co., 1995).

the inimitable Marael Johnson

Before—and after—taking up travel writing full-time, the author designed and stitched clothing for rock stars, sold love beads outside American Express offices in Europe, worked as a barmaid in Spain, an artist's model in California, a set dresser, art catalog publisher, vintage clothing collector, and flea-market wheeler and dealer. She is also a published poet. She has lived in paisley-painted communes in Santa Cruz, elegant Victorians in San Francisco, squats in London, handmade tents in Spain, chateaus in France, and monasteries along the Pacific Ocean, and owns a home in Yuppieville, California. She has completely disproven her mother's theory that "you can't run away," as well as Thomas Wolfe's, who swore "you can never go home again." She does both—very successfully.

The author is currently working on Moon's *Louisiana Handbook*. The first edition of *Outback Australia Handbook* won a Society of American Travel Writer's Lowell Thomas Award.

MOON TRAVEL HANDBOOKS — THE IDEAL TRAVELING COMPANIONS

Moon Travel Handbooks provide focused, comprehensive coverage of distinct destinations all over the world. Our goal is to give travelers all the background and practical information they'll need for an extraordinary travel experience.

Every Handbook begins with an in-depth essay about the land, the people, their history, art, politics, and social concerns—an entire bookcase of cultural insight and introductory information in one portable volume. We also provide accurate, up-to-date coverage of all the practicalities: language, currency, transportation, accommodations, food, and entertainment. And Moon's maps are legendary, covering not only cities and highways, but parks and trails that are often difficult to find in other sources.

Below are highlights of Moon's Asia and Pacific Travel Handbook series. Our complete list of Handbooks covering North America and Hawaii, Mexico, Central America and the Caribbean, and Asia and the Pacific, are listed on the order form on the accompanying pages. To purchase Moon Travel Handbooks, please check your local bookstore or order by phone: (800) 345-5473 Monday-Friday 8 a.m.-5 p.m. PST.

MOON OVER ASIA
THE ASIA AND THE PACIFIC TRAVEL HANDBOOK SERIES

> "Moon guides are wittily written and warmly personal; what's more, they present a vivid, often raw vision of Asia without promotional overtones. They also touch on such topics as official corruption and racism, none of which rate a mention in the bone-dry, air-brushed, dry-cleaned version of Asia written up in the big U.S. guidebooks."
> —*Far Eastern Economic Review*

AUSTRALIA HANDBOOK
by Marael Johnson, Andrew Hempstead, and Nadina Purdon,
800 pages, **$21.95**
Explore the "land down under" with Moon's *Australia Handbook*,
providing comprehensive coverage of outdoor recreation, the
hottest sights, and detailed travel practicalities.

BALI HANDBOOK
by Bill Dalton, 800 pages, **$19.95**
"This book is for the in-depth traveler, interested in history and art,
willing to experiment with language and food and become
immersed in the culture of Bali."

— *Great Expeditions*

BANGKOK HANDBOOK
by Michael Buckley, 221 pages, **$13.95**
"Helps make sense of this beguiling paradox of a city . . .
very entertaining reading."

—*The Vancouver Sun*

FIJI ISLANDS HANDBOOK
by David Stanley, 275 pages, **$13.95**
"If you want to encounter Fiji and not just ride through it, this book
is for you."

—*Great Expeditions*

HONG KONG HANDBOOK
by Kerry Moran, 347 pages, **$15.95**
"One of the most honest glimpses into Hong Kong the Peoples
Republic of China would like never to have seen."

—*TravelNews Asia*

INDONESIA HANDBOOK
by Bill Dalton, 1,351 pages, **$25.00**
"Looking for a fax machine in Palembang, a steak dinner on
Ambon or the best place to photograph Bugis prahus in Sulawesi?
Then buy this brick of a book, which contains a full kilogram of
detailed directions and advice."

—*Asia, Inc. Magazine*

"The classic guidebook to the archipelago."

—*Condé Nast Traveler*

JAPAN HANDBOOK
by J.D. Bisignani, 952 pages, **$22.50**
Winner: Lowell Thomas Gold Award, Society of American Travel
Writers
"The scope of this guide book is staggering, ranging from an
introduction to Japanese history and culture through to the best
spots for shopping for pottery in Mashie or silk pongee in
Kagoshima."

—*Golden Wing*

"More travel information on Japan than any other guidebook."

—*The Japan Times*

MICRONESIA HANDBOOK
by Neil Levy, 330 pages, **$13.95**
"Remarkably informative, fair-minded, sensible, and readable . . ."

—*The Journal of the Polynesian Society*

NEPAL HANDBOOK
by Kerry Moran, 428 pages, **$18.95**
Winner: Lowell Thomas Gold Award, Society of American
Travel Writers
"This is an excellent guidebook, exploring every aspect of the
country the visitor is likely to want to know about with both wit
and authority."

—*South China Morning Post*

NEW ZEALAND HANDBOOK
by Jane King, 544 pages, **$19.95**
"Far and away the best guide to New Zealand."

—*The Atlantic*

OUTBACK AUSTRALIA HANDBOOK
by Marael Johnson, 432 pages, **$18.95**
Winner: Lowell Thomas Silver Award, Society of American
Travel Writers
"Well designed, easy to read, and funny"

—*Buzzworm*

PAKISTAN HANDBOOK
by Isobel Shaw, 660 pages, **$22.50**
Pakistan Handbook guides travelers from the heights of the
Karakorams to the bazaars of Karachi, from sacred mosques in
Sind to the ceasefire line of Azad Kashmir. Includes a detailed
trekking guide with several itineraries for long and short treks
across the Hindu Kush, Karakorams, and Himalayas.

PHILIPPINES HANDBOOK
by Peter Harper and Laurie Fullerton, 638 pages, **$17.95**
"The most comprehensive travel guide done on the Philippines.
Excellent work."

—*Pacific Stars & Stripes*

PRACTICAL NOMAD
by Edward Hasbrouck, 200 pages, **$13.95**
The Practical Nomad is a planning guide for travelers considering
extended, multi-stop international trips, including around-the-
world journeys. This how-to handbook features essential
information on understanding airfares and ticketing, working with
a travel agent, and handling required documentation such as
passports and visas.

ROAD TRIP USA by Jamie Jensen, 800 pages, **$22.50**
Road Trip USA is a comprehensive travel guide to the "blue
highways" that crisscross America between and beyond the
interstates. This guide provides 11 cross-country, non-interstate
routes, many of which intersect, allowing travelers to create their
own driving adventure.

SOUTHEAST ASIA HANDBOOK
by Carl Parkes, 1,103 pages, **$21.95**
Winner: Lowell Thomas Bronze Award, Society of American
Travel Writers
"Plenty of information on sights and entertainment, also provides
a political, environment and cultural context that will allow visitors
to begin to interpret what they see."

—*London Sunday Times*

SOUTH PACIFIC HANDBOOK
by David Stanley, 900 pages, **$22.95**
"Moon's tribute to the South Pacific, by David Stanley, is next to none. "

—*Ubique*

TAHITI-POLYNESIA HANDBOOK
by David Stanley, 243 pages, **$13.95**
"If you can't find it in this book, it is something you don't need to know. "

—*Rapa Nui Journal*

THAILAND HANDBOOK
by Carl Parkes, 800 pages, **$19.95**
"Carl Parkes is the savviest of all tourists to Southeast Asia."

—*Arthur Frommer*

TASMANIA HANDBOOK
by Jane King, 300 pages, **$16.95**
Tasmania Handbook is a comprehensive travel guide to Australia's island-state, covering sights and travel practicalities in a cultural context.

TIBET HANDBOOK
by Victor Chan, 1,103 pages, **$30.00**
"This is the most impressive travel handbook published in the 20th century."   —*Small Press Magazine*

"Shimmers with a fine madness."

—*Escape Magazine*

VIETNAM, CAMBODIA & LAOS HANDBOOK
by Michael Buckley, 650 pages, **$18.95**
The new definitive guide to Indochina from a travel writer who knows Asia like the back of his hand. Michael Buckley combines the most current practical travel information—much of it previously unavailable—with the perspective of a seasoned adventure traveler. Includes 75 maps.

STAYING HEALTHY IN ASIA, AFRICA, AND LATIN AMERICA
by Dirk G. Schroeder, ScD, MPH, 197 pages, **$11.95**
"Read this book if you want to stay healthy on any journeys or stays in Asia, Africa, and Latin America."

—*American Journal of Health Promotion*

PERIPLUS TRAVEL MAPS

Periplus Travel Maps are a necessity for traveling in Southeast Asia. Each map is designed for maximum clarity and utility, combining several views and insets of the area. Transportation information, street indexes, and descriptions of major sites are included in each map. The result is a single map with all the vital information needed to get where you're going. No other maps come close to providing the detail or comprehensive coverage of Asian travel destinations. All maps are updated yearly and produced with digital technology using the latest survey information. **$7.95**

Periplus Travel Maps are available
to the following areas:

Bali	**Kuala Lumpur**
Bandung/W. Java	**Ko Samui/S. Thailand**
Bangkok/C. Thailand	**Lombok**
Batam/Bintan	**N. Sumatra**
Cambodia	**Penang**
Chiangmai/N. Thailand	**Phuket/S. Thailand**
Hong Kong	**Sabah**
Indonesia	**Sarawak**
Jakarta	**Singapore**
E. Java	**Vietnam**
Java	**Yogyakarta/C. Java**

MOONBELT

A new concept in money-belts. Made of heavy-duty Cordura nylon, the Moon-belt offers maximum protection for your money and important papers. This pouch, designed for all-weather comfort, slips under your shirt or waistband, rendering it virtually unde-tectable and inaccessible to pickpockets. It features a one-inch high-test quick-release buckle so there's no more fumbling around for the strap or repeated adjustments. This handy plastic buckle opens and closes with a touch, but won't come undone until you want it to. Moonbelts accommodate traveler's checks, passports, cash, photos, etc. Size 5 x 9 inches. Available in black only. **$8.95**

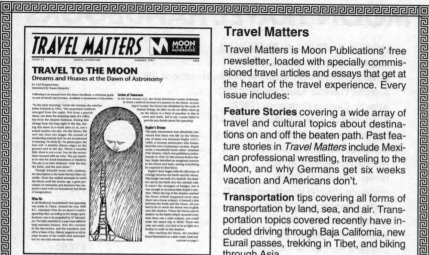

MOON TRAVEL HANDBOOKS

NORTH AMERICA AND HAWAII

Alaska-Yukon Handbook (0161) $14.95
Alberta and the Northwest Territories Handbook (0676) $17.95
Arizona Traveler's Handbook (0714) $17.95
Atlantic Canada Handbook (0072) $17.95
Big Island of Hawaii Handbook (0064) $13.95
British Columbia Handbook (0145) $15.95
Colorado Handbook (0447) $18.95
Georgia Handbook (0390) $17.95
Hawaii Handbook (0005) $19.95
Honolulu-Waikiki Handbook (0587) $14.95
Idaho Handbook (0617) $14.95
Kauai Handbook (0013) $13.95
Maui Handbook (0579) $14.95
Montana Handbook (0498) $17.95
Nevada Handbook (0641) $16.95
New Mexico Handbook (0153) $14.95
Northern California Handbook (3840) $19.95
Oregon Handbook (0102) $16.95
Road Trip USA (0366) $22.50
Texas Handbook (0633) $17.95
Utah Handbook (0684) $16.95
Washington Handbook (0455) $18.95
Wyoming Handbook (3980) $14.95

ASIA AND THE PACIFIC

Australia Handbook (0722) $21.95
Bali Handbook (0730) $19.95
Bangkok Handbook (0595) $13.95
Fiji Islands Handbook (0382) $13.95
Hong Kong Handbook (0560) $15.95
Indonesia Handbook (0625) $25.00
Japan Handbook (3700) $22.50
Micronesia Handbook (0773) $13.95
Nepal Handbook (0412) $18.95
New Zealand Handbook (0331) $19.95
Outback Australia Handbook (0471) $18.95
Pakistan Handbook (0692) $22.50
Philippines Handbook (0048) $17.95

Southeast Asia Handbook (0021)	$21.95
South Pacific Handbook (0404)	$22.95
Tahiti-Polynesia Handbook (0374)	$13.95
Thailand Handbook (0420)	$19.95
Tibet Handbook (3905)	$30.00
Vietnam, Cambodia & Laos Handbook (0293)	$18.95

MEXICO

Baja Handbook (0528)	$15.95
Cabo Handbook (0285)	$14.95
Cancún Handbook (0501)	$13.95
Central Mexico Handbook (0234)	$15.95
Mexico Handbook (0315)	$21.95
Northern Mexico Handbook (0226)	$16.95
Pacific Mexico Handbook (0323)	$16.95
Puerto Vallarta Handbook (0250)	$14.95
Yucatán Peninsula Handbook (0242)	$15.95

CENTRAL AMERICA AND THE CARIBBEAN

Belize Handbook (0307)	$15.95
Caribbean Handbook (0277)	$16.95
Costa Rica Handbook (0358)	$18.95
Jamaica Handbook (0706)	$15.95

INTERNATIONAL

Egypt Handbook (3891)	$18.95
Moon Handbook (0668)	$10.00
Moscow-St. Petersburg Handbook (3913)	$13.95
Staying Healthy in Asia, Africa, and Latin America (0269)	$11.95
The Practical Nomad (0765)	$13.95

PERIPLUS TRAVEL MAPS
All maps $7.95 each

Bali	Jakarta	Phuket/S. Thailand
Bandung/W. Java	E. Java	Sabah
Bangkok/C. Thailand	Java	Sarawak
Batam/Bintan	Kuala Lumpur	Singapore
Cambodia	Ko Samui/S. Thailand	Vietnam
Chiangmai/N. Thailand	Lombok	Yogyakarta/C. Java
Hong Kong	N. Sumatra	
Indonesia	Penang	

WHERE TO BUY MOON TRAVEL HANDBOOKS

BOOKSTORES AND LIBRARIES: Moon Travel Handbooks are sold worldwide. Please contact our sales manager for a list of wholesalers and distributors in your area.

TRAVELERS: We would like to have Moon Travel Handbooks available throughout the world. Please ask your bookstore to write or call us for ordering information. If your bookstore will not order our guides for you, please contact us for a free catalogue.

> Moon Publications, Inc.
> P.O. Box 3040
> Chico, CA 95927-3040 U.S.A.
> tel.: (800) 345-5473
> fax: (916) 345-6751
> e-mail: travel@moon.com

IMPORTANT ORDERING INFORMATION

PRICES: All prices are subject to change. We always ship the most current edition. We will let you know if there is a price increase on the book you order.

SHIPPING AND HANDLING OPTIONS: Domestic UPS or USPS first class (allow 10 working days for delivery): $3.50 for the first item, 50 cents for each additional item.

EXCEPTIONS: *Tibet Handbook, Mexico Handbook,* and *Indonesia Handbook* shipping $4.50; $1.00 for each additional *Tibet Handbook, Mexico Handbook* or *Indonesia Handbook.*

Moonbelt shipping is $1.50 for one, 50 cents for each additional belt.

Add $2.00 for same-day handling.

UPS 2nd Day Air or Printed Airmail requires a special quote.

International Surface Bookrate 8-12 weeks delivery: $3.00 for the first item, $1.00 for each additional item. Note: Moon Publications cannot guarantee international surface bookrate shipping. Moon recommends sending international orders via air mail, which requires a special quote.

FOREIGN ORDERS: Orders that originate outside the U.S.A. must be paid for with either an international money order or a check in U.S. currency drawn on a major U.S. bank based in the U.S.A.

TELEPHONE ORDERS: We accept Visa or MasterCard payments. Minimum order is US$15. Call in your order: (800) 345-5473, 8 a.m.-5 p.m. Pacific standard time.

ORDER FORM

Prices are subject to change without notice. Be sure to call (800) 345-5473 for current prices and editions or for the name of the bookstore nearest you that carries Moon Travel Handbooks • 8 a.m.–5 p.m. PST. (See important ordering information on preceding page.)

Name: _____ Date: _____

Street: _____

City: _____ Daytime Phone: _____

State or Country: _____ Zip Code: _____

QUANTITY	TITLE	PRICE

Taxable Total _____

Sales Tax (7.25%) for California Residents _____

Shipping & Handling _____

TOTAL _____

Ship: ☐ UPS (no P.O. Boxes)　☐ 1st class　　　☐ International surface mail

Ship to: ☐ address above　☐ other _____

Make checks payable to: **MOON PUBLICATIONS, INC.**, P.O. Box 3040, Chico, CA 95927-3040 U.S.A. We accept Visa and MasterCard. **To Order**: Call in your Visa or MasterCard number, or send a written order with your Visa or MasterCard number and expiration date clearly written.

Card Number: ☐ **Visa**　　　☐ **MasterCard**

☐ ☐ ☐ ☐　☐ ☐ ☐ ☐　☐ ☐ ☐ ☐　☐ ☐ ☐ ☐

Exact Name on Card: _____

Expiration date: _____

Signature: _____

THE METRIC SYSTEM

1 inch = 2.54 centimeters (cm)
1 foot = .304 meters (m)
1 mile = 1.6093 kilometers (km)
1 km = .6124 miles
1 fathom = 1.8288 m
1 chain = 20.1168 m
1 furlong = 201.168 m
1 acre = .4047 hectares
1 sq km = 100 hectares
1 sq mile = 2.59 square km
1 ounce = 28.35 grams
1 pound = .4536 kilograms
1 short ton = .90718 metric ton
1 short ton = 2000 pounds
1 long ton = 1.016 metric tons
1 long ton = 2240 pounds
1 metric ton = 1000 kilograms
1 quart = .94635 liters
1 US gallon = 3.7854 liters
1 Imperial gallon = 4.5459 liters
1 nautical mile = 1.852 km

To compute celsius temperatures, subtract 32 from Fahrenheit and divide by 1.8. To go the other way, multiply celsius by 1.8 and add 32.

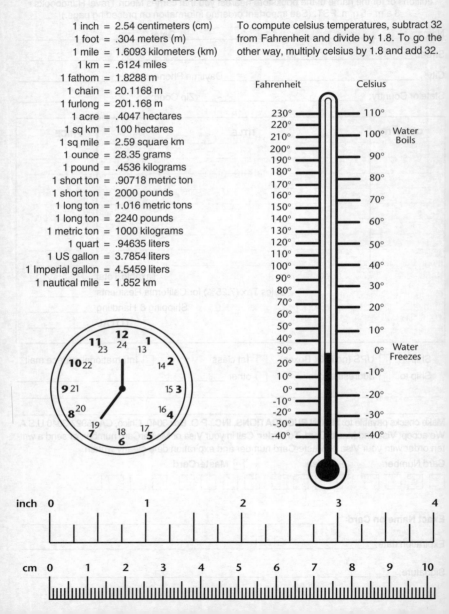

www.moon.com

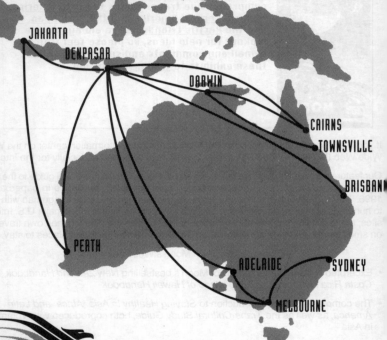

CONVENIENT CONNECTIONS FROM BALI

JAKARTA
DENPASAR
DARWIN
CAIRNS
TOWNSVILLE
BRISBANE
PERTH
ADELAIDE
SYDNEY
MELBOURNE